LEMON-AID
NEW CARS
2001

LEMON-AID
NEW CARS
2001

PHIL EDMONSTON

Published in 2000 by Stoddart Publishing Co. Limited
34 Lesmill Road, Toronto, Canada M3B 2T6

Distributed by:
General Distribution Services Ltd.
325 Humber College Boulevard, Toronto, Canada M9W 7C3
Tel. (416) 213-1919   Fax (416) 213-1917
Email cservice@genpub.com

Canadian Cataloguing in Publication Data

The National Library of Canada has catalogued this publication as follows:

Edmonston, Louis-Philippe, 1944–
Lemon-aid new cars

1998–
Annual.
Continues: Edmonston, Louis-Philippe, 1944–   .
Lemon-aid new car guide, ISSN 0714-5861.
ISSN 1481-4188
ISBN 0-7737-6164-0 (2001)

1. Automobiles — Purchasing — Periodicals. I. Title.

TL162.E3396   629.2'222'05   C98-901177-1

Cover design: Bill Douglas @ The Bang
Typesetting and text design: Wordstyle Productions
Editorial services: Greg Ioannou, Colborne Communications

THE CANADA COUNCIL | LE CONSEIL DES ARTS
FOR THE ARTS | DU CANADA
SINCE 1957 | DEPUIS 1957

We acknowledge for their financial support of our publishing program the Canada Council, the Ontario Arts Council, and the Government of Canada through the Book Publishing Industry Development Program (BPIDP).

Printed and bound in Canada

CONTENTS

Part Three/NEW-VEHICLE RATINGS
139

American Vehicles
149

Asian Vehicles
282

European Vehicles
412

Appendix/HELPFUL INTERNET GRIPE SITES
454

Key Documents

The following photos, charts, documents, memos, court filings and decisions, and service bulletins are included in this index so that you can easily find and photocopy whichever document will prove helpful in your dealings with automakers, government agencies, dealers, or service managers. Most of the service bulletins outline repairs or replacements that should be done for free.

Part One

Part Two

Part Three

Appendix

Introduction
STEALS AND DEALS

Lemon-Aid New Cars 2001 is unlike any other auto book on the market. Its main objective—to inform and protect consumers in an industry known for its dishonesty and exaggerated claims—remains unchanged. However, this guide also focuses on secret warranties and confidential service bulletins that automakers swear don't exist, but may be applicable to your trade-in or the new vehicle you wish to buy. That's why you'll be interested in the "Key Documents" list found on the previous pages. From there you'll be able to find the exact bulletin, memo, or news clipping reproduced from the original so neither the dealer nor the automaker can weasel out of its obligations.

The book's information is culled mostly from Canadian and U.S. sources and is gathered throughout the year from owner complaints, whistle blowers, lawsuits, and judgments, as well as from confidential manufacturer service bulletins.

Lemon-Aid not only targets abusive auto industry practices, it also lobbies automakers for changes. For example, earlier this year we downgraded the ratings on many Ford models due to what we perceived to be the automaker's poor warranty performance characterized by the incompetent and unfair handling of 1993–99 Taurus, Sable, and Windstar claims (primarily engine and transmission failures). Shortly after our ratings were published, Ford began giving refunds to owners of the above vehicles up to 7 years/160,000 km (see Part Two).

We have also blown the whistle on Chrysler's biodegradable automatic transmissions, 4-cylinder engine head gaskets, brakes, and paint. Following *Lemon-Aid*'s downgrading of Chrysler's minivans and cars, company officials met with me and agreed to reconsider previously rejected claims up to 5 years/100,000 km through an ad hoc Warranty Review Committee. This year, we tackle Firestone "killer" tires and GM's Saturn models for engine, drivetrain, and body defects that no amount of hype can hide. Front and side airbags also come under close scrutiny because they can severely injure children, women, seniors, and tall drivers. And don't forget ABS brakes that don't.

Lemon-Aid uses test results, owner complaints, scientific studies, Internet postings, and surveys to determine its ratings and then makes a critical comparison of 2000 and 2001 cars and minivans. Safer, cheaper, and more reliable alternatives are given for each vehicle.

What better way to separate the steals from the deals?

Phil Edmonston
www.lemonaidcars.com
October 2000

1

Part One
CAR WARS

"Thirty-seven percent of millionaires buy used cars, which is one reason
why they're so well off..."

Getting Rich in America
Dwight R. Lee and
Richard B. McKenzie

Three decades of *Lemon-Aid*

It's hard to believe I've been writing *Lemon-Aid* guides for almost 29
years. Imagine, when the first guides were written, car buying was seen
as a man's responsibility, auto safety was dependent upon the "nut
behind the wheel," and Volkswagen had a monopoly on cold, slow, and
unsold Beetles and minivans, while its Audi division was just beginning
to churn out "suddenly accelerating" vehicles that would almost bankrupt the company. Ford was selling biodegradable cars and trucks (and
denying they had a J-67 secret warranty to cover rust repairs) and "You
Light up my Life" fire-prone Pintos. Chrysler "muscle" cars put out
impressive performance scores, while the company's other passenger
vehicles would stall out whenever the weatherman hinted at high
humidity or rain. Plus—and this is the best part—the average new car
could be found for less than $3,000.

*2001 Chrysler PT Cruiser: A Neon-based (aargh!) mini-minivan with both
a 1930s delivery van and a 1950s hot rod styling that's a hit with nostalgic baby-boomers.*

But times have changed. Women now influence—and make—the
majority of car-buying decisions and are extremely thorough in their

2

research, much to the consternation of sellers who see them walk into their showrooms armed to the teeth with *Lemon-Aid, Consumer Reports,* CAA's *Autopinion* magazine, and reams of Internet printouts. Automakers have redesigned their vehicles to make them more crash-worthy, have added front and side airbags, and this year will install infrared windshield sensors to enable drivers to see in the dark. Volkswagen and Audi models top the recommended rating charts, and the average price of a new car or minivan now tops $27,000, says the Automotive Industries Association of Canada.

A good time to buy

Throughout the 1980s, the quality of imports improved dramatically, with Toyota, Nissan, and Honda leading the pack. American quality, on the other hand, improved at a snail's pace over the same period, because Japanese competition was minimal. Today, the Big Three automakers' quality control is about where the Japanese automakers' was in the mid-'80s. Where the gap hasn't narrowed (and a case can be made that it has actually gotten wider) is in powertrain, brakes, and AC reliability and fit and finish quality.

In spite of the persistent quality shortcomings noted above that will likely afflict many of this year's models from Ford, Chrysler, and GM, now is a good time to take the plunge and buy a new car or minivan. Stable foreign currencies, a glut of new models on the market, reluctant buyers pummelled by high fuel prices, and GM's and Chrysler's efforts to gain back market share by offering substantial rebates will likely keep prices relatively low throughout 2001.

With gasoline prices hovering around 75 cents a litre, Canadians are downsizing their vehicle choice in order to save on fuel expenses without necessarily changing the kind of vehicle they buy. For example, sales of small sport-utilities, trucks, and minivans are likely to gather momentum at the expense of large-scale versions of these same vehicles. Hence the continued popularity of the Ford Ranger, Mazda B-series, and Nissan Frontier pickups and the Honda CR-V, Subaru Forester, and Toyota RAV4. Even Chrysler's small minivan, the PT Cruiser, is likely to attract even more buyers due to its large storage capacity combined with better-than-average fuel economy. Ford's fuel-efficient Focus small compact is also a sure winner.

Shoppers can also expect to see a few all-new models that show considerable promise, like the Ford Focus, and a lineup of carried-over 2001 models with more standard convenience and safety features. For example, cars and minivans must now be equipped with similar standard safety features, depowered airbags are used more extensively, child safety seat tethers have been made more user-friendly, and overall crashworthiness has improved. All these factors mean that buyers can purchase a safer, upgraded new car or minivan this year for the same amount or about 2 percent more than what a 2000 model would have fetched.

Ford's 2001 Focus is nicely appointed and reasonably priced. Let's hope early reports of automatic transmission and electrical problems and parts shortages are not a harbinger of future deficiencies.

Stick to the essentials (bring your spouse, Mom, or Dad along)
There are about 4,000 vehicle dealerships in Canada fighting for your business. Before even going into the showroom, you should know what your real needs are and how much you can afford to spend. Don't confuse needs with styling (Do you transport the neighbourhood hockey team? Do you take long holiday trips?) or the trendy with the essential (Can you really fit into a Miata? Are you serious about 4X4 off-roading? Will you be towing a trailer?). Visiting the showroom with your spouse, a relative, or a friend will help you steer a truer course among all the non-essential options you'll be offered. Most sales agents admit that women shoppers are far more knowledgeable about what they want and more patient in negotiating the contract's details than males, who tend to be mesmerized by many of the techno-toys available and often skip over the fine print.

Only $599 a month! But did you spot the $475 "administration fee" and $895 "transportation and preparation" charge? Shame on you, BMW!

Many car buyers don't have a clue what they really want, and automakers are cashing in on their confusion by stuffing their cars and minivans with enough extra equipment to overwhelm most mortals— all in order to squeeze as many dollars as possible out of every sale. The automakers load their vehicles up with costly, complicated mechanical and electronic components that compromise the vehicles' original simplicity and easy repairability. Or buyers are forced to purchase vehicles that are over-engineered for their driving requirements, or equipped with expensive options needed only for hauling heavy cargo or extended driving vacations. Don't fall for the dealer's "must have" song and dance. Instead, ask yourself the following questions about the kind of vehicle you want and at what price.

What can I afford?
Have several models in mind so that you won't be tempted by one that may be overpriced. Use as your benchmark the ratings, alternative models, estimated purchase cost, and residual value figures shown in Part Three. Remember, logic and prudence are the first casualties of showroom hype, so carefully consider your actual requirements and how much you can budget to meet them before comparing models and prices at a dealership. Write down your first, second, and third choices relative to each model and the equipment offered. Browse the automaker websites for the manufacturer's suggested retail price (MSRP), promotions, and package discounts. Look for special low prices that may only apply to Internet-generated referrals—in Ford's case, the "E-Price." Then call the dealership and ask for an appointment to be assured of getting a sales agent's complete attention and take along the downloaded info from the automaker's website to avoid arguments.

Car ownership is astoundingly expensive in Canada and is directly affected by the choice of vehicle and where you live. Among year 2000 models, the Saturn sedan and Chevy Cavalier cost less than half as much to own and operate on an annual basis as either the Cadillac DeVille or Lincoln Town Car, and less than one-third as much as the Mercedes-Benz 500S, according to a November 29, 1999, analysis by Runzheimer Canada, the Toronto-based management consulting firm. Note substantial fuel price increases since then push these estimated costs even higher.

Out of 25 cars, light trucks, vans, and sport-utility vehicles considered, the Saturn shows annual operating or running costs of $3,248 and annual fixed or ownership costs of $7,214, for total annual costs of just over $10,000. Annual costs for the Cavalier are just under $11,000. The Lincoln Town Car Executive and Cadillac DeVille show annual operating costs of $4,464 and $4,896, respectively, and annual fixed costs of $17,718 and $17,168, for total annual costs of more than $22,000 each. Annual costs for the Mercedes 500S are $39,820 (see the table on the next page).

Lemon-Aid

Operating costs include fuel, oil, tires, and maintenance. Ownership costs include insurance, depreciation, financing, taxes, and licensing. Runzheimer Canada examines costs of nearly every domestic and foreign vehicle sold in Canada (see *www.runzheimer.com*).

Vehicles with annual costs exceeding $16,000 yearly include the Mercury Grand Marquis and Buick LeSabre LTD. Some cars with annual costs in the $11,000 range include the Toyota Camry and Mercury Mystique.

When you make a list of the cars or minivans you might buy, remember it is not enough to compare only sticker prices; instead, you should consider how much your car will cost over the life of the vehicle. This must include all the expenses you incur once you drive off the lot, such as finance payments, insurance, fuel, annual depreciation, and the cost of repairs and maintenance.

That's why the study is so useful.

Make & Model	Cylinder	(Litres) Displace	Annual Costs Operating	Fixed	Total
Mercedes 500	8	5.0	$5,072	$34,748	$39,820
Lincoln Town Car Exec.	8	4.6	4,464	17,718	22,182
Cadillac DeVille	8	4.6	4,896	17,168	22,064
Mercury Grand Marquis GS8		4.6	4,432	11,714	16,146
Buick LaSabre Ltd.	6	3.8	4,336	11,720	16,056
Nissan Maxima GXE	6	3.0	3,600	10,349	13,949
Chrysler Intrepid	6	2.7	3,712	9,763	13,475
Ford Taurus SE	6	3.0	4,144	9,032	13,176
Honda Accord LX	4	2.2	3,440	9,570	13,010
Buick Century Custom	6	3.1	3,840	8,815	12,655
Mercury Mystique LS	6	2.5	3,824	8,166	11,990
Toyota Camry CE	4	2.2	3,360	8,400	11,760
Chevrolet Cavalier LS	4	2.2	3,472	7,316	10,788
Saturn SL2	4	1.9	3,248	7,214	10,462

Projected Ownership and Operating Costs for Selected 2000 Cars—Canadian

All four-door vehicles similarly equipped including auto transmission, power steering, power disc brakes, air conditioning, tinted glass, AM/FM stereo, body side moldings, speed control, left-hand remote control mirror, rear window defogger, pulse windshield wipers, anti-lock brakes, driver & passenger airbags and tilt steering.

Costs include operating expenses (fuel, oil, maintenance & tires), fixed expenses (insurance, depreciation, financing, taxes and licensing) and are based on a 36-month/96,000 kilometre retention cycle.

All values expressed in Canadian dollars.

Among Canada's major cities, Montreal and St. John's are the most expensive places to own and operate a typical 1999 mid-sized vehicle, with yearly costs exceeding $9,000, says a 1999 study done by Runzheimer Canada Inc. Driving a typical mid-sized car (represented by a Ford Taurus four-door sedan) in the Montreal area costs the owner $9,874 per year, with St. John's close behind at $9,840 (see the table below).

Expenses include operating costs and fixed (or ownership) costs. In sharp contrast, driving this same vehicle in Winnipeg, Regina, or Edmonton costs the owner only slightly over $8,000.

The high-cost cities share one common liability—high auto insurance rates. For example, Toronto rates for liability, comprehensive, and collision insurance ("business use" classification, principal operator over age 25, clean driving record) are nearly $1,900 annually, and Montreal rates are about $1,750.

Runzheimer Canada Analyzes Costs for Mid-Size 1999 Vehicle	
Location	**Total Annual Costs**
Montreal, PQ	C$9,874
St. John's, NF	9,840
Toronto, ON	9,655
Halifax, NS	9,293
Ottawa, ON	8,863
Moncton, NB	8,842
Vancouver, BC	8,563
Charlottetown, PE	8,558
Regina, SK	8,333
Edmonton, AB	8,278
Winnipeg, MB	8,198

The costs above are based on a 1999 Ford Taurus SE 3.0 litre, 6-cylinder, 4-door sedan equipped with automatic transmission with overdrive, power steering, power disc brakes, tinted glass, AM-FM stereo, speed control, air conditioning, engine block heater, heavy-duty battery, driver's air bag, and anti-lock brakes. Costs include operating costs: fuel, oil, tires, and maintenance; and fixed costs: insurance, depreciation, taxes, and licence fees. Factors are based on 4-year/96,000 kilometre retention cycle. Vehicles are driven within an 80-kilometre radius of the city. All costs are shown in Canadian dollars. Increased fuel costs of about 30 percent over the past year aren't included in these cost estimates.

Will it suit my driving requirements?

In the city, a small wagon is more practical and less expensive than a minivan. However, if you're going to be doing a lot of highway driving, transporting small groups of people (especially kids), and loading up on accessories, a medium-sized wagon or a minivan like the Toyota Sienna could be the more logical choice, considering price, comfort, and reliability. You need an extended minivan or van only if you have to carry at least seven occupants, haul supplies, or get a better view of the road.

Most families should avoid the smallest and largest engines available with a given model. If you're travelling less than 20,000 km per year, your driving needs can be accommodated by a smaller engine that offers both economy and performance. More than 20,000 km of driving per year demands the cruising performance, extra power for additional accessories, and durability of a larger engine (a 6-cylinder, perhaps). If you spend lots of time on the road or plan on buying a minivan or van, you'll definitely need a large 6- or 8-cylinder power-plant to handle the AC and other power-hungry accessories essential to your driving comfort and convenience. Believe me, fuel savings will be the last thing on your mind if you buy an underpowered car or van.

What about short-term and long-term comfort?
The advantages of many sports cars and vans quickly pale in direct pro-portion to your tolerance for a harsh ride, noise, a claustrophobic inte-rior, and limited visibility. Minivan and van owners often have to deal with a high step-up, a cold interior, lots of buffeting from wind and passing trucks, and limited rear visibility. With these drawbacks, many buyers find that after falling in love with the showroom image, they end up hating their purchase—all the more reason to test-drive your choice over a period of several days to get a real feel for its positive and nega-tive characteristics. Each year I get dozens of complaints from owners who didn't test-drive their choice sufficiently and must trade in their almost-new vehicle because the seats are torture after a half-hour com-mute, or the headlights are too dim for night driving.

Does it respond to my special needs?
Auto designers have been more preoccupied with putting cupholders in their minivans, for example, than designing them to be safer, more convenient to use, and more comfortable for women, families, and an aging population.

A survey of 2,400 women by *Chatelaine* magazine concluded that 77 percent play a role in car buying, and 52 percent feel that manufac-turers don't adequately consider women's needs in designing vehicles. For example, some women remarked that if men wore skirts, it's doubt-ful that minivans and vans would have such a high step, and if more men hauled their children around, it's likely that standard seats would more easily accommodate child safety seats.

Will I have to change my driving habits?
Front-drive braking is quite different from braking with a rear drive, and braking efficiency on ABS-equipped vehicles is compromised if you pump the brakes. Also, rear-drive minivans and vans handle like trucks, and will scrub the right rear tire during sharp right-hand turns until you get the hang of making wider turns.

What safety features do I want?
Anti-lock brakes and airbags have proven to be of limited effectiveness in certain kinds of accidents, and downright deadly for inexperienced driv-ers or occupants who aren't of ideal stature (yes, even the new depow-ered airbags have been fatal). If you're of small size, a senior, likely to carry someone small in the front seat, or have recently had upper torso surgery, airbags may pose a serious safety hazard. Since you can't buy a new car or minivan without airbags, you'll want to choose a vehicle with

an adjustable seat that can travel far enough backwards to keep you at a safe distance (about a foot) from the airbag's explosive 300 km/h deployment or a model like the Ford Taurus that provides extendable pedals. (Some models come equipped with "second generation" airbags, which will deploy with a third less force.) Children's safety can be assured by getting a vehicle with an airbag shut-off switch, or by having them sit in the rear middle seat position or the right rear passenger seat, as long as the front seat isn't occupied (front seatbacks often collapse in rear-end collisions, crushing children sitting in the rear).

One safety feature that continues to be a lifesaver is a high crash-protection rating. Since some vehicles are more crashworthy than others, and size doesn't always guarantee crash safety, it's important to buy the vehicle that gives you the best protection from a frontal collision. For example, the Chrysler Caravan and Ford Windstar minivans are similarly designed, but your chances of surviving a high-speed collision with the Windstar are far greater than if you were riding in a Caravan or any other Chrysler minivan. Furthermore, the latest redesigns don't necessarily improve crashworthiness, judging by the abysmal crash ratings given to GM's year 2000 Venture van by the Insurance Institute for Highway Safety (IIHS).

Furthermore, be wary of all of the five-star crash-rating hoopla being raised by Ford and Toyota. There isn't any one vehicle that can claim a prize for being safest. Vehicles that do well in the side and front crash tests done by the National Highway Traffic Safety Administration (NHTSA) may not do very well in the IIHS off-set crash test, or may have poorly designed head restraints that would increase the severity of neck injuries. Or a vehicle may have a high number of airbag failures that cause the bags to deploy when they shouldn't—or not deploy when they should.

Before making a final decision on the vehicle you want, look up its crash rating in Part Three and compare that rating with the ratings of similar vehicles.

Is new better than used?
Probably not if you're buying a rapidly depreciating car. Plus, you may be stuck with a vehicle that has no Canadian track record, an uncertain future, and a weak dealer network making for problematic servicing and warranty support. I'd put Daewoo and Kia, Canada's newest South Korean auto importers, in this category.

You can't lose money, however, if you buy a new minivan, van, pickup, or SUV, which depreciate less rapidly than passenger cars. For example, depreciation will knock off less than one-third of your new minivan's value during the first three years of ownership, whereas the average new car will depreciate far more quickly, losing about half its original value over the same period. Nevertheless, there is an easy way to reduce the depreciation "bite" on a new car: keep it five years or longer and choose a model that is predicted to last that long without requiring expensive repairs.

Keep in mind that you begin to save money from the outset when purchasing any used vehicle—whether you keep it a few months or a few years. Once you add federal and provincial taxes, financing costs, maintenance, and a host of other expenses, you'll find that the yearly outlay for a new car is about twice that of a used car.

Can I get the same vehicle for less elsewhere?
Sure. You can shop on-line and use one dealer's quotes as leverage to get a better deal elsewhere (Hyundai dealers have quoted lower prices to cybershoppers than to walk-ins, and I expect other automakers may attempt the same thing this year under a variety of guises, so as not to rile the dealer body). On the other hand, sometimes a cheaper twin or hybrid model will fit the bill. Twins are those nameplates that are virtually identical in body design and mechanical components, like the Ford Sable/Taurus, GM Camaro/Firebird, and the Chrysler Caravan/Voyager.

You can't lose money buying a Camaro or Firebird twin—especially, if GM carries out its threat to axe one of the models next year.

Perhaps a hybrid or "captive import" will be more to your, and your pocketbook's, liking. American manufacturers have learned to join the Asian automakers instead of competing against them, and vice versa. This has resulted in hybrids whose parentage is impossible to nail down, but that incorporate a high degree of quality control and give owners a wider choice for servicing and competitive warranty programs. Ford's Villager/Quest minivan has been one successful Nissan co-venture that will end next year with the dropping of both models.

Sometimes choosing a higher trimline will cost you less when all the standard features are considered. (General Motors "special edition" vehicles, for example, could give you all the options you need for much less than if you ordered them separately on a cheaper model.) It's hard to compare value prices with the manufacturer's base price, though, because the base prices are inflated and can be negotiated downward, while cars that are value priced are offered as a "take it or leave it" proposition.

Twins and hybrids are only two of the many money-saving options available. Minivans, for example, come in two versions: a base commercial version and a more luxurious model for private use. The commercial version doesn't have as many bells and whistles, but it's more likely to be in stock and will probably cost much less. And if you're planning to convert it, all the extras may just get in the way.

Leasing is an alternative often used to make vehicles appear to be more affordable, but it's more expensive than buying, and for most people the pitfalls will far outweigh any advantages. Jim Davidson of Car Smart, a Toronto company that helps people lease new cars, says leasing has grown to 50 percent of total new vehicle transactions in Canada, but feels it's suitable for only 20 percent of drivers. If you have to lease, keep your losses to a minimum by leasing only for the shortest time possible, and by making sure that the lease is closed-ended (meaning that you walk away from the vehicle when the lease period ends).

If long-term leasing looks too expensive, consider purchasing a 3- to 5-year-old vehicle with 60,000–100,000 km on the clock and some of the original warranty left. Such a vehicle is likely to be just as reliable for less than half the cost of one bought new. Parts will be easier to find, independent servicing should be a breeze, insurance premiums will come down from the stratosphere—and if you get a lemon, your financial risk will be lessened considerably.

Hidden costs
There are a lot of hidden costs in owning a new car or minivan. Automotive magazines don't provide many details about these costs because they don't want to anger their industry sponsors or undercut new-car sales by directing buyers to used cars. Car columnists in particular don't want to offend the manufacturers who supply them with free test cars. This is why most of the motoring press ignore crashworthiness, parts costs and availability, warranty complaints, and depreciation in their new-car ratings. Yet this is precisely the information that most buyers want. Fortunately, there are some exceptions, such as *AutoWeek*, a spinoff of the fiercely independent *Automotive News*; *Mechanics Illustrated* and its quarterly spinoff *CarSmart*, which have always taken an independent line; and *Consumer Reports*, which spurns paid advertisements.

Don't be taken in by gas mileage figures trumpeted by the manufacturers, either. They're exaggerated by about 10 percent because vehicles are run under optimum conditions by automakers who submit their test results to the government. Sure, good fuel economy is important, but it's hardly worth a harsh ride, highway noise, sidewind buffeting, anemic acceleration, and a cramped interior. You may end up with much worse gas mileage than advertised—as well as a vehicle that's underpowered for your needs.

Tax advantages

Tax rules for cars and minivans are very complex. Nevertheless, whether you have a full-time job or are self-employed, there's a good chance that you can deduct some of your transportation expenses on your income tax return. It all hinges on the quality of your record-keeping—not whether you buy or lease, as some salespeople would lead you to believe. If the dealer promises you tax savings with a particular purchase, ask that the amount be included in your contract and verify it with an accountant.

"New" isn't always new

Sorry to burst your bubble, but it's quite probable that the vehicle you bought isn't really new. The odometer may have been disconnected and the vehicle could have been involved in an accident, as was the case with Chrysler cars sold in the late 1980s. Chrysler admitted to disconnecting the odometers on more than 60,000 vehicles. Some of these had been involved in serious accidents, and were repaired and sold as new to unsuspecting Canadian and American buyers. Or the dealer may have disconnected the odometer and driven the car for several thousand kilometres as a demonstrator. And even if the vehicle hasn't been used, it may have been left outdoors for a considerable length of time, causing the deterioration of rubber components; rusting of internal mechanical parts, which leads to brake malfunction and fuel line contamination (hard starting, stalling); and premature body and chassis rusting.

There's also the very real possibility that the new vehicle you've just purchased was damaged while being shipped to the dealer, and was fixed by the dealer during the pre-delivery inspection. It's estimated that this happens to about 10 percent of all new vehicles. There's no specific Canadian legislation allowing buyers of vehicles damaged in transit to cancel their contracts. However, in a more general sense, Canadian common-law jurisprudence does allow for cancellation or compensation whenever the delivered product differs markedly from what the buyer expected to receive.

Most vehicles assembled between September and February are called "first series" cars because they were the first off the assembly line for that model year. "Second series" vehicles, made between March and August, incorporate more assembly-line fixes and are built better than the earlier models, which depend on ineffective "field fixes" that may only mask the symptoms until the warranty expires. Both vehicles will sell for the same price, but the post-February one will be a far better buy since it benefits from assembly-line upgrades and rebates.

This is particularly true of GM's entire '99 model production, which was delayed several months in the fall of '98 during its model-year changeover due to strike action. Not only did first-series vehicle quality suffer due to the changeover, but the ensuing rushed production forced dealers to repair assembly-line goofs and replace substandard parts from suppliers who weren't "validated" through GM's quality control cycle.

The driver-side doorplate tells you the month and year of manufacture; try to get an upgraded second-series car. This '91 Ford Probe was a first-series model built in February 1991.

You can check a vehicle's age by consulting the date of manufacture plate found on the driver's side door pillar. If the date of manufacture is 7/99, your car was one of the last 1999 models made before the September changeover to the 2000 models. Exceptions to this rule are those vehicles that are redesigned or new to the market, arriving at dealerships in early spring or mid-summer. They're considered to be next year's models, but depreciate more quickly owing to their earlier launching (a difference that narrows over time).

Carryovers from previous years generally have fewer problems than vehicles that have been significantly reworked or just introduced to the market. This fact is borne out by a J.D. Power study of 74 vehicle launches from 1989–96, which showed that the Big Three's relaunched models had an 8 percent decline in quality, which turned around to a 19 percent quality improvement in the second year. Among Japanese automakers, Honda, Toyota, and Nissan posted an average 17 percent decline in their first-year offerings (mostly small problems), although this decline was wiped out by an average 19 percent improvement in the next year.

Who Can You Trust?

Car columnists: hear no evil, see no evil

I still find it hard to accept the passivity of Canadian automotive journalists, who by and large have been bought by the Canadian automobile industry through trips and trinkets—or cowed by their editors and producers into believing that their job hinges on how well they kiss advertisers' butts. Unlike the American press, which boasts a number of principled investigative auto writers, few members of the Canadian automotive press will stand up for their constituents. To do so would mean exposing such truths as the outrageously high cost of auto ownership; unsafe safety features like airbags and anti-lock brakes that are poorly designed, prone to malfunction, and capable of killing or maiming drivers or passengers; and national dealer/automaker sales scams, such as leasing, which annually bilk millions out of motorists' pockets. Their silence adds to their complicity.

If you're still not convinced, go ahead and try to decipher the fine print in most newspapers' leasing ads, or better yet, tell me what the fine print scrolled after a national television ad really says. It's probably something to the effect that "everything said or shown before in this ad may or may not be true."

Although car columnists claim that their integrity is not for sale, there's no doubt that it can be rented. Travel junkets, public relations, and advertising contracts all sweeten the honey pot for these pseudo-journalists. Five years ago, CTV's *W5* newsmagazine show ran an exposé on Canadian car columnists and broadcasters ripping off automakers by demanding $3,000 in corporate membership fees to join their Automobile Journalists Association. (Individual memberships cost $100 at the time.) Following the CTV broadcast, the *Toronto Star* required its columnists to indicate in a footnote to their articles, when applicable, that their information came from a travel junket or that a manufacturer-supplied vehicle was used. Interestingly, although the CBC and the *Globe and Mail* don't accept automaker junkets or free loaners, these not-so-pristine news organs do hire freelance automotive writers, who solicit the free wheels, meals, and travel deals in their own name.

'Forget Paris,' GM Tells Journalists; Instead, They Get to Visit Detroit

By ROBERT L. SIMISON
Staff Reporter of THE WALL STREET JOURNAL

DETROIT—The fallout from the recent strike at General Motors Corp. included a surprise victim: Cadillac's press junket to the Paris auto show next month.

To generate ink back home about their latest new cars and trucks, the Big Three auto makers routinely host expense-paid trips for U.S. journalists to foreign auto shows—most often in Paris, Frankfurt, Geneva and Tokyo. (Some news organizations, including this one, reimburse their reporters' hosts.)

So it was hardly surprising that GM's luxury division invited a score of auto writers and business reporters to join its executives on a five-day Paris fling in late September. After all, Cadillac is trying to position itself as GM's global luxury marque.

But two weeks after the invitations went out, GM management decreed deep cuts in all discretionary spending.

Cadillac won't say how much it had budgeted for plane fare, hotel rooms, meals, wine and its special briefings, but Detroit public-relations veterans say the tab would hit $10,000 to $12,000 per journalist pretty quickly.

All at once, what had seemed like a good idea started to look fiscally irresponsible, says J. Christopher Preuss, the Cadillac communications director. Cadillac decided its Paris activities could wait until January and the at-home Detroit auto show. The invitees who had accepted were quietly informed that because of the strike, the trip was off. "It's embarrassing," Mr. Preuss says.

GM cancelled its 1998 press junket to Paris for a score of auto writers during the UAW/CAW strike because the company felt it would look "fiscally irresponsible." In doing so, the automaker saved $10,000 to $12,000 per journalist earmarked for the planned five-day stay.

Nevertheless, there are some Canadian auto writers who have distinguished themselves by writing balanced investigative reports on the auto industry. Interestingly, most of them are women, and most hail from Toronto. John Terauds, formerly, the *Toronto Star* "Wheels" editor, has written many in-depth profiles of the auto industry using a variety of consumer-based resources. Although he's been called on the carpet repeatedly for his jaundiced eye for industry pap and for denouncing dealer sales scams, his tenure as editor made the "Wheels" section more consumer-friendly and relevant to the average automobile owner. *Toronto Star* business columnist Ellen Roseman is also particularly thorough in unearthing stories often missed by others. Denyse O'Leary is a dedicated Toronto-based freelance journalist who's quite resistant to government and corporate BS; she recently dug in her heels when the Ministry of Transport stonewalled her research into the dangers of airbags. There's Maryanna Lewyckyj, a *Toronto Sun* consumer columnist who has taken advanced auto repair classes and won't take any guff from incompetent or evasive automaker PR staffers. They liken being called by her as somewhat akin to a visit to the dentist. And finally, there is Gillian Shaw, a business and consumer reporter for the *Vancouver Province*. Four years ago, she single-handedly forced Chrysler Canada to restructure its customer relations unit and refund thousands of dollars to her readers following their transmission and paint delamination complaints. The Chrysler Lemon Owners Group (CLOG) in B.C. and CLOG Alberta (see Appendix) would never have been so successful if it weren't for Shaw's early consumer advocacy.

Unreliable ratings
Once you've established a budget and selected some vehicles that interest you, the next step is to ascertain which ones are rated as reliable and safe. Be wary of the ratings found in some enthusiast magazines; their supposedly independent tests are a lot of baloney. Their test car is supplied by the manufacturer and tuned to just the right specifications. Of course, servicing will be impeccable. Finally, the manufacturer will probably load the car with an assortment of expensive options to compensate for any design faults. Another very important reason for discounting these tests is that they don't predict a car's vulnerability to rust, poor servicing, crash forces, or inadequate parts distribution.

Automakers can't lose with these rigged tests. And if the tester wants other free courtesy cars to drive, the published report had better gloss over the vehicle's defects and hype its mediocre features. Also, if the magazine or newspaper receives advertising from the manufacturer, any criticism that gets through the driver's own self-censorship will be muted by the editor.

Take the *Windsor Star*'s strange, unnecessary, and exaggerated apology to car dealers four years back, made by that paper's publisher, James Bruce. Bruce ran a three-column apology to Windsor-area car dealers for having run a Canadian Press story criticizing Montreal car dealers (that's right, *Montreal* car dealers). The story, based on a survey done by APA president George Iny, questioned the honesty of nine auto dealerships that were surveyed in Montreal. Bruce felt that the story might reflect badly on local dealers and insisted that the following apology be run.

Story Failed to Meet *Star's* Standards

"On rare occasions a story finds its way into the newspaper which does not meet the high ethical and journalistic standards of balance, fairness and factual accuracy which we set for ourselves at the *Windsor Star...* Although the story did not involve any Essex County dealers, it may have by implication, cast aspersions on their business practices. The story was a discredit to the dealers and employees of members of the Windsor Essex County Dealers Association, who adhere to the highest of ethical standards and provide their customers with first rate standards of service...."

Handling information overload

Funny, as soon as they hear that you're shopping for a new car, everybody wants to tell you what to buy—relatives, co-workers, and friends all think they know what's best for you. After a while you'll get so many conflicting opinions that it'll seem as if any choice you make will be the wrong one. Before making your decision, remember that you should invest a month of research in your $27,000-plus new-car buying project. This includes two weeks for basic research (see the following) and another two weeks to actually bargain with dealers to get the right price and equipment. The following sources provide a variety of useful information that will help you ferret out what vehicle best suits your needs and budget.

"Web" shopping

Anyone with access to a computer and a modem can now obtain useful information relating to the auto industry in a matter of minutes and at little cost. This can be accomplished in two ways: by subscribing to one of the two main American on-line services that offer everything from consumer forums to easy Internet access; or by going directly to the Internet through a low-cost Canadian "server" (service provider) and cruising the thousands of sites that interactively summarize the subject matter that's covered or the services offered.

New-car shopping through automaker and independent websites is a quick and easy way to compare prices and model specifications. In fact, buyers now have access to information they once were routinely denied or had trouble finding, such as manufacturers' suggested retail prices, invoice prices, promotional offers, rebates, the book value for trade-ins, and safety data. Canadian shoppers can contact the Automobile Protection Association by phone or fax, while American shoppers can access invoice data on-line by surfing the Kelly and Edmunds websites.

There are other advantages to on-line shopping. Some manufacturers offer a lower price to on-line shoppers; the entire transaction, including financing, can all be done on the Net; and, finally, buyers don't have to haggle, but merely post their best offer electronically to a number of dealers in their area code (for more convenient servicing of the vehicle) and await counteroffers. Four caveats: You will have to go to a dealer to finalize the contract and be preyed upon by the Financing & Insurance sales agents; as far as bargains are concerned, *Consumer Reports* says its test shoppers found that lower prices are more frequently obtained by first visiting the dealer showroom and concluding the sale there; only a third of on-line dealers respond to customer queries; and most of the online sales outfits use American agencies and data, as the following Canadian cyber-shopper found much to his dismay:

> I have a complaint regarding the service provided on your website, *www.autobytel.ca*. I had just filled out the New Purchase Request form on your Canadian site and was presented with an option to obtain a free insurance quote from AIG. I clicked on this link and found that I was redirected to an American insurance company. Obviously this is not acceptable. If you are seriously planning on doing business in Canada, you must provide Canadian information, with Canadian prices and Canadian insurance companies.
>
> As a matter of fact, your whole "Canadian" site is riddled with American references and American links. Why is there a field called "zip/postal code" when this is a "Canadian" site? Why do I get sent to CarPrice.com, a site with American prices and American information after clicking on the "Canadian Pricing" link?
>
> I am a firm believer in good customer service, and to be honest, this lack of consideration and respect on your part has turned me away from buying through your service. Don't claim to be a Canadian site if you're not prepared to offer Canadian services; you're wasting your time and mine.
>
> I will be telling my friends that you are not serious about the Canadian market and to try someone else. This e-mail is being cc'd to *Lemon-Aid* as well.
>
> I will be buying a new Toyota Corolla within the month, and regret not being able to use your service.
>
> T. B. Web Programmer

On-line services

If you're new to cruising the Internet, try the two major American on-line services accessible to Canadians—America Online and its affiliated company, CompuServe. Except for minor differences in the way fees are collected, the services are similar.

After only a few days, you will acquire the skills needed to access the Internet on your own, browse the various consumer-advocacy message areas (called forums) and shop the hundreds of auto-related services that simplify buying and owning a car. With the click of a button you can cruise forums; download (transfer data from a host computer via an electronic link) government auto safety defect probes, recall campaigns, and crashworthiness ratings; and find out what dealer incentives and customer rebates are being paid out by automakers. Subscribers can also access sites in order to shop for a new vehicle or accessories; read on-line versions of popular American auto magazines, including *Car and Driver* and *Consumer Reports;* and get industry news and reviews. Without a doubt, the liveliest and most informative sites are the forums on cars and consumer rights. Watched over, but not censored, by a volunteer system operator (sysop), members post hundreds of messages each week responding to questions ranging from how to keep cats off your car (use an open box of mothballs) to what the particulars are of GM's secret paint warranty (a Chevrolet dealer's warranty administrator actually gave out all the details).

Internet
After having their hands held by AOL for a few months, many on-line service subscribers jump ship and strike out on their own by switching to an Internet service provider that doesn't have all the razzle-dazzle of AOL and CompuServe, but provides easier, quicker Internet access at more competitive prices.

A server will give you unlimited access to the Internet at an average cost of $25 a month. Most servers provide test accounts so that you can try out the service before signing up. This allows you to check the number of phone lines your service provider has and the accessibility of phone-in technical support.

Local newspapers or computer publications are a good place to comparison shop for servers in your area. Before signing up, though, talk to your local college, university, or library to find out if they offer free Internet connections to outsiders, or if they can put you in touch with a "freenet" system run largely by volunteers.

Surfing the web requires an entry-level computer ($800–$1,000) and software such as Netscape Navigator, along with a "dial-up" program, both of which can be loaded without much trouble. Your service provider (if it's a good one) will have a technical service line you can call for step-by-step help in downloading the software you need. There are also search engines that will list sites on the web according to subject or name. For example, if you want to find sites related to Chrysler cars, a web search using Google, Northern Light, or Alta Vista will come up with hundreds of sites.

The first website you should access is *www.lemonaidcars.com,* the official site for the *Lemon-Aid* guides. It carries updates and important links to other sites of particular interest to new- and used-car shoppers as well as car owners seeking refunds for factory-related defects.

Consumer Reports and CAA's *Autopinion*

Consumer groups and auto associations are your best bet for the most unbiased auto ratings. They're not perfect, however, so it's a good idea to consult several and look for ratings where they agree. My favourites are *Consumer Reports* and the Canadian Automobile Association's *Autopinion*. Both publications list the Manufacturer's Suggested Retail Price (MSRP), not the invoice price; and most prices may have been boosted by the time these magazines hit the newsstands.

Invoice prices

There are three places in Canada where invoice prices can be obtained— for a price. They are Toronto Metro Credit Union, the Automobile Protection Association, and Car Cost Canada.

One of the most convenient and reasonably priced places to get the invoice price is Car Cost Canada (*carcostcanada.com*) at 1-800-805-2270. This company will give you the invoice price, less holdbacks, disclose the subsidized financing and leasing rates, and show what rebates and dealer incentives apply. Furthermore, you are also given a dealer invoice break-down for all major options.

Cost of the service for one quote by phone (you have the option of getting the info faxed back to you) is $29. If ordered through the company's online website, the cost drops to $19. Three vehicles quoted online cost $29, and a "six-pack" request runs $39.

Consumer Reports is an American publication that has a tenuous affiliation with the Consumers Association of Canada. Its ratings, extrapolated from Consumers Union's annual U.S. member survey, accurately mirror the Canadian experience. There are two exceptions, however. Components that are particularly vulnerable to our harsher climate usually perform less well than the *CR* reliability ratings indicate; and poor servicing caused by a weak dealer body in Canada can make some service-dependent vehicles a nightmare to own in Canada, whereas the American experience may have been benign.

Based on 600,000-plus American and Canadian member responses, *CR* lists vehicles that are better or worse than average if owner reports vary from the industry average. Statisticians agree that *CR*'s sampling method has some room for error, but the ratings are good conservative guidelines for buying a new vehicle that hasn't changed much from year to year, and the ratings have stood up to court challenges from automakers. My only criticism is that many models—like Lada and Jaguar—are excluded from *CR*'s ratings, and its frequency-of-repair ratings for certain components aren't specific enough (a failing of CAA ratings, as well). For example, don't just tell me there are problems with the fuel, or the electrical system. Rather, let me know about specific components—is it the fuel pumps that are failure-prone, or the injectors that clog up, or the battery that suddenly dies?

Consumer Reports *and CAA's* Autopinion *are two excellent sources for consumer information on the best and worst car buys.*

There's also the Canadian Automobile Association's *Autopinion* magazine (published every January), available from CAA and newsstands for $6. Kind of like CARP (Canadian Association of Retired Persons) on wheels, CAA is an efficient, competent organization that has reluctantly stuck its big toe into the hot water of consumer advocacy, mostly through promoting auto safety. The group spends much of its time starting and towing cars, selling vacations and preparing trip maps, and decrying gasoline taxes. Much like Canada's Better Business Bureaus, whose noble intentions were compromised early on by a mixture of business-led intimidation, the threat of lawsuits, and the withdrawal of financial support, CAA has traditionally treated consumer advocacy with a mixture of fear and benign neglect.

That said, I must add that some provincial CAA-affiliated groups, such as the Alberta Automobile Motorists Association and Quebec's Club d'automobile du Quebec, take their consumer advocacy roles quite seriously, and have vigorously defended their members' rights. Too bad they're the exception, not the rule.

Autopinion mostly contains general-interest articles, as well as a summary listing of new cars and trucks. Its used-vehicle ratings are based on an owner sampling that's less than 5 percent of *Consumer Reports'*, but at least you know they're all from Canadian drivers. *Autopinion* gives you a good general idea of those vehicles that have generated the most problems for CAA members, but its conclusions should be compared with *CR's* recommendations. In some cases, CAA editors paint too broad a stroke for vehicles and model years that have an insufficient number of responses.

AutoWeek and *Automotive News* are the best trade and special-interest magazines for objective car-buying information. These publications accept automaker ads, but they remain relatively independent. Canadian Tire's *Autoroute* magazine is jam-packed with helpful do-it-yourself information and used-car tips targeted to Canadian drivers. *Popular Mechanics* is a similar publication for Americans.

Look Before You Lease

Canadians are reluctant to buy new vehicles because they cost too darned much. Instead of doing the right thing—reducing prices—automakers are offering deceptive buy-back leases that hide padded list prices through longer monthly payments. And the tactic is working—leasing has never been more popular, or more lucrative, for dealers and automakers alike.

Leasing costs more

Lessees pay the full manufacturer's suggested retail price on a vehicle loaded with costly options, plus hidden fees and interest charges that wouldn't be included if the vehicle were purchased instead (see the chart on page 75 listing Honda's MSRP markup for cars and minivans). But you can forget about getting clear information that would permit you to compare the costs of leasing and financing, says DesRosiers Automotive Research Inc., a Toronto consulting firm that studies the leasing industry. DesRosiers found that cheaper cars often cost more to lease than some luxury models. This was confirmed by the Canadian Bankers Association (CBA) after it blasted dealers' leasing contracts for charging interest rates as high as 34 percent and called for consumer protection legislation to regulate the industry. In another survey carried out five years ago by Les Affaires, a Montreal-based business weekly, mid-range cars and minivans were shown to cost about $3,000 more if leased rather than financed, and luxury cars about $7,000–$9,000 more.

Rob Lo Presti, a Toronto-based consumer advocate and leasing consultant, has campaigned tirelessly for more disclosure in leasing contracts. He says a few provinces have legislation that requires disclosure and limits contract cancellation penalties, but they don't go far enough. This allows leasing agencies to get away with legalized highway robbery through outrageously excessive hidden leasing charges and loan rates that are practically usurious (see Appendix, under the Carcalculator website).

Most people don't have the time or patience to do the complex calculations that leasing contracts require. For them, Lo Presti has created CarCalculator, an easy-to-use program that runs on most computers. It takes the mystery out of leasing, giving you the annual interest rate you are paying, the total cost of the lease, and how it compares to financing—facts guaranteed to frustrate any fast-talking dealer or leasing agent. Check out their Internet site at *www.carcalculator.com*. OrangeSoft Corp. will also check a lease quote for $20 ($10 for each additional quote). For more info call 1-800-647-8693 (toll-free in Canada). Another useful site that takes the mystery out of leasing is run by the United States Federal Reserve Board at *www.federalreserve.gov/pubs/leasing/*. The FRB goes into incredible detail comparing leasing versus buying and has a handy dictionary of terms you're most likely to encounter.

Sure, you get zero freight, PDI, air tax, and licence transfer—as long as you pay full MSRP and accept an annual limit of 18,000 km.

Leasing advantages

Leasing can be worthwhile for people who frequently trade in their cars, since it's more convenient and results in less sales tax. (This advantage is wiped out, however, if you lease for longer than three years or buy back the car at the end of the lease.) In some cases, you may be paying too much if you don't lease, since leasing enables you to drive a new vehicle without tying up a bundle of money that you could otherwise invest or use to pay down more costly debts. Leasing may also offer some tax advantages if your car expenses are deductible from gross income. However, the savings may be minimal. According to the accounting firm of PricewaterhouseCoopers, in 99 percent of the cases it examined, there wasn't much difference in the tax liability if the vehicle was bought or leased. Your chief consideration shouldn't be the tax savings, but rather the difference between the implicit interest rate in the lease and the financing charge.

Leasing disadvantages

Leased vehicles are usually overpriced, jam-packed with nonessential options, and accompanied by a hefty upfront fee. A leased vehicle's residual value gives the leasing agent another avenue to rip you off by setting the vehicle's buy-back value at much more than it's likely to be worth. (Check the "Residual Values" section found in Part Three for a realistic buy-back price for the car or minivan you're thinking of leasing.) It's also a smart idea to buy additional "gap" insurance to cover the balance owed on the lease if the vehicle is stolen or written off in an accident, but most lessors charge too much for it (about $200 is fair). In some cases, the leasing company will throw in gap insurance at no extra cost.

Ask the leasing firm what it's prepared to do if the car turns out to be a lemon. Most companies accept that this happens from time to time, and will simply return the car to the manufacturer and get a replacement. But that's not part of the standard agreement, so be sure that such a clause is included in your lease before you sign it.

Here are two other reasons why you may not wish to lease:
- If you drive more than 18,000–20,000 km a year (you may be charged from 6 to 15 cents per extra kilometre over that limit).
- If you always seem to have dents or scrapes on your car and can't be bothered getting regular maintenance. The vehicle's value at the end of the lease period is probably the single most important factor in computing whether leasing is to the driver's advantage or not. Responsible leasing firms allow for reasonable wear and tear on the vehicle during the leasing contract, but rip-off companies count every scratch and you may have to pay a grossly inflated repair bill.

Ford has recently responded to owner and dealer complaints about the definition of "normal" wear and tear with the following memo to dealers, telling them exactly what should be considered "normal" and "excessive" when a leased vehicle is returned.

Ford Defines "Normal" Wear and Tear

Normal Wear and Tear	Excess Wear and Tear
• Dings • Minor dents • Small scratches • Stone chips in the paint finish • Reduced tread on tires	• Broken or missing parts • Dented body panels or trim • Damaged fabric • Cracked or broken glass • Poor-quality repairs • Unsightly alterations • Tire/wheel damage or less than $1/8$ inch of tread remaining • Mechanical and electrical malfunctions

About 7 percent of consumers who try leasing don't lease again following disputes over "excess wear and tear" charges, says Art Spinella, vice president of CNW Marketing/Research, a Brandon, Oregon, consulting firm. Two years of study by CNW concluded that one in five leased vehicles were charged an average of $1,647 (U.S.) for excess wear. Mercedes-Benz Credit Corp, the leasing arm of DaimlerChrysler in the States, uses a "credit card test" to determine if charges apply: if the interior or exterior stain, scratch, or blemish can be physically covered by a credit card, there will be no extra charge. In the States, Chase Auto Finance has eliminated large end-of-lease damage charges by

waiving excess wear-and-tear costs of up to $1,500 on new leases.
Canadian leases can save money by getting an independent garage to
correct any excessively worn areas or by insisting that an independent
arbitrator decide which repairs must be done under the wear-and-tear
contract provisions.

Unfair lease restrictions

Make sure that the lease allows you to service the vehicle yourself at an
independent repair facility. A maintenance lease that ties you to the
leasing firm's repair shop can lead to outrageous service charges. Use
a less expensive independent repair shop for routine servicing, and
keep all your receipts to prove that proper maintenance (as required
by the manufacturer) was carried out should a warranty dispute arise.

Be wary of unfair restrictions, excessive penalties, and hidden damage charges. Excessive penalty charges for early cancellation of the contract are horrendous and usually require a payout of three to six
months' lease payments. Sometimes lessors will put you on a leasing
treadmill by waiving the penalty only if another vehicle is leased. Most
impose a 20,000 km per year mileage limit and charge a whopping sur-
charge on the excess. Also, you may be restricted from driving your
vehicle outside Canada or lending it to a third party.

Decoding leasing ads

Take a close look at the small print found in most leasing ads. Pay particular attention to the model year, kind of vehicle (demonstrator or
used), equipment, warranty, interest rate, buy-back amount, down payment, security payment, monthly payment, transportation and preparation charges, administration fee ("acquisition" fee), insurance
premium, number of free kilometres, and excess kilometre charge.

The Obscure Language of Leasing

Acquisition fee: Frequently hidden in the body of the contract, this is a $300–$450 extra charge for what is essentially overhead covered in the monthly payment. It's 100 percent profit for the dealer. Save it as the last item to discuss and then refuse to pay it.

Closed-end lease: This lease protects you from a decline in the vehicle's value when the lease expires. Useful with some cars, but a waste of money with slow-depreciating MPVs.

Disposition fee: Another abusive "extra" for preparing the vehicle for resale at the end of the lease. Don't accept this charge.

Early termination penalty: The fee paid by the customer when the lease is broken (see previous comments).

Excess mileage charge: This fee is charged for mileage that exceeds the cap set in the contract. Try to get a cap of 20,000–30,000 km per lease year and a rate that's less than 6 cents per kilometre.

Open-end lease: This lease holds the customer responsible for the difference should a vehicle's value fall below the residual value pre-set when the contract was signed. Not a likely prospect with most sport-utilities, minivans, vans, and pickups that usually depreciate slowly over the years.

Residual value: Think of it as the pre-set trade-in value for a leased vehicle. The lower the residual value, the greater your chance of making money if you purchase the vehicle at the expiration of the lease and then sell it privately a year or two later. Unfortunately, dealers routinely exaggerate the estimated residual value at lease end in order to keep monthly lease payments low. Keep in mind this is a resale value and aggressively bargain it down.

One final point about leasing. When you take your leased vehicle back at the end of an open lease, and neighbours or relatives have shown interest in buying it, find out how much they're willing to offer and make sure that you get the leasing company or dealer to call them. This could save you thousands of dollars by preventing the leasing agency from making a "lowball" bid and forcing you to make up the difference between the residual value and what the leasing company actually gets for the vehicle. (See "Leasing" jurisprudence in Part Two.)

When and Where to Buy

When to buy
Your first good opportunity to buy a discounted new car or minivan is in the winter, between January and March, when you get the first series of rebates and dealer incentives, and production quality begins to improve. Try not to buy when there's strike action—it will be especially tough to get a bargain because there's less product to sell and the dealer has to

make as much profit as possible on each sale. Furthermore, work stoppages increase the chances that on-line defects will go uncorrected, and the vehicle will be delivered, as is, to product-starved dealers.

Instead, lie low for a while and then return in force in the summer, when you can double dip from additional automakers' dealer incentive and buyer rebate programs, which can average about a thousand dollars each. Remember, too, that vehicles made between March and August offer the most factory upgrades, based on field reports from those unfortunate owners who bought the vehicles when they first came out (fleet managers and rental car agencies fall into this category).

Since dealers have very few customers in the dead of winter, and most buyers are on vacation or moving in the month of August, dealers are anxious to cut prices substantially during these times to keep their inventory and financing costs low. Some automakers cut special deals in December to boost year-end numbers for specific models—as Ford once did with its Sable and Taurus so that it could then proclaim them as outselling Honda's Accord, their closest competitor.

Allow yourself at least two weeks to finalize a deal if you're not trading in your vehicle, and longer if you sell your vehicle privately. Visit the dealer at the end of the month just before closing, when the salesperson will want to make that one last sale to meet the month's quota. If sales have been terrible, the sales manager may be willing to do some extra negotiating.

Where to buy
Good dealers aren't always the ones with the lowest prices. Dealing with someone who gives honest and reliable service is just as important as getting a good price. Check a dealer's honesty and reliability by talking with motorists who drive vehicles purchased from that dealer (identified by the nameplate on the trunk). If these customers have been treated fairly they'll be glad to recommend him. You can also ascertain the quality of new-car preparation and servicing by renting one of the dealer's minivans or pickups for a weekend, or by having him service your trade-in.

How can you tell which dealers are the most honest and competent? Well, judging from the many complaints I receive each year, dealerships in small suburban and rural communities are fairer than big city dealers, because they're more vulnerable to negative word-of-mouth advertising and poor sales. When their vehicles aren't selling, good service takes up the slack. Prices may also be more competitive because overhead is often much lower than in metropolitan areas.

Dealers selling more than one manufacturer's product line present special problems. Overhead can be quite high, and cancellation of a dual dealership in favour of an exclusive franchise elsewhere is an ever-present threat. Parts availability may also be a problem, because a dealer with two separate car lines must split his inventory, and so may have an inadequate supply on hand.

The quality of new-car service is linked directly to the number and competence of dealerships within the network. If the network is weak, parts are likely to be unavailable, repair costs can go through the roof, and the skill level of the mechanics may be questionable. Among foreign manufacturers, the Japanese automakers have the best overall dealer representation across Canada.

European automakers are almost all crowded into Quebec, Ontario, and British Columbia, leaving car owners in other provinces to fend for themselves. This is particularly troublesome, given that most European imports are highly dependent on dealers for parts and servicing.

Patronize dealers that shun "shop supplies" charges and give you the choice of hourly rather than flat-rate time in calculating repair charges. Twenty-four-hour servicing, free loaner cars, and/or a downtown shuttle service make for more convenient servicing. (Make sure the free loaner car is spelled out in the sales contract.)

It's also a good idea to patronize dealerships that are accredited by auto clubs such as the Canadian Automobile Association affiliates, or consumer groups like the Automobile Protection Association (look for the accreditation symbol in their phone book ads, or affixed to the shop window). Auto club accreditation is not an iron-clad guarantee of honest or competent business practices, but if you're cheated or become the victim of poor servicing from one of their recommended garages, you can take your complaint to them to apply additional mediation pressure. As you'll see under "Repairs" in Part Two, plaintiffs have won in court by pleading that the auto club is legally responsible for the consequences of the recommendations it makes.

New-car dealers an endangered species?
You bet!

Auto retailing is a marketing disaster. Vehicles distributed through dealers add over $1,500 to their cost, servicing is an after-thought, poorly compensated by the factory warranty, and customers find their showroom experience akin to having their fingernails pulled out. At a time when Dell Computer ships orders within days, dealers have to finance a 60- to 70-day inventory of many cars they didn't want in order to get a few of the vehicles that are hot-sellers. And when they do order vehicles, customers must wait 1–3 months for delivery, due to inefficient ordering systems (GM is the biggest offender).

Dealer servicing is another nightmare. Over 85 percent of the highly profitable non-warranty service revenues go to independent garages. Warranty work is often poorly done because automakers don't pay enough or force dealers to pay for factory mistakes. No wonder customer dealer loyalty measured by automaker surveys is less than 20 percent.

Will this lousy distribution system ever change?

Yes, it will, but it'll take lots of deception, intimidation, blackmail, and bribing of dealers and legislators. The deception part involves automakers assuring dealers their franchises are safe, while buying up as many as they can and operating "factory" stores. Once Internet sales really take off, these automaker-run stores will get the most referrals, the better-selling models, the lowest invoice prices, and the fewest warranty audits. Recalcitrant dealers who refuse to sell out their businesses will be both intimidated and bribed to leave the business. Provincial and federal legislators, sensitive to dealer lobbying in their ridings, will be bribed through campaign donations to treat automaker takeovers of their dealer market with benign neglect, while extolling the process as further proof that the free market is working.

After the automakers restructure the distribution system, we'll see the establishment of a two-tier system with a half-dozen huge national one-stop chains like Auto Nation and many smaller independent, specialized dealers. New car purchases will be made direct through third-party or manufacturer-owned distribution centres serving regional markets and dealers serving as order and pickup points.

Automobile brokers/vehicle-buying services
Throughout this book I've tried to give you all the key information you need to get a good deal when buying a new or used vehicle. I understand that this kind of negotiation isn't for everyone, and offer you the following alternative: an auto broker.

Brokers are independent agents who try to find the new or used vehicle you want at a price below what you'd pay at a dealership (including the extra cost of the broker's services). Broker services appeal to buyers who want to save time and money while avoiding most of the stress and hassle associated with the dealership experience, which for many people is like a swim in shark-infested waters.

Brokers get new cars through dealers, while used cars may come from automobile dealers, auctions, private sellers, and leasing companies. Basically, brokers find an appropriate vehicle that meets the client's expressed needs, and then negotiate the purchase (or lease) on behalf of their client. The majority of brokers tend to deal exclusively in new cars, with a small percentage dealing in both new and used vehicles. Ancillary services vary among brokers, and may include such things as comparative vehicle analysis and price research.

The cost of hiring a broker ranges anywhere from a flat fee of a few hundred dollars to a percentage of the value of the car (usually one to two percent). A flat fee is usually best because it encourages the broker to keep the selling price low. Reputable brokers are not beholden to any particular dealership or make, and will disclose their flat fee up front or tell the buyer the percentage amount they charge on a specific vehicle.

Finding the right broker
This is a toughie, because good brokers are hard to find, particularly in Western Canada and British Columbia. Buyers who are looking for a broker should first ask friends and acquaintances if they can recommend one. Word-of-mouth referrals are often the best, because people

won't refer others to a service with which they were dissatisfied. Your local credit union and the regional CAA office are good places to get a broker referral from people who see their work on an everyday basis.

Toronto's Metro Credit Union has its vehicle counseling and purchasing service (Auto Advisory Services Group, comprising CarFacts and AutoBuy) where members can hire an expert "car shopper" who will do the legwork—including the tedious and frustrating dickering with sales staff—and save members time and hassle. This program can also get that new or used vehicle at a reduced (fleet) rate, arrange top-dollar prices for trade-ins, provide independent advice on options like rustproofing and extended warranties, carry out lien searches, and even negotiate the best settlement with insurance agents. The Credit Union also holds regular car-buying seminars throughout the year in the Greater Toronto Area.

Rosemary Edwards, a CarFacts advisor, says Metro's CarFacts program has saved members over $600,000 since its inception. For information on how you can join Metro or start up a similar program with your credit union, contact Rosemary Edwards or David Lawrence at 1-800-777-8507 or 416-252-5621.

Buying clubs: watch out for kickbacks
Be wary of buying clubs or referrals that aren't backed by a national organization. Except for Price Costco, the Internet's Autobytel, and some auto associations, buying clubs that promise huge savings on purchases or claim to get new vehicles at dealer's cost seldom survive close scrutiny. The savings they promote are often illusory at best, because the so-called wholesale or dealer's cost price is usually no different than the regular retail price suggested by the manufacturer. Furthermore, many referral agencies make "sweetheart" deals with dealers that send them "under-the-table" kickbacks or predetermined commissions. Whether dealing with the APA, a credit union, or an on-line referral service, find out first if there is a fee received by the agency for giving out referrals to particular sellers. To its credit, Autobytel is upfront with the fact that it gets a commission from dealers it promotes.

Some credit unions or union-buying clubs do a very good job in cutting prices on all vehicles. They use their buying clout in a particular region to exact substantial concessions from local dealers. They generally charge minimal membership fees, and they don't get too "chummy" with the local dealers because they put their members' interests first.

Safety First

How popular are safety features?
Don Esmond, general manager of Toyota's U.S. sales unit, says Toyota market research shows that consumers in the mid-sized family sedan market rank safety features ninth among the top 10 reasons for choosing a car. Minivan buyers apparently place a higher premium on safety,

although firm statistics aren't available. That's why you see Ford, Honda, and Toyota touting their five-star ratings in minivan ads. On the other hand, it's obvious that the public has become wary of airbags, and anti-lock brakes, as the chart below clearly shows.

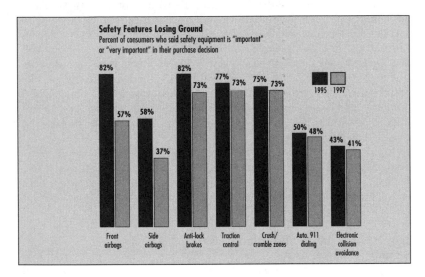

Safety improvements
Important safety improvements, once found only on luxury vehicles, are working their way down to popular mid-sized family sedans. The 2000 Ford Taurus, for example, has seatbelt pretensioners, which tighten the seatbelt against the chest, and "thinking" seatbelts that can detect whether a driver has buckled the belt, and can prevent the airbag from deploying in "fender-bender" accidents (or cause it to deploy more slowly in high-speed impacts). The airbags themselves have also been made more benign; they'll come in two parts to protect the head/shoulder area and upper torso area separately. Furthermore, the car's sides have been reinforced to prevent intrusion into the interior, and the Taurus's armrests have been redesigned to crumple, protecting passengers from possibly severe internal injuries arising from a side-impact.

Canadian and U.S. legislation
Canada's safety legislation is generally a weakened mirror image of U.S. federal regulations. When a recall occurs in Canada, the onus is placed upon automakers to notify owners of a defect, but they do not necessarily have to follow the notice up with a free repair. Canadian regulations are also backwards in another way: they require daylight-running lights, for instance, but don't require airbags or regulate how they should deploy (you won't find an airbag-equipped Lada—you won't find a Lada anymore, for that matter).

Why not? Here's what Brian Jonah, Transport Canada's director of motor vehicle standards and research, told the *Ottawa Citizen* a few years ago: "We don't dictate the solution when it comes to occupant protection. We don't want to limit a manufacturer's ability to innovate in vehicle design when it comes to protecting passengers." How limp. How Canadian.

If Transport Canada had been on the ball a decade ago, it could have forced automakers to initially make airbags less dangerous to women, seniors, and children. This would have saved over a hundred motorists' lives in North America taken by airbag deployment in fender-bender accidents and reduced the more than 25,000 reports of airbag-induced occupant injuries recorded up to 1991. "We" (read: Canadians) don't dictate, indeed.

Active and passive safety

How safe a vehicle is depends on its active and passive safety features. Active safety components, like high-performance, four-wheel disc brakes, and 4X4 capability, help drivers to avoid accidents. Advocates of active safety stress that accidents are caused by the proverbial "nut behind the wheel" and believe that safe driving courses are the key to fewer accidents.

The theory of active safety has several drawbacks. There is no independent proof that safe driving can be taught successfully. Even if one learns how to master defensive driving techniques, there's still no assurance that this training will be of any use in an emergency situation, where panic reflexes kick in (look at the disappointing ABS findings, discussed in the ABS section on page 32). And what about NHTSA's 1994 study estimating that 41 percent of all fatal accidents are caused by drivers who are under the influence of alcohol or drugs? All the high-performance options and specialized driving courses in the world won't provide much protection for such drivers or their victims.

While professional drivers extol the virtues of active safety features, everyday drivers know their limitations, and feel safer with passive safety protection. Passive safety systems, like three-point seatbelts and chassis designed to absorb crash forces and direct them away from a vehicle's occupants, work just as well with skilled and unskilled drivers. Of all the passive safety features one can choose, traction control seems to be the least important because it's so rarely used and its advantages aren't apparent. Interestingly, anti-lock brake systems (ABS), both an active and passive safety item, have been discredited of late—primarily because drivers use them improperly.

Two accidents per vehicle

According to NHTSA, a new vehicle will be in an average of two accidents from the time it leaves the assembly line (10 percent of all new vehicles sustain some transport damage) to the day it's towed to the junkyard. So crash safety is a major factor that must be taken into consideration when purchasing a new vehicle. NHTSA data show that 51 percent of deaths occur in head-on collisions, 27 percent in side impacts, and barely 4 percent in rear impacts. Rollovers—a frequent occurrence with small sport-utility vehicles—are particularly lethal, especially for occupants who are ejected because they're not wearing their seatbelts. They face a fatality rate 25 times greater than passengers who remain strapped into the vehicle. On the other hand, sport-utilities, trucks, and vans protect passengers better than passenger cars in most collisions.

Traffic safety studies show that women are particularly vulnerable to traffic fatalities and injuries (wait until you read what airbags do to them). The number of women who die behind the wheel has increased 62 percent since 1975, while highway deaths among men are dropping. The reasons given for this difference include the fact that women are driving more, they drive smaller cars, they drive more aggressively, are less tolerant of alcohol than men, and tend to drive on local roads where accident rates are higher. I would also add airbags as a factor.

Distracted drivers are also estimated to be the cause up to half of all crashes—more than impaired drivers—says the U.S. Network of Employers for Traffic Safety. In addition to drunks, we now have to worry about drivers who drive while they read, shave, apply makeup, fiddle with the radio or AC, reach for items on the floor of the car, or talk with passengers, chat on the cell phone, and do other stupid things instead of paying attention to driving.

Anti-lock brake system (ABS)

Anti-lock brakes are impressive on the test track but not on the road. In fact, the Insurance Institute for Highway Safety says that cars with anti-lock brakes are more likely to be in crashes where no other car is involved but a passenger is killed. Insurance claim statistics show that anti-lock brakes aren't producing the overall safety benefits that were predicted by the government and automakers. The latest IIHS study found that a passenger has a 45 percent greater chance of dying in a single-vehicle crash in a car with anti-lock brakes than in the same car with old-style brakes. On wet pavement, where ABS supposedly excels, the chance of being killed increased to 65 percent. In multi-vehicle crashes, ABS-equipped vehicles have a passenger death rate 6 percent higher than vehicles not equipped with ABS.

Essentially, ABS prevents a vehicle's wheels from locking when the brakes are applied in an emergency situation, thus reducing skidding and the loss of directional control. When braking on wet and dry roads, your stopping distance will be about the same as with conventional braking systems. But in gravel, slush, or snow, your stopping distance will be greater.

Automakers have created the impression that cars equipped with ABS will stop on a dime, but they don't fully explain how ABS should be used. For example, many drivers don't know that anti-lock brakes require that they do what driving schools have told them not to do: slam on the brakes in a skid.

The high cost of ABS maintenance is one disadvantage that few safety advocates mention. Consider the following: 1) original equipment parts can cost five times higher than regular braking components, and 2) many dealers prefer to replace the entire ABS unit rather than troubleshoot its very complex system.

Insurance claims aren't very supportive of assertions that ABS prevents collisions. The Washington-based Highway Loss Data Institute's study of identical vehicles equipped and not equipped with ABS found that the frequency and cost of collision claims were not reduced with ABS. Other studies do show a decrease in crashes, varying between 8 percent (the Markham, Ontario–based Vehicle Information Centre) and 3 percent (General Motors) depending on road conditions. In view of these conflicting studies, insurance companies are backing away from premium reductions for ABS-equipped vehicles.

Transport Canada is concerned about the hype surrounding ABS effectiveness. Its tests indicate that the safety benefits may be compromised by drivers who are less cautious and who tend to drive more aggressively than others. They accelerate more quickly, drive faster, and apply the brakes later than do drivers using vehicles without anti-lock brakes (paper presented at the 1993 Multidisciplinary Road Safety Conference).

Airbags

Airbags are killers. Granted, they save lives in high-speed collisions, but they also take lives—or leave occupants horribly scarred—in fender-benders. Millions of vehicles have been recalled because their airbags go off when they shouldn't and don't go off when they should. Latest research reports show that even depowered and side airbags are also hazardous.

I have read the stats and they *are* scary.

Two startling studies conducted by Transport Canada were uncovered last October as part of a CBC *Marketplace* investigation into airbag safety. They show airbags reduce the risk of injury by only 2 percent for adults who wear seatbelts.

The studies also confirm earlier findings that airbags decrease the rick of injury for men by 11 percent, but increase the risk of injury to women by 9 percent.

Children are the most vulnerable. The study shows airbags increase the risk of death for children by 21 percent.

The studies were completed in 1996 and 1998. It took four months for Transport Canada to release them to *Marketplace*. The government has yet to release the findings publicly.

Lemon-Aid lists in Part Three which vehicles have airbags that have severely injured occupants or deployed inadvertently because we know the severe injuries an airbag firing can cause.

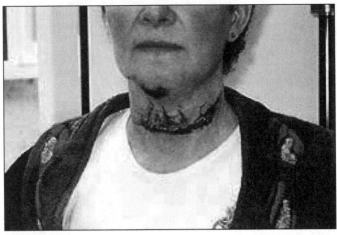

This woman had just negotiated a traffic circle on a busy, single lane road when her airbag exploded. "I was doing about 60 km/h, no more. The road was straight and I hadn't hit anything." She managed to stop her car at a nearby bus stop. "A lady stopped and ran back to ask if I needed any help, but I couldn't hear her: it felt as though my hearing had been reduced by 75 percent, like being in a box." Nor could she speak. "My voice was stunned, faint and tight, I was straining to even speak, although I hadn't started bleeding at that stage." (I'm aware of the graphic nature of this photo, but I feel it's essential to show the trauma airbag victims routinely sustain.)

True, well-publicized American and Canadian safety studies show convincingly that airbags save lives in high-speed collisions in excess of 39 km/h, but equally thorough, though little-publicized, government–university studies show airbags can maim or kill through inadvertent deployment (1 chance in 30) or in low-speed collisions at speeds as low as 20–39 km/h—particularly if you're a woman, a senior, not of average size, have had upper torso surgery, or use a tilt steering wheel. In fact, the dangers are so great that a little-publicized 1996 Transport Canada and George Washington University study of 445 drivers and passengers concludes:

> While the initial findings of this study confirm that belted drivers are afforded added protection against head and facial injury in moderate to severe frontal collisions, the findings also suggest that these benefits are being negated by a high incidence of bag-induced injury.... The incidence of bag-induced injury was greatest among female drivers.... Furthermore, the intervention of the airbag can be expected to introduce a variety of new injury mechanisms such as facial injuries from "bag slap," upper extremity fractures, either directly from the deploying airbag module or from arm flailing, and thermal burns to the face and arms.

**AirBag Deployment Crashes
in Canada**

**Dainius J. Dalmotas
Jean Hurley
Alan German**
Transport Canada
Canada

Kennerly Digges
George Washington University
USA

Preprint

Paper Number 96-S1-O-05

**Fifteenth International Technical Conference
on the Enhanced Safety of Vehicles
Melbourne, Australia,
May 13–16, 1996**

*Don't look for the above study on Transport Canada's website. It's not there.
Other supporting studies can be accessed from NHTSA at*
www.nhtsa.dot.gov/esv/search.html *or at the* lemonaidcars.com *websites.*

Transport Canada covered up the above-mentioned research findings because they contradict the government's contention that airbags are intrinsically safe and injuries are caused by drivers' failing to buckle up. On the contrary, recent fatalities show that even depowered airbags (phased in some vehicles since 1997) are killers and that women in particular are still at risk.

As I fit together all the recent accident reports and emergency-room studies, it's obvious that for over two decades engineers, automakers, and government bureaucrats have lied to us about airbag dangers. Instead of the promised billowing protective cloud that would gently cushion us in an accident, we discover that the airbag's 330 km/h deployment is more like a Mike Tyson right cross. Front airbags have killed 158 people, 92 of them children, in low-speed collisions or otherwise survivable accidents since 1990. All these deaths came from accidents with speeds as slow as 11 to 12 km/h, and three-quarters of the adults killed were women. Seven of the first 28 recorded deaths involved 1994–96 Chrysler minivans.

Sexist federal regulations governing automobile airbag design are the main reason why the safety devices put women, children, and the aged at risk. Consider this: while Canadian legislators were asleep at the switch in the late '80s, the American auto industry, government engineers, and public safety groups lobbied for airbags that would deploy with sufficient strength to protect an average-sized 5'8", 172-pound unbelted man in a 30 mph frontal crash. Meeting that rule requires that the airbag inflate with sufficient force to kill or seriously injure anyone not fitting the engineering norm.

If our government in Ottawa had rejected these regulations a decade ago, Karol Steinhouse would be alive today. Last March as Karol waited at a stoplight in Toronto, her 2000 Acura Integra was nudged from behind and her front bumper hit the car in front of her. Her airbag exploded, rupturing her aorta. She bled to death at the scene of the accident. Following her death, the supervisor of traffic safety and training for the Canada Safety Council commented, "really short people should not have airbags in their cars."

What a dumb, insensitive statement. Short, tall, big, or small, motorists cannot order new vehicles without airbags.

A campaign of misinformation
North America's safety "establishment," composed of government, automakers, and safety advocates, hasn't levelled with the public about airbag dangers inherent in the 60 million airbag-equipped vehicles found on U.S. and Canadian highways. For example, their admonition that children under the age of 13 should sit in the rear is nonsense, since it's a question of size, not age (a small 18-year-old could be more vulnerable). Actually, no one who is of small stature, child or adult, should sit behind an airbag, unless they can put at least 25 centimetres between their body and the airbag. The government also hasn't explained why airbags are of little benefit to seniors 70 and older, and why there have been more than 25,000 injuries resulting from airbag deployment between 1988 and 1991 recorded by NHTSA. There have also been thousands of incidences of airbag malfunctions—causing late deployment or inadvertent deployment—reported to American federal safety regulators, resulting in the recalls of millions of vehicles (1 out of every 30 on the road) since 1993.

Federal regulators' efforts to explain away airbag hazards have been a deliberate policy decision: they didn't want to lose their own credibility, alarm the public, or undermine the acceptance of airbags as a supplementary restraint. Well, guess what? The public is more than alarmed; in fact, it's clamouring for retrofitted cut-off switches and looking for new vehicles equipped with depowered airbags. Recent surveys show that the public's confidence in airbags has plummeted from 82 to 57 percent following the spate of news stories reporting airbag-induced deaths and injuries.

Inadvertent airbag deployment
Airbags frequently go off for no apparent reason due to what Ralph Hoar, a Virginia-based safety adviser to plaintiffs' attorneys, blames on "cheap sensors." Other causes of inadvertent deployment: passing over a bump in the road in your GM Cavalier or Sunfire, slamming the car

door, having wet carpets in your Cadillac or, in some Chrysler minivans, simply putting the key in the ignition. This happens more often than you would imagine, judging by the frequent recalls and thousands of complaints recorded on NHTSA's website at *www.nhtsa.dot.gov/cars/problems/complain/compmmy1.cfm.* Incidentally, insurers are refusing to pay for car damage or airbag replacements unless there has been a collision. Automakers deny responsibility on the grounds that the vehicle collided with "something." In the end, the driver is faced with a hefty repair bill and no means of proving the automaker's liability.

Airbag deployment—for no apparent reason—is bad enough if the vehicle is parked. However, if it explodes while the vehicle is being driven, it will likely cause an accident and then be of no use during the ensuing impact, as it has already deflated. Says Michael Leshner, a U.S. forensic engineer, "The airbag knocks them silly. Then they have an accident."

THE WALL STREET JOURNAL FRIDAY, APRIL 9, 1999

Side Air Bags Coming Under Scrutiny
For Potential to Hurt Kids in Back Seat

By ANNA WILDE MATHEWS
Staff Reporter of THE WALL STREET JOURNAL

WASHINGTON — Federal regulators have expressed concern that three auto manufacturers' side air bags may deploy with enough force to injure children sitting in the back seat.

The National Highway Traffic Safety Administration believes that, based on test results, side air-bag systems provided by Audi, Mercedes and BMW may be too powerful for the rear seat, where childr— supposed to sit, according + iar with the matt— known +— '

vices, which are an optional feature, in the rear seats of model year 2000 cars. Buyers will have the choice to turn them back on, the spokesman said. Previously, cars were shipped with the rear side air bags activated, and customers could request that they be turned off.

A spokesman for Merce— of **DaimlerChrys**— concern—

Automakers are rushing side airbags into production without fully evaluating their danger to children and small adults. Frankly, I wish manufacturers would prioritize the redesign of head restraints to make them more effective and install safety glass in side windows to reduce occupant ejection and head trauma.

Side airbags

Side airbags are designed to protect drivers and passengers in side-impact crashes, estimated to account for 30 percent of vehicular deaths. About three-quarters of automakers offer them on some of their models. Unfortunately, because side airbags aren't required by federal regulation in the States or in Canada, neither government has developed any tests to measure their safety to children and small adults.

Yet, preliminary safety studies show side airbags may be killers to children or any occupant not sitting in the correct position. Research carried out in 1998 by safety researchers Anil Khadikar (Biodynamics Engineering Inc.) and Lonney Pauls (Springwater Micro Data Systems), "Assessment of Injury Protection Performance of Side Impact Airbags," show there are four hazards that have yet to be addressed by automakers. They are:

1. Inadvertent airbag firing (short circuit, faulty hardware, or software)
2. Unnecessary firing (sometimes opposite side airbag will fire; airbag may deploy when a low-speed side-swipe wouldn't have endangered occupant safety)
3. A 3-year-old restrained in a booster seat could be seriously injured
4. Out-of-position restrained occupant could be seriously injured

The researchers conclude with the following observation: "Even properly restrained vehicle occupants can have their upper or lower extremities in harm's way in the path of an exploding [side] airbag."

The above study and dozens of other scientific papers confirm that small and tall restrained drivers face death or severe injury from frontal and side airbag deployments for the simple reason that they are outside of the norm of the 5-foot-8 172-pound, male test dummy. These studies also debunk the safety merits of ABS, so it's no surprise they go unheralded by Transport Canada and other government and private safety groups. You can find them at: *www.nhtsa.dot.gov/esv/*. Also, if you'd like to see a government video showing a side airbag's devastating effect upon a child dummy, go to the following web page and click on Real NHTSA Video: *www.nhtsa.dot.gov/nhtsa/announce/press/ca101499.html.*

In the meantime, let's heed the NHTSA's side airbag warning issued on October 14, 1999:

> Side impact air bags can provide significant supplemental safety benefits to adults in side impact crashes. However, children who are seated in close proximity to a side airbag may be at risk of serious or fatal injury, especially if the child's head, neck, or chest is in close proximity to the airbag at the time of deployment...

NHTSA has confirmed that rear side airbag systems offered by Audi, BMW, and Mercedes may be too powerful for rear seat occupants—notably children who must sit in the back to escape the deployment dangers of front seat airbags. Following these findings, BMW has turned off the rear airbags prior to delivery, although it offers owners the option of having them reconnected by the dealer.

Protect yourself
You should take the following steps to lessen the danger from airbag deployment:
• Don't buy a vehicle with side airbags until the federal government comes up with standards.

- Make sure that seatbelts are buckled and all head restraints are properly adjusted (at about ear level).
- Make sure the Insurance Institute for Highway Safety rates the head restraints as "good."
- Insist that passengers who are frail, short, or have recently had surgery sit in the back.
- Make sure that the driver's seat can be adjusted for height and has tracks with sufficient rearward travel to allow short drivers to remain a safe distance away from the bag's deployment and still reach the accelerator and brake. Buy pedal extensions, if needed.
- Have a retrofitted cut-off switch installed by a dealer for your make of vehicle. Canadian federal motor vehicle safety regulations don't require the installation of airbags in motor vehicles. However, because the airbag is an integral part of the vehicle restraint system, provincial statutes in Nova Scotia, P.E.I., New Brunswick, and Alberta may make airbag deactivation or removal illegal, unless there are mitigating circumstances or Transport Canada permission has been obtained.
- Buy a vehicle that comes with passenger-side airbag disablers.
- Buy a vehicle that uses sensors to detect the presence of an electronically tagged child safety seat in the passenger seat, and disable the airbag for that seat (already used in the Mercedes SLK).
- If you are of short stature, consider the purchase of aftermarket pedal extensions from auto parts retailers or optional adjustable accelerator and brake pedals from Ford to keep you a safe distance away from a deploying airbag.
- If you feel at risk and live near the American border, you may have your airbag deactivated by an American dealer or independent garage, following factory-approved guidelines (in some cases, it may involve simply removing a fuse). An extensive listing of garages willing to perform this service is available from NHTSA's website found in the Appendix. Cost: about $100 (U.S.). Keep in mind, however, that you may be violating provincial statutes. On the other hand, inspectors can't easily check for compliance, and penalties for deactivation are practically nonexistent.

NHTSA's 25 mph barrier test promulgated in Washington, D.C., last April is much better than the 30-mph test in that it should lead to less powerful deployments and fewer driver injuries from fender-bender accidents and inadvertent deployment. There is still a problem with the millions of vehicles equipped with full-strength airbags already on our roads and the high cost of airbag on-off switches needed to make these vehicles safe for small-statured drivers, seniors, and children. Although the U.S. government maintains to install these switches should cost between $38–$63 U.S. each, real world experience shows most car owners are charged $200–$300 each.

Childproof locks
Especially important in sport-utility vehicles, minivans, and vans, child-proof locks consist of a special control that the driver can trip to prevent the rear doors from being unlocked from the inside while the vehicle is in motion. They offer extra safety and convenience.

Child restraint systems
Every year, car accidents in Canada kill almost 70 youngsters under age five and injure another 4,000. The tragedy of this statistic is that parents ignore it; half of the children riding in vehicles still aren't properly secured compared to the 87 percent of adults who wear seatbelts. Seventy percent of these deaths and injuries could have been prevented if children had been properly belted into a safety seat. In recognition of this fact, safety authorities and the courts are cracking down on negligent parents. Provinces with seatbelt laws now require that children, especially infants, travel in an approved safety seat. Drivers who don't protect young passengers may face criminal charges or be held liable for civil damages if a youngster is injured or killed.

Contrary to popular belief, carrying young children on laps in a moving vehicle is not safe. A 9 kg (20 lb.) child will be pulled away with a force of over 270 kg (600 lb.) in a 48 km/h crash. Accident studies show that unrestrained adults can crush their children against the dashboard during a crash. Even in a relatively minor accident or panic stop, a child can be pulled away with surprising force and hit the dashboard or the floor hard enough to be seriously injured or killed.

There are three types of safety seats for children: infant-only carriers for newborns up to about 9 kg (20 lb.) or 69 cm (27 in.) in height; convertible carriers for children from birth up to 18 kg (40 lb.) or 1.02m (40 in.) in height; and booster seats for kids weighing between 18 and 27 kg (40–60 lb.). If you're not sure which seat fits your child's weight and height, check the Transport Canada compliance label affixed to the seat.

There are two sizes of infant carriers—those that are designed only for infants weighing up to 7.9 kg (17 lb.) and others that can handle up to 9 kg (20 lb.). Infant carriers often do double-duty as rockers and baby feeders. The typical carrier is lined with soft padding, has an internal safety harness, and is anchored by the vehicle's safety belt in the rear seat. Extra padding (a rolled-up towel or baby blanket) can be added between the legs or on the sides as long as it's not placed under the harness straps. The baby faces backwards in a semi-reclining position. In an accident, the baby's back absorbs the crash forces rather than its delicate chest and abdomen. These rear-facing infant safety seats should never be used in the front seat of a vehicle equipped with a passenger-side airbag, unless the airbag has a disabler. The force of the airbag inflating is the equivalent of being hit by a vehicle travelling 320 kilometres per hour (200 mph). Put the carrier in the rear outboard seats.

Forward-facing seats are anchored to the vehicle's frame by a tether strap, and they too should always be used in the rear seat. The U.S.

Department of Transportation estimates that 80 percent of all child safety seats are improperly secured, so take the extra care needed to make sure that the seat is installed properly. Convertible models are bulky and much less portable than infant seats, but they can be used for a much longer time. Chrysler's built-in child safety seats are an innovative optional safety feature patented by Ontario-based Magna International Ltd., and are now offered by many other automakers. They're convenient to use and may spare you the expense of a convertible or booster seat. Since they can't be faced to the rear, don't use them to carry infants.

A booster seat bridges the gap between a forward-facing seat and the vehicle's standard seatbelt. It consists of a firm cushion that incorporates its own restraining system, which ensures the lap belt doesn't ride up. Instead, the belt fits snugly over the child's lap and the shoulder harness doesn't touch the neck. Remember, booster seats designed for use around the house cannot protect your child in a collision.

Booster seats are needed for children weighing 40–60 pounds, roughly ages four to eight, as they are too big for baby car seats and too small for adult seatbelts. You can discontinue use of the booster seat when the child's height or weight exceeds the compliance label's limits. Safety experts and physicians recommend booster seats be installed in the rear seat, a location considered one-third safer for children. But the problem with this is that if you own a vehicle made before 1988, you won't likely have a rear-seat shoulder belt essential for the proper installation of a booster seat.

As children outgrow the safety seat, well-meaning parents are tempted to strap them in with seatbelts, bypassing the use of a booster seat—producing tragic results. According to a study published in the June 2000 edition of *Pediatrics*, the medical Journal of the American Academy of Pediatrics, less than 1 percent of children older than age five use booster seats, significantly increasing their risk of death and serious injury.

> This inappropriate [seatbelt] restraint resulted in a 3.5-fold increased risk of significant injury and a more than fourfold increased risk of significant head injury for the 2- to 5-year-olds studied, say the report's authors. These injuries were mostly caused by the child "submarining" or sliding out of the lapbelt during a crash. Rapid, jackknife bending about a poorly positioned vehicle seatbelt increases the risk of intra-abdominal and spinal cord injuries, also known as seatbelt syndrome, and brain injury resulting from the impact of the head with the child's knees or the vehicle interior...

NHTSA says 85 percent of child safety seats may be incorrectly installed. In an attempt to ensure the seats are safely installed, in September 1999, the federal government forced automakers to phase into production a new seat design to make latching the seats much easier.

Called Isofix, the new car seats will have metal bars mounted between the vehicle's rear seatback and cushion. Latches on the child safety seat will snap onto the bars. Phase one required that forward-facing child safety seats have a redesigned top-tether system that limits forward motion. Phase two, starting in September 2000, requires that 20 percent of all passenger cars have an improved lower mounting system, and that by 2002, all vehicles are so equipped.

Some vehicles that already have the redesigned top and lower mounts are the Ford Windstar and Focus, Chrysler PT Cruiser, Volvo V70 wagon, and VW New Beetle, Golf, Jetta, and Cabriolet. 2001 GM and Chrysler minivans are expected to adopt the safer seats this fall.

A variety of child safety seats can be rented from hospitals and provincial safety groups. If you decide to purchase one, be sure to ask the retailer for a registration card. The card will enable the manufacturer to notify you of a recall that you otherwise might not learn about.

Ergonomics

One of the new catchphrases used in rating vehicles is "ergonomics." Simply put, it means making the vehicle's interior user-friendly. For example, can you reach the controls you'll need without strain, or without taking your eyes off the road? Are the controls just as easy to operate by feel as they are by sight? Can rear-seat passengers enter or exit without becoming contortionists, as is the case with many two-door sport-utility vehicles?

To answer these questions, you need to drive the vehicle over a period of time to test how well it responds to the diversity of your driving needs. If this can't be done, you may find out too late that the climate control system keeps you cold in the winter and hot in the summer, or that the handling is more truck-like than you'd wanted. But you can conduct the following showroom test. Adjust the seat to a comfortable setting, buckle up, and settle in. Can you sit a foot away from the steering wheel and still reach the accelerator and brake pedals? When you look out the windshield and use the rear- and side-view mirrors, do you detect any serious blind spots? Will optional mirrors give you an unobstructed view? Does the seat feel comfortable enough for long trips? Can you reach important controls without moving off the seatback? If so, then your vehicle has been ergonomically designed. If not, shop for something that better suits your requirements.

Head restraints

Offered as a standard feature on all front and some rear seats, the main function of head restraints is to prevent neck whiplash injuries during a rear collision when the impact forces snap your head back. Whiplash injuries are not only literally a pain in the neck, they're affecting younger, female drivers more than ever before. According to a 1999 joint study carried out by IIHS and State Farm insurance (yep, the same insurance company fined for refusing claims in the United States), over a quarter of accident claims involve neck injury. The study also revealed that in mid-sized vehicle accidents women have more neck injuries than men (30 percent versus 23 percent) and, surprisingly, drivers 65 years and older had lower neck injury rates than younger drivers.

Whiplash injuries are also closely related to head restraint design. Your vehicle's head restraints may be either fixed or adjustable. Fixed restraints are preferred, but adjustable ones are acceptable as long as they're adjusted high enough (at ear level). Make sure that rear visibility isn't obstructed by the front or rear restraints. The State Farm study showed that drivers struck in the rear in cars with head restraints rated "Good" by IIHS are 24 percent less likely to sustain neck trauma than drivers using head restraints rated "Poor." Unfortunately, 70 percent of head restraints are rated "Poor" by IIHS; only three percent are rated "Good." Current ratings can be found at the IIHS website: *www.highwaysafety. org/vehicle_ratings/head_restraints/head.htm.*

Seats and seatbacks
Seat anchorages have to conform to government load regulations, but the regulations are so minimal that seats can easily collapse or tear loose from their anchorages, leaving drivers and passengers vulnerable in accidents. NHTSA's complaint database is replete with instances in which occupants report severe injuries caused by collapsing seatbacks that have injured front seat occupants or crushed children in safety seats placed in the rear seat.

Seatbelts
Apart from airbags, seatbelts provide the best means of reducing the severity of injury arising from both low- and high-speed frontal collisions. In order to be effective, however, seatbelts must be adjusted properly and feel comfortably tight without undue slack. Unfortunately, this is not always the case, and seatbelts rank high in customer complaints: they don't retract enough for a snug fit, are too tight, chafe the neck, and don't properly fit children. Some automakers have corrected these problems with adjustable shoulder-belt anchors that allow both tall and short drivers to raise or lower the belt for a snug, more comfortable fit. Another important seatbelt innovation is front seatbelt pretensioners, devices that automatically tighten the safety belt in the event of a crash. They are offered only as original equipment on a limited number of vehicles and must be replaced once deployed.

Crashworthiness (size matters)
All things being equal, a heavier vehicle—except for compacts and mid-size sport-utilities—will fare better in a crash than a light one. GM's recent two-car crash tests dramatically confirm this fact. Its engineers concluded that if two cars collide, and one weighs half as much as the other, the driver in the lighter car is ten times as likely to be killed as is the driver in the heavier one.

NHTSA says GM's Cavalier and Sunfire give average driver protection in frontal collisions, but score poorly in protecting side front- and side-rear seat passengers.

Washington-based IIHS says that vehicles in the mid-size and large car class are far safer than smaller ones when crashed at 65 km/h (40 mph)— 8 km/h (5 mph) more than in government tests. The IIHS figures show that the fatality rate for the occupants in a small car is roughly twice that of a mid-size car, and three times as high as a big car. What's the cutoff point? A wheelbase of at least 105 inches. Vehicles with wheelbases of 105 inches or more have 1.4 or fewer deaths per 10,000 registered vehicles, while those with 104-inch wheelbases or less have 2.1 or more deaths for the same number of registered vehicles.

The IIHS and NHTSA crashworthiness ratings don't usually differ all that much. However, there are some other factors that can skew both groups' scores: size, height, and frame rail placement, for example. If your Ford Taurus (five-star rating) is clobbered by a Dodge Durango 4X4 (two stars), chances are you'll fare much worse than the sport-utility's occupants simply because it's so much heavier (15,792 kg vs. 2,148 kg) and may ride over the Taurus' protective frame. On the other hand, some small vehicles are designed better than larger ones to absorb crash forces. VW's New Beetle is a good example. It's one of the few small cars to win a "good" crash rating from IIHS, while a handful of sport-utilities and even some Cadillacs don't do as well. Other factors include whether or not occupants are wearing seatbelts, and airbag and head restraint design.

Owners of imports that haven't been crash-tested in the States or Canada may access the Federation internationale de l'automobile website (*www.fia.com*) for European crash test scores. Interestingly, the crash data is posted in English, although the website is clearly oriented to the French driver.

Choosing an Inexpensive Vehicle

Know your warranty

There's a big difference between warranty promises and warranty performance. All major automakers offer bumper-to-bumper warranties good for the first 3 years/60,000 kilometres. It's becoming an industry standard for car companies to also pay for roadside assistance, a loaner car, or hotel accommodations if your vehicle breaks down under warranty while you're away from home.

Luxury makes like Lincoln and Cadillac and South Korean automakers are using more comprehensive 5- and 10-year warranties as important marketing tools to give their cars a luxury cachet or allay buyers' fears of poor quality/reliability. But, like the performance ads you see on TV, what you think you see isn't always what you get. For example, bumper-to-bumper coverage usually excludes tires (GM vehicles are an exception in that they allow you to claim a refund through the dealer), stereo components, brake pads and rotors, clutch disks, and many other expensive components. Furthermore, Canadian warranties aren't always honoured in the United States. To really know what the warranty covers on your vehicle, you have to read the fine print. Chrysler, for example, offers a fairly comprehensive powertrain warranty, but major items are excluded and Chrysler is very tightfisted in the interpretation of its obligations (exemplified by its frequent refusal to pay air conditioning, ABS brakes, automatic transmission, and paint delamination claims, or put many of its "goodwill" programs in writing). Ford has made considerable progress in facing up to its warranty and post-warranty obligations and treating its customers responsibly during the last six months. The company has publicly extended its engine and automatic transmission goodwill warranties up to 7 years or 160,000 km, and energized its customer assistance centres by hiring staffers as Ford employees. GM also has extended engine goodwill warranties on Cavaliers, Sunfires, and Saturns, but the company still remains saddled with sub-par customer relations and a "What, me worry?" attitude that has already cost the automaker almost half its market share.

Look for "secret" warranties

Automobile manufacturers are reluctant to publicize their secret warranty programs because they feel that such publicity would weaken consumer confidence in their products and increase their legal liability. The closest they come to an admission is to send out a "goodwill policy," "special policy," or "product update" letter or service bulletin for first owners' or dealers' eyes only. These bulletins admit liability and propose free repairs for defects running the gamut from fishy-smelling headliners on Chrysler sport-utilities and minivans to engine failures on Chrysler, Ford, and GM cars and minivans (see Part Two for a summary of current goodwill programs).

When faced with repairs for what is clearly a factory mistake, the only motorists who get compensated are the ones who yell the loudest or threaten to go to small claims court. Uninformed customers who hesitate to complain are forced to pay for the same repairs.

If you're refused compensation, keep in mind that secret warranty extensions are, first and foremost, an admission of manufacturing negligence. You can usually find them in dealer service bulletins that are sent out weekly by automakers through on-line updates or mail. Your bottom-line position should be to accept a pro-rata adjustment from the manufacturer, whereby you share a third of the repair costs with the dealer and automaker. If polite negotiations fail, challenge the refusal in court on the grounds that you should not be penalized for failing to make a reimbursement claim under a secret warranty that you never knew existed!

Getting all your vehicle's service bulletins

Free summaries of automotive recalls and technical service bulletins are listed by year, make, model, and engine can be found at the ALL-DATA (*www.alldata.com/consumer/TSB/yr.html*) and NHTSA websites. Like the NHTSA summaries, ALLDATA's summaries are so short and cryptic, they're of limited usefulness. You can't see the contents of individual bulletins unless you purchase for about $30 (U.S.) a CD-ROM that holds all the bulletins that pertain to your vehicle. Considering that many vehicles have over three hundred bulletins, the ALLDATA fee is a real bargain.

2000 Chrysler 300M, Concorde, Intrepid, and LHS
Technical Service Bulletins

Number	Date	Name
19-03-00	Jun 00	Loose steering
23-20-00	May 00	Body Mounted Door Opening Weatherstrip Loose
07-01-00	Mar 00	Cold off-idle engine growl sounds
24-02-00	Mar 00	A/C and Heater Performance Complaints
08-08-00	Mar 00	Inoperative or Intermittent Keyless Entry Transmitter
23-07-00	Feb 00	Wind noise
08-02-00	Feb 00	Headlamp Welt Service
23-02-00	Feb 00	Internal Emergency Trunk Release
02-01-00	Feb 00	Squeaking Noise Coming From Front Strut(s)
863	Feb 00	Safety Recall #863 - Stop Sale Order
866	Feb 00	Recall 866 Shoulder Belt Height Adjuster Bolt
19-01-00	Jan 00	Steering Gear/Front Suspension Rattle
857	Jan 00	Customer Satisfaction Notification No. 857 - Reprogram PCM
858	Jan 00	Safety Recall No. 858 - Passenger Airbag Module
02-16-99	Dec 99	Vehicle Leads or Pulls
23-54-99	Dec 99	Flag Speaker Screw Contacts Door Seal
08-40-99	Dec 99	Window Motor Service
08-37-99	Nov 99	Airbag On/Off Switches
21-17-99	Oct 99	Reduced Differential Fill Level
22-04-99	Oct 99	Steering Wheel Vibration
08-26-99	Aug 99	Erroneous Heated Seat Switch Missing/Shorted to Ground
08-14-99	May 99	Vehicle Start and Stall or Vehicle No Start

These Chryslers and the GM Saturn have an inordinate number of service bulletins issued to correct 2000 model defects. Interestingly, GM's Cavalier and Sunfire and Ford's Taurus, Sable and Windstar have fewer bulletins this year, hopefully indicating improved quality control.

Service bulletins are great guides for warranty inspections (especially the final one) and they're useful in helping you decide when it's best to trade in your car. They're written by automakers in "mechanic-speak" because service managers relate better to them that way, and manufacturers can't weasel out of their obligations by claiming that they never wrote such a bulletin.

If your vehicle is out of warranty, show these bulletins to less expensive independent garage mechanics, so they can quickly find the trouble and order the most recent *upgraded* part, ensuring that you don't replace one defective component with another.

Because these bulletins are sent out by U.S. automakers, Canadian service managers and automakers may deny, at first, that they even exist (are you listening, Honda and Nissan?). However, when they're shown a copy they usually find the appropriate Canadian part number or bulletin in their files. The problem and its solution doesn't change from one side of the border to another. Imagine American and Canadian

tourists being towed across the border because each country's technical bulletins were different. Mechanical fixes do differ in cases where a
bulletin is for California only, or relates to a safety or emissions component used only in the U.S. But these instances are rare indeed.

The best way to get bulletin-related repairs carried out is to visit the
dealer's service bay and attach the specific service bulletin covering
your vehicle's problems to a work order. If you're refused help:

• Fax the automaker in Canada a copy of the bulletin and ask for the
  appropriate kit or upgraded part number for Canada.

• If the dealer and automaker say that Canadians are excluded, ask why
  Canadians don't have the same rights as Americans.

• Complain to Transport Canada and your provincial consumer affairs
  department about being refused corrective repairs that are given routinely to American customers.

• Finally, you could visit an American dealer to have the repair carried
  out during a regularly scheduled vacation trip. Once back in Canada,
  you can sue the Canadian automaker and its dealer for your costs
  (including ALLDATA bulletin costs) in small claims court, because
  they gave you the runaround in the first place.

Fuel economy fantasies
Fuel economy figures are published by Natural Resources Canada (a
free copy of its Fuel Consumption Guide can be obtained by calling
1-800-387-2000 or accessing *autosmart.nrcan.gc.ca/home*) and are based
on data supplied by the automakers who follow U.S. Environmental
Protection Administration testing guidelines. These figures can be off
by 10 to 20 percent depending on the testing method chosen. In fact,
a recent Ford bulletin warns dealers that "very few people will drive in
a way that is identical to the EPA tests…. These [fuel economy] numbers are the result of test procedures that were originally developed to
test emissions, not fuel economy."

If you never quite got the hang of metric fuel economy measure-
ments (like me), use the fuel conversion table that follows to establish
how many miles to a gallon of gas your vehicle provides.

Fuel Economy Conversion Table					
L/100 km	m.p.g.	L/100 km	m.p.g.	L/100 km	m.p.g.
5.0	56	7.4	38	12.5	23
5.2	54	7.6	37	13.0	22
5.4	52	7.8	36	13.5	21
5.6	50	8.0	35	14.0	20
5.8	48	8.5	33	15.0	19
6.0	47	9.0	31	15.0	18
6.2	46	9.5	30	17.0	17
6.4	44	10.0	28	18.0	16
6.7	43	10.5	27	19.0	15
6.8	42	11.0	26	20.0	14
7.0	40	11.5	25	21.0	13
7.2	39	12.0	24	23.0	12

A handy metric conversion Internet site for weight, capacity, volume, length, area, speed, pressure, temperature, circular measure, and time, can be found at www.ur.ru/nsg/trans/. *Click on the unit and the conversion is done automatically.*

Insurance costs

Insurance costs can vary between $500 and $5,000 per year, depending on the type of vehicle you own and your personal statistics and driving habits. Multi-purpose vehicles are usually classed in the high-risk category (accident and theft) and therefore usually cost more than passenger cars to insure.

Now that banks are getting into the insurance business, they're heating up the competition by offering lower premium payments through independent agents whom they use as go-betweens. The Canadian Imperial Bank of Commerce, for example, says that it offers low insurance premiums by selling directly to the Ontario public, avoiding the 10–12 percent commission that most insurance brokers charge.

Insured depreciation savings

High depreciation losses can be avoided during the first few years by purchasing insurance coverage for an extra $25 a year that will give you the actual purchase price of the vehicle and its equipment. Depreciation charges are limited by a special endorsement on the automobile policy called "Removing Depreciation Deduction" (OPCF43). With this policy rider the insurance company won't charge depreciation within the time specified (usually 24 months). So, if you have an accident, you are refunded the amount you originally paid in addition to all sales taxes—or the Manufacturer's Suggested Retail Price (MSRP) at the time of purchase, whichever amount is lower.

This endorsement can save you thousands of dollars during the first few years if your vehicle is written off in an accident. Unfortunately, few motorists are aware that this cheap extra protection is available. Since

these endorsements change periodically and coverage cost may fluctuate, contact your local insurance broker or the Insurance Bureau of
Canada (1-800-387-2880) for the latest details.

The dealer network

A weak dealer network drives up maintenance costs, adds to a vehicle's
downtime, and makes it difficult for you to go elsewhere when servicing is poor. Also, the more sophisticated and complicated a vehicle's
engineering and the farther away its manufacturing plant, the more
important it is to have strong dealer service support. Ford Aerostar and
GM Astro and Safari minivans, for example, use mostly old truck technology and so can often be repaired anywhere using parts from independent suppliers. The more complicated VW EuroVan, on the other
hand, is severely handicapped by a lack of extensive dealer support.

Sometimes good parts availability exists within a weak dealer network. This occurs when a vehicle has sold quite well or has been on the
market for a long time with few changes, thereby creating a good supply of replacement parts and creating a reservoir of experienced independent mechanics (common with European makes).

Parts and service

Parts for imports are generally no more expensive than parts sold by
the major American automakers. But when it comes to captive imports,
some American automakers have been known to charge twice as much
for the same part sold by their Japanese partners.

Here are two tips that may help cut the high cost of repair parts:
• Try to find good quality rebuilt parts whenever possible. Generally,
  rebuilt parts cost anywhere from one-third to one-half the price of
  new parts and last just as long. A vehicle has to be on the market for
  at least two years before rebuilt or remanufactured parts become
  available in sufficient quantities.
• Before authorizing non-warranty repairs at an independent shop, ask
  the mechanic to compare the parts prices charged by different manufacturers selling the same basic vehicle. For example, a Tracker part
  may be cheaper at a Suzuki dealership under the Sidekick name than
  one bought from General Motors.

Even when parts costs aren't deliberately "boosted" by American car
manufacturers, prices are unacceptably high. For example, according
to the Alliance of American Insurers, the price of original-equipment
replacement parts needed to rebuild a vehicle is about 2.5 times the
original retail price. In an annual study, a 1999 Ford Taurus SE retailing for $25,000 was rebuilt with Ford-supplied replacement parts. Total
cost? More than $72,000 for the parts alone. No labour was included in
the estimate.

Consumers have found that automakers are more interested in sales
than in ensuring that their dealers give honest, competent service. In

fact, I can't recall a single occasion where an automaker terminated a dealership's franchise because of odometer tampering or other dishonest dealings, yet the RCMP reports dozens of odometer fraud convictions every year.

A vehicle can incorporate the best engineering in the world, but it will quickly deteriorate and fall into the lemon category if the servicing is lousy, a problem more acute with vehicles that are new on the market, part of a recent acquisition, like Ford Jaguars and GM Saabs, and with South Korean imports. American manufacturers are generally weak in service support—General Motors is the best example of this deficiency. Its own records show that 70 percent of its customers switch to other repair outlets when their vehicle warranty expires.

Servicing among European importers has much improved, although customers still complain about the abrasive, arrogant attitude typified by some German and Swedish automakers and dealer service outlets. Fortunately, a rather large network of less expensive, independent mechanics who service European imports has sprung up across the country.

Check servicing costs and the quality of repairs with owners who drive similar models, fleet administrators, and rental car counter attendants. They'll be glad to tell you about servicing problems they've encountered. Be sure to question consumer protection groups about which vehicles generate the most complaints and what mechanical components are the most failure-prone and covered by secret warranties. Owner comments found on the Internet (see Appendix), service bulletin summaries from ALLDATA, owners' groups listed in collectors' publications, and car buff magazines are also helpful in giving you a picture of the overall reliability, parts availability, servicing, and price range for specific models.

Finding a Reliable Vehicle

American or Esperanto?

A lot of controversy surrounds the relative quality control of North American and imported vehicles. Before deciding which manufacturer provides the best quality, forget all the popular mythology about what is made in North America and what is "foreign" made. The seesaw value of the dollar and the yen has led to a rush of foreign and American automakers moving production facilities to the U.S., Canada, and Mexico. Surprisingly, this has been accomplished without a corresponding drop in quality control. J.D. Power and Associates for example, have rated Toyota's Corolla assembly plant in Cambridge, Ontario, as the highest quality production facility in North America.

Despite their improvements over the past several years, American vehicles still don't measure up to the Japanese in quality and technology, especially when it comes to engines, transmissions, brakes, body construction, and paint quality. Take brake rotors, for example. Over the past decade,

American automakers have downsized their brake rotors, causing the following problems: rotors, which once lasted an average of 3 years or 60,000 km, now may last only a third as long; the smaller, thinner rotors fail to dissipate heat and therefore soon warp, producing brake vibration or pulsation within the first year or 20,000 km (sometimes, much sooner than that). Adding to the expense, repairers can't resurface the disk because the disks are too thin to begin with, and, therefore, the entire unit has to be replaced at a cost of $400 or more. Automakers routinely try to blame the problem on maintenance, but owners who stand fast usually get the repair done the first time free of charge.

Japanese vehicles aren't made better or more quickly because of robotics or overworked, low-salaried workers, as American automakers would like us to believe. Actually, American production costs are now lower than what the Japanese and Europeans pay at home. High manufacturing costs in Japan and Europe (due mostly to high taxes and workers' benefits) are forcing European and Japanese automakers to locate plants in Canada and the U.S., where skilled workers are plentiful. The real reasons for the poor quality of American cars are the automakers' blind price-cutting at the expense of quality, and their preference for style over substance. For the past three decades, Chrysler, Ford, and GM has been telling us they can produce cars that can compete directly with the Japanese and Europeans.

But they can't.

In fact, importers are setting up their own factories in North America and building high quality cars in Canada, the United States, and Mexico with indigenous workers.

Proof positive poor quality isn't a worker thing.

Consider this: GM's Saturn division was started up almost a decade ago to prove to the world that GM could make high-quality small cars. Unfortunately, GM's advertising hype was the best part of the car, which quickly gained a reputation for overall poor reliability and biodegradable engine head gaskets (covered by a "goodwill" warranty).

Next year GM is powering its Saturns with Honda engines.

European quality varies

Motorists' complaints, dealer service bulletins, and auto association membership surveys, like those sent out by CAA, confirm that the quality of European vehicles like Audi, BMW, Volvo, and VW remains quite high, while other European automakers like Saab and Jaguar produce vehicles of lesser quality.

Most European automakers are breaking sales records due to their cars' impressive driving performance and comfort. Volkswagen and Audi have become top sellers by dramatically improving the quality of their vehicles over the past few years, offering comprehensive warranties, and holding the line on prices in the mid-range. In comparison, Japanese imports are too pricey and American cars don't perform as well. Luxury and sports car importers, like BMW and Porsche, have also made a remarkable comeback through price cuts and inexpensive new products, and in BMW's case, selling its money-losing Rover acquisition. Unfortunately, what these companies give they also take away—the last few years have seen steep price increases by both Audi and VW.

Other Buying Considerations

Front-wheel drive

Front-wheel drives direct engine power to the front wheels, which pull the vehicle forward while the rear wheels simply support the rear. The biggest benefit of front-wheel drive (FWD) is foul weather traction. With the engine and transmission up front there's lots of extra weight pressing down on the front-drive wheels, increasing tire grip in snow and on wet pavement. But when you drive up a steep hill or tow a boat or trailer the weight shifts, and you lose the traction advantage.

Although I recommend a number of FWD vehicles in this guide, I don't like them as much as rear-drives. Granted, front-drives provide a bit more interior room (no transmission hump), more car-like handling, and better fuel economy than do rear-drives, but damage from potholes and fender-benders is usually more extensive, and maintenance costs (especially premature front tire and brake wear) are much higher than with rear-drives.

Servicing front-wheel drives can be a real nightmare—and a walletbuster. Entire steering, suspension, and drivetrain assemblies have to be replaced when only one component is defective. Downtime is considerable, the cost of parts is far too high, and the drivetrain and its components aren't designed for the do-it-yourself mechanic. A new FWD transmission assembly (called a transaxle) can cost about $2,000 to repair, compared to $700 for a rear-drive transmission. And having to make such a repair isn't that remote a possibility, particularly if you own a 1989–96 Chrysler minivan or a Ford Taurus or Sable.

Accident repairs are a unique problem. Front-wheel-drive transmissions and steering and suspension components are easily damaged, and alignment difficulties abound. Repair shops need expensive, specialized equipment to align all four wheels and square up a badly smashed unibody chassis—and even if you manage to get all four wheels tracking true, the clutch and transaxle can still be misaligned. No wonder many insurance companies prefer to write off an FWD car rather than repair it. And when that happens, you wind up eating the difference between what you paid for the vehicle and what the insurance company says your vehicle is worth—minus your deductible, of course.

Rear-wheel drive

Rear-drives direct engine power to the rear wheels, which push the vehicle forward. The front wheels steer and also support the front of the vehicle. With the engine up front, the transmission in the middle, and the drive axle in the rear, there's plenty of room for larger and more durable drivetrain components. This makes for less crash damage, lower maintenance costs, and higher towing capacities than front-drives.

On the other hand, rear-drives don't have as much weight over the rear wheels as do the front-drives (no, putting concrete blocks in the bed or trunk will only void your transmission warranty), and therefore they can't provide as much traction on wet and icy roads unless they're equipped with an expensive traction-control system.

Finally, rear-drives are scarcer than hens' teeth, so much of the foregoing dissertation may be of little practical value if all you have to pick from are front-wheel drives.

Four-wheel drive

Four-wheel drives direct engine power through a transfer case to all four wheels, which *pull* and *push* the vehicle forward, giving you twice as much traction. The system is activated with either a floor-mounted shift lever or a dashboard button. When the 4X4 drive isn't engaged, the vehicle is essentially a rear-drive truck. The large transfer case housing makes the vehicle sit higher, giving you additional ground clearance. The most fuel-efficient systems disengage the four-wheel drive when extra traction isn't needed. Rear-drives, though, have some of the highest payload and towing capabilities, usually slightly higher than four-wheel drives.

Encouraged by the popularity of 4X4 vehicles in North America, many automakers now offer optional four-wheel drive or all-wheel drive (AWD) on their more moderately priced family sedans, pickups, and minivans—at jacked-up prices. Nevertheless, despite reports of high repair costs, low rust resistance, fragile mechanical components, and government studies that show poor crashworthiness and an increased risk of rollover accidents, 4X4 and AWD sport-utilities, pickups, and vans are hotter than ever.

All-wheel drive

Essentially, this is four-wheel drive all the time. Used mostly in minivans, AWD never needs to be deactivated when running over dry pavement and doesn't require a heavy transfer case (although some sport-utilities and pickups do use a special transfer case) that raises ground clearance and cuts fuel economy. AWD-equipped vehicles aren't recommended for off-roading because of their lower ground clearance and their fragile driveline parts that aren't as rugged as four-wheel drive components.

Diesel power

Diesel engines become more efficient, and gasoline engines less so, as the engine load increases. This is the main reason why diesels are best used when the driving cycle includes a lot of city driving, with its slow speeds, frequent stops, and long idling times. At full throttle, both engines are essentially equal from a fuel-efficiency standpoint. The gasoline engine, however, leaves the diesel in the dust when it comes to high-speed performance.

Electric cars: plug and pray

Electric cars have been around for nearly 170 years. In fact, Thomas Davenport, a Brandon, Vermont, blacksmith, built the first battery-powered, self-contained electric vehicle in North America in the early 1830s. In 1893, Canadian patent attorney Frederick Featherstonhaugh took delivery of our country's first electric vehicle, built in John Dixon's Toronto carriage shop by English electrician William Sill. It was later exhibited that year at Toronto's Canadian National Exhibition.

Since those early years, electric-car popularity has waned due to the obvious advantages of gasoline-powered vehicles. There has been some renewed interest during the past three decades, spurred on by restricted fuel supplies, high prices, and government legislation (mostly from California). But this alternative hasn't really caught on with the average motorist, particularly in view of the electric car's short driving range, large, heavy, expensive batteries, cramped interior, and safety deficiencies (electrical fires were commonplace).

Now automakers are looking to hybrid vehicles like the Toyota Prius and Honda Insight that use an engine/electric motor for maximum fuel economy and low emissions while providing the driving range of a comparable small car. Yet, this latest iteration of the electric car still has serious drawbacks that compromise its future.

The hybrid cars' battery components such as lead and cadmium can be toxic to the environment, safety in crashes is not assured, price isn't competitive, reliability and repairs may be problematic, and interior room is cramped. Hybrid cars are usually lighter than their non-hybrid predecessors—the Honda Insight is 1,645 lb. less—though some hybrids, like the Toyota Prius, may be heavier (302 lb. more). This could put them at a safety disadvantage if hit by a larger vehicle.

Be wary of electric car rentals. Some rental agencies in the States, will rent you an electrically powered car for about $49–$89 (about what a medium-sized SUV would cost) a day compared with about $30 a day for a gasoline-powered Cavalier. First off you'll notice a confusing array of buttons scattered around the driver's console where numbered keypads abound. You'll need to do some careful planning for any trip longer than a simple commute, since charging stations are scarce. Put into your schedule a four- to five-hour wait for each battery recharge. And remember, most electric cars have a theoretical 193-kilometre range before recharge, but hilly terrain can cut that range by a third, unless you stay between 90–100 km/h (55–60 mph), coast downhill, and use the car's "regenerative braking" (a generator helps recharge the battery while slowing the car).

Surviving the Options Jungle

Dealers make three times as much profit selling options as they do selling most cars (50 percent vs. 15 percent). No wonder their eyes light up when you start perusing their options list. If you must have some options, compare prices with independent retailers and buy where the price is lowest and the warranty is the most comprehensive. Buy as few options as possible from the dealer, since you'll get faster service, more comprehensive guarantees, and lower prices from independent suppliers. Remember, extravagantly equipped vehicles hurt your pocketbook in three ways: they cost more to begin with, they cost more to maintain, and they often consume extra fuel.

Before buying options separately, consider getting a vehicle in a higher trimline or in a "special edition" format, where the options package includes what you want for a lower price. Another possibility is "value pricing," where automakers like GM will offer a package of options on a bare-bones model. Whichever choice you make, don't buy any unnecessary options if the total cost of the package exceeds what you'd pay for the options if purchased separately.

A heavy-duty battery and suspension and perhaps an upgraded sound system will generally suffice for American-made vehicles; most imports already come well equipped. An engine block heater with a timer isn't a bad idea, either. It's an inexpensive investment that ensures winter starting and reduces fuel consumption by allowing you to start out with a semi-warm engine. Factory installed in-line heaters are usually more efficient and durable.

It's hard to buy and even harder to lease a new vehicle that isn't loaded with unnecessary options. This is particularly evident with medium-size vehicles and minivans. If you're unsure as to what optional equipment like sound systems and anti-theft devices should cost, shop around and compare prices with independent suppliers like J.C. Whitney. Their mail-order parts catalogue can be ordered by calling 312-431-6102 (Visa and Mastercard accepted).

Smart Options

Adjustable pedals and extensions
Offered with the Ford Taurus, Sable, Expedition, Navigator, and Windstar, this device moves the brake and accelerator pedals forwards or backwards about four inches. This is an excellent safety feature that reduces the dangers of airbag deployment for short-statured drivers. If the manufacturer of your vehicle doesn't offer optional power-adjustable pedals, there are several companies selling inexpensive pedal extensions by mail order through the Internet; go to *stores.yahoo.com/hdsmn/pedex.html.* If you live in the Toronto or London, Ontario, check out *www.kinomobility.com.* A *Lemon-Aid* reader sent back this report:

> Kino is located in midtown Toronto, just west of the Allan Expressway at 1140 Sheppard Ave. West, Unit 3, Toronto M3K 2A2; tel: 416-635-5873: fax: 416-635-5910; toll free: 1-888-495-4455; contact person is Garry Ladner. There is also an outlet in London,

Ontario. They have a showroom in the front and what seems to be the working area in the rear, opening garage-like to a rear roadway. I was given some excellent tips as to how to improve some of my problems, i.e. get a seatbelt clip at Canadian Tire to stop the belt rubbing my neck, use a wedge shaped cushion instead of the one I have so there would not be so much pressure on the underthigh... and they are all working. However, the cost for the extensions and slight raising of the car floor would be between $250 and $350. I must say he took good 20 minutes checking my posture, knee height in relation to hips, etc. before he made the recommendations...

Air conditioning

Whether or not you choose air conditioning should depend more on where you live and your comfort requirements than on saving money. Just like buying an underpowered car to save on fuel costs and then regretting its poor performance, your savings will be the last thing on your mind when you're sweltering in your vehicle some summer day.

Air conditioning costs between $800 and $1,650, plus a $100 federal excise tax, and may reduce fuel economy by as much as 10 percent in stop-and-go traffic. At highway speeds, air conditioning increases fuel consumption by 3 to 4 percent. It provides extra comfort, reduces wind noise from not having to roll down the windows, and improves window defogging. But because air conditioning units aren't used year-round, they're failure-prone (expect repairs of about $1,000 around the 5-year mark), easy prey for premature corrosion, and an excellent incubator for airborne bacteria and allergens. If you must have air conditioning, opt for a factory-installed unit. You'll get a longer warranty and reduce the chance that other mechanical components will be damaged during installation.

Anti-theft systems

Car break-ins and thefts cost Canadians more than $400 million annually, meaning that there's a 1 in 130 chance that your car will be stolen and only a 60 percent chance that you'll ever get it back. It's no wonder that over one-third of new vehicles are equipped with standard or optional alarms, with a clear preference for fuel cut-off devices and electronic alarms among the four main types of security systems: active and passive units either armed by the driver or are self-arming, ignition disablers, parts identification, and security keys.

Some automakers have more effective standard alarm systems than others. The Canadian Crime Prevention Bureau, for example, recently singled out Volkswagen for praise after its new anti-theft devices and car-parts marking resulted in a 75 percent drop in VW thefts.

The most effective theft-deterrent systems aren't always the most expensive ones. Don't waste your money on costly anti-theft devices that depend solely upon your car's horn or lights to scare thieves away. They often go off at the wrong time and can be easily deactivated.

Furthermore, they frighten the thief away only after the vehicle has
been damaged. When it comes to stealing your car's contents, no alarm
system can resist a brick through a side window. It takes just twelve minutes for thieves to strip a car seat, radio, and body parts, and few citi-
zens are brave enough to personally stop a theft or testify in court.

Since most cars are stolen by amateurs, the best theft deterrent is a
visible device that complicates the job while immobilizing the vehicle
and sounding an alarm. For less than $150, you can install both a steer-
ing wheel lock and a hidden remote-controlled ignition disabler. These
clublike devices cost between $50 and $75, and deter thieves by forcing
them to carry a hacksaw and adding about a half-minute to the time it
takes to steal the average car or make off with the airbag (they have to
cut through the steering wheel or bust the lock). Ignition disablers are
also inexpensive and very effective. They sell for $30–$90, depending
on their sophistication.

Battery (heavy-duty)
The best battery for northern climates is the optional heavy-duty type
offered by many manufacturers for about $80. It's a worthwhile pur-
chase, especially for vehicles equipped with lots of electrical options.
Most standard batteries last only two winters; heavy-duty batteries give
you an extra year or two for about 20 percent more.

Block heater
A block heater is an inexpensive investment at about $75. Factory-
installed in-line models are effective and durable. Cheaper ($40
installed) dipstick or freeze plug models are not recommended.

Cellular telephone
This is a recommended option mainly because it provides a greater
degree of safety for drivers stuck on the side of the road or threatened
by smash-and-grab artists. Buy the cheapest hands-free model available
from an independent retailer.

Cellular phones can be expensive to operate due to the high rates
charged by the phone companies to "carry" calls. Because calls are billed
by the minute and according to the distance the caller or receiver is
from a given site, charges can vary from $30–$75+ a month for a sales
agent who uses it extensively. This is in addition to $50–$150 for the
phone itself. The temptation to use the car phone for nonessential calls
is also hard to resist, and expensive in the long run. And remember
that what's said on a cellular phone can be heard by anyone.

Three independent studies have shown that car phones are a safety
hazard. Drivers whose attention is distracted while talking on a cellular
telephone have four times as high a risk of having an accident, says a
recent University of Toronto study of 699 car crashes reported in the
February 1997 issue of *The New England Journal of Medicine*. That's about
the same risk as driving while intoxicated.

Drivers using hands-free phones were just as likely as people holding a receiver to be involved in an accident while on the phone or shortly after having used it. The American Automobile Association Foundation for Traffic Safety says that a road hazard is 20 to 30 percent more likely to go unnoticed by someone using a car phone than by a driver who gives full attention to driving. This warning is buttressed by another study done at the Rochester Institute of Technology in Rochester, New York, which found that drivers with cellular phones installed in their vehicles run a 34 percent greater risk of having an accident than other motorists.

Legislation is inevitable. Already thirteen countries, including England, Germany, and Japan, have prohibited the use of hand-held cell phones by drivers.

If the possibility of crashing into someone isn't scary enough, how about cellular phones that are real heart-stoppers? The U.S. government is looking into allegations that people with heart pacemakers implanted in their chests may experience pacemaker malfunctions as a result of their cell phones. Safety researchers say that if the phone is placed in close proximity to the chest it may cause the pacemaker to stop, restart, or recalibrate itself. The problem is more apparent with the new digital cellular phones than with the older analog models.

One last thing: cellular phones aren't particularly efficient in placing emergency calls through the 911 exchange. Rather than going to a central dispatch centre where the caller's location is indicated on-screen, cell phone calls are often routed to other, distant places where staffers may be unfamiliar with the area from which the call originates.

Central locking control

Costing around $200, this option is most useful for families with small children, car-poolers, or drivers of pickups, minivans, and vans who can't easily slide across the seat to lock the other doors. Look for a remote feature that provides automatic locking and then unlocking when the inside door handle is pulled.

Child safety seat (integrated)

One of the best child safety innovations to come along in decades, integrated safety seats are designed to accommodate any child more than one year old or weighing over 9.09 kilograms (20 lb.). Since it's permanently integrated into the seatback, it takes the fuss out of installing and removing the safety seat and finding some place to store it. When not in use, it quickly folds away out of sight, becoming part of the seatback. Two other safety benefits: you know the seat has been properly installed (which is not the case with 80 percent of the bolt-ons), and your child gets used to having his or her "special" seat in back where it's safest to sit.

Courtesy lights

This option permits the car's lights to stay on a few seconds after the doors are closed. This is particularly convenient when entering your home if the only outside source of illumination is your car's headlights. Another variation is having the interior lights come on when you pull the door handle. This should allay your fear that someone is lurking in the back seat.

Engines

Choose the most powerful 6- or 8-cylinder engine available if you're going to be doing a lot of highway driving, plan to carry a full passenger load and luggage on a regular basis, or intend to load up the vehicle with convenience features like air conditioning. Keep in mind that multipurpose vehicles with larger engines are easier to resell and retain their value the longest. For example, Honda's '96 Odyssey minivan was a sales dud despite its bulletproof reliability, mainly because buyers didn't want a minivan with an underpowered 4-cylinder powerplant. Some people underpower their vehicles in the mistaken belief that increased fuel economy is a good trade-off for decreased engine performance. It isn't.

Engine and transmission cooling system (heavy-duty)

This relatively inexpensive option provides extra cooling for the transmission and engine. It can extend the life of these components by preventing overheating when heavy towing is required.

Extended warranties

A waste of money for vehicles recommended in *Lemon-Aid*, or vehicles sold by automakers that have written goodwill warranties extending the parameters for engine and transmission durability (Ford and GM) to 7 years/ 100,000 km. If you can get a great price for a vehicle rated just Acceptable, but want to protect yourself from costly repair bills, by all means buy an extended warranty. Remember, though, these warranties carry a high markup and you should bargain down the cost accordingly.

HOW CAN WE OFFER SUCH GOOD COVERAGE AT THIS LOW PRICE? IT'S SIMPLE!!! A CAR DEALER CAN GET AS MUCH AS 60% COMMISSION OR AS MUCH AS $240 ON A $400 WARRANTY, WHICH MEANS THAT ONLY $160.00 OF THE TOTAL COST ACTUALLY IF FOR THE PURCHASE OF THE WARRANTY. AT WARRANTY ACCEPTANCE CORPORATION, WE AVOID THOSE MARKUPS AND PASS THE SAVINGS TO YOU – OUR CUSTOMERS.
THIS MAKES SENSE – DON'T YOU AGREE?

This independent warranty company confirms that much of the warranty's cost is pure profit for the seller—in this case 60 percent.

Keyless entry (remote)

A safety and convenience option. You don't need to fiddle with the key in a dark parking lot or take off a glove in cold weather to unlock/lock the vehicle. Try to get a keyless entry system combined with anti-theft measures that include an ignition kill-switch or some other disabler.

Mirror options

Power mirrors are particularly convenient on vehicles that have a number of drivers, or on large sedans and wagons, minivans, vans, or trucks.

Navigation aids

Both GM and Ford offer an optional navigation aid, called OnStar and RESCU respectively, which links a GPS satellite unit to the vehicle's cellular phone and electronics. For a monthly fee of about $25, GM's OnStar unit connects Cadillac drivers to live operators who will help them with driving directions, give repair or emergency assistance, or relay messages. And if the airbag deploys or the car is stolen, satellite-transmitted signals are automatically sent from the car to operators who will notify the proper authorities of the vehicle's location.

Paint colour

Choosing a popular colour can make your vehicle easier to sell at a good price. J.D. Power recommends metallic silver, but adds that black, white, blue, and green are also popular with car buyers.

Power-assisted windows and seats

Merely a convenience feature with cars, power-assisted windows and seats are a necessity with minivans—crawling across the front seat a few times to roll up the passenger-side window or to lock the doors will quickly convince you of their value. Power seats with memory are particularly useful if more than one person drives the vehicle. Automatic window and seat controls currently have few reliability problems, and they're fairly inexpensive to install, troubleshoot, and repair.

Running boards

Rather than returning you to '50s styling, running boards are practically essential for climbing into some minivans. They can be purchased from independent suppliers for $65–$200, which is much less than the $500–$700 charged by some automakers.

Seats

Make sure the driver's seat has sufficient rearward travel to keep you out of harm's way (about a foot) should the airbag deploy. Also look for a height adjustment so that you can still see over the hood as the seat is pushed rearward. Make sure the head restraints are properly adjusted and don't block your rear vision. Finally, rent the vehicle overnight to determine if the seats are comfortable after an hour or two of driving.

Keep in mind that an uncomfortable seat is one of the most frequent complaints heard from new-car buyers.

Sound system

Remember when it was just called a radio?

Three criteria must be considered when buying a sound system: your overall budget, the make of car, and the kind of music that's likely to be played. A simple AM/FM stereo radio with a stereo cassette tape player is sold by GM for less than $500, but most independent after-market stores can easily beat GM's price. Sophisticated, personalized car stereos may cost between $500 and $1,000, and hi-fi fanatics can spend between $2,000 and $9,000 for a "total sound system" that'll likely get ripped off shortly after leaving the showroom. In addition to getting the best quality sound for the cheapest price, the stereo buyer should look for features that make it easy and safe to operate—for example, radios that automatically seek out stations and cassette decks with automatic reverse, play, and eject.

In budgeting for a stereo sound system, allocate half the money for the speakers. Pare down the scores of available features to what's essential, like a strong FM receiver (under two decibels), separate controls for treble and bass, auto reverse, and a key-auto-eject to protect the tape when the ignition is turned on and off.

Factory-installed speakers are usually lousy performers, and options are outrageously priced by automakers. For example, an after-market CD player priced at $400 would cost about $1,200 if installed by the factory or dealer. Dealers often say that only the factory's original equipment can overcome electrical interference or provide the appropriate sound for a vehicle's particular interior configuration. This is baloney.

There are, however, some advantages to having a factory-installed sound system. It's usually guaranteed for a much longer period than an independently installed unit, and the dealer is better equipped than a retailer to remove, ship, and reinstall it. A factory unit will also be more cosmetically attractive and less prone to rattle because it fits better when mounted in the dash and door panels.

Once a stereo system has been purchased, it must be protected from theft. Experts recommend the installation of a slider box for about $80–$100. It's the size of a textbook and connects the cassette player and radio to the car's wiring when pushed into place. When the car is parked, the box and unit stereo can be removed from the vehicle.

CD players

Sales of car CD players exceed a million units annually, including at least 140 separate models. Mail-order discount houses offer them for less than $300. Improved vibration dampening has made the players impervious to potholes. Look for:
- repeat functions that allow you to select a mixture of tracks or repeat a particular track;
- anti-theft features that include removing the faceplate or unit; and

• single-slot CD changers offered by a few automakers (Ford, Acura, Subaru, and Volkswagen). These changers do away with glovebox- or trunk-mounted devices and flimsy plastic trays.

Suspension (heavy-duty)
Always a good idea, this inexpensive option pays for itself by providing better handling, additional ride comfort (though a bit on the firm side), and extending shock life an extra year or two.

Tires
There are three rules to remember when purchasing tires. First, neither brand nor price is a reliable gauge of performance, quality, and durability. Second, choosing a tire recommended by the automaker may not be in your best interest, since traction and long tread life are often sacrificed for a softer ride and maximum EPA mileage ratings. And third, don't buy any new tire that's older than two years, since the rubber compound may have deteriorated due to poor handling and improper storage (near electrical motors). You can check the date of manufacture on the sidewall.

There are two types of tires: all-season and performance. Touring is just a fancier name for all-season tires. All-season radial tires cost between $90 and $150. They're a compromise, since according to Transport Canada they won't get you through winter with the same margin of safety as will snow tires, and they don't provide the same durability on dry surfaces as do regular summer tires. In low to moderate snowfall areas, however, these tires are adequate as long as they're not pushed beyond their limits.

Mud or snow tires provide the best traction on snowy surfaces, but traction on wet roads is actually decreased. Tread wear is also accelerated by the use of softer rubber compounds. Beware of using wide tires for winter driving; 70-series or wider give poor traction and tend to "float" over snow. Consumers report good performance with Nokia Hakkapellitas snow tires imported from Finland.

Performance tires have a low sidewall profile and a wider and shallower tread. They give good wet and dry traction, but perform poorly on snow and ice. They also wear quickly and tend to give a hard ride. Remember, some sports cars can't be fitted with snow tires unless the rims are changed or a more expensive brand is chosen.

It's a good idea to purchase tires that provide a road hazard warranty. Under the terms of this guarantee, the tire dealer or manufacturer will provide compensation for any tire that's found to be defective. Also, don't pay full list for any tire; just as with cars, prices may vary by as much as 40 percent among retailers. Make sure, though, that the price includes mounting and balancing. Tire dealers are the best place to find a wide selection of tire brands, models, and sizes, and their salespeople are usually more knowledgeable than they are at dealerships, discount houses, or gas stations. Mail-order tire distributors are also quite price competitive and will often deliver your tires to the garage of your choice within a few days of purchase.

Spare tires
Be wary of space-saver spare tires. They often can't match the promised mileage and seriously degrade steering control. Furthermore, they are usually stored in spaces inside the trunk that won't hold a normal sized tire. Where the spare is stored can also have safety implications. Watch out for spares stowed under the chassis or mounted on the rear hatch on some sport-utilities. Frequently, the attaching cables and bolts rust out or freeze permitting the spare to fall off or making it next to impossible to access when needed.

Self-sealing tires
A good idea if you don't mind spending from $130–$200 per tire. Uniroyal has introduced its NailGuard tire, available in over 22 different sizes, that can seal up to a 5 mm puncture once the puncturing object has been removed. Remember, self-sealing tires generally don't perform well in wet snow and slush.

Which tires are best?
There is no independent Canadian agency that evaluates tire performance and durability. However, NHTSA, a Washington-based government agency, rates tread wear, traction, and resistance to sustained high temperatures. It posts its findings on the Internet (just enter "NHTSA" after locating the Alta Vista search engine). The tread wear grade is fixed at a base 100 points and the tire's wear rate is measured after the tire is driven through a course that approximates most driving conditions. A tire rated 300 will last three times as long as one rated 100.

I've come up with the following tire ratings after researching government tests, consumer comments, and industry insiders.

Dunlop D65 and D60 A2: Treadware rated 520, this tire is the bargain of the group. It corners well and provides excellent wet braking and good steering response. Cost: $146 list; sells for $100.
Goodrich Comp T/A HR4: Treadwear rated 360, this tire excels at cornering and is bargain priced at $120.
Goodyear Aquatred: Treadware rated 340, this tire is a bit noisy and its higher-rolling resistance cuts fuel economy. Still, it's an exceptional performer on wet roads, and works especially well on front-drive cars where the weight is over the front tires. Average performance on dry pavement. Costs about $130; no discounts.
Goodyear Regatta: Treadware rated 460, this $100 tire does everything well, including keeping tire noise to a minimum.

Michelin MX4: Treadware rated 320, this tire gives a smoother ride and a sharper steering response than the Aquatred. Cost: $144 list; often discounted to $100.

Pirelli P300 and P400: Treadware rated 460 and 420, these are two of the best all-around performing all-season tires. Cost: $173 list; sells for about $120.

Yokohama Avid MD-H4: Treadware rated 300, this is another Aquatred knock-off that performs almost as well for half the price.

Other good tire choices: Goodrich Touring T/A HR4, Goodyear Eagle LS, and Pirelli P6000. Winter tires: Bridgestone Blizzak WS-15, Goodyear Ultra Grip Ice, Michelin Arctic Alpin, and Pirelli Winter Ice Assimmetrico.

The following tires aren't recommended: Bridgestone Potenza RE 92, Cooper Lifeline Classic II, all Firestone makes, Hydro 2000 and Ameri G4S, Goodyear Eagle GA and WeatherHandler, Goodrich Advantage, Michelin XGT H4, XW4, and MXV4 Green X, Pirelli P4000 Super Touring (not to be confused with the recommended P400), and the Toyo 800 Plus.

Trailer-towing equipment

Just because you need a vehicle with towing capability doesn't mean that you have to spend big bucks. The first thing you should do when choosing a towing option is determine if a pickup or small van will do the job and if your tires will handle the extra burden. For most towing needs (up to 900 kg or 2,000 lb.), a passenger vehicle, small pickup, or minivan will work just as well and cost much less than a full-size pickup or van. But if you're pulling a trailer that weighs more than 900 kg, most passenger vehicles won't handle the load, unless they've been specially outfitted according to the automaker's specifications. Pulling a trailer that weighs more (up to 1,800 kg or 4,000 lb.) will likely require a compact passenger van. A full-size van can handle up to 4,500 kg (10,000 lb.), and may be cheaper and more versatile than a multipurpose vehicle that would have to be equipped with a V8 engine and heavy-duty chassis components.

Automakers reserve the right to change limits whenever they feel like it, so make any sales promise an integral part of your contract (see "Misrepresentation" in Part Two). A good general rule is to reduce the promised tow rating by 20 percent. In assessing towing weight, consider the cargo, passengers, and equipment of both the trailer and the tow vehicle. Keep in mind that five people and their luggage add 450 kg (1,000 lb.) and that a full 227-litre (50-gallon) water tank adds another 225 kg (500 lb.) to the load. The manufacturer's gross vehicle weight rating (GVWR) takes into account the anticipated average cargo and supplies that your vehicle is likely to carry.

Automatic transmissions are fine for trailering, although there's a slight fuel penalty to pay. Manual transmissions tend to have greater clutch wear from towing than do automatic transmissions. Both transmission choices are equally acceptable if the driver is competent. Ford and Chevrolet/GMC give higher tow ratings to their trucks with automatics than to those with manual transmissions—they know that drivers tend to ride the clutch and generally mess up shifting with a manual. Remember, the best compromise is to shift the automatic manually for maximum performance going uphill, and to maintain control while not overheating the brakes when descending.

Unit-body vehicles (without a separate frame) can handle most trailering jobs as long as their limits aren't exceeded. Front-drives aren't the best choice for pulling heavy loads in excess of 900 kg since they lose some steering control and traction with all the weight concentrated in the rear.

Whatever vehicle you choose, keep in mind that the trailer hitch is crucial. It must have a tongue capacity of at least 10 percent of the trailer's weight, otherwise it may be unsafe to use. Hitches are chosen according to the type of tow vehicle and, to a lesser extent, the weight of the load. They fall into the following four classes depending on the weight they can pull:

- Class 1: loads up to 900 kg (2,000 lb.); hooked to the frame or rear bumper of most passenger cars, small pickups, and small vans.
- Class 2: loads up to 1,600 kg (3,500 lb.); attached to a car or MPV frame.
- Class 3: loads up to 3,400 kg (7,500 lb.); also attached to a car or MPV frame.
- Class 4: loads up to 4,500 kg (10,000 lb.); attached to a pickup or MPV frame or incorporated as fifth-wheel hitches used in the beds of large pickups.

Most hitches are factory installed, even though independents can put them on more cheaply. Expect to pay about $200 for a simple boat hitch and a minimum of $600 for a fifth-wheel version.

Equalizer bars and extra cooling systems for the radiator, transmission, engine oil, and steering are a prerequisite for towing anything heavier than 900 kg. Heavy-duty springs and brakes are a big help, too. Separate brakes for the trailer may be necessary to increase your vehicle's maximum towing capacity.

Transmissions: automatic, manual, 5-speed, and overdrive automatic
A transmission with four or more forward speeds is usually more fuel efficient than one with three forward speeds, and manual transmissions are usually more efficient than automatics, although this isn't always the case. Nevertheless, most motorists prefer to pay extra to have a transmission that shifts by itself, even though this convenience saps the performance of small engines, requires expensive repairs, and makes you less alert to driving conditions. This last point is particularly important, because a manual transmission makes you aware of the traffic flow and requires that you shift gears in anticipation of changes.

But, if you want a stick shift, you'd better act quickly. Aging knees, cheap gasoline, and the increasing popularity of cell phones have led automakers to curtail their production of stick shift–equipped cars. In fact, J.D. Power & Associates says the percentage of cars and light trucks with manual transmissions has dropped from 17.5 percent in the 1989 model year to 13.6 percent in 1997. Even sports cars have been affected—only 30 percent of GM's Corvettes are ordered with a manual transmission, Ford's Taurus SHO only comes with an automatic, and both the Porsche 911 and Ferrari F1 are clutchless. Industry experts predict that in the future, manual transmissions may only be offered in a small number of economy cars, trucks, and high-priced sports cars.

Dumb Options

Adjustable steering wheel
This option can be deadly in an airbag-equipped vehicle, since it can tilt the steering so that the deployed airbag could cause severe or fatal head and neck injuries. On the plus side, this option facilitates access to the driver's seat and permits a more comfortable driving position. It's particularly useful if more than one person will drive the vehicle.

Automatic level control
A useless option, unless you're planning to carry heavy loads or pull a trailer. It's expensive to repair and not easily adjusted.

Cruise control
Mainly a convenience feature, automakers provide this $250–$300 option to motorists who use their vehicles for long periods of high-speed driving. Some fuel is saved owing to the constant rate of speed, and driver fatigue is lessened during long trips. Still, the system is particularly failure-prone and expensive to repair, and it can lead to driver inattention and make the vehicle hard to control on icy roadways. Malfunctioning cruise control units are also one of the major causes of sudden acceleration incidents. At other times cruise control can be just plain annoying, as is the case with Chrysler's current crop, which often "hunt" for the right gear when traversing hilly terrain.

Electronic instrument read-out
If you've ever had trouble reading a digital-watch face or re-setting your VCR you'll feel right at home with this electronic gizmo. Gauges are presented in a series of moving digital patterns that are confusing, distracting, and unreadable in direct sunlight. It's often accompanied by a trip computer and a vehicle monitor that computes fuel use and kilometres to empty, indicates average speed, and signals component failures. Figures are frequently in error or slow to catch up.

Foglights
A pain in the eyes for other drivers, foglights aren't necessary for most drivers with well-aimed original-equipment headlights.

GPS navigation systems

Many of the systems are obtrusive, distracting, washed out in sunlight, and hard to calibrate by the passenger since controls are on the steering wheel (Volvo). Audi's system has no screen, has confusing controls, doesn't always give accurate read-outs, and uses an antenna that looks like a hockey puck glued to the trunk sill.

ID etching

This $150–$200 option is a scam. The government doesn't require it and thieves and joyriders aren't deterred by the etchings. If you want to etch your windows for your own peace of mind, several private companies will sell you a $15–$30 kit that does an excellent job (*www.autoetch.net*) or you can wait for your municipality or local police agency to conduct one of their periodic free VIN ID etching sessions in your locality.

Leather upholstery

An expensive option that's too hot in summer, too cold in winter, too slippery, and tough to clean or repair.

Night Vision

Cadillac's DeVille Night Vision uses an infrared camera to project the heat images of animals, pedestrians, and other cars on your windshield that may be just beyond the reach of your headlights. In theory, the $2000 option is a significant safety improvement. In practice, however, it's distracting, works poorly on twisting, mountainous roads, and presents a grainy, ill-defined image.

Paint and fabric protectors

Paint protectors sold by auto dealers aren't just overpriced—they also don't work. The auto industry's equivalent of the "Emperor's New Clothes," I wouldn't give two cents for paint protector products sold by auto dealers. This is said with the knowledge that Chrysler, Ford, and GM factory paint jobs have become less and less durable over the years. Selling for $200–$300, these "sealants" are a waste of money and add nothing to a vehicle's resale value. Although paint lustre may be temporarily heightened, this treatment is less effective and more costly than regular waxing, and may also invalidate the manufacturer's guarantee at a time when the automaker will look for any pretext at all to deny your paint claim.

According to tests carried out by the Consumers' Association of Canada and the Quebec Consumer Protection Bureau, waxing your vehicle regularly is a much better idea than investing in paint protectors. Certain waxes are better than others, as shown in CAC field tests; Nu Finish gave good paint protection for three to six months after each application and did very well in bringing out paint lustre. Surprisingly, Turtle Wax was one of the poorer performers in the CAC study.

Consumer Reports and the Canadian Automobile Protection Association believe that auto fabric protection products are nothing more than Scotchguard variations, which can be bought in aerosol cans for a few dollars, instead of the $50–$75 charged by dealers. Still, if you want someone else to do the spraying, offer the dealer half of what he asks. Even at that, he should make a small profit.

Power-assisted minivan sliding doors

Not a good idea if you carry children. These doors have a high failure rate: opening or closing for no apparent reason and injuring children caught between the door and post.

Radar detectors and "stealth" devices

Another product that targets van vacationers and sports car enthusiasts, radar detectors are a dumb idea for two reasons: they're illegal in most provinces and most U.S. states and, like so-called paint protectors, they aren't always effective. The newest wrinkle is an electronic "stealth" cloaking device that claims to generate a frequency that confuses police radar and laser guns. Mounted on the front end of the vehicle, the $400 (tax and installation included) device failed every test carried out by the *Vancouver Province*. Even if it were effective, motorists would have to buy one for the rear end as well since many laser guns are trained on vehicles after they've gone by.

Roof-top carrier

Although this inexpensive option provides additional baggage space and may allow you to meet all your driving needs with a smaller vehicle, a loaded roof rack can increase fuel consumption by as much as 5 percent. An empty rack cuts fuel economy by about 1 percent.

Rustproofing

The high profits earned from rustproofing cars (over 75 percent in some cases) encourage dealers to sell aftermarket rustproofing, even though automakers like GM and Nissan threaten to void the rust warranty if critical drain holes are plugged. Most automakers will reject all rust warranty claims where holes have been drilled into their cars by aftermarket rustproofers.

Nevertheless, rustproofing is no longer necessary now that the automakers have extended their own rust warranties. In fact, you have a greater chance of seeing your rustproofer go belly-up than having your untreated vehicle ravaged by premature rusting. Even if the rustproofer stays in business, you're likely to get a song and dance about why the warranty won't cover so-called internal rusting, or why repairs will be delayed until the sheet metal is actually rusted through.

If you live in an area where roads are heavily salted in winter, or in a coastal region, have your vehicle washed every few weeks and undercoated frequently—paying particular attention to rocker panels (door bottoms) and wheelwells. Also, keep your car away from a heated garage in winter; Canadian studies show that a heated garage will accelerate the damage caused by corrosion.

Sunroof
Unless you live in a temperate region, the advantages of a sunroof are far outweighed by its disadvantages. You're not going to get better ventilation than a good air conditioning system would provide, and you'll appreciate that your highway trips aren't accompanied by wind noises, water leaks, and road dust accumulation. Gas consumption is increased, night vision is reduced by overhead highway lights shining through the roof opening, and several inches of headroom can be lost, forcing tall drivers to adopt a hunched-over driving position. Flip-up styles are particularly leak-prone, while electronically controlled sliding sunroofs often fall prey to short circuits. And without a manual override, your car will be vulnerable to theft and the weather.

Factory installation of a sunroof is far more costly than having it done by an independent—$1,000 vs. $250, with little difference in the quality of the job or the warranty.

Tinted glass
Tinting jeopardizes your safety by reducing night vision. On the other hand, it does keep the interior cool in hot weather, reduces glare, and hides the car's contents from prying eyes. Factory applications are worth the extra cost because cheaper aftermarket products (costing about $100) distort visibility and peel away after a few years. Some tinting done in the U.S. can run afoul of provincial highway codes that require more transparency.

Wheels (aluminum)
Standard equipment on many sporty models, alloy wheels are optional on other cars ($150–$300). They're fragile, frequently leak, corrode easily, and aren't always compatible with snow tires. Unpainted wheels require regular cleaning with acetone and an annual coating with a protective clear spray.

Cutting the Price

Buy by Internet or fax—no more "showroom shakedown"

Even though most auto buyers use the Internet primarily for price and feature comparison shopping, many cybershoppers use the info to order directly off the Net. For example, of the 15.1 million new vehicles sold in 1998 in North America, 2 million were sold over the Internet. This figure isn't all that surprising when you consider that hundreds of Internet-based new-car shopping services (like Autobytel) have sprung up to channel customers to participating dealers. For a service fee, these firms encourage dealers to bid against each other for your business through electronic mail. In other cases, you can go directly to a number of dealer websites and initiate the bidding process on your own. So far, shoppers report impressive savings, particularly in regions where there aren't that many dealers and the local dealer has a "take it or leave it" attitude.

Encouraged by the success of these "shop by email" firms, automakers have begun to offer similar services guaranteeing low prices through specially selected dealers. Ford in Arizona and Ford Canada in Ontario have begun two pilot projects where customers can log on the automaker's website and get "e-price promise" prices. In Arizona, these prices are about 10 percent *below* Ford's own suggested retail prices (MSRP).

If you don't have a computer or aren't Internet-savvy, don't despair. You can get the same results by using a fax machine. Simply fax an invitation (a cover letter with your company logo would help) for bids to area dealerships, asking them to give their bottom-line price for a specific make and model and clearly stating that all final bids must be faxed within a week. Because no salesperson is acting as a commission-paid intermediary, the dealers' first bids are likely to start off a few hundred dollars less than advertised. When all the bids are received, the lowest bid is faxed to the other dealers to give them a chance to beat that price. After a week of bidding, the lowest price gets your business.

Dozens of *Lemon-Aid* readers have told me how effective buying by fax was in keeping the price down and preventing the showroom song-and-dance routine between the sales agent and sales manager ("he said, she said, they said").

Here's how one Downsview, Ontario, *Lemon-Aid* reader got the bidding started and subsequently paid 18 percent, or $1,995.47, less than the list price of a Nissan Sentra.

FAX TRANSMISSION
Date: November 30, 1994
To: Joe Blow Motors
Att: President

Dear Sir,
    I have decided to buy a new car. What and from whom I buy depends on the
responses to this fax.
    I have visited dealerships and have brochures for every car I am consider-
ing, and am sending this fax to other dealers. It is now a matter of finding the
best deal.
    I will buy either a Nissan Sentra, Honda Civic, Toyota Corolla, or Mazda
Protegé. I would like the base model, and the only options that interest me are
a full-size spare tire and a block heater. I will accept other features that are
already installed, but my decision is going to be based on price. I want a manual transmission, will take either two or four doors, and will accept any color.
I will pay by cheque and will not trade in my current car.
    Please fax me an offer. Include the price of the car, the price of all options,
PDI, freight, GST, PST, all surtaxes (fuel, etc.), your administration fee, and
the licence transfer fee. You should specify the total amount and include the
name of the person I should contact if I accept the offer.
    Today is November 30, 1994. I will make my selection at the end of the
business day on December 7th. When faxing your offer, please phone me first
at 555-1212 so I may connect my modem.
    I want to buy a car. Do you want to sell one?
    Awaiting your earliest convenient response, I remain

Sincerely,
Jane Customer

    Several hours after sending this fax, our reader got her first quote.
She also received additional bids by phone and mail, including one
dealer's promise to beat the lowest price offered. That dealer gave the
best price, drove the customer to his dealership, and sold the Sentra.

The myth of "no haggle" pricing
New cars and minivans have no "official" selling price, and most dealers will charge as much as the market will bear. If you let them, they'll
use any pretext they can to boost prices, including a "no dicker sticker"
policy. They'll pretend to have abandoned negotiated prices and high-
pressure sales tactics in favour of "no haggle prices," where they give
the buyer a better deal.
    Don't believe dealers who say they won't negotiate the MSRP. In
effect, all dealers bargain. They hang out the "NO DICKERING, ONE
PRICE ONLY" sign simply as a means to discourage customers from
asking for a better deal. Like parking lots and restaurants that claim
they won't be responsible for lost or stolen property, in the end they're

bluffing. Still, you'd be surprised by how many people believe that if it's posted, it's non-negotiable. Industry figures show that "no dicker" dealers average a 14 percent markup over their cost.

There are several price guidelines, however, and dealers use the one that will make the most profit on each transaction. Take, for example, the following experience one Vancouver shopper relates when he dealt with a major Chevrolet-Oldsmobile dealer in that city:

> Here's one to put in your "Things dealers do to sell cars" file (although you have probably seen this before): [this] Chev Olds [dealer] in Vancouver has been advertising that they are selling Chevrolet Ventures at one dollar below invoice plus freight (which is in fine print). Seeing this, I decided to go down and check out what they are doing to maintain their profit margin. They gladly show you the invoice, which I looked at and confirmed that it was the factory price (based on the APA dealer prices). However, the "invoice price" includes the $840 freight charge and the $100 air conditioning levy. Then they take a dollar off that price and add freight and the levy AGAIN. When I pointed this out to them he said that this was their profit margin (he was quite candid about it). So I said it was a bit of stretching the truth about "a dollar below invoice," why didn't they just advertise that they would sell the vehicle at $840 above invoice? And why did he want to charge me a second air conditioning levy? I didn't get a straight answer on that one, so I left shaking my head at the things dealers do to sell cars...!

Two of the more common prices quoted are the Manufacturer's Suggested Retail Price (what the carmaker advertises as a fair price) and the dealer's invoice cost, which is supposed to indicate how much the dealer paid for the vehicle. Both price indicators leave considerable room for the dealer's profit margin, along with some extra padding in the form of inflated transportation and preparation charges. If presented with both figures, go with the MSRP because it can be verified by calling the manufacturer. Any dealer can print up an invoice and swear to its veracity. If you want an invoice price from an independent source, contact Car Cost Canada (*carcostcanada.com*) at 1-800-805-2270.

Residents of rural and western Canada are often faced with car prices that are grossly inflated compared to those charged in major metropolitan areas. A good way to beat this scam without buying out of province is to buy a couple of out-of-town newspapers (the Saturday *Toronto Star* "Wheels" section is especially helpful) and demand that your dealer bring his selling price, preparation, and transportation fees into line with the costs as advertised.

Getting a Fair Price

What's the dealer's cut?

Most new-car salespeople are reluctant to give out information on the amount of profit figured into the cost of each new car, but a few years back *Automotive News* gave the following markups based on the Manufacturer's Suggested Retail Price (MSRP). These percentages may vary a bit from year to year, but they're fairly accurate.

Dealer Markup (American Vehicles)

small cars: 10–12%
mid-size cars: 15–18%
large cars: 20%
sports cars: 17–20%
high-end sports cars: 20+%
luxury cars: 25+%
high-end luxury cars: 20+%
minivans: 18+%
high-end minivans: 21+%
base pickups: 14+%
high-end pickups: 16+%
vans and sport-utility vehicles: 16+%
fully equipped, top-of-the-line vans and SUVs: 21+%

Dealer Markup (Japanese Vehicles)

small cars: 8–12%
midsize cars: 10–15%
large cars: 15–17%
sports cars: 15–17%
high-end sports cars: 18+%
luxury cars: 20%
high-end luxury cars: 20+%
minivans: 15+%
high-end minivans: 17+%
base pickups: 12+%
high-end pickups: 16+%
sport-utility vehicles: 15+%
fully equipped, top-of-the-line vans and SUVs: 18+%

2000 HONDA AUTOMOBILE PRICE LIST (Confidential)			
MODEL CODE	MODEL	DEALER NET (Exc. Taxes)	SUGGESTED RETAIL (Exc. Taxes)
EJ612YPB	CIVIC COUPE DX 5-SPEED	14,996	16,300
EJ622YPB	CIVIC COUPE DX 4-SPEED AUTO	15,916	17,300
EJ616YE	CIVIC COUPE DX-G 5-SPEED	16,376	17,800
EJ626YE	CIVIC COUPE DX-G 4-SPEED AUTO	17,292	18,800
EJ812YF	CIVIC COUPE SI 5-SPEED	17,368	18,900
EJ822YF	CIVIC COUPE SI 4-SPEED AUTO	18,308	18,900
EJ817YJ	CIVIC COUPE SI-G 5-SPEED	18,768	20,400
EJ827YJ	CIVIC COUPE SI-G 4-SPEED AUTO	19,688	21,400
EM115YJ	CIVIC COUPE SIR 5-SPEED	21,528	23,400
EJ632YB	CIVIC HATCHBACK CX 5-SPEED	13,299	14,300
EJ642YPB	CIVIC HATCHBACK CX 4-SPEED AUTO	14,415	15,500
EJ633YPB	CIVIC HATCHBACK DX 5-SPEED	14,229	15,300
EJ643YPB	CIVIC HATCHBACK DX 4-SPEED AUTO	15,159	16,300
EJ653YX	CIVIC SEDAN LX 5-SPEED	14,812	16,100
EJ663YX	CIVIC SEDAN LX 4-SPEED AUTO	15,782	17,100
EJ651YXV	CIVIC SEDAN SPECIAL EDITION 5-SPEED	15,717	16,900
EJ661YXV	CIVIC SEDAN SPECIAL EDITION 4-SPEED AUTO	16,647	17,900
EJ650YX	CIVIC SEDAN EX 5-SPEED	16,008	17,400
EJ660YX	CIVIC SEDAN EX 4-SPEED AUTO	16,928	18,400
EJ658YX	CIVIC SEDAN EX-G 5-SPEED	17,388	18,900
EJ668YX	CIVIC SEDAN EX-G 4-SPEED AUTO	18,308	19,900
CG314YPB	ACCORD COUPE LX 5-SPEED	21,777	23,800
CG324YPB	ACCORD COUPE LX 4-SPEED AUTO	22,692	24,800
CG315YJN	ACCORD COUPE EX LTH 5-SPEED	25,437	27,800
CG325YJN	ACCORD COUPE EX LTH 4-SPEED AUTO	26,352	28,800
CG225YJN	ACCORD COUPE EX V6 4-SPEED AUTO	28,640	31,300
CF854YPB	ACCORD SEDAN DX 5-SPEED	20,130	22,000
CF864YPB	ACCORD SEDAN DX 4-SPEED AUTO	21,045	23,000
CG554YE	ACCORD SEDAN LX ABS 5-SPEED	22,235	24,300
CG564YE	ACCORD SEDAN LX ABS 4-SPEED AUTO	23,150	25,300
CG556YJN	ACCORD SEDAN EX LTH 5-SPEED	25,437	27,800
CG566YJN	ACCORD SEDAN EX LTH 4-SPEED AUTO	25,352	28,800
CG165YJN	ACCORD SEDAN EX V6 LTH 4-SPEED AUTO	28,640	31,300
RL185YE	ODYSSEY LX-CAPTAIN AUTO	28,182	30,800
RL186YPK	ODYSSEY EX-CAPTAIN AUTO	30,927	33,800
BB614YJ	PRELUDE 5-SPEED	25,529	27,900
BB624YJ	PRELUDE 4-SPEED AUTO	26,444	28,900
BB615YJ	PRELUDE TYPE SH 5-SPEED	29,189	31,900
Issue Date:	September 1, 1999		

European vehicle markups are slightly lower than the markups charged by American dealers. In addition to the dealer's markup, some previous-year Big Three vehicles may also have a 3 percent carryover allowance paid out in a dealer incentive program.

Holdback

Ever wonder how dealers who advertise vehicles for "a hundred dollars over invoice" can make a profit? They are counting mostly upon the manufacturer's holdback.

In addition to the MSRP, the invoice price, dealer incentives, and customer rebates (available to Canadians from the *www.apa.org* website), another key element in every dealer's profit margin is the manufacturer's holdback—quarterly payouts dealers depend upon when calculating gross profit.

The holdback was set up almost 40 years ago by General Motors as a guaranteed profit for dealers tempted to bargain away their entire profit to make a sale. It usually represents 1–3 percent of the sticker price (MSRP) and is seldom given out by Asian or European automakers, who use dealer incentive programs instead. There are several free Internet sources for holdback information: the most recent and comprehensive are *www.edmunds.com* and *www.kelley.com,* two websites geared towards American buyers. Although there may be a difference in the holdback percentage between American automakers and their Canadian subsidiaries, it's usually not significant.

Some GM dealers maintain that they no longer get a holdback allowance. They are being disingenuous, I suspect, as the holdback has been added to their annual "incentive" programs, which won't show up on the dealer's invoice. Options are the icing on the cake, with their average 35–65 percent markup.

What's a fair price?
New-car negotiations aren't wrestling matches where you have to pin the sales agent's shoulders to the mat to win. If you feel that the overall price is fair, don't jeopardize the deal by giving no quarter. For example, if you've brought the contract price 10 percent or more below the MSRP and the dealer sticks you with a $200 "administrative fee" at the last moment, let it pass. You've saved money and the sales agent has saved face.

To come up with a fair price, subtract one-half the dealer markup from the MSRP and trade the carryover and holdback allowance for a reduced delivery and transportation fee. Compute the options separately and sell your trade-in privately. Buyers can more easily knock $1,000–$2,000 off a $20,000 base price if they wait until January or February when sales are stagnant, choose a vehicle in stock, and resist unnecessary options.

Once you and the dealer have settled on the vehicle's price, you aren't out of the woods yet. Like a tag-team wrestling match, you'll then be handed over to an F&I (financing and insurance) specialist, whose main goal is to convince you to buy additional financing, loan insurance, paint and seatcover protectors, rustproofing, and extended warranties. These items will be presented on a computer screen as costing only "a little bit more each month." Compare the dealer's insurance and financing charges with an independent agency that may offer better rates and better service. Often the dealer gets a kickback for selling insurance and financing, and guess who pays for it? Additionally, remember that if the financing rate looks too good to be true, you're probably paying too much for the vehicle. The F&I closer's hard-sell approach will take all your willpower and patience to resist, but when F&I gives up, your trials are over.

Add-on charges are the dealer's last chance to stick it to you before the contract is signed. Dealer preparation PDI and transportation charges, "documentation" fees, and extra handling costs are ways that the dealer gets extra profits for nothing. Dealer preparation is a once-over-lightly affair, with a car seldom getting more than a wash job and a couple of dollars of gas in the tank. It's paid for by the factory in most cases and, when it's not, should cost no more than 2 percent of the car's selling price. Reasonable transportation charges are acceptable, although dealers who claim that the manufacturer requires the payment often inflate them.

Dealer incentives and customer rebates

When vehicles are first introduced in the fall, they're generally over-priced. Later on, near the end of summer, automakers offer customer cash rebates of $750–$3,000, and increased dealer cash incentives for almost as much. Incentives are first offered during the winter months and boosted in late summer or early fall when dealer showroom traffic has fallen off. Smart shoppers who buy during these months can shave an additional 10 percent off a vehicle's list price by double-dipping from both of these automaker rebate programs.

In most cases, the manufacturer's rebate is straightforward and mailed directly to the buyer from the automaker. But there are other rebate programs that require a financial investment on the dealer's part. These shared programs tempt dealers to offset losses by inflating the selling price or pocketing the manufacturer's rebate. Therefore, when the dealer participates in the rebate program, demand that the rebate be deducted from the suggested selling price and not from some inflated invoice price concocted by the dealer.

Some rebate ads will include the phrase "from dealer inventory only." If your dealer doesn't have the vehicle in stock, you won't get the rebate. Keep in mind that the manufacturer's rebate is considered to be part of the fair value and is not deductible from the purchase price prior to determining the retail sales tax payable.

Sometimes automakers will suddenly decide that a rebate no longer applies to a specific model, even though their ads continue to include it. If this happens, take all brochures and advertisements showing your eligibility for the rebate plan to provincial consumer protection officials. They can use false advertising statutes to force automakers to give rebates to every purchaser who was unjustly denied one.

When buying a heavily discounted vehicle, be wary of "option packaging" by dealers who push unwanted protection packages (rust-proofing, paint sealants, and upholstery finishes) or levy excessive charges for preparation, filing fees, loan guarantee insurance, and credit life insurance.

Rebate savings

To come out ahead, you have to know how to play the rebate game. Customer and dealer incentives are frequently given out to stimulate sales of year-old models that are unpopular, scheduled to be redesigned, or headed for the axe. By choosing carefully which rebated models you buy, it's easy to achieve important savings with little downside risk. For example, GM's $1,000 incentive on its Cavalier and Sunfire models is a great deal on these inexpensive, slow-depreciating, well-equipped small cars that are also reasonably reliable. On the other hand, GM's Tahoe, Yukon, and Catera rebates ($1,500–$3,000) will barely cover these vehicles' poor fuel economy and high maintenance costs. The same can be said of Ford's $1,500–$2,000 rebates on the Taurus, Sable, Contour, and Mystique. These four vehicles have had serious reliability problems, and the Contour and Mystique were dropped last year.

False bargains, indeed.

Prevailing market value

Generally, vehicles are priced according to what the market will bear. Therefore, a vehicle's stylishness, scarcity, or general popularity can inflate its value considerably. For example, the Dodge Sebring convertible and Ford Explorer sport-utility have a prevailing market value that's higher than their suggested selling price, mainly because they're part of a hot market segment and in short supply. Once sales slow down later in the new year, popular vehicles will sell at a discount. A good general rule for vehicles that have a high prevailing market value is to wait for their popularity to subside, or to purchase the previous year's version. Don't try this with a Honda Accord or Toyota Camry, however. Their market value generally stays constant throughout the year. On the other hand, if a vehicle has an unusually low market value (like the Chevrolet Astro and Safari), find out why it's so unpopular before buying it. (In the GM example, both minivans have a worse-than-deserved reputation for being unreliable.)

Vehicles that don't sell because of their weird styling are no problem, but reports of poor quality control can send prices plummeting. Already, Ford Taurus and Sable owners are finding that dealers are reluctant to take their cars in trade due to reports of serious engine and transmission defects afflicting the 1991–95 models. This perceived lack of quality has carried over to the automaker's new models and resulted in lower-priced '98 models. If consumer confidence isn't restored, buyers will likely see these two Ford models drastically reduced in price this year through rebates and dealer incentives.

Leftovers: false bargains?

In the fall, at the beginning of each new model year, most dealers still have a few of last year's cars left. Some are new, some are demonstrators. The factory gives the dealer a 3–5 percent rebate on late-season cars, and dealers will often pass on some of these savings to clients. But are these leftovers really bargains?

They might be, if you can amortize the first year's depreciation by keeping the vehicle for 6–10 years. But if you're the kind of driver who trades every two or three years, you're likely to come out a loser by buying an end-of-season car. The simple reason is that as far as trade-ins are concerned, a leftover is a used car that has depreciated at least 10–15 percent. The savings the dealer gives you may not equal that first year's depreciation, a cost you'll incur without getting any of the first year's driving benefits. If the dealer's discounted price matches or exceeds the depreciation, then you're getting a pretty good deal. But if the next year's model is only a bit more expensive, and has been substantially improved or is covered by a more extensive, comprehensive warranty, it could represent a better buy than a slightly cheaper leftover.

Ask the dealer for all work orders relating to the car and make sure that the odometer readings follow in sequential order. Remember as well that most demonstrators have less than 5,000 km on the ticker, and the original warranty has been reduced from the day the vehicle was first put on the road. Have the dealer extend the warranty or lower the price accordingly—about $100 for each month of warranty that has expired. If the vehicle's file shows that it was registered to a leasing agency or any other third party, you're definitely buying a used vehicle disguised as a demo. You should walk away from the sale because you're dealing with a crook.

Mid-year models

Entirely new models often make their debut in mid-summer, and getting any kind of a discount from the dealer for mid-year models is like pulling teeth. Dealers know that a seller's market exists during the first few months of a model's launch, and they're not likely to sell their few sample cars for anything less than full price. Furthermore, you're likely to lose an extra year of depreciation since, over time, mid-year vehicles are depreciated back to the beginning of the model year in which they were introduced.

Paying Cash vs. Getting a Loan

About 8 percent of new car buyers pay cash—they may be making a big mistake. Financial planners say it may be smarter to borrow the money to purchase a new vehicle even if you can afford to pay cash, because if you use the vehicle for business a portion of the interest may be tax deductible. The cash that you free up can then be used to repay debts that aren't tax deductible (mortgages or credit card debt, for example). Paying cash is not advantageous to the dealer, though, since kickbacks on finance contracts represent an important part of the F&I division's profits.

Hidden loan costs

Decide how much you want to spend and then pre-arrange your loan before you buy the car, so that you'll know in advance if your credit is good enough to qualify for the amount you need. In your quest for an auto loan, remember that the Internet offers help for people who need an auto loan, want quick approval, but don't like to face a banker. The Bank of Montreal (*www.bmo.com*) was the first Canadian bank that accepted loan applications on its website, and claims to send a loan response within 20 seconds. Other banks, such as Royal Bank, offer a similar service. Loans are available to any web surfer, including those who aren't current Montreal or Royal customers.

Be sure to call various financial institutions to find out:

• the annual percentage rate on the amount you want to borrow and for the duration of your repayment period;
• the minimum down payment that the institution requires;
• whether taxes and licence fees are considered part of the overall cost, and thus covered by part of the loan;
• whether lower rates are available for different loan periods or for a larger down payment; and
• whether discounts are available to depositors, and if so, how long you must be a depositor before qualifying.

When comparing loans, consider the annual rate and calculate the total cost of the loan offer; that is, how much you'll pay above and beyond the total price of the vehicle.

Don't dismiss dealer financing out of hand. Dealers can finance the cost of a new car at interest rates that are competitive with the banks because of the rebates they get from the manufacturers and some lending institutions. Some dealers, though, mislead their customers into thinking they can borrow money at as much as 5 percentage points below the prime rate. Actually, they're jacking up the retail price to more than make up for the lower interest charges. Sometimes, instead of boosting the price, dealers reduce the amount they pay for the trade-in. In either case, the savings are illusory.

When dealing with banks, keep in mind that the traditional 36-month loan has now been stretched to 48 and 60 months. Longer payment terms make each month's payment more affordable, but over the long run they increase the cost of the loan considerably. Therefore, take as short a term as possible.

Be wary of lending institutions that charge a "processing" or "document" fee, ranging from $99–$150. Sometimes consumers will be charged an extra 1–2 percent of the loan up front in order to cover servicing. This is similar to lending institutions adding "points" to mortgages, and it's totally unjustified.

Some banks will cut the interest rate if you're a member of an automobile owners association, or if loan payments are automatically deducted from your chequing account. This latter proposal may be costly, though, if the chequing account charges exceed the interest rate savings.

Finance companies affiliated with GM, Ford, and Chrysler have been offering low-interest loans many points below the prime rate. In many cases, this low rate is applicable only to hard-to-sell models or vehicles equipped with expensive options. The low rate frequently doesn't cover the entire loan period. If vehicles recommended in this book are covered by low-interest loans, then the automaker-affiliated finance companies become a useful alternative to regular banking institutions.

Loan protection
Credit insurance guarantees that the car loan will be paid if the borrower becomes disabled or dies. There are three basic types of insurance that can be written into an installment contract: credit life, accident and health, and comprehensive. Most bank and credit union loans are already covered by some kind of loan insurance, but dealers sell the protection separately at an extra cost to the borrower. For this service the dealer gets a hefty commission that may vary from 10 to 20 percent. The additional cost to the purchaser can be significant. The federal 7 percent GST is applied to loan insurance, but provincial sales tax is exempted in provinces such as Ontario.

Collecting on these types of policies isn't easy. There's no payment if your illness is due to some condition that existed prior to your taking out the insurance. Nor will the policy cover strikes, layoffs, etc. Generally, credit insurance is unnecessary if you're in good health, have no dependents, and your job is secure.

The Royal Bank has two interesting loan programs. One protects motorists from depreciation losses arising from an accident. For example, if a vehicle is scrapped after an accident, the Royal Bank will reimburse its depreciated value. The other program keeps monthly payments low, except for a final balloon payment.

There are plenty of advantageous programs available elsewhere. Personal loans from financial institutions now offer lots of flexibility. Most offer 100 percent financing (with no down payment), fixed or variable interest rates, a choice of loan terms, and no penalties for prepayment. Precise conditions depend on your personal credit rating. Leasing contracts are less flexible. There's a penalty for any prepayment, and rates aren't necessarily competitive. Finally, credit unions can also underwrite new-car loans that combine a flexible payment schedule with low rates.

Negotiating the Contract

Any document that requires your signature is a contract. Don't sign anything unless all the details are clear to you and all the blanks have been filled in. Don't accept any verbal promises. Remember, too, that your contract doesn't have to include all the clauses found in the dealer's preprinted form. You and the sales representative can agree to strike some clauses and add others. It's up to you to negotiate the best deal for yourself.

When the sales agent asks for a deposit, make sure that it's stated on the contract as a deposit and try to keep it as small as possible (a couple of hundred dollars at the most). If you decide to back out of the deal on a vehicle taken from stock, let the seller have the deposit as an incentive to cancel the contract (believe me, it's cheaper than a lawyer and probably equal to his or her commission).

Scrutinize all references to prices and delivery dates. Delivery can sometimes be delayed three to five months, and you'll have to pay all price increases announced during the interim (3–5 percent) unless you specify a delivery date in the contract that protects the price.

Make sure that the contract indicates your new vehicle will be delivered to you with a full tank of gas. At one time, this was the buyer's responsibility, however, with drivers spending almost $30,000 for the average new vehicle, dealers usually throw in a free tank of gas in the process. In fact, a 1998 Maritz New Vehicle Buyer Study that polled 31,763 Canadian buyers found that 72 percent of buyers left the dealership with a free full tank of fuel (Toyota Canada insists upon it).

Finally, don't let the dealer put his decal on your car. It can mar the finish or cause premature rusting. Plus, why should you give him the free publicity?

Additional clauses

You can put things on a more equal footing by negotiating the inclusion of as many clauses as possible from the sample additional contract clauses found on page 84. To do this, write in a "Remarks" section on your contract, and add "See attached clauses, which form part of this agreement." Then attach a photocopy of the "Additional Contract Clauses" and have the sales agent initial as many of the clauses as you can. Although some clauses may be rejected, the inclusion of just a couple of these clauses can have important legal ramifications later on if you want a full or partial refund. For example, as a result of GM's recent two-month strike, many GM dealers will experience two- and three-month delivery delays and may try to pass on to their customers any price increases announced in the interim. Clauses #2 and #4 will protect you from these delays and price increases.

Don't take the dealer's word that "we're not allowed to do that," heard most often in reference to your cancelling the sale or reducing the PDI/transportation fee. Sales are cancelled all the time. In fact, Saturn made a big deal of its money-back warranty in which only a few dozen purchasers sought refunds over the several years the program was in effect. If Saturn dealers can do it, other dealers can, too. As far as PDI/transportation fees are concerned, some dealers have been telling *Lemon-Aid* readers that they are "obligated" by the automaker to charge a set fee and could lose their franchise if they charge less. This is pure hogwash. No dealer has ever had their franchise licence revoked for cutting prices, and the automakers clearly state that they don't set a bottom-line price, since that would violate Canada's Competition Act—that's why you always see them putting disclaimers in their ads saying the dealer can charge less.

The pre-delivery inspection

Many new vehicle orders are screwed up by the factory, so the pre-delivery inspection (PDI) is critical for making sure that corrections are made before taking delivery. Also, because about 10 percent of new vehicles are damaged in transit from the factory, the PDI can spot the damage and the extent of repairs needed. If the repair costs are substantial, the dealer can be forced to exchange the vehicle or give the buyer a rebate. Every auto manufacturer expects the dealer to carry out a PDI on each vehicle sold.

The PDI allowance is figured into the suggested retail price, so whatever you pay the dealer is profit. Dealers who don't get top dollar for a vehicle are tempted to skip the PDI. According to testimony before the U.S. Federal Trade Commission and the U.S. Senate Subcommittee on Antitrust and Monopoly, many dealers deliver vehicles straight from the factory to their customers with only a cursory inspection. This practice wouldn't have such serious consequences if vehicles were delivered from the factory in reasonably good shape. The PDI serves as a last stop to catch the three or so major and minor defects that *Consumer Reports* estimates afflict most new vehicles. If they aren't corrected before delivery, there's a good chance the dealer will charge to fix them later. And if these minor defects aren't caught in time, they can quickly become major failures.

The best way to ensure that the PDI will be done is to write in the sales contract that you'll be given a copy of the completed PDI sheet when the vehicle is delivered to you. Then, with the PDI sheet in hand, verify some of the items that were to be checked. If any items appear to have been missed, refuse delivery of the vehicle. Once you get home, check out the vehicle more thoroughly and send a registered letter to the dealer if you discover multiple major defects.

Additional Contract Clauses

1. Financing: This agreement is subject to the purchaser obtaining financing at a rate of _____% or less within _____ days of the date below. Failing notification in writing confirming approval of this financing, the contract is automatically cancelled.

2. Delivery: The vehicle is to be delivered by _____, failing which the contract is cancelled and the deposit will be refunded.

3. Cancellation: (a) The purchaser retains the right to cancel this agreement without penalty at any time before delivery of the vehicle by sending a notice in writing to the vendor.

(b) Following delivery of the vehicle, the purchaser shall have two days to return the vehicle and cancel the agreement in writing, without penalty. After two days and before thirty-one days, the purchaser shall pay the dealer $25 a day as compensation for depreciation on the returned vehicle.

(c) Cancellation of contract can be refused where the vehicle has been subjected to abuse, negligence, or unauthorized modifications after delivery.

(d) The purchaser is responsible for accident damage and traffic violations while in possession of the said vehicle. The purchaser is also responsible for re-registering the vehicle traded in and obtaining reimbursement of the sales tax. If the traded vehicle has been resold, the vendor will remit the monetary value attributed to the vehicle when it was delivered to the vendor.

4. Protected Price: The vendor agrees not to alter the price of the new vehicle, the cost of preparation, or the cost of shipping.

5. Trade-in: The vendor agrees that the value attributed to the vehicle offered in trade shall not be reduced. An exception may be made when the said vehicle has been significantly modified or has suffered from unreasonable and accelerated deterioration since the signing of the agreement.

6. Courtesy Car: (a) In the event the new vehicle is not delivered on the agreed-upon date, the vendor agrees to supply the purchaser with a courtesy car at no cost. If no courtesy vehicle is available, the vendor agrees to reimburse the purchaser the cost of renting a vehicle of equivalent or lesser value than the new car purchased.

(b) If the vehicle is off the road for more than five days for warranty repairs, the purchaser is entitled to a free courtesy vehicle for the duration of the repair period. If no courtesy vehicle is available, the vendor agrees to reimburse the purchaser the cost of renting a vehicle of equivalent or lesser value.

7. Work Orders: The purchaser will receive duly completed copies of all work orders pertaining to the vehicle, including warranty repairs and the original pre-delivery inspection (PDI).

8. Dealer Stickers: The vendor will not affix any dealer advertising, in any form, on the purchaser's new vehicle.

9. Fuel: Vehicle will be delivered with a free full tank of gas.

| _____ | _____ | _____ |
| Date | Vendor's Signature | Buyer's Signature |

Selling Your Trade-In

Buy, sell, or hold?

It doesn't take a genius to figure out that the longer one keeps a vehicle, the less it costs to own—up to a point. The Hertz Corporation has estimated that a small car equipped with standard options, driven 10,000 miles (16,000 km), and traded each year, costs 9.6 cents more a mile than a comparable car traded after five years. That same car kept for ten years and run 10,000 miles a year would cost 10.8 cents less a mile (6.75 cents less a kilometre) than a similar vehicle kept for five years, and a whopping 20.38 cents less a mile (12.75 cents a kilometre) than a comparable compact traded in each year. That would amount to a savings of $20,380 over a 10-year period.

If you're happy with you vehicle's styling and convenience features and it's safe and dependable, there is no reason to get rid of it. But when the cost of repairs becomes equal to or greater than the cost of payments for a new car, then you need to consider trading it in. Shortly after your vehicle's fifth birthday (or whenever you start to think about trading it in), ask a mechanic to look at it to give you some idea of the repairs, replacement parts, and maintenance work it will need in the coming year. Find out if dealer service bulletins show that it will need extensive repairs in the near future. (See Appendix, under ALLDATA, on how to order a bulletin summary.) If it's going to require expensive repairs, you should trade the vehicle right away, but if expensive work isn't necessary you may want to keep your vehicle. Auto owner associations provide a good yardstick. They estimate that the annual cost of repairs and preventive maintenance for the average car is between $500 and $600. If your vehicle is five years old and you haven't spent anywhere near $3,000 in maintenance, it would pay to invest in your old car and continue using it for another few years.

Consider whether your car can still be serviced easily. If it's no longer on the market, the parts supply is likely to dry up and independent mechanics will be reluctant to repair it.

Don't trade for fuel economy alone. More fuel-efficient vehicles, such as front-wheel drives, offset the savings through higher repair costs. Also, the more fuel-efficient cars may not be as comfortable to drive due to excessive engine noise, lightweight construction, and stiff suspension and torque steer.

Reassess your needs. Does your family growth require a different vehicle? Are you driving less? Are long trips taken less frequently? Let your car rust in peace and pocket the savings if its deteriorating condition doesn't pose a safety hazard or isn't too embarrassing. On the other hand, if you're in sales and are constantly on the road, it makes sense to trade every few years—in that case mechanical reliability becomes a prime consideration, and the increased depreciation costs are mostly tax deductible.

Getting the most for your trade-in

Customers who are on guard against paying too much for a new car often sell their trade-ins for too little. Before agreeing to any trade-in amount, read Part Three of *Lemon-Aid Used Cars 2001* if your trade-in is a passenger car or minivan. For prices on used pickups, vans, or sport-utilities, consult *Lemon-Aid Used 4X4s, Vans and Trucks 2001*. Both guides give your vehicle's dealer and private selling price, and offer a formula to figure out regional price fluctuations. For a small fee, you can also obtain new- and used-car prices by calling the Montreal or Toronto office of the Automobile Protection Association (514-273-1733 or 416-964-6774). Keep in mind, however, that the APA can't guarantee that you'll always get the lowest price possible. In fact, some buyers tell me that they've done better buying a new or used car on their own.

Now that you've nailed down your trade-in's approximate value, here are some tips on selling it with a minimum of stress:
- Don't sign a new-car sales contract unless your trade-in has been sold—you could end up with two cars.
- Negotiate the price from retail (dealer price) down to *wholesale* (private sales).
- If you haven't sold your trade-in after two weekends, you might be trying to sell it at the wrong time of year or have it priced too high.

Private sales
If you must sell your vehicle and want to make the most out of the deal, consider selling it yourself and putting the profits towards your next purchase. You'll likely come out hundreds or thousands of dollars ahead—buyers will pay more for your vehicle, since they won't have to pay the 7 percent GST on a private sale. The most important thing to remember is that there's a large market for used vehicles in good condition in the $7,000–$10,000 range. Although most people prefer buying from individuals rather than from used-car lots, they may still be afraid that the vehicle is a lemon. The following suggestions should enable you to assuage that fear and sell your vehicle quite easily:
1. Know its value. Study dealers' newspaper ads and compare them with the prices listed in this book. Undercut the dealer price by $300–$800, and be ready to bargain down another 10 percent for a serious buyer. Remember that prices can fluctuate wildly depending on which models are trendy, so watch the want ads carefully.
2. Enlist the aid of the salesperson who is selling you your new car. Offer him a couple of hundred dollars if he finds you a buyer. The fact that one sale hinges on the other, and the prospect of making two commissions, may work wonders.
3. Post notices on bulletin boards at your office or local supermarkets, and place a "For Sale" sign in the window of the car itself. Place a newspaper ad only as a last resort.
4. Don't give your address right away to a potential buyer responding to your ad. Instead, ask for the telephone number where you may call that person back.
5. Don't sell to friends or family members. Anything short of perfection, and you can forget Christmas dinner with the family.
6. Don't touch the odometer. You may get a few hundred dollars more—and a criminal record.
7. Paint the vehicle. Some specialty shops charge only $300 and give a guarantee that's transferable to subsequent owners.

8. Make minor repairs. This includes a minor tune-up and patching up the exhaust. Again, if any repair warranty is transferable, use it as a selling point.

9. Clean the vehicle. Go to a reconditioning firm or spend the weekend scrubbing the interior and exterior. First impressions are important. Clean the chrome, polish the body, and peel off old bumper stickers. Remove butts from the ashtrays and clean out the glove compartment. Make sure all tools and spare parts have been taken out of the trunk. Don't remove the radio or speakers. The gaping holes will make the vehicle worth much less than the radio or speakers cost. Replace missing or broken dash knobs and window cranks.

10. Change the tires. Recaps are good buys.

11. Let the buyer examine the vehicle. Insist that the vehicle be inspected by an independent garage, and accompany the prospective buyer to the garage.

12. Keep important documents handy. Show prospective buyers the sales contract, repair orders, owner's manual, and all other documents that show how the vehicle has been maintained. Authenticate your claims about fuel consumption.

13. Don't mislead the buyer. If the vehicle was in an accident, or some financing is still to be paid, admit it. Any misleading statements may be used later in court against you. It's also advisable to have someone witness the actual transaction in case of a future dispute.

14. Sell to a dealer who sells the same make. He'll give you more because he can easily sell your trade-in to customers who are interested only in that make of vehicle.

15. Write an effective ad.

Selling to dealers

Selling to a dealer means that you're likely to get 20 percent less than if you sold your vehicle privately, unless the dealer agrees to participate in an accommodation sale. Most sellers will gladly pay some penalty to the dealer, however, for the peace of mind that comes with knowing that the eventual buyer won't lay a claim against them. This assumes that the dealer hasn't been cheated by the seller—if the car is stolen, isn't paid for, has had its odometer spun back (or forward to a lower setting), or is seriously defective, the buyer or dealer can sue the original owner for fraud.

Drawing up the contract

Draw up a bill of sale in duplicate and date it (photocopy the following sample bill of sale on the following page). Identify the vehicle (including the serial number), its price, whether a warranty applies, and the nature of the examination made by the buyer. The buyer may ask you to put in a lower price than what was actually paid in order to reduce the sales tax. If you agree to this, don't be surprised when a Ministry of Revenue agent comes to your door. Although the purchaser is ultimately the responsible party, you're an accomplice in defrauding the government. Furthermore, if you turn to the courts for redress your own conduct may be put on trial.

Bill of Sale

1. The seller agrees to sell, and the buyer agrees to buy a:
   a) _____ , b) _____ .
       Year   Serial Number

2. The seller is selling the motor vehicle:
   ❑ without a warranty
   ❑ with the following warranty _____ .

3. The buyer:
   ❑ has test driven the motor vehicle
   ❑ has not test driven the motor vehicle.

4. The purchase price in full is $_____ .

5. The seller acknowledges receiving from the buyer a deposit in the amount of $_____ .

6. The seller warrants and guarantees that there are no liens, chattel mortgages, or security agreements outstanding with respect to the motor vehicle or any equipment and/or accessories, and that the motor vehicle and any equipment and/or accessories has/have not been given as collateral on any loan.

7. The seller and the buyer agree that the buyer was allowed to take the motor vehicle for an inspection by a mechanic before the signing of this agreement.

8. The seller warrants to the buyer that to the best of his knowledge:
   a) the odometer reading on the motor vehicle is accurate,
   b) the motor vehicle has not been damaged in a collision, and
   c) there are no outstanding traffic violations with respect to the motor vehicle.

_____	_____
Date	City
_____	_____
Buyer	Seller

Summary

Purchasing a vehicle used saves you the most money. Paying cash or with the biggest down payment you can afford, and piling up as many kilometres and years as possible on your trade-in, are the next best ways to save money. Remember, too, that safety is another consideration largely dependent on the type of vehicle you choose. Focus on the following objectives.

Buy smart

1. Take your time. Price comparisons and test drives may take a month, but you'll get a better car and price in the long run.
2. Buy in winter or later in the new year to double-dip from dealer incentive and customer rebate programs.
3. Sell your trade-in privately.
4. Arrange financing before buying your vehicle.
5. Test-drive your choice by renting it overnight or for several days.
6. Buy through the Internet, by fax, or use an auto broker if you're not confident in your own bargaining skills, lack the time to haggle, or want to avoid the "showroom shakedown."
7. Ask for at least a 5 percent discount off the MSRP and cut pre-delivery inspection and freight charges by at least 50 percent. Insist on a specific delivery date written in the contract as well as a pro-tected price, in case there's a price increase from the time the con-tract is signed and when the vehicle is delivered. Plus, ask for a free tank of gas.
8. Order a minimum of options and seek a 30 percent discount on the entire option list. Try not to let the total option cost cxcccd 15 per-cent of the vehicle's MSRP.
9. Try to avoid leasing. If you must lease, choose the shortest time pos-sible, drive down the MSRP, and refuse to pay an "acquisition" fee.
10. Japanese vehicles made in North America, co-ventures with American automakers, and re-badged imports often cost less than imports, and are just as reliable.

Buy safe

Look for:

1. A high crashworthiness rating and low rollover potential
2. Good quality tires—be wary of "all-season" tires and Firestone makes
3. Three-point belts with belt pretensioners and adjustable shoulder belt anchorages
4. Integrated child safety seats and seat anchors
5. Depowered dual airbags with a cutoff switch highly rated, unobtru-sive head restraints, and pedal extenders
6. Front driver's seat with plenty of rearward travel and a height adjustment
7. Good all-around visibility
8. An ergonomic interior with an efficient heating and ventilation system
9. Headlights that are adequate for night driving
10. Dash gauges that don't wash out in sunlight or produce windshield glare

Now that you know what the rules of the game are, Part Two will show you how to fight back if that dream car turns into a nightmare.

Part Two
GETTING HELP AND GETTING EVEN

Firestone Firestorm
"It was a textbook case of boardroom bozos choosing profits over the safety of their customers. Whether it was 50 or 500 motorists who'd died on defective Firestones, the company obviously wasn't going to make a peep unless the story broke. Meanwhile, astoundingly, it kept selling the three suspect types of tires to unknowing buyers.

One tragedy followed another. Then came the lawsuits, the head-lines, the predictable corporate denial followed by the predictable corporate retreat.

Oops, said Bridgestone/Firestone last week. It seems our tires do sometimes unspool. Stop by a dealer and we'll give you some new ones. Yet days earlier, a company spokesperson confidently had stated: 'These are safe tires...'"

Carl Hiaasen
Miami Herald
August 13, 2000

"Only" 10% of Chrsylers Cause Repeat Problems
"Out of 100 vehicles, we're apt to build 10 that are as good as any that Toyota has ever built, 80 that are okay and 10 that cause repeated problems for our customers."

Robert Lutz, President
Chrysler U.S.
Chrysler Times, July 17, 1995

Both Chrysler and Runzheimer Consultants estimate that 1 out of every 10 American vehicles produced by the Big Three is a "lemon." If you've bought an unsafe tire or a lemon, or if you've been forced to pay for repairs that shouldn't be your responsibility, this section will help you get your money back—without going to court or getting frazzled by the broken promises or "benign neglect" of the dealer or private party who sold you the vehicle. But if going to court is your only recourse, you'll find the jurisprudence you need to get an out-of-court settlement or to win your case without spending a fortune on lawyers and research.

These owners formed the first Chrysler Lemon Owners Group (CLOG) in Eastern Canada four years ago. Most got their money back. Since then, CLOG B.C. and CLOG Alberta have secured substantial refunds for their members. Now that Daimler has ordered Chrysler to cut back $2 billion in costs for the year 2000, you can be sure post-warranty assistance will be cut and CLOGs will proliferate.

Four Ways to Get Your Money Back

Remember the "money-back" guarantee? Well, with the exception of Saturn, automakers are reluctant to offer any warranty that requires them to take back a defective new car or minivan. Nevertheless, our provincial consumer protection laws have filled the gap so that now any sales contract for a new or used vehicle can be cancelled—or free repairs can be ordered—if the vehicle:

• is misrepresented;
• is unfit for the purpose for which it was purchased;
• hasn't been reasonably durable, considering how well it was maintained, the mileage driven, and the type of driving done (particularly applicable to engine, transmission, and paint defects); or
• was covered by a secret warranty, without your knowledge.

Subject: Re: defective Chrysler Transaxle
Date: Thu, 12 Feb 1998 19:14:36 –0500

Hi Phil,

Just thought that I would let you know that I received a "goodwill" cheque from Chrysler Canada today in the amount of $1977.34 to cover the cost of transmission parts on my 91 Dodge Caravan. Thanks again for your advice—it sure was worthwhile pursuing the matter!!!

Sincerely,

Wayne Sockovie
Port Robinson, Ont. Canada.

Here's what the four legal concepts enumerated above mean in real-life situations: if the seller says that a minivan can pull a 900 kg (2,000 lb.) trailer and you discover that it can barely tow half that weight, you can cancel the contract for misrepresentation. The same principle applies to a seller's exaggerated claims concerning a vehicle's fuel economy or reliability, as well as to "demonstrators" that are in fact used cars with false (rolled back) odometer readings.

It's essential that printed evidence and/or witnesses (relatives are not excluded) are available to confirm that the false representation actually occurred. These misrepresentations must concern an important fact that substantially affects the vehicle's performance, reliability, or value.

When their products fail to live up to the advertised hype, automakers often blame the owner for having pushed the vehicle beyond its limits. Therefore, when you seek to set aside the contract by claiming that the vehicle is unfit for your needs, it's essential that you get the testimony of an independent mechanic and co-workers in order to prove that the vehicle's poor performance isn't caused by negligent maintenance or abusive driving.

The reasonable durability claim is probably the easiest allegation to prove, since all automakers have benchmarks as to how long body components, trim and finish, and mechanical and electronic parts should last (see the durability chart on pages 106–7). New and used vehicles are expected to be reasonably durable and merchantable. What is reasonably durable depends on the price paid, kilometres driven, purchaser's driving habits, and how well the vehicle was maintained by the owner. Judges carefully weigh all these factors in awarding compensation or cancelling a sale.

As mentioned in Part One, automobile manufacturers are reluctant to make secret warranty extensions public because they feel it would weaken confidence in their product and increase their legal liability. The closest they come to an admission is sending a "goodwill policy," "product improvement program," or "special policy" service bulletin to dealers or first owners of record. Consequently, the only motorists who get compensated for repairs to defective parts are those who are the original owners, who haven't moved or leased their vehicle, or who yell the loudest and present automaker service bulletins (to order your own bulletins, see Appendix, under the ALLDATA website).

If you're refused compensation, keep in mind that secret warranty extensions are an admission of manufacturing negligence. Try to compromise with a pro rata adjustment from the manufacturer. A good bottom-line position is to suggest the dealer and manufacturer each pay a third of the cost. If polite negotiations fail, challenge the refusal in court on the grounds that you should not be penalized for failing to make a reimbursement claim under a secret warranty you never knew existed!

Whatever reason you use to get your money back, don't forget to conform to the "reasonable diligence" rule that requires you to file suit within a reasonable time after purchase or after you've discovered the defect. If there have been no negotiations with the dealer or automaker, this delay cannot exceed a few months. If either the dealer or the automaker has been promising to correct the defects for some time, or has carried out repeated unsuccessful repairs, the delay for filing the lawsuit can be extended.

Consequential damages

It's a lot easier to get the automaker to pay to replace a defective part than it is to obtain compensation for a missed day of work or a ruined vacation. Manufacturers hate to pay for consequential expenses under the basic warranty, supplementary warranty, or extended warranty because they can't control the amount of the refund. (Towing expenses, however, are usually accepted.) Courts are more generous, having ruled that all expenses (damages) flowing from a problem covered by a warranty or service bulletin are the manufacturer's/dealer's responsibility under both common law (all provinces except Quebec) and Quebec civil law. Fortunately, when legal action is threatened—usually through small claims court—automakers quickly back down from their refusal to pay consequential damage claims.

Warranties

In addition to the automakers' and dealers' *expressed* warranty, every vehicle sold new or used in Canada is covered by an *implied* warranty— a collection of federal and provincial laws and regulations that protect you from misrepresentation and a host of other evils. Furthermore, Canadian law presumes that car dealers, unlike private sellers, are aware of the defects present in the vehicles they sell. That way, dealers can't just pass the ball to the automakers and walk away from the dispute.

The manufacturer's warranty is a legal promise that its product will perform in the normal and customary manner for which it was designed. Regardless of the number of subsequent owners, this promise remains in force as long as the warranty's original time/kilometre limits haven't expired.

Treacherous tires (Firestone)

Tires and batteries aren't covered by most car manufacturers' warranties (except for GMs), and are warranted instead by the manufacturer on a pro-rated basis. This isn't such a good deal, because the manufacturer is making a profit by charging you the full list price. If you were to buy the same replacement tire from a discount store you'd likely pay less, even without the pro-rated rebate. Tiremakers give a pro-rated rebate on the suggested list price, which almost nobody pays.

Tire recalls, however, are a different matter. Bridgestone/Firestone has just announced a massive recall of 6.5 million ATX II and Wilderness tires, used mainly on sport-utilities trucks, minivans, and

vans. Due to the confusion and chaos surrounding Firestone's handling of the recall, Ford's 575 Canadian dealers have stepped into the
breech and are exchanging the recalled tires for any equivalent tires
dealers have in stock.

No questions asked.

Blowout

How the Tire Problem
Turned Into a Crisis
For Firestone and Ford

Lack of a Database Masked
The Pattern That Led
To Yesterday's Big Recall

The Heat and the Pressure

Attorney Jay Halpern has been suing
tire makers for more than a decade, targeting different manufacturers for various
problems on a range of models. But in
1998, he got a case involving the failure of
a Firestone tire on a Ford Explorer. Then
he saw another. And another.

Mr. Halpern says he sent a damaged
Firestone tire from one of his client's vehicles to a tire expert who consults with
plaintiffs' lawyers. "I have a room full of
them." the expert, Dick Baumgardner,

This is an important precedent
that tears down the corporate wall sep-
arating tire and battery manufacturers from automakers in product
liability claims. In essence, whoever
sells the product can be held liable for
damages. In the future, Canadian
consumers will have an easier time
holding the dealer, automaker and
the tire or battery manufacturer
liable, not just for recalled products,
but for any defect that affects the
safety or reasonable durablilty of
that product. This is particularly
true, now that the Supreme Court of
Canada (*Winnipeg Condominium v.
Bird Construction* [1995] 1S.C.R.85)
has ruled that defendants are liable
in negligence for any designs that
resulted in a risk to the public for
safety or health. The Supreme Court
reversed a long-standing policy and
provided the public with a new cause
of action that had not existed before
in Canada. Prior to this Supreme Court ruling, companies dodged liability for falling bridges and crashing planes by warranty exclusion and
entire-agreement contract clauses.

In the Winnipeg Condominium case, the Supreme Court held that
repairs made to prevent serious damage or accident could be claimed
from the designer/builder for the cost of repair in tort, from any
subsequent purchaser.

Consumers with tire or other safety-related claims would be wise to
insert the above court decision (with explanation) in their claim letter
and mail or fax it to the automaker's "legal affairs" or "product liability"
department. A copy should be also deposited with the clerk of the small
claims court if you have to use that recourse.

Safety restraints, such as airbags and safety belts, usually mirror the
basic warranty, with coverage extended for the lifetime of the vehicle.

Aftermarket products and services—such as gas-saving gadgets,
rustproofing, paint protectors, air conditioning, and van conversions—

can render the manufacturer's warranty invalid, so be sure to check with your dealer before purchasing any optional equipment or services from an independent supplier.

How fairly a warranty is applied is more important than how long it remains in effect. The new warranties are useful to consumers who are making claims before provincial small claims courts, because they prove that the technology exists to make powertrain components and rust resistance/paint adhesion last far longer than admitted in the past. Once you know the normal wear rate for a mechanical component or body part, you can demand proportional compensation when you get less than normal durability—no matter what the original warranty said.

Some dealers tell customers that they need to have original equipment parts installed in order to maintain their warranty. A variation on this theme requires that routine servicing—including tune-ups and oil changes (with a certain brand of oil)—be done by the selling dealer, or the warranty is invalidated.

Nothing could be further from the truth. Canadian law stipulates that whoever issues a warranty cannot make that warranty conditional on the use of any specific brand of motor oil, oil filter, or any other component, unless it's provided to the customer free of charge.

Sometimes dealers will do all sorts of minor repairs that don't correct the problem, and then, after the warranty runs out, they'll tell you that major repairs are needed. You can avoid this nasty surprise by repeatedly bringing in your vehicle to the dealership before the warranty ends. During each visit, insist that a written work order include the specific nature of the problem, *as you see it*, and that it carries the notation that this is the second, third, or fourth time the same problem has been brought to the dealer's attention. Write it down yourself, if need be. This allows you to show a pattern of non-performance by the dealer during the warranty period and establishes that it's a serious and chronic problem. When the warranty expires, you have the legal right to demand that it be extended on those items consistently reappearing on your handful of work orders.

Extended (supplementary) warranties

Supplementary warranties providing extended coverage may be sold by the manufacturer, dealer, or an independent third party and are automatically transferred when the vehicle is sold. They cost between $500 and $1,500 and should be purchased only if the vehicle you're buying is off its original warranty or has a poor repair history (see Part Three), or if you're reluctant to use the small claims courts when factory-related trouble arises. Don't let the dealer pressure you into deciding right away. Generally, you can purchase an extended warranty anytime during the period in which the manufacturer's warranty is in effect.

Because up to 60 percent of the warranty's cost represents dealer markup, dealers love to sell extended warranties, whether you need them or not. Out of the remaining 40 percent comes the sponsor's administration costs and profit margin, calculated at another 15 percent. What's left to pay for repairs is a minuscule 25 percent of the original amount. The only reason why automakers and independent warranty companies haven't been busted for operating this warranty Ponzi scheme is because only half of the car buyers who purchase extended service contracts actually use it.

It's often difficult to collect on supplementary warranties, because independent companies not tied to the automakers frequently go out of business. When this happens, and the company's insurance policy won't cover your claim, take the dealer to small claims court and ask for the repair cost and a refund of the original warranty payment. Your argument for holding the dealer responsible is a simple one: by accepting a commission for acting as an agent of the defunct company, the selling dealer took on the obligations of the company as well.

Emissions control warranties
These little-publicized warranties can save you big bucks if major engine or exhaust components fail prematurely. They come with all new vehicles and cover the emissions control system for up to 8 years/130,000 km. Unfortunately, although owners' manuals vaguely mention the emissions warranty, most don't specify which parts are covered. Fortunately, the U.S. Environmental Protection Agency has intervened on several occasions with hefty fines against Chrysler and Ford and ruled that all major motor and fuel-system components are covered. These include fuel metering, ignition spark advance, restart, evaporative emissions, positive crankcase ventilation, engine electronics (computer modules), and catalytic converters, as well as hoses, clamps, brackets, pipes, gaskets, belts, seals, and connectors. Canada, however, has no government definition, and it's left up to each manufacturer and the small claims courts to decide which components are covered.

Article No.
97-9-5
04/28/97
LONG CRANK - STICKING IDLE AIR CONTROL (IAC) VALVE - VEHICLES BUILT FROM 11/1/94 THROUGH 3/30/96 STALL - AFTER STARTING WHEN ENGINE ALLOWED TO SOAK FROM 1-4 HOURS - STICKING IDLE AIR CONTROL (IAC) VALVE - VEHICLES BUILT FROM 1/11/94 THROUGH 3/30/96
1995–96 CONTOUR, CROWN VICTORIA, ESCORT, TAURUS, THUNDERBIRD
1996 MUSTANG
LINCOLN-MERCURY:
1995–96 CONTINENTAL, COUGAR, GRAND MARQUIS, MARK VIII, MYSTIQUE, SABLE, TOWN CAR, TRACER
LIGHT TRUCK:
1995–96 AEROSTAR, BRONCO, ECONOLINE, F-150-350 SERIES, RANGER, WINDSTAR
1996 EXPLORER
ISSUE:
After a 1–4 hour engine soak time, long crank times and/or long crank to start followed by a stall may occur on some vehicles. No further stalling or rough idle will occur after the engine is running. The long crank and/or stall may be due to the Idle Air Control (IAC) Valve sticking.
ACTION:
Replace the AC Valve with a revised AC Valve if no Diagnostic Trouble Codes (DTCs) are present.
WARRANTY STATUS: Eligible Under The Provisions Of Bumper to Bumper Warranty Coverage And Emissions Warranty

This fuel system repair would cost you several hundred dollar, if you didn't have this bulletin in your possession.

97-16-6
08/04/97
• EXHAUST SYSTEM - LOOSE CATALYST OR MUFFLER HEAT SHIELDS
• NOISE - "BUZZING" OR "RATTLING" - LOOSE CATALYST OR MUFFLER HEAT SHIELDS
FORD:

1985–94 TEMPO	1986–97 TAURUS
1985–97 CROWN VICTORIA, MUSTANG, THUNDERBIRD	1988–93 FESTIVA
1985–98 ESCORT	1989–97 PROBE

LINCOLN-MERCURY:

1985–92 MARK VII	1987–89 TRACER
1985–94 TOPAZ	1991–94 CAPRI
1985–97 CONTINENTAL, COUGAR, GRAND MARQUIS, TOWN CAR	1991–98 TRACER
1986–97 SABLE	

MERKUR:

1985–89 XR4TI	1988–89 SCORPIO

LIGHT TRUCK:

1985–90 BRONCO II	1986–97 AEROSTAR
1985–96 BRONCO	1988–97 F SUPER DUTY
1985–97 ECONOLINE, F-150, F-250, F-350, RANGER	1991–97 EXPLORER

This TSB article is being republished in its entirety to Include vehicles built through the 1997 model year.
ISSUE:
A "buzzing or rattling" noise from the exhaust system may be caused by a loose heat shield attachment to the muffler or catalyst. The noise is noticeable during normal driving conditions or at engine idle.
ACTION:
Install worm clamps to secure the heat shield attachments.
WARRANTY STATUS: Eligible Under Basic Warranty Coverage For 1991 And Prior Models, Bumper to Bumper Warranty Coverage For 1992–97 Models, And Emissions Warranty Coverage For Catalytic Converters With Welded Heat Shields For All Model Years

Many problems related to the exhaust system are also covered by the emissions warranty.

Make sure you get your emissions system checked out thoroughly by a dealer or independent garage before the emissions warranty expires and before having the vehicle inspected by provincial emissions inspectors. In addition to ensuring you pass provincial tests, this precaution could save you up to $1,000 if both your catalytic converter and your other emissions components are faulty, as the following *Lemon-Aid* reader relates:

Knowing my '96 Pontiac Grand Am has "second level diagnostics" (OBD 2) and has the ability to store intermittent code alerts in its computer, I phoned my brother-in-law, who is an Ontario licenced mechanic (I'm an Ontario licenced auto body repairer), and asked him to "scan" my car with his Snap-On scanner for any hidden trouble codes.

He did, and sure enough, he found that it had a defective oxygen sensor that never triggered the CHECK ENGINE light to come on. How long it had been defective, I have no idea. But, I knew it was using more gas than it should because I was filling it up every week. (Now a tank of gas lasts two weeks since it's been fixed.)

So I took it to the dealer and explained what we did and showed them the data from the scanner. They fixed it for free, right away. (If they didn't, I was advised to contact Environment Canada.)

Phil, please urge people to have their "second level diagnostics" scanned by an independent garage before the warranty expires, because the cost of the check-out is small compared to the cost of replacing emissions components out of warranty, not to mention the hassle if their cars won't pass an emissions test because of failed components that nobody knew about.

D.R.
St. Catharines, Ontario

Thanks for the tip. By the way, the Check Engine or Service Engine lights are notorious for coming on for no apparent reason; GM estimates that 99% of car owners can expect one false warning during the first 16,000 km (10,000 miles). Most motorists ignore the warning since it usually only shows a glitch in the emissions system—not some major engine failure. Common causes are a loose gas cap or failure of an oxygen sensor—a device that double-checks that the emissions controls are working properly.

Secret warranties

Secret warranties have been around since automobiles were first mass-produced. They're set up to provide free repairs of performance-related defects caused by substandard materials, faulty design, or assembly-line errors. In 1974, *Lemon-Aid* exposed Ford's secret J-67 7-year rust warranty, which covered the company's 1970–74 models. After first denying that it had such a warranty, Ford admitted two years later that it was indeed in place, and negotiated a $2.8 million settlement with this author to compensate owners of rust-cankered Fords. And you know what? Twenty-six years later, hundreds of secret warranties continue to exist among automakers. *Lemon-Aid* is still the only consumer publication blowing the whistle on hundreds of current programs that secretly allocate funds for the repair of engine, transmission, fuel pump, and paint defects on cars, sport-utilities, trucks, minivans, and vans.

Secret warranties go through four stages:

1st stage—Service advisories are posted on an automaker's internal computer network. They offer troubleshooting tips and allow the dealer to bill the manufacturer for the repair. This information is never shared with the customer.

2nd stage—If the defect grows in scope and a more involved solution, requiring upgraded parts, is needed, automakers then draw up a technical service bulletin (TSB), sometimes called a dealer service bulletin (DSB), and distribute the bulletin to dealers and U.S. and Canadian government agencies. The service bulletin is only issued after the manufacturer has what it thinks is the solution for the defect. TSBs issued by Chrysler, Ford, and GM will usually spell out clearly which base warranty will cover the repair (emissions warranty, bumper-to-bumper, etc.). Interestingly, Asian and European automakers are vague in their description of their warranty obligations. Honda, for example, uses the term "goodwill" as a euphemism to describe its warranty extensions.

3rd stage—As more and more customers hear through *Lemon-Aid*, ALLDATA-published service bulletins, friends, and relatives that some TSBs recognize that a factory-related defect exists, and find that the base warranty is clearly inadequate to deal with the scope of the problem, pressure is exerted by dealers and customers for additional after-warranty-assistance. This, in turn, results in a second TSB, sent only to dealers, extending the warranty for the defects' correction and leaving to the dealer's discretion the amount of the customer's refund.

Customer dissatisfaction is now building into a crescendo, since the dealers and automakers keep the extended guidelines to themselves and customers get widely divergent refunds, which only angers the owners more, brings in the media, and leads to a proliferation of Internet gripe sites and lawsuits (small claims and class actions).

4th stage—Finally, the aggravation is too great and the automaker decides to make a press release followed by an owner notification letter (sent to first owners only, at their last known address) which clearly spells out what all owners will get and which vehicles are involved. A special bulletin or letter is also sent out to dealers to ensure they follow the guidelines 100 percent. Ford calls these "Owner Notification Policies," GM calls them "Special Policies," and Chrysler calls them "Owner Satisfaction Notifications." No matter the euphemism, they are an extension of the original warranty, applied to vehicles that may have been bought new or used. Even mundane little repairs that can still cost you a hundred bucks or more are covered. Take, for example, the elimination of foul, musty, or mildew odours emitted by the air conditioning unit. Despite what the dealer may say, GM, Ford, and Chrysler service bulletins clearly show automakers will pay for AC service adjustments for a reasonable period of time.

Here are a few examples of the latest and most comprehensive secret warranties that have come across my desk in the last several years. Keep in mind that an up-to-date listing of other secret warranties and service programs for every vehicle *Lemon-Aid* rates can be found in Part Three under "Secret Warranties/Service Tips" in *Lemon-Aid Used Cars 2001*.

Chrysler, Ford, General Motors: All models, all years
- **Problem:** Faulty paint jobs that cause paint to turn white and peel off of horizontal panels. GM and Ford documents show that the problem is a factory defect.
- **Warranty coverage:** Vehicle will be repainted free for up to six years with no mileage limitation. Thereafter, the automakers usually offer 50–75 percent refunds. Lots of Internet documentation is available to help you win these paint claims (see Appendix).

 PONTIAC

PONTIAC DIVISION
GeneralMotors Corporation
One Pontiac Plaza
Pontiac, Michigan 48340-2952
October 16, 1992

TO: All Pontiac Dealers

SUBJECT: Partners in Satisfaction (PICS)
            Dealer Authorization

Pontiac continually reviews the Warranty Management System to ensure that Warranty Administration achieves its purposes, including high levels of customer satisfaction with after sale treatment.

Following a recent review, Pontiac has decided to provide dealers authorization for cases involving paint repairs for vehicles up to six (6) years from the date of delivery, without regard for mileage. This is a change from the current PICS dealer self-authorization which allows paint repair goodwill adjustments to be made up to 6 years/60,000 miles. Dealers who have a deductible override capabilities may also waive deductibles as they see appropriate on this type of repair.

Paint repairs are only to be authorized beyond the warranty period by the Dealership Service Manager on a case-by-case basis as with any other goodwill policy adjustment.

Assistance should only be considered for cases involving evidence of a defect in materials or workmanship by the manufacturer. Assistance should not be considered for conditions related to wear and tear and/or lack of maintenance (such as fading, stone chips, scratches, environmental damage, etc.).

Please contact your Zone representative if you have specific questions.

Perry S. White
Director of Service/
Customer Satisfaction

GM says it has no secret paint warranty, so what's this? The GM 6-year benchmark is usually followed by Chrysler and Ford; however, small claims court judges have awarded paint refunds going back 10 years.

Chrysler: 1991–99 cars, minivans, vans, sport-utilities, and trucks

- **Problem:** Defective engine head gaskets, automatic transmissions, air conditioners, and brakes; delaminated paint that turns a chalky colour and then peels off.
- **Warranty coverage:** Chrysler has offered full or partial refunds for claims that are within the durability guidelines set out on pages 106–7.

Chrysler set up a special Warranty Review Committee in February 1998 in response to the bad publicity and threats of court action coming from *Lemon-Aid* and the approximately 600 Chrysler owners who helped form Chrysler Lemon Owners Groups (CLOG) in British Columbia and New Brunswick. If you have had any of these problems and want "goodwill" repairs (or a refund for repairs already carried out), go through Chrysler's regular customer relations hotline. If you're not satisfied by the response you get, then phone the Review Committee at 519-973-2300 or fax Lou Spadotto, National Service Manager: tel.: 519-973-2890; fax: 519-973-2318. If you cannot get in touch with Lou Spadotto, phone or fax Larry Latta, Vice President Sales and Marketing: tel.: 519-973-2947; fax: 519-973-2799. Mr. Latta confirmed to me earlier this year that the Review Committee will continue to review all claims, including those that were previously rejected by customer relations staffers.

Unlike Ford and GM, Chrysler rarely publishes its goodwill warranty parameters, preferring, instead, to deal with each claim individually. This creates a climate of secrecy where customers aren't told post-warranty assistance is available and results in claimants being treated unfairly. What Chrysler reps trumpet as a more efficacious refund procedure is actually an administrative attempt to reduce claims costs. In the absence of written guidelines, I see no reason why Chrysler shouldn't be held accountable for powertrain (engines and automatic transmissions) failures to the same extent that Ford and GM have voluntarily accepted—that is, up to 7 years or 160,000 km.

Three suggestions if you plan to contact the Review Committee: send Chrysler copies of all your repair bills or independent garage estimates; don't accept a refusal based on the fact that you're not the first owner; and finally, don't let Chrysler turn your claim down because the repairs were carried out by an independent repair facility (see the following letter):

Dear Phil,

   I thought you might be interested to learn of the outcome of my troubles with a transmission failure on my 1993 Plymouth minivan. I requested a faxed dealer service bulletin summary from you on August 21 this year. You added a note that I should call a Bob Renaud at Chrysler and start the claim process.

   We phoned this gentleman's office and spoke with Sharon McDonald, who assigned us a claim file number and asked that we fax her our bill and a covering letter outlining the circumstances. We sent that off on September 4, and heard nothing until today, the 25th of September. We were actually going through our copy of *Lemon-Aid*, reading up on our next step (threaten court action?) when the mail arrived containing a letter from Chrysler Canada and a $2,885.73 cheque to reimburse us for our costs.

   We were stunned! Surely it couldn't be this easy! We hadn't even trotted out our list of DSB numbers yet, nor had we mentioned lawyers or Small Claims Court. Chrysler obviously knew they had a problem with the transmissions....

   I hope my experiences can be used to help other motorists. They can be summarized thusly:

   1. Don't let the dealer brush you off (this is their job)—go to the factory.

   2. Just because you chose the short-term warranty option doesn't mean you aren't covered by the long-term—if you fight for it.

   Thank you very much for the excellent advice in your book: it gave us the determination to keep on at the problem when it would have been all too easy to let go. Thanks especially for the phone contact at Chrysler. I'm sure that one little piece of information saved us hours of time and many dollars in phone calls to Ontario. Our local dealer certainly wasn't forthcoming with stuff like that. We are definitely a lot more satisfied with Chrysler now, thanks to their willingness to promptly settle a fair claim....

Yours sincerely,
Wally James & Barb Steele

Chrysler: 1995–98 Neon, Cirrus, and Stratus with 4-cylinder engines
- **Problem:** Engine head gasket failure.
- **Warranty coverage:** Chrysler Canada reps have indicated that 5 years/100,000 km was the limit where claims would be looked upon "favourably" and owners would be reimbursed for previous engine repairs. Unfortunately, there is no written record of this secret warranty; the details we have amassed come from discussions with Chrysler executives, service manager whistleblowers, and owners who have gotten refunds. Apparently, Chrysler pays 100 percent of the claim unless repairs were done by an independent garage. In that case, the claim may be reduced to 75 or even 50 percent. I suggest you fight any payout of less than 100 percent with a small claims action reinforced by Ford's 7-year/100,000 mile (160,000 km) extended warranty benchmark, and Chrysler's engine head gasket service bulletin, downloaded from *neons.org/neonstsb/TSB/09/090598.htm*.

Ford: 1994–98 all front-drive vehicles

Problem: Automatic transmission failures that involve the forward clutch piston, planetary gear lube, and clutch slave cylinder. Bulletins show problems are factory related.

Warranty coverage: Ford will repair or replace the transmission at no charge up to 7 years/160,000 km and then offer 50–75 percent refunds for vehicles exceeding these parameters. Ford also has promised to reconsider all claims that were previously denied because they were out of warranty (see Ford Transmission Victims website in the Appendix).

Ford: 1996–97 Taurus and Sable with 3.0L engines

• **Problem:** Blown head gasket, engine failure, lack of heat, coolant smell, coolant overflow, contaminated/corroded coolant, fluctuating or high temperature readings, chronic blown hoses, and hose leaks.

• **Warranty coverage:** Installation of a free coolant by-pass kit to prevent the above-noted problems. This bulletin gives owners additional rights if their engines require major repairs up to 7 years/160,000 km (simply extrapolate the 3.8L warranty extension provisions and get a copy of the ALLDATA service bulletin #97-24-16, issued 11/24/97.

Ford: 1996–97 Mustang, Thunderbird, and Cougar and 1997 F-Series trucks with 3.8L and 4.2L engines

• **Problem:** Engine coolant leaks.

• **Warranty coverage:** Ford dealers will replace the engine front cover gasket at no charge until March 31, 2001; there is no mileage limitation. See service bulletin #99-20-7 for details of the defect Ford is correcting and the other models and years that are affected, but have been conveniently left out of this program.

Ford/Lincoln: 1994–95 Taurus, Sable, and Windstar; 1994 Lincoln Continental

• **Problem:** Defective 3.8L engine head gaskets may cause loss of coolant, overheating, or destruction of the engine.

• **Warranty coverage:** Ford will replace the defective components at no charge up to 7 years/160,000 km. Claims for pre-1994 vehicles and independent repairs carried out after the above date will be reviewed on a case-by-case basis.

A.R. O'Neill   Ford Motor Company
Director   P.O. Box 1904
Vehicle Services and Programs   Dearborn, MI 48121-1904
Ford Customer Service Division

January, 2000

Ford Motor Company is providing a no-charge Service Program, Number 99B29, to owners of certain 1996 and 1997 model year Mustang, Thunderbird, Cougar, and 1997 F-Series vehicles equipped with 3.8L or 4.2L engines.

What Is The Reason For This Program?
The affected vehicles may experience engine coolant leaks at the engine front cover gasket; this could cause severe engine damage if not corrected. To avoid engine damage, you should make an appointment to have this service performed on your vehicle at your Ford or Lincoln Mercury Dealer as soon as possible.

No Charge Service:
At no charge to you, your dealer will replace the engine from cover gasket with a redesigned gasket and change the engine oil and filter. This service will reduce the likelihood of coolant leaks at the engine front cover, and will help avoid the potential inconvenience of breakdowns and costly engine repairs.

Your vehicle is eligible for this program until March 31, 2001, regardless of mileage.

How Long Will It Take?
The time needed for this repair is less than one day. However, due to service scheduling issues, your dealer may need your vehicle for a longer period of time. To avoid engine damage, inconvenience, and costly repairs please schedule a service date as soon as possible.

Call Your Dealer:
Call your dealer without delay. Ask for a service date and whether parts are in stock for Owner Notification Program 99B29.

If your dealer does not have the parts in stock, they can be ordered before scheduling your service date. Parts would be expected to arrive within a week after the order is placed.

When you bring your vehicle in, show the dealer this letter. If you misplace this letter, your dealer will still do the work, free of charge.

Refund:
If you paid for engine repairs caused by a front cover gasket leak on this vehicle *before* the date of this letter, Ford is offering a refund. For the refund, please give your paid original receipt to your Ford or Lincoln Mercury dealer. To avoid delays, do not send receipts to Ford Motor Company.

Ford Motor Company
P.O. Box 1904
Dearborn, Michigan 48121
1-800-392-3673

Owner Notification Program - 00M09   March, 2000

Ford Motor Company is committed to becoming the world's leading consumer company of
automotive products and services and is dedicated to pursuing customer satisfaction. Our goal,
together with your local Ford dealer, is to earn your continued loyalty by providing consumer
focused service and support.

In support of this commitment, Ford Motor Company is providing additional warranty coverage
under Service Program Number 00M09, to owners of 1994 and 1995 model year Ford Taurus and
1995 model year Ford Windstar vehicles equipped with a 3.8L engine.

The additional warranty covers potential engine head gasket failures, which may be experienced
by some owners of these vehicles, and will be in effect for 7 years or 100,000 miles, from the
vehicle's original warranty start date, whichever comes first.

If you have already paid to have the head gasket repaired, prior to the date of this letter, you may
be entitled to a refund of your repair costs, or, for a limited time, an option to purchase a new
Ford, Mercury, or Lincoln vehicle under a special marketing program. Please refer to the next
page for additional details of coverage. This program is offered in addition to other excellent new
vehicle incentives Ford Motor Company has available in the marketplace currently. If you are
interested in a new vehicle, please contact your dealer for details.

We apologize for problems you may have with your vehicle. Ford Motor Company is committed
to maintaining satisfying and long-term relationships with our valued customers, and demonstrat-
ing that commitment through actions such as this. Thank you.

*General Motors: 1992–94 Cavalier/Sunbird with 4-cylinder engines; 1995–96
Cavalier/Sunfire;1996 Chevrolet S-10 and GMC Sonoma pickups with two-
wheel-drive and 2.2-litre 4-cylinder engines*

• **Problem:** Faulty head gaskets may cause loss of engine coolant,
engine overheating, or destruction of the engine. GM's letter shows
problem is a factory defect, but only mentions the Cavalier's 2.2L
engine, and apparently only applies to Canada. Owner feedback,
however, tells me the Sunbird's 2.0L engine repairs are covered on a
case-by-case basis.

• **Warranty coverage:** GM will replace the faulty head gasket or repair the
engine damage caused by head gasket failure at no charge up to
7 years/160,000 km. As for the '94 model engine, Chris Jensen, automotive columnist for the *Cleveland Plain Dealer* disclosed in a June 3, 2000
article that GM spokesman Greg Martin confirmed that the '94s were
also part of the Special Policy, but this policy only applied to Canadians.

Consumers who already paid for repairs at a dealership should contact the dealership to be reimbursed. Consumers who did not have a
GM dealership do the work aren't excluded from the refund program
and should contact the toll-free customer assistance number in the
owner's manual. Future repairs, however, must take place at a GM dealership. The program is not a recall, and owners should take their vehicles to a dealership only if it appears they have a problem. Remember,
if you have an engine head gasket failure on a GM vehicle or engine
not included in the above-noted programs, don't despair. Simply use
the same benchmarks for your own vehicle and threaten small claims
action on those grounds.

GM Saturn: 1994–96 Saturn SOHC engines
- **Problem:** Faulty head gaskets may overheat and cook the engine.
- **Warranty coverage:** GM will replace the defective head gasket or repair the engine damage caused by head gasket failure at no charge up to 6 years/160,000 km.

How Long Should Parts/Repairs Last?

Let's say you can't find a service bulletin that says your problem is factory related or covered by a special compensation program. Or a part lasts just a little longer than its guarantee, but not as long as is generally expected. Can you get a refund if the same problem reappears shortly after it has been repaired? Yes—if you can prove the part failed prematurely.

Automakers, mechanics, and the courts have their own benchmarks as to what a reasonable period of time or amount of mileage is during which one should expect a part or adjustment to last. The following table shows what most automakers consider to be reasonable durability as expressed by their original warranties, as well as their secret warranties (often called "goodwill" or "special policy" programs).

Estimated Part Durability

ACCESSORIES

Air conditioner	7 years
Cellular phone	5 years
Cruise control	5 years/ 100,000 km
Power antenna	5 years
Power doors, windows	5 years
Radio	5 years

BODY

Paint (peeling)	7 years
Rust (perforations)	7 years
Rust (surface)	5 years
Water/wind/air leaks	5 years

BRAKE SYSTEM

Brake drum	120,000 km
Brake drum linings	35,000 km
Brake rotor	60,000 km
Disc brake calipers	30,000 km
Disc brake pads	30,000 km
Master cylinder, rebuild	100,000 km
Wheel cylinder, rebuild	80,000 km

ENGINE AND DRIVETRAIN

Constant velocity joint	7 years/ 160,000 km
Differential	7 years/ 160,000 km
Engine (gas)	7 years/ 160,000 km
Radiator	4 years/ 80,000 km

Transfer case	7 years/ 150,000 km
Transmission (auto.)	7 years/ 160,000 km
Transmission (man.)	7 years/ 200,000 km
Transmission oil cooler	5 years/ 100,000 km

EXHAUST SYSTEM

Catalytic converter	5 years/ 100,000 km or more
Muffler	2 years/ 40,000 km
Tailpipe	3 years/ 60,000 km

FUEL SYSTEM

Fuel filter	2 years/ 40,000 km
Fuel pump	5 years/ 80,000 km
Injectors	5 years/ 80,000 km

IGNITION SYSTEM

Cable set	60,000 km
Electronic module	5 years/ 80,000 km
Retiming	20,000 km
Spark plugs	20,000 km
Tune-up	20,000 km

SAFETY COMPONENTS

Airbags	life of vehicle
ABS brakes	7 years/ 160,000 km
ABS computer	10 years/ 160,000 km
Seatbelts	life of vehicle

STEERING AND SUSPENSION

Alignment	1 year 20,000 km
Ball joints	80,000 km
Power steering	5 years/ 80,000 km
Shock absorber	2 years/ 40,000 km

Struts	5 years/ 80,000 km
Tires (radial)	5 years/ 80,000 km
Wheel bearing	3 years/ 60,000 km

VISIBILITY

Halogen/fog lights	3 years/ 60,000 km
Sealed beam	2 years/ 40,000 km
Windshield wiper motor	5 years/ 80,000 km

The previous guidelines are extrapolated from Ford and Chrysler goodwill payouts to claimants over the past three years. Other sources for this chart were the Ford and GM transmission warranties as outlined in their secret warranties, and GM, Mercury, Nissan, and Toyota engine "special programs" laid out in their internal service bulletins.

Safety features generally have a lifetime warranty, with the exception of ABS brakes, which are a wear item. Nevertheless, the Chrysler 10-year "free service program" portion of its ABS recall, announced several years ago, can serve as a handy benchmark as to how long one can expect these components to last.

Airbags are a different matter. Those that deploy in an accident, as well as the personal injury and interior damage their deployment will likely have caused, are covered by your accident insurance policy. However, if there is a sudden deployment for no apparent reason, the automaker and dealer should be held jointly responsible for all injuries and damages caused by the airbag. This will likely lead to a more generous settlement from the two parties and prevent your insurance premiums from being jacked up. Inadvertent deployment may occur after passing over a bump in the road, slamming the car door, having wet carpets in your Cadillac (no kidding), or, in some Chrysler minivans, simply putting the key in the ignition. This happens more often than you might imagine, judging by the hundreds of recalls and thousands of complaints recorded on the U.S. National Highway Traffic Safety Administration's website at *www.nhtsa.dot.gov/cars/problems/complain/compmmy1.cfm*.

Finally, the manufacturer's emissions warranty serves as the primary guideline governing how long a vast array of electronic and mechanical components should last. Look first at your owner's manual for an indication of which parts on your vehicle are covered. If you come up with few specifics, use the provincial government's guidelines in provinces where emissions testing is mandatory. Keep in mind that these durability benchmarks, secret warranties, and emissions warranties all apply to subsequent owners.

Recall Campaigns

Safety- and emissions-recall campaigns confer warranty benefits on owners whereby the manufacturer and dealer are obligated to repair a defect at no charge, no matter how often the vehicle has been sold or what its mileage is. Furthermore, Transport Canada monitors how well automakers carry out recall campaigns and will intervene if any company stonewalls a legitimate request.

Recall repairs

Let the automaker know who and where you are. If you've bought a used vehicle, or if you've moved, it's a smart idea to pay a visit to your local dealer and get a "report card" on which recalls, free service campaigns, and warranties are listed. Simply give the service advisor your vehicle identification number (VIN)—found on the dash just below the windshield on the driver's side, or on your insurance card—and have the number run through the automaker's computer system ("Function 70" for Chrysler, "OASIS" for Ford, and "CRIS" for GM). Ask for a computer printout of the vehicle's history (have it faxed to you, if you're so equipped) and make sure you're listed in the automaker's computer as the new owner. This ensures that you'll receive notices of warranty extensions and emissions and safety recalls.

Still, don't expect to be welcomed with open arms when your vehicle develops a safety- or emissions-related problem that's not yet part of a recall campaign. Automakers and dealers generally take a restrictive view of what constitutes a safety or emissions defect and frequently charge for repairs that should be free under federal safety or emissions legislation. To counter this tendency, look at the following list of typical defects that are clearly safety related, and if you experience similar problems, tell the dealer you expect your repair to be paid by the manufacturer:

• airbag malfunctions
• corrosion affecting safe operation
• disconnected or stuck accelerators
• electrical shorts
• faulty windshield wipers
• fuel leaks
• problems with original axles, drive shafts, seats, seat recliners, or defrosters
• seatbelt problems
• stalling or sudden acceleration
• sudden steering or brake loss
• suspension failures
• trailer coupling failures

U.S. recall campaigns force automakers to pay the entire cost of fixing a vehicle's safety-related defect. This includes used vehicles, and has no cut-off limitation. Recalls may be voluntary or ordered by the U.S. Department of Transportation. Canadian regulation has an added twist: Transport Canada can only order automakers to notify owners that their vehicles may be unsafe; it can't force them to correct the problem. Fortunately, most U.S.-ordered recalls are carried out in Canada, and when Transport Canada makes a defect determination on its own, automakers generally comply with an owner notification letter.

Voluntary recall campaigns are a real problem, though. They aren't as rigorously monitored as government-ordered recalls, and dealers and automakers routinely deny there's a recall. Also, the company's so-called "fix" often doesn't correct the hazard. Take, as an example, Chrysler's voluntary recall to strengthen the rear latches on as many as 4.5 million 1984–95 minivans. Almost 50 percent of affected owners were still waiting for Chrysler to fix their minivans nearly two years after the company volunteered to correct the defect.

Safety defect information

If you wish to report a safety defect or want recall info, you may access Transport Canada's website: *www.tc.gc.ca/roadsafety/Recalls/search_e.asp.* You'll get recall information in French or English, as well as general information relating to road safety and importing a vehicle into Canada. Cybersurfers can now access the recall database for 1970–2000 model vehicles, but unlike NHTSA's website, owner complaints aren't listed, defect investigations aren't disclosed, and service bulletin summaries aren't provided. You can also call Transport Canada at 1-800-333-0510 (toll-free within Canada) or 613-993-9851 (within the Ottawa region or outside Canada) to get additional information.

Unfortunately, there are some problems with Ottawa's database—and attitude. First, when calling Ottawa through the toll-free line, Transport Canada bureaucrats insist that the dealer must already have refused you the recall info before they will give it to you. You won't be told if others have reported similar safety problems affecting your vehicle. And more often than not, if you suspect your car has a safety defect, you'll be asked to take it to the dealer for a safety exam (where there's a good chance the problem will be covered up or you'll be blamed for the malfunction).

If you're not happy with Ottawa's treatment of your recall inquiry, try the U.S. government's NHTSA website. It's more complete than Transport Canada's site (NHTSA's database was established in 1972 and is updated daily). You can search the database specific to your vehicle and be thoroughly briefed on recalls, crash ratings, safety and performance defects reported by other vehicle owners, and a host of other safety-related items. The NHTSA website is *www.nhtsa.dot.gov/cars/ problems/recalls/recmmy1.cfm* for recalls and *www.nhtsa.dot.gov/cars/ problems/complain/compmmy1.cfm* for the complaint database.

NHTSA's fax-back service provides the same info through a local line that can be accessed from Canada—although long-distance charges will apply (most calls take 5–10 minutes to complete). For calls placed within the U.S., the toll-free hot line is 1-800-424-9393 (1-800-424-9153 for the hearing impaired). The following local numbers get you into the automatic response service just as quickly, and can be reached 24 hours a day: 202-366-0123 (202-366-7800 for the hearing impaired).

Three Steps to a Settlement

Step 1: informal negotiations

If your vehicle was misrepresented, has major defects, or wasn't properly repaired under warranty, the first thing you should do is give the seller (the dealer and automaker or a private party) a written summary (by registered mail or fax) of the outstanding problems and stipulate a time period in which they will need to be corrected or your money will be refunded. Keep a copy for yourself along with all your repair records. Be sure to check all of the sales and warranty documents you were given to see if they conform to provincial laws. Any errors, omissions, or violations can be used to get a settlement with the dealer in lieu of making a formal complaint.

When negotiating with the seller, speak in a calm, polite manner and try to avoid polarizing the issue. Talk about how "we can work together" on the problem. Support your position with independent garage reports, service bulletins, and maintenance records. Let a compromise slowly emerge—don't come in with a hard-line set of demands. Don't demand the settlement offer in writing, but make sure you're accompanied by a friend who can confirm the offer in court if it's not honoured (relatives can testify in court). Be prepared to act on the offer without delay, so that you won't be blamed for its withdrawal.

Service managers

Service managers are directly responsible to dealers and manufacturers and make the first determination of what work is covered under warranty. They are paid to save the dealers and automakers money and to mollify irate clients—almost an impossible balancing act, wherein my sympathies are more with the dealers than with the automakers. When service managers agree to warranty coverage, it's because you've convinced them that they must do so. This can be done by getting them to access the vehicle's history from the manufacturer's computer and by presenting the facts of your case in a confident, forthright manner with as many dealer service bulletins and NHTSA owner complaint printouts as you can find for support.

If the service manager can't or won't set things right, your next step is to convene a mini-summit with the service manager, the dealership principal, and the automaker's rep. By getting the automaker involved, you run less risk of having the dealer fob you off on the manufacturer and you can often get an agreement in which the seller and automaker pay two-thirds of the repair cost.

Dealers/automakers

Check all of the sales and warranty documents you were given to see if they conform to provincial laws. Any errors, omissions, or violations can be used to clinch a deal with the dealer in lieu of making a formal complaint, because the dealer could be fined if he has violated provincial protection laws.

You have to make the case that the vehicle's defects were present during the warranty period, or that the vehicle doesn't conform to the way it was represented when it was purchased. Emphasize that you intend to use the courts if necessary to obtain a refund—most dealers would rather settle than risk a lawsuit with all the attendant publicity. An independent estimate of the vehicle's defects and cost of repairs is essential if you want to convince the seller that you're serious in your claim and stand a good chance of winning your case in court. The estimated cost of repairs is also useful in challenging a dealer who agrees to pay half the repair costs and then jacks up the costs a hundred percent so that you wind up paying the whole shot.

If the dealer won't talk with you, write or call the nearest regional office or the manufacturer's head office. The address and telephone numbers can be found in the owner's manual. Often, addressing your letter to "Legal Affairs" will ensure your complaint is kicked upstairs and handled expeditiously by more competent staffers who have been empowered with more latitude in granting goodwill payouts. Many companies have a telephone centre to handle customer concerns—General Motors, for example, has a toll-free customer hot line (1-800-263-3777) that operates out of Oshawa, Ontario, and employs over 30 people (one-third of whom are bilingual) to answer customer inquiries. Don't expect miracles from these people. Each staffer has a guidebook showing the appropriate, corporate-approved response for the most frequently asked consumer questions. If you dig too deeply, you'll likely get the cold shoulder or, as one GM owner wrote me, get the receiver hung up in your ear.

If there's a warranty dispute, or if you've found that your service manager can't correct a persistent problem, GM customer relations staff will intervene to set things right, if possible, at the dealership level. Once your name, vehicle identification number (VIN), and dealer's name are punched into the computer, the customer relations rep can tell you if you're eligible for free repairs under a special (i.e., secret) warranty or through a safety/emissions recall campaign. The telephone staff will never mention the phrase "secret warranty," nor will they ever pass you on to someone else in charge. Since they were hired to reduce the number of calls their bosses receive, every call that gets through their screening is a black mark against their job performance.

Lemon-Aid readers tell me that automaker telephone staffers try to "barter down" owners' requests for warranty compensation involving paint defects and other secret warranty-related problems. Using the pretexts that the vehicle was repaired by an independent garage, the customer didn't buy the extended warranty, or Phil Edmonston is out to unfairly punish car companies, they initially offer to pay only 50 percent of the repair bill—an offer that is often boosted to 75 percent compensation if the customer will agree—at that very moment—to pay 25 percent of the repair.

Factory reps
The factory rep is directly responsible to the manufacturer and has the last word on what work is covered under warranty. Not unlike the customer relations staff, he's paid to save the company money. Every time he says no, he docs his job. When he says yes to warranty coverage, it's because you've convinced him he must. Should you see that you're getting nowhere with the factory rep, give him one last chance to make a reasonable offer. Don't threaten him or tip him off to your next move.

Step 2: send a registered letter, fax, or email
This is the next step to take if your claim is refused. Send the dealer and manufacturer a polite registered letter or a fax that asks for compensation for repairs that have been done or need to be done, insurance costs while the vehicle is being repaired, towing charges, supplementary transportation costs like taxis and rented cars, and damages for inconvenience.

Specify five days (but allow ten) for either party to respond. If no satisfactory offer is made, file suit in small claims court. Make the manufacturer a party to the lawsuit, especially if the emissions warranty, a secret warranty extension, a safety-recall campaign, or extensive chassis rusting is involved. Use the sample complaint letter on the following page as a guide for getting compensation. Include a reference in your letter to any court decisions you find in this section of the book that support your claim.

Step 3: mediation and arbitration
If you have a new- or used-vehicle complaint and the formality of a courtroom puts you off, or if you're not sure your claim is all that solid and don't want to pay legal costs to find out, consider using mediation or arbitration sponsored by the Better Business Bureau, the Automobile Protection Association, the Canadian Automobile Association, or provincial and territorial governments.

New-Car Complaint Letter/Fax/Email

Without Prejudice

Date: _____
Name and address of dealer: _____
Name and address of manufacturer: _____

Please be advised that I am not satisfied with my _____ (indicate year, make, model, and serial number of vehicle). The vehicle was purchased on _____ (indicate date) and currently indicates _____ km on the odometer. The vehicle presently exhibits the following defects:

      1. Premature rusting
      2. Paint peeling/discoloration
      3. Water leaks
      4. Other defects (explain)

(List previous attempts to repair the vehicle. Attach a copy of a report from an independent garage, showing cost of estimated repairs and confirming the manufacturer's responsibility.)

I hereby request that you correct these defects free of charge under the terms of the implied warranty provisions of provincial consumer protection statutes as applied in *Kravitz v. General Motors* (1979), I.S.C.R., and *Chabot v. Ford* (1983), 39 O.R. (2d).

If you do not correct the defects noted above to my satisfaction and within a reasonable length of time, I will be obliged to ask an independent garage to _____ (choose [a] estimate or [b] carry out) the repairs and claim the amount of $_____ (state the cost, if possible) by way of the courts without further notice or delay.

I have dealt with your company because of its competence and honesty. I close in the hope of hearing from you within five (5) days of receiving this letter, failing which I will exercise the alternatives available to me. Please govern yourself accordingly.

Sincerely,

(Signed, with telephone number)

CAMVAP
Except for Quebec, all provinces and the Northwest Territories adhere to the Canadian Motor Vehicle Arbitration Plan (CAMVAP), which arbitrates disputes between consumers and automakers that result from

alleged manufacturing defects. Before you decide to use CAMVAP to resolve your dispute, there is one thing you must keep in mind. Once the CAMVAP arbitrator has made a decision, that decision is final. This means that both you and the manufacturer are subject to very limited rights to have the decision reviewed by a court through judicial review. In applying for judicial review, you should keep in mind that you must pay the costs of initiating this process. Neither party can appeal or seek judicial review just because you do not agree with the arbitrator's decision.

The Provincial and Territorial Arbitration Acts allow judicial review of the arbitration process. This takes place before a judge. If the judge rules that the arbitrator made a mistake or error in law at your hearing, the decision can be set aside or a new hearing may be ordered. The Arbitration Acts also allow the arbitrator to correct minor errors or omissions in the award. The time limit for referring the matter back to the arbitrator varies by province and territory. To be safe, if you believe there is an error or omission in the decision made by the arbitrator, you should communicate your concern in writing to the CAMVAP Administrator for your region within 15 days of receiving the arbitrator's decision.

Arbitrating about 350–400 cases a year, out of a total of 8,000 annual complaints, CAMVAP offers its services free of charge to new- and used-car owners. Lawyers aren't usually involved (so no awards need to be split); binding arbitration by a neutral third party can be arranged within a 6- to 8-week period; and all negotiations are carried out informally, allowing plaintiffs to bring along anyone they wish to represent them.

CAMVAP won't consider claims for personal injury, tire defects (except on GM's models), third-party rustproofing or paint protection failure, motor homes, or vehicles used primarily for business purposes, unless the plaintiff owns the business and the vehicle is driven by that person or a member of his or her family.

CAMVAP arbitration is worth serious consideration, particularly now that its rules have been become more user-friendly as a result of *Lemon-Aid* and other consumer group pressures. Access to the program is now much easier and compensation guidelines for plaintiffs have been enhanced. For example, consumers who use the CAMVAP process are no longer sworn to secrecy; plaintiffs may appear with an advocate at the hearing; the formula for automaker buy-backs now includes freight charges, administration fees, and fuel and tire conservation taxes which could add as much as $1,000 to the award; a new buy-back formula for leased vehicles includes the reimbursement of the down payment and security deposit; and the arbitrator can award out-of-pocket expenses up to $500.

Under CAMVAP's present rules, Canadian residents who own or lease a defective 1996 or later model vehicle with less than 160,000 km must first contact their dealer and automaker to settle the dispute before asking for arbitration. If this doesn't take care of the problem, ask the dealer for the regional CAMVAP phone number and call for an arbitration application form. If the dealer is uncooperative, call CAMVAP toll-free at 1-800-207-0685 or access the group on the Internet at *www.camvap.ca.* If the vehicle has been in service longer than three years or 36,000 km, only repair or repair compensation can be awarded. No buy-backs are possible.

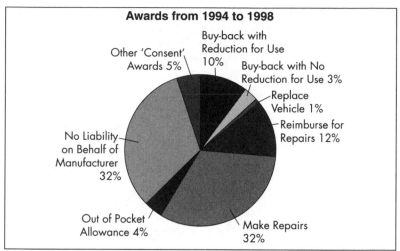

Awards from 1994 to 1998

Buy-back with Reduction for Use 10%

Other 'Consent' Awards 5%

Buy-back with No Reduction for Use 3%

Replace Vehicle 1%

Reimburse for Repairs 12%

No Liability on Behalf of Manufacturer 32%

Out of Pocket Allowance 4%

Make Repairs 32%

CAMVAP's 1999 case decisions are so sketchy, it's impossible to find any meaningful information. Plus the group's Internet site's "tip-toeing through the tulips" introduction is embarrassingly pro-automaker.

CAMVAP claims that through 1994 to 1998 it has ruled in the consumer's favour 68 percent of the time. Of course, this self-serving figure can't be checked, because CAMVAP put a gag order on all claimants prior to relaxing its rules in June 1999. Nevertheless, the organization says in 1998 it heard 463 cases and ordered the manufacturer to buy back 63 vehicles and repair most of the others.

Getting outside help
Don't lose your case due to poor preparation. Ask government or independent consumer protection agencies to evaluate how well you're prepared before going to your first hearing. Also use the Internet to ferret out additional facts and gather support (*www.lemonaidcars.com* is a good place to start).

On-line services/Internet/websites
America Online and CompuServe are two on-line service providers with active consumer forums that use experts to answer consumer queries, and to provide legal and technical advice. The Internet offers the same information using a worldwide database. If you or someone you know is able to create a website, you might consider using this site to attract atten-

tion to your plight and arm yourself for arbitration or court. You may wish to follow the example of some existing websites I've listed in the

Appendix. A few of my favourites are: Chrysler Peeling Paint, Neon Enthusiasts (engine head gaskets), Dead Ford, Ford Automatic Transmission Victims, Ford Suckz, and GM Saturn Exposed. I don't know why, but Ford seems to attract the most web-savvy complainers.

DO NOT BUY A KIA!!!!!
Note: In an effort to get this website highly ranked on search engines (and save people from buying a lemon), I have replaced Kia with K--, Sportage by Sport--- and Sephia by Seph---. This is because too many occurences of the same keyword is considered

spamming and can hurt your website ranking. You can avoid these replacements by clicking here to visit my mirror site.

I bought a new 1997 K-- Seph--- that I was happy with at first. However, in the last month it's been in the repair shop 5 times and I've had over $1000 in repairs done (the cars is barely 2 years old!). I've had the alternator ($236), the battery ($70), the idle motor/throttle assembly ($687), and the pcm (the main computer that controls everything - luckily this was covered under warranty) replaced. I also had to take it to a mechanic who specialized in electrical problems so he could make sure that the K-- dealership I took the car to didn't mess anything up ($65). Aside from these recent repairs, I have also had to replace all four tires ($280), another battery ($60), the PC valve ($55), and I've had assorted repairs done that were covered under warranty. Part of the problem this last month could have been with the Sante Fe Dodge/K-- dealership, but a K-- repair shop should know how to fix it's own cars. I've done some checking around and having to do this many repairs does not seem to be anything out of the ordinary for K-- cars. I've talked to several repair shops and have been told that K--'s are good for about 1-2 years, after which time they start to fall apart. This car has left my fiance and me stranded on the highway 4 times in the last month. Once it almost cost my fiancee her life (the car died at night on a 2 lane highway with no shoulder and she had no power at all - she couldn't even turn on the hazzard lights) Buying this car has been the worst mistake of my life, and I want to prevent other people from making the same mistake. If you are planning on buying a K--, please read some of the many bad reviews and horror stories that I have found on the internet. If you would like to add your review to this site, please email me. To read some of the many reviews that other unsatisfied K-- owners have emailed me, click here. Most of these reviews make the problems with my K-- seem very minor

Acura was one of the first targets of a successful consumer protest using the Internet. Michael Hos, a dissatisfied Acura owner from the United States, became fed up with what he felt was Acura's stonewalling of his complaints. Rather than getting angry, he got organized and set up a website called "Acura 1997 CL 3.0L: My Lemon" to collect other owners' comments and list some of the most common Acura problem areas. Within six months, Acura settled. Here's what Hos wrote me:

As far as my website goes, I think it was a major part of them settling early. I had a counter placed on it that showed them how many people had visited the site. Anyone can set up a web page like mine pretty easily. I have web space on my university's computer, so it was free for me to use. Folks without space should expect to spend about $20 a month for space, or if they have their own e-mail account, web space is usually provided for free. If they don't know how to set up their web page, paying someone to do it will be kinda pricey, a few hundred bucks should cover it. The main thing it needs to have is the counter, and it also needs to be slander free. I had only facts on my web page as I didn't want to get involved in a slander suit. They also need to register the site with all the major search engines so it comes up when looking for the manufacturer. *Submitit.com* offers such services for free. Putting in a <Meta> tag into the page also helps move it up the search engines' list of hits. Posting to newsgroups also is helpful. I also wrote to J.D. Power, NHTSA, *Consumer Reports*, and any other consumer-oriented agency I could think of.

When we settled for $4,000 before going to court, I had to sign the settlement papers saying I would pull down my site. They would not settle with me until I did that. This shows how much power the site can have. I also put the manufacturer's phone number and address on it so viewers of the site could contact the manufacturer...

PROJECTS AND CAUSES

A BAD FIRE occured in our 1994 Jeep Cherokee because of driving with a compact spare tire while in 4WD (could not get out of 4WD). Compact spare is standard equipment but appropriate warning not in Owners Manual. No appropriate answers from Chrysler Canada yet. Seeking others with similar experience.

Classified ads
Use your local paper's classified section or *The Globe and Mail*'s "National Personals" column to gather data from others who may have experienced a problem similar to your own. This alerts others to the potential problem, helps build a core base for a class action or group meeting with the automaker, and puts pressure on the dealer or manufacturer to settle. Sometimes the paper's news desk will assign someone to cover your story after your ad is published.

Federal and provincial consumer affairs
The wind left the sails of the consumer movement over a decade ago, leaving provincial consumer affairs offices understaffed and unsupported by the government. This has created a passive mindset among many staffers, who are tired of getting their heads kicked in by businesses and budget-cutters.

Consumer affairs offices can still help with investigation, mediation, and some litigation. Strong and effective consumer protection legislation has been left standing in most of the provinces, and resourceful consumers can use these laws in conjunction with media coverage to prod provincial consumer affairs offices into action. Furthermore, provincial bureaucrats aren't as well shielded from criticism as are their federal counterparts. A call to your MPP or MLA, or to the minister's executive assistant, can often get things rolling.

Federal consumer protection is a government-created PR myth. Don't expect the reorganized Consumer and Corporate Affairs staffers to be very helpful—they've been de-fanged and de-gummed through budget cuts and a succession of ineffective ministers. Although the revised Competition Act has some bite concerning misleading advertising and a number of other illegal business practices, the federal government has watered down the act's applicability to consumer groups and individual consumers.

Nevertheless, when used creatively, the recently beefed-up Competition Act can be a powerful tool for forcing a formal government investigation and prosecution, attracting media attention, and obtaining individual and collective compensation.

Getting a Secret Warranty Settlement

The following settlement advice applies mainly to paint defects, but you can use these tips for any other vehicle defect that you believe is the automaker's or dealer's responsibility. If you're not sure that the problem is a factory-related deficiency or a maintenance item, have it checked out by an independent garage or get a dealer service bulletin summary for your vehicle. The summary may include specific bulletins relating to the diagnosis, correction, and ordering of upgraded parts needed to fix your problem.

1. If you know the problem is factory related, take your vehicle to the dealer and ask for a written, signed estimate. When you're handed the estimate, ask that the paint job be done for free under the manufacturer's "goodwill" program. (Ford's euphemism for this secret warranty is "Owner Dialogue Program," GM's term is "Special Policy," and Chrysler just calls it "goodwill." Don't use the term "secret warranty" yet, you'll just make the dealer and automaker angry and evasive.)

2. Your request will probably be met with a refusal, an offer to repaint the vehicle for half the cost, or, if you're lucky, an agreement to repaint the vehicle free of charge. If you accept half-cost, make sure that it's based on the original estimate you have in hand, since some dealers jack up their estimates so that your 50 percent is really 100 percent of the true cost.

3. If the dealer/automaker has already refused your claim and the repair hasn't been done yet, get an additional estimate from an independent garage that shows the problem is factory related.

4. Again, if the repair has yet to be done, send a registered claim letter or fax to the automaker (send a copy to the dealer), claiming the average of both estimates. If the repair has been done at your expense, send a registered claim letter or fax with a copy of your bill.

5. If you don't receive a satisfactory response within a week, deposit a copy of the estimate or paid bill and letter before the small claims court and await a trial date. This means that the automaker/dealer

will have to appear, no lawyer is required, costs should be reasonable ($95–$125), and a mediation hearing or trial will be scheduled in a few months followed by a judgment a few weeks later (the time varies among different regions).

Things that you can collect to help your case include photographs, maintenance work orders, previous work orders dealing with your problem, dealer service bulletins, and an independent expert (the garage or body shop that did the estimate or repair is best, but you can also use a local teacher who teaches automotive repair).

Other situations

- If the vehicle has just been repainted but the dealer says that "goodwill" coverage was denied by the automaker, pay for the repair with a certified cheque and write "under protest" on the cheque. Remember, though, if the dealer does the repair, you won't have an independent expert who can affirm that the problem was factory related or that it was a result of premature wearout. Plus, the dealer can say that you or the environment caused the paint problem. In these cases, internal service bulletins can make or break your case.
- If the dealer/automaker offers a partial repair or refund, take it. Then sue for the rest, including any "deductible" you were forced to pay; GM's own memo says the deductible can be waived (see page 100). Remember, if a partial repair has been done under warranty, it counts as an admission of responsibility, no matter what "goodwill" euphemism is used. Also, the repaired component/body panel should be just as durable as if it were new. Hence, the clock starts ticking again until you reach the original warranty parameter—again, no matter what the dealer's repair warranty limit says.
- It's a lot easier to get the automaker to pay to replace a defective part than it is to be compensated for a missed day of work or a ruined vacation. Manufacturers hate to pay for consequential expenses apart from towing bills because they can't control the amount of the refund. Fortunately, the courts have taken the position that all expenses (damages) flowing from a problem covered by a warranty or service bulletin are the manufacturer's/dealer's responsibility under both common law and Quebec civil law. Nevertheless, don't risk a fair settlement for some outlandish claim of "emotional distress," "pain and suffering," etc. If you have invoices to prove actual consequential damages, then use them. If not, don't be greedy.

Very seldom do automakers contest these paint claims before small claims court, opting instead to settle once the court claim is bounced from their customer relations people to their legal affairs department. At that time, you'll probably be offered an out-of-court settlement for 50–75 percent of your claim.

Stand fast and make reference to the service bulletins you intend to subpoena in order to publicly contest in court the unfair nature of this

"secret warranty" program (automaker lawyers cringe at the idea of trying to explain why consumers aren't made aware of these bulletins).
One hundred percent restitution will probably result. A good example
is the *Shields v. General Motors of Canada* judgment rendered January 6,
1998 (found on the *www.lemonaidcars.com* website).

*Bentley v. Dave Wheaton Pontiac Buick GMC Ltd. and General Motors of
Canada*, Victoria Registry No. 24779, British Columbia Small Claims
Court, December 1, 1998, Judge Higinbotham. This is the third, and
most recent, small claims judgment against GM. It builds upon the
Ontario *Shields v. General Motors of Canada* decision and cites other
jurisprudence as to how long paint should last. If you're wondering why
Ford and Chrysler haven't been hit by similar judgments, remember
that they usually settle.

Reasons for Judgment

In this case the claimant purchased a vehicle, a pickup truck, from
a dealership, Dave Wheaton Pontiac Buick G.M.C. Ltd., a new vehicle, in 1991. There was an admitted defect in the paint which did
not become apparent until later. General Motors is also a defendant in this action and discovered in a general sense this problem
of delamination in the paint on some vehicles in 1992, about one
year after the claimant purchased the vehicle in question.

The specific problem with this vehicle was observed early in
1994. It was brought to the attention of Wheaton when the vehicle was brought in for other maintenance two weeks after the
warranty expired. At that time the problem was relatively minor.
I say relatively in the sense that compared to what later occurred
it was minor.

Mr. Palfry, who is the manager of the paint and body shop
for the retailer Wheaton, was made aware of the problem.
There is no dispute about that, and he sold the claimant a tub
of touch-up paint.

The paint continued to deteriorate and in late 1996 was
severely peeled.

In January of 1997, the claimant became aware that this
problem was general to certain GM vehicles, vehicles of certain
colours produced at a certain time by the defendant company.

The claimant took the vehicle back in but was told that it was
too late. The warranty had expired and even the discretionary
goodwill warranty was over. I do not think the claimant was told
about the discretionary goodwill warranty, but in fact it was a policy of GM to extend the warranty for this sort of claim in certain
circumstances, but it was discretionary. In any case, the claimant
was told that it was too late for it to be fixed under warranty.
Neither the dealership nor the manufacturer would accept
responsibility at that time. As a result, this action was commenced.

I make the following findings: There was a latent defect in the vehicle relating to the paint, which revealed itself over time and in far less time than a good paint job would be expected to last.

The dealer or the manufacturer, had the manufacturer been informed by the dealer, ought to have advised the claimant in May of 1994 that they were aware of this general delamination problem and ought to have advised as to what warranty extension might be available. I will say more about this in a moment. In any event, the dealer and the manufacturer, if the dealer had notified the manufacturer of the problem, would have known that the delamination commenced within the three year period and ought to have honoured the warranty.

Despite my findings, as I said earlier that the dealer and manufacturer ought to have given guidance to the claimant in May of 1994 as to a possible warranty claim, I do not find any cause of action arising directly from this finding. It would simply have been good business practice for them to have advised the claimant.

If liability is to be found against General Motors, it must be for a breach of the warranty. On the other hand, if liability is to be found against Dave Wheaton, it must be because as a seller the dealership breached an implied condition of the Sale of Goods Act.

On the issue of the warranty supplied by General Motors, I note that it covers "repairs, or adjustments to correct any vehicle defect related to material or workmanship occurring during the warranty period." It appears from the evidence that General Motors' major concern with this particular case was that the problem with this specific vehicle was not brought to their attention during the warranty period, not that the problem with the paint did not actually arise within the warranty period.

I find the claimant has established that the paint problem was brought to the attention of the dealer in mid-May of 1994. The warranty had expired two weeks earlier. I accept that the defect occurred during the warranty period on two bases. First, as submitted by the claimant, Ms. Bentley, the defect occurred at the time of manufacture and continues to this day.

Similar finding was made in *Shields v. General Motors of Canada*, a decision of the Ontario Court, General Division, number 1398 of 1996.

Secondly, in any event, based on the condition of the paint in mid-May 1994, the defect likely became apparent during the three year warranty period. I therefore find that General Motors has breached the warranty and the claimant is entitled to damages.

As for the dealership, defendant's counsel argues that there has been no breach of the Sale of Goods Act in that the vehicle when sold was of merchantable quality and reasonably fit for the purpose for which it was intended.

I agree as to merchantable quality. And as to the other implied condition, I also agree if what is meant by "reasonably fit for the purpose" is that it was a truck that operated and was capable of hauling cargo and passengers, but I am of the view that every seller of new vehicles knows that the purchaser expects the vehicle to be reasonably fit for the purpose of resale at some future time, depending upon the age and quality of the vehicle. This vehicle was not and is not reasonably fit for resale given those factors. It is not reasonably fit due to the latent defect in its quality, a defect which existed in incipient form at the time of sale.

I note that in *McCready Products v. Sherwin-Williams*, (1984) 53 A.R. 304, a decision of the Alberta Queen's Bench, referred to in the article by Fridman submitted by counsel, in that case paint that weathered and faded in less than three years was found unfit for its purpose. That was house paint. The same is true here. Even though the paint in question here was only a component of the item purchased, it was a very important component having a great deal to do with the value of the vehicle.

I therefore find the defendant Dave Wheaton Pontiac Buick G.M.C. Ltd. also liable for damages. The liability of both defendants is joint and several.

I turn now to the question of damages. The claimants have averaged three estimates they have placed before the court and claim the amount of twenty-three hundred seventy-three dollars and sixty-one cents.

The defendant says damages are lower as a different allowance to dealers are made under the warranty. The defendants cannot now get the benefit of this, in my opinion, as responsibility under the warranty was denied by them.

I prefer to assess damages by taking the defendant's estimate or figure of fifteen hundred eighty-eight dollars twenty-six cents, a sum which the dealer could charge under the warranty to GM, and multiply that figure by a factor admitted to by the defendant as to what another body shop would—the number of hours another body shop would employ in order to obtain a realistic assessment.

It was stated in evidence that twenty-two to twenty-five hours is required to repair this damage, of which two hours are the actual painting.

The defendant's estimate is based on sixteen point one hours, because that's all they can claim under the warranty. There is therefore a difference of approximately nine hours in the estimates based on the upper level of twenty-five hours required by another body shop. I accept the proportion of paint to labour as stated by the witness and therefore accept that the defendant's estimate is based on fourteen point one hours of labour.

I also accept that the acceptable labour rate is fifty dollars and fifty-five cents and the painting rate is twenty-three dollars and seventy-one cents. It is the nine hours of labour that is in issue here in the assessment of damages.

The costs of the paint and materials I accept is two hundred and sixty-two dollars and forty-two cents.

I am therefore going to base damages on the defendant's estimate of one thousand eight hundred and ten dollars and sixty-two cents, which includes taxes, plus an additional nine hours labour at fifty dollars and fifty-five cents per hour, plus taxes, or an additional five hundred eighteen dollars eighty-four cents, bringing the total to two thousand three hundred and twenty-nine dollars and forty-six cents, very close to the estimate given by the claimant.

I am making no adjustment for betterment as it is known because, in my opinion, this is offset by the fact that for seven and a half years, or at least most of those seven and a half years, the vehicle was essentially unmarketable, unsaleable without substantial loss.

The claimant will therefore have judgment against both defendants, joint and several, in the amount of two thousand three hundred twenty-nine dollars forty-six cents, plus costs. No interest is awarded as it is inapplicable to this type of claim.

Launching a Lawsuit

When to sue

If the seller you've been negotiating with agrees to make things right, give him or her a deadline and then have an independent garage check the repairs. If no offer is made within 10 working days, file a suit in court. Make the manufacturer a party to the lawsuit only if the original, unexpired warranty was transferred to you, your claim falls under the emissions warranty, a secret warranty extension or a safety recall campaign exists, or extensive chassis rusting is involved.

There are small claims courts in most counties of each province, and you can make a claim either in the county where the problem occurred or where the defendant lives and carries on business. The first step is to make sure that your claim doesn't exceed the dollar limit of the court. You should then go to the small claims court office and ask for a claim form. (The form includes instructions on how to properly fill it out.) Keep in mind that you must identify the defendant correctly. It's a practice of some dishonest firms to change a company's name in order to escape liability. For example, it would be impossible to sue Joe's Garage (1991) if your contract is with Joe's Garage Inc. (1984).

You're entitled to bring any evidence to court that's relevant to the case, including such written documents as a bill of sale or receipt, a contract, or a letter. If your car has developed severe paint problems, take a photograph to court. Have the photographer sign and date the photo. You may also have witnesses testify in court (a family member may act as a witness). It's important to discuss a witness's testimony prior to the court date. If a witness can't attend the court date, he or she can write a report and sign it for representation in court. This situation usually applies to an expert witness, such as the independent mechanic who evaluated your car's problems.

Be sure to organize your evidence, prepare questions for the witnesses, and write down what you want to tell the court.

Choosing the Right Court

You must decide which remedy to pursue; that is, whether you want a partial refund or a cancellation of the sale. To determine the refund amount, add the estimated cost of repairing existing mechanical defects to the cost of prior repairs. Don't exaggerate your losses or claim for repairs that are considered routine maintenance.

Generally, if the cost of repairs falls within the small claims court limit (discussed later), the case should be filed there to keep costs to a minimum and to obtain a speedy hearing. Small claims court judgments aren't easily appealed, lawyers aren't necessary, filing fees are minimal (about $125), and cases are usually heard within a few months.

If the damages exceed the small claims court limit and there's no way to reduce them, or if you want to cancel the sale, you'll have to go to a higher court—where costs quickly add up and lengthy delays of a few years or more are commonplace. However, some lawyers may take your case on a "contingency fee" basis, where they get nothing if you lose, but take up to a third of the award if you win.

A suit for cancellation of sale involves practical problems. The court requires that the vehicle be "tendered" back to the seller at the time the lawsuit is filed. This means you are without transportation for as long as the case continues, unless you purchase another car in the interim. If you lose the case, you must then take back the old car and pay storage fees. You could go from having no car to having two, one of which is a clunker. For these reasons, try to stay out of the higher courts if at all possible and plead the case yourself (after getting legal advice).

Small claims court
Canadian small claims courts offer simple claim forms, and actions cost only about $50–$125 for a $6,000 claim and take only a few months to be heard. The beauty of a small claims action is that most provincial courts force the automaker into a mediation session with you before proceeding to trial. Many claims are settled through mediation for one-half to two-thirds of the amount demanded in the action.

Small claims court clerks can be helpful in giving you general information, like how long is the wait before trial or who is the automaker's mandated representative to receive lawsuits for that province. But the degree of help provided varies considerably from court to court. Some clerks may simply be too busy to go into much detail, others may be afraid of giving out what could be construed as legal advice. If you find it difficult to get your questions answered, ask the clerk where else you may go. Spending a half-hour with a lawyer with small claims court experience may be helpful, and sitting in on a few cases one afternoon can be quite illuminating.

Sometimes, small claims courts can be used creatively to get as much compensation as would be given by a higher court. For example, the hardship of owning a $6,000 lemon can be eased if the owner sues the dealer in small claims court for the maximum to cover repairs, insurance, rental cars, inconvenience, etc., which may total $3,000. If the court awards this amount, the car can then be sold without the repairs done for about $3,000. Thus, the customer gets back the $6,000 with few legal fees to pay after a delay of only a few months. Furthermore, the car can still be used during the lawsuit, because the plaintiff isn't seeking to set the sale aside.

If the damages exceed the small claims court limit and there is no way to reduce them, you'll have to go to a court with a higher claim limit. This will be costly. Before rushing off to file a lawsuit, consider the following ways in which you can win your case in a higher court and still wind up losing your shirt.

- For a simple case that comes to a short trial, lawyers' fees can vary between $500 and $1,000. These fees must be paid whether the case is won or lost. If you lose, you may have to pay court costs as well.
- The first trial isn't likely to take place for two or three years. Then, even if you win, the judgment is likely to be appealed, thus delaying final judgment for another two to four years, and boosting each side's legal fees.
- Once appeals are exhausted and you've won, the judgment will be paid in depreciated dollars supplemented by a low interest rate—if you can collect.
- Car dealers can avoid judgment by disappearing or closing down and reopening under a new name. It happens quite often, and the courts can do little to stop it.

Class actions

Class action lawsuits allow a single individual to sue a company, government, or other entity on behalf of hundreds or even thousands of others with similar claims. Although class action suits have been used for three decades in the United States, they are a recent arrival in Canada. Quebec was the first province to adopt this legal remedy in the early '80s, and Ontario and British Columbia followed suit in 1992 and 1995, respectively. In fact, both Chrysler and General Motors are facing class action lawsuits in British Columbia, where plaintiffs are seeking compensation for paint-delaminated 1986–97 vehicles.

Class actions allow for contingency fees, where consumers can enter into no-win-no-pay agreements with lawyers. If you lose, you usually pay reasonable court expenses and move on. However, Ontario judges can require that losing class action plaintiffs pay the defendant's fees as well, a chilling thought for most plaintiffs. (B.C. legislation requires that both sides pay their own legal costs.)

One of the more recent successful class actions in Canada concerned the recovery of condo owner deposits in Toronto. In *Windisman v. Toronto College Park Ltd.*, 544 condominium residents recovered $2.6 million, representing the interest earned on their deposit payments for apartments, parking spaces, and storage lockers.

If the class wins, individual cases may then be heard to assess damages, or a notification may be sent to each member to apply for their part of the settlement or award. It may take from three to five years before a final judgment is rendered, and appeals may double that time. Lawyers typically charge the class one-third of the amount obtained.

Trial conduct

Because the cost of defence would be prohibitive and the bad publicity could ruin the dealer's business, lawyers often tell their dealer-clients to settle a small claims case out of court. Lawyers also know that urging their clients to settle out of court means they never lose a case.

Sometimes a dealer's lawyer will threaten to sue the plaintiff for libel or slander if the case is taken to court. This is a move designed to intimidate. No one can be sued for libel or slander merely for exercising his or her rights before the courts. The dealer, however, can be sued for harassment, and the lawyer can be cited for unprofessional conduct if the threat is carried out.

On the day of the trial, bring in a mechanic to confirm that the defects exist and to estimate the cost of repairing them. If the repairs have already been carried out, the mechanic can explain what caused the defects and justify the bill for repairing them. This should be done by presenting the defective parts, if possible. He must convince the judge that the defects were present at the time the car was sold, and that they were not caused by poor maintenance or abusive driving habits.

Before the dealer leaves the stand, get him to confirm any representations he or his salespeople made, either verbally or through a newspaper ad, extolling the vehicle's qualities. With witnesses excluded, it's quite likely that the dealer's witnesses will contradict him when their turn comes to testify because they didn't hear the previous testimony. Your own co-workers or friends can testify as to how well you maintained the vehicle and how it was driven, as well as describe the seriousness of the defects.

Dos and don'ts

- Do complain to the provincial Transport and Consumer Affairs ministries about possible violations of provincial laws.
- Do contact local consumer groups and the Automobile Protection Association for recent jurisprudence and help in mediating the complaint.
- Do publicize any favourable court judgment as a warning to other dealers and as encouragement for other consumers.

- Don't sue a car dealer if he is bankrupt, or is willing to negotiate a settlement.
- Don't threaten or insult the dealer. This will only gain sympathy for him and hurt your own credibility.

Remember not to delay in filing a claim once it's obvious that no settlement is forthcoming. A lawsuit should be filed no later than three months after the final registered claim letter has been sent.

Collecting Your Winnings

Settlements

You may be asked to sign a document called a "release," which proves that a final settlement has been made. Generally, once you sign the release you can't sue the other person for that particular debt or injury. If you're the debtor, it's very important that you make sure the other person signs the release when you pay him or her. If you're the creditor collecting on the debt, you must sign the release, but don't do so until you've received the money or verified that the cheque is good. Also, don't give up any more rights than you have to. Release the debtor from that particular debt, but don't release him or her from all future debts.

Sample Settlement Form

I, John Doe, hereby acknowledge the receipt of $300 plus $10 interest from Jane Smith, in full and final satisfaction of all claims, which I may have against her arising from a sale of a used Ford Mustang by her to me on June 30th, 1996, and from all claims arising from a cheque for $300 dated November 30th, 1993, signed by her and payable to me, which was returned to me marked "Not Sufficient Funds."

_____   _____
Date   John Doe

Name of Witness: _____

Helpful Court Decisions

The following Canadian lawsuits and judgments cover typical problems that are likely to arise. Put any relevant case in your claim letter as leverage when negotiating a settlement, or as a reference should your claim go to trial. I've chosen these court judgments to cover most of the problems that are likely to arise. Legal principles are similarly applicable to Canadian and American law. Quebec court decisions, however, may be based on legal principles that don't apply outside that province.

Therefore, do what most lawyers do: present all the court judgments that may be helpful and let the presiding judge or the defendant's lawyer sort out those that are most pertinent.

Additional court judgments can be found on my *lemonaidcars.com* website, or in the legal reference section of your city's main public library or at a nearby university law library. Ask the librarian for help in choosing the legal phrases that best describe your claim.

Drivers who have been charged with a traffic offence and who wish to mount a spirited and well-researched defence should ask the librarian for a copy of *The Law of Traffic Offences (Second Edition)*, by Scott Hutchison, David Rose, and Philip Downes and published by Carswell. Written by three Toronto lawyers, this guide covers radar challenges, fatal prosecutorial flaws, court procedure, objections, appeals, witnesses, and expert testimony, giving relevant case law for almost any situation. First published in 1988, this is an excellent reference guide for laypersons and legal practitioners alike.

Damages (Punitive)

Punitive damages (also known as exemplary damages) allow the plaintiff to get compensation that exceeds his or her losses. In Canada, judges sometimes award punitive damages as a deterrent to those who carry out dishonest or negligent practices; however, these kinds of judgments are more common in the U.S. For example, last July both Ford and GM were hit with huge punitive judgments: the GM plaintiffs were given $4.9 billion by a California jury as compensation for burns sustained when a speeding Mustang rear-ended their 1972 Malibu; and Ford plaintiffs were awarded $295 million for injuries sustained from a Bronco rollover.

Vlchek v. Koshel (1988), 44 C.C.L.T. 314, B.C.S.C., No. B842974. The plaintiff was seriously injured when she was thrown from a Honda all-terrain cycle on which she had been riding as a passenger. The Court allowed for punitive damages because the manufacturer was well aware of the injuries likely to be caused by the cycle. Specifically, the Court ruled that there is no firm and inflexible principle of law stipulating that punitive or exemplary damages must be denied unless the defendant's acts are specifically directed against the plaintiff. The Court may apply punitive damages "where the defendant's conduct has been indiscriminate of focus, but reckless or malicious in its character. Intent to injure the plaintiff need not be present, so long as intent to do the injurious act can be shown."

See also:
- *Granek v. Reiter*, Ont. Ct. (Gen. Div.), No. 35/741.
- *Morrison v. Sharp*, Ont. Ct. (Gen. Div.), No. 43/548.
- *Schryvers v. Richport Ford Sales*, May 18, 1993, B.C.S.C., No. C917060, Judge Tysoe.
- *Varleg v. Angeloni*, B.C.S.C., No. 41/301.

Furthermore, a slew of cases cover specifics in damage claims. Provincial business practices acts cover false, misleading, or deceptive representations, and allow for punitive damages should the unfair practice toward the consumer amount to an unconscionable representation. (See C.E.D. (3d) s. 76, pp. 140–45.) "Unconscionable" is defined as "where the consumer is not reasonably able to protect his or her interest because of physical infirmity, ignorance, illiteracy, or inability to understand the language of an agreement or similar factors."

- Exemplary damages are justified where compensatory damages are insufficient to deter and punish. See *Walker et al. v. CFTO Ltd. et al.* (1978), 59 O.R. (2nd), No. 104 (Ont. C.A.).
- Exemplary damages can be awarded in cases where the defendant's conduct was "cavalier." See *Ronald Elwyn Lister Ltd. et al. v. Dayton Tire Canada Ltd.* (1985), 52 O.R. (2nd), No. 89 (Ont. C.A.).
- The primary purpose of exemplary damages is to prevent the defendant and all others from doing similar wrongs. See *Fleming v. Spracklin* (1921).
- Disregard of the public's interest, lack of preventive measures, and a callous attitude all merit exemplary damages. See *Coughlin v. Kuntz* (1989), 2 C.C.L.T. (2nd) (B.C.C.A.).
- Punitive damages can be awarded for mental distress. See *Ribeiro v. Canadian Imperial Bank of Commerce* (1992), Ontario Reports 13 (3rd) and *Brown v. Waterloo Regional Board of Comissioners of Police* (1992), 37 O.R. (2nd).

Defects (Body/Performance Related)

What's a lemon?
The definitive description of a "lemon" is found in U.S. state law, in which it's defined as a vehicle with problems that can't be repaired after four attempts, keep the vehicle out of service for more than 30 days, or render it unfit for the purpose for which it was purchased.

When a vehicle no longer falls within the limits of the warranty expressed by the manufacturer or dealer, it doesn't necessarily mean that the manufacturer can't be held liable for damages caused by defective design. As mentioned before, the manufacturer is always liable for the replacement or repair of defective parts if independent testimony can show that the part was incorrectly manufactured or designed, and that this "mistake" affects its reliability or durability. The existence of service bulletins indicating upgrades or a secret warranty extension will usually help to prove that the part was poorly made (or the paint process was flawed). For example, in *Lowe v. Chrysler*, internal service bulletins were instrumental in showing an Ontario small claims court judge that Chrysler had a history of automatic transmission failures since 1989.

In addition to replacing or repairing the part that failed, an automaker can be held responsible for any damages arising from the part's failure.

This means that loss of wages, supplementary transportation costs, and damages for personal inconvenience can be awarded.

Paint delamination or peeling, and rusting

Although this was once a problem with early Hondas, Mazdas, and Nissans, premature paint delamination and peeling now mostly afflicts the Big Three American automakers. Chrysler, Ford, and GM 1984–97 models are equally affected. Each company, however, has responded differently to owners' requests for compensation. To help you prepare the best arguments for negotiations or court, read the following court judgments carefully and frame your claim accordingly.

Chrysler
Because Chrysler has settled most of its paint claims out of court, there aren't many recent judgments against the company. There is, however, a 29-page class action lawsuit filed in the state of Washington which seeks damages for all Chrysler owners who have owned or leased paint-delaminated 1986–97 models: *Schurk, Chanes, Jansen, and Ricker v. Chrysler*, No. 97-2-04113-9-SEA, filed in the Superior Court of King County, Washington on October 2, 1997 (contact Steve Berman or Clyde Platt with the Seattle, Washington, law firm of Hagens and Berman at 206-623-7292). *Lemon-Aid Used Cars 1999* has much of the text, as does the Chrysler Paint Peeling website in Appendix AA.

Canadian lawyers have filed a class action seeking damages for paint delamination from Chrysler on behalf of British Columbia owners of 1986–97 Chrysler vehicles. What makes this lawsuit particularly important is that the plaintiffs are suing under the provincial Trade Practice Act, alleging that Chrysler and its dealers engaged in a deceptive trade practice due to their knowledge that

> ...the two-stage paint process was defective. In particular, prior to 1986 the defendants knew that exposure to sunlight caused the electrocoat layer to deteriorate and result in failure of the bond between the paint finishes and the vehicle body....

The lawsuit concludes:

> ...the failure to disclose the defective nature of the two-stage process to the class plaintiffs and, in particular, the representative plaintiffs, constitutes a deceptive trade practice pursuant to section three of the Act...

B.C. residents who want to join this class action may contact the plaintiffs' attorneys: Joe Fiorante or J.J. Camp at 1-800-689-2322, or *jcamp@campchurch.com* and *jfiorante@campchurch.com*. In the States, Paul Weiss, who is coordinating his efforts with the Canadian lawyers, has already filed similar paint delamination class actions against Chrysler,

Ford, and GM on behalf of American owners. Paul Weiss can be reached at *jandpw@ix.netcom.com.*

Ford

Faced with an estimated 13 percent failure rate, Ford repainted its delaminated 1983–93 cars, minivans, vans, F-Series trucks, Explorers, Rangers, and Broncos free of charge under a secret "Owner Dialogue" program. Ford whistle blowers say the company discontinued the program in January '95 because it was proving to be too costly. Nevertheless, post-1993 owners who threaten small claims action are still routinely given initial offers of 50 percent compensation, and eventually complete refunds if they press further.

General Motors

Confidential U.S. dealer service bulletins and memos confirm the 6-year/unlimited mileage benchmark that GM uses to accept or reject secret warranty paint claims (see page 100). As with Ford and Chrysler, GM customers seeking paint compensation are thrust into a "Let's Make a Deal" scenario, where they're usually first offered a 50 percent refund.

In addition to their Chrysler paint lawsuit, British Columbia lawyers Joe Fiorante and J. J. Camp (see "*Chrysler*," above, for contact information) also filed a class action against General Motors last May seeking damages for paint delamination from Chrysler on behalf of 1986–97 GM vehicle owners in B.C. Again, they contend that GM violated the provincial Trade Practice Act, claiming the automaker and its dealers engaged in a deceptive trade practice.

Why no Ford class action in Canada? Apparently, Ford Canada is smart enough to settle most cases before they go that far.

Other paint and rust cases won by consumers can be found on the *lemonaidcars.com* website.

Defects (Safety Related)

More than 300 million cars have been recalled since the late '60s to correct safety-related defects. Under Canadian federal legislation (Canadian Motor Vehicle Safety Act, 1971), car companies don't have to recall their cars, or fix them free of charge within a certain period of time. The law stipulates only that companies have to notify owners that their cars can kill them. American legislation requires notification and free correction unless NHTSA's defect determination is challenged in the courts.

Motor murder, the perfect crime. Although it's quite common for American juries to award multi-million dollar judgments against automakers for defective components that have killed or injured plaintiffs, you won't find similar judgments in Canada. Blame it on no-fault insurance.

In provinces where no-fault insurance has been adopted, both consumers and bar associations have discovered that insurance companies or the province—not automakers—must pay for the injuries and deaths caused by defective vehicles. It also shields governments responsible for public roadways.

Says the Saskatchewan Branch of the Canadian Bar Association:

> Given that vehicle manufacturers contribute nothing towards the Saskatchewan insurance system and that their defective products cause serious injury and financial loss to motorists and the health care system, lawyers' organizations have taken particular offence to this aspect of the law....

They must have been clinking champagne glasses in Detroit!

Although your rights to claim for death or injury are limited, use the following court decisions in your claim letter and as a guide to what you can expect when filing a lawsuit against an automobile manufacturer for safety-related defects.

Airbags

The National Highway Traffic Safety Administration says that airbags have saved 2,500 lives and reduce moderate and severe injuries in auto accidents by 25 percent. Unfortunately, says the *Wall Street Journal*, these figures are shaky and not based on real-world experiences.

THE WALL STREET JOURNAL.

WEDNESDAY, JANUARY 22, 1997 **B1**

MARKETPLACE

FLORIDA JOURNAL *(Follows Page B10)*

Rx for HMOs: *Managed health-care industry faces some changes in the Legislature.*

Royal Feud: *Bond forged by King of Beers and home-run king starts to break apart.*

Shaky Statistics Are Driving the Air Bag Debate

By ASRA Q. NOMANI
And JEFFREY TAYLOR
Staff Reporters of THE WALL STREET JOURNAL

How many lives have air bags saved? At a recent Senate hearing, Ricardo Martinez, chief of the National Highway Traffic Safety Administration, had a fairly

AUTOS

precise answer: more than 1,700. In the highly emotional debate over air bags, that number purports to provide a degree of comfort. Auto makers and federal regulators use it frequently to counter concerns about the 55 people killed since 1990 by the explosive force of air bags.

In fact, no one can say with certainty how many lives air bags have saved -- or how many lives they have claimed. Was the air bag really to blame in each of the deaths or were other factors involved? Moreover, the 1,700 figure for lives saved is an estimate, generated by a computer model developed by the NHTSA. And the estimate isn't very specific; those who crunch the numbers say the actual tally

could be anywhere from 1,039 to 2,437.

As uncertain as they are, the figures show how pivotal statistics can be in a red-hot safety debate. They also demonstrate how estimates can create a public perception of precision and certainty when neither exist.

"It's a numbers game," says Idaho Republican Sen. Dick Kempthorne, who has been calling for new testing procedures since November, when an infant in his state was decapitated by an air bag in a low-speedfender bender. Both the number of lives saved and lives lost are likely to increase as air bags become more prevalent. By law, all new cars will be equipped with both driver-side and passenger-side bags by next fall.

Even NHTSA officials concede that their air bag "save" figures are far from precise. They are based on an August 1996 report in which a team of researchers used two different methods to estimate fatalities prevented by air bags, then averaged them together. First, the NHTSA researchers looked at how many drivers and front-seat passengers had died in crashes of

KEY DATA MEASURING the efficacy of air bags in a crash often ignore whether passengers were using seat belts.

2,880 cars equipped with air bags, compared with fatalities in crashes of 5,237 cars without air bags. After accounting for the difference in the sample size, they found 10% fewer fatalities in cars with air bags.

The NHTSA researchers also compared survival rates with and without air bags in frontal and nonfrontal crashes, and concluded that air bags reduced fatalities by 12%. Then they averaged the two results to derive a best estimate: that air bags bring 11% fewer fatalities. From actual accident statistics, they calculated that there would have been 1,136 additional fatalities between 1986 and 1996 if air bags did not exist. Finally, they estimated the number of 1996 fatalities, factored in the number of new cars equipped with air bags that have

entered the market and projected that the number of lives saved through last year was 1,703.

Still, in calculating those numbers, government researchers don't know for sure whether or not the people "saved" by air bags had been wearing seat belts. If they had been belted, they would have faced less risk of death in the first place, saftey experts say. But the federal accident database the researchers used "does not contain accurate information about the belt use of crash survivors, especially in recent years," the report notes.

The seat belt question complicates the count of people "killed" by air bags, as well. Of the 55 people who died, 35 were children sitting on the passenger side. In each case, NHTSA investigators culled accident reports and determined that the air bag itself caused the fatal injuries. But 24 of the 35 children were not wearing seat belts or were improperly restrained. In nine cases, the children were in rear-facing child-seats, which are not supposed to be placed in a front seat.

"The greatest threat to children isn't *Please Turn to Page B11, Column 1*

Although safety experts agree that you are likely to need anti-lock brakes 99 times more often than an airbag, the bag's advantage is that it doesn't depend upon driver skill or reaction time and it deploys when it's too late for braking. Nevertheless, there have been thousands of reports of airbags that have failed to deploy or have accidentally gone off and caused massive injuries. In fact, General Motors recalled almost a million Cadillacs, Cavaliers, and Sunfires for the problem of accidental deployment—caused by wet carpeting in Cadillacs and passing over a bump in the road for the other vehicles.

Safety experts at NHTSA once estimated that 25,000 people were injured by airbags between 1988 and 1991. Additionally, recent NHTSA-run crash tests indicate that all of Chrysler's minivan airbags produced in 1997 and earlier deploy with such excessive force they may cause disabling or fatal injuries. In February 1999 crash tests, the deploying passenger-side airbag in a 1997 Caravan caused neck injuries to a small, belted, female dummy that, according to the agency would have disabled or killed a person. The suspect airbags may be in as many as 1.9 million minivans. Coincidentally, a U.S. national auto safety group, the Insurance Institute for Highway Safety (IIHS), has launched an exhaustive investigation into reports that inflating airbags have seriously injured motorists.

Hundreds of lawsuits have been filed claiming airbags don't function as designed (not deploying when they should, or deploying when they shouldn't) and over 60 suits have been filed claiming the device caused or aggravated injuries after actually deploying as designed. Chrysler, the first automaker to install airbags as standard equipment, is the target of most of these lawsuits. So far, the successful suits against Chrysler relate to poor design rather than malfunctions and fall into two categories: severe burns and premature deployment at low speeds.

Severe burns

Claimants have won substantial jury awards for first- or second-degree burns caused by the Thiokol-designed airbag directing hot gases at the driver's hands and wrists. Used on Chrysler's 1988–91 models, these airbags have vent holes that direct hot gases at the three o'clock and nine o'clock hand positions. In late 1990, the vent holes were relocated to the twelve o'clock position. A class action lawsuit asking for damages arising from the earlier Thiokol design was filed in Philadelphia County and has recently resulted in a verdict of $60 million in compensatory damages, and another $3.75 million in punitive damages, for 80,000 Pennsylvania Chrysler owners who purchased their vehicles between 1988 and 1990. The jury ruled that vehicles sold during that time came with airbags that, when deployed, could severely burn the hands and wrists of drivers. Owners were awarded $730 each to replace the defective airbags, although Pennsylvania's Consumer Protection Law could triple the damages. Martin D'Urso from the law firm of Kohn, Swift & Graf and Isaac Green from Moody & Anderson pleaded the case for the plaintiffs.

Collazo-Santiago v. Toyota, July 1998, The United States' First Circuit Court of Appeals. The driver of a 1994 Corolla suffered minor facial burns and abrasions when her airbag deployed as her car was rear-ended. The court concluded that the airbag's design caused the injuries. Toyota maintained that the airbag deployed as it should, and that it couldn't change the design without reducing the airbag's effectiveness. The plaintiff was awarded $30,000 compensation.

Premature airbag deployment
All automakers are worried they may face a slew of huge damage awards in the future following a $750,000 jury award for damages in the death of a five-year-old from a deploying airbag. In *Crespo v. Chrysler*, a New York jury concluded that the 1995 minivan's airbag design contributed to the child's death because it deployed too early (at a speed of between 9 and 12 mph). Safety experts contend that the airbag should deploy within a range of 15–20 mph (24–32 km/h). Chrysler submitted, however, that there are no standards as to what speeds should trigger the airbag's deployment, and claimed most automakers program their airbags to deploy at crash speeds of 8–14 mph (13–23 km/h). The jury rejected Chrysler's argument and awarded half the damages sought by the child's family, despite the fact that the child was unbelted and not seated in a safety seat.

Failure to deploy
Taylor v. Ford, Wayne County Circuit Court. American courts are taking a harder look at the automakers' liability when airbags fail to deploy, following a recent Michigan Court of Appeals decision to uphold a lower court's $292,000 verdict against Ford. Although the 1990 Lincoln Continental's driver-side airbag failed to deploy during a frontal collision, the jury found no design defect, but awarded damages against Ford for breach of an implied warranty based on defective manufacturing.

Inadvertent deployment
Perez-Trujillo v. Volvo Car Corp. (*www.law.emory.edu/1circuit/mar98/97-1792.01a.html*). This lawsuit involves injuries suffered by a dockworker while parking a Volvo on the dock. The case has just been reinstated by a U.S. Appeals Court and provides an interesting, though lengthy, dissertation on the safety hazards that airbags pose and why automakers are ultimately responsible for the injuries and deaths caused by their deployment.

False Advertising

Odometer tampering
Odometer tampering is a criminal offence under the federal Weights and Measures Act. The Department of Consumer and Corporate Affairs uses the RCMP to investigate all such cases. Many violators have been caught and successfully prosecuted. Nevertheless, the federal law is weak because fines are so low that they practically represent a licence to operate illegally, and an individual can escape prosecution by pleading that the odometer was broken and had to be changed.

Bouchard v. South Park Mercury Sales (1978), 3 W.W.R., No. 78. The odometer figure written on the contract was incorrect. The dealer pleaded ignorance, but the judge ruled that the car's owner should receive damages to compensate for the extra mileage.

Used car sold as new (demonstrator)
Leblanc v. Frenette and Chrysler Credit, May 27, 1971, Quebec Provincial Court, No. 279-772, Judge Laurier. The plaintiff's "new" demonstrator was actually a used car with a rolled-back odometer. It had also been in an accident. The Court held the dealer responsible and ordered him to refund the purchase price.

Leasing

Canadian courts have made several significant rulings that give lessees added clout when seeking refunds for deceptive practices and defective vehicles.

Ford Motor Credit v. Bothwell, December 3, 1979, Ontario County Court (Middlcscx), No. 9226-T, Judge Macnab. The defendant leased a 1977 Ford truck that had frequent engine problems, characterized by stalling and hard starting. After complaining for one year and driving 22,000 miles (35,000 km), the defendant cancelled the lease. Ford Credit sued for the money owing on the lease. Judge Macnab cancelled the lease and ordered Ford Credit to repay 70 percent of the amount paid during the leasing period. Ford Credit was also ordered to refund repair costs, even though the corporation claimed that it should not be held responsible for Ford's failure to honour its warranty.

Salvador v. Setay Motors/Queenstown Chev-Olds, Hamilton Small Claims Court, No. 1621/95. Robert Salvador, an Ontario consumer advocate and founder of the Consumer Action Group (CAG), was awarded $2,000 plus costs from Queenstown Leasing. The Court found that the company should have tried harder to sell the leased vehicle, and for a higher price, when the "open lease" expired.

Salvador gave Queenstown a list of offers from independent buyers when he returned the vehicle, but they were never contacted. Instead, the leasing agency auctioned off the van to the highest bidder. You guessed it—Queenstown Leasing.

This judgment can also be helpful in cases where a repossessed vehicle is sold or auctioned off for far less than what it's worth, or where the seller is in a conflict of interest by being the buyer as well.

Schryvers v. Richport Ford Sales, May 18, 1993, B.C.S.C., No. C917060, Justice Tysoe. The Court awarded $17,578.47 (including $6,000 in punitive damages) plus costs to a couple who paid thousands of dollars over the purchase price for their Ford Explorer and Escort in unfair and hidden leasing charges. The Court found that this price difference constituted a deceptive, unconscionable act or practice in contravention of the Trade Practices Act, R.S.B.C. 1979, c. 406.

Judge Tysoe concluded that the total of the general damages awarded to the Schryvers for both vehicles would be $11,578.47. He then proceeded to give the following reasons for awarding an additional $6,000 in punitive damages:

> Little wonder Richport Ford had a contest for the salesperson who could persuade the most customers to acquire their vehicles by way of a lease transaction. I consider the actions of Richport Ford to be sufficiently flagrant and high-handed to warrant an award of punitive damages.
>
> There must be a disincentive to suppliers in respect of intentionally deceptive trade practices. If no punitive damages are awarded for intentional violations of the legislation, suppliers will continue to conduct their businesses in a manner that involves deceptive trade practices because they will have nothing to lose. In this case I believe that the appropriate amount of punitive damages is the extra profit Richport Ford endeavoured to make as a result of its deceptive acts. I therefore award punitive damages against Richport Ford in the amount of $6,000...

See also:
- *Barber v. Inland Truck Sales,* 11 D.L.R. (3rd), No. 469.
- *Canadian-Dominion Leasing v. Suburban Super Drug Ltd.* (1966), 56 D.L.R. (2nd), No. 43.
- *Neilson v. Atlantic Rentals Ltd.* (1974), 8 N.B.R. (2nd), No. 594.
- *Volvo Canada v. Fox,* December 13, 1979, New Brunswick Court of Queen's Bench, No. 1698/77/C, Judge Stevenson.
- *Western Tractor v. Dyck,* 7 D.L.R. (3rd), No. 535.

Misrepresentation

Late delivery
When the delivery of a new car is delayed, the customer can either demand that the contract be cancelled or ask for special damages. If the delay was caused by the seller's or manufacturer's negligence, both the contract's cancellation and compensating damages can be claimed.

Manery v. Kampe (1943), 3 W.W.R., No. 687 (B.C.C.A.). The seller delivered the goods 18 days after the contracted delivery date. The buyer refused the merchandise and sued for cancellation of the contract. The Court ordered that the buyer's money be refunded.

"New" car really a used car
Bilodeau v. Sud Auto, Quebec Court of Appeal, No. 09-000751-73, Judge Tremblay. This appellate Court cancelled the contract, and held that a

car can't be sold as new or as a demonstrator if it has ever been rented, leased, sold, or titled to anyone other than the dealer.

Rourke v. Gilmore, January 16, 1928 (*Ontario Weekly Notes,* vol. XXXIII, p. 292). Before discovering that his new car was really used, the plaintiff drove it for over a year. For this reason, the contract couldn't be cancelled. However, the Appeals Court instead awarded damages for $500, which was quite a sum in 1928!

Vehicle not as ordered

Whether you're buying a new or used vehicle, the seller can't misrepresent the vehicle. Anything that varies from what one would commonly expect, or from the seller's representation, must be disclosed prior to signing the contract. Typical scenarios involve odometer turnbacks, accident damage, used or leased cars sold as new, new vehicles that are the wrong colour and the wrong model year, or vehicles that lack promised options or standard features.

Chenel v. Bel Automobile (1981) Inc., August 27, 1976, Quebec Superior Court (Quebec City), Judge Desmeules. The plaintiff didn't receive his new Ford truck with the Jacob brakes essential for transporting sand in hilly regions. The Court awarded the plaintiff $27,000, representing the purchase price of the vehicle less the money he earned while using the truck.

Lasky v. Royal City Chrysler Plymouth, February 18, 1987, Ontario High Court of Justice, 59 O.R. (2nd), No. 323. The plaintiff bought a 4-cylinder 1983 Dodge 600 that was represented by the salesman as being a 6-cylinder model. After putting 40,000 km on the vehicle over a 22-month period, the buyer was given her money back, without interest, under the provincial Business Practices Act.

White v. Munn Motors (1960), 45 M.P.R., No. 253 (Nfld. T.D.). The dealer misrepresented a half-ton truck as having a three-quarter-ton capacity. The buyer was given his money back because he didn't get what he paid for.

Secret Warranties

It's common practice for manufacturers to extend their warranties secretly to cover components with a high failure rate. Customers who complain vigorously get extended warranty compensation in the form of "goodwill" adjustments.

François Chong v. Marine Drive Imported Cars Ltd. and Honda Canada Inc., May 17, 1994, British Columbia Provincial Court (Small Claims Division), No. 92-06760, Judge C.L. Bagnall. Mr. Chong is the first owner of a 1983 Honda Accord with 134,000 km on the odometer. He's had six engine camshafts replaced—four under Honda "goodwill"

programs, one where he paid part of the repairs, and one via the small
claims court judgment below.

In his ruling, Judge Bagnall ordered Honda and the dealer to each
pay half of the $835.81 repair bill, for the following reasons:

> The defendants assert that the warranty which was part of the con-
> tract for purchase of the car encompassed the entirety of their obli-
> gation to the claimant, and that it expired in February 1985. The
> replacements of the camshaft after that date were paid for wholly
> or in part by Honda as a "goodwill gesture." The time has come for
> these gestures to cease, according to the witness for Honda....
>
> The claimant has convinced me that the problem he is having
> with rapid breakdowns of camshafts in his car is due to a defect,
> which was present in the engine at the time that he purchased the
> car. The problem first arose during the warranty period and in my
> view has never been properly identified nor repaired.

Repairs

Faulty diagnosis

Let's say that before taking a holiday you have your van checked out
and are assured that it's in good condition. While en route to your vacation spot, it dies on the highway and ruins your holiday. When the
check-up is incorrect and leads to financial losses (damages), the
garage owner is responsible for those losses, as well as for refunding the
diagnostic costs. Of course, you'd better show that the defect that
caused your troubles was present and detectable at the time the
vehicle was checked.

Davies v. Alberta Motor Association, August 13, 1991, Alberta Provincial
Court, Civil Division, No. P9090106097, Judge Moore. The plaintiff had
a used 1985 Nissan Pulsar NX checked out by the AMA's Vehicle
Inspection Service prior to buying it. The car passed with flying
colours. A month later the clutch was replaced and numerous electrical problems ensued. At that time, another garage discovered that the
car had been involved in a major accident, had a bent frame, a leaking
radiator, and was unsafe to drive. The Court awarded the plaintiff
$1,578.40 plus three years of interest. The judge held that the AMA set
itself out as an expert and should have spotted the car's defects. The
AMA's defence—that it was not responsible for errors—was thrown
out. The Court held that a disclaimer clause could not protect the
Association from a fundamental breach of contract.

Part Three
NEW-VEHICLE RATINGS

Chrysler's Lament: Fewer Stupid Customers

"Information technology plays a bigger role than ever before. Customers are armed with better and more complete information. And they're getting it online, they're getting it instantaneously.

At Chrysler I was once talking about the sales department's failure to achieve their sales objectives in one particular vehicle. I said, 'Why is it?' And one of my colleagues said, 'The problem is, we're running out of stupid customers.' You can't screw people anymore. They are no longer happy with dealers who don't provide outstanding service. They are demanding alternatives—and they're getting them."

From an address by Robert Lutz,
former Chrysler Corp. vice chairman,
delivered to the Society of Automotive Engineers
January 28, 1999

That's right, Robert, and it's *Lemon-Aid*'s job to educate buyers so they'll steer clear of all vehicles that pack an airbag "surprise" or are equipped with "biodegradable" engines, automatic transmissions, ABS brakes, air conditioners, and paint jobs.

What Makes a Good Car or Minivan?

Your new car or minivan must first live up to the promises made by the manufacturer and dealer. It must be safe, crashworthy, reasonably durable (lasting at least 10 years), cost no more than CAA's estimated $800 a year to maintain, and provide you with a fair resale value a few years down the road. Parts should be reasonably priced and easily available, and servicing shouldn't be delayed or incompetent.

Lemon-Aid guides try to publish up-to-date photographs of each new model rated, but some automakers disagree with our ratings and refuse to cooperate with us in any manner whatsoever, including sending us recent photos and current technical specifications. We regret any errors or omissions that may result. Our independence is more important than an all-inclusive book with pretty pictures.

Definitions of Terms

Ratings

This edition makes use of owner complaints, confidential dealer service bulletins (TSBs), and test-drives to expose serious factory-related defects, design deficiencies, or servicing glitches. It should be noted that customer complaints alone do not make a scientific sampling, and that's why they are used in conjunction with other sources of information. On the other hand, owner complaints combined with inside information found in dealer service bulletins are a good starting point to cut through the automakers' hyperbole and get a glimpse of reality. Since ratings can change dramatically from one year to the next, depending upon the manufacturer's warranty performance, you will want to keep abreast of these changes between editions by logging onto *www.lemonaidcars.com.*

This edition emphasizes important new features that add to a vehicle's safety, reliability, road performance, and comfort, and points out those changes that are merely gadgets and styling revisions. Also noted are important improvements to be made in the future, or the dropping of a model line. In addition to the "Recommended" or "Not Recommended" rating, each vehicle's strong and weak points are summarized.

Unlike most auto guides, *Lemon-Aid* isn't bedazzled by high-tech wizardry. Almost 30 years of consumer advocacy in the auto industry have taught me that complex components are usually quite troublesome during their first few years on the market (airbags, faulty tires, and anti-lock brakes can be particularly dangerous, as GM's recent 3.5 million vehicle recall on 1991–96 pickups, SUVs, and vans for defective ABS brakes and Firestone's 6.5 million tire buy-back show). Complexity drives up ownership costs, reduces overall reliability, and puts extra stress on such expensive major parts as the powertrain, fuel system, and emissions components.

Depreciation is the biggest—and most often ignored—expense you encounter when you trade in your vehicle, or when an accident forces you to buy another vehicle before the depreciated loss can be amortized. Most new cars depreciate a whopping 30–40 percent during the first two years of ownership. Fortunately, minivans, vans, trucks, and sport-utilities lose their value at a much slower rate. The best way to use depreciation rates to your advantage is to choose a vehicle listed as being both reliable and economical to own and keep it for 5 to 10 years. Alternatively, you may buy insurance to protect you from depreciation's bite (see page 49).

During a car or minivan's first year on the market it takes about six months to acquire enough information for a fair-minded evaluation, unless it's a hybrid that has been in service under another name or has only been re-badged. Most new cars hit the market before all of the bugs have been worked out, so it would be irresponsible to recommend them before they've been owner-driven, or before the quality of service from the dealer and manufacturer has been customer-tested. The Chrysler Neon is a case in point. Hailed as "Car of the Year" by the motoring press in 1995, it's now noted mostly for its costly engine, AC, electrical, and body deficiencies. The kicker: the Neon may be axed next year.

Recommended
This rating indicates a best buy. This category includes new vehicles that combine a high level of crashworthiness with good road performance,

few safety-related complaints, decent reliability, and better than average resale value. Servicing must be readily available, and parts inexpensive and easy to find.

A vehicle may lose its "Recommended" rating from the previous edition of *Lemon-Aid* whenever NHTSA-registered complaints increase as with Honda and Toyota, its price becomes unreasonable, or its warranty performance falters.

Above Average
Vehicles in this class exhibit quality construction, durability, and safety features as standard equipment. They may have expensive parts and servicing, safety-related complaints, an unreasonably high price tag, or only satisfactory warranty performance, one or all of which may have disqualified them from the "Recommended" category.

Average
Vehicles in this group have some deficiencies or flaws that make them a second choice. In many cases, certain components are prone to premature wear or breakdown, or some other positive aspect of long-term ownership is lacking. An "Average" rating can also be attributed to such factors as substandard assembly quality, lack of a solid long-term reliability record, a substantial number of safety-related complaints, or some flaw in the parts and service network.

Below Average
This rating category denotes a vehicle that may have had a poor safety or reliability record, but where improvements have been made with regard to durability and/or safety features. Ensure you get an extended warranty with a vehicle in this category.

Not Recommended
Buy at your own risk. Substandard crashworthiness, poor overall reliability and safety, inadequate road performance, and poor dealer service, among other factors, can make owning one of these vehicles a traumatic and expensive experience. It doesn't necessarily follow that every single vehicle produced in a "Not Recommended" model line will have exactly the same reliability shortcomings, but chances of having trouble are higher than normal.

Vehicles that have not been on the road long enough to assess, or that are sold in such small numbers that owner feedback is insufficient, are "Not Recommended" or left unrated.

Cost analysis/best alternatives
Following an incredibly successful 2000 model year, fall price increases for the 2001 models are expected to be relatively restrained, ranging 1–2 percent for the Big Three and only slightly higher for most Asian and European makes. Be wary, though, of subsequent price increases

throughout next year that may boost selling prices several thousand dollars. Also, popular models may have MSRPs that are 5–10 percent higher than last year's version.

Each model's cost is analyzed in light of cheaper earlier models eligible for substantial rebates, PDI and destination charges, insurance costs, parts costs, depreciation, and fuel consumption. A listing of some competing recommended models is also included.

Quality/reliability/safety

Lemon-Aid bases its quality and reliability evaluations on owner comments, confidential manufacturer service bulletins, and government reports from the NHTSA safety complaint files, among other sources. This year's edition also draws on the knowledge and expertise of professionals working in the automotive marketplace, including mechanics and fleet owners. The aim is to have a wide range of unbiased (and irrefutable) data on quality, reliability, durability, and ownership costs. Allowances are made for the number of vehicles sold versus the number of complaints, as well as for the seriousness of problems reported and the average number of problems reported by each owner.

Manufacturer service bulletins listed in this section give the most probable cause of factory-related defects on year 2000 models that will likely be carried over to the 2001 version, because manufacturers depend on the dealer corrections outlined in their bulletins until a permanent, cost-effective engineering solution is found at the factory. This sometimes takes several model years with lots of experimentation.

Many of the bulletins listed in this edition come from American sources and often differ from Canadian bulletins where part numbers are concerned. Nevertheless, the problems and defects they treat are exactly the same on both sides of the border. Some vehicles have more TSBs than others, but this doesn't necessarily mean they're lemons. It may be that the listed problems affect only a small number of vehicles, or are minor and easily corrected. TSBs should also be used to verify that a problem was correctly diagnosed, the correct upgraded replacement part was used, and the billed labour time was fair.

As you read through the quality and reliability ratings (safety is more of a mixed bag) you'll quickly discover that most Japanese automakers are far ahead of Chrysler, Ford, GM, and South Korean manufacturers in maintaining a high level of quality control in their vehicles. What once was a small-car phenomenon, has spread to mid-size, luxury, minivan, truck, and sport-utility production, say both *Consumer Reports* and J.D. Power and Associates.

Quality Vehicles: Detroit in Decline

Toyota Avalon   **Nissan Pathfinder**

Top vehicles by segment according to
J.D. Power and Associates 2000 initial quality study:

Cars		Trucks	
Compact	Toyota Corolla	**Compact pickup**	Mazda B-Series
Entry midsize	Plymouth Breeze*	**Fullsize pickup**	Toyota Tundra
Premium midsize	Toyota Avalon*	**Mini SUV**	Honda CR-V
Sporty	Acura Integra	**Compact SUV**	Nissan Pathfinder
Entry luxury	Lexus ES 300	**Fullsize SUV**	Toyota Land Cruiser
Premium luxury	Lexus LS 400	**Luxury SUV**	Lexus LX 470
Sports	Porsche 911	**Compact Van**	Toyota Sienna
* To be discontinued			

The above study says poor engineering, not assembly-line mistakes, causes two-thirds of quality defects.

Warranty performance

I'm more impressed by performance than promise. A manufacturer's warranty is a legal commitment that the product it sells will perform in the normal and customary manner for which it is designed. It's an important factor in this edition's ratings, and is judged by how fairly it's applied—not by what's promised. Extended or supplementary warranties provide extended coverage and may be sold by the manufacturer, dealer, or an independent third party. If a part malfunctions or fails (not owing to owner negligence), the dealer will fix, repair, or replace the defective part or parts and bill the automaker or warranty company for the cost.

Most new-vehicle warranties fall into two categories: bumper-to-bumper for a period of three to five years, and powertrain for up to 6 years/130,000 km. Automakers sometimes charge an additional $50–$100 fee for repairs requested by purchasers of used vehicles with unexpired base warranties. For snowbirds, the federal and provincial governments can charge GST and sales tax on warranty and non-warranty repairs done south of the border. Beware.

Also keep in mind that some automakers, like Honda, won't honour your warranty if a vehicle is purchased in Canada and registered in the United States.

After using longer, more comprehensive warranties to successfully sell its cars and minivans, in 1995 Chrysler dropped its generous 7-year warranty in favour of rebates and low interest rates, even though its cars and minivans aren't sufficiently reliable to forego the extra protection. Now, much like Ford and GM, Chrysler uses secret warranties to pay for factory defects. Unlike other automakers, however, you rarely see written confirmation of this fact in a Chrysler service bulletin or dealer memo.

ADDENDUM TO BASIC WARRANTY

The following applies to 1993 through 1997 New Yorker, LHS, Concorde, Intrepid, Vision and Grand Cherokee vehicles equipped with factory-installed air conditioning:

> *The Basic Warranty coverage for the air conditioner evaporator has been extended to 7 years or 115,000 kilometres, whichever occurs first, from the vehicle's warranty start date.*
>
> *This extended coverage applies to all owners of the vehicle. All of the other warranty terms apply to this extension.*

We suggest that you keep this addendum card
in your warranty information booklet.

AD9502-B

The above little-known warranty extension was sent to all owners on record, says Chrysler. It's the first time I've seen it. Be that as it may, this special policy confers rights on owners of other Chrysler vehicles with AC problems because it establishes a seven-year benchmark as to what Chrysler sees as normal AC durability.

Chrysler is also unique among automakers in having set up a special Review Committee several years ago to give out compensation to owners who were refused help through normal warranty channels. That committee, available only to Canadians, is still operating today, and is mostly preoccupied with automatic transmission, brake, and paint delamination claims, often channelled through Chrysler Lemon Owners Groups (CLOG) set up in New Brunswick, British Columbia, Alberta, and Saskatchewan (see Appendix).

Ford's warranty performance in Canada (not in the States, where owners are treated as serfs) has improved considerably since I called attention to the company's shamefully arrogant and insensitive customer relations staff in last year's *Lemon-Aid*. The company has settled most of the hundreds of cases I sent to it, and there have been fewer complaints in the last six months. Additionally, Ford has formally extended its engine warranty goodwill assistance up to 7 years/160,000 km. Informally, the company has given the same post-warranty consideration to automatic transmission failures—often going as far back as 1993 models for both engine and transmission claims. Finally, Ford has improved its customer assistance centre by purchasing a controlling interest in the company running the centre, raising salaries, and making the staffers Ford employees, under the direction of John Vernile.

On the other hand, I'm still not pleased with the powertrain defects I'm encountering with Ford's newest vehicles and I'm disappointed that Ford hasn't yet formally extended its warranty on past models to cover automatic transmission failures, caused by an aluminum piston, that affect over a decade's worth of its entire vehicle line. I was told there would be an announcement by year's end. I'll report that news in the upcoming *Lemon-Aid Used Cars* and on the *www.lemonaidcars.com* website.

General Motors is tougher to deal with than Chrysler or Ford. Once it rules on a customer's complaint, the file is closed and won't be reopened unless there's a threat of court action or the media becomes interested in the case. Like other automakers, GM informs its dealers and customers selectively of its goodwill policies through bulletins and memos. Nevertheless, the automaker likes to see its customers squirm, urging dealers to give them the third degree before warranty assistance is forthcoming.

Road performance

The main factors considered in this rating are acceleration and torque, transmission operation, routine handling, emergency handling, steering, and braking.

Every vehicle must at minimum be able to merge safely onto a highway and have adequate passing power for two-lane roads. Steering feel and handling should inspire confidence. The suspension ought to provide a reasonably well-controlled ride on most road surfaces. Ideally, the passenger compartment will be roomy enough to accommodate passengers comfortably on extended trips. The noise level should not become tiresome and annoying. As a rule, handling and ride comfort are inversely proportional—good handling requires a stiff suspension, which pounds the kidneys. Variations from this pattern are reflected in the ratings.

Comfort/convenience

Here we rate a vehicle based on the level of standard equipment offered, driving position comfort, effectiveness of controls, displays, and climate control, ease of entry/exit without running boards, amount of front and rear interior space/comfort, cargo space, trunk space and liftover, and degree of interior quietness.

Driving pleasure is hard to define, but a cramped interior, controls that are hard to see or reach, poor climate control systems, and excessive engine, road, and wind noise can turn that pleasure into a distressing experience.

Cost

Here we list the manufacturer's suggested retail price (MSRP) in effect at press time and applicable to standard models, that price's negotiability, the range of the dealer's markup, and the vehicle's estimated residual value over the next five years (particularly helpful when leasing). Undoubtedly, the MSRP will be a bit higher when the fall prices are announced. However, if the dealer's price is more than 3 percent higher than the price indicated in *Lemon-Aid*, ask for a copy of the manufacturer's notice to the dealer of the MSRP increase. You can confirm the MSRP figure by accessing each manufacturer's website.

Once you discover the latest MSRP, negotiate a reduction of the MSRP of at least half the indicated markup percentage, keeping in mind whether the price is "firm" or "negotiable."

With all the attention given to so-called "no haggle" sticker prices, keep in mind that all dealers haggle in one way or another. The substantial gap between the cost of the vehicle to the dealer ("invoice") and the manufacturer's suggested retail price (the "sticker" price) allows for such bargaining. This difference represents the dealer's markup (or gross profit), which is usually augmented by other incentive programs and holdbacks. To help you negotiate the best price, this edition indicates those MSRP prices that are firm and those that are negotiable, and gives the approximate price markup percentage in parentheses.

Destination charges and the PDI fee are outrageous $500–$850 add-ons that you shouldn't pay. In fact, last year Infiniti dealers were ordered by Nissan/Infiniti to forego both the delivery and preparation charges on all new models, and Land Rover has these costs built into the selling price (where they belong). If you get tired of haggling with the dealer, agree to pay no more than 2 percent of a vehicle's MSRP for these extra charges. Also, don't fall for the $99–$475 "administration fee" scam, unless the bottom line price is so attractive, it won't make much difference. Principle is one thing; not losing an attractive deal is another.

Technical data
Note that towing capacities differ depending on the kind of power-train/suspension package or towing package you buy. Remember that there's a difference between how a vehicle is rated for cargo capacity or payload and how heavy a boat or trailer it can pull. Do not purchase any new vehicle without receiving from the dealer very clear information, in writing, about a vehicle's towing capacity and the kind of special equipment you need to meet your requirements. Have the towing capacity and necessary equipment written into the contract.

In the ratings, cargo capacity is expressed in cubic feet with the rear seat up. With the rear seat folded or removed, cargo capacity obviously becomes quite larger.

Study: Car crashes riskier for elderly

LOS ANGELES TIMES

WASHINGTON — A study showing that the elderly are dying in traffic accidents at twice the rate of other adults, often in easily survivable crashes, is prompting a re-examination of auto safety devices, from seat belts to test dummies.

Safety experts and automakers alike are saying that protecting the brittle bones of America's growing population of older adults may be the greatest challenge of the next 20 years for the industry.

"We are asking people to sit up and take notice that this is going to be a growing problem," said Dr. Stewart Wang, a surgeon at the University of Michigan's Trauma Burn Center in Ann Arbor, Mich., who was a lead researcher for the study. "We can chalk it up to frailty and say there is nothing we can do, or we can raise the bar on vehicle design and testing."

The Michigan center is one of nine trauma centers that form the Crash Injury Research and Engineering Network, a partnership created in 1996 that connects the federal government, major hospitals and some automakers.

Network researchers discovered that rib fractures — painful but not life-threatening for most adults — are killing older crash victims. The findings, which have been quietly circulating for months, could prompt action from federal regulators who set vehicle-safety standards for the automobile industry.

While making vehicles safer for children has become an urgent priority of regulators and automakers, network cases show that older people are dying of chest injuries — rib fractures, collapsed lungs, damaged hearts and ruptured arteries — at markedly higher rates than younger adults.

Despite promising ideas and initiatives from individual automakers, there is no consensus about how to improve the odds of survival for the elderly. The AARP (formerly the American Association of Retired Persons) supports the development of a crash-test dummy that could model the effects of aging on the human body.

"The primary model that has been used in safety has been a healthy young adult," said Dr. Jeffrey Augenstein of the William Lehman Injury Research Center in Miami. "But increasingly, older people are behind the wheel."

Older people are dying of chest injuries— rib fractures, collapsed lungs, damaged hearts, and ruptured arteries—in otherwise survivable crashes. Researchers blame safety devices as the principle cause.

Safety features/crashworthiness
Some of the main features weighed in the safety ratings are a model's crashworthiness and the availability of seatbelt pretensioners, depowered airbags, airbag disablers, anti-lock brakes (rear-wheel-only systems aren't as effective as the four-wheel ABS), integrated child safety seats, effective head restraints, traction control, and front and rearward visibility.

Side airbags won't be considered a safety plus until real-world crash findings prove their worth and confirm that they're not a danger to children, women, seniors, or small-statured adults, as a number of safety researchers have postulated.

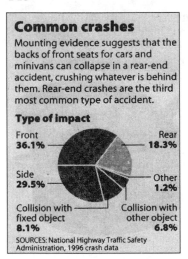

Common crashes

Mounting evidence suggests that the backs of front seats for cars and minivans can collapse in a rear-end accident, crushing whatever is behind them. Rear-end crashes are the third most common type of accident.

Type of impact

Front
36.1%

Rear
18.3%

Side
29.5%

Other
1.2%

Collision with fixed object
8.1%

Collision with other object
6.8%

SOURCES: National Highway Traffic Safety Administration, 1996 crash data

Crash protection figures are taken from NHTSA's New Car Assessment Program. Vehicles are crashed into a fixed barrier, head-on, at 57 km/h (35 mph), in order to evaluate the effects of the consequent forces exerted on the specially constructed dummies placed in the two front seats. The latest results—even if they may be several years old—have been included in the ratings.

NHTSA shows a vehicle's level of crashworthiness by the likelihood, expressed as a percentage, of the belted occupants being seriously injured. The higher the number of stars, the greater the protection:

NHTSA Front Collision Ratings

★★★★★   — a 10% or less chance of serious injury
★★★★   — an 11% to 20% chance of serious injury
★★★   — a 21% to 35% chance of serious injury
★★   — a 36% to 45% chance of serious injury
★   — a 46% or greater chance of serious injury

NHTSA tests don't necessarily provide an accurate picture of how a given model will perform in every accident; test figures are only valid if they're used to compare vehicles that are of the same size (i.e., compact, mid-size, or large). It's also unfortunate that vehicles aren't tested twice to confirm the validity of the first test.

Mercedes-Benz, proud of its reputation for building crashworthy vehicles of all sorts, hasn't always fared well in the NHTSA head-on collisions, and questions the validity of the ratings. The company claims that its own crash data show that most frontal collisions occur at an angle (off-set), and that that's the kind of test wherein its vehicles excel. The Insurance Institute for Highway Safety (IIHS) sides with Mercedes, and crash-tests at an angle and at 64 km/h (40 mph). NHTSA doesn't do front off-set testing, but it has tested many 1997–2001 cars for side-impact protection.

NHTSA Side Collision Ratings

★★★★★   — a 5% or less chance of serious injury
★★★★   — a 6% to 10% chance of serious injury
★★★   — an 11% to 20% chance of serious injury
★★   — a 21% to 25% chance of serious injury
★   — a 26% or greater chance of serious injury

American Vehicles
DAIMLERCHRYSLER

The honeymoon's over

Except for a few years of record profits, Chrysler's shotgun marriage to Daimler-Benz hasn't improved the American automaker's profits, product mix, quality control, or warranty performance. Although the company plans to introduce a number of new vehicles during the next five years, its 2001 products consist mainly of modest redesigns of the Sebring, Stratus, and minivans. Popular models like the PT Cruiser minivan, Prowler two-seat hot rod, and Viper sports car return relatively unchanged.

This year you won't see the Plymouth nameplate, Cirrus (the Stratus twin), the Avenger (which will be renamed the Stratus), or Jeep's long-awaited redesigned Cherokee (delayed until the 2002 model year to correct powertrain problems). In fact, most of Chrysler's small and mid-sized car plans are on hold, now that the company has bought a controlling interest in Mitsubishi. And at the other end of the scale, you can wave goodbye to Chrysler's 25-year-old full-sized vans; this will be their last model year.

Lots of sizzle, little substance

Chrysler's vehicles *do* look good. Whether it's the bold and quirky styling of its sports cars or PT Cruiser, or simply the sleek "cab forward" styling of the 300M, Charger R/T, Intrepid, or Concorde large sedans, the automaker's vehicles seldom go unnoticed. And when it comes to convenience, you can't beat the company's minivans for providing oodles of convenience features packaged in an attractive box on wheels.

But what good is smart styling or extra cupholders, if your vehicle's unreliable or your paint job becomes two-tone after a few years?

In almost every car quality survey I can think of, Chrysler products anchor the bottom ratings. Most car columnists, consumer advocates, and owners can recite the same litany of quality shortcomings found year after year throughout the automaker's line-up of vehicles—like failure-prone engine head gaskets, automatic transmissions that "limp" home, or shift erratically, ABS brakes that don't, and inoperative air conditioners that can cost as much as $1,500 to fix. Owners will also point out Chrysler's sub-par finish and build quality that produces excessive noise, vibration and harshness, in addition to water/air leaks and paint delamination.

There are no signs whatsoever that Chrysler's poor quality control has been addressed in its year 2000 model and 2001 models—judging by the automaker's own service bulletins and press statements. Apparently, DaimlerChrysler bean-counters in Stuttgart still reign supreme—"get the dollars first; repair the defects later." And now that Chrysler has extended

the 2001 powertrain warranty to 5 years/100,000 km, its warranty performance *better* match its warranty promise.

The company's warranty performance (the manner in which it handles customer complaints) is presently stagnating, after initially improving during 1997–99. Administrative improvements that were put in
place following angry car owner protests that led to CLOGs (Chrysler
Lemon Owners Groups) sprouting up in British Columbia and New
Brunswick are no longer adequate. Chrysler owners are now demanding fairer treatment through newly organized Alberta and
Saskatchewan CLOGs (see Appendix).

Price war?

After announcing early in the year that it was abandoning its costly
rebate programs to boost sales, Chrysler made an about-face in August
with its announcement that all rebate programs would be substantially
enhanced. This return to its old rebate strategy to goose sales (at an
estimated rebate of $2,000 per vehicle) comes at a time when the
automaker has suffered a decline in minivan sales of 10% and Jeep
Grand Cherokee sales down by 12% for the first half of the year. Until
the end of the year, the company is offering for the first time, rebates
of $1,500 on all Cherokee models, an additional $500 rebate to all
other existing programs, plus low financing.

By firing the first salvo in what looms as a rebate war, Chrysler is forcing Ford and GM to respond with their own discount programs, which
will surely include additional rebates and dealer incentives. For the
average buyer, this turnaround in Chrysler's strategy means vehicles
will become less costly as we move into the new year, making patience
more of a virtue than ever before.

Prowler

Prowler

RATING: Recommended. One of Chrysler's few concept cars to make it into mass-production, the Prowler is, nevertheless, more show than go. Even last year's 3.5L 253-hp V6 engine upgrade can't hide the car's floppy chassis and poor handling. A chick magnet, you bet. **Strong points:** Attractive styling, good acceleration, reasonably priced, and slow to depreciate. **Weak points:** Mediocre handling, ABS is unavailable, limited visibility, difficult entry/exit, limited storage space, and the car shakes and rattles.

NEW FOR 2001: Carried over virtually unchanged.

OVERVIEW: An aluminum and plastic, rear-drive, two-seat pseudo–hot rod that isn't for introverts. With a $61,000 base price, the Prowler, much like the Viper (another head-turner), is one of Chrysler's most unusual cars. Despite its racy styling, the Prowler's no high-performance muscle car, even though it posts impressive 0–100 km/h acceleration times. With a 253-hp 3.5L V6 engine, the 4-speed automatic comes with AutoStick (also available on the Vision, Intrepid, and Stratus), allowing you to shift the transmission as you would with a manual gearbox. On climbs, it prevents the transmission from changing gears back and forth, and on the downhill you can keep the car in a lower gear to prevent picking up excess speed. An airbag cut-off switch and side airbags are also available.

On the downside, the Prowler has a kidney-pounding, stiff ride; no trunk (you have to buy an optional purple mini-trailer); no spare tire; and room only for two—as long as they're not too tall. **Best alternatives:** Mercedes-Benz SLK230, Chevrolet Corvette convertible, and Porsche Boxster.

Viper GTS, RT/10

✓ **BEST BUY**

Viper

RATING: Recommended. **Strong points:** Good acceleration and handling. **Weak points:** No ABS, poor fuel economy, and passenger comfort is compromised by excessive wind noise.

NEW FOR 2001: Nothing of importance.

OVERVIEW: This red-hot $107,920 (RT/10: $104,150), mid-sized, two-door, rear-drive roadster breaks all the marketing rules—and wins. Its awesome 450-hp 8.0L V10 engine, 6-speed manual gearbox, and "in your face" styling aren't equalled by any vehicle in its class. It features depowered airbags and an airbag cut-off switch. Service bulletins and owner comments paint a positive picture of the Viper's overall dependability. **Best alternatives:** Acura NSX, Chevrolet Corvette, and Porsche Boxster.

Neon

✗ **RISKY BUY**

Neon

RATING: Not Recommended. **Strong points:** Plenty of interior space, good handling, and a thrifty engine. **Weak points:** Wimpy failure-prone engine; imprecise manual shifter; clunky 3-speed automatic; mediocre braking; excessive engine, road, and body noise; and a history of failure-prone powertrain, electrical, and body components. Log onto *www.neons.org* for updated reports from owners.

NEW FOR 2001: Carried over relatively unchanged.

OVERVIEW: The Neon, Chrysler's homegrown small car, is roomy and reasonably powered for urban use. Recent refinements have given the Neon a mini-Intrepid styling and a softer, quieter ride while enhancing the car's handling. Interior room is where the Neon shines, though, with front and rear seating that easily accommodates 6-footers. Chrysler has tried to make its low-end Neons more appealing by loading up on features that are usually only seen with higher-priced vehicles.

Cost analysis/best alternatives: Feel free to buy a discounted year 2000 version; it's practically identical to this year's version. Other cars worth considering are the Ford Focus, Honda Civic, Mazda Protegé, and Suzuki Swift. If you're in the market for a sport coupe, check out the VW Golf GTi. **Options:** Built-in child safety seats (if available) and height adjustment for the steering wheel (for short drivers). ABS is one safety option that hasn't got the bugs worked out yet. **Rebates:** $1,000–$1,500. **Delivery/PDI:** $800. **Depreciation:** About average. **Insurance cost:** Average. **Parts supply/cost:** Average. **Annual maintenance cost:** Higher than average. **Warranty:** Bumper-to-bumper 3 years/60,000 km; powertrain 5 years/ 100,000 km; rust perforation 5 years/160,000 km. **Supplementary warranty:** A definite plus. A bumper-to-bumper extended warranty would be advisable, but this takes away the car's price advantage. **Highway/city fuel economy:** 7–9.5L/100 km with the base 2.0L engine.

Quality/Reliability/Safety

Pro: Apparently, the 4-cylinder engine faulty head gaskets, present since 1995, have been remedied with improved gaskets on most Chrysler 2000 models (Sebring excepted) and all 2001 models, says TSB #09-08-99. Keep your fingers crossed. Front adjustable shoulder belt anchors.

Con: Quality control: Pressed by Daimler to cut $2 billion from its budget this year, I doubt there will be sufficient funds to fix the Neon's factory-related deficiencies. *Consumer Reports* says that its member survey found that first-year (1995 model) Neons had nearly twice the problems of the average 1995 model car. **Reliability:** When *Autoweek*, an American car enthusiast magazine, tested a '96 Neon Sport Coupe with only 16,566 miles (26,506 km) on the odometer for its March 4th edition, it concluded that "aliens" had invaded the test car. **Warranty performance:** Chrysler's 5-year powertrain warranty is far from reassuring when one considers how tough Chrysler has been in interpreting its warranty obligations, and that Ford gives owners up to 7 years/160,000 km. You can always appeal any warranty repair refusal to the company's Review

Committee (see Appendix), but this is a shot in the dark without written guidelines as to what Chrysler considers a valid goodwill claim. Ford and GM, on the other hand, have publicly announced they'll accept powertrain claims up to 7 years or 160,000 km. **Owner-reported problems:** A perusal of owner comments confirms that these cars continue to have lots of serious factory-related defects, including engine head gasket failures, an air-conditioning system that often requires expensive servicing, lots of interior noise and leaks, interior window film buildup, exposed screw heads, uneven fit and finish, and poor quality trim items that break or fall off easily. The finish isn't as good as most other subcompacts either. **Service bulletin problems:** AC compressor locks up at low mileage; harsh AC engagement and clunk noise; measures to reduce steering wheel column clunks and rattles; front suspension creaking; remote keyless transmitter failure; front door water leaks; power-steering moan; steering wheel/column clunk and rattle; shake in steering wheel and/or seat at idle; poorly seated instrument panel top cover; instrument panel creaks; rear door glass won't roll down all the way; high window cranking effort or slow power window operation; blower motor noise or vibration; front suspension snapping noise; from deck lid rattle and water/dust intrusion past the deck lid seal; difficulty moving front seats forward; discoloured B-pillar appliqué.

2000 Dodge Neon 4-122 2.0L SOHC
Technical Service Bulletin

Number	Date	Name
23-06-00	Feb 00	Water Leak From Top Edge Of Right Or Left Front Door
23-02-00	Feb 00	Internal Emergency Trunk Release
23-55-99	Dec 99	B-Pillar Applique On Doors Brown Haze/Appears Discolored
19-07-99	Dec 99	Power Steering Moan Noise
23-51-99	Nov 99	Instrument Panel Top Cover Not Properly Seated At Edges
24-23-99	Nov 99	Revised A/C Suction Line And Unified Line Installation
23-50-99	Nov 99	Instrument Panel Creak
08-37-99	Nov 99	Airbag On/Off Switches
23-46-99	Nov 99	High Effort Required To Adjust The Front Seats Forward
23-45-99	Nov 99	Deck Lid Rattle, Water/Dust Leak Past Deck Lid Seal
19-02-99A	Oct 99	Clunking Or Rattle In Steering Wheel/Steering Column
08-33-99	Oct 99	Gauge Pointers On Wrong Side Of Pointer Stops
23-35-99A	Oct 99	Child Seat Tether Anchor
09-08-99	Sep 99	Multi-Layer Steel Head Gasket Installation Procedures.
24-17-99	Aug 99	Vibration Or Noise From HVAC Blower Motor
18-20-99	Aug 99	Harsh A/C Initial Engagement - Clunk Noise
13-01-99	Jul 99	Snapping Noise From Front Suspension Area
24-15-99	Jul 99	A/C Compressor Lock-up At Low Mileage
23-23-99	Jul 99	Rear Door Glass Will Not Roll Down All The Way
08-16-99A	Jun 99	Inoperative Or Intermittent RKE Transmitter
23-16-99	May 99	Decklid Does Not Open With First Cycle Of Key Fob
09-01-99A	May 99	Shake In Steering Wheel And/Or Seat at Idle
826	May 99	Safety Recall # 826 - Lower Control Arms
23-13-99	Apr 99	High Window Cranking Effort Or Slow Power Window Opp.
821	Mar 99	Safety Recall # 821 - Passenger Airbag Module

NHTSA safety complaints/safety: Airbags fail to deploy or deploy inadvertently; Michelin tires fail prematurely; engine head gasket, intake manifold, front-end suspension, and drivetrain failure; front and rear head restraints are set too low; headlight switch is a "hide-and-go-seek" affair; ventilation system doesn't contain a mechanism to shut off exterior air flow to prevent exhaust fumes from entering the cabin; horn failures. Two safety recalls: lower control arms may fail (replace both); passenger airbag may not deploy (replace module).

Road Performance

Pro: Better than average acceleration (0–100 km/h: 8.1 sec) with plenty of low-end torque. The 2.0L engine's 132 horses and the Neon's low weight give it acceptable performance in lower gear ranges, but restrict it to mainly urban use. **Emergency handling:** Better than average. **Steering:** Precise and easy to control on smooth roads.

Con: Acceleration/torque: Base engine runs out of steam in high gear and is buzzy from 4,000 rpm on up. It runs particularly roughly after 5,000 rpm. This is especially irritating because horsepower and torque peak at 5,000 and 6,000 rpm. Even with the manual transmission, highway passing requires downshifting from fifth gear to third, with the 2.0L engine crying all the way. The optional 150-hp 4-cylinder engine only available on last year's model isn't much better. **Transmission:** The manual transmission is harsh and noisy—no comparison with Honda and Toyota vehicles. The manual gearbox also requires lots of downshifting when going over small hills. The 3-speed automatic transmission lacks sufficient torque in high gear, and shifts abruptly and often. The car cries out for a more economical and efficient 4-speed electronic transmission. **Routine handling:** Definitely improved over last year, but the jittery ride becomes fairly rough when traversing anything but the smoothest roads. Ride deteriorates and the suspension bottoms with a vengeance with a full load. **Braking:** Worse than average (100–0 km/h: 143 ft.).

Comfort/Convenience

Pro: Driving position: Good driving position. The bucket seats are comfortable and there's plenty of head room. **Controls and displays:** Easy-to-operate controls and clear gauges. Easy-to-use and effective heating and ventilation system. **Climate control:** Everything's within easy reach and easily read. **Entry/exit:** Good up front; large door openings for long legs. **Interior space/comfort F/R:** The Neon seats five adults and has a spacious interior. Practical cloth bucket seats. Seats are firmer and more comfortable than one would expect. Plenty of rear leg room and elbow room. Rear seat is roomy enough for three adults. Rear seatbacks can be folded down to increase trunk space. **Cargo space:** Lots of little storage areas. Upgraded radio antenna reduces wind noise.

Con: Standard equipment: Low-quality interior appointments. Rear visibility compromised by high rear parcel shelf. Gauges lose contrast in dim light with headlights on. Door-mounted power window switches press uncomfortably against the driver's leg. Rear door shape makes for difficult entry and exit. Hard-to-access rear seat doesn't provide enough thigh support. Inadequate rear head room and toe space. Hard-to-operate window cranks and only the front windows are power-assisted. Short, flimsy trunk lid restricts trunk access. **Trunk/liftover:** Narrow trunk with a low sill. Trunk hinges eat up lots of storage space as well as possibly damaging your luggage. **Quietness:** Plenty of engine boom and growling, automatic transmission whine, and tire thumping.

COST

List Price (negotiable)	Residual Values (months)			
	24	**36**	**48**	**60**
LE 4d: $18,375 (13%)	$9,800	$7,900	$6,700	$4,900
LX 4d: $20,230 (14%)	$11,000	$9,000	$7,500	$6,000

TECHNICAL DATA

Powertrain (front-drive)
Engine: 2.0L 4-cyl. (132 hp)
Transmissions: 5-speed man.
• 3-speed auto.
Dimensions/Capacity
Passengers: 2/3
Height/length/width:
53/171.8/67.5 in.

Head room F/R: 39.6/36.5 in.
Leg room F/R: 42.5/35.1 in.
Wheelbase: 104 in.
Turning circle: 35.4 ft.
Cargo volume: 42.6 cu. ft.
Tow limit: 1,000 lb.; 2,000 lb. (manual)
Fuel tank: 47L/reg.
Weight: 2,400 lb.

SAFETY FEATURES/CRASHWORTHINESS

	Std.	Opt.
Anti-lock brakes	❑	■
Seatbelt pretensioners	—	—
Side airbags	❑	■
Traction control	❑	■
Head restraints F/R	*	*
Visibility F/R	*****	*
Crash protection (front) D/P	****	****
Crash protection (side) D/P	***	***
Crash protection (off-set)	**	

Sebring, Stratus

Sebring

RATING: Above Average. **Strong points:** Comfortable ride, adequate interior room, and optional ABS. **Weak points:** Mediocre engine performance, lots of engine and road noise, and sub-par warranty performance.

NEW FOR 2001: First a couple of name games and plant changes: The Avenger coupe and sedan will be renamed the Stratus, and the Cirrus coupe, sedan, and convertible will, henceforth, go under the Sebring moniker. The Sebring sedan and convertible will be built at Chrysler's plant in Michigan, along side the Stratus sedan; the Sebring and Stratus coupes will be built by Mitsubishi in Illinois, where a Stratus R/T coupe should appear later this year. The Plymouth Breeze, as with Plymouth, has been discontinued. Other improvements this year: measures to reduce vibration, noise, and a harsh ride and the addition of a 2.7L engine.

OVERVIEW: These coupes, sedans, and convertibles are good buys mainly because they've had fewer new-model "teething" problems than other Chrysler-built vehicles. Sebring is a reasonably priced luxury model equipped with standard amenities, including AC, bucket seats, and a tilt steering wheel, while the Stratus fills the sporty Avenger niche with standard tinted glass and an awesome sound system.

These front-drive replacements for the failure-prone Dodge Daytona and LeBaron coupes share most safety features and mechanical components, including standard dual airbags and a 150-hp 2.4L 4-banger along with an optional 200-hp 3.0L V6. An optional 200-hp 2.7L V6 will also be offered with the four-door version of either car.

Cost analysis/best alternatives: The 2000 Sebring, Stratus, or Avenger should be heavily discounted and represent the better buy. Also, it's not a good idea to buy a model that's just changed its manufacturing plant. Finally, any models built at the Mitsubishi plant in Illinois seem to have fewer factory-related glitches. Avenger shoppers should take a look at other sporty coupes, including the Honda Accord and Toyota Celica. Convertibles worth a glance: Ford Mustang and Chevrolet Camaro. **Options:** These cars come well-appointed. **Rebates:** $1,500 rebates on all models. **Delivery/PDI:** $350. **Depreciation:** A bit slower than average. **Insurance cost:** Average. **Parts supply/cost:** Reasonably priced parts are easily found. **Annual maintenance cost:** Average. **Warranty:** Bumper-to-bumper 3 years/60,000 km; powertrain 5 years/100,000 km; rust perforation 5 years/160,000 km. **Supplementary warranty:** Not needed for the Mitsubishi-built cars; a wise precaution for those models made in Michigan. **Highway/city fuel economy:** 7.3–11.2L/100 km with the base 4-cylinder; 8–12L/100 km with the V6.

Quality/Reliability/Safety

Pro: Quality control: Quality control is unusually good. Body construction and assembly are solid, with few gaps. **Reliability:** Better than average. **Warranty performance:** Average, of course with few claims it's difficulty to get a complete picture. Remember, you can always appeal any warranty repair refusal to the company's Review Committee (see Appendix).

Con: Owner-reported problems: Premature brake wear and some electrical glitches. **Service bulletin problems:** *Coupe* and *sedan:* Steering wheel/column clunk or rattle; plugged windshield washer nozzle. *Convertible:* Steering wheel/column clunk or rattle; plugged windshield washer nozzle; peeling or blistering quarter window weatherstrip coating; seatbelt appears twisted. **NHTSA safety complaints/safety:** Electrical system fire; several brake system failures due to loss of vacuum; space-saver spare tire is only good for a few miles and at slow speeds; seatbelts too tight; chronic dead battery.

Road Performance

Pro: Emergency handling: Better than average. **Steering:** Steering is responsive and light. **Acceleration/torque:** Adequate, but far from sporty acceleration (0–100 km/h: 10 sec. with the V6). The base 4-cylinder is thrifty and adequate for most driving tasks. It works well with both the manual and automatic transmission. **Transmission:** Smooth and quiet operation in all gear ranges. **Routine handling:** Handling is exceptional with either engine, and there's little body lean when cornering under speed. The ride deteriorates only slightly on bad surfaces due to the car's compliant suspension. Jarring is reduced as the weight of passengers is added.

Con: The base 2.4L engine loses power when mated to the 4-speed automatic and, when pushed, it's noisy and less responsive than the V6. Some front-end plow in turns. The car's large turning circle makes parking a chore. **Braking:** Unimpressive (100–0 km/h: 141 ft.).

Comfort/Convenience

Pro: Standard equipment: Well-appointed with many standard features. **Controls and displays:** Controls and gauges are easily reached and seen. **Entry/exit:** Large doors facilitate entry and exit. **Interior space/comfort F/R:** The rear seating area is more adult-friendly than most sport coupes. Three tall passengers can sit in the rear for short trips, but the seating is really designed for two. **Cargo space:** Limited trunk cargo area can be extended by folding the split seatback. **Trunk/liftover:** Average trunk space with a low liftover. Rear seatback and remote trunk release can be locked.

Con: Driving position: Front seats need additional lateral support, and the seatback bulge is annoying to some drivers. The tilt steering wheel is set too low (almost in the driver's lap). Short drivers may have difficulty with forward vision, even with the seat raised to its maximum setting. **Climate control:** The climate control system is hampered by a noisy fan and uneven air distribution. The rear defroster leaves some of the glass untouched. With rear-quarter windows that won't open and the optional rear deck-lid spoiler cutting rear visibility, it's not hard to feel a bit claustrophobic. **Quietness:** Excessive tire/road noise intrudes into the passenger compartment.

COST

List Price (very negotiable)	Residual Values (months)			
	24	36	48	60
Sebring 4d: $23,240 (19%)	$16,000	$15,000	$13,500	$12,000
Stratus: $23,380 (19%)	$16,000	$15,000	$13,500	$12,000

TECHNICAL DATA

Powertrain (front-drive)
Engines: 2.4L 4-cyl. (147 hp)
• 2.4L 4-cyl. (150 hp)
• 2.7 L V6 (200 hp)
• 3.0L V6 (200 hp)
Transmissions: 5-speed man.
• 4-speed auto.
Dimensions/Capacity
Passengers: 2/3
Height/length/width:
53.3/187.2/70.3 in.

Head room F/R: 37.6/36.5 in.
Leg room F/R: 43.3/35 in.
Wheelbase: 103.7 in.
Turning circle: 33.6 ft.
Cargo volume: 13.1 cu. ft.
Tow limit: 1,000 lb.
Fuel tank: 60L/reg.
Weight: 3,012 lb.

SAFETY FEATURES/CRASHWORTHINESS (2000)

	Std.	Opt.
Anti-lock brakes	■	■
Seatbelt pretensioners	—	—
Side airbags	—	—
Traction control	■	❑

Sebring		
Head restraints F/R	*****	**
Visibility F/R	****	*****
Crash protection (front) D/P	*****	*****
Convertible	****	****
Crash protection (side) D/P	N/A	N/A
Crash protection (off-set)	N/A	
Stratus		
Head restraints F/R	**	*
Visibility F/R	*****	*****
Crash protection (front) D/P	***	****
Crash protection (side) D/P	***	**
Crash protection (off-set)	*	

300M, Concorde, Intrepid, LHS

300M

RATING: *Concorde* and *Intrepid:* Average. These cars give you more room than dependability. *300M* and *LHS:* Below Average. These over-priced, stylish sedans offer a nicely packaged depository of generic components used on the Concorde and Intrepid. This means they will have generic Chrysler-type problems compromising reliability and safety. **Strong points:** *Concorde* and *Intrepid:* Attractive styling, nice riding, easy entry/exit, and lots of passenger and cargo room. *300M* and *LHS:* Attractive styling, good acceleration and handling, plenty of passenger and cargo room, and reasonable price. The LHS also has a large trunk with a wide opening. **Weak points:** *Concorde* and *Intrepid:* Excessive road and wind noise, vague steering, optional ABS, limited rear visibility caused by the cars' high rear end, impractical trunk, poor reliability, and sub-par warranty performance on Chrysler's part. *300M* and *LHS:* Rough-running engine and transmission, excessive road and wind noise, five-passenger capacity, the 300M has limited rear leg room, a narrow rear windshield reduces rear visibility and carries a smaller trunk with a smaller opening than the LHS, mediocre fit and finish, and questionable reliability.

NEW FOR 2001: Optional front side airbags.

OVERVIEW: *Concorde* and *Intrepid:* These full-sized cars share the same chassis and offer most of the same standard and optional features. Both cars have loads of passenger space and many standard features that usually sell as options, such as four-wheel disc brakes and an independent rear suspension. The Concorde is marketed to the more conservative buyer. The Intrepid, the more popular model, is the entry-level version. Base models are equipped with a 2.7L V6 aluminum engine that delivers 200 hp. Higher line variants get a more powerful 3.2L V6 225-hp powerplant, or a 242-hp 3.5L V6.

300M and *LHS:* These two models represent the near-luxury and sport clones of the Chrysler Concorde. Although they use the same front-drive platform as the Concorde, their bodies are shorter and they're styled differently. In fact, the 300M is the shortest of Chrysler's mid-sized sedans. Both cars are powered by a 253-hp 3.5L V6 and mated to Chrysler's AutoStick semi-automatic transmission. Only a few months after their launch in the summer of '98, Chrysler made engineering changes to reduce noise and vibration and smooth out what was thought to be an overly harsh ride. Automatic headlights were added as well.

Cost analysis/best alternatives: Look for a 15 percent discount on the year 2000 versions before any rebates are applied. If you want first-class quality, though, an Acura RL, Audi A6, Lexus GS 300, Nissan Maxima, or a fully loaded Toyota Camry or Avalon should be your first choice. **Options:** You'd be smart to get any of the two larger V6 engines. Goodyear GA tires provide better handling, but they're noisy. The harsh sports suspension, however, is a waste of money. Opt for the handling package and you get crisper steering response, better brakes and tires, and stiffer springs that eliminate much of the body roll. The large rear windshield may need tinting to protect rear-seat passengers from the sun. **Rebates:** All four models will have $1,500–$2,000 rebates coming into the year 2001. **Delivery/PDI:** $800. **Depreciation:** Average. The Intrepid suffers from a low level of owner loyalty—industry stats show that about nine out of ten Intrepid owners walk away from the model when considering their next vehicle purchase. **Insurance cost:** Higher than average. **Parts supply/cost:** Reasonably priced and easily found. **Annual maintenance cost:** Much higher than average. **Warranty:** Bumper-to-bumper 3 years/60,000 km; powertrain 5 years/100,000 km; rust perforation 5 years/160,000 km. **Supplementary warranty:** Don't leave home without it. A wise investment, judging from the serious problems reported on previous models. **Highway/city fuel economy:** 7.2–11.3L/100 km with the 2.7L engine; 7.6–12.5L/100 km with the 3.2L engine; 8.0–13L/100 km with the 3.5L engine.

Quality/Reliability/Safety

Pro: Plastic front fenders are dent- and corrosion-resistant. Platinum-tipped spark plugs are expected to last 160,000 kilometres. Improved headlights really illuminate the road, and the upgraded defroster now clears the entire windshield.

Con: Quality control: Below average. **Reliability:** Poor overall. **Warranty performance:** Worse than average. You can always appeal any warranty repair refusal to the company's Review Committee (see Appendix). But without knowing Chrysler's benchmarks for goodwill assistance, your appeal will be like a shot in the dark. **Owner-reported problems:** Glitches in the computerized transmission's shift timing, which cause driveability problems (stalling, hard starts, and surging). Amazingly, the 4-speed LE42 automatic transmission—a spin-off of Chrysler's failure-prone A604—appears to be just as problem-plagued as its predecessor, with reports of driveline shudder during three to four shifts and frequent transmission defaults into second gear (limp-in mode). Other owner-reported defects include premature brake wear and brake malfunctions, electrical problems, and sloppy body construction. For example, owners complain of water and air leaks into the interior, uneven fit and finish, poor quality trim items that break or easily fall off, exposed screw heads, faulty door hinges that make the doors rattle and hard to open, windows that come off their tracks or are misaligned, and power-window motor failures. **Service bulletin problems:** Front strut noise; front suspension or steering gear rattle; vehicle leads or pulls speaker screw contacts door seal. **NHTSA safety complaints/safety:** Transmission won't shift to reverse, engine stalls; headlights sometimes shut off on their own; side seatbelts don't retract; front and rear windshields distort view; there may be an annoying reflection on the inside of the windshield, particularly evident on vehicles with beige interiors. 300M and LHS rear visibility compromised by narrow rear windows.

Road Performance

Pro: Emergency handling: Steering is a bit vague and ponderous with some tire squealing, but no worse than the competition. **Acceleration/torque:** The 3.2L and 3.5L V6 engines provide plenty of low-end torque and acceleration (0–100 km/h: 9 sec.). **Routine handling:** Good or better handling and steering response than the Taurus, and the optional AutoStick clutch-less manual transmission available with the Intrepid sports package improves overall performance even more. Independent suspension also maximizes control and provides lots of suspension travel so that you don't get bumped around on rough roads. The ride doesn't deteriorate as the load is increased. The best balance between performance and ride is found with the mid-level touring suspension. It's not as harsh as the optional sport suspension, and it's firmer than the standard settings. **Braking:** Good braking performance with standard brakes (100–0 km/h: 125 ft.).

Con: The traction control system is noisy when activated. The smaller, 2.7L V6 engine is inadequate to handle a fully loaded Concorde or Intrepid. The 300M and LHS 3.5L V6 isn't as smooth a performer as the Lexus GS 300 or the Acura TL powerplants. **Transmission:** The 4-speed automatic transmission shifts in and out of overdrive with a jolt. A considerable amount of body roll occurs in tight manoeuvring.

Comfort/Convenience

Pro: Standard equipment: Loaded with standard features. A sleeker, more aerodynamic body than the Taurus/Sable, the Honda Accord, and Chevrolet's Lumina. Excellent front visibility due to the large windshield and low front end. **Controls and displays:** Very user-friendly. Analogue instruments are clearly laid out. **Climate control:** Automatic climate-control system is much improved. Efficient and easy to adjust. **Entry/exit:** Excellent front and rear access. The user-friendly interior features passenger grab handles for easy access. **Interior space/comfort F/R:** Extended front seat tracks for long-legged drivers or simply for people wanting to sit away from the airbag. Comfortable front bucket seats and rear seat sits three abreast. **Cargo space:** Lots of storage space, including map pockets in the door.

Con: Driving position: Front seat lacks lateral support and the adjustable lumbar support is uncomfortable. Instrumentation illumination could be brighter and more distinct on the LHS and 300M. **Truck/liftover:** The trunk has a high deck lid, making for difficult loading and unloading, and there's no inside access by folding down the rear seat, as in the Camry. **Quietness:** All four vehicles have excessive engine, road, and wind noise that comes mainly from the tires and poor sealing around the doors and windows.

COST				
List Price (very negotiable)	**Residual Values (months)**			
	24	**36**	**48**	**60**
Intrepid SE: $25,910 (21%)	$16,000	$13,000	$11,000	$9,000
Concorde LX: $28,485 (22%)	$17,000	$14,000	$12,000	$10,000
300M: $40,900 (22%)	$28,000	$23,000	$18,000	$15,000
LHS: $41,655 (22%)	$28,500	$23,500	$18,500	$15,500

TECHNICAL DATA	
Powertrain (front-drive)	Head room F/R: 38.3/37.2 in.;
Engines: 2.7L V6 (200 hp)	38.3/37.7 in.
• 3.2L V6 (225 hp)	Leg room F/R: 42.2/41.6 in.;
• 3.5L V6 (242 hp)	42.2/39.1 in.
• 3.5L V6 (253 hp)	Wheelbase: 113 in.
Transmissions: 5-speed man.	Turning circle: 35.4 ft.; 37.6 ft.
• 4-speed auto.	Cargo volume: 18.7 cu. ft.; 16.8 cu. ft.

Dimensions/Capacity (Concorde; 300M)	Tow limit: 2,000 lb.
Passengers: 3/3; 2/3	Fuel tank: 68L/reg.; 65L/reg.
Height/length/width:	Weight: 3,550 lb.; 3,567 lb.
55.9/209.1/74.4 in.;	
56/197.8/82.7 in.	

SAFETY FEATURES/CRASHWORTHINESS

	Std.	Opt.
Anti-lock brakes	■	■
Seatbelt pretensioners	—	—
Side airbags	❑	■
Traction control	■	■
Head restraints F/R		
Concorde and Intrepid	*****	**
300M and LHS	**	**
Visibility F/R		
Concorde and Intreprid	*****	*****
300M and LHS	*****	*
Crash protection (front) D/P	****	****
300M	***	****
Crash protection (side) D/P	****	***
Crash protection (off-set)	N/A	

PT Cruiser

PT Cruiser

RATING: Average. A Neon clone, cobbled together with Neon parts and engineering and assembly processes. The PT Cruiser is essentially a fuel- and space-efficient hatchback mini-minivan that uses the same nostalgic hot rod flair that's been so successful with the Prowler. **Strong points:** Excellent fuel economy, nimble handling around town, good braking, lots of interior space, easy access, versatile cargo area, many thoughtful interior amenities, slow depreciation, and unforgettable styling. **Weak points:** Outrageously high-priced, failure-prone Neon DNA, lethargic engine, poor crashworthiness rating (driver), first year on the market, mediocre highway performance and handling, a firm ride, lots of road noise in cabin area and unforgettable styling. Log onto *www.ptcruiser.org* for the latest owners' comments.

NEW FOR 2001: The Cruiser, launched last spring, is carried over with no substantive changes. Don't expect any changes until the 2003 model year when a panel version may appear along with GPS navigation, an optional 2.4L inline 4-banger, a flexible-fuel option for the base 2.4L, some engineering improvements, and a freshened interior.

OVERVIEW: The PT Cruiser doesn't look like any other vehicle on the market. Even the U.S. federal government can't agree upon its classification. Its Neon platform and spacious interior have resulted in one government agency (the Environmental Protection Agency) calling it a car while NHTSA—impressed by its cargo-carrying ability—rates it as a truck. This confusion is presently playing out in underground parking lots and condo associations where trucks pay additional fees or are simply banned.

I call it a mini-minivan with 1930s delivery van and 1950s hot rod styling, that's more of a hit with nostalgic baby-boomers than with younger buyers.

The Cruiser is ideal for buyers tired of the truckish handling of rear-drive minivans, and who are willing to risk the Neon component failures in exchange for good passenger/cargo flexibility. True, its bold styling is an attention-getter, but the basic configuration has been used in other countries for years by Asian and European automakers and in North America with the bland-looking Mitsubishi Expo LRV/Eagle Summit, popular in the early '90s.

The Cruiser comes with a nice assortment of new parts that includes attractive chrome door handles, a four-spoke steering wheel, and a cue-ball shifter for the 5-speed manual that sits atop a chrome stalk with a vinyl boot. It carries a Dodge Stratus 150-hp 2.4L 16-valve engine, although in international markets, a 1.6L and 2.0L 4-cylinder will be offered.

Cost analysis/best alternatives: There is no real alternative to the uniquely designed Cruiser. That's why you should either expect to get hosed in buying one this year, or patiently wait until the end of 2001, when prices will stabilize as they did with the VW New Beetle. In a pinch, you may wish to consider these wagons: VW's Passat GLS 4, the Ford Focus SE Wagon, Subaru Legacy Outback Limited, or the Volvo V40. Sport-utilities worth considering are: the Subaru Forester, Honda CR-V EX, GM Tracker, Suzuki Grand Vitara, and Isuzu Rodeo S. **Options:** The optional front folding rear seatback allows objects up to 2.4 m (8.0 ft.) long to fit inside the vehicle. The same option permits the back of the front passenger seat to be used as a table for the driver.

Stay away from the side airbag and ABS brakes—neither safety item is worth the extra risk they pose. Although the disc brakes have been improved, Chrysler's large number of ABS failures is worrisome. It would be a good idea to replace the rear drum brakes with discs; however, that option is only available with the expensive, and still unproven, four-wheel ABS option coupled with electronic traction control. Gotcha! **Rebates:** Forget it. Chrysler dealers expect *you* to pay them extra for the opportunity to buy a Cruiser. Price gouging is rampant with some dealers getting $3,000–$10,000 over the Manufacturer's Suggested Retail Price (MSRP). Chrysler has refused to intervene, blaming the problem on the car's popularity and impatient buyers. **Delivery/PDI:** Supposedly $800; but you'll likely pay more. **Depreciation:** Practically non-existent. Expect ten percent depreciation per year to kick in after the second year. **Insurance cost:** Higher than average, because many insurance companies impose the higher rates they use for trucks. **Parts supply/cost:** Predicted to be average since many parts come from the Neon generic parts bin. Body parts are another matter. Expect long delays and high costs until independent suppliers and Chrysler's own distribution network come up to speed. **Annual maintenance cost:** Average, until the 3-year mark, when poor durability, first-year glitches, and the warranty's expiration hike maintenance and repair costs. **Warranty:** Bumper-to-bumper 3 years/60,000 km; powertrain 5 years/100,000 km; rust perforation 5 years/160,000 km. **Supplementary warranty:** A bumper-to-bumper extended warranty is essential if you plan on keeping your Cruiser longer than three years. Paying over $1,000 for this protection is ridiculous; settle for a third or half as much, and take solace in knowing the Cruiser's low depreciation will make up for the initial extra cost. **Highway/city fuel economy:** 8.3–11.7L/100 km.

Quality/Reliability/Safety

Pro: The Neon platform has been strengthened, and Chrysler's Toluca, Mexico, plant has been upgraded to reduce engine and transmission vibration and noise. About 800 pounds heavier than a Neon, the Cruiser uses larger brake rotors and drums to carry the extra weight. Head restraints have a locking feature for added protection during a crash. There are three-point safety belts for four passengers, and a rear lap belt for the centre rear passenger. Extra measures taken to prevent window fogging.

Con: **Quality control:** There is nothing in the press releases I received from Chrysler or the service bulletins I accessed that reassures me that the Cruiser won't have the same powertrain and body deficiencies that have been seen on Chrysler's other first-year vehicles. **Reliability:** Predicted to be below average. **Warranty performance:** Average to below average. Chrysler showed considerable promise when it restructured its in-house customer relations department (it stank three years ago) to handle warranty and post-warranty complaints in a fair and efficient manner. However, now, one gets the impression the company's Review Committee (see Appendix) simply endorses what has previously been decided. **Owner-reported problems:** Water leaks through the side passenger window, and drivetrain whine. **Service bulletin problems:** Fuel gauge needle doesn't reach the full mark with the fuel tank full; wind buffeting with the windows and/or sunroof open or partially opened; the front door water dam may contact the speaker and create a buzzing or humming.

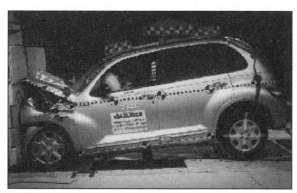

It's interesting to note that despite front airbags and side airbags, the driver would have sustained severe or fatal head and leg trauma in this crash test.

NHTSA safety complaints/safety: NHTSA crash tests have determined the driver would possibly sustain severe or fatal injuries in a frontal collision. Some sidewind instability. Tall drivers beware: the windshield is uncomfortably close, and its styling makes it difficult to see overhead traffic lights. The three small and recessed instrument pods are difficult to read in the daylight. Wide pillars obstruct one's view.

Road Performance

Pro: Steering: Acceptable, with good road feedback. Good acceleration with a manual transmission; times from 0–100 km/h should average in the 8-second range. **Transmission:** Precise manual shifter. Optional automatic gearbox has four forward gears rather than the Neon's primitive three-speed automatic. **Routine handling:** Getting around town is easy. **Braking:** Acceptable ABS braking when it functions as it should.

Con: Emergency handling: Slow and sloppy. The turning diameter seems excessive for such a short vehicle. Hard cornering produces an unsteady, wobbly ride due to the car's height. **Acceleration/torque:** Forget about hot rod power. The 2.4L 150-hp, 4-cylinder engine is not very smooth running and when matched to the automatic transmission struggles when going uphill or merging with freeway traffic. This requires frequent downshifting and lots of patience—accelerating to

100 km/h takes about nine seconds. The 4-banger was originally developed by Mitsubishi and used as the base minivan engine and as an upgrade for the Stratus. Automatic transmission doesn't have much low-end torque, forcing early kickdown shifting and deft manipulation of the accelerator pedal. **Braking:** The Cruiser has rear drum brakes, instead of more efficacious disc brakes.

Comfort/Convenience

Pro: **Standard equipment:** Very well-appointed with lots of innovative convenience features. Standard AM/FM/cassette stereo with six speakers. Front passengers have two 12-volt power plug-ins. **Controls and displays:** User-friendly rotary ventilation and heater controls. Centre dash area has buttons for the defogger, rear wiper/washer, and (optional) traction control on/off button. Easy access to all gauges and controls. **Climate control:** Efficient system that's easily understood and accessed. **Entry/exit:** Getting in and out is quite easy because of the Cruiser's tall roof, big doors, and elevated seats. The rear doors in particular open about 10 degrees more than most cars. **Interior space/comfort F/R:** Slightly smaller than the Neon in wheelbase and overall length, the Cruiser's about three inches shorter than the base minivan. But its additional ten inches of height over the Neon provides lots of room for tall passengers in front and rear. Seating is midway between a Caravan and a Neon, also making access quite easy. Tall, chair-like seats provide lots of leg room, and there's also generous head room, although the Cruiser is a bit narrower than the Neon. The front and rear seats have a reasonable amount of bolster to keep occupants from sliding side to side. **Cargo space:** Storage spaces include two large front door pockets, an underseat drawer, and a small glovebox. Removable seats and a flat floor put the PT into the truck class for government taxonomists. Folding front passenger seat is a nice touch, though it's hardly innovative—Volvo wagons have had it since the mid-'90s. Rear seats can be easily folded, flipped forward, and unlatched for quick removal. They have easy-to-carry handles, and wheels for rolling away. The seats aren't light, though, with the 65-pound right rear seat weighing about twice as much as the left. Another innovative feature is the car's (truck's?) rigid cargo hold cover that can double as a tailgate-party table. **Trunk/liftover:** The rear hatch door has a very low 632 mm (25.0 in.) liftover height, and is easy to open and close.

Con: Controls and displays: Left side of the tachometer not easily seen. Front power window switches are found at the top of the dashboard; rear window switches are inconveniently located on the back of the centre console. **Quietness:** Some drivetrain, wind, tire, and road noise intrudes into the interior.

COST

List Price (firm)	Residual Values (months)			
	24	**36**	**48**	**60**
PT Cruiser: $23,665 (15%)	$21,000	$19,000	$16,000	$14,000
Limited: $27,180 (17%)	$23,000	$21,000	$18,000	$16,000

TECHNICAL DATA

Powertrain (front-drive)
Engine: 2.4L 4-cyl. (150 hp)
Transmissions: 5-speed manual
• 4-speed auto.
Dimension/Capacity (base)
Passengers: 2/3
Height/length/width:
63/168.8/67.1 in.

Head room F/R: 40.4/39.6 in.
Leg room F/R: 41/40.8 in.
Wheelbase: 103 in.
Turning circle: 36.5 ft.
Cargo volume: 64 cu. ft.
Tow limit: 1,000 lb.
Fuel tank: 57L/reg
Weight: 3,123 lb.

SAFETY FEATURES/CRASHWORTHINESS

	Std.	Opt.
Anti-lock brakes (4W)	❏	■
Seatbelt pretensioners	❏	❏
Side airbags	❏	■
Traction control	❏	■
Head restraints F/R	**	*
Visibility F/R	****	*****
Crash protection (front) D/P	*	*****
Crash protection (side) D/P	*****	***
Crash protection (off-set)	N/A	

Caravan, Grand Caravan, Town & Country

Town & Country

RATING: Average. Compromised by a history of poor quality control and worse than average reliability, particularly since 1991. Recent service bulletins on the '99 model indicate fewer problems than have been seen on past versions. Not to be bought without an extended warranty, which should be bargained down to about half the asking price. **Strong points:** Comfortable ride, excellent braking, lots of innovative convenience features, user-friendly instruments and controls, driver-side sliding door, and plenty of interior room. **Weak points:** Poor acceleration with the base engine and mediocre handling with the extended versions. Both automatic transmissions perform poorly in different ways. Headlight illumination is inadequate. Skimpy storage compartments. A chintzy base warranty is inadequate to deal with serious powertrain, ABS, and body defects, and is exacerbated by the automaker's hard-nosed attitude in interpreting its warranty obligations. Crashworthiness has declined.

NEW FOR 2001: Six-cylinder engines get a horsepower boost; a 3.5L V6 will be added early in 2001. Other additions: adjustable pedals; front side airbags; larger, more effective headlights; a centre console with power ports that can be moved between the front and rear passengers; and a power-operated rear lift gate for easier cargo loading.

OVERVIEW: These versatile and stylish minivans return with a wide array of standard and optional features that include AWD, anti-lock brakes, child safety seats integrated into the seatbacks, flush design door handles, and front windshield wiper/washer controls located on the steering column lever for easier use. Childproof locks are standard and the front bucket seats incorporate vertically adjustable head restraints. The Town & Country, a luxury version of the Caravan, comes equipped with a 3.8L V6 and standard luxury features that make the vehicle more fashionable for upscale buyers.

Cost analysis/best alternatives: Chrysler is expected to keep 2001 model price increases within 1 percent through January. If this actually pans out, as I suspect it will, the redesigned 2001 models will represent the better buy. Don't look for any bargains among the Japanese imports. The red-hot Honda Odyssey and Toyota Sienna minivans will likely cost much more by year's end, and Mazda's MPV (redesigned last year) isn't even in the running. Although the Nissan Quest is scheduled to bow out by the end of 2001, vehicles remaining in stock will likely be deep-discounted to make way for new products. You also may have better luck bargaining down the Quest's price since Nissan is desperate to make a profit this year. Some full-sized GM or Chrysler rear-drive cargo vans, ripe for conversion, might be a more affordable and practical buy if you intend to haul a full passenger load, do some regular heavy hauling, use lots of accessories, or take frequent motoring excursions. **Options:** As you increase body length you lose manoeuvrability. Don't even consider the 4-cylinder engine—it has no place in a minivan, especially when hooked to the automatic transmission. If you buy a Grand version, stay away from the inadequate 3.0L V6 mated to the 3-speed automatic. That transmission lacks an Overdrive and will shift back and forth as speed varies, and it's slower and noisier than the other optional 6-cylinders when accelerating from a standing start. The 3.3L V6 is a better choice for most city-driving situations, but don't hesitate to get the 3.8L if you're planning lots of highway travel or carrying four or more passengers. Since its introduction, it's been relatively trouble-free, plus it's more economical on the highway than the 3.3L, which strains to maintain speed. The sliding side doors make it easy to load and unload children, install a child safety seat in the middle, or remove the rear seat. On the downside, they expose kids to traffic and are a costly option. Child safety seats integrated into the rear seatbacks are convenient and reasonably priced, but Chrysler's versions have had a history of tightening up excessively or not tightening enough, allowing the child to slip out. Try the seat with your child before buying it. Other important features to consider are the optional defroster, power mirrors, power door locks, and power driver's seat (if you're shorter than 5' 9" or expect to have different drivers using the minivan). You may wish to pass on the tinted windshields; they seriously reduce visibility. Town & Country buyers should pass on the optional all-wheel drive coupled with four-wheel disc brakes (instead of the standard rear drums). Although the disc brakes have been improved, Chrysler's large number of ABS failures is worrisome. **Rebates:** Now that foreign minivans are red hot (read Honda Odyssey and Toyota Sienna), look for both year 2000 and 2001 models getting rebates that top $1,500 to $2,500, depending upon the model year. **Delivery/PDI:** $855. **Depreciation:** Slightly slower than average, but not as slow as pickups, SUVs, or the PT Cruiser. **Insurance cost:** Higher than average, but about average for a minivan. **Parts supply/cost:** Average. Chrysler says that its 3.3L and 3.8L engines won't require tuneups before 160,000 kilometres. Prepare to be disappointed; many owners have had to tune up their minivans way before then. **Annual maintenance cost:** Repair costs are average during the warranty period. Now that the base warranty has been cut back, owners won't have the luxury of time to get proper warranty servicing through repeat repair-bay visits. If your dealer or Chrysler starts to play the waiting game—waiting for the warranty to expire—don't hesitate to use an independent garage if that's where good service can be found, and take the dealer and Chrysler to small claims court if the defect is factory related. **Warranty:** Base warranty is inadequate, if you plan to keep your minivan more than five years. Bumper-to-bumper 3 years/60,000 km; powertrain 5 years/100,000 km; rust perforation 5 years/160,000 km. **Supplementary warranty:** A musthave—preferably a 7-year powertrain warranty (the bumper-to-bumper extended warranty is simply too expensive). Paying over $1,000 for this protection is ridiculous; settle for a third or half as much. **Highway/ city fuel economy:** *Caravan:* 9–13L/100 km; *Grand Caravan AWD:* 10–14L/100 km; *Town & Country:* 9–14L/100 km; *Town & Country AWD:* 10–15L/100 km.

Quality/Reliability/Safety

Pro: Depowered front airbags. Power adjustable pedals are an important upgrade to be phased in by mid-2001. ABS improvements made three years ago are promising in that consumer complaints have gone down—though they have not been eliminated entirely. It will take several more years to be sure that these systems are functioning as they should. Dual airbags include knee bolsters to prevent front occupants from sliding under the seatbelts. Side-impact protection has been increased with steel beams in door panels. An innovative engine compartment layout also makes for a larger "crumple zone" in the event of collision. Remote-control power door locks can be programmed to lock when the vehicle is put in gear. Chrysler has developed a mechanism that releases the power door locks and turns on the interior lights when the airbag is deployed. The rear wiper is extraordinarily efficient and front wipers have been improved for better de-icing effectiveness.

Con: Quality control: Nothing reassures me that the year 2001 minivans won't continue to have chronic powertrain, fuel system, brake, electronic, and body deficiencies. Although *Consumer Reports* rates only the extended versions as worse than average, Canadian *Lemon-Aid* readers report that the base versions are just as failure-prone. This isn't surprising—quality control has been below average since these vehicles were first launched 15 years ago, and got much worse after the '90 model year. Quality has improved a bit over the last two years; we no longer have an unending stream of automatic transmission, ABS, and paint delamination complaints. Interestingly, the British Columbia class action against Chrysler for paint delamination includes vehicles only up to the 1997 model year. Hopefully, the worst is behind us—once the warranty expires, these common problems can collectively produce repair bills that will easily reach $5,000. **Reliability:** Has improved of late; approaching average. **Warranty performance:** It had improved to above average, but now it's stagnating around below average. True, Chrysler has come a long way in restructuring its customer relations department (it was the pits three years ago) to handle warranty and post-warranty claims, but the company's Review Committee (see Appendix) fails to render consistent decisions, due to a lack of written guidelines. Although many owners have been compensated by the Committee, that compensation appears to be hit or miss, and cannot replace better quality control and the need for a more comprehensive base warranty. **Owner-reported problems:** Most owner complaints focus on electrical glitches, premature brake wear, poor body construction, and body creaks, rattles, moans, and groans. Premature wear-out was reported on these parts: cooling system, clutch, front suspension components, wheel bearings, air-conditioning, and body parts (trim, weatherstrip becomes loose and falls off, plastic pieces rattle and break easily). In spite of improvements over the years, the front brakes need constant attention, if not to replace the pads or warped rotors, then to silence the excessive squeaks when braking. Premature wearout of the front brake rotors within two years or 30,000 km is a common Chrysler minivan failing that also has serious safety implications. **Service bulletin problems:** Loud moaning and groaning sound from the compressor and reports of low-mileage AC compressor lockup, a honking or squealing noise during parking lot manoeuvres, front door weatherstrip falls off, suspension strut tower chirping or squeaking, excessive engine ticking, CV boot grease seepage, engine gasket oil seepage, front door glass misadjustment causes excessive wind noise, ticking noise emanating from the top of the left B-pillar, whirling noise coming from the front or side sliding door power lock motors, and faulty transmission range sensors. Speed control doesn't hold while climbing a grade; poor radio reception due to ignition noises; right side sliding door rubs quarter panel; steering wheel click or rattle; snow or water ingestion into the rear brake drum (see following TSB).

Snow/Water Ingestion Into Rear Brake Drum
NUMBER: 05-10-99
GROUP: Brakes
EFFECTIVE DATE: Jan.31, 2000
SUBJECT:
Snow/Water Ingestion Into Rear Brake Drum
OVERVIEW:
This bulletin involves installing a revised rear brake drum support (backing) plate and possible replacement of the rear brake shoes and drums.
MODELS:
1996-2000 (NS) Town & Country/Caravan/Voyager
1996-2000 (GS) Chrysler Voyager (International Model)
SYMPTOM/CONDITION:
While driving through deep or blowing snow/water, the snow/water may enter the rear brake drums causing rust to develop on the rear brake drum and shoe friction surfaces. This condition can lead to temporary freezing of the rear brake linings to the drums. This symptom is experienced after the vehicle has been parked in below freezing temperatures long enough for the snow/water to freeze inside of the rear brake drums. If the parking brake has been applied the symptom is more likely to occur.

This factory-related mistake is covered under warranty and should be also eligible for post-warranty goodwill in view of Chrysler's bulletin listing it under its FAILURE CODE: P8 category.

NHTSA safety complaints/safety: Sudden acceleration, first in Reverse and then in Drive; stalling while cruising on the highway; van parked with gear in Park with the ignition off rolled backwards, crashed through a fence and hit a mobile home; 5-year-old pulled vehicle shift lever out of Park and into Drive and vehicle took off; sliding door opens when passing over bumps; side power door switch burns out prematurely; right rear brake lockup when backing up.

Road Performance

Pro: Emergency handling: Slow, but acceptable. **Steering:** Precise and predictable. **Acceleration/torque:** The most versatile, though a bit underpowered, powertrain for short-distance commuting is the 3.3L V6 engine coupled with the 4-speed automatic transmission (0–100 km/h: in about 10.8 sec. with a 3.3L-equipped Grand Caravan). Chrysler's top-of-the-line 3.8L engine is a better choice if you intend to do a lot of highway cruising: it's smooth and quiet with lots of much-needed low-end torque. The AWD transfers 90 percent of the engine power to the front wheels during normal driving conditions. It's easy to use and performs well. As the front wheels lose traction, the rear wheels get additional power until traction has been stabilized or the 55/45 percent front-to-rear limit is reached. **Routine handling:** These minivans are the closest thing to a passenger car when it comes to ride and handling. The redesigned chassis and improved steering provide a comfortable, no-surprise ride. Stiff springs greatly improve handling and comfort. Manoeuvrability around town is easy. Remember, the Grand version sacrifices handling for extra interior room. **Braking:** Acceptable ABS braking when it functions as it should (100–0 km/h: 118 ft. with the base Caravan and 132 ft. with the Grand Caravan).

Con: Acceleration/torque: Sluggish highway acceleration until you move up to the upgraded V6 engines. **Transmission:** The 3-speed automatic transmission accelerates poorly and is noisy, while the optional 41TE 4-speed automatic transmission with Overdrive shifts slowly and imprecisely. Excessive transmission whine. It's hard to use engine compression to slow down by "gearing down." Downshifting from the electronic gearbox provides practically no braking effect. **Routine handling:** Although it works well, the all-wheel drive option is overrated and not worth the fuel penalty for most driving situations. The stretched wheelbase version gives less-than-nimble handling. A large turning radius and long nose can make parking difficult. Power steering is vague and over-assisted as speed increases. **Braking:** Brake pedal feels mushy and the brakes tend to heat up after repeated applications, causing considerable loss of effectiveness (fade) and warping of the front discs. The ABS system has proved unreliable on older vans and repair costs are astronomical. Furthermore, the ABS control unit is located behind a front wheel, where it's susceptible to contamination by road salt and dirt.

Comfort/Convenience

Pro: Standard equipment: This is where Chrysler minivans shine. They offer plenty of standard comfort and versatility features. **Driving position:** Drivers are treated to a car-like driving position. Good overall view of the road. **Controls and displays:** The instrument panel features easy-to-read gauges and warning lights, and radio and heater controls are set close to the driver. The location of the turn signal indicators is particularly well thought out—they're in the lower portion of your field of vision. Lots of cupholders and interior reading lights. **Climate control:** Adequate. Triple-zone AC allows for different temperature settings for the driver and rear-seat passenger. Overhead heating and ventilation ducts to the rear seat are well placed. **Entry/exit:** Easy. The step-up height isn't too high for most people. Another nice touch: grab handles on the rear hatch and sliding door. There's convenient "walk through" access to the rear seating area. **Interior space/comfort F/R:** Minivan doesn't mean "mini" in terms of passenger space. The aerodynamic exterior design, increased window area, and lower sills make for an attractive, roomier-feeling vehicle, and the interior is large and versatile with excellent outward visibility. Chrysler has copied the Windstar in providing theatre-type seating; each row is set a little higher than the row in front, giving most passengers a better view. A fairly high roofline—about four inches taller than the Ford Windstar—means that a six-foot-tall passenger will sit comfortably in the back seat, but would touch the roof in a Windstar. The rear seat will accommodate three adults. Chrysler's integrated child safety seat has a reclining back. An optional "Convert-a-Bed" package is available with the seven-passenger seating configuration. **Cargo space:** Plenty and practical. This is where the dual sliding doors come in handy. No longer do you have to walk around to the passenger side to load or unload cargo. Rear seatbacks fold down, and removing the centre and rear seats is a "snap," thanks to the addition of little wheels on the base of the rear seat. Snap them down and you can roll the seat anywhere. Lifting them is a chore, though. **Trunk/liftover:** Easy to load and unload 4' x 8' sheets of plywood thanks to the wide doors and low floor. Courtesy lights in front and on the liftgate are an added convenience. Interestingly, with the rear seat removed, the regular-sized Caravan provides more cargo space than the Grand Caravan. **Quietness:** Better than average, thanks to better body soundproofing with polyurethane foam injected into body cavities (watch those allergies).

Con: Controls and displays: Driver is faced with 44 switches, dials, and buttons on the dash/door panel/console. Centre console is way too low and console storage bin for small objects is sometimes hard to open and close, and the panel dimmer is hidden behind the steering wheel. Wipers obstruct forward vision. **Entry/exit:** Both sliding side doors are unwieldy to slide and it takes lots of effort to push the buttons that unlatch them. Rear hatch door is hard to close. **Interior space/comfort F/R:** Front seats lack sufficient lumbar support and the seatback comes up short against the shoulder blades. Tall drivers will find leg room a bit tight without an adequate left footrest. Three adults will find the third-row bench seat a bit cramped and the head restraints set too low. **Cargo space:** Storage space is squandered by an absence of door pouches; skimpy, poorly accessible storage compartments, like the tiny glove compartment; a lack of storage shelves; and coat hooks that can't support a hanger. Removable seats, which weigh 50 to 100 pounds, aren't as easy to remove as Chrysler would have you believe. **Quietness:** Some wind noise intrudes into the interior.

COST				
List Price (very negotiable)	**Residual Values (months)**			
	24	**36**	**48**	**60**
Base Caravan: $24,885 (19%)	$18,000	$15,000	$13,000	$10,000
G. Caravan: $29,505 (20%)	$19,000	$16,000	$14,000	$11,500
Town & Country LXI:				
$41,150 (22%)	$27,000	$24,000	$21,000	$18,000

TECHNICAL DATA

Powertrain (front-drive)
Engines: 2.4L 4-cyl. (150 hp)
• 3.0L V6 (150 hp)
• 3.3L V6 (180 hp)
• 3.8L V6 (215 hp)
Transmissions: 3-speed auto.
• 4-speed auto.
Dimension/Capacity (base)
Passengers: 2/2/3
Height/length/width:
68.5/186.3/76.8 in.

Head room F: 39.8/R1: 40.1/R2: 38.1 in.
Leg room F: 41.2/R1: 36.6/R2: 35.8 in.
Wheelbase: 113.3 in.
Turning circle: 39.5 ft.
Cargo volume: 64 cu. ft.
GVWR: 3,536–3,851 lb.
Payload: N/A
Tow limit: 2,000–3,500 lb.
Fuel tank: 76L/reg.
Weight: 3,985 lb.

SAFETY FEATURES/CRASHWORTHINESS

	Std.	Opt.
Anti-lock brakes (4W)	❑	■
Seatbelt pretensioners	❑	❑
Side airbags	■	■
Traction control	■	■
Head restraints F/R	**	*
Visibility F/R	****	*****
Crash protection (front) D/P		
Caravan	***	***
G. Caravan	****	****
Town & Country	****	****
Crash protection (side) D/P		
G. Caravan	*****	***
Town & Country	*****	***
Crash protection (off-set)	**	

FORD

Ford is well positioned this year to continue earning substantial profits in spite of its buying back millions of faulty Firestone tires and loss of Explorer sales. This is due to the large variety of vehicles it sells and its successful transition to the lucrative sport-utility market, in addition to its substantial number of products in other market niches. Its vehicles appeal to buyers wanting a stylish, inexpensive, and roomy front-drive econobox like the Focus; those opting for imported and domestic front-drive mid-sized sedans and coupes; muscle-car enthusiasts who want a rear-drive machine; and those wanting the comfort and power of traditional rear-drive luxury cars. Die-hard Brits can get their Jaguar fix and fixed by Ford, and minivan aficionados can get their fill with the Windstar.

The only fly in Ford's product ointment is Land Rover. What could Ford have been thinking when they bought this turkey that nearly bankrupted BMW? Actually, Ford was thinking globally, knowing that it couldn't sell luxury cars throughout the world with just its Lincoln models. Therefore, Ford has acquired those companies that already have a worldwide luxury cachet. So, Land Rover will become part of Ford's Premier Automotive Group, where it'll join Aston Martin, Jaguar, Lincoln, and Volvo.

Pricing and dealer relations
Ford says it has held its 2001 model price increases to an average of only 1 percent by making some options standard equipment and restricting the number of vehicle combinations customers can order. The company will also use discriminatory pricing this year to reward top-rated Blue Oval dealers through lower invoice prices.

Ford Canada dealer relations are tense following the automaker's decision to separate Lincoln from the Ford franchise, axe its Mercury division, and sell cars for less to its top-performing dealers. In fact, for the second year in a row, Ford comes in last place in the Canadian Automobile Dealers Association annual survey rating dealers satisfaction with automakers. Dealers explain that the low ratings are also due to Ford's "chaotic" new ordering system, the lack of new passenger car products, and a new parts pricing system.

New products: trucks and SUVs
Unlike Chrysler, Ford's passenger car sales are quite good (especially with the Focus, Taurus, Sable, Crown Victoria [fleet sales only], and Mercury Grand Marquis); therefore, few model changes are planned for the 2001 model year, except for a freshening of the Cougar and Windstar.

Actually, the small Focus and large-sized Crown Victoria/Marquis have been particularly successful in fighting imports at both ends of the market while keeping Chrysler and GM on their toes. This is all the more ironic because neither of these vehicles is all that new. The Focus is a European-designed carryover, and the rear-drive Crown Victoria and Grand Marquis are restyled 1970s products. The not-so-new Taurus and Sable models have also done very well against Toyota's Camry, Honda's Accord, and Mazda's 626.

Truck and sport-utility sales have been declining during the past few months, though, so Ford is hopeful its new Escape and Explorer Sport, and Explorer Sport Trac SUVs will boost sales despite rising fuel prices. On the truck side, this year will see the debut of the F-150 SuperCrew and the re-skinning of the small Ranger pickup.

A number of slow-moving models like the Contour and the Contour SVT may no longer be sold in Canada by the end of the 2000 model year. Also, some more familiar Mercury nameplates will disappear (Mystique and Sable), as Ford further consolidates its distribution after keeping the Mountaineer out of the country and dropping the Villager and Sable. Only the Mercury Cougar and Grand Marquis will remain in Canada, but all Mercury models will continue to be sold in the States.

Warranty performance

I am much happier with Ford's warranty performance this year than last.

Why? Simply because the company followed through on a number of my suggestions in overhauling its customer assistance centre, then publicly announced the setting up of a new post-warranty "goodwill" program for engine defects. Ford officials have also reassured me that the company will consider setting up Owner Notification Programs to pay all claims for 1994+ automatic transmission failures as well, though this was not announced publicly. I'm also pleased that John Vernile, the head of the centre, and Pamela Kueber, vice president of Ford public relations, have both followed through assiduously on the several hundred customer complaints I brought to their attention over the past 12 months.

Qualms About Changing Tires

Congress begins hearings today aimed at learning when Ford and Firestone executives knew of defects in Firestone tires.

Firestone legal has some major reservations about the plan to notify customers and offer them an option... They feel that the U.S. D.O.T. will have to be notified of the program, since the product is sold in the U.S.

—*Excerpt from a March 1999 Ford memo discussing a potential replacement of Firestone tires in Saudi Arabia*

Ford's Firestone firestorm

As a test (I know better than to buy Firestones), I called Ford's regular customer assistance line three days after the defective Firestone tire story hit the news. My concern was that Ford Explorer and Ranger owners would find busy signals or staffers not knowledgeable enough about the problem to make a decision, as had been my experience with Firestone's telephone lines and customer relations people.

What a surprise. After a 10-second wait, a staffer (Carl) came on line and offered to find me a dealer who would quickly replace my tires, free of charge, with another tire maker's products, if needed.

I understand that Ford—after replacing the tires for free in a handful of other countries, years ago—bears some of the responsibility for allowing this tire problem to fester in North America. However, at this point I'm more concerned with the company's efforts to satisfy owners who want their tires replaced now. At the moment, Ford seems to be moving in the right direction and its newly restructured owner assistance centre is holding up well under the onslaught of owners angered by Firestone's confusion and chaos.

As a consequence of Ford's improved owner relations, I'm upgrading the ratings on the company's Taurus and Windstar with the expectation that the company's goodwill in applying warranty assistance and post-warranty help won't waver during the coming year. I'm also confident that should Ford backslide in its warranty performance relating to any engine or transmission defect, claimants seeking small claims refunds now have a powerful new weapon in their argument for extra-warranty assistance: namely, Ford's 7-year/160,000 km engine goodwill warranty Owner Notification Program. It would be silly for Ford to argue that engines should last as long, but that transmissions (the other part of the powertrain setup), shouldn't.

Automatic transmission problems remain

Meanwhile, cognizant that Ford's automatic transmission deficiencies are broadly based and have existed for over a decade, I intend to continually petition Ford to publicly acknowledge the problem and provide a remedy through an Owner Notification Program. It should be identical to the 3.8L and 4.2L engine ONPs, with seven years and 160,000 km as the benchmarks for full repair refunds. In September 2000, under ONP#00B51, Ford extended its transmission warranty 100 percent, no mileage or ownership restrictions, on 1999 Tauruses, Sables, and Windstars. Clearly, it's a step in the right direction, but 1994–98 models must also be included.

Ford's quality control of mechanical and electronic components and body construction is still sub-par. As mentioned previously, automatic transmission failures and chronic malfunctions apparently afflict the company's entire model line to such an extent that Chrysler and GM's transmission problems pale in comparison.

I am particularly concerned that the 2000 and 2001 models may continue to have premature transmission failures, judging by NHTSA complaints and confidential Ford internal documents cited by *www.blueoval.com.*

Premature brake wear and brake failures are other areas where Ford needs immediate improvement and a more generous policy in handling customer complaints. The quality of body components also remains far below Japanese and European standards.

I'll continue monitoring Ford's treatment of its customers this year through *Lemon-Aid* reader feedback and email reports. If I detect any change in its policies before next year's edition, I'll post the information on *www.lemonaidcars.com.*

Focus

Focus

RATING: Above Average. **Strong points:** Excellent handling and road holding, impressively good fuel economy, plenty of interior space for occupants and cargo—well-appointed for an entry-level vehicle. **Weak points:** Mediocre acceleration, excessive engine and road noise, difficult rear seat access with the hatchback version, and a large number of safety-related complaints.

NEW FOR 2001: The ZTS and ZX3 get Ford's AdvanceTrac vehicle stability system, and a manual transmission will be offered with the wagon. Since last June, a ZX3 Kona Mountain Bike edition is available with a special carrier holding a Kona Blast bike (bike has just been recalled).

OVERVIEW: Hailed as Europe's 1999 Car of the Year, Ford's sleek Focus came to North America last November as an uplevel, premium small car, positioning itself between the entry-level four-door Escort and Contour (both cars soon to be discontinued). Two inches taller and almost seven inches longer than the Escort, and embodying Ford's "new edge" styling (read less aero, more creases), are three body styles: a two-door hatchback in sporty ZX3 trim; LX, SE, and upscale ZTS four-door sedans; and a four-door SE wagon. The Escort's base engine, a 110-hp 2.0L 4-banger, is carried over to the Focus LX and SE, while the 130-hp twin-cam 2.0L (also used on the Escort ZX2 coupe) is standard on the ZTS and ZX3 and optional on the SE. Either engine can be hooked to a manual or an optional 4-speed automatic transmission. Safety features include standard head/chest front airbags, optional side airbags, optional anti-lock brakes (standard only on the ZTS), and rear child safety seat anchors.

Cost analysis/best alternatives: Ford says it won't increase the Focus price by more than a few hundred dollars. If so, the 2001 model represents the better buy because you'll avoid some of the first-year glitches that have afflicted last year's version. Other viable alternatives include this or last year's Honda Civic (it's softer riding, quieter, and has a smoother-running engine), GM Cavalier and Sunfire, Hyundai Accent, or Toyota Echo. **Options:** Go for the $300 upgraded, twin-cam engine; the extra horsepower is sorely needed. Stay away from the cruise control, it's been failure-prone and still may malfunction, despite recall repairs. Don't go for the side airbags until more is known about their overall effect. **Rebates:** None expected. **Delivery/PDI:** $700. **Depreciation:** Expected to be slower than average as fuel costs drive buyers toward more fuel-efficient vehicles. **Insurance cost:** Average. **Parts supply/cost:** A 2- or 3-week wait for parts was reported by Focus owners in the States. Parts cost expected to be average. **Annual maintenance cost:** Too early to tell. **Warranty:** Bumper-to-bumper 3 years/60,000 km; rust perforation 5 years/unlimited km. **Supplementary warranty:** A good idea, until Ford shows that it has remedied the many factory-related deficiencies reported with its 2000 version. **Highway/city fuel economy:** 6.5–9.4L/100 km with a manual transmission; 6.9–9.4L/100 km with the automatic.

Quality/Reliability/Safety

Pro: Warranty performance: In spite of the many owner complaints registered with NHTSA, there have been few complaints reported in Canada from *Lemon-Aid* readers or from other sources. This indicates that Ford Canada is attending to the problems under warranty and that the owner body will remain relatively quiet as long as repairs are covered by the warranty and parts replaced expeditiously.

Con: Quality control: Worrisome. A disturbingly large number of first-year glitches (brakes, body and moulding, transmission, fuel pump, power control module, and ignition switch) have been reported, yet few service bulletins offering remedies have been found. **Reliability:** Predicted to be worse than average on leftover 2000 models, particularly in view of the many stalling and hard starting complaints. **Owner-reported problems:**

Ignition switch failure (18 days for part arrival); seatback bar digs into driver's back (3-week wait for part); power window failure; excessive vibration when underway; excessive engine, brake, steering column, suspension, and wheel noise; trunk lid won't open; passenger side carpet wet from AC; AC leaks coolant; driver's door won't open from the inside; fuel door lid broke in half; hood latch broke off when closing hood; right rear door moulding fell off, and interior panels are poorly fitted. **Service bulletin problems:** Engine malfunction light comes on for no apparent reason, and a fluttering noise that comes from the PCV when the car is turned off. **NHTSA safety complaints/safety:** Airbag deploys for no apparent reason or after hitting a pothole; several complaints of second- and third-degree facial and hand burns arising from airbag deployment; airbag light remains on for no reason; sudden brake loss; differential fluid leaks on brake components (right side) causing brake loss; defective speed control causes sudden acceleration in spite of corrective recall; other sudden acceleration incidents ascribed to faulty power control module (PCM) and driver's shoe being caught under the plastic console; sudden acceleration in Reverse; chronic stalling with loss of brakes and steering, believed to be caused by faulty fuel pump; collapse of tie-rod and axle leading to loss of control; defective axle wheel bearing; sudden pull to the left when turning left; clutch pedal spring pops out, injuring driver; pedal fell on floorboard; transmission slippage and failure; inaccurate fuel gauge sender and fuel pump replaced; windshield cracks for no reason; AC condensation drips on accelerator pedal; exhaust fumes enter passenger compartment.

Road Performance

Pro: Emergency handling: Very good. Good tire grip and little body lean under power when going into corners. Automatic transmission was smooth and quiet; however, it did compromise performance a bit and long-term durability is still undecided. **Steering:** Precise with good road feedback. **Routine handling:** Excellent. **Braking:** Good, but some brake fade.

Con: Acceleration/torque: Not good with either engine, although the optional engine gives you a bit more power. Expect a ho-hum 0–100km/h time of about 9.6 seconds. **Transmission:** Manual's short gearing requires frequent shifting.

Comfort/Convenience

Pro: Standard equipment: Very well appointed for an entry-level Ford. Height-adjustable driver's seat provides good outward visibility. **Driving position:** Comfortable, with good all-around visibility. **Controls and displays:** Easy to find and very user friendly. **Climate control:** AC works well and is easily adjusted for almost any setting. **Interior space/comfort F/R:** Passenger comfort has been enhanced with the high roofline, raised seating position, and tall, wide doors. Pasengers sit comfortably high with lots of head room and an acceptable amount of leg room (for a small car). **Entry/exit:** No problem; the large front doors are helpful, but the rear doors could open wider. **Cargo space:** Best in class. The wagon version, for example, has plenty of cargo space and rear seats that fold or flip flat for additional room. **Trunk/liftover:** Low, making for easy luggage loading and unloading. Plus, trunklid hinges are luggage friendly.

Con: Controls and displays: Could use a tachometer to keep the engine on track. Crank handle for seat adjustments is both primitive and annoying. Air vents could be more conveniently placed. **Quietness:** Excessive engine and wind noise at higher speeds (especially, around the front side windows).

COST

List Price (very negotiable)	Residual Values (months)			
	24	36	48	60
Focus 4d: $16,015 (15%)	$13,000	$11,000	$9,500	$8,000
ZX3: $16,970 (15%)	$13,500	$11,500	$10,000	$8,500

TECHNICAL DATA

Powertrain (front-drive)
Engines: 2.0L 4-cyl. (110 hp)
• 2.0L DOHC 4 (130 hp)
Transmissions: 5-speed man.
• 4-speed auto.
Dimensions/Capacity
Passengers: 2/3
Height/length/width:
56.3/168.1/66.9 in.

Head room F/R: 39.3/38.7 in.
Leg room F/R: 43.1/37.6 in.
Wheelbase: 103 in.
Turning circle: 36. ft.
Cargo volume: 13 cu. ft.
Tow limit: 1,000 lb.
Fuel tank: N/A/reg.
Weight: 2,551 lb.

SAFETY FEATURES/CRASHWORTHINESS

	Std.	Opt.
Anti-lock brakes	❏	■
Seatbelt pretensioners	■	❏
Side airbags	❏	■
Traction control	❏	■
Head restraints F/R	N/A	N/A
Visibility F/R	*****	*****
Crash protection (front) D/P	*****	*****
4d	****	****
Crash protection (side) D/P	****	*
4d	***	****
Crash protection (off-set)	N/A	

Cougar

RATING: Average, for what is essentially a Contour spin-off. **Strong points:** Attractive styling and pleasant handling. **Weak points:** So-so acceleration with the base models, problematic transmission performance, a four-seater with a narrow, claustrophobic interior, limited rear-seat room, obstructed rear visibility, an ugly and superfluous trunklid spoiler, and excessive interior noise.

NEW FOR 2001: A modest refreshening of the interior and exterior. A high-performance 200-hp S model, with a manual transmission and special sports suspension and trim, joins the lineup later this year.

OVERVIEW: Part Contour and part Probe, the 2001 Cougar, like the Contour and Mystique, is based on the European Mondeo sedan and is built at the Mazda-run Auto Alliance plant in Flat Rock, Michigan, once home to the Probe, MX-6, and Mazda 626. The front-drive Cougar, restyled as a hatchback, is equipped with a 16-valve, 125-hp 2.0L inline-four and a 24-valve, 170-hp 2.5L V6, soon to be replaced with an upgraded 200-hp powerplant. ABS and side airbags are optional.
    Although the Cougar shares the Contour's chassis (with an inch added), base 4-banger, and V6, its suspension and steering are much tighter.

Cost analysis/best alternatives: There are two reasons to turn a thumbs down on a leftover 2000 version: Mercury says it'll hold the line on 2001 prices, and this year's model offers a 200-hp V6. Alternatives: Acura CL; GM Cavalier, Sunfire; Honda Accord or Prelude; Mazda 626; or the Toyota Camry. **Options:** Overall performance can be improved with the Sport Group option which gives you rear disc brakes and larger wheels on the V6 version. You'll have to put up with a harder, noisier ride, though. Don't waste your money on the silly rear spoiler or the unproven side airbags and ABS. **Rebates:** Sales have been disappointing; expect $2,000 rebates on last year's models and half as much on the 2001. **Delivery/PDI:** Around $800. **Depreciation:** Average. **Insurance cost:** A bit higher than average. **Parts supply/cost:** Parts are easy to find and reasonably priced, although body parts may be in short supply. **Annual maintenance cost:** Predicted to be average. **Warranty:** Bumper-to-bumper 3 years/60,000 km; rust perforation 5 years/unlimited km. **Supplementary warranty:** A good idea. **Highway/city fuel economy:** 6.4L–9.7L/100 km with the 4-cylinder; 7.5–11.8L/100 km with the 6-cylinder.

Quality/Reliability/Safety

Pro: Quality control: Very good. Not sure if these vehicles are better built or Ford is more attentive to owner complaints during the initial warranty period. **Reliability:** Owners are positive about the overall reliability and durability of these vehicles. **Warranty performance:** Better than average, but keep in mind that the Cougar hasn't been on the market long enough to generate much warranty feedback.

Con: Owner-reported problems: Premature brake wear and stalling. **Service bulletin problems:** Low coolant lamp on for no apparent reason, automatic transmission fluid leakage, and water leak or wind noise at the upper corner of the B-pillar. **NHTSA safety complaints/safety:** Tire sidewall failure; airbag failed to deploy; engine increases rpms when shifting; sudden stalling with locked up steering; engine and airbag service lights stay on for no apparent reason; key won't work in the ignition; hard to find a child safety seat that fits in the rear. The silly, non-functional rear spoiler is both distracting and cuts rearward vision.

Road Performance

Pro: Emergency handling: Acceptable, but not in the same league as Japanese sedans. The firm suspension and quick, responsive steering make the Cougar both nimble and stable when cornering under speed (especially with the optional Sport Group's wider tires) as long as it's not pushed very hard. **Acceleration/torque:** Peppy around town, with good amount of low-end torque. **Braking:** Braking is quite good with little fading after successive stops.

Con: Steering: Steering is a bit heavy in city traffic. **Acceleration/torque:** Acceleration is only so-so with the base four or V6 engine and they both run roughly. Base 4-cylinder engine is not as refined or fun to push as the Japanese competition. 170-hp V6 lacks passing or merging power; 0–100 km/h takes about 10 seconds. **Transmission:** The automatic transmission tends to "hunt" the proper gear when going over hilly terrain and there's no way to lock out Overdrive in fourth gear. The 5-speed hooked to the V6 also shifted roughly. **Routine handling:** The base suspension doesn't absorb bumps very well and the optional Sports Group tires produce a busy, jostling ride on any surface that's less than perfect.

Comfort/Convenience

Pro: Standard equipment: Acceptable, though lacks many standard features found on competitors' products. Comfortable bucket seats and seatbacks. **Climate control:** Efficient and user-friendly. **Cargo space:** A split-fold rear seatback makes cargo hauling a breeze.

Con: Driving position: The interior feels narrow and small—the Accord gives a much roomier impression. Short front seat cushions don't give enough thigh support. **Controls and displays:** The tacky-looking cabin houses an overstyled dashboard with controls that are confusing and cheap-looking. The radio is mounted too low and uses small buttons that are the antithesis of user-friendly. **Entry/exit:** Rear-seat access takes some acrobatic prowess. **Interior space/comfort F/R:** Rear seating is cramped and uncomfortable. **Trunk/liftover:** Cargo loading is made difficult by the high liftover. **Quietness:** Excessive road rumble and exhaust noise and annoying body squeaks and groans.

COST				
List Price (very negotiable)	**Residual Values (months)**			
	24	**36**	**48**	**60**
Cougar: $23,655 (18%)	$15,500	$13,500	$11,500	$9,500

TECHNICAL DATA	
Powertrain (front-drive)	Head room F/R: 37.8/34.6 in.
Engines: 2.0L 4-cyl. (125 hp)	Leg room F/R: 42.5/33.2 in.
• 2.5L V6 (170 hp)	Wheelbase: 106.4 in.
• 2.5L V6 (200 hp)	Turning circle: 39 ft.
Transmissions: 5-speed man.	Cargo volume: 14.5 cu. ft.
• 4-speed auto.	Tow limit: 1,000 lb.
Dimensions/Capacity	Fuel tank: 60L/reg.
Passengers: 2/2	Weight: 2,892 lb.
Height/length/width:	
52.2/185/69.6 in.	

SAFETY FEATURES/CRASHWORTHINESS		
	Std.	Opt.
Anti-lock brakes (4W)	❏	■
Seatbelt pretensioners	—	—
Side airbags	❏	■
Traction control	❏	■
Head restraints F/R	N/A	N/A
Visibility F/R	*****	*****
Crash protection (front) D/P	N/A	N/A
Crash protection (side) D/P	N/A	N/A
Crash protection (off-set)	N/A	

Mustang

RATING: Recommended. **Strong points:** Fast acceleration, impressive handling, braking, and resale value. Better-than-average crashworthiness and overall reliability. **Weak points:** Insufficient rear seat room, limited cargo space, fishtails easily when accelerating upon a wet surface or cornering under moderate speed.

NEW FOR 2001: Re-skinned and re-engineered in 1999, this year's Mustang is mostly a carryover with only a few changes. For example, the interior console will be upgraded, and new hood and side scoops will distinguish the V8 GT from the V6 model. Production of the 2001 SVT Mustang Cobra convertible will resume by year's end.

OVERVIEW: While GM considers dropping its sporty Camaro, Ford has renewed its commitment to the Mustang through a "retro" restyling, using sharp exterior creases that harken back to the pony car's early years. In 1999 the Mustang's length and width were increased by almost two inches. The car also got a 40-hp boost to its 3.8L V6 (also used in the Taurus and Windstar) and 25 extra horses to its 4.6L V8 engine. Optional all-speed traction control is also available. A new Cobra with independent rear suspension made its debut in mid-'99, then was taken off the market because it couldn't produce the advertised 320 hp.

The Mustang carries a base 3.8L V6 and offers an optional 4.6L V8 along with a high performance, limited-edition Cobra variation that delivers 60 more horses than the stock 4.6L V8. The single- and twin-cam V8 options make the Mustang a powerful street machine that has far more brawn than finesse (one of its failings when compared with its GM rivals). V6 models are an acceptable compromise, even though the engine fails to deliver the gobs of power expected of a Mustang by most performance enthusiasts. Base models come equipped with a host of luxury and convenience items. Furthermore, the price is hard to beat, and resale value stays relatively high through the fifth year of ownership.

This is definitely not a family car. But for those who want a sturdy and stylish second car, or who don't need room in the back or standard ABS, the Mustang is a less risky buy than most of the Big Three sports cars.

Cost analysis/best alternatives: Get a 2000 model discounted in the $1,500–$2,000 range on V6-equipped versions. Discounts are rare on the GT and convertible "muscle" variants. Other cars worth considering are the GM Camaro/Firebird (ample stock of year 2000s available) and Toyota Celica. **Options:** Traction control, considering this rear-drive's tendency to "spin out" when pushed, and an anti-theft system that includes an engine immobilizer. **Rebates:** $1,500 rebates to clear out year 2000 V6-equipped leftovers. **Delivery/PDI:** $500. **Depreciation:** Much slower than average. **Insurance cost:** Way higher than average. **Parts supply/cost:** Inexpensive and easily found among independent suppliers. **Annual maintenance cost:** Lower than average: any mechanic is able to fix a Mustang. **Warranty:** Bumper-to-bumper 3 years/60,000 km; rust perforation 5 years/ unlimited km. **Supplementary warranty:** Not necessary; put your money into making the car safe from thieves. **Highway/city fuel economy:** 7–12L/100 km with the 3.8L; 9–14.5L/100 km with the 4.6L.

Quality/Reliability/Safety

Pro: Quality control: Better than average. The Mustang's repair history has improved greatly and this is likely to continue with the 2001 models. **Reliability:** Very good. The engines and transmissions are durable, as are most other components. Body assembly has improved of late, with fewer rattles and a more solid feeling. **Warranty performance:** Much improved: few warranty complaints.

Con: Owner-reported problems: The front suspension, brakes, and steering components remain the only consistent weak spots. The engine computer can be temperamental, and electrical problems are common. Keep an eye on the 3.8L engine: head gasket failures may be in the offing. Body assembly quality is not up to the level of Japanese vehicles. Numerous complaints of convertible door and trunk water leaks. **Service bulletin problems:** Automatic transmission fluid leak near the radiator; faulty key fob transmitter; premature wearout of some vinyl-covered items like dash cover and door panels; exhaust system "buzzing" or "rattling." **NHTSA safety complaints/safety:** Sudden acceleration; sudden loss of steering when making a left hand turn; car left on an incline with transmission in Park and motor shut off rolled down after 10 minutes and hit a tree; airbags failed to deploy in a frontal collision; emergency brake ratchet assembly broke, making mechanism inoperable; gas spills out of fuel tank due to clamps not sufficiently tightened; left front wheel fell off when the lower control arm and ball joint became loose; defective transmission spider gear; seat ratchet assembly teeth broke; chronic stalling; engine produces an annoying "harmonic vibration." A light rear end makes the car dangerously unstable on wet roads or when cornering at moderate speeds.

Road Performance

Pro: Emergency handling: Slow but predictable. **Steering:** Quick and responsive. **Acceleration/torque:** The V8 provides very quick acceleration and smooth power delivery (0–100 km/h: 7.1 sec.), while the V6 performs fairly well with the automatic 4-speed transmission. **Transmission:** The clutch is reasonably smooth and the automatic shifts reasonably well most of the time. **Routine handling:** Models equipped with the sport suspension (which includes larger tires) provide sure and predictable handling on dry roads. The upgraded base suspension also makes the car more stable and controllable on most roads. **Braking:** Excellent braking performance for a car this heavy (100–0 km/h: 123 ft.).

Con: Emergency handling: The 3.8L V6 is rough and noisy when pushed. The V8s are a bit too powerful for the amount of traction available to the rear wheels, making for lots of wheelspin and instability on slippery surfaces. **Transmission:** The manual transmission is notchy at times and the automatic sometimes hesitates between gears. **Routine handling:** The rear end tends to slip out under hard cornering. The GT rides harshly on rough roads. These cars are a bit clumsy around town because of a wide turning circle.

Comfort/Convenience

Pro: Standard equipment: Even the base Mustangs come well equipped with lots of standard features. **Driving position:** Excellent, with plenty of head and leg room for tall drivers. **Controls and displays:** First class. Complete and well laid-out dual-cowl dashboard and controls. **Climate control:** Efficient, easy to adjust, and quiet. **Interior space/comfort F/R:** Comfortable front seats on all models. **Cargo space:** The split folding rear seat frees up much-needed trunk storage space. Easy loading, thanks to the low liftover. **Quietness:** Improved body rigidity has reduced interior noise somewhat.

Con: Rear visibility is obstructed by the roof pillars and high parcel shelf. **Interior space/comfort F/R:** Front seats need at least an inch more travel, and the rear seat is best left to children, especially with the convertible version. **Entry/exit:** The wide doors make for clumsy entry and exit in tight spots. GT ride comfort is below average. **Trunk/liftover:** Very shallow trunk with a small opening. Low liftover.

COST				
List Price (negotiable)	**Residual Values (months)**			
	24	**36**	**48**	**60**
Mustang: $22,275 (18%)	$17,000	$14,000	$11,000	$9,000
Cvt.: $26,945 (20%)	$20,000	$16,000	$14,000	$12,000
GT: $30,525 (21%)	$22,000	$19,000	$17,000	$15,000
Cvt.: $34,490 (22%)	$24,000	$21,000	$19,000	$17,000

TECHNICAL DATA

Powertrain (front-drive)
Engines: 3.8L V6 (190 hp)
• 4.6L V8 (260 hp)
• 4.6L V8 (320 hp)
Transmissions: 5-speed man.
• 4-speed auto.
Dimensions/Capacity
Passengers: 2/2
Height/length/width:
53.4/181.5/71.8 in.

Head room F/R: 38.2/35.9 in.
Leg room F/R: 42.9/31.3 in.
Wheelbase: 101.3 in.
Turning circle: 35.4 ft.
Cargo volume: 10.3 cu. ft.
Tow limit: 1,000 lb.
Fuel tank: 58L/reg.
Weight: 3,300 lb.

SAFETY FEATURES/CRASHWORTHINESS

	Std.	Opt.
Anti-lock brakes	❑	■
Seatbelt pretensioners	—	—
Side airbags	—	—
Traction control	—	■
Head restraints	*	*
Visibility F/R	*****	**
Crash protection (front) D/P	****	****
Convertible	*****	*****
Crash protection (side) D/P	***	***
Crash protection (off-set)	N/A	

Taurus

Taurus

RATING: Average. Last year's additional safety features and restyling are a nice touch but they fail to convince me that this car's horrendously poor reliability record won't continue. Your best bet is to buy only with an extended bumper-to-bumper warranty and trade in at the 5-year mark— just before the extended warranty expires. **Strong points:** Quiet running, good handling, comfortable ride, better-than-average crash protection, improved warranty performance, and bargain prices (we know why). **Weak points:** Insufficient storage space, limited rear head room and access, and a history of serious mechanical and body deficiencies.

NEW FOR 2001: Recently restyled and given important safety improvements last year, the Taurus soldiers on relatively unchanged this year. The Sable will be phased out in Canada as Mercury dealers are shut down.

OVERVIEW: Despite their deficiencies, the Taurus and Sable are Ford's most popular family cars due to their attractive combination of safety, performance, handling, and comfort. The base 3.0L Vulcan V6 is adequate, though dated, and the high-performing 24-valve V6 provides plenty of power for most driving needs. Other nice standard features include heated outside mirrors, a 60/40 split-fold rear seatback for additional cargo space, a driver's foot rest, and reserve power to operate the power windows and moon roof after the engine is shut off.

The SHO high-performance version returns this year with a 3.4L, 32-valve V8 engine. It delivers sparkling performance and sports car handling—at a price. Acceleration rivals the Mustang GT with a top speed of over 225 km/h, and it comes with an automatic transmission.

Cost analysis/best alternatives: If Ford keeps prices in check, get the 2001 model in the hope for more durable mechanical and body components. A year 2000 version discounted by $2,000–$3,000 could be a false bargain for the following reasons: the extra year's depreciation will take over five years to amortize; and once you get to that fifth year, you're risking expensive powertrain, AC, brake, computer, suspension, and body repairs. Wagons are competent performers, but they're outclassed by some imports and most minivans as far as reliability and overall performance are concerned. The SHO has become a cult car for high-performance fans and its slow depreciation reflects this fact. Other sedans worth considering are the Honda Accord, Mazda 626, Toyota Camry, and Volvo S70. Wagons worth considering are the Honda Accord EX, Subaru Legacy, Toyota Camry LE V6, and Volvo V90. **Options:** Expect to spend about $300 more for the flexible-fuel Taurus (ethanol or methanol), currently sold only to fleets. The automatic climate control system, a rear integrated child safety seat, power seats, and a heavy-duty suspension are wise choices. Get the optional DOHC V6 variation, but tell the dealer to forget the wagon's uncomfortable rear-facing third seat. Don't buy the optional leather seats, either; they're slippery and not all that durable. The digital instrumentation is another useless option; it's gimmicky and distracting. On the other hand, Ford's optional pedal extensions minimize the danger from airbag deployments and the InstaClear windshield is a boon in Canadian winters. **Rebates:** As the Toyota Camry and Honda Accord eat into Ford's sales and stock continues to pile up in dealers' lots, generous dealer incentives and customer rebates will start kicking in before the year is up. Expect at least $2,000 rebates on the 2000s and half as much on this year's models. **Delivery/PDI:** $500. **Depreciation:** Higher than average. **Insurance cost:** Higher than average. **Parts supply/cost:** Parts are easily found, and they are reasonably priced. **Annual maintenance cost:** Average to higher than average as the vehicle ages. **Warranty:** Bumper-to-bumper 3 years/60,000 km; rust perforation 5 years/unlimited km. **Supplementary warranty:** A wise investment, particularly when you replace the AC, automatic transmission, or fuel pump around the fifth year of use. **Highway/city fuel economy:** 7.7–12L/100 km with the 3.0L; 8.5–14.5L/100 km with the SHO V8.

Quality/Reliability/Safety

Pro: Reliability: The SHO engine has been particularly reliable. Important safety improvements, once found only on luxury vehicles, are working their way down to Ford's popular mid-sized family sedans. The 2000 and 2001 Taurus, for example, has standard "thinking" seatbelts and airbags that come in two parts to protect head and shoulders and upper torso separately. Optional adjustable pedals, needed by short-statured drivers to avoid airbag injury, are also a worthwhile safety feature first offered with the year 2000 model. Test-drive a vehicle with the extensions, though, before ordering the option.

Con: Quality control: Below average for an American car. Ford promises that many of its quality problems have been corrected with its year 2000 redesign. But I've heard that before. As you will see below, service bulletin-related defects and safety complaints called into NHTSA still show a disturbing pattern of fuel system, powertrain, and body component deficiencies. Ford officials also once reassured me that many of the Taurus defects would be corrected when the car was reworked for 1996. Guess what? Most of the factory-related defects remained practically unchanged. Paint and body assembly is still sub-par and body squeaks and rattles are omnipresent. **Reliability:** Mediocre long-term reliability, highlighted by an automatic transmission that Ford apparently still can't build to last or even shift properly. Latest "goodwill" adjustment: '99 Taurus, Sable, and Windstar transmissions (ONP#00B51). **Warranty performance:** Much better than average. Ford has improved its handling of engine and automatic transmission post-warranty claims during the past year, after *Lemon-Aid* blasted the company both publicly and in private meetings with Ford executives. Nevertheless, the safety risk, outrageously expensive repair costs, and chronic inconvenience and anxiety that these defects create cannot be imagined or easily assuaged merely with "goodwill" reimbursements. **Owner-reported problems:** Automatic transmission shifts out of 1st gear too soon, shifts slowly, constantly bangs through the gears, and often chooses the wrong gear; AC, electrical system (lots of blown fuses), steering, fuel system, fuel pumps, front suspension, and ignition problems are frequently reported on these cars. There have been lots of complaints concerning poor gas mileage, paint delamination (fading, chalking, and peeling), and, surprisingly, premature rusting. **Service bulletin problems:** Many bulletins concern various driveability and shift-related problems. Harsh 3–2 downshift when coasting and then accelerating and frequent automatic transmission fluid leaks, particularly near the bellhousing area. Troubleshooting tips on correcting brake vibrations. 3.0L engine hiss, growl, scraping, and exhaust ringing noise. With the same engine, a chronically overrich fuel mixture may be the cause of hard starts, poor idling, and the engine malfunction light's being activated. Both 3.0L and 4.0L engines may experience backfire on startup. Moon roof may bind, rattle, or not work at all. Buzzing, rattling, and groaning from the rear suspension area and front stabilizer link noise. Possible causes and remedies for malfunctioning door, ignition, and decklid locks and headlamp, taillamp condensation. Water intrudes through windows and door sills. **NHTSA safety complaints/safety:** Sudden acceleration; vehicle often surges and then shuts off when fuel tank is filled; frequent stalling, hard starts, and poor idle caused by chronic fuel pump failures or a contaminated fuel pressure sensor; fuel gauge stuck on FULL; interior rear view mirror location obstructs visibility; airbag light comes on for no reason; excessive steering vibration.

Taurus has "thinking" seatbelts that can detect whether a driver has buckled the belt, and prevent the airbag from deploying in "fender-bender" accidents, or cause it to deploy more slowly in high-speed impacts. The airbags now come in two parts to protect head and shoulders and upper torso separately. Furthermore, the car's sides have been reinforced to prevent intrusion into the interior, and the Taurus's armrests have been redesigned to crumple, thereby protecting passengers from possibly severe internal injuries in a side impact. As for the adjustable brake and accelerator pedals, while most people agree they are helpful in avoiding airbag-induced injuries, some owners have complained they are set too close together and are often too loose.

Adjustable pedals aren't for everyone. Some owners say pedals are set too close and are often loose. Take a test-drive before making your choice.

Road Performance

Pro: Emergency handling: Better than average. **Steering:** The speed-sensitive variable-assist power steering makes the car easier to handle, but not as much as Ford claims. **Acceleration/torque:** Better than average with the 3.0L engine (0–100 km/h: 8.7 sec.). The base 3.0L V6 is a decade-old engine that offers adequate power for most driving situations, while the twin-cam Duratec version provides exhilarating, quiet acceleration equal to the European-influenced chassis dynamics. **Transmission:** The 4-speed automatic transmission shifts smoothly and responsively. **Routine handling:** The sedan's handling, both around town and on the highway, is better than average due primarily to its solid suspension and stiff body construction.

Con: Ford's 3.0L Vulcan V6 is okay for rentals and city commuting, but it's unable to take full advantage of the car's excellent handling characteristics. Wagons handle poorly in turns and over uneven terrain. The high-performance SHO doesn't handle well in tight spaces, requiring four more feet to make a U-turn. **Braking:** Unimpressive braking (100–0 km/h: 134 ft.). ABS produces strong pedal pulsations.

Comfort/Convenience

Pro: Standard equipment: Nicely restyled last year with plenty of convenience features, but four-wheel disc anti-lock brakes are still optional. The three-way front-seat console is a nice touch. It's a flip-fold affair that's a regular seat, an armrest, or a cup- and coin-carrying console. Armrest switches make it easy to activate the door locks and power windows. Efficient and quiet climate control system. **Interior space/comfort F/R:** Loads of room both in the front and in the rear. The standard seats are comfortable for most people, but the wagon's fabric-covered seats are more comfortable and supportive than the leather-covered sedan seats. The sedans will seat five in comfort, while the wagons offer an optional third seat. **Cargo space:** There's lots of cargo area in the wagon, and its innovative two-way tailgate allows the entire unit to swing out for large cargo or just the window glass to open for small packages. **Trunk/liftover:** The sedan's huge trunk has a low liftover and split rear seatbacks to facilitate easier loading.

Con: The SHO sedan is loaded with exterior styling gimmicks that may not be to everyone's taste. The wagon's interior plastic trim is cheap. **Driving position:** Short drivers will have to strain to reach the accelerator and see over the dash and tall drivers will find thigh support lacking. Leather seats offer little lateral support. **Controls and displays:** The massive dash and digital treatment are gimmicky and take getting used to. The radio is set too low and too far forward, and the JBL Premium Sound System's push-button controls require a Ph.D. to understand. Radio reception quality is disappointing. The low-fuel warning light comes on with enough fuel to travel 160 km. The wagon's liftgate doesn't rise high enough to clear most people's heads. **Climate control:** The rear window defroster is hard to find on the left side of the steering column. Air conditioning push buttons are difficult to understand and manipulate. **Entry/exit:** Difficult third seat access and limited head room for the third seat passenger. **Quietness:** Both the sedan and wagon's noise levels are unusually high, with lots of wind noise and tire drumming from the rear.

COST				
List Price (negotiable)	**Residual Values (months)**			
	24	**36**	**48**	**60**
Taurus LX: $24,820 (17%)	$14,000	$12,000	$10,000	$7,500

TECHNICAL DATA

Powertrain (front-drive)
Engines: 3.0L V6 (145 hp)
• 3.0L V6 (200 hp)
• 3.4L V8 (235 hp)
Transmissions: 5-speed man.
• 4-speed auto.
Dimensions/Capacity (LX)
Passengers: 2/3
Height/length/width:
55.1/197.5/73.1 in.

Head room F/R: 39.2/36.2 in.
Leg room F/R: 42.2/38.9 in.
Wheelbase: 108.5 in.
Turning circle: 35.4 ft.
Cargo volume: 15.8 cu. ft.
Tow limit: 1,750 lb.
Fuel tank: 60L/reg.
Weight: 3,350 lb.

SAFETY FEATURES/CRASHWORTHINESS

	Std.	Opt.
Anti-lock brakes	❏	■
Seatbelt pretensioners	■	❏
Side airbags	❏	■
Traction control	—	—
Head restraints F/R	*	*
Visibility F/R	*****	*****
Crash protection (front) D/P	*****	*****
Crash protection (side) D/P	***	***
Crash protection (off-set)	*****	

Crown Victoria, Grand Marquis, Town Car

✓ BEST BUY

Grand Marquis

RATING: Recommended. Best suited for highway cruising and trailer towing. The Crown Victoria has been relegated mostly to fleets and police work. **Strong points:** Lots of interior room, quiet running, easy entry/exit, reliable, and excellent resale value. A natural gas V8 engine is available. **Weak points:** Difficult trunk access and terrible fuel economy.

NEW FOR 2001: The addition of adjustable pedals (optional on the Crown Victoria, standard with the Grand Marquis LS Premium) and optional ABS (it was standard last year), dual-stage airbags, crash-severity and seat-position sensors, and safety belt pretensioners. Engine gets a 25-hp boost. Town Car may offer a voice-activated telecommunication service that includes a wireless telephone, roadside emergency assistance, and optional Web access. Ford plans to stretch the platform in 2002 to appeal more to fleet buyers, cab companies, and police departments.

OVERVIEW: The industry's lowest-priced six-passenger V8 sedans, the Crown Victoria and Grand Marquis have always been a favourite with police, taxi drivers, farmers, and retirees. Now, with the addition of a 4.6L OHC V8 several years ago, they're likely to stay around a relatively long time without many other changes.

Although some fleets and police departments have replaced their Crown Victorias with 200-hp, 3.8L V6-equipped Impalas to save fuel costs, the rank and file don't like the change. This is even though acceleration tests conducted by the Michigan State Police concluded that the Ford's additional fifteen horses (215-hp, 4.6L V8) didn't result in significant performance improvements when compared with the more fuel-efficient and smaller front-drive Impala: the Ford accelerated 0 to 60 mph in an average of 8.75 seconds; the Impala took 8.99 seconds. The Impala actually beat out the Crown Vic in 0 to 100 mph acceleration tests, taking 24.92 seconds, compared with 26.09 seconds for Ford.

But cops place acceleration a distant third after handling and comfort, which gives the Crown Victoria (and the identical Mecury Grand Marquis) two advantages over the Impala:

> ...We're adamant about a rear-drive car...especially for pursuit situations. On snow and ice, you can pull a rear wheel car around; you can spin it around, but when you accelerate a fwd car, the front end will go right out from under you...It will slide sideways and you will lose control...

Aside from the sheer wastefulness of the design and the high fuel cost of running one of these boats, they're fairly reliable and predictable highway cruisers. Handling isn't very responsive, but everyone is going to be comfortable inside. The mechanical design is straightforward and easy to troubleshoot (electronic gizmos excepted). The Crown Victoria and Grand Marquis have consistently come out on top in quality surveys of North American cars.

Speed-sensitive, variable-assist power steering is a standard feature, as it is with most of Ford's luxury cars. The base model and LX are joined by the Touring Sedan, which offers a firmer ride, a more responsive handling package, and different exterior and interior styling touches. An electronically controlled automatic transmission has been around since early 1992.

The Lincoln Town Car is still, to many people, the epitome of large car luxury, and it's a popular rear-drive base for Ford's luxury cars. A stretched version of the Crown Victoria/Marquis, its air-spring rear suspension provides a smooth ride and prevents tail-dragging, even when fully loaded.

Cost analysis/best alternatives: Get the year 2001 model for the upgraded engine and safety features. The Marquis is a slightly more luxurious version of the Crown that costs more, but gives little of consequence for the extra expense. Other cars worth considering are the Nissan Maxima, Mazda Millenia, Toyota Avalon, and Volvo S90 series. **Options:** Invest in the "Handling and Performance" option to reduce body roll and increase traction, and consider a power seat. **Rebates:** In the late fall expect $2,000 rebates on the Grand Marquis. **Delivery/PDI:** $800. **Depreciation:** Slower than average. **Insurance cost:** Higher than average. **Parts supply/cost:** Parts aren't hard to find, but may be more expensive than parts for most other cars in this class. **Annual maintenance cost:** A bit higher than average. Although repairs are relatively easy to carry out, these cars have complicated brake, fuel, and electronic systems that are a pain in the butt—and wallet—to troubleshoot. **Warranty:** *Crown Victoria* and *Grand Marquis:* Bumper-to-bumper 3 years/60,000 km; rust perforation 5 years/unlimited km. *Town Car:* Bumper-to-bumper 4 years/ 80,000 km; rust perforation 5 years/unlimited km. **Supplementary warranty:** A good idea as protection from costly diagnostic procedures. **Highway/city fuel economy:** 9.2–13.9L/100 km.

Quality/Reliability/Safety

Pro: Quality control: Body components and construction are first rate. **Reliability:** Overall reliability has been above average for the past several years. **Warranty performance:** Very good. Ford staffers are more cooperative and reasonable than last year; Lincoln customer assistance has always been first-rate.

Con: Owner-reported problems: Main problem areas are the engine computer module, air-conditioning compressor, prematurely worn brakes, and the fuel system. **Service bulletin problems:** After a cold start, vehicle idles roughly and Check Engine light comes on; vehicle may miss, buck or jerk due to a surge in the ignition coil/spark plug boot; inoperative keyless entry pad; malfunctioning door, ignition, and trunk locks; jammed CD changer; increased radio static when defroster is activated; AC thump noise shortly after compressor engages; sagging headliner; excessive brake vibration; steering wheel clicks; and vehicle wanders at highway speeds. Crown Victoria police vehicles may experience erratic shifting. Town Car may have a defective AC blower, slow-moving front power windows, and a moon roof that booms or is buffeted by the wind. **NHTSA safety complaints/safety:** Fire ignited in engine compartment after car sat parked; vehicle struck from behind and exploded in flames; missing upper control arm bolt; horn "sweet spot" too small and takes too much effort to sound; sunlight causes a reflection of the defrost vents onto the windshield.

Road Performance

Pro: Emergency handling: A bit slow, but predictable and sure-footed. Less body lean in corners thanks to the upgraded suspension. **Steering:** Improved steering transmits more road feel than before. **Acceleration/torque:** Respectable, though not impressive, acceleration with plenty of low-end torque (0–100 km/h: 10.2 sec.). The smooth, quiet-running 4.6L V8 provides more than enough power for a comfortable ride. Towing capacity is 2,250 kg (5,000 lb.) with the Class III Towing or Handling and Performance packages offered with the Grand Marquis. **Transmission:** Flawless, most of the time. **Routine handling:** Fairly good for vehicles this large. Ride isn't overly soft. A '98 improvement smoothed out the ride and revised the steering to upgrade the handling. In effect, the rear end no longer sways when you turn the steering wheel. **Braking:** Better-than-average braking with the four-wheel disc brakes (100–0 km/h: 124 ft.).

Con: Transmission: sometimes hesitates between gear changes. Handling still takes a backseat to ride quality. Despite improvements, steering is still rather vague.

Comfort/Convenience

Pro: Standard equipment: Lots of standard convenience features. **Driving position:** Very comfortable. **Controls and displays:** Everything is within easy reach and well presented. **Climate control:** Powerful, quiet ventilation system. **Entry/exit:** Large doors make entry/exit a breeze. **Interior space/comfort F/R:** Spacious interior: three passengers are comfortable in the back, where there's lots of head, leg, and shoulder room. The individual front seats are large, comfortable, and supportive (the power seat option is recommended), particularly in the lumbar region. **Cargo space:** Plenty of storage areas. **Trunk/liftover:** Huge trunk. The Town Car's trunk, for example, is an impressive 22 cubic feet, with a low liftover. **Quietness:** Very quiet interior.

Con: Conservative styling. The driver's right knee frequently hits the dashboard/radio housing. Seatbelt anchor pokes into driver's right hip. Distracting continuous digital readout of your fuel economy. Poor rear visibility. The Town Car's electronic dash is too gimmicky. **Controls**

and displays: Confusing power seat and controls. **Climate control:** Slow to warm up. **Interior space/comfort F/R:** The split-bench front seat in the Crown Victoria isn't very comfortable due to its insufficient seat-back padding and side support. Town Car's moon roof cuts down on rear head room. Rear seats also lack sufficient seatback padding. **Trunk/liftover:** Deep-dish trunk is not very practical for everyday baggage. You have to do some acrobatics to get at the full-sized spare tire, which is placed far forward in the trunk.

COST

List Price (negotiable)	Residual Values (months)			
	24	36	48	60
Grand Marquis:				
$34,730 (20%)	$23,000	$18,000	$15,000	$13,000
Town Car Executive:				
$52,445 (22%)	$37,000	$28,000	$24,000	$20,000

TECHNICAL DATA

Powertrain (rear-drive)
Engine: 4.6L V8 (225 hp)
  natural gas
Transmission: 4-speed auto.
Dimensions/Capacity
  (Crown Victoria)
Passengers: 3/3
Height/length/width:
56.8/212/77.9 in.

Head room F/R: 39.4/38 in.
Leg room F/R: 42.5/39.6 in.
Wheelbase: 114.4 in
Turning circle: 35.4 ft.
Cargo volume: 20.6 cu. ft.
Tow limit: 2,000 lb.
Fuel tank: 75L/reg.
Weight: 3,800 lb.

SAFETY FEATURES/CRASHWORTHINESS

	Std.	Opt.
Anti-lock brakes (4W)	❑	■
Seatbelt pretensioners	■	❑
Side airbags	■	❑
Traction control	■	■
Head restraints F/R	*	*
Visibility F/R	*****	**
Crash protection (front) D/P		
Crown Victoria and Gr. Marquis	*****	*****
Town Car	****	*****
Crash protection (side) D/P	****	****
Crash protection (off-set) D/P	N/A	

Lincoln LS

Lincoln LS

RATING: Below Average. Lincoln handles complaints well, but factory-related deficiencies are simply too numerous to recommend the LS this year. **Strong points**: Impressive V8 acceleration, comfortable ride, crisp handling, comfortable interior, and good warranty performance. **Weak points**: Erratic automatic transmission shifting, confusing climate controls, poor quality mechanical, electrical and body components.

NEW FOR 2001: A carried-over model that may offer a voice-activated telecommunication service featuring a wireless telephone, roadside emergency assistance, and optional Web access. A redesign is planned for the 2005 version.

OVERVIEW: Lincoln's LS rear-drive sedan comes with a high-performance 210-hp variant of the Taurus 3.0L V6 mated to an optional manual or a standard automatic gearbox. Also available: a 252-hp 3.9L V8 based on the Jaguar XK8 coupe coupled to a semi-automatic transmission. Both engines are identical but produce 30 less horses than the Jag equivalent.

Cost analysis/best alternatives: The LS offers a lot for what is a reasonable base price. The V6 version is priced in the BMW 3 Series, Lexus ES 300, and Mercedes C-Class territory while delivering standard equipment and interior space that rivals the 5 series, GS, and E-Class. **Options:** Traction control is a worthwhile option on the V6 version. Another option worth considering: the optional sports package which includes thicker anti-roll bars, upgraded brake pads, recalibrated variable-ratio steering, an automanual shifter (if ordered with an automatic), body-coloured bumper trim, a full-sized spare, and bigger wheels and tires. **Rebates:** Sales have been slow; expect rebates of $3,000 for a 2000 version and half as much for a 2001. **Delivery/PDI:** $855 **Depreciation:** Average. **Insurance cost:** Higher than average. **Parts supply/cost:** Parts availability hasn't been a problem and parts cost has been reasonable. **Annual maintenance cost:** Predicted to be average. **Warranty:** Bumper-to-bumper 4 years/80,000 km; rust perforation 5 years/unlimited km. **Supplementary warranty:** Not necessary. Lincoln customer relations staffers treat you as a VIP. **Highway/city fuel economy:** 8.9–13.8L/100 km with the 6-cylinder; 9.1–14.2L/100 km with the 8-cylinder.

Quality/Reliability/Safety

Pro: Warranty performance: Hard to believe, but Lincoln owners haven't complained about Ford's servicing the many aforementioned defects under warranty.

Con: Reliability: In spite of Ford's good warranty performance noted above, the powertrain and electrical problems still compromise the LS's overall reliability. **Quality control:** Below average. Apparently, Lincoln's return to rear-drive has opened up a Pandora's box of powertrain, AC, and body glitches. **Owner-reported problems:** Poor transmission shifting, excessive drivetrain and body noise and vibrations, inconsistent braking response, and faulty AC performance. **Service bulletin problems:** Frequent bulletin references to automatic transmission defects producing: delayed engagement (PCM module seen as likely culprit), driveline vibration and buzz/clunk/drone, and fluid leakage. Other problems: trunk may suddenly open; inaccurate ambient temperature display; inoperative AC dual zone heater; ABS, airbag, and engine service lights come on for no apparent reason; noisy front power windows; and steering wheel "nibble," hum, or boom noise. With the 3.9L engine: oil leak from the bellhousing area; poor braking on V6-equipped models; V6 engine noise on acceleration; highway drone noise; hard start or no starts; and instrument panels squeaks and rattles. **NHTSA safety complaints/safety:** Sudden acceleration in Forward or Reverse gear; airbag deployment for no reason; airbag failed to deploy; lurching, hesitating automatic transmission shifting; brakes fail during the first five minutes after a cold start; brake pedal becomes hard and resists application or mushy and goes to the floor; faulty airbag monitor; all kinds of warning lights come on for no reason; defective steering causes violent swerving from side to side; automatic door locks engage by themselves, locking out driver.

Road Performance

Pro: Emergency handling: Traction control works quite well in emergency situations. **Acceleration/torque:** The V8 is the engine of choice for moving the LS (0-100 km/h: 7.3 sec.). **Steering:** Acceptable, but not as responsive as European and Japanese luxury vehicles. **Routine handling:** Pretty good, despite the soft suspension. **Braking:** Quite good.

Con: The V6's performance is seriously compromised by the Lincoln's heft, and turns in 0–100 km/h times that are one to two seconds slower than V6 competitors'. **Transmission:** The 5-speed automatic shifts slowly, not as decisively as competitors' gearboxes, and far less smoothly than Lexus drivetrains. A manual transmission (first one since 1951) is available only with the V6-equipped LS. Suspension provides a soft ride and is not as sporty as the competition.

Comfort/Convenience

Pro: Standard equipment: Very well appointed for the price. **Climate control:** Confusing and not very accessible. **Interior space/comfort F/R:** The LS is roomier than both the Bimmer and Mercedes E-Class, and a bit longer and taller than the Jaguar S-type. Comfortable seats. **Trunk/liftover:** Easy to load or unload.

Con: Driving position: In spite of the many seat adjustments available, it's hard to find a comfortable driving position. Don't believe the hype that this is a five-seater. **Entry/exit:** Rear access is awkward. **Cargo space:** Small trunk and limited interior storage space. **Quietness:** Tire noise intrudes the interior.

COST				
List Price (very negotiable)	**Residual Values (months)**			
	24	36	48	60
Lincoln LS: $42,765 (21%)	$29,000	$25,000	$21,000	$17,000

TECHNICAL DATA	
Powertrain (rear-drive)	Head room F/R: 40.4/37.5 in.
Engines: 3.0L V6 (210 hp)	Leg room F/R: 42.6/37.7 in.
• 3.9L V8 (252 hp)	Wheelbase: 115. in.
Transmissions: 5-speed man.	Turning circle: 39 ft.
• 5-speed auto.	Cargo volume: 14 cu. ft.
Dimensions/Capacity	Tow limit: 2,000 lb.
Passengers: 2/2	Fuel tank: 55L/prem.
Height/length/width:	Weight: 3,655 lb.
56.1/194/73 in.	

SAFETY FEATURES/CRASHWORTHINESS		
	Std.	**Opt.**
Anti-lock brakes (4W)	■	❏
Seatbelt pretensioners	—	—
Side airbags	■	❏
Traction control	■	❏
Head restraints F/R	*	*
Visibility F/R	*****	*****
Crash protection (front) D/P	N/A	N/A
Crash protection (side) D/P	N/A	N/A
Crash protection (off-set)	*****	

Lincoln Continental

Lincoln Continental

RATING: Average. Think of the Continental as a larger, fully loaded Ford Taurus. **Strong points:** Many standard features, comfortable ride, easy access, and lots of cargo room. **Weak points:** Limited rear seat room, delayed transmission engagement, and uncertain long-term reliability.

NEW FOR 2001: A carryover model that may offer a voice-activated telecommunication service. That includes a wireless telephone, roadside emergency assistance, and optional Web access. A complete redesign is due in 2002.

OVERVIEW: The Continental rests on a modified front-wheel drive Taurus chassis, which is one of the most up-to-date designs on the road. With the addition of a depowered 4.6L V8 once used in the Mark VIII as the standard powerplant, performance has improved immeasurably, to the point that it's now comparable to other Lincolns. One of the Continental's strong selling points is its large array of standard features that would cost extra on many other luxury sedans.

Cost analysis/best alternatives: Get a discounted year 2000 version unless you must have the new wireless telecommunication gizmos. Other cars worth considering: the Mercury Grand Marquis (Crown Vics are now mostly used for police work), Lincoln Town Car, Nissan Maxima, Mercedes-Benz 300 series, or Toyota Avalon. The Continental is less expensive than imported luxury sedans, and doesn't sacrifice luxury features or innovative technology. On the other hand, German and Japanese models leave the Continental far behind in handling, braking, engine smoothness, and overall reliability. **Options:** A one-touch panic button (RESCU) that alerts the police, ambulance, or tow truck to your whereabouts through a patch between the cellular phone network and global satellites; and run-flat Michelin ZP tires that can be driven up to 80 km (50 miles) without tire pressure. **Rebates:** Expect $3,000 dealer incentives on the 2000 version early in the year 2001. **Delivery/PDI:** $800. **Depreciation:** Faster than average. **Insurance cost:** Higher than average. **Parts supply/cost:** Parts are easy to come by and reasonably priced. **Annual maintenance cost:** Higher than average. The fuel-injection system is difficult and costly to service when problems arise. **Warranty:** Bumper-to-bumper 4 years/80,000 km; rust perforation 5 years/unlimited km. **Supplementary warranty:** A good idea, not just because of the Continental's uncertain long-term reliability, but because the complicated mechanical and electrical components cost so much to troubleshoot and replace. **Highway/city fuel economy:** 8.8–13.9L/100 km.

Quality/Reliability/Safety

Pro: Quality control: Overall quality control is the best of Ford's domestic luxury cars, which is far from complimentary. **Reliability:** Average. The front brakes and suspension system aren't very durable. **Warranty performance:** Better than average. Lincoln owners are given a special VIP number to call.

Con: Owner-reported problems: AC, automatic transmission, and fuel pump failures and lots of body squeaks and rattles. The added complexity of ABS, an electronic air suspension, and all the other high-tech items found on these cars are likely to cause some headaches with age, which is reason enough to buy an extended warranty. **Service bulletin problems:** Transmission hesitation caused by incorrect power control module setting; transmission fluid leakage; brake vibration; and front stabilizer link clunk or rattle. **NHTSA safety complaints/safety:** Airbags deployed for no apparent reason; frequent transmission malfunctions and failures; right side view mirror hard to adjust to satisfy short-statured drivers.

Road Performance

Pro: Emergency handling: Better than average. **Steering:** The variable-ratio, power steering gives the right amount of road feel and control. **Acceleration/torque:** Brisk and smooth acceleration with lots of low-end torque (0–100 km/h: 8 sec.). **Routine handling:** Air suspension helps both ride and handling; the car is smooth on all but the worst roads, and cornering at highway speeds remains precise and predictable. **Braking:** Acceptable braking, considering the Continental's size (100–0 km/h: 130 ft.).

Con: Transmission: The automatic transmission is sometimes slow to downshift and occasionally has trouble deciding if it wants to be in Overdrive or third gear. Despite its good handling, the Continental feels clumsy around town. The computer-controlled air suspension emits an irritating hissing sound when it settles after parking. Some torque steer (steering twists a bit) when the accelerator pedal is floored.

Comfort/Convenience

Pro: Standard equipment: A sophisticated air cushion suspension allows the driver to dial in different suspension settings for all driving conditions. **Driving position:** Comfortable seating and good all-around visibility. **Entry/exit:** Easy front and rear access. **Interior space/comfort F/R:** Better than average. The interior is narrower than other domestic cars in this class, but it's plush and comfortable. **Trunk/liftover:** Large trunk and low liftover facilitate loading. **Quietness:** Very little engine, road, or wind noise.

Con: Ford's chintzy side is evident when you open the spacious trunk and find that it houses a temporary-service spare tire. Handset cradle is not user-friendly. The standard leather upholstery is slippery, and it's hot in summer and cold in winter. **Controls and displays:** The digital dash is hard to read, and some operating controls are inconvenient and illogical. For example, you'll have to shut off the ignition and blindly grope inside the glove compartment for the trunk lid remote release, hoping you don't hit the fuel-filler door release instead. Confusing power window switches. Plus, it takes far too many buttons to set the trip computer, suspension mode, and steering effort. Seats aren't as comfortable as the competition's and only two can sit up front. Loading the trunk is made difficult by the protruding rear bumper. **Climate control:** Fresh air ventilation is adequate, but the automatic climate controls tend to overcompensate and perform erratically. The rear seats need more side and lower back support. **Cargo space:** The interior lacks storage bins for small objects.

COST				
List Price (negotiable)	**Residual Values (months)**			
	24	**36**	**48**	**60**
Continental: $53,705 (23%)	$40,000	$28,000	$23,000	$20,000
Note: Price includes PDI, freight.				

TECHNICAL DATA	
Powertrain (front-drive)	Head room F/R: 39/38 in.
Engine: 4.6L V8 (275 hp)	Leg room F/R: 41.9/38.9 in.
Transmission: 4-speed auto.	Wheelbase: 109 in.
Dimensions/Capacity	Turning circle: 35.4 ft.
Passengers: 2/3	Cargo volume: 18.1 cu. ft.
Height/length/width:	Tow limit: 2,000 lb.
56/206.3/73.6 in.	Fuel tank: 67L/reg.
	Weight: 3,900 lb.

SAFETY FEATURES/CRASHWORTHINESS

	Std.	Opt.
Anti-lock brakes	■	❑
Seatbelt pretensioners	■	❑
Side airbags	■	❑
Traction control	■	❑
Head restraints F/R	*	*
Visibility F/R	*****	*****
Crash protection (front) D/P	***	N/A
Crash protection (side) D/P	N/A	
Crash protection (off-set)	***	

Note: NHTSA rating applies to the '94 model.

Windstar

Windstar

RATING: Average. Factory defects are still omnipresent, however, Ford's benchmark 7-year/160,000 km extended engine "goodwill" protects owners from engine and transmission failures. **Strong points:** Comfortable ride; good instrument/controls layout; plenty of passenger space; and a five-star crashworthiness rating. Much-improved warranty performance. **Weak points:** Mediocre handling and restricted side and rear visibility. Automatic transmission and other mechanical components don't hold up well from day one; many electrical and body glitches.

NEW FOR 2001: An upgraded transmission, a freshened interior and exterior along with "smart" airbags that adjust deployment speed according to occupant weight; a sliding door warning light; an upgraded rear-seat entertainment system (would you believe wireless headsets that work in and outside the vehicle?); and an optional AdvanceTrac traction control system and adjustable pedals for shorter drivers.

OVERVIEW: Windstar is a front-drive minivan that looks a bit like a stretched Mercury Villager. It's longer, larger, and lower than most other minivans. It's also one of the few minivans not built on a truck platform (it uses the Taurus platform instead), and as such it has some of the car-like handling characteristics of Chrysler's minivans and some of the engine and automatic transmission problems experienced by Taurus and Sable owners. It's offered in two body styles—a seven-passenger people-hauler and the less expensive basic cargo van. Buyers have the choice of two 6-cylinder engines: a standard 147-hp 3.0L V6 or a 200-hp 3.8L V6. Both motors are hooked to a 4-speed electronic automatic transmission.

Cost analysis/best alternatives: Forget the rebates and discounts, the 2001 model is the better buy. You'll benefit from a number of upgrades and safety features. Honda Odyssey (Nissan Quest Villager has been dropped in Canada) and the Toyota Sienna are recommended alternatives. **Options:** Automatic levelling suspension ($385); dual integrated child safety seats for the middle bench seat; power side windows; and rear air conditioner, defroster, and heater. Be careful before choosing the optional adjustable pedals; some drivers have found them set too close together and say they often felt loose. Test-drive before you buy. Don't spring for the centre console option unless you're prepared to sacrifice rear seat access. Most Windstars are the LX, costing about $30,000 with a carefully prepared list of options. Since the 1999 version, both sliding side doors are powered and include an override circuit to prevent the door from closing on a hand. This overpriced convenience feature is failure-prone and a bit slow in operation. On the other hand, it's amazing the reaction this gadget engenders—buyers' eyes light up when they see the door open automatically with the remote control fob. An argument can be made for the added convenience, but I suspect its chief attraction is to gadget-hungry males who must have the latest eye-popping innovation. Another overpriced feature that has a dubious safety value is Ford's $338 optional reverse sensing system that alerts you to an object behind the vehicle when backing up. Four sonar sensors in the bumpers detect—starting at 1.8 m—large stationary objects and emit warning beeps that increase to a steady tone as you get within 25 cm of the object. **Rebates:** $2,500 on the last year's models; $1,500 on the 2001 by early spring. With minivan sales slowing down, heftier rebates won't be far behind. By the end of the year, look for more generous rebates and dealer incentives. **Delivery/PDI:** $900. **Depreciation:** Much slower than average. **Insurance cost:** Above average. **Parts supply/cost:** Parts are widely available and reasonably priced. **Annual maintenance cost:** Above average. **Warranty:** Bumper-to-bumper 3 years/60,000 km; rust perforation 5 years/unlimited km. **Supplementary warranty:** An extended warranty is a good idea. **Highway/city fuel economy:** With the 3.0L V6: 9.3–14L/100 km; with the 3.8L V6: 9.5–13.3L/100 km.

Quality/Reliability/Safety

Pro: Warranty performance: Improved considerably over the past six months. Ford has extended "goodwill" coverage for tranny defects on the '99 model without mileage or prior ownership limitations under ONP#00B51.

Con: Quality control: Average for American-made minivans; below average when compared with the Japanese competition (Mazda excepted). The last five years have been a disaster from a quality control standpoint. "Goodwill" payouts have been used as a substitute for better quality control. **Reliability:** Serious problems affecting the automatic transmission, which continues to shift erratically and is failure prone. Ford insiders and service bulletins confirm that this transmission problem is both hardware and software related and affects most of Ford's model lineup—it's a chronic complaint from owners reporting to NHTSA (see below). Electrical system and brake defects also frequently sideline the Windstar. **Owner-reported problems:** Not as many as reported in previous years. Either quality is improving, warranty repairs are more generous, or the 2000 vehicles haven't been on the road long enough to generate many complaints. Nevertheless, as stated above, transmission defects lead the list of factory-related problems, but there have also been a number of complaints concerning computer modules, AC failures, and premature brake rotor and caliper wear. **Service bulletin problems:** Harsh 3–2 shifting when coasting then accelerating. Transmission fluid leakage. 3.8L engine hum, moan, drone, spark knock, and vibration. Vibration under light acceleration. Power steering grunt or shudder during slow turns. Instrument panel popping; snapping at the lower centre bin area; rattling, clunking noise from front of vehicle; suspension noise, squeaks and rattles from the exterior right rear and liftgate areas. Faulty self-activating wipers, and door, trunk, and ignition locks. Centre storage bin binds and door glass may bind or travel slowly. Discharged battery after extended parking. Instrument panel chimes continually. Malfunctioning indicator lights. Dust enters into AC auxiliary air distribution system. **NHTSA safety complaints/safety:** Vehicle caught on fire while parked; sudden acceleration; hood flew up while under power; lug nuts failed causing front right wheel to fall off; sliding door makes noises as if it were loose, won't hold in place when opened, and suddenly pops open; with ignition switched ON, transmission can be shifted without pressing the brakes; automatic door lock pinches your arm if it's near the locks; joints not connected under the quarter wheel weld; driver's seat cross bar pops in and out; Check Engine light constantly comes on for no reason; Reverse sensing chime can't be heard over the radio; excessive steering vibrations when turning; vehicle sways from side to side when passing over bumps; when interior rearview mirror is set for night vision, it gives a distorted view, making objects hard to see.

Road Performance

Pro: Emergency handling: High-speed handling is acceptably stable and predictable, and the steering is particularly precise and light. **Steering:** Light and responsive, though not as effortless as the competition. **Acceleration/torque:** The 3.8L V6 is usually competent and smooth, with lots of low-end torque (0–100 km/h: 10.7 sec.). **Transmission:** The electronic 4-speed automatic responds well and shifts smoothly, when it's working properly (see "Con"). Fourth gear can be locked out for towing. **Routine handling:** Easy to drive. Smooth and supple ride under most driving conditions; ride improves as the load increases.

Con: Engine frequently stalls due to fuel pump, computer module, and electrical system glitches. Erratically performing automatic gearbox often slips out of gear, lurches into gear, or simply refuses to engage whichever gear you choose. The Windstar's city manners aren't impressive: excessive body swish and sway takes its toll on tires and makes highway driving less car-like than the shorter base Chrysler minivans. It also has a large turning radius. Lots of wind noise on the highway. **Braking:** Average braking that's a bit difficult to modulate.

Comfort/Convenience

Pro: Standard equipment: Comfortable and well-appointed interior. Superior sound system. One innovative touch that many families will appreciate: a wide-angle mirror housed in the ceiling console lets the driver watch the little darlings in the rear without turning around. **Driving position:** Excellent driving position gives most drivers a commanding view of the road. **Controls and displays:** Well laid-out instrument panel with easy-to-read gauges. **Climate control:** Adequate and easily adjusted. **Entry/exit:** Acceptable. **Cargo space:** Lots of small storage spaces in addition to the large amount of space for larger items. Another nice touch is the optional power lock switch just inside the rear hatch, which saves you from having to walk to the front of the van to lock up. **Trunk/liftover:** Rear hatch is easy to open and shut, and the low floor improves cargo handling.

Con: There's not a lot of choice when it comes to engine, body format, and cabin layout. Restricted side/rear visibility. **Controls and displays:** Headlight switch is partly obscured by the steering wheel. Tiny, flat buttons on the Windstar's radio make it hard to calibrate. **Climate control:** Weak AC and heater airflow to the floor makes an auxiliary heater a good idea. **Interior space/comfort F/R:** The Windstar's driver's seat isn't comfortable for big, tall drivers, who complain of the lack of leg room, seat contouring, and lower back support. The driver's shoulder belt can ride uncomfortably on a tall driver's collarbone because it's anchored too far back. It's also a long reach to put on. Middle seating behind the driver provides less leg and knee room than Chrysler mini-vans. Middle and rear seatbenches use short cushions and the rear seat is practically inaccessible. **Entry/exit:** Although the seats are easily removed, getting them in and out of the vehicle is more of a chore than Ford lets on (the rear bench seat alone weighs 110 lb., or almost 50 kg). The right sliding door takes a lot of effort to open and close. **Cargo space:** Unlike Chrysler, Ford still hasn't figured out a way to reconfigure the Windstar's storage space so that it will hold bulky items like 4' x 8' sheets of building material. **Quietness:** An abundance of clunks, rattles, and wind and road noise.

COST

List Price (negotiable)	Residual Values (months)			
	24	36	48	60
LX: $26,950 (20%)	$18,500	$15,500	$13,000	$11,000
SEL: $33,745 (21%)	$22,000	$19,000	$16,000	$14,000

Note: Price includes PDI, freight.

TECHNICAL DATA

Powertrain (front-drive)
Engines: 3.0L V6 (147 hp)
• 3.8L V6 (200 hp)
Transmission: 4-speed auto.
Dimension/Capacity
Passengers: 2/2/3
Height/length/width:
66.1/200.9/76.6 in.

Head room F: 39.3/R1: 41.1/R2: 37.9 in.
Leg room F:40.7/R1: 36.8/R2: 35.6 in.
Wheelbase: 120.7 in.
Turning circle: 42 ft.
Cargo volume: 66.5 cu. ft.
GVWR: 5,540 lb.
Payload: 1,800–1,831 lb.
Tow limit: 3,400 lb.
Fuel tank: 75/94L
Weight: 4,150 lb.

SAFETY FEATURES/CRASHWORTHINESS

	Std.	Opt.
Anti-lock brakes (4W)	■	❑
Seatbelt pretensioners	—	—
Side airbags	—	■
Traction control	❑	■
Head restraints F/R	****	*
Visibility F/R	*****	**
Crash protection (front) D/P	*****	*****
Crash protection (side) D/P	*****	*****
Crash protection (off-set)	*****	

JAGUAR

Jaguar's name conjures up images of posh sedans and fast sports cars rolling through the English countryside. Jaguars reek of elegance, taste, and money. The car's styling, ride, handling, and comfort still entice motorists full of nostalgia for British cars of the 1960s, but mechanical, electronic, and body problems persist—though there aren't as many as a decade ago. Interestingly, that may explain why Jaguars have such a high rate of depreciation, and why 70 percent of buyers prefer to lease rather than purchase their "Jag."

There are three models to choose from: the XJ8, the XK8, and the entry-level S-Type. XJ8s have four variations to choose from: the entry-level XJ8 ($79,950), the long-wheelbase XJ8L, the luxurious long-wheelbase Vanden Plas ($90,950), and the standard-length, supercharged XJR ($94,950). XK8 models are available as coupes or convertibles ($91,950 and $99,950, respectively).

Caught in a dilemma similar to that of the Corvette, the Jaguar has excess weight that makes it necessary to install lots of complicated and difficult-to-troubleshoot devices, as well as larger engines, in order to make these cars decent highway performers.

Even though Ford has taken over the company, long-term reliability is still a rather large question mark; however, recent studies show considerable improvement in quality control. Confident that its poor quality cars are ancient history, Jaguar offers a 30-day, money-back guarantee and a comprehensive 4-year/80,000 km base mechanical warranty. The automaker also provides a 6-year/unlimited km rust perforation warranty, and Jaguar Club benefits that include no-cost maintenance, roadside assistance, and trip interruption services.

Spotty servicing quality is still a problem, however. Owners report long delays for service appointments and then even longer waits for the right parts to arrive. Unfortunately, there aren't many Jaguar dealers to choose from, so if you don't find a competent and conscientious one, it's doubtful that you'll be able to go elsewhere for a second opinion.

S-Type

RATING: Below Average. On sale since the summer of 1999 and sharing its rear-drive platform with Ford's new Lincoln LS sedan, the S-Type is Jaguar's smallest luxury car. **Strong points:** Impressive engine performance, superb handling and roadholding, quiet-running, improved reliability, and a well-appointed interior. **Weak points:** Erratic-shifting manual-automatic transmission, not much room for cargo, a cramped interior, limited dealer network, Ford mechanics unfamiliar with this new model, some parts delay, and accelerated depreciation.

NEW FOR 2001: Carried over with few significant changes.

OVERVIEW: Finally, Ford comes out with a mid-priced Jaguar, the first product built upon Ford's shared platform concept that was also used with the 2000 Lincoln LS sedan. So, what's there not to like? How 'bout a transmission that's more suitable to John Deere? Interior room that won't hold three rear occupants in comfort? Plastic trim instead of real wood?

Seen as a "baby Jag," the S-Type has a longer wheelbase than the XJ sedans and is wider and taller. It's just a bit shorter in length, however. Retro styling continues at Ford with the oval grill vertical bars, four round headlights, and bland, pinched-looking taillights. From the side, this Jag looks like an Infiniti J30.

Quality control, although improved of late, is likely to still be a long-term problem, particularly in view of this being a new model churned out by Jaguar's old manufacturing complex near Birmingham, England. The car does have four-wheel ABS, traction control, front head/chest side airbags, Ford's Duratec-based 240-hp 3.0L V6, and an optional Jaguar 281-hp 4.0L V8. The only transmission offered, a 5-speed automatic, is a Ford-Jaguar joint venture. It's slow to react to a throttle-induced downshift. Stomp all you want on the gas pedal, the transmission still takes its own sweet time to engage. It also seems to hunt for the proper gear (more pronounced with the V6) and often changes gears for no apparent reason, after hesitating a few seconds.

Other deficiencies: steering is a bit over-assisted for high speeds (the optional Sport Package will help), limited passenger (rear passengers sit knees-to-chin with scrunched toes) and cargo space, an inaccessible glovebox, restricted rear visibility, and a confusing array of audio and climate controls.

Aimed at the BMW 5-series, Mercedes E-Class, and Lexus GS crowd, the S-Type is pricier than its Lincoln LS twin at $59,250 for the V6 and $11,000 more for the V8. This price puts it a few thousand dollars below the Benz, and on par with Lexus and BMW.

Cost analysis/best alternatives: Although sales have been much better than last year, Jaguar still is a low volume seller, and discounting is quite common. There isn't any compelling reason to buy or lease a year 2000 or 2001 Jaguar when the car is compared with less expensive convertibles/roadsters like the BMW Z3, Mercedes SLK, and Porsche Boxster. Other more reliable luxury cars you may wish to consider, with as much or more cachet, are the Lexus models, the Lincoln Town Car, Infiniti models, Mercedes S-Class, Nissan Maxima, and the Toyota Camry or Avalon. **Options:** The voice-activation system is a pricey gadget that adds to complexity without providing the convenience promised. **Rebates:** Although you can expect $2,000–$3,000 rebates on other unsold Jags, don't expect any on the S-Type. **Delivery/PDI:** $600. **Depreciation:** Resale values plummet about as quickly as Bre-X stock on most of Jaguar's models; the S-Type may hold its value better during its first year on the market. **Insurance cost:** Higher than average, close to usurious. **Parts supply/cost:** Parts are often back-ordered because not a lot of Ford dealer inventory goes into stocking Jaguar parts. The S-Type will be able to benefit from Ford's generic chassis components, but other components will still likely be back-ordered. Parts are moderately expensive as well, and there aren't any independent suppliers to inject price competition into the equation. **Annual maintenance cost:** Predicted to be higher than average. **Warranty:** Bumper-to-bumper 4 years/80,000 km; rust perforation 6 years/unlimited km. **Supplementary warranty:** Don't leave home without it. **Highway/city fuel economy:** 8.9–13.8L/100 km with the 3.0L V6 and 9.1–14.2L/100 km with the V8.

SAFETY FEATURES/CRASHWORTHINESS		
	Std.	**Opt.**
Anti-lock brakes	■	❑
Seatbelt pretensioners	■	❑
Side airbags	■	❑
Traction control	■	❑
Head restraints F/R	**	**
Convertible X	*	*
Visibility F/R	*****	**
Crash protection (front) D/P	N/A	
Crash protection (side) D/P	N/A	
Crash protection (off-set)	N/A	

GENERAL MOTORS

Ever since GM switched to mostly front-drives over 16 years ago, it began losing market share and earning a reputation for making look-alike, low-quality vehicles. This helps account for GM's U.S. market share plummeting from nearly 50 percent in the late '70s to its current 28 percent.

GM knows it has become the marginal car champ, with too many nameplates for models that are both identical and bland. Its various divisions are in serious need of pruning and restructuring. While axing the Olds Cutlass and Riviera was a smart move, GM's entire Olds division should be dropped—it makes no sense at all to have so many Olds nameplates on different model platforms.

Actually, experts agree that GM could make more money by shutting down its small cars and trucks. But union contracts would never let this happen. Plant workers' wages are guaranteed whether they work or not, so GM keeps pumping out cars even if they are low-profit, or even no-profit (insiders estimate GM loses $1,000 U.S. for every Cavalier it sells).

At a time when it could use all the dealer goodwill it could get, GM's dealer relations are tumultuous. The manufacturer's dealers are angry with the company for the following three reasons: the company's attempts to take over the retailing end by buying up dealerships through GM Retail Holdings and inching toward direct Web sales; the company's dysfunctional vehicle ordering system; and the lack of hot products.

New products: daring or dumb?

GM has delayed the redesign of its best-selling Cavalier/Sunfire until 2004, and says it will put the hundreds of millions of dollars saved into faster production and daring new designs. But, except for its new butt-ugly Aztek SUV and a freshening of the Aurora, GM's new designs appear to be more of the "same ol', same ol'." DaimlerChrysler's Viper, Prowler, and PT Cruiser make GM's designers look like the bland leading the bland.

No one would call GM's new Aztek sport-utility bland, least of all the originators of the "kill the Aztek" website.

Desperate to get new products onto the market, General Motors says it will reinvent its Cadillac and Saturn divisions over the next five years by converting most Cadillacs back to rear-drive and expanding the Saturn model lineup with larger cars, a sport-utility, and a minivan. The automaker will also add a small sport-utility division that will develop SUTs—sport-utility trucks with pickup beds (remember the El Camino?), and bring new sport wagons to the market. Surprisingly, a number of GM's once-popular cars and minivans are scheduled to be dropped within the next few years. They are the Metro, Camaro, Firebird, Park Avenue, Catera, Lumina, Astro, and Safari.

Specifically, here's what we can expect this year:
- Redesign of the Aurora.
- Slight restyling of the Grand Prix.
- Slight restyling of the Intrigue.
- Slight restyling of the Malibu.
- Slight restyling of the Saturn S-series.
- Slight restyling of the Venture minivan.
- Slight restyling of the Montana minivan.
- Debut of the Aztek.
- Debut of the Silverado HD.
- Redesign of the Denali sport-utility.
- GM dealers selling the Hummer H1 sport-utility.

Incidentally, last March GM formed a partnership with Fiat and plans to sell Alfa Romeos in North America through its existing Cadillac and Saab dealerships. This may mark the return of Fiat to North America (Oh, happy day! Fix it again, Tony!).

Warranty performance, quality control
GM has put more money into warranty repairs and continues to let its dealers make most post-warranty decisions. So it's not surprising to see that GM warranty complaints have moderated a bit over the years. The company has also been more upfront in admitting its vehicles' failures, like its announcement to extend its "goodwill warranty" to six years on 1994–96 Saturns that overheat and blow their engine head gaskets.

GM's quality control has improved as well. This is particularly evident in the better-made, redesigned Silverado and Sierra full-sized pickups, and the fewer complaints relating to Cadillac and Saab models. Front-drive powertrain and other mechanical and electronic components still aren't as reliable or durable as those produced by the Japanese automakers, but this is a problem shared by all three American automakers. The quality of body components and their assembly also remain far below Japanese and European standards. Poor paint quality, a Ford problem for over a decade, was addressed in 1995 by a changeover in suppliers. Apparently, GM has yet to make that move, in spite of a Canadian class action launched against the company in British Columbia two years ago—as well as a handful of lengthy, though well-reasoned, small claims court judgments targeting GM paint delamination.

I'll continue monitoring GM's quality control and treatment of its customers this year through Lemon-Aid reader feedback and email reports. If I detect any change in GM's policies before next year's edition, I'll post the information on *www.lemonaidcars.com.*

Metro, Firefly, Swift (2000)

Firefly

RATING: Average. Acceptable only for bare-bones city commuting, where fuel savings and agility are paramount. Rating would have been above average or better, except for safety-related complaints that include poor braking and inadvertent airbag deployment. **Strong points:** Cheap to buy and cheap to run; better-than-average quality control; above average crashworthiness; fun to drive with a manual shifter. **Weak points:** Anemic, noisy engine makes these cars the antithesis of "swift"; harsh, choppy ride; lots of interior noise; a spartan interior; poorly performing original equipment tires; safety-related failures; and inadequate braking.

NEW FOR 2001: No significant changes, except that these models may only be sold to fleets this year, prior to their being dropped in 2001.

OVERVIEW: These are good city and commuter cars, capable of fitting into the tiniest of parking spaces and nipping through narrow city streets, with sufficient room inside for two adults and their cargo. Interestingly, only GM offers optional power steering.

These cars deliver outstanding fuel economy because of an unusual aluminum 1.0L 3-cylinder engine, which is a little rough around the edges but gets the job done efficiently. People who'd like a little more zest from their city scooter can order the fuel-injected 1.3L 4-banger.

Cost analysis/best alternatives: Get the year 2000 model if it's discounted by at least $1,000. The XFi bare-bones Metro is the fuel economy champion, but it sacrifices an automatic transmission and a host of other amenities. Actually, a better-equipped model would be almost as economical. Convertibles are the best choice for ragtop thrills that won't break your budget. Compare prices with the Suzuki Swift, the Metro's twin; it may offer a longer warranty and more standard features for less. On the other hand, Suzuki dealership servicing and Suzuki's warranty performance are not as good as GM's and its dealers. Other cars to consider are the Honda Civic, Hyundai Accent, and Toyota Tercel. **Options:** The larger engine with fuel injection, a remote trunk release, split folding rear seats (sedans), and premium tires. **Rebates:** $1,000 on year 2000 Metros and Fireflys; Swifts may get a $750 dealer incentive. **Delivery/PDI:** $525. **Depreciation:** Faster than average at first, then it levels off. Convertibles depreciate very slowly. **Insurance cost:** Lower than average; convertibles, average. **Parts supply/cost:** Above average availability and reasonably priced (powertrain components tend to be pricey). Shop around for the best price among GM and Suzuki dealers. **Annual maintenance cost:** Less than average. Maintenance is made simple by an uncluttered under-hood layout and the availability of two dealer networks for servicing. **Warranty:** *Metro, Firefly:* Bumper-to-bumper 3 years/60,000 km; rust perforation 6 years/160,000 km. *Swift:* Bumper-to-bumper 3 years/80,000 km; rust perforation 5 years/unlimited km. **Supplementary warranty:** Not needed. **Highway/city fuel economy:** 6.2–7.8L/100 km with the 1.3L and 3-speed automatic.

Quality/Reliability/Safety

Pro: Quality control: Better than average. This is a low-cost and low-maintenance econobox with a better-than-average repair record that goes back many years. The trend seems to be continuing, judging by the absence of significant problems reported by owners. **Reliability:** Fairly good, except for some fuel-injection glitches and engine head gasket failures. If not checked often for corrosion and leaks, the cooling system could eventually fail, causing serious damage to the aluminum engine. **Warranty performance:** Average at GM and Suzuki. **Service bulletin problems:** Nothing reported. Chassis rigidity and crash safety have been enhanced by the placement of a steel beam behind the instrument panel.

Con: Owner-reported problems: Premature brake wear (the front discs warp easily), and the front metallic brake pads are noisy. Some owners complain about fragile body hardware. Stopping distances are greater than average and the car is very sensitive to crosswinds and passing trucks on the highway. **NHTSA safety complaints:** Several incidents of sudden acceleration; inadvertent airbag deployment; airbags failed to deploy; fuel tank fuel hose leak; taillight failure when daylight running lights are on; strut, transmission, and clutch failures; brakes are noisy and make for extended stopping distances; emergency brake applied, but vehicle still rolled backwards.

Road Performance

Pro: The tiny 1.0L 3-cylinder powerplant has no trouble keeping up with city traffic, but the optional 1.3L 4-cylinder handles the automatic gearbox and highways much better. **Steering:** The non-power steering is fairly precise and always predictable. **Transmission:** The 5-speed manual with Overdrive shifts easily. **Routine handling:** Handling is nimble and stable most of the time, thanks in part to the independent suspension.

Con: Emergency handling: Cornering becomes sloppier and less predictable as speed increases. The added weight of the 4-cylinder engine makes for hard steering while parking. **Acceleration/torque:** Very slow and without much torque (0–100 km/h: 12.3 sec.), which means that you'll quickly become expert at using the manual shifter—and get just as quickly fed up with the constant shifting of the 3-speed automatic. Even with the optional 4-cylinder engine, these cars are not great highway or long-distance cruisers. There is some stalling and hesitation under full throttle. If you hear a constant knocking when accelerating or decelerating, blame it on the unusually pliable engine mounts that allow the engine and exhaust system to knock against the floor pan. The clutch is abrupt, and the automatic transmission robs the engine of what little power it produces. The absence of an Overdrive gear on the automatic makes for excessive engine noise at highway speeds. The suspension thumps and bounces in hard turns. Cheap original-equipment tires compromise handling, ride, and braking. **Braking:** Incredibly bad without ABS (100–0 km/h: varies between 139 and 152 ft.).

Comfort/Convenience

Pro: Standard equipment: Well-appointed interior with complete instrumentation. The plunging hood, sweeping window glass, and thin side pillars give the interior an airy look that heightens visibility in all directions. **Driving position:** Good. **Controls and displays:** Convenient, easy-to-read controls. **Interior space/comfort F/R:** Despite their diminutive proportions, these cars will easily accommodate tall occupants in front. Standard seats are reasonably comfortable for short rides. **Cargo space:** The area behind the front seats is a compromise; either you get limited space for two people and no room for cargo, or a spacious cargo area with the rear seat folded down. **Trunk/liftover:** Fairly large trunk with a low liftover to facilitate loading.

Con: Coupes don't offer power steering. Some radios furnished by GM dealers are poorly calibrated, producing an irritating, tinny sound. **Climate control:** Mediocre heating and ventilation. Seats become cramped and generally uncomfortable during long trips. **Entry/exit:** Very difficult rear access. Not much room for your feet in the rear. **Quietness:** The interior is quite noisy, due mainly to poor soundproofing and the car's small size.

COST

List Price (firm)	Residual Values (months)			
	24	**36**	**48**	**60**
Metro: $10,795 (10%)	$8,000	$6,000	$4,000	$3,000
Swift DLX: $11,595 (9%)	$8,500	$7,000	$5,000	$4,000

TECHNICAL DATA

Powertrain (front-drive)
Engines: 1.0L 3-cyl. (55 hp)
• 1.3L 4-cyl. (70 hp)
Transmissions: 5-speed man. OD
• 3-speed auto.
Dimension/Capacity (Metro LSi)
Passengers: 2/2
Height/length/width:
55.4/164/62.6 in.

Head room F/R: 39.3/37.3 in.
Leg room F/R: 42.5/32.2 in.
Wheelbase: 93.1 in.
Turning circle: 35 ft.
Cargo volume: 10 cu. ft.
Tow limit: Not recommended
Fuel tank: 39L/reg.
Weight: 1,792 lb.

SAFETY FEATURES/CRASHWORTHINESS

	Std.	Opt.
Anti-lock brakes	❑	■
Seatbelt pretensioners	—	—
Side airbags	—	—
Traction control	—	—
Head restraints F/R	*	*
Visibility F/R	*****	*****
Crash protection (front) D/P	****	****
Crash protection (side) D/P	N/A	N/A
Crash protection (off-set)	N/A	

Saturn S-series, L-series

Saturn LS

Rating: Below Average. There have been some improvements, but Saturn's long-term reliability and uneven servicing trail its Asian competitors, and even make GM's ubiquitous Cavalier and Sunfire look good. **Strong points:** *S-series:* Comfortable driving position, adequate instrumentation and controls, unobstructed visibility, good braking, dent-resistant body panels, and better-than-average crashworthiness scores. *L-series:* Well appointed; comfortable driving position; and a roomy interior with a full range of convenience features, instruments, and controls. Excellent powertrain matchup with the V6; firm European ride; impressive high speed stability; and excellent braking. Effective soundproofing and lots of storage areas, including a large accessible trunk. **Weak points:** *S-series:* Excessive engine noise with the base engine; limited rear seat room; optional ABS and traction control; window of coupe's third door doesn't roll down. *L-Series:* Interior isn't as refined as what you would find in a Toyota or Honda; optional ABS and traction control; limited rear visibility; steering feels heavy at low speeds and too light at higher speeds; small audio controls; and wagons give a jarring ride over bumps.

NEW FOR 2001: No significant changes with the L-series; S-series coupe gets a slight restyling.

OVERVIEW: Remember the hype? Saturn would be GM's *different* car company. Quality would match or exceed anything offered by the Japanese. Customers would be coddled and dealers would offer fair, "no haggle" prices. Sales would soar.

Unfortunately, Saturn never did meet these expectations. Instead, the company has produced poor-quality, overpriced cars that have sold poorly, now that their novelty has worn off. Customers who didn't walk out of showrooms when faced with a "take it or leave it" attitude, found inflated "no haggle" prices that could be whittled down by hard bargaining. And, Saturn's response to complaints over its poor quality powertrains?

A rush order for new engines from—Honda!

Saturn has redesigned the body panels and cabin of its S-series sedan and wagon, giving the vehicles a more angular look and sharing many cockpit components with the new LS-series. These changes give the S-series a bit over 1.2 inches in extra length, a quieter twin-cam 1.9L engine, door panel-integrated beverage holders, a more user-friendly horn, more front seat travel, better lumbar support, and top tether anchors for child safety seats.

In an attempt to save money by adapting a European car to the American market, Saturn's LS sedan and LW wagon are products of a whole series of cost-cutting compromises since they are spun off the Vectra, made by GM's Opel subsidiary. Some major differences, however, include a lengthened body to give the Saturns additional crashworthiness, a standard ignition theft-deterrent system, a re-engineered chassis to give a more comfortable ride, the continued use of Saturn dent-resistant polymer body panels, the substitution of a Saturn space frame, and the use of a homegrown 137-hp 2.2L 4-banger constructed with aluminum components (remember the Vega?). Other components lifted directly from the European parts bin are Opel's 3.0L V6 engine, a manual transmission from Saab, and German-made braking systems.

Cost analysis/best alternatives: Buy whichever model year is the cheapest; however, in view of the problems generally experienced after the third year of ownership, a "walk-away," 3-year lease may be a better alternative (but not always, as the owner's report below shows). The L-series is way overpriced, particularly in view of Saturn's bogus no-haggle policy; only consider a better-made, second-series model made after March 2000. As alternatives to the S-series, the Honda Civic and Toyota Corolla perform better and offer higher quality vehicles. The Hyundai Tiburon compares well with the Saturn SC. Alternatives to the L-series: GM Cavalier or Sunfire, Honda Accord, Mazda 626, and the Toyota Camry. **Options:** Traction control is a wise choice. **Rebates:** Nothing reported yet, but expect $1,000–$1,500 rebates on the S-series models by year's end. Rebates on the more popular L-series aren't likely to kick in until early 2001. **Delivery/PDI:** $500. **Depreciation:** Slower than average. **Insurance cost:** Average. **Parts supply/cost:** Parts are easily found and reasonably priced. **Annual maintenance cost:** Average. Estimated to increase dramatically after the third year of ownership. **Warranty:** Bumper-to-bumper 3 years/60,000 km; rust perforation 6 years/160,000 km. **Supplementary warranty:** A good idea in view of Saturn's poor quality control and hard-nose attitude in treating post-warranty repair claims. **Highway/city fuel economy:** *SC:* 5.8–8.7L/100 km with the 1.9L engine and an automatic transmission; *LS:* 7.2–10.5L/100 km with the 2.2L engine and an automatic transmission; 8.2–11.8L/100 km with the 3.0L engine and an automatic transmission.

Quality/Reliability/Safety

Pro: There have been fewer serious complaints registered against the new L-series than the S-series. The installation of Honda engines next year should eliminate one of the traditional problem areas plaguing Saturn since the first models were launched in 1992. Unfortunately, this will be too late for owners already paying huge bills for premature engine failures, like the following Ontario owner of a 1997 Saturn SC1 reports:

> ...My grievance is with Saturn Motors. It appears to me that they are manufacturing automobiles powered by less than reliable engines. I have suffered 63,508 km of what I call a 'complete engine meltdown'! Where I live, I have heard of at least five other such engine failures and if you research the net, the problem seems almost epidemic.
>
> These engine failures seem to stem from problems with excess oil consumption and a problem with the oil properly lubricating the engine.
>
> So to summarize, Mr. Edmonston, I am paying $324 a month for a car I cannot drive, which means I cannot afford to get

another one. As well, they want between $3000–$5000 to repair a
car that will be returned in four months. Also, since I definitely
do not want to use my option to purchase at the end of the lease,
I have lost $10 000 in equity...

Con: Reliability: Below average, particularly after the third year of
ownership—two years earlier than when most vehicles start needing
major repairs. **Quality control:** Not up to Japanese car standards.
Saturn has always been afflicted by serious quality control problems.
During its first year of production, for example, the company had to
buy back 1,836 vehicles because improper coolant would have ruined
the cars' engines. **Warranty performance:** Great, as long as the warranty
is in force. Afterwards, customers report they feel abandoned.
Sample the Saturn complaint site at *www.pedsweb.com/saturn/*. **Owner-
reported problems:** Engine; transmission; electrical and fuel system;
brake and body defects. **Service bulletin problems:** *S-series:* Delayed,
harsh engagement into Reverse or Drive; erratic shifting between first
and second gear; no second or third gears; AC odours upon startup;
AC sizzling or hissing type noise heard when the AC has been used;
Check Engine light comes on for no reason; front door outside handle
may come in contact with the front door outer panel; steering column
popping noise during low-speed turns; steering wheel shake or vibration
at highway speeds (see following bulletin);

Steering Wheel Shake/Vibration at Highway Speeds
Issue Date: November, 1999
Group/SEQ. No.: Chassis-05
Corporation No.: 99-00-91-002
Subject:
Steering Wheel Shake or Vibration at Highway Speeds
(Balance Tire/Wheel Assemblies and Replace Tires if Necessary)
Models Affected:
2000 Saturn L-Series Sedans and Wagons
Condition:
Some customers may comment regarding a steering wheel shake or vibration felt
when driving vehicle at highway speeds. This condition is more noticeable on smooth
road surfaces at vehicle speeds above 65 mph (105 km/h).
Cause:
Vehicle sensitivity to out-of-balance tire/wheel assemblies or excessive force variation
within the tire/wheel assembly.
Correction:
Balance all four tire/wheel assemblies, evaluate, and if necessary replace two or four
tires with qualified tires.

Take note: this problem may involve replacing all four tires, at Saturn's
expense, *during the warranty period.*

dome lamp, sunroof or headliner rattling; muffler assembly rattling or clunk noise; defective sunroof sunshade fabric; inoperative driver's side window; rear compartment side carpet falls down at deck-lid hinge area; bumps or iron dust on paint surface; and intermittent operation or difficulty in programming remote keyless entry transmitter. *L-series:* No third and fourth gear (replace direct clutch piston assembly); steering wheel shake or vibration at highway speeds; Service Engine and engine coolant temperature gauge needle in the red zone (see following service bulletin);

Bulletin No.: 00-T-04
January, 2000
Category Type: Engine-02
Category: Cooling
Corporation No.: 99-06-02-020
Models Affected:
2000 Saturn L-Series vehicles
Condition
Some customers may comment on any of the following conditions:
o Service Wrench telltale is On
o Engine Coolant Temperature telltale is On
o Coolant temperature gauge needle is in the red zone
o 30A COOL FAN #1 fuse located in under hood fuse block (UHFB) is open
Cause
Puller fan (driver side) wiring harness, which contains three wires, may chafe on aluminum upper radiator mount.
Correction
Repair chafed engine cooling fan wire(s)

What may, at first, appear to be a major engine or electrical problem is actually a simple warranty-covered short-circuit.

faulty, noisy cooling fan operation; front doors re-lock after being unlocked with key; intermittent operation or difficulty in programming remote keyless entry transmitter; inoperative power windows and sunroof; rattle from behind the right-hand side of the instrument panel; wind whistle from the front door glass area and from the outside rear view mirror; door glass may bind and distort outer window run channel weather stripping; headliner sagging; and windshield wiper chatter or hop. **NHTSA safety complaints/safety:** *L-series:* Transmission can't be shifted into a forward gear; location of power seat button allows it to be accidentally activated, causing seat to suddenly recline; power door locks short out; electrical short causes all lights and gauges to suddenly come on; faulty evaporator surge solenoids; and seatbelt won't lock up at sudden stops. *SC1:* When applying brakes, there's excessive noise coming from the rear end; fuel sloshing sound when fuel tank is half full. *SC2:* Seatbelt tightens on any sudden movement, however slight; the small, recessed horn buttons make the horn hard to find and activate without looking down. *SL:* Steering wheel came apart while driving; total loss of steering when the retaining clip was omitted during assembly. *SL1:* Windshield wipers fail to adequately clean the windshield; defrosting system doesn't work properly, causing moisture damage and poor visibility. *SL2:* Sudden acceleration; turn signal indicator sticks in the resume position; seatbelts are hard to engage; when driving at night, one sees multiple lights when looking through the rear view mirror at the vehicle in back; during rainy weather, rear windshield view is distorted or wavy; sudden brake failure. *SW2:* Automatic transmission slippage caused collision, and film collects on interior of windshield.

Road Performance

Pro: Emergency handling: Good with the S-series; first class with the L-series. **Steering:** On the S-series it's fairly precise and predictable, with plenty of assist and road feedback. There's no torque steer, owing to the use of equal-length driveshafts. **Acceleration/torque:** Brisk acceleration with both the V6 and the DOHC 124-hp 4-banger (0–100 km/h: 8.5 sec.). The smaller engine delivers excellent fuel economy as well. **Transmission:** The manual transmission is precise and easily shifted. The automatic shifts smoothly. **Routine handling:** Better than average. The firm suspension gives a comfortable ride. Nimble handling with only a slight tendency to understeer. **Braking:** Fairly good; excellent braking with the optional four-wheel ABS (100–0 km/h: 124 ft.).

Con: Noisy S-series base engine. The 1.9L 100-hp 4-cylinder engine found on the sporty SC coupe gives barely adequate acceleration times (11.5 seconds to reach 100 km/h) with the manual transmission. This time is increased to a near-glacial 13.7 seconds with the 4-speed automatic gearbox, which robs the engine of what little power it produces. Excessive automatic gearbox shudder when the kickdown is engaged while passing. There is some wallowing in tight turns, and ride quality deteriorates if the car is loaded. L-series steering could be better tuned and the suspension may be too firm, especially on the wagon.

Comfort/Convenience

Pro: Standard equipment: Base Saturns come with a wide range of standard equipment. Large glove box and convenient door pockets. **Driving position:** Very good. Good all-around visibility on the S-series. **Controls and displays:** Most everything's within easy reach and well presented. **Climate control:** Efficient, quiet, and easy to adjust. **Interior space/comfort F/R:** Comfortable front seats, with a fair amount of head and leg room. **Cargo space:** Plenty of trunk space and storage compartments, particularly with the LS-series. Rear seatbacks fold down 60/40 for cargo flexibility. **Trunk/liftover:** Huge trunk has a large opening and low liftover height.

Con: Interior isn't as refined as that found on the Accord or Camry. GM's too cheap to make ABS a standard feature (ABS is, however, a standard feature with the Cavalier and Sunfire). Steering wheel is too close for comfort and the radio controls are tiny and distracting. LS-series visibility hampered by the high rear deck. Rear fold-down armrest isn't very useful. Coupe's third door window doesn't roll down. **Entry/exit:** Difficult rear access with the S-series. The rear is not the place to be—door sills are high, seat cushions are short, low, and too soft. **Quietness:** Lots of rattles and road and wind noise. Some engine noise at cruising speed.

COST

List Price (negotiable)	Residual Values (months)			
	24	36	48	60
SL1: $14,523 (11%)	$10,000	$9,000	$7,000	$5,500
LS: $19,255 (14%)	$14,000	$12,000	$10,000	$8,500
LS1: $21,620 (17%)	$15,500	$13,500	$11,500	$9,500
LS2: $26,120 (17%)	$17,000	$15,000	$13,000	$11,000
LW1: $24,400 (18%)	$16,500	$14,500	$12,500	$10,500
LW2: $27,810 (18%)	$18,000	$16,000	$13,500	$12,000

TECHNICAL DATA

Powertrain (front-drive)
Engines: 1.9L 4-cyl. (100 hp)
• 1.9L 4-cyl. (124 hp)
• 2.2L 4-cyl. (137 hp)
• 3.0L V6 (182 hp)
Transmissions: 5-speed man.
• 4-speed auto.
Dimension/Capacity (SL; SC)
Passengers: 2/3; 2/2
Height/length/width:
55/178.1/66.4 in.

Head room F/R: 39.3/38 in.
Leg room F/R: 42.5/32.8 in.
Wheelbase: 102.4 in.
Turning circle: 41 ft.
Cargo volume: 12 cu. ft.
Tow limit: 1,000 lb.
Fuel tank: 46–49L/reg.
Weight: 2,400 lb.

SAFETY FEATURES/CRASHWORTHINESS

	Std.	Opt.
Anti-lock brakes (4W)	❏	■
Seatbelt pretensioners	—	—
Side airbags	—	—
Traction control	—	■
Head restraints F/R	**	*
Visibility F/R		
All excl. L-Series and Saturn SC	*****	*****
L-series	*****	***
Crash protection (front) D/P	*****	*****
Crash protection (side) D/P	***	***
Crash protection (off-set)	***	

Note: Only the visibility rating applies to the L-series.

Cavalier, Sunfire

Cavalier

RATING: Above Average. **Strong points:** Very reasonably priced; good acceleration with the 2.4L engine; plenty of front passenger and cargo room; comfortable riding; well appointed for an entry-level vehicle; and good fuel economy. **Weak points:** Noisy engine and mediocre steering and handling. Limited rear passenger room. Crash safety and quality control still need some improvement.

NEW FOR 2001: Nothing significant. Biggest disappointment: the absence of a 6-cylinder engine.

OVERVIEW: These twins are two of the lowest-priced cars to come equipped with standard ABS and dual airbags (GM claims to lose $1,000 U.S. on each Cavalier and Sunfire it sells). They have exceptional styling (especially the coupe) and lots of interior room, with a nicely tuned suspension. The ride and handling have also improved markedly over the past three years, with power rack-and-pinion steering, a longer wheelbase, and a wider track. The Sunfire is identical to the Cavalier, except for its more rakish look.

The Cavalier Z24/Sunfire GT are performance versions of the compacts introduced four years ago. They use a reworked version of the failure-prone Quad 4 2.4L DOHC 16-valve 4-cylinder powerplant.

Cost analysis/best alternatives: Get a second-series (made after March 2000), discounted 2000 model for the upgrades. Also look at the Honda Civic, Hyundai Tiburon, Mazda Protegé, or Nissan Sentra. **Options:** 3-speed automatic transmission, which will reduce engine noise and make for more responsive performance; a suspension upgrade; traction control; and air conditioning. If you want more performance, and don't mind a bit more noise, the best combination is the 2.4L engine hooked to a 5-speed manual transmission. Of course, you'll have to deal with the engine's uncertain reliability. **Rebates:** $1,500 rebates on the year 2000 convertibles and $750–$1,000 rebates on the sedans and coupes. **Delivery/PDI:** $620. **Depreciation:** Slower than average. **Insurance cost:** Average. **Parts supply/cost:** Parts are easy to find and they're reasonably priced, with heavy discounting by dealers. **Annual maintenance cost:** Average. Maintenance on 4-cylinder models is reasonably straightforward. **Warranty:** Bumper-to-bumper 3 years/60,000 km; rust perforation 6 years/160,000 km. **Supplementary warranty:** A wise investment. **Highway/city fuel economy:** 7.5–10.4L/100 km with the 2.2L and automatic 3-speed; 7.4–11L/100 km with the 2.4L and automatic 4-speed. Interestingly, the larger engine doesn't impose much of a fuel penalty.

Quality/Reliability/Safety

Pro: Reliability: Overall reliability has been average. **Warranty performance:** Better than average. Important safety features include a new remote keyless entry with a panic button, top child-seat anchors for all three rear positions, and power door locks that prevent accidental lockout with the key in the ignition.

Con: Failure-prone Getrag manual gearbox. **Quality control:** Quality control is variable, often leading to poor paint application, inside and outside body panel gaps, and lots of exposed screw heads. Most body hardware is fragile. **Owner-reported problems:** Head gasket failures have been a frequent problem. Computer modules have also been one of the most common sources of complaints; symptoms include stalling and a shaky idle. Fuel-injection and cooling systems are temperamental as well. The power steering may lead or pull, and the steering rack tends to deteriorate quickly, usually requiring replacement some time shortly after 80,000 km. The front MacPherson struts also wear out rapidly, as do the rear shock absorbers. Many owners complain of rapid front brake wear and warped brake discs after a year or so. One owner reported the following brake repairs to NHTSA:

> ...Front brake rotors are warping and had to be turned at 1,600 miles and 1,800 miles. They then were replaced at 2,800 miles. They would cause the vehicle to jump when braking...

Service bulletin problems: Snow may intrude into the rear brake drum assembly; premature connecting rod failure if engine run at high rpms at low mileage; rough engine idle, misfire, Check Engine light all due to poorly calibrated computer module; possibility of engine coolant leaks caused by the upper radiator hose rubbing against the battery tray; automatic transmission may not go into third or fourth gear (see the following bulletin);

No Third and Fourth Gear

File In Section: 07-Transmission/Transaxle
Bulletin No.: 99-07-30-031
Date: December, 1999
Technical
Subject:
No Third and Fourth Gear (Replace Direct Clutch Piston Assembly)
Models:
1999–2000 Chevrolet Cavalier, Malibu
1999 Oldsmobile Cutlass
1999–2000 Oldsmobile Alero
1999–2000 Pontiac Grand Am, Sunfire
with Hydra-Matic 4T40-E, 4T45-E Transaxle (RPOs MN4, MN5) and 2.2 L, 2.4 L, 3.0 L,
3.1 L or 3.4 L Engine (VINs 4, F, T, R, M, E - RPOs LN2, L61, LD9, L81, L82, LA1)
Condition
This condition may be caused by the molded seal portion of the direct clutch piston
assembly delaminating from the steel housing eventually causing the outer lip of the
piston seal to cut or tear. This cut or tear prevents the direct clutch piston assembly
from applying causing the loss of both third and fourth gear.
Correction
To correct the above condition, install a Tech 2 to the vehicle and command third
gear. If third gear does not exist, proceed with an inspection of the direct clutch piston assembly for the cause listed above. If the direct clutch piston has a torn seal,
replace it with a new piston that has been released to prevent this condition. Inspect
and replace any other parts that show potential damage or quality concerns.

mismachined sealing surface on forward clutch housing (4T40-E
transmission); grinding or growling from transmission when in Park
on an incline. Vehicles equipped with a 2.2L engine may produce an
annoying engine or transmission whine; door rattles when closing;
driver-side manual mirror doesn't adjust when the adjusting lever is
moved. **NHTSA safety complaints/safety:** *Cavalier:* Engine fires; leaking fuel tank; plastic fuel tank is easily punctured; right wheel axle
twisted off vehicle; chronic hesitation, stalling, and surging; sudden
acceleration; clutch will not disengage, causing sudden acceleration;
faulty ABS; brake failure due to leaking master cylinder fluid; ABS
locked up, causing vehicle to go into a skid; airbags failed to deploy;
seatbelt failed to retract; transmission wouldn't go into Reverse; transmission failed to engage upon startup; automatic transmission locks
up in second gear; vehicle rolled away even though parked with parking brake engaged; when vehicle is in Drive with foot on the brake it
lurches forward, stalls, and produces a crashing sound; during highway driving the vehicle suddenly accelerated without steering control;
rear leaf spring U-bolts broke, causing entire rear end to drop; front
right side of the vehicle collapsed due to wheel bolts shearing off, causing the wheel to detach completely; springs are too weak, causing poor
stability and control; floor mat impedes clutch pedal travel; sudden
brake cable breakage while driving; brake grinding noise; warping of
the front and rear brakes; when stopping, vehicle makes a thumping

noise; when driving with door locked, it came ajar; hood flew up while driving; misaligned driver's door; windshield water leaks; Check Engine light came on due to loose fuel cap. *Sunfire:* Chronic stalling and brake failures; brake master cylinder leaks; when brakes are applied, all the interior lights go out; dash warning light indicating time to upshift comes on at the wrong time; sudden transmission failure; fuel tank leakage; AC fumes enter the interior at idle; airbags failed to fully inflate; horn only works intermittently; annoying squeak from both doors. On both cars, the trunk lid remains open at such a low angle that it's easy to hit your head.

Road Performance

Pro: Acceleration/torque: Acceptable acceleration with the 2.2L (0–100 km/h: 9.6 sec.), but the 2.4L is a much better performer. The fuel-injected 2.2L 4-cylinder engine provides adequate power when used with the manual transmission or with the smoother, more responsive 4-speed automatic. The 150-hp 2.4L Quad 4 produces lots more torque, shaving 0–100 km/h times by over a second (to 8 seconds). Models equipped with an optional suspension package offer the best handling at highway speeds and the best ride control on bad roads. **Braking:** Acceptable (100–0 km/h: 131 ft.).

Con: Even with the torque upgrade this year, when hooked to the 3-speed transaxle the 2.2L 4-cylinder lacks sufficient power to distinguish these J-cars from the competition. **Emergency handling:** Excessive lean when cornering under power and standard tires corner poorly. **Steering:** Power steering feels over-assisted, resulting in insufficient road feel. **Transmission:** The 5-speed manual transaxle has an abrupt clutch. The 3-speed automatic strains to get into the proper gear range. **Routine handling:** Base models don't handle as well as do most other vehicles in this class.

Comfort/Convenience

Pro: Standard equipment: Nicely equipped with standard AC and rear defroster, upgraded ABS, a Getrag 5-speed manual transmission, a redesigned instrument panel and centre console. **Driving position:** Generous up-front head room, although tall drivers may find the driving position a bit confining. **Controls and displays:** Well laid-out dashboard and controls. **Entry/exit:** Lots of foot space and large door openings make for easy access into the front or rear areas. **Interior space/comfort F/R:** Interior room will seat four adults comfortably. **Cargo space:** Fairly generous for a compact. **Trunk/liftover:** Good-sized trunk with a low liftover. **Quietness:** Quiet interior with minimal road/wind noise intrusion.

Con: Poor visibility on the Z24. **Climate control:** Interior ventilation is feeble without the air conditioning option. Rear seat room is skimpy. Lots of engine resonance invades the car's interior. Watch out for the low-hanging trunk lid.

COST

List Price (firm)	Residual Values (months)			
	24	36	48	60
Cavalier VL: $15,865 (12%)	$11,000	$8,000	$6,000	$4,500
Sunfire SL: $14,755 (12%)	$11,000	$7,500	$6,500	$5,000

TECHNICAL DATA

Powertrain (front-drive)
Engines: 2.2L 4-cyl. (120 hp)
• 2.4L 4-cyl. (150 hp)
Transmissions: 5-speed man. OD
• 3-speed auto.
• 4-speed auto.
Dimension/Capacity
Passengers: 2/3
Height/length/width:
54.8/180.3/67.4 in.

Head room F/R: 38.9/37.2 in.
Leg room F/R: 42.3/34.6 in.
Wheelbase: 104.1 in.
Turning circle: 38 ft.
Cargo volume: 14 cu. ft.
Tow limit: 1,000 lb.
Fuel tank: 58L/reg.
Weight: 2,700 lb.

SAFETY FEATURES/CRASHWORTHINESS

	Std.	Opt.
Anti-lock brakes (4W)	■	❑
Seatbelt pretensioners	—	—
Side airbags	—	—
Traction control	❑	■
Head restraints F/R	*	*
Visibility F/R	*****	*****
Crash protection (front) D/P		
2d	***	****
4d	****	****
Crash protection (side) D/P		
2d	*	**
4d	*	***
Crash protection (off-set)	*	

Grand Am, Alero

Alero

RATING: Below Average. Rating downgraded due to large number of serious safety-related complaints. Nevertheless, performance and quality control are no match for the Honda and Toyota competition. **Strong points:** *Grand Am:* Competent V6, good steering and handling, standard traction control, and average quality control. **Weak points:** *Grand Am:* Mediocre ride over rough terrain; excessive 4-cylinder noise; noisy interior; a four-seater with barely enough room in the coupe. Difficult rear seat access (coupe); awkward radio controls; rear visibility obstructed by spoiler; problematic trunk access; annoying body creaks and rattles; and long-term powertrain reliability is still a question mark. **Strong points:** *Alero:* Impressive V6 acceleration; even though it's the same engine found in the Grand Am, it performs better in the Alero. Logical, user-friendly gauges and controls; fairly spacious interior for cargo and passengers; standard traction control; and quiet running. **Weak points:** *Alero:* Excessive 4-cylinder engine noise and torque steer, steering isn't as crisp as the Grand Am's. Difficult rear seat access (coupe), and long-term powertrain reliability is still questionable.

NEW FOR 2001: Nothing significant for either model.

OVERVIEW: Taking its styling cues from GM's redesigned Grand Prix, the Grand Am offers a roomy, comfortable interior in two- and four-door body styles. Sharing its platform and mechanical components with the Oldsmobile Alero, which targets a slightly more upscale and performance-minded clientele, the base Grand Am uses a 150-hp Quad DOHC engine; a 170-hp 3.4L V6 engine is optional on the SE1 and standard on the SE2.

The upscale Alero, Oldsmobile's entry-level model, debuted in 1999 as the replacement for the slow-selling Achieva—often referred to as the "under-Achieva." Alero shares the Grand Am's chassis and powertrains.

Cost analysis/best alternatives: Get a year 2000 model if it's discounted by at least 15 percent. Other cars worth considering are the Honda Accord, Mazda 626, Nissan Altima, Subaru Legacy, Toyota Camry and Avalon, or VW Passat. **Options:** The best engine choice for power, smoothness, and value retention is the 170-hp 3.4L V6; it gives you much-needed power and costs only $60 extra per year in fuel. Stay away from the Computer Command Ride option: true, it allows you to choose your own suspension setting, but the settings aren't quite what they pretend to be. **Rebates:** $2,000 on both year 2000 models; about half as much for the 2001 versions early in the new year. **Delivery/PDI:** $650. **Depreciation:** Faster than average. **Insurance cost:** Higher than average. **Parts supply/cost:** Easy to find parts at reasonable prices. **Annual maintenance cost:** Average. **Warranty:** Bumper-to-bumper 3 years/60,000 km; rust perforation 6 years/160,000 km. **Supplementary warranty:** A good idea. **Highway/city fuel economy:** 7.5–11.1L/100 km with the 2.4L and automatic 4-speed, and 7.8–11.8L/100 km with the 3.4L.

Quality/Reliability/Safety

Pro: Quality control: The 4-speed automatic and 5-speed manual have had few major mechanical problems. **Warranty performance:** Average. Rear cornering lights shine at a 45 degree angle and make backing up both easier and safer.

Con: Reliability: The Getrag manual transmission and Quad 4 engine have proven to be unreliable in the past, and parts are often in short supply. **Owner-reported problems:** Powertrain malfunctions, including sudden transmission failure and poor shifting; vehicle runs hot; premature brake pad and rotor wear; electrical problems; suspension squeaks; and substandard body assembly producing squeaks and rattles, water leaks, and poor paint adhesion. Rear visibility obstructed by spoiler. **Service bulletin problems:** *Grand Am and Alero:* No starts or hard starts; rough idle or Check Engine light comes on; engine connecting rod bearings may fail if a low-mileage engine is run at high rpms; automatic transmission may not shift into third or fourth gear; creaks and squeaks heard from the rear when passing over rough pavement; and wet front or rear carpets. *Alero:* Check Engine and generator lights come on; engine cranks slowly and no-starts. **NHTSA safety complaints/safety:** *Grand Am:* Transmission suddenly failed while cruising at speeds over 100 km/h; chronic stalling; vehicle continued accelerating after passing another car on the highway; airbags failed to deploy; inadvertent airbag deployment; inadequate headlight illumination; vehicle pulls to one side when accelerating; power steering fluid leakage; steering shudders upon braking; faulty power steering pump; excessive steering vibration when accelerating; ABS light comes on, followed by brake failure; brake pedal set too low; premature wearout of the front and rear brake pads and rotors; front brake pads wear out every 5,000 km; shoulder belts twist in their housing; power door locks lock on their own; headlights blink on and off, and theft alarm sounds for no reason; middle rear lap seatbelt is too short to secure a child safety seat and GM says an extension isn't available; head restraints and optional rear spoiler blocks rear vision; side door glass shattered behind mirror for no reason; slight front impact causes the battery tray to either break off, or results in the battery sliding off the tray. *Alero:* Engine compartment fire; right front wheel separated because the lug nuts and bolts sheared off; tapped brakes to turn cruise control off and vehicle accelerated; rear main oil seal leak blew oil onto exhaust pipe; water leakage onto the back of the instrument panel causes the instruments and gauges to malfunction; other electrical shorts cause instrument panel gauges and controls to fail; windshield water leaks cause electrical shorts; hard to find horn "sweet spot" in an emergency; side mirror spring mounts break when passing over unpaved roads; seat latch doesn't lock immediately when moved.

Road Performance

Pro: Emergency handling: Better than average. **Steering:** Steering is predictably responsive, less so with the Alero. **Acceleration/torque:** Fair acceleration (0–100 km/h: 9.9 sec.) with the 4-cylinder engine. V6 acceleration is impressive, delivering power smoothly and quietly. **Transmission:** Well suited to the V6. **Routine handling:** Better than average on the highway. Suspension improvements have made for better handling and have smoothed out the ride considerably. **Braking:** Reasonably good (100–0 km/h: 121 ft.) with some brake fade after repeated stops.

Con: Transmission: There's been a lot of hype about the Quad 4 engine, but little of this translates into benefits for the average driver. Multi-valve motors produce more power than a standard engine, but always at higher rpms and with a fuel penalty. The Quad 4 is rougher than most multi-valve engines when revved to cruising speed, and so does little to encourage drivers to get the maximum power from it. The Quad 4 powerplant also accentuates the harsh shifting of the 4-speed automatic; it's overeager to enter lockup mode in high gear, causing sluggish response in city driving. Impact of rough roads isn't completely absorbed by the suspension.

Comfort/Convenience

Pro: Standard equipment: Well appointed. Nice, heavily padded interior. Good interior and exterior styling. **Driving position:** Comfortable cockpit with an easily adjusted, supportive driver's seat and plenty of head and leg room for two. Alero's bucket seats are particularly comfortable.

Climate control: Efficient heating/defrosting and ventilation system. Rear windows roll all the way down. **Interior space/comfort F/R:** Sedan has better-than-average room in front and back. Standard split folding rear seats are quite useful. **Trunk/liftover:** Standard split folding rear seatbacks expand cargo space.

Con: Alero's dash vents are rather crude and the seat fabric feels cheap. **Controls and displays:** Not user-friendly. **Entry/exit:** The doors on two-door models are heavy and awkward to open in tight spaces. The front seatbelts interfere with getting in and out. **Interior space/comfort F/R:** *Coupe:* Back seat will only hold two adults comfortably, due to its narrower seats and reduced head room. Rear visibility is also somewhat limited. **Cargo space:** Limited storage space. **Trunk/liftover:** High sill and small opening makes loading difficult. **Quietness:** Excessive road noise, interior creaks and rattles, and annoying exhaust drone.

COST				
List Price (negotiable)	**Residual Values (months)**			
	24	**36**	**48**	**60**
Grand Am 2d: $20,725 (16%)	$15,000	$12,000	$9,500	$7,500
Alero: $21,325 (17%)	$16,000	$13,000	$10,500	$8,500
GLS: $27,335 (18%)	$19,000	$16,000	$13,500	$11,000

TECHNICAL DATA

Powertrain (front-drive)
Engines: 2.4L 4-cyl. (150 hp)
• 3.4L V6 (170 hp)
Transmissions: 5-speed man.
• 4-speed auto.
Dimension/Capacity
Passengers: 2/3
Height/length/width:
55.1/186.3/70.4 in.

Head room F/R: 37.8/36.5 in.
Leg room F/R: 43.1/33.9 in.
Wheelbase: 107 in.
Turning circle: 39 ft.
Cargo volume: 14/15 cu. ft.
Tow limit: 1,000 lb.
Fuel tank: 47L/reg.
Weight: 3,066 lb.

SAFETY FEATURES/CRASHWORTHINESS

	Std.	Opt.
Anti-lock brakes (4W)	■	❑
Seatbelt pretensioners	—	—
Side airbags	—	—
Traction control	■	❑
Head restraints F/R	**	**
Visibility F/R	*****	***
Coupe	*****	*
Crash protection (front) D/P	****	****
Crash protection (side) D/P	***	***
Crash protection (off-set)	*	

Malibu

Malibu

RATING: Average. **Strong points:** Good V6 powertrain setup. Well appointed, comfortable ride, easy handling, and plenty of passenger and luggage space. **Weak points:** Mediocre high-speed handling; no traction control; mediocre seats; stiff suspension may be too firm for some; excessive interior noise premature wearout of Firestone affinity tires; and uneven quality control.

NEW FOR 2001: A slight restyling.

OVERVIEW: The Malibu is a small front-drive, mid-sized sedan that replaces the long-discontinued Celebrity and Ciera. It's a conventionally styled (boring?) car that uses a rigid body structure to cut down on noise and improve handling. Standard mechanical components include a standard 3.1L V6 coupled to a 4-speed, floor-mounted automatic transmission. The ignition switch is mounted on the dash (a throwback to your granddad's Oldsmobile).

Cost analysis/best alternatives: Go for the 2001 model to avoid getting stung by last year's quality glitches. Other cars worth considering: Toyota Camry, Honda Accord, or Mazda 626. **Options:** The LS package and premium tires. **Rebates:** $1,000–$2,000 rebates on unsold year 2000 models and similar rebates on the 2001 models by mid-2001. **Delivery/PDI:** $750. **Depreciation:** Average. **Insurance cost:** Higher than average. **Parts supply/cost:** Malibu uses GM generic parts that are found everywhere and are reasonably priced. **Annual maintenance cost:** Average. **Warranty:** Bumper-to-bumper 3 years/60,000 km; rust perforation 6 years/160,000 km. **Supplementary warranty:** A wise investment. **Highway/city fuel economy:** 7.4–11.8L/100 km with the 3.1L.

Quality/Reliability/Safety

Pro: Quality control: Average quality control. **Reliability:** Nothing of a serious nature, although chronic brake rotor warpage is both annoying and time-consuming, as the following email from *Lemon-Aid* reader Ron Phillips relates:

> ...I have a '99 Chevrolet Malibu and I am having nothing but problems with the brakes. The car in general is a very good car but today is the second time that I have brought my vehicle in for new or machined rotors. The service advisor at the dealership that I took it to said that this is a problem for all '99 Chevy Malibu's as the rotors are made from a lighter material and they warp instantly. If I hit the brakes on the highway (at higher speeds) the whole vehicle shakes very erratically and it becomes a safety concern. It does shake as well in the city but not nearly as bad. I have discussed these concerns with GM Canada via email and they said it is up to the service managers of the specific dealerships to advise them on a defect on a particular vehicle. Could you please publish my concerns in an upcoming issue...

Warranty performance: Nothing negative, yet. **Safety:** The automatic headlight control that turns on at dusk is a useful feature.

Con: Owner-reported problems: Some hard starting and stalling; malfunctioning theft lock prevents the car from starting; leaking steering rack; glove box door won't close; faulty window control pod; and sticking power windows. **Service bulletin problems:** Automatic transmission may not shift into third or fourth gear; cold air enters vehicle from around the door handles; and rear-end squeal/creak when passing over uneven pavement. **NHTSA safety complaints:** Sudden brake loss; premature warpage of the brake rotors; loose tie rod nut caused steering loss; sudden steering lockup; chronic steering shimmy; frequent stalling for unexplained reasons; stalling caused by fuel line leak; hit a small bump in road and vehicle stalled with a complete loss of electrical power; tire blew and cruise control wouldn't disengage; fuel tank filler tube is loosely connected to the frame; excessive vibration at any speed; engine rattle caused by defective piston; transmission doesn't lock when the key is in the accessory position; very loose steering; faulty high-beam switch; original equipment tires don't have gripping power; outside mirrors are too small.

Road Performance

Pro: Emergency handling: Acceptable. Cornering under speed is well controlled, with little front-end plowing or excessive body roll. **Steering:** Acceptable for everyday driving. **Acceleration/torque:** Brisk acceleration and plenty of low-end torque with the V6 engine (0–100 km/h:

8.8 sec.); the V6 has the same horsepower as the '99's 4-banger, but delivers it in a smoother, quieter manner. **Transmission:** Smooth and predictable shifting, most of the time. **Routine handling:** Better than average, thanks to an independent suspension that doesn't sacrifice solid handling for passenger comfort.

Con: Hard cornering produces considerable body lean and numb steering. Push-rod V6 is a bit rougher than the overhead-cam V6 used by the competition. Downshifting is a bit slow when passing other vehicles. **Braking:** Antiquated rear drum brakes provide mediocre braking with standard ABS (100–0 km/h: 128 ft.). Some brake fade after repeated stops.

Comfort/Convenience

Pro: Standard equipment: Well appointed for the price, but the better-equipped LS version has more of what you need. **Driving position:** Seating is adequate, though a bit low. Large side mirrors help provide good all-around visibility. **Controls and displays:** Very well thought out instrumentation with gauges that are easy to access and read. For example, the ignition switch is located on the instrument panel, a radical departure for GM. **Climate control:** Excellent ventilation system and first-class controls that are easy to use. AC vents are mounted high enough to direct cool air at your face. **Entry/exit:** Easy access to both front and rear interiors. **Interior space/comfort F/R:** More head and leg room than the Chrysler Stratus. Unusually spacious rear seat area can accommodate three adults. **Cargo space:** Lots of interior storage space. **Trunk/liftover:** Plenty of trunk space that can be expanded through the split folding rear seatbacks. Low liftover and practical cargo net.

Con: Bland styling. Seats could use better side bolstering and lumbar support. Some gauges are hard to read in direct sunlight. Outside mirrors are too small. Heating to the floor area is a bit slow. Door checks may not hold the doors open when parked facing uphill. Rear bench seat is hard and flat. Rear seatbacks don't lie flat when folded. Trunk hinges intrude into the trunk area, possibly damaging contents in a stuffed trunk. Parcel shelf compromises rear visibility. The 2.4L engine's noise intrudes into the passenger compartment. **Quietness:** Excessive engine, tire, and suspension noise.

COST				
List Price (negotiable)	**Residual Values (months)**			
	24	**36**	**48**	**60**
Malibu Sedan: $22,495 (18%)	$16,000	$14,000	$12,000	$10,000

TECHNICAL DATA

Powertrain (front-drive)
Engine: 3.1L V6 (170 hp)
Transmission: 4-speed auto.
Dimension/Capacity
Passengers: 2/3
Height/length/width:
56.7/190.4/69.4 in.

Head room F/R: 39.4/37.6 in.
Leg room F/R: 41.9/38 in.
Wheelbase: 107 in.
Turning circle: 40 ft.
Cargo volume: 16 cu. ft.
Tow limit: 1,000 lb.
Fuel tank: 58L/reg.
Weight: 3,051 lb.

SAFETY FEATURES/CRASHWORTHINESS

	Std.	Opt.
Anti-lock brakes	■	❑
Seatbelt pretensioners	—	—
Side airbags	—	—
Traction control	—	—
Head restraints F/R	**	*
Visibility F/R	*****	*****
Crash protection (front) D/P	****	****
Crash protection (side) D/P	**	****
Crash protection (off-set)	***	

Century, Grand Prix, Impala, Intrigue, Monte Carlo, Regal

Monte Carlo

RATING: *Century, Grand Prix, Impala, Monte Carlo* and *Regal:* Average buys; *Intrigue:* Above Average buy. **Strong points:** Nice array of standard features on the Impala and Intrigue, good choice of powertrains, comfortable ride, easily accessed, and roomy interior. **Weak points:** Excessive engine noise at high speeds, rear seating uncomfortable for three, bland styling, and obstructed rear visibility due to high-tail rear end.

NEW FOR 2001: The Intrigue and Grand Prix will be slightly restyled. The Regal Olympic and Joseph Abboud editions debut.

OVERVIEW: These front-drive, mid-sized cars share the same platform and mostly exhibit the same performance characteristics with similar powertrains—except for the Intrigue's 3.5L twin-cam V6, which is in a class by itself. *Century:* This is a bland, unexciting sedan, loaded with convenience features and powered by a 3.1L V6. One gets the impression the Century targets young retirees who prefer to be driven, rather than drive. *Grand Prix:* The new sport sedan, it comes as a two- or four-door model and is powered by the Chevy Lumina's 3.1L V6 and an optional 3.8L V6—or supercharged variation—borrowed from the Pontiac Bonneville. Larger brakes, upgraded power steering, and a 2-inch longer body, a 3-inch longer wheelbase, and a 2-inch wider track are also featured. *Impala and Monte Carlo:* Positioned to replace the slightly smaller Lumina sedan (sold only to fleet buyers this year), Impala is a more upscale, nicely appointed sedan that seats six and comes equipped with a base 3.4L and an optional 3.8L engine. Surprisingly, ABS is optional on the base model, yet the base Cavalier (a much cheaper car) has it as a standard feature. The Monte Carlo is a mid-sized sport coupe that incorporates more creases in its styling, along with round taillights, a longer wheelbase, and shorter length. Four-wheel ABS is standard, along with a host of other features. Only bucket seats are offered (five-passenger limit) and side airbags aren't available. *Intrigue:* Oldsmobile's near-luxury-class sedan is a much better performer than any of the others. It's got plenty of interior room, a competent base 3.8L V6, and a more powerful optional 3.5L 215-hp 24-valve V6, as well as knockout styling. It garners high marks for handling and ride comfort, exceptional braking with the AutoBahn package, and a superb suspension that provides a firm, though not unpleasant, ride. *Regal:* GM says the Regal is designed to appeal to younger, more sport-oriented buyers who will appreciate the car's high-performance add-ons. Buick has enlisted the aid of special edition versions to appeal to a younger crowd.

Cost analysis/best alternatives: Get discounted 2000 models, since this year's restyling efforts aren't worth a higher price. There are plenty of more reliable, better-performing vehicles available from the competition. Consider the Acura Integra, Honda Accord, Mazda 626, Nissan Altima and Maxima, and Toyota Camry and Avalon. Intrigue shoppers should also look at the redesigned BMW 3-series. **Options:** The rear-mounted child safety seat. The Intrigue's AutoBahn package with larger brake rotors and better-performing tires, or the GL version, both of which offer lots of useful features for only $2,000 more. Stay away from the Impala's rear spoiler; it obstructs rear visibility and is of doubtful utility. **Rebates:** $2,000 on all year 2000 models. Expect $1,000 customer rebates in the year 2001 on this year's models. **Delivery/PDI:** $800. **Depreciation:** Average. **Insurance cost:** Higher than average. **Parts supply/cost:** Moderately priced parts that aren't hard to find. **Annual maintenance cost:** Higher than average. Most non-emissions servicing can be performed by independent garages. **Warranty:** Bumper-to-bumper 3 years/60,000 km; rust perforation 6 years/160,000 km. **Supplementary warranty:** Essential, especially after the third year of ownership. **Highway/city fuel economy:** 7.4–11.8L/100 km with the 3.1L for the base sedan; 7.2–12L/100 km with the 3.4L; 8–12.7L/100 km with the 3.5L; 7.6–12.3L/100 km with the 3.8L.

Quality/Reliability/Safety

Pro: Warranty performance: Average; above average for the Intrigue. Apparently, GM wants to keep the Intrigue's image "clean," since it counts on the model to draw in a younger crowd. Once the base warranty is over, though, owners will be on their own with GM's less-than-generous assistance. **Safety:** Standard tire-inflation monitor is a good idea.

Con: Quality control: Below average for powertrain and body construction, which puts it on par with Chrysler and Ford. Go to *www.execpc.com/~thor101/impala/* for details as to the kinds of problems you'll likely encounter with your Impala. **Reliability:** The 3.1L V6 engine has had more than its share of fuel system and engine computer module problems, and the 3.4L engines found in the Impala and Monte Carlo this year have yet to prove themselves. **Owner-reported problems:** Electrical system problems are common on cars loaded with power accessories. The front brakes wear out early and the discs warp far too easily. Shock absorbers and MacPherson struts wear out or leak prematurely. The power rack-and-pinion steering system degenerates quickly after three years and is characterized by chronic leaking. Poor body fit, particularly around the doors, leads to excessive wind noise and water leaks into the interior. Door locks freeze up easily. **Service bulletin problems:** *All models:* Poor AC performance; cupholder separates from the armrest; complaints that the driver and passenger seatbelts are uncomfortable; power windows chatter or squeal when activated; creak-type noise from door glass when driving over bumpy roads. *Regal:* Harsh upshifts; harsh garage shifts; soft shifts; shudders on hard acceleration; erratic shifting; windshield wiper fluid may leak from the under-hood washer reservoir area; voluntary emission campaign requires that the supercharged engine's spark plug be changed. *Grand Prix:* Service Engine or generator light may come on for no reason; engine cranks slowly; car won't start, or may stall suddenly. *Intrigue:* ABS and Service Engine light come on for no reason. **NHTSA safety complaints:** (Keep in mind that the safety problems noted below may apply to any one of the following practically identical cars.) *Impala:* Airbags failed to deploy; frequent complaints of dash area and engine compartment fire; front harness wires overheat; excessive current load from fuel pump may burn the ignition block wire terminal; inhalation injuries caused by the melting of the wiring harness plastic; electrically heated seat burned the driver's back; the connection which goes to the brake pedal piston collapsed, causing total brake failure; chronic stalling; engine sputters, hesitates; Service Engine and battery lights come on (dealer unable to correct problem); when traction control is activated, wheel slip computer is also activated and security system kills the engine and prevents it from being restarted; driver's side wheel fell off; vehicle jerks when passing over rough pavement; car rolls back at a stop; excessive steering wheel vibration; excessive front end vibration; fuel sloshes in tank when accelerating or stopping; brake rotors had to be replaced at 7,500 km; aluminum subframe "flexes," causing a clicking sound when turning; popping sound upon stopping, starting, and turning; transmission line broke and poured fluid all over the road; transmission centre support bearing was put in backwards, causing the transmission to fail; left and right control arm, lower control arm, balljoint, and steering failure; AC R-134A refrigerant leaks into car interior; driver's seat adjuster failed, causing seat to suddenly move backwards, causing loss of vehicle control; the rubber seal on the windows, which sometimes acts as a squeegee when lowering and raising the window, has been removed with a new design, which allows road salt to enter and short-circuit the window mechanism; front driver's side windshield wiper doesn't clean the windshield completely; poor design allows dirty windshield washer fluid to be deflected off the windshield and cut the view out of the side windows; a hazy film collects on the inside of all the windows (dealer says it's normal). *Monte Carlo:* Engine cradle mounting welds came apart from the steering gear, and driver's and passenger's seatbelts tighten up progressively to the point where they are extremely uncomfortable. *Century:* Sudden brake failure; car rolls backward when stopped in gear on an incline; constant reflection of curved dashboard in windshield with or without sunlight; passenger-side windshield wiper channels water directly in the line of vision on the upstroke, temporarily blocking driver's vision; front seat head restraints won't stay in raised position; vent behind shifter handle becomes very hot when heater is on; gear shift lever continually sticks; water leaks onto the interior carpet; air dam deflector on the front of the vehicle is mounted too low and hits the road on dips; defective radio volume control; horn is hard to find. *Grand Prix:* Chronic stalling; false airbag deployment; airbag failed to deploy; seatbacks designed with an inertia lock that only locks when braking aggressively, allowing unoccupied seatback to flop around and distract driver; ABS failure; prematurely worn rear brake pads create excessive metal-to-metal grinding noise; wheel lug nuts and bolts sheared off causing wheel to fall off; windshield wipers malfunction; windshield wiper system freezes up in cold weather; lap/shoulder seatbelts become twisted when reaching up and pulling down from the guide loop; cruise control suddenly engaged on its own and wouldn't release; sometimes cruise control causes the vehicle to suddenly accelerate and then slow down; right door speaker and dash rattling. *Intrigue:* Fuel leak caused by loose fuel line; cruise control doesn't maintain speeds when going up or down hill; windows fog easily. *Regal:* Vehicle was on a medium incline, with the ignition on and the shift indicator in the Drive position, when driver took foot off the brake pedal and the vehicle rolled backward; excessive shaking on smooth roads; audio speaker failure; loose power steering; passenger-side airbag cover came loose.

Road Performance

Pro: Emergency handling: Better than average, thanks to standard traction control. **Steering:** Precise and predictable. **Acceleration/torque:** The 3.1L and 3.4L V6 engines produce sufficient power for smooth acceleration and work well with the 4-speed automatic transmission (0–100 km/h: 10.5 sec.), but could use more high-speed torque. For extended highway use, you'll find the 3.8L powerplant better suited to your needs. Intrigue buyers will want to get the 3.5L engine; it's generally smooth and quiet-running (except for some cycling), and has plenty of high-speed torque when you need it. **Transmission:** The automatic transmission is quiet and smooth under most conditions. **Routine handling:** Handling and ride are better than average due to recent suspension and steering refinements. **Braking:** Better than average.

Con: There's excessive engine noise intrusion into the interior. The 3.5L twin-cam V6 cruising at 100–110 km/h tends to cycle annoyingly. The automatic 4-speed transmission is sometimes slow to downshift.

Comfort/Convenience

Pro: Standard equipment: Reasonably well appointed, with such innovative features as automatic headlights that turn on at dusk and a system that prevents the doors from locking automatically if the key is in the ignition. Large side mirrors help to overcome the obstructed rear view. **Driving position:** The cockpit area is much more user-friendly this year; lots of room; good all-around visibility; optional power driver's seat is a boon for short drivers. A tilt steering wheel is standard. **Controls and displays:** Improved instrumentation and easy-to-read gauges and controls. **Climate control:** Excellent heating-defrosting-ventilation system that even includes a pollen filter. **Entry/exit:** Not difficult. **Interior space/comfort F/R:** Front bench seats accommodate two with plenty of head and leg room. Rear seats have enough space for three adults. Grand Prix seating is quite firm, but not uncomfortable. **Trunk/liftover:** Large trunk and a low liftover. **Quietness:** Fairly quiet, except for some engine noise.

Con: Luxury models use tacky imitation wood and cheap cloth covers. Flimsy cupholders. Climate controls are set too low, interfering with middle passenger's knees, and low dash vents can chill a driver's hands. The Grand Prix sport sedan's head room has been sacrificed to give the car a sleeker appearance. Seats are too soft and lack support on all models, with the exception of the Grand Prix. Insufficient rear leg room. **Cargo space:** Absence of truly functional interior storage areas. There are lots of little storage spaces, but they're generally small and narrow. **Trunk/liftover:** *Century:* Quite a stretch to get over the wide, bumper-level shelf. *Grand Prix:* High trunk sill and narrow opening make for difficult loading and unloading, and large deck-lid hinges reduce usable trunk space. Rear seatbacks don't fold down to increase trunk space.

COST

List Price (negotiable)	Residual Values (months)			
	24	36	48	60
Century: $25,200 (22%)	$16,000	$13,000	$11,000	$8,000
Grand Prix SE Sedan: $26,130 (22%)	$16,500	$13,500	$11,500	$8,500
Intrigue: $28,450 (23%)	$18,000	$15,000	$13,000	$10,500
Impala: $24,490 (21%)	$16,000	$13,000	$12,000	$9,000
Monte Carlo: $26,195 (22%)	$16,000	$13,000	$11,000	$8,000
Regal: $28,895 (22%)	$17,500	$14,500	$12,500	$9,500

TECHNICAL DATA

Powertrain (front-drive)
Engines: 3.1L V6 (170 hp)
• 3.4L V6 (180 hp)
• 3.8L V6 (200 hp)
• 3.5L V6 (215 hp)
• 3.8L V6 SC (240 hp)
Transmissions: 5-speed man.
• 4-speed auto.
Dimension/Capacity (Grand Prix)
Passengers: 2/3
Height/length/width:
54.7/196.5/72.7 in.
Head room F/R: 38.3/36.7 in.
Leg room F/R: 42.4/35.8 in.
Dimension/Capacity (Century)
Passengers: 3/3
Height/length/width:
56.6/194.6/72.7 in.
Head room F/R: 39.3/37.4 in.
Leg room F/R: 42.4/36.9 in.

Dimension/Capacity (Regal)
Passengers: 2/3
Height/length/width:
56.6/196.2/72.7 in.
Head room F/R: 39.3/37.4 in.
Leg room F/R: 42.4/36.9 in.
Dimension/Capacity (Intrigue)
Passengers: 2/3
Height/length/width:
56.6/195.9/73.6 in.
Head room F/R: 39.3/37.4 in.
Leg room F/R: 42.4/36.9 in.
Wheelbase: Grand Prix: 110.5 in.;
Century, Intrigue, and Regal: 109 in.
Turning circle: 40 ft.
Cargo volume: 16/17 cu. ft.
Tow limit: 1,000 lb.
Fuel tank: 62L/reg./prem.
Weight: approx. 3,400 lb.

SAFETY FEATURES/CRASHWORTHINESS

	Std.	Opt.
Anti-lock brakes (4W)	■	❑
Seatbelt pretensioners	—	—
Side airbags	❑	■
Traction control	■	❑

Head restraints F/R	*	*
Grand Prix	***	*
Visibility F/R	*****	***
Crash protection (front) D/P		
All excl. Grand Prix and Impala	****	***
Grand Prix	****	*****
Impala	*****	*****
Crash protection (side) D/P		
Century, Monte Carlo,		
and Regal	***	***
Impala	****	****
Intrigue	***	*
Crash protection (off-set)	***	

Aurora

Aurora

RATING: Average, during the first year of its redesign. **Strong points:** V8 provides impressive acceleration; plenty of passenger room; comfortable ride on smooth terrain; good steering and handling; and well-appointed interior. **Weak points:** Stiff, jostling suspension over rough pavement; uncomfortable rear seating; obstructed rear visibility; complicated radio and climate controls; poorly assembled body components; and traditional first-series redesign glitches.

NEW FOR 2001: Totally redesigned.

OVERVIEW: The Aurora is a five-passenger front-drive sports sedan that targets Lexus ES 300, Infiniti I30, Mazda Millenia, and Toyota Avalon. This year's model is a slightly downsized version of its former self. It uses the same platform as the Cadillac DeVille, Pontiac Bonneville, and Buick LeSabre and takes its 215-hp V6 engine from the Intrigue. A 250-hp 4.0L V8 Northstar engine—a smaller version of the Cadillac powerplant—is also available. The only transmission offered is a floor-mounted, 4-speed automatic—putting the Aurora at a disadvantage with its competitors who mostly offer 5-speeds. Standard features include dual airbags, four-wheel ABS, traction control, adjustable shoulder height manual seatbelts, cruise control, keyless remote entry and security system, and power-assisted everything.

Cost analysis/best alternatives: The 2001 Aurora is the better buy; last year's version isn't worth what discounts may be offered. Other cars worth considering are the Acura TL, Ford Crown Victoria and Mercury Marquis, Infiniti I30, Lexus ES 300, Lincoln Town Car, Mazda Millenia, Nissan Maxima, and Toyota Avalon. **Options:** The traction control and anti-skid system. Bucket seats provide more comfortable support. **Rebates:** Not likely until well into the new year, if then. **Delivery/PDI:** $895. **Depreciation:** Faster than average. **Insurance cost:** Higher than average. **Parts supply/cost:** Moderately priced parts that aren't hard to find. **Annual maintenance cost:** Above average. **Warranty:** Bumper-to-bumper 3 years/60,000 km; rust perforation 5 years/160,000 km. **Supplementary warranty:** A good buy. **Highway/city fuel economy:** 8.4–13.6L/100 km.

Quality/Reliability/Safety

Pro: Quality control: It's been spotty so far, but no worse than GM's other models. **Reliability:** Few major reliability problems reported, due to the short time this reworked version has been on the market. **Service bulletin problems:** N/A. **NHTSA safety complaints/safety:** N/A. Standard rear fog lamps.

Con: Warranty performance: Predicted to be below average during the Aurora's first year on the market. **Owner-reported problems:** The failure-prone front-drive (based on past complaints) competes poorly in a market that has more reliable powertrains. Exterior fit and finish just don't measure up to the competition; creaks, squeaks, and rattles are common.

Road Performance

Pro: Steering: Crisp and direct, with good road feel. **Acceleration/torque:** Impressive acceleration with both the base V6 and optional V8 engines, although the larger engine makes for easier merging with traffic and passing. **Transmission:** Smooth and quiet shifting. **Routine handling:** Better-than-average handling and ride quality. **Braking:** Excellent braking, although pedal effort is a bit high.

Con: Emergency handling: Some excessive body lean and jostling when pushed; not as nimble as the competition. Firm suspension may be uncomfortable for some. Brake pedal may be hard too modulate due to its firmness.

Comfort/Convenience

Pro: Standard equipment: Very well appointed. Impressive styling combined with a roomy interior. Well thought-out interior ergonomics. Plush interior includes comfortable front seats and generous amounts of head and leg room. **Driving position:** Excellent. **Controls and displays:** User-friendly, except for radio controls. **Climate control:** Efficient and quiet. **Interior space/comfort F/R:** Roomy interior provides generous room for five adults. Front seating is exceptionally comfortable, with just the right amount of thigh and lumbar support. **Cargo space:** Lots of storage areas that are easily accessed. **Trunk/liftover:** Large trunk also offers a large and low opening. **Quietness:** Excellent soundproofing keeps out engine, wind, and tire noise.

Con: Rear visibility is obstructed by the high tail and centre-mounted brakelight. Audio system and climate controls aren't easily adjusted. **Entry/exit:** Five-passenger seating can't compete with Avalon's six-passenger capacity, and the middle occupant won't be comfortable for long. Rear seat cushion is too small and not sufficiently padded.

COST				
List Price (firm)	**Residual Values (months)**			
	24	**36**	**48**	**60**
Aurora: $39,035 (25%)	$28,000	$24,000	$22,000	$19,000

TECHNICAL DATA

Powertrain (front-drive)
Engines: 3.5L V6 (212 hp)
• 4.0L V8 (250 hp)
Transmission: 4-speed auto.
Dimension/Capacity
Passengers: 2/3
Height/length/width:
56.7/199.3/72.9 in.

Head room F/R: 38.6/37.7 in.
Leg room F/R: 42.5/38 in.
Wheelbase: 112.2 in.
Turning circle: 43 ft.
Cargo volume: 14.9 cu. ft.
Tow limit: 3,000 lb.
Fuel tank: 76L/prem.
Weight: 3,627 lb.

SAFETY FEATURES/CRASHWORTHINESS

	Std.	Opt.
Anti-lock brakes (4W)	■	❑
Seatbelt pretensioners	■	❑
Side airbags	■	❑
Traction control	■	❑
Head restraints F/R	****	****
Visibility F/R	*****	*****
Crash protection (front) D/P	N/A	N/A
Crash protection (side) D/P	N/A	N/A
Crash protection (off-set)	*****	

Bonneville, LeSabre, Park Avenue, Ultra

Bonneville

RATING: Below Average. Rating has been downgraded due to the large number of safety-related failures. **Strong points:** *All models:* Great powertrain performance and comfortable ride. *Park Avenue:* Good handling, good passenger and cargo room. **Weak points:** *All models:* Fuel thirsty; a plethora of safety-related complaints, including airbag-induced injuries and chronic stalling; and poor quality mechanical and body components. *LeSabre:* Uncomfortable rear seating. *Bonneville:* Some torque-steer on the SSEi; braking sometimes hard to modulate; lots of wind and road noise; cramped seating for five; uncomfortable front seats (SSEi); rear bench seat lacks support; and the tacky-looking dash isn't well laid out. *Park Avenue:* Ponderous handling, caused partly by a mediocre suspension and over-assisted steering with the base model; obstructed rear visibility; Ultra requires premium fuel.

NEW FOR 2001: Nothing significant. GM may drop the Park Avenue in the near future.

OVERVIEW: Full-size luxury sedan aficionados love the flush glass, wraparound windshield and bumpers, and clean body lines that make for an aerodynamic, pleasing appearance. But these cars are more than a pretty package; they provide lots of room, luxury, style, and—dare I say—performance. Plenty of power is available with the 205-hp 3.8L V6 engine and the 240-hp supercharged version of the same powerplant. It does a 0–100 km/h time in under 9 seconds (an eternity for a Miata, but impressive considering the heft of these vehicles), and improves low- and mid-range throttle response. Power is transmitted to the front wheels through an electronically controlled transmission that features "free-wheeling" clutches designed to eliminate abrupt gear changes. Although the Park Avenue is a bit larger and more expensive than the Bonneville and LeSabre, its mechanicals, performance, and overall reliability are quite similar to those of its smaller brethren.

Cost analysis/best alternatives: Get a discounted 2000 model. Other vehicles worth considering: the Ford Crown Victoria and Mercury Grand Marquis, Infiniti I30, Lexus ES 300, or Nissan Maxima. **Options:** StabiliTrak and the tire pressure monitor are also useful features. On the other hand, the moisture-sensing wipers and EyeCue windshield display are more of a gimmick than anything else. The Grand Touring suspension creates a jittery ride and compromises control. **Rebates:** $2,000 applicable to the base 2000 Park Avenue, Ultra, Bonneville, and LeSabre by mid-summer. **Delivery/PDI:** $900. **Depreciation:** Faster than average. **Insurance cost:** Higher than average. **Parts supply/cost:** Parts aren't hard to find, but they can be pricey (particularly the supercharged engine components). **Annual maintenance cost:** Higher than average. **Warranty:** Bumper-to-bumper 3 years/60,000 km; rust perforation 5 years/160,000 km. **Supplementary warranty:** It'll come in handy after the third year of use. **Highway/city fuel economy:** 7.8–12.4L/100 km; 7.7–13.2L/100 km with the High Output engine. Supercharged V6 sips fuel, unlike the V8-equipped competition.

Quality/Reliability/Safety

Pro: Quality control: Average. **Warranty performance:** Better than average. **Safety:** A personalized vehicle security system disables the starting and fuel systems if a non-matching key is used. Rear shoulder belts have a strap to pull the belt away from the neck of small passengers and children. Right-side mirror tilts down when Reverse is engaged (standard on the Ultra). Safety belts mount to the outboard front seats for better neck protection.

Con: Reliability: Mediocre. **Owner-reported problems:** Engine, transmission, brake, and electronic module malfunctions. Safety-related failures are disturbingly common. **Service bulletin problems:** *Bonneville* and *LeSabre:* Harsh, erratic shifting; generator whine, hum, moan, or vibration; steering vibration, shudder, or moan during parking manoeuvres; garage door opener has a limited range; wrong radio may have been installed in the LeSabre; security indicator may malfunction; manually adjusted front seat may take too much effort to adjust; door creaks when closing or when car passes over bumpy roads; door glass binds in the run channel; and excessive wind noise. *Park Avenue:* malfunctioning seat or seatback heating element; front seat rocking; harsh shifting; hard-to-move gearshift control lever; steering vibration, shudder, or moan during parking manoeuvres. **NHTSA safety complaints:** *Bonneville:* Battery located in the back of the rear seat has gone bad, causing sulfuric acid fumes to escape into the passenger's compartment, making passengers ill; weak spring design allowed trunk lid to fall on person's head, causing injury; automatic trunk lid flies up and then comes down on customer's head. *LeSabre:* Under-hood fire erupted as driver was parking car; when the fuel tank is full, fuel leaks from the top; false airbag deployment injured driver; airbag deployed when key was inserted into the ignition; airbag failed to deploy in an accident;

sudden, unintended acceleration; many complaints of sudden stalling while driving on the highway; while driving on the highway, vehicle stalled due to excessive leaking in the fuel lines; cruise control cable disconnects from cruise control module, jamming the accelerator cable to full throttle; accelerator cable popped out of its bracket, causing vehicle to go to full throttle; brake pedal went all the way to the floor due to missing brake shaft retainer clip; when applying brakes, pedal becomes very hard and results in extended stopping distance; sudden steering loss; excessive highway wander; seatbelt crosses at driver's neck; hard-to-read speedometer; difficult to see dashboard controls due to dash-top design; a reflection in the windshield coming from the dashboard obstructs view; ABS and service light come on for no reason; engine head gasket failure; intermittent windshield wiper failure; horn is hard to operate, unless driver balled her hand into a fist and pounded on it; water leaks into interior through the dash; cupholders will hold nothing; a cup of hot coffee could result in severe injuries; headlight design creates a shadow, impeding visibility; windshield design and colour of the dashboard creates annoying reflection, making it hard to see through the windshield. *Park Avenue:* Airbags failed to deploy; horn is hard to activate; poor middle seat design makes the seat off-line and puts the armrest too far rearward, providing no support to the occupant; front lap seatbelts are too short in length. Dealer gives extension but makes owner sign a waiver absolving GM and dealer of all liability.

Road Performance

Pro: Acceleration/torque: The 3.8L V6 engine is competent, quiet, and smooth running, with lots of low-end torque. Impressively fast with the supercharged engine (0–100 km/h: 8 sec.). **Transmission:** The F31 electronic 4-speed transmission works imperceptibly. Cruise control is much smoother without all those annoying downshifts we've learned to hate in GM cars. **Routine handling:** Acceptably predictable, though quite slow with variable-assist power steering and shocks that are a bit firmer than usual. Body roll has been reduced, thanks to the re-tuned suspension. With its stiffer suspension, the Ultra performs well on winding roads, while the softly sprung Park Avenue is best for city use. **Emergency handling:** Fairly quick and sure footed. **Braking:** Good braking with or without ABS (100–0 km/h: 135 ft.).

Con: Acceleration/torque: Acceleration isn't breathtaking with the base 3.8L engine; at higher revs, torque falls off quickly. **Steering:** Power steering is a bit vague at highway speeds. Panic braking causes considerable nosediving that compromises handling.

Comfort/Convenience

Pro: The entire body has a more solid feel than what one normally finds with GM. **Standard equipment:** Very well equipped, with many performance and convenience features included as standard equipment. **Controls and displays:** Complete and easy-to-read instruments and gauges, except for the Bonneville. **Climate control:** Much improved interior ventilation and AC performance. **Entry/exit:** No problem. **Interior space/comfort F/R:** Exceptionally spacious and comfortable front seating. **Cargo space:** Plenty of storage areas that are easily accessible. **Trunk/liftover:** Huge trunk has a low liftover.

Con: Driving position: Driver seat lacks lateral support. Wide rear pillars block visibility, but large side mirrors compensate. Rear seating lacks adequate leg room and there's no rear centre armrest (LeSabre). **Quietness:** Excessive wind and road noise.

COST

List Price (negotiable)	Residual Values (months)			
	24	36	48	60
LeSabre: $32,120 (22%)	$27,000	$23,000	$19,000	$16,000
Bonneville: $32,065 (22%)	$27,000	$23,000	$19,000	$16,000
Park Avenue: $43,000 (23%)	$35,000	$31,000	$27,000	$22,000
Park Avenue Ultra:				
$48,520 (23%)	$38,000	$34,000	$30,000	$25,000

TECHNICAL DATA

Powertrain (front-drive)
Engines: 3.8L V6 (205 hp)
• 3.8L V6 (240 hp)
Transmission: 4-speed auto.
Dimension/Capacity
Passengers: 3/3
Height/length/width:
57/200/73.5 in.

Head room F/R: 38.8/37.8 in.
Leg room F/R: 42.4/39.9 in.
Wheelbase: 112.2. in.
Turning circle: 43 ft.
Cargo volume: 18 cu. ft.
Tow limit: 3,000 lb.
Fuel tank: 68L/reg./prem.
Weight: 3,567 lb.

SAFETY FEATURES/CRASHWORTHINESS

	Std.	Opt.
Anti-lock brakes	■	❑
Seatbelt pretensioners	—	—
Side airbags	■	❑
Traction control	■	❑
Head restraints F/R	*	*
LeSabre	****	****
Park Avenue	*	*
Visibility F/R	*****	***
Crash protection (front) D/P	*****	*****
Crash protection (side) D/P	****	****
Crash protection (off-set)	*****	

Cadillac Catera

Catera

RATING: Average. If Cadillac is to once again lure luxury buyers into the GM fold, the automaker has to copy its European competitors with something more substantial than a warmed-over Opel. **Strong points:** Well appointed; good brakes; a comfortable ride; and remarkably few reliability problems. **Weak points:** Merely adequate acceleration, mediocre handling, numb steering, ponderous cornering, limited rear visibility, bland styling, excessive interior noise, and an uncertain future.

NEW FOR 2001: Nothing significant; a new, U.S.-assembled model will debut for 2002.

OVERVIEW: Assembled in Germany and based on the Opel Omega, the rear-drive, mid-sized Catera comes with a 200-hp V6 engine, a 4-speed automatic transmission, 16-inch alloy wheels, four-wheel disc brakes, a limited-slip differential, traction control, and standard dual side airbags. The Sport package includes heated sports seats, a firmer suspension, a different grille, rear spoiler (are you kidding?), and alloy wheels.

Cost analysis/best alternatives: Look for a discounted year 2000 version, it's no different than the 2001 and will likely cost about 20 percent less. Other "driver's" cars worth considering: Acura TL, Audi A6, BMW 3-series, Infiniti I30, Lexus ES 300, and Mercedes Benz C-Class. **Options:** The Sport package option isn't worth the extra money. **Rebates:** $3,000 on 2000 models; 2001 models will likely get as much by mid-2001. **Delivery/PDI:** $900. **Depreciation:** Higher than average. **Insurance cost:** Also higher than average. **Parts supply/cost:** Parts are expensive and not easily found. **Annual maintenance cost:** Predicted to be higher than average after the fourth year—when the warranty expires. **Warranty:** Bumper-to-bumper 4 years/80,000 km; rust perforation 6 years/160,000 km. **Supplementary warranty:** A toss-up, mainly because long-term reliability has still to be determined. **Highway/city fuel economy:** 8.8–13.1L/100 km.

Quality/Reliability/Safety

Pro: Quality control: Average. Just a few computer module and body problems have been reported. **Reliability:** Reliability hasn't been a concern. **Warranty performance:** Unblemished. Now if only all of GM's customers were treated so well. **Service bulletin problems:** Nothing significant.

Con: GM dealers are notoriously bad when it comes to understanding and repairing European-transplanted cars (just ask any Saab owner), so expect to return often to correct the same problem. **Owner-reported problems:** Premature front brake wear, electrical glitches, and some body imperfections. **NHTSA safety complaints/safety:** When fueling up, gas spews out of the fuel filler pipe; front seatbelts malfunction; airbag failed to deploy; brakes squeal and pull vehicle sharply to the right when applied; rear visibility is obstructed by a narrow window and large rear head restraints.

Road Performance

Pro: Acceleration/torque: German-built V6 engine has plenty of low-end torque and accelerates smoothly (0–100 km/h: 8.9 sec.). **Transmission:** Smooth and quiet, and the automatic transmission allows for third-gear starts for maximum traction on snow or ice. **Braking:** Respectable for a vehicle this heavy (100–0 km/h: 129 ft.).

Con: Engine runs out of steam in higher gear ranges. **Emergency handling:** Surprisingly slow for a European-bred luxury car. **Steering:** Vague, with little road feel. **Transmission:** The transmission has to kick down two gears to achieve adequate highway passing power. **Routine handling:** Though the "European" ride is comfortable, it has its problems. When you pass over a large expansion joint, the floor pan vibrates annoyingly; drive over a bump when turning and the steering wheel kicks back in your hands.

Comfort/Convenience

Pro: Standard equipment: Loaded with convenience and performance features that would be optional on other cars. **Driving position:** Excellent, with good front and rear visibility. **Controls and displays:** Complete, logically presented, and easy to read. **Climate control:** Quite efficient and quiet. **Entry/exit:** Wide door openings make for easy front and rear access. **Interior space/comfort F/R:** Plush interior will seat four adults comfortably. **Cargo space:** Split-folding rear seatbacks increase storage capability. **Trunk/liftover:** The large trunk has a low liftover.

Con: The uninspired styling has Lumina written all over it. Unmarked power window switches are mounted on the centre console, where they are less convenient. **Quietness:** Lots of road and wind noise at highway speeds.

COST

List Price (very negotiable)	Residual Values (months)			
	24	**36**	**48**	**60**
Catera Sedan: $42,785 (30%)	$25,000	$21,000	$17,000	$13,000

TECHNICAL DATA

Powertrain (front-drive)
Engine: 3.0L V6 (200 hp)
Transmission: 4-speed auto.
Dimension/Capacity
Passengers: 2/3
Height/length/width:
57.4/193.8/70.3 in.

Head room F/R: 38.6/37.8 in.
Leg room F/R: 42/36.2 in.
Wheelbase: 107.4 in.
Turning circle: 37 ft.
Cargo volume: 14 cu. ft.
Tow limit: 2,000 lb.
Fuel tank: 68L/prem.
Weight: 3,800 lb.

SAFETY FEATURES/CRASHWORTHINESS

	Std.	Opt.
Anti-lock brakes	■	❑
Seatbelt pretensioners	■	❑
Side airbags	■	❑
Traction control	■	❑
Head restraints F/R	**	**
Visibility F/R	*****	*
Crash protection (front) D/P	N/A	N/A
Crash protection (side) D/P	N/A	N/A
Crash protection (off-set)	****	

DeVille DHS, DTS

DeVille

RATING: An Average buy. **Strong points:** Good handling, well appointed, spacious interior, easy rear access, quiet running, lots of passenger and cargo room, and gadgets galore. Well-matched engine and transmission, comfortable riding, better-than-average body assembly, and many standard safety features. **Weak points:** Many complex and fragile electronic systems that have yet to prove themselves. Poor fuel economy (premium fuel) and mediocre body assembly quality.

NEW FOR 2001: Nothing significant, except for a few additional bells and whistles.

OVERVIEW: The d'Elegance and Concours have been replaced by the DHS (DeVille High Luxury Sedan) and DTS (DeVille Touring Sedan), respectively. The shorter, narrower body uses a front-drive powertrain that includes a 275-horsepower and 300-horsepower V8 Northstar engine coupled to a 4-speed automatic transmission. Other standard features: front side airbags with a head/chest bag for the driver, Cadillac's StabiliTrak anti-skid system, Variable Road Sensing Suspension, traction control, four-wheel anti-lock brakes, steering wheel audio controls, and separate rear seat temperature controls. Cadillac has also added some rather innovative optional features: rear side torso airbags; a GPS navigation system with touch-screen display; GM's OnStar communication and assistance system; Night Vision—a device that uses infrared technology to detect road hazards beyond headlight range; and Ultrasonic Parking Assist, which uses sensors to warn you both audibly and visually that there's an object behind you when backing up.

Acceleration remains strong with the Northstar—it's still posting 0–100 km/h times under 7 seconds, with regular fuel. The ride is soft, comfortable, and quieter than before, thanks to Cadillac's new engine intake system, a tighter chassis, and additional sound-deadening measures. Handling is also much more responsive, particularly with the sportier DTS.

One would think this year's smaller DeVille would sacrifice passenger and storage space—however, this is clearly not the case. There is plenty of room for six passengers (the front middle passenger may be squeezed a bit), the rear bench seat provides loads of head and leg room, and is slightly raised to provide "theatre-like" seating for better visibility. Entry and exit is exceptionally easy due to the large doors that open wide. And as for storage space, the large trunk is easily accessible and opens at bumper level to make loading and unloading a breeze.

Cost analysis/best alternatives: Consider an identical year 2000 model only if the price is cut at least 20 percent. Other big, traditional luxury cars worth considering: the Ford Crown Victoria and Lincoln Town Car. **Options:** Stay away from the optional digital cluster; all you get are large digital read-outs and bar graphs. Buy the optional firmer suspension to counteract the base suspension's unsettling jiggle. It includes quicker-ratio steering, firmer shocks, thicker sway bars, and high-performance Goodyear tires. **Rebates:** Up to $3,000 for either year by next summer. **Delivery/PDI:** $900: **Depreciation:** Predicted to be faster than average. **Insurance cost:** Higher than average. **Parts supply/cost:** Except for engine components, most parts are easily found, though a bit expensive. **Annual maintenance cost:** Average during the first four years of ownership. Engine control and electrical systems are too complicated for most garages to service. **Warranty:** Bumper-to-bumper 4 years/80,000 km; rust perforation 6 years/160,000 km. **Supplementary warranty:** If you plan to keep the car after the fourth year, an extended warranty is essential. **Highway/city fuel economy:** 8.1–13.9L/100 km.

Quality/Reliability/Safety

Pro: **Warranty performance:** Better than average. This isn't surprising in view of the fact that these Cadillacs are barely halfway through their original base warranty.

Con: **Quality control:** Assembly quality isn't anywhere near luxury car standards, and paint is often poorly applied. Fragile body hardware. Large gaps between sheet metal panels and doors. **Reliability:** Long-term ownership of any of these models doesn't look promising. Reliability histories are replete with major faults, constant malfunctions, and mind-spinning depreciation. **Owner-reported problems:** The front brakes and shock absorbers wear out quickly. Serious fit and finish deficiencies. Intermittent stalling, rough idling, hesitation, and no-starts. **Service bulletin problems:** Customer service campaign to repair inoperative climate control/display modules; vehicle battery may continually run down. **NHTSA safety complaints/safety:** Vehicle suddenly stalls on the highway; vehicle stalled while driving uphill and then started rolling backwards; airbags failed to deploy in an accident; sudden brake failure; premature brake wear; traction control light comes on for no reason; ignition and electronic control module failures; seats protrude out too far in the back area, preventing passengers from sitting back—and making head restraints too far back; sudden headlight failure; horn location makes it very difficult to press it in an emergency; power door locks won't open with remote control device; windshield wipers won't activate unless turned on high; visor hides overhead traffic lights.

Road Performance

Pro: **Emergency handling:** Very good. Road Sensing suspension prevents excessive body lean when cornering at high speed. **Steering:** Speed-sensitive power steering is precise, with lots of road feel. **Acceleration/torque:** Plenty of power and torque with the base 275-hp 4.6L V8 engine, delivered with minimal harshness, vibration, and noise (0–100 km/h: 7.6 sec.). The 300-hp variant is even more impressive. **Transmission:** The 4-speed automatic with Overdrive is responsive, smooth, and quiet. **Routine handling:** Very good. Little body roll and crisp handling. **Braking:** Best in its class (100–0 km/h: 120 ft.).

Con: The 4.6L V8 overpowers the front-drive chassis. Some torque steer is evident. The 44-foot turning radius can make parking a chore.

Comfort/Convenience

Pro: Standard equipment: These cars come equipped with just about every imaginable electrical and power-assisted gadget, in addition to an ultra-plush interior. **Driving position:** Excellent. **Climate control:** Efficient and quiet, though the controls may be hard to reach (DTS). **Entry/exit:** Easy front and rear access. **Interior space/comfort F/R:** This is one huge front-drive Cadillac. Impressively large interior easily accommodates six adults in comfort. **Cargo space:** Lots of storage areas. **Trunk/liftover:** Fairly large trunk has a low liftover. **Quietness:** Very little engine or road noise seeps into the interior.

Con: Tacky imitation wood dash. All seats lack sufficient lumbar support and the front seats lack adequate thigh support. Rear visibility is blocked by wide rear roof pillars, and rear view mirrors are too small to be of much help. **Controls and displays:** Dashboard controls are too fussy for safe operation; the driver must often look away from the road to do such simple things as tune the radio or adjust the climate controls.

COST				
List Price (very negotiable)	**Residual Values (months)**			
	24	36	48	60
DeVille: $52,770 (23%)	$39,000	$28,000	$24,000	$21,000

TECHNICAL DATA	
Powertrain (front-drive)	Head room F/R: 39.1/38.3 in.
Engines: 4.6L V8 (275 hp)	Leg room F/R: 43.2/43.2 in.
• 4.6L V8 (300 hp)	Wheelbase: 115.3 in.
Transmission: 4-speed auto.	Turning circle: 43 ft.
Dimension/Capacity	Cargo volume: 19 cu. ft.
Passengers: 3/3	Tow limit: 3,000 lb.
Height/length/width:	Fuel tank: 76L/prem.
56.7/207/74 in.	Weight: 3,978 lb.

SAFETY FEATURES/CRASHWORTHINESS		
	Std.	**Opt.**
Anti-lock brakes	■	❑
Seatbelt pretensioners	■	❑
Side airbags	■	❑
Traction control	■	❑
Head restraints F/R	**	**
Visibility F/R	*****	**
Crash protection (front) D/P	***	****
Crash protection (side) D/P	****	****
Crash protection (off-set)	N/A	

Eldorado, Seville

Eldorado

RATING: *Eldorado:* Below Average; *Seville:* An Average buy. **Strong points:** *Eldorado:* Impressive engine performance, good handling, and a comfortable ride. *Seville:* Good powertrain match-up, excellent handling, taut ride, responsive steering, lots of storage space, and many standard safety features. **Weak points:** *Eldorado:* Limited rear visibility; rear seating for two; climate controls hard to find on the base model; sloppy body assembly; and poor fuel economy. *Seville:* Limited rear visibility and poor fuel economy.

NEW FOR 2001: The Seville gets an upgraded sport package and enhanced communications/entertainment features. Poor sales may force GM to drop the Eldorado after the 2003 model year.

OVERVIEW: The front-drive Eldorado shares the same chassis, engine and mechanical parts with the Seville. Both models are equipped with the Northstar V8 and use the same powertrain components. This provides a quiet, comfortable ride along with impressive acceleration.

Three years ago, the Seville was dramatically restyled and adopted GM's G-body, the stiffened chassis created for the Oldsmobile Aurora and Park Avenue. This gave it a wider stance, longer wheelbase, and a bit shorter length.

On the safety front, seatbelts are attached to the seat itself rather than the B-pillar, the tires and rear brakes have been upgraded, and seat-mounted side airbags are standard. Other standard safety features include: traction control, an anti-skid system, and anti-lock brakes.

Most Cadillacs offer some sort of performance package, usually in a special model, and the Eldorado and Seville are no different. Granted, this makes them more pleasant to drive, but these are usually only half-hearted, bolt-on efforts when compared to the sterling performance built into the Japanese and German imports.

Cost analysis/best alternatives: Get the year 2000 version of either model—if the price is cut by at least 20 percent. Other cars worth considering: a BMW 5-series, Infiniti Q45, Lexus LS 400, or Mercedes-Benz E-Class. **Options:** Be wary of the hard-riding ETC package; the base model's standard suspension gives a more comfortable ride and better low-speed performance. **Rebates:** *Eldorado:* $2,500–$3,500 on last year's models; $1,500 on the 2001 version by spring of next year. **Delivery/PDI:** $900. **Depreciation:** Faster than average. **Insurance cost:** Higher than average. **Parts supply/cost:** Parts aren't hard to find, and they're reasonably priced. **Annual maintenance cost:** Average. **Warranty:** Bumper-to-bumper 4 years/80,000 km; rust perforation 6 years/160,000 km. **Supplementary warranty:** Not necessary. **Highway/city fuel economy:** 8.3–13.9L/100 km.

Quality/Reliability/Safety

Pro: Warranty performance: Better than average. All Cadillacs come with GM's PASS KEY theft-deterrent system that shuts down the starter and fuel system if the right key isn't used. Plastic fuel tanks improve Seville and Eldorado crashworthiness.

Con: Quality control: Assembly quality isn't anywhere near luxury car standards, and paint is often poorly applied. **Reliability:** If you're planning to spend big bucks on either the Eldorado or the Seville, the likelihood of multiple reliability and body problems should make you think twice. Like most of GM's front-drives, these models have amassed a terrible reputation for being unreliable and expensive to maintain. In all, there is little to recommend them; there are cheaper vehicles that offer better performance and interior comfort. Nevertheless, if you have to choose one of the two, go for the Seville—it promises to be around longer than the Eldorado and should have its new platform bugs worked out over the last two years. **Owner-reported problems:** Intermittent stalling, rough idling, hesitation, and no-starts. The front brakes and shock absorbers wear out quickly. Serious fit and finish deficiencies, windshield and trunk leaks, and poorly fitting rear door seals. **Service bulletin problems:** *Eldorado:* Battery may run down and crankshaft position sensors may fail causing engine chuggle, stall, or possible hard starts or no-starts. *Seville:* A coolant leak at the engine heater inlet pipe connector/fitting; loss of driver seat, mirror, and steering column memory settings; and front or rear side door lower mouldings may fall off. **NHTSA safety complaints/safety:** *Eldorado:* Shoulder belt chafes the neck and is too tight; *Seville:* Excessive vibrations when turning; headlights on high beam cause a shadow at an approximately 60 degree angle from the hood, which causes poor visibility; water filters in through the headlight and taillight lens, causing poor illumination and electrical shorts.

Road Performance

Pro: Emergency handling: Average. Suspension improvements make for much less body roll, more responsive handling, and a softer ride. **Steering:** Steering is crisp and predictable. **Acceleration/torque:** Tire-burning acceleration (0–100 km/h: 7.1 sec.) with gobs of torque and minimal harshness, vibration, and noise. **Transmission:** The 4-speed automatic with Overdrive is responsive, despite occasional confusion about which gear it should be in. **Routine handling:** Better than average, although it floats a bit. Road Sensing suspension prevents excessive body lean in turns. **Braking:** Acceptable, though not impressive (100–0 km/h: 134 ft.).

Con: The 4.6L V8 engine overpowers the Eldorado's front-drive chassis. Some torque steer is evident on both vehicles, but it's particularly strong on the Seville STS. Seville's STS suspension is jarring when passing over bumps.

Comfort/Convenience

Pro: Standard equipment: These cars come equipped with just about every imaginable electrical and power-assisted gadget. **Controls and displays:** Most controls are within easy reach, and instruments aren't hard to decipher. **Interior space/comfort F/R:** Spacious seating due to the Seville's extra length and width, which gives rear passengers considerable room and easy access. The Eldorado also has a surprisingly spacious interior for a coupe, and it actually offers more head room in the rear than up front. **Cargo space:** Plenty of small storage areas that are easily accessed. **Trunk/liftover:** Large trunk with a low liftover. **Quietness:** Better than average. Almost no engine, road, or wind noise finds its way into the passenger compartment.

Con: Driving position: Though the Seville's driving position is quite good, both cars' wide rear pillars obstruct the driver's view to the right rear; front seats lack adequate thigh and lumbar support. **Climate control:** Efficient and quiet, but the climate control system has limited manual override and the steering wheel blocks the view of the controls. **Entry/exit:** *Eldorado:* Getting to the back seat requires very inelegant contortions. **Interior space/comfort F/R:** *Eldorado:* Rear seat won't accommodate three adults comfortably.

COST				
List Price (very negotiable)	**Residual Values (months)**			
	24	**36**	**48**	**60**
Eldorado: $58,225 (25%)	$42,000	$37,000	$32,000	$27,000
Seville SLS: $58,710 (25%)	$45,000	$39,000	$34,000	$29,000

TECHNICAL DATA

Powertrain (front-drive)
Engines: 4.6L V8 (275 hp)
• 4.6L V8 (300 hp)
Transmission: 4-speed auto. OD
Dimension/Capacity (Eldorado;
  Seville)
Passengers: 2/2; 2/3
Height/length/width:
  53.6/200.6/75.5 in.;
  55/201/75 in.

Head room F/R: 37.8/38.3 in.;
  38/38.3 in.
Leg room F/R: 38/38.3 in.;
  43/39.1 in.
Wheelbase: 108/112 in.
Turning circle: 42/44 ft.
Cargo volume: 15/16 cu. ft.
Tow limit: 3,000 lb.
Fuel tank: 76L/prem.
Weight: 3,900/4,010 lb.

SAFETY FEATURES/CRASHWORTHINESS

	Std.	Opt.
Anti-lock brakes	■	❑
Seatbelt pretensioners	—	—
Side airbags	■	❑
Traction control	■	❑
Head restraints F/R	*	*
Visibility F/R	*****	**
Crash protection (front) D/P	N/A	N/A
Crash protection (side) D/P	N/A	N/A
Crash protection (off-set)	****	

Camaro, Firebird

✓ BEST BUY

Camaro

RATING: Recommended. Firebird shares the Camaro's mechanical components, but is styled differently. Keep in mind these are not collectors' cars. If taken off the market, they won't increase in worth— before twenty years, at least. **Strong points:** High-performance muscle cars with above-average crash protection, a reasonably good reliability record, and high resale value. Good engine performance (Z28) and crisp handling. **Weak points:** Poor wet-weather traction without traction control; limited rear seat room; hard riding; difficult access; wide rear pillars impede rear visibility; and limited cargo space.

NEW FOR 2001: Nothing significant. The Camaro and Firebird will be dropped after the 2002 model year. GM says it has great plans for the St. Therese, Quebec plant, but I'm betting it's all bull. Predict the union will get wise halfway through this model year and make noises to keep the cars in Canada. Cars' future will hinge upon how much corporate welfare Quebec/Ottawa will dole out.

OVERVIEW: These sporty convertibles and coupes are almost identical in the features they offer and in their pricing. Both cars were extensively upgraded several years back, making them more powerful and aerodynamic with less spine-jarring performance.

Moving up the scale, overall performance improves considerably. The aluminum-block LS1 V8 engine gives these cars lots of sparkle and tire-spinning torque, but there's a fuel penalty to pay. A 4-speed automatic transmission is standard on the 5.7L-equipped Z28; other versions come with a standard 5-speed manual gearbox or an optional 6-speed. All cars can be ordered with lots of extra performance and luxury options, including a T-roof package guaranteed to include a full assortment of creaks and groans.

Cost analysis/best alternatives: Last year's models are the better buy if they're discounted by at least 15 percent. Convertibles and V8-equipped models are the best choice for retained value a few years hence. But you can do quite well with the base coupe equipped with the Performance Handling Package (about $800) and 235 tires. Base Camaros usually outperform V6-equipped Mustangs and they get better gas mileage as well. Other cars worth considering are the Ford Mustang, Honda Prelude, and Toyota Celica. **Options:** Go for GM's Performance Handling Package and 235/55 tires on 16-inch aluminum wheels. Most drivers will find the optional traction control system more useful than the limited-slip differential. **Rebates:** $1,000 rebate for year 2000 V6 models. **Delivery/PDI:** $800. **Depreciation:** Much slower than average. **Insurance cost:** Much higher than average. **Parts supply/cost:** No problem finding reasonably priced parts. **Annual maintenance cost:** Average. Servicing the fuel-injection system is an exercise in frustration and drives up maintenance costs. **Warranty:** Bumper-to-bumper 3 years/60,000 km; rust perforation 6 years/ 160,000 km. **Supplementary warranty:** Not needed. **Highway/city fuel economy:** 7.5–12.4L/100 km with the base 3.8L and automatic; 8.8–14.1L/100 km with the 5.7L and 4-speed automatic.

Quality/Reliability/Safety

Pro: Quality control: Above average. Plastic body panels are dent and rust resistant. **Warranty performance:** Above average. Most repairs are simple to perform and relatively inexpensive. **Service bulletin problems:** Nothing significant. Both cars are equipped with an impressively effective PASS KEY theft-deterrent system similar to the one used successfully in the Corvette. A resistor pellet in the ignition disables the starter and fuel system when the key code doesn't match the ignition lock.

Con: Reliability: Powertrain components frequently fail, causing extended periods of downtime while they're repaired. **Owner-reported problems:** The 5.7L V8 fuel and electrical systems have been troublesome in the past. Engine cooling and ignition systems are also bug-plagued. Poor air conditioner performance is a common complaint. The front brakes and MacPherson struts wear out quickly. Body problems include door rattles, poor fit and finish, misaligned doors and hatch, and a sticking hatch power release. **Service bulletin problems:** Rear brake noise, chirp, or groan; front brake squealing noise; anti-theft alarm may be too sensitive; squeak or chirp noise coming from the accessory drive serpentine belt; loose moulding at sides of windshield. **NHTSA safety complaints/safety:** *Camaro:* Airbags failed to deploy; driving down the highway, locked T-top flew off. *Firebird:* Airbags failed to deploy; headlights suddenly go out.

Road Performance

Pro: Steering: The rack-and-pinion steering is responsive and precise, with lots of road feedback. **Acceleration/torque:** Better-than-average acceleration with the base V6. Thrilling performance with either the base 305-hp V8 or the optional 320-hp 5.7L V8. Engines start well in cold weather and give ample pulling power. In fact, these cars have so much power in reserve that the automatic transmission doesn't compromise fuel economy or performance. **Routine handling:** Handling is best on the sports models, but even the base coupes perform respectably on the road, and the stiffer suspension makes for much tighter cornering. **Braking:** Much better than average, due primarily to the standard four-wheel anti-lock brakes (100–0 km/h: 117 ft.).

Con: Emergency handling: Without traction control the tires lose traction, and directional stability is compromised on wet pavement. Due to the rear axle suspension, the ride is constantly busy and particularly bouncy on poor roads. A stiffer suspension adds to this effect. These cars cry out for independent rear suspension. **Transmission:** The 6-speed manual transmission's clutch is heavy and gets tiring in city driving—the shifter takes getting used to, due to the pattern of the gear throws. Furthermore, it has a fuel-saving feature that automatically shifts to fourth from first gear if you're not driving aggressively enough.

The upgraded 4-speed automatic with Overdrive tends to shift late, putting extra strain on the engine.

Comfort/Convenience

Pro: Standard equipment: Even the base models come loaded with such useful features as anti-lock brakes. Most people find the Firebird's front seats more comfortable, but they're comfortable and supportive on both cars. **Controls and displays:** Dash is well laid-out with easy-to-read gauges and complete instrumentation. **Climate control:** Good fresh-air ventilation system. **Cargo space:** Quite limited, but folding back seat expands cargo storage capability. **Quietness:** A tighter chassis has eliminated most of the creaks and groans that have accompanied these cars for decades.

Con: Driving position: Driving position is too low for short drivers and rear visibility is compromised by wide roof pillars and the high rear end. The obtrusive centre console gets in the way when shifting. The front windshield has only a single de-mister vent. **Entry/exit:** Large doors make access into the interior a breeze, but they're a bit unwieldy, especially in tight parking spaces. Very difficult rear seat access. Door detents are too weak to keep the heavy doors open. **Interior space/comfort F/R:** Limited leg room for the front seat passenger. The rear buckets are just that—buckets. Consider this car a two-seater: the split rear seat is a joke (or a place to put people you don't like). **Cargo space:** The cargo area is small and awkwardly shaped. Large objects won't fit under the hatch. **Trunk/liftover:** Small trunk with a high liftover; the convertible has 40 percent less trunk space. Excessive tire, road, and engine noise.

COST				
List Price (very negotiable)	**Residual Values (months)**			
	24	**36**	**48**	**60**
Camaro: $26,065 (18%)	$18,000	$16,000	$13,000	$11,000
Firebird: $26,010 (19%)	$18,700	$16,700	$13,700	$12,000

TECHNICAL DATA	
Powertrain (front-drive)	Head room F/R: 37.2/35.3 in.
Engines: 3.8L V6 (200 hp)	Leg room F/R: 42.9/26.8 in.
• 5.7L V8 (305 hp)	Wheelbase: 101.1 in.
• 5.7L V8 (320 hp)	Turning circle: 42 ft.
Transmissions: 5-speed man.	Cargo volume: 13 cu. ft.
• 6-speed man.	Tow limit: 1,000 lb.
• 4-speed auto.	Fuel tank: 59L/reg.
Dimension/Capacity (Z28)	Weight: 3,600 lb.
Passengers: 2/2	
Height/length/width:	
52/193.2/74.1 in.	

SAFETY FEATURES/CRASHWORTHINESS

	Std.	Opt.
Anti-lock brakes	■	❏
Seatbelt pretensioners	—	—
Side airbags	—	—
Traction control	❏	■
Head restraints F/R	*	*
Visibility F/R	**	**
Crash protection (front) D/P	****	*****
Crash protection (side) D/P	***	****
Crash protection (off-set)	N/A	

Corvette

Corvette

RATING: Average. A brawny sport coupe that's slowly evolving into a more refined machine. **Strong points:** Powerful powertrain; easy handling; supple ride; attractively styled; user-friendly instruments and controls; and lots of standard convenience features. **Weak points:** Poorly performing "skip shift" manual gearbox; hard ride (Z51 or FE4 suspension); limited rear visibility; inadequate storage space; no spare tire (you get a can of tire sealant); poor quality fit and finish; large number of complaints of sudden steering wheel lockup; and no crashworthiness or insurance claim data.

NEW FOR 2001: All Corvettes get improved rear brake proportioning to prevent wheel lockup; enhanced side-slip angle control to prevent skidding; and better traction control. Base engine gets five more horses and additional torque, plus revamped electronic driver aids. Convertible tops get more material and better soundproofing. The renamed Z06 hardtop gets a high performance version of the 5.7L LS1 engine, upgraded brakes and suspension; revamped suspension; and larger tires.

OVERVIEW: Introduced in 1953 as a futuristic show car, and the first American car to use fuel-injection (in 1957), Chevrolet has sold more than a million Corvettes over the past 45 years, with an estimated 600,000 still on the roads. Its peak year was 1984, when over 84,000 coupes and convertibles were sold in North America, for about a third of today's price.

This year's Corvette returns with its 345-hp 5.7L LS1 powerplant, harnessed to either a 4-speed automatic or a 6-speed manual transmission. The engine is made from aluminum, and most transmission components have been shifted to the rear for better handling and increased passenger room.

The high-performance hardtop version returns along with additional options for the coupe and convertible that include a head-up display that projects instrumentation readouts onto the windshield; a power telescoping steering column; and an active handling system.

Cost analysis/best alternatives: Get the 2001 model for the upgrades. Keep in mind that premium fuel and astronomical insurance rates will further drive up your operating costs. Other sporty models worth considering are a "loaded to the gills" Chevy Camaro or Pontiac Firebird, a Dodge Viper, or a Porsche Boxster. **Options:** The 6-speed manual transmission and Z51 suspension, if you want the extra performance thrills, but you may find the suspension a bit harsh. Run-flat tires from Goodyear are an excellent investment. A dash indicator tells you when the tire is flat, even though you can continue to drive at a steady 90 km/h for 85 kilometres and the only noticeable change you'll feel will be a stiffer ride and less steering response. Forget about the head-up instrument display that projects speed and other data onto the windshield; it's annoyingly distracting. **Rebates:** The Corvette is so popular that GM doesn't have to offer rebates to boost sales, but dealers have a wide margin for discounting. **Delivery/PDI:** $820. **Depreciation:** A bit slower than average, but nowhere near the resale prices often quoted by sales people. For example, a 1993 ZR1 that originally sold for $78,898, is now worth barely $25,000. **Insurance cost:** Astronomical. **Parts supply/cost:** Good availability, but parts are pricey. **Annual maintenance cost:** Higher than average. **Warranty:** Bumper-to-bumper 3 years/60,000 km; rust perforation 6 years/160,000 km. **Supplementary warranty:** A smart idea. **Highway/city fuel economy:** 8.8–14.1L/100 km with the automatic.

Quality/Reliability/Safety

Pro: Warranty performance: Above average. GM has beefed up its warranty and given more authority to its dealers to resolve warranty disputes. Key-controlled lockout feature discourages joy riding by cutting engine power in half. Both Corvette versions are equipped with an impressively effective PASS KEY theft-deterrent system that uses a resistor pellet in the ignition to disable the starter and fuel system when the key code doesn't match the ignition lock. **Safety:** The tires have built-in low-pressure sensors that warn the driver by way of a light on the centre console. Run-flat tires eliminate the need for a spare tire.

Con: Quality control: Below average, especially body construction. **Reliability:** Spotty. The Corvette's sophisticated electronic and powertrain components have low tolerance for real-world conditions. Expect lots of visits to the dealer's repair bays. **Owner-reported problems:** Electronically controlled suspension systems have been glitch-plagued over the past several years. Squeaks and rattles due to the car's structural deficiencies. The car was built as a convertible, and therefore has too much body flex. Servicing the different sophisticated fuel-injection systems isn't easy, even (especially) for GM mechanics. **Service bulletin problems:** Failure of the engine serpentine belt and tensioner; inoperative window motor; growling-type noise from inside the door, as the glass is raised or lowered; tire pressure monitor shows incorrect pressure. **NHTSA safety complaints/safety:** Catalytic converter caught fire; when fuel tank is full, full leaks from the top of the vent; frequent reports of steering wheel lockup while driving on the highway (tow required); steering wheel locked up upon startup; steering wheel locked up in Reverse gear and was corrected only when transmission was put into Park and key re-inserted into the ignition; "SERVICE COLUMN LOCK" indication has been a common problem on 1997–2000 Corvettes (service manager); faulty fuel line clip may cause chronic stalling; fuel-injector failures cause vehicle to shudder and stall; engine dies while driving in the rain and brakes don't work; brakes drag and lock up; overheated rotors; car is nearly uncontrollable at time of brake lockup; early failure of the engine serpentine belt and tensioner; intermittent electrical problems degrade computer operation; if one wheel loses traction, the throttle closes, starving the engine; excessive cabin heat, even with AC set to MAX; driver's seat moves while driving; warped trunk door; seatbelts twist easily and tend to pull down uncomfortably against the shoulder; passenger seatbelt jams and won't extend or retract; smelly fumes enter the cabin, causing watery eyes and dizziness; the glass rear view window limits rear vision; front and rear wheel weights fly off the wheels.

Road Performance

Pro: Emergency handling: Very good, especially with this year's enhanced side-slip angle control to prevent skidding, and provide better traction control. No oversteer, wheel spinning, breakaway rear ends (are you listening, Ford?), or nasty surprises. **Steering:** Predictable, with good road feel. **Acceleration/torque:** Gobs of torque and horsepower with a top speed of 172 mph. Base engine is fast (0–100 km/h: 5 sec.), but this year's Z06 is faster (0–100 km/h: 4+ sec.). **Transmission:** The 6-speed gearbox performs well in all gear ranges and makes shifting smooth with short throws and easy entry into all gears. **Routine handling:** Above average. The car is so low that its front air dam scrapes over the smallest rise in the road, but still gives no-surprise handling and responds quickly to the throttle. The Bilstein FX-3 Selective Ride Control suspension can be pre-set to Touring, Sport, or Performance. Under acceleration, an electronic module automatically varies the suspension as the speed increases. **Braking:** Better than average. This year's upgraded ABS-vented disc brakes are easy to modulate and fade-free.

Con: Optional Z51 suspension's ride is too firm for some. This is one large and heavy sports car, whose weight compromises its fuel economy. True, the 6-speed manual does provides quicker acceleration and better fuel economy, but it's not particularly user-friendly.

Comfort/Convenience

Pro: Standard equipment: Attractively styled and full of power-assisted accessories. Defrosted rear glass window. Rust-resistant fibreglass body. Simple-to-operate convertible top. Innovative Passive Keyless Entry System. **Driving position:** Excellent, with everything within easy reach, good front and rear visibility, and a roomy cockpit for average-statured adults. **Controls and displays:** Complete instrumentation that's easy to decipher, and user-friendly controls. **Climate control:** Easy to adjust and quiet. **Interior space/comfort F/R:** Snug, but not uncomfortable for two adults.

Con: How chintzy can you get? GM gives you a can of tire sealant instead of a spare tire, or run-flat tires, provided by competitors. Steering wheel hides some controls. No room in the engine compartment for a sophisticated climate control system. Dual-zone climate control system takes time to warm up. Lowering the top takes patience: you release two latches, lift the plastic panel, and manually fold the top into its storage compartment. **Entry/exit:** Crouch and crawl; like getting into a space capsule. Tall drivers will find the interior confining. **Cargo space:** Insufficient storage space, which is no surprise to sports car enthusiasts. The lowered top cuts trunk space in half. **Trunk/liftover:** Skimpy storage space; high sill makes loading baggage difficult. **Quietness:** In addition to an irritating engine boom, there's excessive tire noise, wind whistling through the car's A- and C-pillars, and the all-too-familiar fibreglass body squeaks caused by excessive body flexing on rough surfaces.

COST				
List Price (negotiable)	**Residual Values (months)**			
	24	**36**	**48**	**60**
Corvette: $56,585 (25%)	$41,000	$36,000	$31,000	$26,000

TECHNICAL DATA

Powertrain (rear-drive)
Engines: 5.7L V8 (350 hp)
• 5.7L V8 (385 hp)
Transmissions: 6-speed man.
• 4-speed auto.
Dimension/Capacity
Passengers: 2/0
Height/length/width:
47.7/179.7/73.6 in.

Head room: 37.8 in.
Leg room: 42.7 in.
Wheelbase: 104.5 in.
Turning circle: 42 ft.
Cargo volume: 11 cu. ft.
Tow limit: N/A
Fuel tank: 72L/prem.
Weight: 3,245 lb.

SAFETY FEATURES/CRASHWORTHINESS

	Std.	Opt.
Anti-lock brakes	■	❑
Seatbelt pretensioners	—	—
Side airbags	—	—
Traction control	■	❑
Head restraints F/R	*****	N/A
Visibility F/R	*****	**
Crash protection (front) D/P	N/A	N/A
Crash protection (side) D/P	N/A	N/A
Crash protection (off-set)	N/A	

Montana, Silhouette, Venture

Venture

RATING: Above Average, if you don't overwhelm the engine. **Strong points:** A comfortable ride, easy handling, dual sliding doors, plenty of comfort and convenience features, flexible seating arrangements, and good crash scores. **Weak points:** Average acceleration with a light load; optional traction control; uncomfortable, low rear seats; excessive brake fading; a high number of safety-related failures that involve the sliding doors and dangerous airbags; and disappointing fuel economy.

NEW FOR 2001: A slight restyling of the front and rear end, optional AWD in 2002. Both the Montana and Venture get a fold-flat third-row seat.

OVERVIEW: This practically identical threesome of front-drive minivans comes in regular and extended wheelbase versions. The extended wheelbase models get more bells and whistles, including optional power slide-open passenger- and driver-side doors. The Venture and Silhouette seat seven, while the Montana manages to squeeze in one more passenger. Longer versions have dual sliding doors with optional power assist.

Cost analysis/best alternatives: Get a 15–20 percent discounted year 2000 minivan if you don't care about the fold-flat rear seat or this year's restyling. These minivans are a definite step up from the GM minivans they replaced several years ago. Other vehicles worth considering: Honda Odyssey, Nissan Quest, and Toyota Sienna. **Options:** Integrated child safety seats are generally a good idea, but make sure your child can't slip out—parents report that this has happened. The power-assisted passenger-side sliding door is both convenient and dangerous (see NHTSA, following section)—despite its override circuit that prevents the door from closing on a hand, a number of injuries have been reported. Furthermore, with most sliding doors, mechanical and electronic glitches allow the doors to open when they shouldn't, and they are difficult to close. Overall, this $1,200 convenience feature is overpriced, failure-prone, and a bit slow in operation. An argument can be made for the added convenience, but I suspect its chief attraction is to gadget-hungry males. The same goes for GM's video entertainment system (read VCR player) sold in almost 28 percent of last year's Silhouettes. Consider the $235 load-levelling feature—a must-have for front-drive minivans. It keeps the weight on the front wheels, giving you better steering, traction, and braking. Other options that are worth buying: General XP2000 tires (about $100 for all four), traction control, power side windows, and rear air conditioner, defroster, and heater. The Montana Package offers a firmer suspension and self-sealing tires. **Rebates:** $1,500 on the 2000 models. **Delivery/PDI:** $840. **Depreciation:** A bit slower than average. **Insurance cost:** High, but about average for a minivan. **Annual maintenance cost:** Average during the warranty period. Transmission, ABS, and electrical malfunctions will likely cause maintenance costs to rise after the third year of ownership. **Parts supply/cost:** Parts are generic to GM's other models, so they should be reasonably priced and not hard to find. Body parts are likely to be more problematic and costly. **Warranty:** Bumper-to-bumper 3 years/60,000 km; rust perforation 6 years/160,000 km. **Supplementary warranty:** An extended warranty is a good idea until long-term reliability has been assessed. **Highway/city fuel economy:** 9.3–13.5L/100 km.

Quality/Reliability/Safety

Pro: Quality control: Average. Less rattle-prone due to a more rigid body structure than that of their predecessors. **Reliability:** Average. **Warranty performance:** Average.

Con: Fit and finish is still not up to the Asian competition. Chassis could still use reinforcing to mute the rattles heard when passing over rough roads. **Owner-reported problems:** Electrical glitches, windshield wiper motor failures, excessive front brake noise, power sliding door malfunctions, and assorted body deficiencies. Windshield wipers are frequently frozen into place and the under-hood climate control vents, found at the base of the windshield, freeze up as well. Seatbelts often won't hold child safety seats. **Service bulletin problems:** Poorly performing AC, faulty power sliding door control module, excessive side-to-side movement with certain child safety seats placed in second- and third-row bucket seats; chronic driveline clunk (see following bulletin). **NHTSA safety complaints/safety:** Airbag deployed when door was slammed; airbags failed to deploy; windshield suddenly exploded outward while driving with wipers activated; brakes activate on their own, making it appear as if van is pulling a load; steering idler arm fell off due to missing bolt; loose fuel tank due to loose bolts/bracket; fuel tank cracked when passing over a tree branch; plastic tube within heating system fell off and wedged behind the accelerator pedal; bracket weld pin that secures the rear split seat sheared off; faulty fuel pump causes chronic stalling; no starts; surging; sudden acceleration; vehicle suddenly lost power while going uphill, slid back, and stalled; van will roll back while in gear on an incline; Service Engine light comes on constantly; Service Engine light remains on due to transmission bearing assembled backwards in the transmission box; premature transmission failures; power sliding door has a gap at the base large enough to trap a child; when reversing, the door will not stop; sliding door slams shut on an incline; person's wrist broken when power sliding door opened; broken sliding door track trim panel; centre rear lap seatbelt isn't long enough to secure a rear-facing child safety seat; middle-row passenger-side seatbelts jam in the retracted position; front passenger shoulder belt cuts into passenger's neck; children can slide out of the integrated child safety seat; electrical harness failures result in complete electrical shutdown; headlights, interior lights, gauges, and instruments fail intermittently (electrical cluster module is the prime suspect); excess padding around horn makes it difficult to depress horn button in an emergency; weak-sounding horn; loud noise emanating from underneath the vehicle; frequent windshield wiper motor failures; heater doesn't warm up vehicle sufficiently; anti-freeze smell intrudes into the interior.

Driveline Clunk

File In Section: 04-Driveline Axle

Bulletin No.: 99-04-20-002

Date: December, 1999

Information

Subject:

Driveline Clunk

Models:

2000 and Prior Chevrolet and GMC Light Duty Truck Models

This bulletin is being revised to update the models section and add information to the Important statement. Please discard Corporate Bulletin Number 56-44-01A (Section 4 - Drive Axle and Section 7 - Transmission).

Important:

The condition described in this bulletin should not be confused with Driveline Stop Clunk, described in Corporate Bulletin Number 964101R (Chevrolet 92-265-7A, GMC Truck 91-4A-77, Oldsmobile 47-71-20A, GM of Canada 93-4A-100) or Bump/Clunk Upon Acceleration, described in Corporate Bulletin Number 99-04-21-004.

Some owners of the light duty trucks equipped with automatic transmission may comment that the vehicle exhibits a clunk noise when shifting between Park and Drive, Park and Reverse, or Drive and Reverse. Similarly, owners of vehicles equipped with automatic or manual transmissions may comment that the vehicle exhibits a clunk noise while driving when the accelerator is quickly depressed and then released.

Whenever there are two or more gears interacting with one another, there must be a certain amount of clearance between those gears in order for the gears to operate properly. This clearance or freeplay (also known as lash) can translate into a clunk noise whenever the gear is loaded and unloaded quickly, or whenever the direction of rotation is reversed. The more gears you have in a system, the more freeplay the total system will have.

The clunk noise that owners sometimes hear may be the result of a buildup of freeplay (lash) between the components in the driveline.

For example, the potential for a driveline clunk would be greater in a 4-wheel drive or all-wheel drive vehicle than a 2-wheel drive vehicle. This is because in addition to the freeplay from the rear axle gears, the universal joints, and the transmission (common to both vehicles), the 4-wheel drive transfer case gears (and their associated clearances) add additional freeplay to the driveline.

In service, dealers are discouraged from attempting to repair driveline clunk conditions for the following reasons:

- Comments of driveline clunk are almost never the result of one individual component with excessive lash, but rather the result of the added affect of freeplay (or lash) present in all of the driveline components.
- Because all of the components in the driveline have a certain amount of lash by design, changing driveline components may not result in a satisfactory lash reduction.
- While some owners may find the clunk noise objectionable, this will not adversely affect durability or performance.

Just when I thought GM had licked this problem, here's proof that the decade-old clunk lives on. No wonder Honda Odyssey and Toyota Sienna minivans are so popular. They don't have "driveline clunk," and their dealers aren't "discouraged from attempting to repair driveline clunk."

Road Performance

Pro: Emergency handling: Better than average, due to the responsive powertrain, steering, and ABS. **Steering:** The steering takes some effort, but it's responsive and fairly predictable. Longer, loaded versions have a smoother ride than the base versions, which tend to be choppier. **Acceleration/torque:** Nice powertrain setup with smooth acceleration for most light-duty work. The 3.4L engine is smooth and responsive (0–100 km/h: 10.7 sec.). These minivans use the same quiet-running V6 powerplant that harnesses a few more horses than the Chrysler minivans' top-line 3.8L 6-cylinder, providing good mid-range and top-end power. Chrysler's engines do have a bit more torque, however. **Transmission:** The electronically controlled 4-speed automatic transmission shifts smoothly and quietly—another advantage over Chrysler. **Routine handling:** Pretty good. Sedan-like handling is better than most of the competition, particularly when equipped with the load-levelling option. **Braking:** Unimpressive for the Venture (100–0 km/h: 147 ft.), much better with the Montana (100–0 km/h: 134 ft.) and Silhouette (100–0 km/h: 135 ft.).

Con: Some body roll in hard turns. Powertrain isn't suitable for heavy towing or carrying a full passenger load. **Acceleration/torque:** The GM engine is hampered by less torque, making for less grunt when accelerating and frequently downshifting out of Overdrive when climbing moderate grades (there's no Overdrive on/off switch). This is the main reason why owners feel that the GM minivans are underpowered when compared with Chrysler's. **Braking:** Watch out for excessive brake fading; the brakes progressively lose their effectiveness after repeated application.

Comfort/Convenience

Pro: Standard equipment: Fairly well equipped. **Driving position:** Drivers are treated to a car-like driving position. Comfortable left footrest. Concealed windshield wipers, a large windshield, and larger side mirrors enhance visibility fore and aft. **Controls and displays:** Everything is easy to read and within reach. **Climate control:** Efficient and easy to use. AC has a pollen control feature. **Entry/exit:** Easy, especially with the low interior step-in, side interior door handles, power remote sliding door on the curb side and a manual sliding door on the street side of extended-wheelbase models. **Interior space/comfort F/R:** Plenty of room in the first two rows, while the third row is more problematic. Comfortable seats, particularly on the Venture. There are two reclining bucket seats in the front row, and the second and third rows can accommodate modular or bench seats. Easy-to-fold seats drop down to increase storage space; the second seat flips forward for access to the third seat. **Cargo space:** Lots of storage bins and compartments. **Trunk/liftover:** A breeze. Dual sliding doors mean that you no longer have to walk around to the passenger side to load or unload cargo. Rear seats can be flipped down to carry a 4' x 8' sheet of plywood. **Quietness:** One of the quietest minivans in its class.

Con: Tacky plastic interior. **Driving position:** Tall drivers will find insufficient head room and short drivers may find it hard to see where the front ends. **Controls and displays:** Steering column stalk controls are confusing. **Climate control:** These minivans take a while to warm up the interior. **Interior space/comfort F/R:** Uncomfortable centre and rear bench seats; cushions are hard, flat, and too short; and the seatbacks lack sufficient lower back support. Low rear seats force passengers into an uncomfortable knees-up position. **Cargo space:** One convenience item that can easily become an inconvenience: the two cargo nets found between the front seats and behind the rear seat are easily entangled and complicate the removal of the rear seats. Also, eight of the twelve cupholders are only usable if the seats are folded down. **Trunk/liftover:** Cargo may not slide out easily due to the rear sill sticking up a few inches. **Quietness:** Some wind noise.

COST

List Price (negotiable)	Residual Values (months)			
	24	36	48	60
Montana: $26,755 (20%)	$19,000	$16,000	$14,000	$12,000
Silhouette: $31,105 (20%)	$22,000	$18,000	$16,000	$14,000
Venture SW: $25,230 (20%)	$18,000	$15,000	$11,000	$11,000

TECHNICAL DATA

Powertrain (front-drive)
Engine: 3.4L V6 (185 hp)
Transmission: 4-speed auto.
Dimension/Capacity (Silhouette; Montana and Venture)
Passengers: 2/2/3; 2/3/3
Height/length/width:
  67.4/186.9/72 in.;
  68.1/187.3/72.7 in.

Head room F: 39.9/R1: 39.3/R2: 38.8 in.;
  F: 39.9/R1: 39.3/R2: 38.9 in.
Leg room F: 39.9/R1: 36.9/R2: 34 in.;
  F: 39.9/R1: 39/R2: 36.7 in.
Wheelbase: 112 in.
Turning circle: 42 ft.
Cargo volume: 76 cu. ft.
GVWR: 5,357 lb.
Payload: 1,415–1,577 lb.
Tow limit: 3,500 lb.
Fuel tank: 76/95L
Weight: 3,890 lb./4,005 lb.

SAFETY FEATURES/CRASHWORTHINESS

	Std.	Opt.
Anti-lock brakes (4W)	■	❏
Seatbelt pretensioners	■	❏
Side airbags	■	❏
Traction control	❏	■
Head restraints F/R	***	*
Silhouette	***	***
Visibility F/R	*****	*****
Crash protection (front) D/P	****	***
Crash protection (side) D/P	*****	*****
Crash protection (off-set)	*	

Astro, Safari

Astro

RATING: Above Average. How come these old dinosaurs rate higher than Ford's and Chrysler's high-tech, front-drive marvels? Simple: the GM rear-drive minivans have fewer problems, and those deficiencies that do appear are easier to diagnose and relatively less expensive to repair. **Strong points:** Standard ABS, brisk acceleration, trailer-towing capability, lots of passenger room and cargo space, and improved reliability and quality control. **Weak points:** Harsh riding, limited front seat room, and excessive fuel consumption made worse by the AWD option.

NEW FOR 2001: Nothing significant; will be put out to pasture after the 2002 model year.

OVERVIEW: More a utility truck than a comfortable minivan, these boxy, rear-drive minivans are built on a reworked S-10 pickup chassis. As such, they offer uninspiring handling, trouble-prone mechanical and body components, and relatively high fuel consumption. Both Astro and Safari come in a choice of either cargo or passenger van. The cargo van is used either commercially or as an inexpensive starting point for a fully customized vehicle. The Safari is identical to the Astro, except for a slightly higher base price.

The engine is a 4.3L 190-hp V6. Dual airbags are standard. Also offered are an optional rear door and rear bench seats that can be adjusted fore and aft. Carried-over standard features are a 4-speed automatic transmission with Overdrive, power steering, a front stabilizer bar, a 95L fuel tank (a Lumina offers 76L), and anti-lock brakes. All-wheel drive with a single-speed transfer case with viscous-controlled differential (no switches to throw) is available on the regular length and extended models. The Sport package includes louvred rear-quarter body panels, two-tone paint, fog lights, and a front air dam. With the right options, the Astro and Safari have the advantage of being versatile cargo haulers when equipped with a heavy-duty suspension. In fact, Astro's 5,500-lb. trailer-towing capability is 2,000 lb. more than that of the front-drive Venture.

Cost analysis/best alternatives: Get the year 2000 minivans if they're discounted $2,000–$3,000. Front-drive minivans made by Nissan and Toyota have better handling, and are more reliable and economical people carriers; unfortunately, they lack the Astro's considerable grunt, essential for cargo hauling and trailer towing. **Options:** Integrated child safety seats, rear AC, and rear Dutch doors. Be wary of the AWD option; it exacts a high fuel penalty. **Rebates:** About $2,000 before year's end on the 2000s and possibly half as much on this year's models by mid-summer. **Delivery/PDI:** $900. **Depreciation:** Average. **Insurance cost:** Slightly higher than average. **Annual maintenance cost:** Average. **Parts supply/cost:** Good supply of cheap parts. A large contingent of independent parts suppliers keeps repair costs down. Parts are less expensive than they are for other vehicles in this class. **Warranty:** Bumper-to-bumper 3 years/60,000 km; rust perforation 6 years/160,000 km. **Supplementary warranty:** A toss-up. Individual repairs won't cost a lot, but those nickels and dimes can add up. **Highway/city fuel economy:** 10.6–14.6L/100 km for two-wheel drive and 11.3–15.3L/100 km with AWD.

Quality/Reliability/Safety

Pro: Quality control: Average. **Reliability:** Average; most of the Astro and Safari's defects are easy to diagnose, leading to a minimum of downtime in the repair bay. **Warranty performance:** Average.

Con: Owner-reported problems: Some problems with the automatic transmission, steering, electrical system, heating and defrosting system, and suspension components. **Service bulletin problems:** Engine crankshaft may have been "mis-machined"; GM will replace it, if necessary. **NHTSA safety complaints/safety:** Rear cargo door latch and hinge slipped off and door flew open; sudden acceleration; chronic stalling; hard starts; cranks, but would not start due to broken electrical connection; sudden total electrical failure, especially when going into Reverse; loss of power steering; sudden steering and brake loss when power-steering pump shaft snapped; when applying brakes, pedal stiffens and then vehicle surges ahead; extended stopping distance with ABS, especially in rainy weather; brake pedal set too high; differential in transfer case locked up while driving; defective axle seals; vehicle rolls backward on an incline while in Drive (dealer adjusted transfer case to no avail); front passenger seatbelt locked up; fuel gauge failure; faulty AC vents; water can be trapped inside the wheels and freeze, causing the wheels to be out of balance.

Road Performance

Pro: Acceleration/torque: The V6 engine is more than adequate for most driving chores and has plenty of reserve power for trailer towing and heavy hauling (0–100 km/h: 11.8 sec.). **Braking:** Excellent braking.

Con: The V6 is thirsty in city driving. **Emergency handling:** Ponderous, but still fairly predictable. **Steering:** Very light power steering, but still handles and manoeuvres like a large truck. **Transmission:** Clunky automatic transmission. **Routine handling:** Handling isn't very precise; overall behaviour is competent, but sloppy. A heavy-duty suspension will improve both ride and handling. Busy, harsh ride caused by stiff springs.

Comfort/Convenience

Pro: Standard equipment: Adequate. **Controls and displays:** Well laid-out instrument panel with easy-to-read gauges. **Climate control:** Very good climate control system. **Interior space/comfort F/R:** Spacious interior provides plenty of room for passengers. All seats are comfortable, although the front two are the best. The rear seat can be removed by a single person. **Cargo space:** An incredible amount of cargo space can handle all kinds of bulky items. **Trunk/liftover:** No problem. In fact, the optional Dutch doors provide better rear-view visibility and include a convenient lift-open glass and defroster.

Con: Driving position: The driving position is awkward for most drivers. Tall drivers will find the pedals too close. Obtrusive engine makes for very narrow front footwells that give little room for the driver's left foot to rest. Some dashboard controls are hard to reach. **Entry/exit:** Difficult due to the high step-up and the intruding wheelwell. **Quietness:** Interior noise levels rise sharply at highway speeds.

COST				
List Price (very negotiable)	**Residual Values (months)**			
	24	36	48	60
Base: $26,440 (19%)	$19,000	$15,000	$13,000	$11,500

TECHNICAL DATA	
Powertrain (rear-drive)	Head room F: 39.2/R1: 37.9/R2: 38.7 in.
Engine: 4.3L V6 (190 hp)	Leg room F: 41.6/R1: 36.5/R2: 38.5 in.
Transmission: 4-speed auto.	Wheelbase: 111.2 in.
Dimension/Capacity	Turning circle: 45 ft.
Passengers: 2/3/3	Cargo volume: 98 cu. ft.
Height/length/width:	GVWR: 5,950–6,100 lb.
74.9/189.8/77.5 in.	Payload: 1,667–1,764 lb.
	Tow limit: 5,500 lb.
	Fuel tank: 95L
	Weight: 4,520 lb.

SAFETY FEATURES/CRASHWORTHINESS		
	Std.	**Opt.**
Anti-lock brakes (4W)	■	❏
Seatbelt pretensioners	—	—
Side airbags	—	—
Traction control (AWD)	❏	■
Head restraints F/R	**	**
Visibility F/R	*****	**
Crash protection (front) D/P	***	****
Crash protection (side) D/P	N/A	N/A
Crash protection (off-set)	*	

SAAB

What's so special about Saabs? Their unusual, aerodynamic styling is (to put it mildly) distinctive; passenger comfort is unbeatable; and they handle very well, with precise steering and lots of road feel. Unfortunately, lots of less expensive cars offer just as much road performance and are more reliable and easier to repair.

No one can accuse GM of opportunism in buying Saab for $600 million in late 1989—just before the Swedish automaker announced a $380-million operating loss for that year, followed by stunning 1990–91 losses exceeding a billion dollars. But, after three straight years of losses, Saab turned a small profit in '99 due to its new products and improved European sales.

Saab's growth has been undeniably slowed by increased competition from European and Japanese luxury sedans that are more smartly styled, have greater market penetration, and are marketed through attractive and innovative leasing plans. Furthermore, Saab's reliability and servicing problems have only begun to be addressed by GM, which is beset by its own quality and servicing deficiencies.

9-3

RATING: Average. **Strong points:** Many standard safety features; a good highway performer with excellent handling, steering, and braking; comfortable seating; and lots of storage capability. Improved build quality and exterior finish. **Weak points:** Turbo lag, and a poor ride with premium tires. Convertible has minimal rear seat room, less comfortable seating, and shakes and rattles. Obstructed rear visibility in both the sedan and convertible, a history of poor quality control, and the servicing network is rather limited.

NEW FOR 2001: Nothing significant.

OVERVIEW: Selling for about $33,500, the 9-3 is essentially the old 900 loaded with lots of engineering upgrades housed in a two- or four-door hatchback or convertible. The base engine is a 185-hp twin-cam 2.0L four that gets 15 additional horses when turbocharged. A 230-hp 2.3L turbocharged version powers the Viggen, a limited edition coupe. The Viggen comes only with a manual transmission.

   Don't expect fast starts uphill. The turbo kicks in at about 3000 rpm (which means lots of time spent in second gear waiting for a much-needed turbo boost), plus, you'll have to contend with a lurching transmission, uncomfortably long passing times, and sudden torque steer that may tug at the steering wheel.

   Notwithstanding the turbo's deficiencies, the 9-3 is a driver's car, with impressive braking performance, sporty handling, and sure-footed cornering. Nevertheless, the SE's high-performance, premium tires accentuate the smallest bumps, and make for a harsh, jiggly ride. The standard V-rated tires give a much smoother ride.

   Safety features abound, including "active" head restraints that minimize whiplash injury and thicker headliner padding as cushioning in rollovers. One obvious deficiency is the absence of traction control, a feature offered by almost all of the 9-3's rivals.

There's plenty of cargo space and room for five adults, except in the convertible version, and the soft top is easily raised or lowered electrically. The narrow two-place rear bench seat and manual front passenger seat, however, move slowly to provide rear-seat access. Climate settings on the SE have to be readjusted between startups, the ignition is still floor-mounted, rear visibility is not very good in the sedans and even worse in the convertible with the top raised, and the convertible's less-rigid chassis tends to shake and rattle.

Cost analysis/best alternatives: for the 9-3 and 9-5: Get the year 2000 Saabs if they're discounted by at least 20 percent. The Acura TL, Audi A4, Infiniti I30, and Volvo 70 series are attractive alternatives to the 9-3 hatchbacks; Mercedes' CLK320, the BMW 3-series, and the 5-cyl. Volvo C70 are credible alternatives to the $53,070 9-3 convertible. Alternatives to the 9-5: Acura RL or Mercedes E-Class. Keep in mind that Saabs may be cheaper than their European counterparts, like the Audi A6 and Volvo S80, but they depreciate far more quickly. **Options:** Integrated child safety seats. The V6 engine isn't worth the extra $5,000. It adds additional weight, is fuel-thirsty, and compromises handling. Plus, it's only available with an automatic gearbox. The GPS navigation aids can be useful, but don't waste your money on the power sunroof, leather upholstery, and heated seats. **Rebates:** About $2,000 before year's end on the 2000s and possibly half as much on this year's models by mid-summer. **Delivery/PDI:** $800. **Depreciation:** Faster than average. If you plan to keep yours for only a few years and don't want to lose much money through depreciation, choose the convertible; it keeps its value longer. **Insurance cost:** Slightly higher than average. **Annual maintenance cost:** Average. **Parts supply/cost:** Not easily found; costly, at times. **Insurance cost:** Higher than average. **Parts supply/cost:** Parts are moderately expensive and servicing is a major liability (the dealership network is weak) due to GM's inept administration of its Saab franchises. GM threw out many Saab dealers when it bought the company, and gave the Saab franchise to inexperienced Passport dealers who primarily serviced Isuzus. After fielding a deluge of customer complaints, GM realized this was a mistake and closed a third of its 60 dealerships. Saab owners are feeling GM's pain. **Annual maintenance cost:** Higher than average. **Warranty:** Bumper-to-bumper 4 years/ 80,000 km; rust perforation 6 years/unlimited km. **Supplementary warranty:** A very good idea, considering that these cars are complicated to diagnose and expensive to repair. **Highway/city fuel economy:** with the 2.3L engine and a manual transmission: 7.4–11.6L/100 km; 2.0L engine and an automatic transmission: 8.5–11.9L/100 km.

Quality/Reliability/Safety

Pro: Warranty performance: Above average. GM has treated Saab owners more generously than its other divisions with the exception of Saturn and Cadillac.

Con: Quality control: Below average. **Reliability:** Average; most of the 9-3's defects are electrical in nature, tending to take lots of diagnostic time. **Owner-reported problems:** Electrical and fuel system malfunctions, premature brake wear, and body defects. **Service bulletin problems:** *9-3:* Vibration during acceleration at 60–90 km/h and details relating to a voluntary safety recall involving the manually adjusted front seats. *9-5:* Seat heater switch or fan switch may not light up or may appear to be inoperative. **NHTSA safety complaints/safety:** *9-3:* Side airbag failed to deploy; aluminum hubs may not support the stress of everyday driving; when passing over grooves in the road, vehicle suddenly jerks to the right or left; driver's door lock won't unlock from the inside. *9-5:* Fuel sloshes around in fuel tank when accelerating or stopping.

SAFETY FEATURES/CRASHWORTHINESS

	Std.	Opt.
Anti-lock brakes	■	❑
Seatbelt pretensioners	■	❑
Side airbags	■	❑
Traction control	❑	❑
Head restraints F/R	*****	*****
Visibility F/R	*****	*
Crash protection (front) D/P	****	****
Crash protection (side) D/P	N/A	N/A
Crash protection (off-set)	***	

Note: Safety features and crash data also apply to the 9-5.

9-5

9-5

RATING: Average. **Strong points:** Good acceleration, handling, road holding, and braking; "smart" head restraints; comfortable seating (lots of room for six-footers plus); lots of storage capability; improved build quality and fit and finish; and good fuel economy. Traction control (V6 only). **Weak points:** Turbo lag, excessive tire and road noise, the steering feels a bit over-assisted and a bit numb, some body lean when cornering, climate controls aren't very user-friendly, and the servicing network is rather limited.

NEW FOR 2001: Nothing significant.

OVERVIEW: The $40,400 base 9-5 replaced the 9000 several years ago. It uses suspension and brake parts taken from GM's Opel Vectra, with a stiffened chassis and added four-wheel independent suspension. It floats less and corners better than the 9000, though there's still too much body lean. Saab has also turbocharged its V6 engine without boosting horsepower, so that it provides lots of low-end torque. It doesn't kick in under 3000 rpm, however, and comes only with an automatic transmission.

There's plenty of cargo space and room for five adults. In addition to providing a spacious trunk, Saab pays lots of attention to detail. For example: work gloves and a plastic bag are provided so you don't soil your hands when changing the tire; the "smart" head restraint is specially designed to prevent neck injuries; the glove box has an air conditioning duct that keeps drinks cold; there are air vents in the back of the centre console for added comfort; rear seats fold flat for added cargo room; and, for added safety, a passenger-side rear-view mirror automatically tilts down so you can get a better view when you engage Reverse.

Some things you won't like about the 9-5: power steering is over-assisted and doesn't transmit sufficient road feel; only two adults can sit comfortably in the rear; the remote lock/unlock key fob won't fit into the average-sized pocket and is hard to decipher; the outside mirrors are unacceptably small; the in-dash cupholder won't support a tall coffee cup; the fan-cooled seats are more gimmicky than practical; climate controls are set too low to be easily adjusted and have to be recalibrated after each startup; the ignition is still floor-mounted; rear visibility is obstructed; and servicing isn't widely available. **Highway/city fuel economy:** with a 2.3L engine and a manual transmission: 7.5–11.7L/100 km; 3.0L engine coupled to an auto transmission: 8.3–12.7L/100 km.

Quality/Reliability/Safety

Pro: Quality control: Average. Saab 9-5 owners report fewer factory-related defects than owners of the entry-level 9-3. **Reliability:** Average; not much downtime in the repair bay reported—so far. **Warranty performance:** Above average.

Con: Owner-reported problems: Electrical, brake, and fuel system glitches; some minor fit and finish complaints.

Asian Vehicles

With just a few exceptions (Mazda, Daewoo, and Kia, for example), Asian automakers have a lock on reliable cars, minivans, sport-utilities, and pickups. Whether the vehicles are built in Japan, Canada, Mexico, or the United States, you usually get much more for your money than if you were to buy the equivalent vehicle made by DaimlerChrysler, Ford, or General Motors. You can also count on Japanese vehicles to be easy to repair and slow to depreciate. They're also terribly overpriced, though they have been made cheaper during the past few years through "content-cutting" (in Toyota's case) and fewer standard features.

On the downside, the past few years have seen an upswing in safety-related defects with Toyota and Honda. I'm not sure whether the cause is the cheapening of the products to keep prices relatively moderate, or if the companies have simply become complacent after winning so many quality awards from CAA and others. Whatever the reason, this year's *Lemon-Aid* has downgraded the ratings of a number of Japanese models due to the safety hazard the alleged defects may pose.

South Korean automakers' vehicles, on the other hand, aren't as reliable as their Japanese competition, even though Hyundai's quality control has risen considerably over the past few years. And Daewoo and Kia's products have an even worse reputation, having been rated by their owners as below average in quality. Nevertheless, this year has seen an increase in sales for all three South Korean automakers, after they shifted their marketing strategy to include rock-bottom prices and generous warranties that promise to make up for the deficiencies in quality. Interestingly, Chrysler made a similar move in the early '90s and successfully won over wary buyers. Then the automaker cut its 7-year warranty, and sales plummeted while customer complaints soared.

Although the Japanese automakers have pledged to keep price increases to a minimum, and in some cases not raise the MSRP on some vehicles, a devalued Canadian dollar plus renewed enthusiasm for fuel-efficient Japanese and Korean vehicles may push prices higher.

Those automakers likely to be involved in the heaviest discounting are Daewoo, Kia, Mazda, Nissan, and Suzuki. Daewoo and Kia are newcomers to Canada and need to capture market share in order to lure more dealers into their network. Mazda, Nissan, and Suzuki are discounting in order to make up for poor previous-year sales—and, in Nissan's case, get some quick cash to pay off huge debts.

ACURA

When Acura first came to Canada in 1986, it did very well in selling reasonably priced compact cars that many considered to be no more than all-dressed Honda clones. Then the company got cocky and, rather than counting on lower profits and more sales, they raised prices (over dealers' objections) to what the market would bear. Fortunately, competitive pressures—not the least from Lexus and Infiniti—forced the automaker to cut Acura prices with cash rebates, low-interest financing programs, and the launching of the 1.6L EL, a Canada-exclusive, entry-level compact. Seven models are sold under the Acura nameplate: the 1.6 EL, Integra, 3.2 CL coupe, 3.2 TL, 3.5 RL, MD-X sport-utility, and NSX sports car. Except for the all new MD-X and redesigned 3.2 CL, all of Acura's models return this year unchanged.

Acura products are generally good buys (even though they're overpriced) because maintenance costs are low and reliability is way above average. What few defects they have are usually related to accessories like the navigation system, creaks and squeaks, and paint problems from environmental causes (still covered under a "goodwill" program).

One caution: I'm very concerned over the recent death of a Toronto driver of a 2000 Intregra. Stopped at a traffic light, Karol Steinhouse was tapped at the rear of her car and pushed into the car ahead. Her airbag exploded and several minutes later she bled to death from a ruptured aorta. She was small statured and had to sit close to the steering wheel.

I cannot in good conscience recommend any new or used Acura model to small-statured drivers, seniors, persons who have had recent surgery, and families with children who must ride up front.

Acura has said its airbags are safe. I'm unconvinced.

Asian Vehicles

1.6 EL

1.6 EL (2000)

RATING: Above Average. **Strong points:** High level of performance and comfort, slow depreciation, and high-quality construction. **Weak points:** Optional anti-lock brakes (inexcusable, when you consider that

GM's $15,865 entry-level Cavalier coupe has standard ABS), no crash-worthiness data, limited rear seat room, and difficult rear access.

NEW FOR 2001: Nothing significant. A mid-year redesign based on the new Civic is scheduled.

OVERVIEW: With a $19,700 base price, the 1.6 EL has sold quite well for what is essentially a restyled, luxury version of the Honda Civic Si with the following features: conservative styling, different bumpers and front headlights, upgraded wipers, heated power door mirrors, restyled dash, different seat covers, upgraded soundproofing, 15-inch wheels, and a rear sway bar.

Taken from the Civic Coupe Si, the VTEC 4-cylinder puts out 127 hp for good all-around acceleration, but without the sports car cachet of the Integra 1.8, which gives you a sportier 142-hp engine in a two-door body style. Consumer feedback notes that the 4-speed gearbox is well designed in that it doesn't "hunt" for the right gear when traversing hilly terrain. On the safety front, anti-lock brakes are optional, child-proof rear door locks are standard, and no crash tests have yet been carried out.

Some of the 1.6 EL's weak points: relatively expensive for what is essentially a four-door Year 2000 Civic (still, a low depreciation rate may give you back a greater portion of your initial investment); a narrow interior, with seats and seatbacks not to everyone's liking; emergency braking that's only average; head restraints rated "poor" by IIHS; an average insurance injury claim rate; and excessive engine noise intruding into the passenger compartment—despite upgraded soundproofing.

Warning: airbag may be deadly to short-statured drivers.

Cost analysis/best alternatives: Get a second-series 2001 model if it incorporates the Civic's redesign and is reasonably priced. Other vehicles worth a look: Acura Integra and Honda Civic Si. **Options:** A block heater. **Rebates:** Not likely, but look for 10–15 percent discounts on last year's models. **Delivery/PDI:** $400. **Depreciation:** Much slower than average. **Insurance cost:** Higher than average. **Parts supply/cost:** Moderately priced parts can be found at Acura or Honda dealers. **Annual maintenance cost:** Lower than average. **Warranty:** Bumper-to-bumper 3 years/60,000 km; powertrain 5 years/100,000 km; rust perforation 6 years/unlimited km. **Supplementary warranty:** Not needed. **Highway/city fuel economy:** 6.5–8.5L/100 km.

CL

RATING: Above Average. The Accord grows up. **Strong points:** Good powertrain setup, steering, and handling; well built; stylish; plenty of standard features; and comfortable riding. **Weak points:** As with most coupes, problematic rear-seat access and limited rear head room. The TL-inspired navigation system is overly complicated.

NEW FOR 2001: Redesigned last spring.

OVERVIEW: Priced about $40,000, this four-passenger luxury coupe is larger, heavier, and more performance-oriented than last year's version, now that it shares the TL's platform and base 225-hp 3.2L V6. A better-performing 260-hp variant powers the Type S. An automatic 5-speed with a manual shift gate is the only transmission offered with either model.

And while other Japanese automakers are taking content out of their vehicles, Acura has put content into the CL, making it one of the most feature-laden cars in its class.

Sure, we all know that the coupe's mechanical components and platform aren't that different from the Accord's, but when you add up all of its standard bells and whistles, you get a fully loaded small car that costs thousands of dollars less than competing luxury coupes. Base models are well appointed with standard four-wheel ABS, a "smart" passenger's side airbag, traction control, heated front seats, leather upholstery, Xenon headlights, power sunroof, remote keyless entry, and a dash-mounted 6-disc CD changer. Type S standard features include all the above, plus an anti-skid system, a stiffer suspension, 17-inch wheels, and upgraded tires.

The CL gets plenty of power from its smooth-running and quiet 3.2L V6. Handling is better than average, thanks to upgraded suspension, variable-assisted steering, and 16-inch wheels. The ride is comfortable and well controlled. Excellent braking (100–0 km/h: 115 ft.).

Front and rear bucket seats are supportive and easily adjusted. There's plenty of room up front, controls and most gauges are user-friendly (the navigation system and tachometer placement are the only exceptions), and the climate controls are efficient and within easy reach. A large trunk with a low liftover and a locking ski pass-through enhances the CL's cargo space.

On the minus side, this is not a car for passengers in the rear. Adults will likely find their heads pressed against the top of the backlight glass, and leg and foot room are at a premium. Rear access is a crouch-and-crawl affair. Trunk lid hinges intrude into the trunk area and risk damaging cargo when the trunk is closed.

Service bulletin problems: Nothing reported due to the short time this vehicle has been on the market. **NHTSA safety complaints/safety:** Short-statured drivers may be seriously injured by the front airbag's deployment. IIHS gives head restraints a "poor" rating. **Cost analysis/best alternatives:** Opt for this year's model; it's leagues ahead of its predecessor. Other vehicles worth considering: the BMW 328Ci, Honda Accord, Lexus IS300, Mercedes-Benz CLK320, Nissan Maxima, Saab Viggen, Toyota Solara, and Volvo C70. **Options:** Don't get the GPS navigation system, unless you're technically inclined and patient. **Rebates:** Not likely. **Delivery/PDI:** $400. **Depreciation:** Much slower than average. **Insurance cost:** Higher than average. **Parts supply/cost:** It's not hard to find moderately priced parts at Acura or Honda dealers. **Annual maintenance cost:** Average. **Warranty:** Bumper-to-bumper 3 years/ 60,000 km; powertrain 5 years/100,000 km; rust perforation 6 years/ unlimited km. **Supplementary warranty:** Not needed. **Highway/city fuel economy:** 7.4–12.2L/100 km with the base 3.2L

3.2 TL

RATING: Above Average. **Strong points:** Impressive acceleration; handles well; rides comfortably; and is well constructed with quality mechanical and body components. **Weak points:** Suspension may be too firm for some; uncomfortable rear seating; excessive road noise; and problematic navigation system controls.

NEW FOR 2001: Carried over unchanged; a slight restyling is scheduled for next year's model.

OVERVIEW: Retailing for about $36,000, the 3.2 TL combines luxury and performance in a nicely styled front-drive five-passenger sedan that uses the same chassis as the Accord and CL coupe. The only engine available, a 3.2L 225-hp V6 mated to a 4-speed automatic transmission, provides impressive acceleration (0–100 km/h in just over 8 seconds) in a smooth and quiet manner. Handling is exceptional with the firm suspension, and responsive, precise steering makes it easy to toss the TL around turns without losing control. Bumps can be a bit jarring, but this is a small price to pay for the car's high-speed stability.

Interior accommodations are better than average up front, but rear occupants may discover that leg room is a bit tight and the seat cushions lack sufficient thigh support. The cockpit layout is very user-friendly, due in part to the easy-to-read gauges and accessible controls (far away climate controls, the only exception). Visibility fore and aft is unobstructed; however, the optional navigation system is tough to read, hard to calibrate, and subject to malfunction. Invest in maps instead.

Standard safety features include ABS, traction control, childproof door locks, three-point seatbelts, and a transmission/brake interlock. Crash tests give four stars for driver and passenger crash protection in a frontal collision. On the other hand, head restraints are given a "poor" rating by IIHS.

Cost analysis/best alternatives: Get the year 2000 model if it's sufficiently discounted; also consider the Audi A4, BMW's redesigned 3-series, Infiniti's redesigned I30, and Lexus' ES 300. You may want to take a look at the CL coupe: it's not as expensive, and is as close as you can get to the Accord with lots of standard bells and whistles thrown in. **Options:** Don't waste your money on the satellite navigation system; it's confusing to calibrate and hard to see. **Rebates:** No incentives or rebates are likely, but some discounting can be expected early next year. **Delivery/PDI:** $400. **Depreciation:** Much slower than average. **Insurance cost:** Higher than average. **Parts supply/cost:** Except for some body parts, parts, especially most mechanical and electronic components, are easily found and moderately priced. **Annual maintenance cost:** Less than average. **Warranty:** Bumper-to-bumper 3 years/60,000 km; powertrain 5 years/100,000 km; rust perforation 6 years/unlimited km. **Supplementary warranty:** Not needed. **Highway/city fuel economy:** 7.4–12.2L/100 km.

Quality/Reliability/Safety

Pro: Quality control: Above average. **Reliability:** Above average. **Warranty performance:** Average.

Con: Owner-reported problems: The only areas that have proven troublesome in the past have been poor body fits, malfunctioning accessories, and premature brake wear. **Service bulletin problems:** ABS warning light may come on; there have been tips about a leaking torque converter; driver's seat squeaks and moon roof creaks; and wrinkled rear door sash trim. **NHTSA safety complaints/safety:** Driver's airbag failed to deploy; complete brake failure; spongy brake pedal feel; design of side view mirrors obscures visibility; dashboard display is unreadable in daylight; in a crash, seatbelt did not restrain driver; defective intake manifold causes the fuel to boil, leading to chronic stalling. Short-statured drivers should be wary of Acura airbag fender-bender deployments; severe injury or death may ensue.

3.5 RL

RATING: Above Average. Basically, a fully loaded, longer, wider, and heavier TL, equipped with a larger engine that produces less horsepower than its smaller brother. **Strong points:** Good acceleration that's smooth and quiet in all gear ranges; exceptional steering and handling; comfortable ride; loaded with goodies; top-quality body and mechanical components. **Weak points:** Numb steering and problematic navigation system controls.

NEW FOR 2001: Relatively unchanged this year.

OVERVIEW: Retailing for about $53,000, the 3.5 RL is Honda's—oh, I mean, Acura's—flagship sedan. It's loaded with innovative high-tech safety and convenience features one would expect to find in a luxury car. These include: heated front seats, front and rear climate controls, rear-seat trunk pass-through, Xenon headlights (get used to oncoming drivers flashing you their headlights), "smart" side airbags, ABS, traction control, and an anti-skid system. No other engine but the 3.5L is available, and the only option offered is Acura's ubiquitous GPS navigation system (see TL comments).

The 3.5L 210-hp V6 mated to a 4-speed automatic transmission provides good acceleration that's a bit slower and more fuel thirsty than the TL, due partly to the RL's extra pounds. Power is nevertheless delivered in a smooth and quiet manner. The car handles nicely with a less firm ride than the TL, although steering response doesn't feel as crisp. Interior accommodations for four occupants are excellent up front and in the rear, due to the RL's use of a larger platform than the TL. All seats are well cushioned and give plenty of thigh support. Cockpit controls and instruments are easily accessed and the climate control system is both efficient and easy to adjust, both fore and aft. Good all-around visibility; however, the optional navigation is annoyingly distracting and not easily mastered.

Crash tests give four stars for driver and passenger crash protection in a frontal collision. On the other hand, head restraints are given a "marginal" rating by IIHS.

Cost analysis/best alternatives: Get the practically identical 2000 model, if it's sufficiently discounted; also consider BMW's 5-series, Infiniti's redesigned I30, and the Lexus GS 300/400. You may want to take a look at the TL sedan: it's not as expensive, and is a better performer, though passenger room is more limited. **Options:** Forget the satellite navigation system; buy maps instead. **Rebates:** Expect discounting of at least 10–15 percent on leftover 2000 models. **Delivery/PDI:** $400. **Depreciation:** Much slower than average. **Insurance cost:** Higher than average. **Parts supply/cost:** Most mechanical and electronic components are easily found and moderately priced. Body parts may be hard to come by and can be expensive. **Annual maintenance cost:** Less than average. **Warranty:** Bumper-to-bumper 3 years/60,000 km; powertrain 5 years/100,000 km; rust perforation 6 years/unlimited km. **Supplementary warranty:** Not needed. **Highway/city fuel economy:** 9.2–13.4L/100 km.

Quality/Reliability/Safety

Pro: Quality control: Above average. **Reliability:** Above average. **Warranty performance:** Average.

Con: Owner-reported problems: The only areas that have proven troublesome in the past have been malfunctioning accessories and premature brake wear. **Service bulletin problems:** Moon roof rattle; driver's seat squeaks; steering wheel may be off-centre; and damaged paint. **NHTSA safety complaints/safety:** Vehicle suddenly stalled while exiting a freeway; dashboard display is unreadable in daylight; in a crash, seatbelt did not restrain driver. Short-statured drivers should be wary of Acura airbag fender-bender deployments; severe injury or death may ensue.

Integra

Integra

RATING: Average. The performance and reliability aren't worth $26,000. **Strong points:** Better-than-average powertrain performance, excellent high-speed handling, good fuel economy, low depreciation, and high-quality construction. **Weak points:** Acceleration compromised by the automatic transmission, skimpy rear seat room, difficult rear access, excessive road noise, and too much low-speed steering effort. Way overpriced; more Honda than Acura.

NEW FOR 2001: No significant changes. A redesign is planned for 2001 when the Integra will be built off of the Civic platform.

OVERVIEW: The base Integra doesn't quite fit into any category; it's a comfortable and practical small sedan with a high price. Its sporty pretensions lack the sizzle you'll find with the Mazda Miata or other more stylish small cars. On the whole, there's little to be said against the Integra and little to be said for it. One can get the same size four-door compact with a bit less performance for a lot less money—or a similar car with a lot more performance for just a little more money.

Type R
If you can afford a lot more money, like an extra $5,000, the well-appointed Integra Type R will give you the high-performance thrills missing in the base Integra. Its rev-happy 195-hp 1.8L 4-cylinder VTEC engine, 5-speed manual transmission, quick steering and shifting, impressive brakes, and performance suspension will give you all the sports car thrills a five-seater can provide. Plus, it doesn't look bad, with its front chin spoiler, large rear spoiler, body cladding, alloy wheels and low suspension. An ignition immobilizer and spark plugs touted to last 160,000 kilometres are also standard.

On the minus side, the Type R's firm shocks make for a harsh ride when passing over rough terrain, and the VTEC engine produces an annoying interior buzz/drone when cruising and requires constant shifting while driving in the city. If you prefer your sports car performance in smaller doses, but still want a well-equipped, comfortable sporty coupe, consider the Integra SE, GS, or GS-R. You'll get a more conventional ride and higher ground clearance for less money.

Cost analysis/best alternatives: A discounted year 2000 model will do, since this year's models don't offer anything to justify a higher price. Other cars worth considering are the Honda Prelude, Mazda Miata, or VW Golf or Jetta. **Options:** Forget the GS leather upholstery and spoiler. Remember, Canadian Type R's may not include the nifty titanium shift knob found on American versions. **Rebates:** Expect sizeable discounts early next year. **Delivery/PDI:** $400. **Depreciation:** Slower than average. **Insurance cost:** Higher than average. **Parts supply/cost:** No problem getting moderately priced parts from Acura or Honda dealers. **Warranty:** Bumper-to-bumper 3 years/60,000 km; powertrain 5 years/100,000 km; rust perforation 6 years/unlimited km. **Supplementary warranty:** Not needed. **Highway/city fuel economy:** 7.0–10L/100 km.

Quality/Reliability/Safety

Pro: Quality control: Typical Honda (oops—I mean Acura): first class. **Reliability:** Few complaints that affect the Integra's overall reliability. **Warranty performance:** Better than average. Acura has a comprehensive standard warranty, and there have been few occasions where warranty disputes have had to be settled by third parties.

Con: Owner-reported problems: Some body fit and finish deficiencies. **Service bulletin problems:** An off-centre steering wheel, and paint damage from environmental fallout. **NHTSA safety complaints/safety:** Steering wheel locked up while driving; sunroof suddenly shattered; key can be removed from the ignition without the transmission lever in Park; distorted front windshield; windshield wipers suddenly stop working until you shut off the ignition and wait a few minutes.

Road Performance

Pro: Emergency handling: Better than average, with little body lean or front end plow. **Steering:** Variable-assisted power steering is quick and precise at high speeds. **Acceleration/torque:** Acceptable acceleration from the base engine; more impressive with the high-performance, 170-hp GS-R powerplant (0–100 km/h: 7.2 sec.). **Transmission:** The standard 5-speed manual transmission shifter and clutch mechanism were substantially beefed up last year, giving slightly higher ratios in third and fourth and a taller fifth gear. An optional electronic 4-speed automatic uses "fuzzy logic" to reduce the annoying shifting back and forth over hilly terrain. **Routine handling:** Good handling under almost

all circumstances. Gas shocks and improved body rigidity create a
smooth and firm ride. Ride doesn't deteriorate as load is increased.
Braking: Quite respectable (100–0 km/h: 118 ft.).

Con: Base engine whines at high speed. The GS-R's VTEC engine
requires expert throttle control, frequent gear shifts, and constant
attention in order to work properly. Some torque steer when accelerating. GS-R is hard riding. Steering exhibits a bit of under-steer and isn't
sufficiently assisted for parking.

Comfort/Convenience

Pro: Driving position: Very good. Comfortable, manually adjusted front
bucket seats. **Controls and displays:** The attractive interior includes an
easy-to-read dashboard layout with large analogue gauges that are complete and clear, and climate controls that are easy to operate. **Climate
control:** The climate control system works flawlessly. **Interior
space/comfort F/R:** Plenty of front head and leg room. The coupe's
seat cushions provide good thigh support; its windows have frames for
better sealing; and a reinforced body makes for a stiffer body shell. The
four-door sedan carries four passengers in comfort. The cloth-covered
seats are fairly comfortable and supportive for short drives. The sedan
has comfortable rear seating for two adults, and the rear seats fold
down completely. **Cargo space:** Average.

Con: Standard equipment: Not impressive. A $25,000 base price and
anti-lock brakes are optional, and traction control is unavailable. The
coupe's four small headlights are a throwback to the Isuzu Impulse,
and the side-view mirrors resemble those of both the Prelude and Civic.
The sunroof switch is too far from the sunroof, the radio controls
aren't easily reached, and the sun visors are cheap looking. The steering column, even when tilted to the max, practically rests on your
kneecaps. Spoiler restricts rear visibility. **Entry/exit:** Entry/exit is made
difficult by the curved windows and the doors' awkward design. The
three-door model's rear seat is cramped and suitable only for luggage.
Seats are lower than usual and tend to be uncomfortable on long trips.
Trunk/liftover: The trunk on the coupe and sedan is awkward to load
because of its narrow opening and high liftover. **Quietness:** Poor sealing around the sedan's side windows. Lots of road and engine noise,
especially at full throttle.

COST				
List Price (negotiable)	**Residual Values (months)**			
	24	36	48	60
Integra GS: $25,500 (20%)	$18,000	$15,000	$12,000	$9,000

TECHNICAL DATA

Powertrain (front-drive)
Engines: 1.8L 4-cyl. (139 hp)
• 1.8L 4-cyl (195 hp)
• 1.8L VTEC (170 hp)
Transmissions: 5-speed man.
• 4-speed auto.
Dimension/Capacity
Passengers: 2/2
Height/length/width:
52.6/172.4/67.3 in.

Head room F/R: 38.6/35 in.
Leg room F/R: 42.7/28.1 in.
Wheelbase: 101.2 in.
Turning circle: 39 ft.
Cargo volume: 13.3 cu. ft.
Tow limit: N/A
Fuel tank: 50L/reg.
Weight: 2,650 lb.

SAFETY FEATURES/CRASHWORTHINESS

	Std.	Opt.
Anti-lock brakes	■	❏
Seatbelt pretensioners	—	—
Side airbags	—	—
Traction control	—	—
Head restraints F/R	***	**
Visibility F/R	*****	**
Crash protection (front) D/P	****	***
Crash protection (side) D/P	N/A	N/A
Crash protection (off-set)	N/A	

DAEWOO

South Korea's bankrupt conglomerate is seen as a poorly managed company, making wild sales predictions that never materialize. In fact, Daewoo has become South Korea's best-known financial basket case, with the company's shipbuilding, commercial vehicle, automotive parts, and electronic businesses on the block. Additionally, there's the very real possibility that GM or Chrysler will acquire the company's auto interests sometime next year.

Although sales have improved of late, Daewoo's 3-year foray in the States has been a public relations disaster, characterized by sales way below expectations, a reputation for low-quality vehicles, and angry dealers who claim they've been misled.

Specifically, American dealers accused Daewoo of undercutting them by selling directly to the public at prices they couldn't match. Soon thereafter, the automaker admitted it had made a mistake and stopped the practice after dealers threatened to walk away from their franchises. After settling with its American dealers, the automaker began retailing cars in French markets for about $5,000 less than dealer prices. Now, these franchisees say they were cheated by the parent company and have asked for compensation. Daewoo claims it was simply a marketing mistake.

"Daewoo Complaints" at *www.badcustomerservice.co.uk/press.htm* is an interesting site set up by the owner of a new 2000 Daewoo Galant that burned to the ground. He details his frustration in dealing with Daewoo in attempting to get a replacement vehicle.

Lanos

✘ RISKY BUY

Lanos

RATING: Not Recommended. Carried over unchanged. **Strong points:** Low base price and relatively fuel efficient. **Weak points:** Poor acceleration; harsh ride; poor handling; automatic transmission eats into performance; and a cramped interior. Long-term quality and reliability has yet to be determined. Also keep in mind the automaker's uncertain future and small dealer network, which can complicate servicing and warranty support.

OVERVIEW: Daewoo's $13,500 ($380 PDI/transport) entry-level, front-drive, subcompact model comes as a five-passenger, two-door hatchback and four-door sedan. The smallest of its three-car lineup, the Lanos is about the size of a VW Golf, with less standard equipment and costing about $6,000 less. The 1.6L 105-hp 16-valve 4-cylinder engine can be mated to a base 5-speed manual transmission or an optional 4-speed automatic. **Highway/city fuel economy:** 5.9–9.9L/100 km with the 1.5L engine; 6.0–9.1L/100 km with the 1.6L engine. Other standard features: power steering, AM/FM cassette, 60/40 split-folding rear seats, and 14-inch tires. The few other options available: a power sunroof, ABS, and air conditioning.

    Service bulletin problems: Nothing published, yet. **NHTSA safety complaints/safety:** Automatic transmission suddenly drops into neutral on the highway; vehicle veers sharply when cruising.

    Even though the Lanos looks like a bargain at first glance, it doesn't have much of a track record in Canada or the United States. You can get the more refined Accent for about the same price.

Nubira

RATING: Not Recommended until the manufacturer, dealer network, and car prove themselves to be more than just hype. This year's models arrive without any significant changes. **Strong points:** Well appointed; good engine performance; relatively fuel efficient; competent handling, adequate interior room, and good braking. **Weak points:** Noisy engine; windshield is too close to the driver; steering is over assisted; predicted rapid depreciation; and weak dealer/manufacturer support.

OVERVIEW: This is a larger, more powerful front-drive (about the Hyundai Elantra's size) that has a few more standard features than the Lanos—as shown by its improved road performance and higher price ($16,500). It's available as a four-door sedan, hatchback, or wagon and will seat five in relative comfort. **Highway/city fuel economy:** 7.1–10.6L/100 km with an automatic gearbox. Standard features include: a twin-cam 129-hp 2.0L, 4-cylinder engine coupled to a 5-speed manual transmission or an optional 4-speed automatic; 4-wheel disc brakes; front and rear anti-sway bars; a fully independent suspension; an AM/FM cassette radio, and fog lights.

The Nubira is a nicely packaged and reasonably priced small car that is outclassed by other small cars with a better track record and a larger dealer network. Alternatives worth considering: the Honda Civic, Mazda Protegé, and Toyota Corolla. **Service bulletin problems:** Nothing published, yet. **NHTSA safety complaints/safety:** Zilch.

Leganza

Leganza

RATING: Not Recommended. You'd have to be crazy to pay $20,300 to $24,200 for a South Korean car that has no past and an uncertain future. The 2001 model returns this year with a slight restyling. **Strong points:** Lots of standard features, adequate acceleration, good braking, and roomy interior. **Weak points:** Noisy engine runs out of steam at higher speeds; mediocre automatic transmission performance; ponderous handling; uncomfortable rear seating; and weak dealer network and warranty support. Power-adjusted driver's seat doesn't adjust the seatback; the leather feels cheap; small vent controls aren't user-friendly; the CD changer skips when the car passes over bumps; and the sound system's graphic equalizer indicator washes out in daylight. Dealers are concentrated in Quebec and Ontario.

OVERVIEW: Daewoo's top-of-the-line luxury sedan, the Leganza is about the size of a Nissan Altima and is loaded to the gills with standard features that enhance performance, convenience, and safety. It uses a 2.2L 131-hp 4-cylinder engine (only two horses more than the Nubira) mated to a standard 5-speed manual transmission or an optional 4-speed automatic. Alternatives worth considering: the Honda Accord, Mazda 626, and Toyota Camry.

Despite its many standard features that would cost extra on its rivals, the Leganza doesn't deliver the performance so apparent with the Accord and Camry. Reliability and durability are also an unknown. **Service bulletin problems:** N/A. **NHTSA safety complaints/safety:** N/A.

HONDA

Honda continues to set sales records with every one of its cars, trucks, and minivans. The best we can hope is that the company holds the line on prices, making the redesigned Civic a bargain.We'll also see two new cars—the Insight, Honda's first hybrid powered vehicle, touted to use only 3.2 litres of gas per 100 kilometres; and the S2000, a limited-production $48,000 roadster that's not as refined as the Mazda Miata.

Insight: A great idea, but a lousy car. Get a new Honda Civic, a 2000 Chevrolet Metro, or Suzuki Swift, or a used 1992–93 Honda Civic VX, instead.

Insight

A low volume hybrid-powertrain two-seater, the Insight is the Toyota Prius's chief fuel economy rival. Not as large or refined as Prius, the Insight's gas engine runs all the time. The Prius is capable of running on battery power alone, engine power alone, or both. Nevertheless, the Insight's 73-hp 1.0L, 12-valve, 3-cylinder engine combines with an electric motor to produce outstanding fuel savings—estimated by Honda to be 3.2 litres of gas per 100 kilometres on the highway and 5.0 L/100 km in the city. Other pluses: crisp handling around town, footwells that provide plenty of leg and foot room, and a fairly large storage area (5.0 cu. ft.). A continuously variable transmission (CVT) will be offered on 2001 models. Safety features include dual airbags and three-point seatbelts with pretensioners and load limiters.

So why isn't everyone buying up this econobox?

A high price and low performance; this great idea for fuel economy makes for a lousy vehicle. The Insight is frighteningly underpowered (freeway travel not recommended), taking over 11 seconds to reach 100 km/h. It only comes with a manual gearbox, gets whipped around by sidewinds, has little soundproofing, provides a harsh, uncomfortable ride on smooth pavement, has a small blind spot to the right-rear, and doesn't offer a centre armrest with storage bin.

By the way, the only option is air conditioning—essential when the beads of sweat pour down as you try to merge or pass on the highway.

At $26,000, the Insight is grossly overpriced for a vehicle that has all the above disadvantages, no reliability track record, and spotty dealer servicing. Plus, I doubt the public wants to sacrifice comfort and safety in exchange for better gas mileage. I remember when Honda launched, with as much "green" fanfare, its $11,995 1992 Civic VX equipped with a lean-burn VTEC engine and touted to only need 5 litres of gas per 100 kilometres. A hit with the Sierra Club, it bombed in dealer showrooms. It got the axe in 1993.

S2000

S2000

This new world-class sport roadster is lightweight, with a peppy though loud 4-cylinder engine that generates 240 hp and 25 mpg. Priced at $48,000, plus $850 PDI/transport, only 5,000 a year are earmarked for North America (expect less than 500 for Canada). Other models worth considering: the BMW Z3 2.3 ($45,900) or the Mazda Miata ($26,995). The S2000 comes fully equipped with limited-slip differential, anti-lock brakes, AC, cruise control, leather seats, 16-inch wheels, high-intensity headlights, remote door locks with an engine immobilizer, a CD player with remote audio controls, power everything, and an air deflector.

Powered by a 2.0-litre, 16-valve, inline four, the S2000 will reach 0–100 km/h in about the same time it takes to close the convertible roof—under six seconds. All this without straining the high-revving VTEC engine (the tachometer has an unbelievable 9000 redline). The 6-speed shifter has short throws helped by a direct link with the gearbox, rather than shift-by-wire units used in other cars. New standard features to be phased in this year: floor mats, a clock, and an emergency trunk release.

Performance drivers will immediately discover that the S2000 excels at acceleration, braking, cornering, and shifting, due in large part to the car's powerful engine, anti-lock brakes, double wishbone body, rigid suspension, and electronically controlled rack-and-pinion steering, which enhances steering response without compromising stability.

Not everything is perfect, though. Rear visibility is cut a bit by the convertible top boot cover, the convertible top, when it's up, and the rear plastic window sans defroster. The small trunk houses a temporary spare tire (shame!) and Honda doesn't include a passenger airbag shut-off switch (double shame!). The ride can be jolting, as with many convertibles: there are quite a few squeaks and rattles; tall drivers won't fit comfortably in the cockpit; and the sound system has Lilliputian controls and sounds cheap.

Civic

Civic

RATING: Above Average. New or used, the Honda Civic is one of the best cars money can buy, and this year, the redesigned model is a particularly good buy. Nevertheless, its rating has been downgraded due to the serious safety-related complaints registered against the year 2000 model. **Strong points:** Good acceleration—better with the 2001, smooth-shifting automatic transmission, great handling, comfortable ride, good front and rear visibility (except for the year 2000 Si's spoiler), more interior and trunk space with the 2001, high-quality construction, excellent resale value, and bulletproof reliability. **Weak points:** Suspension may be too firm for some, difficult rear access, rear seat room limited to two adults, and an unusually large number of safety-related complaints that include airbag malfunctions, sudden acceleration, and complete brake failure.

NEW FOR 2001: A complete redesign giving the Civic more interior and trunk room, a horsepower boost, a firmer strut suspension, more rear passenger room, and styling similar to a small Accord. All references to the hatchback and Si concern year 2000 leftovers; the hatchback has been dropped from the 2001 lineup; the redesigned Si won't arrive until year's end.

OVERVIEW: The Civic is one of the most refined and competent subcompacts on the market today. Few larger and more expensive cars can match its quality, performance, and roominess.

Civic sedans can be found in three trim levels: much like the Accord's sedans, with a base DX, a mid-level LX, and a high-performance EX. In addition to the above trim levels, the HX coupe is offered to buyers who put fuel economy over highway performance.

DX and LX models use either a 5-speed manual or a 4-speed automatic transmission coupled to a 115-hp 4-cylinder engine, while the EX gets 12 more horses, with the emphasis on low-end torque, from its VTEC powerplant. HX versions come with a 117-hp VTEC engine mated to either a manual 5-speed, or a CVT (continually variable transmission) gearbox.

Honda has replaced its front double-wishbone suspension with MacPherson struts in order to shorten the body length and firm up the suspension. Combined with a modified steering linkage, Honda manages to shorten this year's cars, provide additional interior room, and still retain good steering feedback.

New Civics in any form are usually quite expensive when compared with domestic offerings. However, they are easy to resell and always command premium prices that equal or surpass the extra money spent when first bought.

Cost analysis/best alternatives: Get the 2001 model, for the upgrades. If you are looking for a year-old hatchback, go for the reasonably priced Civic CX or DX for the best combination of comfort, performance, and fuel economy. Other cars worth considering are the Mazda Protegé, Nissan Sentra, Hyundai Accent, and Toyota Echo. **Options:** Four-wheel anti-lock brakes are wise buys. Try to get a free extra set of ignition keys written into the contract; Honda's anti-start, theft-protection keys may cost as much as $150 a set. Steer clear of the standard-issue radio and Firestone tires. **Rebates:** Not likely. **Delivery/PDI:** $400. **Depreciation:** Expected to be much slower than average. **Insurance cost:** High insurance costs, wrote one Elmvale, Ontario, shopper: "I was choosing between a Saturn and a Civic and I simply couldn't afford the insurance costs for the Civic. They were almost three times the cost of the Saturn in our area." **Parts supply/cost:** Predicted to be moderately priced and easily found at dealers and independent suppliers. **Annual maintenance cost:** Less than average. **Warranty:** Bumper-to-bumper 3 years/60,000 km; powertrain 5 years/100,000 km; rust perforation 6 years/unlimited km. **Supplementary warranty:** Not necessary. **Highway/city fuel economy:** 6.0–8.6L/100 km with the base engine and 6.0–9.3L/100 km with the Si.

Quality/Reliability/Safety

Pro: Quality control: Assembly, as well as the quality of materials used in these cars, is first class. **Reliability:** Outstanding. Civics have proven to be mostly trouble free. **Warranty performance:** Not generous, but acceptable. **Owner-reported problems:** Minor fit and finish deficiencies.

Con: Service bulletin problems: (previous year's Civics) Steering pull or drifting; whistling or howling noise coming from the top middle of the windshield at highway speeds; moon roof seal sticks up or leaks; key is difficult to remove from the ignition switch; rear door lock tab is hard to open; warped wheel covers; driver's power mirror vibrations; security system LED malfunction. **NHTSA safety complaints/safety:** (previous year's Civics) Airbags failed to deploy; accelerator pedal sticks to cables mounted too tight; accelerator cable got hung up in the cruise control, causing the vehicle to suddenly accelerate; while driving, vehicle suddenly accelerated due to the throttle sticking open, and brakes couldn't stop the car; car suddenly accelerated when passing another vehicle; gas pedal keeps sticking; while driving at a low speed, transmission popped out of gear and brake pedal went right to the floor without any braking effect; brakes locked up and vehicle pulled to the left when coming to an emergency stop; sudden steering loss while driving; excessive vibration due to engine main bearing failure; transmission sometimes fails to change gear; transmission was stuck in Reverse; vehicle suddenly went into Reverse although shift lever was put into Drive; while stopped at a light on a hill, vehicle suddenly shifted into Reverse; another driver had the same thing happen, except this time the transmission shifted into Neutral; faulty power door lock makes it impossible to open door from the inside or outside; dome light won't work when doors are open; taillights don't work when the headlights and dash lights are on; spoiler height prevents a clear line of sight; rear view mirror is poorly located and is non-adjustable, creating a large forward blind spot for tall drivers; sheet metal fatigue on both front fenders; faulty hood support rod causes the hood to come crashing down; exterior rear view mirror becomes loose, despite dealer efforts to tighten it.

Road Performance

Pro: Acceleration/torque: The 1.7L engine is smooth and responsive. Transmission shifting is quiet and effortless with the manual and practically imperceptible with the automatic. The Si's 160-hp 1.6L 4-cylinder is a tire burner. **Routine handling:** Handling is excellent, and the ride, though a bit stiff with this year's front struts, is among the best in the subcompact class. The Si's larger wheels add to its handling prowess. **Braking:** Very good (100–0 km/h: 125 ft.).

Con: The VTEC variant is noisy—get the VTEC option only if you enjoy constant gear shifting and intend to do a lot of highway driving, where it's most useful and less interactive. The HX gets its impressive fuel economy by sacrificing acceleration power through its tall gearing. **Transmission:** The CVT often feels like it's slipping in gear until you get used to its little quirks. **Emergency handling:** Some body roll when cornering at highway speeds. Skinny tires add to overall noise and harshness. **Steering:** Optional power steering could be more precise.

Comfort/Convenience

Pro: Driving position: Very good; seat height is higher in the sedans than in previous years. A large cockpit area, along with interior refinements and the large window area, makes for excellent visibility and a feeling of spaciousness. **Controls and displays:** Excellent dashboard design, with easy-to-read gauges and accessible controls. **Climate control:** Heating and ventilation are first class. **Interior space/comfort F/R:** Spacious front seating, less roomy in the rear. **Cargo space:** Versatile and spacious cargo areas. **Trunk/liftover:** Trunk space is acceptable. **Quietness:** Engine/road noise has been cut considerably.

Con: Standard equipment: Though it's reasonably well appointed, the base Honda has few standard features in order to keep the base price down. Interestingly, the front side airbag feature has a warning device to alert you to the fact that the passenger's head is resting on the airbag. I guess it's there so you can waken the passenger just prior to impact so he or she is properly positioned. Go figure. Coupe's low seating may be troublesome for short-statured drivers. Doors give a "tinny" sound when closed. **Entry/exit:** The small door openings and low seating make for difficult entry and exit, and restrict overall visibility. **Interior space/comfort F/R:** Both front and rear seats are uncomfortable on long trips. Trunk has a high sill, making for difficult loading.

COST				
List Price (firm)	**Residual Values (months)**			
	24	36	48	60
Civic DX: $16,300 (11%)	$12,000	$10,000	$8,000	$6,500

TECHNICAL DATA	
Powertrain (front-drive)	Head room F/R: 38.2/36.2 in.
Engines: 1.7L 4-cyl. (115 hp)	Leg room F/R: 42.7/34.1 in.
• 1.7L 4-cyl. (127 hp)	Wheelbase: 103.1 in.
• 1.7L 4-cyl. (160 hp)	Turning circle: 37 ft.
Transmissions: 5-speed man.	Cargo volume: 11.9 cu. ft.
• 4-speed auto.	Tow limit: N/A
Dimension/Capacity	Fuel tank: 45L/reg.
Passengers: 2/3	Weight: 2,500 lb.
Height/length/width:	
56.7/174.6/67.5 in.	

SAFETY FEATURES/CRASHWORTHINESS

	Std.	**Opt.**
Anti-lock brakes	■	■
Seatbelt pretensioners	—	—
Side airbags	—	■
Traction control	—	—
Head restraints F/R	**	*
Visibility F/R	*****	****
Crash protection (front) D/P		
2d	****	****
4d	****	****
Crash protection (side) D/P		
2d	**	***
4d	***	***
Crash protection (off-set)	***	

Note: Crash data applies to the year 2000 Civic.

Accord

Accord

RATING: Above Average. Having competed toe-to-toe for over a decade with the Camry and Ford Taurus/Sable, the Accord's incremental upgrades put it in the forefront of mid-sized family sedans. Nevertheless, this year's models have been downgraded due to NHTSA-collected safety-related complaints of stalling, automatic transmission failures, brake failures, and airbag malfunctions. **Strong points:** Excellent V6 acceleration, well equipped with user-friendly instruments and controls, easy handling, a comfortable ride, quiet cabin, good craftsmanship, above average reliability, and high resale value. **Weak points:** Low torque base engine makes for constant highway downshifting; problematic automatic transmission shifts harshly and slowly; average braking; rear passenger room is tight; and serious safety-related complaints reported to NHTSA.

NEW FOR 2001: Standard side airbags. Freshened exterior styling with a more aggressive-looking front end and hood, plus, an all-new taillight and rear deck lid.

OVERVIEW: Having undergone a makeover a few years ago, this year's Accord is better than ever. You want performance? Well, you can choose among three engines that include two competent 4-bangers and a powerful V6. You want ride comfort and responsive handling? Accord gives you that too, through a more refined suspension and steering setup. What about space? Look out, Taurus/Sable—the Accord sedans are roomier than ever before, with interior dimension/capacity that provides more interior space than Ford's mid-sized duo. That could be why Honda has regained its lead over Ford in mid-sized sedan sales.

Overall, the Honda Accord is smooth, quiet, mannerly, and predictable. Every time Honda has redesigned this line it not only caught up with the latest advances, but also went slightly ahead. Other strong points are ergonomics that prioritize comfort, easy driveability, high-quality fit and finish inside and out, impressive assembly quality, and outstanding reliability.

Fast and nimble without a V6, this is the mid-sized sedan of choice for drivers who want maximum fuel economy and comfort along with lots of space for grocery hauling and occasional highway cruising. With the optional 16-valve 4-cylinder engine or V6, the Accord is one of the most versatile mid-sized cars you can find. It offers something for everyone, and its top-drawer quality and high resale value mean there's no way you can lose money buying one.

Cost analysis/best alternatives: Only consider a practically identical year 2000 model if the price is cut by at least 10 percent and side airbags aren't your bag. Some other vehicles worth considering: the BMW 3-series, Mazda Protegé and 626, Toyota Camry, and VW Golf and Jetta. **Options:** V6 for a smoother ride. If you're likely to do a lot of driving in the snow or over wet pavement, don't let the dealer sell you Michelin MXV4 tires—they're terrible snow performers. Choose instead one of the brands recommended in Part One. Try to get a free extra set of ignition keys written into the contract; Honda's anti-start, theft-protection keys may cost as much as $150 a set. **Rebates:** Not likely. **Delivery/PDI:** $500. **Depreciation:** Slower than average. **Insurance cost:** Higher than average. **Parts supply/cost:** Good availability and moderately priced. **Annual maintenance cost:** Less than average. **Warranty:** Bumper-to-bumper 3 years/60,000 km; powertrain 5 years/100,000 km; rust perforation 5 years/unlimited km. **Supplementary warranty:** Not needed. **Highway/city fuel economy:** 7.4–10.5L/100 km with the base engine, 7.1–10.5L/100 km with the 16-valve 2.3L, and 7.8–11.5L/100 km with the V6 engine.

Quality/Reliability/Safety

Pro: Quality control: Not perfect, but much better than what you'll get from Chrysler, Ford, GM, the South Koreans, or Ashley, Franz, Jean Pierre, and Guido. These cars are built with care, although occasionally mistakes slip through. Interestingly, quality control in U. S. and Mexican plants appears to be on par with plants in Japan. **Reliability:** Better than average, throughout the life of the car. An increase in transmission and brake failures is worrisome. **Warranty performance:** Average. CAA surveys have shown that customer satisfaction is an impressive 88 percent, compared to 85 percent for both the Toyota Camry and Mazda 626. Keep in mind that Honda puts a "goodwill" clause in almost all of its service bulletins, allowing service managers to submit any claim to the company, long after the original warranty has elapsed.

Con: Owner-reported problems: Transmission failures, transmission slips and surges at 50–70 km/h, clunks and jolts when engaging Reverse and Forward gears (see below), brake failures and premature brake wear, electrical short circuits, malfunctioning accessories, and rattles and squeaks. **Service bulletin problems:** Clunk or bang when engaging Reverse gear (280100 Bulletin, Sequence Number: 135, Date of Bulletin: 0001, NHTSA Item Number: SB61353). This appears to be a generic problem that affects Honda transmissions used in other models, as well. Other bulletin-related problems: Excessive judder or shudder when driving at speeds of 40–80 km/h, vibration is most evident when the torque converter lock-up clutch is in the partial lock-up mode; flickering dash lights; driver's door mirror vibrates when driving on smooth roads; and rear door sash wrinkling. **NHTSA safety complaints:** Airbags failed to deploy; airbag light stays on continually; strong smell of gas fumes in the interior; vehicle hit from behind at stoplight and then suddenly accelerated; brake pedal has to be pushed down with both feet to stop vehicle; brake failure caused lengthy stopping distances; emergency brakes failed on an incline; when braking while going downhill, brakes suddenly failed; loss of brakes as pedal went all the way to the floor. Master cylinder was replaced but failed again. ABS and airbag light continually stays lit; premature brake wear; check engine light stays lit; sudden loss of power steering fluid while driving; loss of power steering fluid when making a U-turn; excessive steering wander that degrades progressively; vehicle pulls severely to the right, without warning, while driving at any rate of speed; during warm days fuel will boil over and flood the engine, causing a no-start condition. Apparently, Honda is aware of this vapour-lock type of problem with their redesigned 2000 V6 engines. Vehicle suddenly stalls while driving, which dealer says is caused by a faulty computer module; engine hesitates when accelerating to merge with traffic; frequent transmission failures; when cruise control is engaged, the transmission suddenly downshifts; chronic transmission leaks leading to replacement; automatic transmission's gears disengage and make a loud noise when engaging; loud thump and jolt when shifting into Reverse; vehicle rolls forward when in Reverse gear; while parked on an incline, vehicle rolled forward, despite having gear lever in the Park position; vertical lines distort windshield view; took key out of the ignition and all the accessories still work; due to the design of the dash lighting, it's hard to read the odometer, clock, and radio indicator; speedometer reads 8–10 percent higher than actual speed; fuel tank never shows more than 2/3 when tank is full; turn signal fails to self-cancel on left turns; horn is very difficult to access in an emergency; poor design of driver's power seat—sits too high in the DOWN position, causing driver's leg to slam against the ignition and steering wheel; driver's side seatback rocks; right front passenger-side window suddenly exploded; windshield whistling after repeated attempts to seal it; rear seatbelts lock too tightly around neck and are difficult to loosen; child pulled shoulder belt around neck and head and it locked up when he let the strap go; difficult to secure child safety seat to middle of rear seat; rear seatbelt fails to retract; defective rear computerized motor mounts; excessive wind noise; doors won't close properly due to misaligned body; radiator is not protected by the front of the body; raised vehicle with jack that came with Accord when it suddenly bent, pinning driver under the vehicle.

Road Performance

Pro: Emergency handling: Very good. A firm but well-controlled ride is achieved through increased body rigidity and a reworked suspension. **Steering:** Improved variable-assist power steering provides excellent road feel. **Acceleration/torque:** Excellent with both the 4- and 6-cylinder engines (0–100 km/h: 7.6 sec. with the V6). The 16-valve 2.3L engine delivers a sportier performance than the more sedate V6. Both engines give sparkling performance with plenty of low-end torque and minimal noise. The new 200-hp V6 doesn't offer a stick shift, but the automatic transmission doesn't sacrifice performance. **Transmission:** The 5-speed manual transmission works very well with smooth and light clutch action. The 4-speed automatic has Overdrive to help save fuel. It also has a Grade Logic feature that reduces gear hunting when climbing hills and automatically downshifts when descending, using engine compression to brake. **Routine handling:** Excellent handling in town and on the highway. It's also amazingly smooth and quiet. There isn't a trace of vibration throughout the operating range, including at idle. Excels in smoothness when passing over freeway expansion joints and potholes, where it damps out the jolts better than most cars in its class. The emphasis on comfort also dominates the Accord's ride and handling. Although its chassis is as good as any, Honda's suspension settings aren't as firm as those of the other cars in this class. **Braking:** Average (100–0 km/h: 133 ft.).

Con: VTEC 150-hp 2.3L engine lacks guts and is a bit buzzy in the higher ranges. Could use a bit more high-end torque. Automatic transmission frequently pops out of gear. Jolts and clunks when engaging Reverse. No all-wheel drive option, which is available on many cars in the Accord class. Sometimes, the tall centre console gets in the way of shifting. The four-doors have a less rigid suspension and softer ride than does the coupe. Standard Bridgestone tires don't grip enough in corners.

Comfort/Convenience

Pro: Standard equipment: A nice array of standard features on the base model. Wood and leather on upper-end models. **Driving position:** Excellent driving position and visibility. Very comfortable, sporty front seats are well padded and supportive. Everything is right where it should be, easily seen and easily reached. **Controls and displays:** The well-designed dashboard looks like it's one big moulding, rather than a lot of pieces thrown together. Clear gauges and instruments. User-friendly controls and instrumentation. The radio and AC controls have been moved closer to eye level. **Climate control:** Very user friendly; quiet, efficient, and easily calibrated. **Entry/exit:** Easy entry and exit. **Interior space/comfort F/R:** More interior space than the BMW 740i, Ford Taurus, or Toyota Camry. Redesigned front seat bases provide more rear foot room. **Cargo space:** The LX and DX sedans' pass-through rear seats allow for more convenient cargo handling. **Trunk/liftover:** Large trunk on sedans and versatile hatchback design; high liftover, however. **Quietness:** Average, with some tire drumming evident.

Con: Si spoiler cuts into rear visibility. Rear seating is too low. Rear room for three is a bit tight. The remote lock key fob is quirky: sometimes it refuses to unlock the doors.

COST				
List Price (firm)	**Residual Values (months)**			
	24	36	48	60
Accord DX Sedan:				
$23,000 (10%)	$19,000	$16,000	$13,000	$10,000

TECHNICAL DATA	
Powertrain (front-drive)	Head room F/R: 40/37.6 in.
Engines: 2.3L 4-cyl. (135 hp)	Leg room F/R: 42.1/37.9 in.
• 2.3L 4-cyl. (150 hp)	Wheelbase: 106.9 in.
• 3.0L V6 (200 hp)	Turning circle: 40 ft.
Transmissions: 5-speed man.	Cargo volume: 14.1 cu. ft.
• 4-speed auto.	Tow limit: 1,000 lb.
Dimension/Capacity (sedan)	Fuel tank: 65L/reg.
Passengers: 2/3	Weight: 3,230 lb.
Height/length/width:	
57.2/188.8/70.3 in	

SAFETY FEATURES/CRASHWORTHINESS

	Std.	Opt.
Anti-lock brakes	■	■
Seatbelt pretensioners	—	—
Side airbags	■	❑
Traction control	—	—
Head restraints F/R	***	**
Visibility F/R	*****	*****
Crash protection (front) D/P	****	****
Crash protection (side) D/P	****	****
Crash protection (off-set)	***	

Prelude

Prelude

RATING: Above Average. **Strong points:** Powerful engine, easy handling, lots of standard features, and impressive reliability and quality control. **Weak points:** A bit hard riding, difficult rear seat access, limited rear seat room, insufficient trunk space, and excessive road noise.

NEW FOR 2001: Floor mats, rear child seat tether anchors, and an emergency trunk opener.

OVERVIEW: This fifth-generation Prelude sport coupe is complete, functional, and rational without any hint of aggression in its styling or performance components. In fact, most of its performance upgrades won't be noticed by the average driver. It comes with a standard 2.2L 200-hp VTEC engine. There are two trim levels available: the base Prelude and the Prelude Type SH.

Cost analysis/best alternatives: If you don't know it already, the 2000 Prelude is practically identical to this year's version, and is a real bargain if you can find a reasonably priced discounted leftover. Other worthwhile cars to consider are the Acura Integra, Ford Mustang, GM Camaro and Firebird, and Mazda Miata. **Options:** Try to get a free extra set of ignition keys written into the contract; Honda's anti-start, theft-protection keys may cost as much as $150 a set. **Rebates:** Not likely. **Delivery/PDI:** $300. **Depreciation:** Slower than average. **Insurance cost:** Higher than average. **Parts supply/cost:** Parts are easily found and moderately priced. Most corner mechanics are ill-equipped to service these cars, and the complex Automatic Torque Transfer System (ATTS) won't make their job any easier. **Annual maintenance cost:** Less than average. **Warranty:** Bumper-to-bumper 3 years/60,000 km; power-train 5 years/100,000 km; rust perforation 5 years/unlimited km. **Supplementary warranty:** Not needed. **Highway/city fuel economy:** 8.2–11.2L/100 km.

Quality/Reliability/Safety

Pro: Quality control: Exceptional quality control. **Reliability:** No problems have been reported that would make the Prelude unreliable. **Warranty performance:** Better than average. **Owner-reported problems:** Preludes usually give their owners excellent service for the first five years. Even later on, the few problems that surface aren't difficult to diagnose or expensive to repair.

Con: Owner-reported problems: Air-conditioner condensers frequently need cleaning to eliminate disagreeable odours. Owners have complained about minor electrical problems and accessory malfunctions. **Service bulletin problems:** Steering wheel column won't hold a set position, the steering pump is noisy, and the upper windshield moulding warps. **NHTSA safety complaints/safety:** Driver's airbag failed to deploy; airbag deployed three seconds late; without ABS, wheels tend to lock up easily during emergency braking; door locks frequently malfunction, causing the driver's door to lock unexpectedly and not unlock.

Road Performance

Pro: Emergency handling: Handling is excellent in all conditions. Suspension travel is long enough to reduce bottoming out when fully loaded or when encountering irregular terrain. Suspension gives a better feel of the road while reducing throttle-lift oversteer, bump, and torque steer (high-performance enthusiasts, rejoice!). **Steering:** Direct and predictable. **Acceleration/torque:** Plenty of power (0–100 km/h: 7 sec.), but insufficient torque means you'll do a lot of shifting to keep pace in traffic or on the highway. The Automatic Torque Transfer System (ATTS) is an interesting gizmo that transfers torque to the outside wheel in a turn, making for quicker high-speed cornering. **Transmission:** The manual and automatic transmissions are precise, smooth shifting, and require little effort. **Routine handling:** Very responsive. The ride is quite comfortable, due mainly to suspension refinements and four-wheel disc brakes. **Braking:** Better than average.

Con: Even though the 200-hp engine is ideal for sporty performance, this car cries out for a V6 powerplant that provides more torque in all gears. It could also use a 6-speed transmission to more efficiently harness the VTEC's high-revving engine.

Comfort/Convenience

Pro: Standard equipment: Lots of standard features. Height-adjustable bucket seat. Excellent visibility. **Controls and displays:** Greatly improved, user-friendly dash. **Climate control:** Competent climate control system is quiet and easy to adjust. **Interior space/comfort F/R:** Last year's extended wheelbase increased rear head room by 1.5 inches, knee room by 2.5 inches, and foot room by almost 3 inches. Comfortable front seats are well-padded and supportive.

Con: Driving position: All drivers may find head room lacking, especially with a sunroof. **Interior space/comfort F/R:** Insufficient rear passenger room. **Entry/exit:** Very difficult for both the driver and passengers. **Cargo space:** Rather limited. **Trunk/liftover:** Small trunk has a low liftover. **Quietness:** Some road noise is still present.

COST				
List Price (negotiable)		**Residual Values (months)**		
	24	36	48	60
Base Prelude: $28,900 (10%)	$20,000	$17,000	$14,000	$11,000

TECHNICAL DATA	
Powertrain (front-drive)	Head room F/R: 37.9/35.3 in.
Engine: 2.2L 4-cyl. (200 hp)	Leg room F/R: 43/28.1 in.
Transmissions: 5-speed man.	Wheelbase: 101.8 in.
• 4-speed auto.	Turning circle: 40 ft.
Dimension/Capacity	Cargo volume: 8.7 cu. ft.
Passengers: 2/2	Tow limit: 1,000 lb.
Height/length/width:	Fuel tank: 60L/reg.
51.8/178/69 in.	Weight: 2,950 lb.

SAFETY FEATURES/CRASHWORTHINESS		
	Std.	**Opt.**
Anti-lock brakes	■	❑
Seatbelt pretensioners	❑	❑
Side airbags	—	—
Traction control	■	❑
Head restraints F/R	**	**
Visibility F/R	*****	*****
Crash protection (front) D/P	N/A	N/A
Crash protection (side) D/P	N/A	N/A
Crash protection (off-set)	N/A	

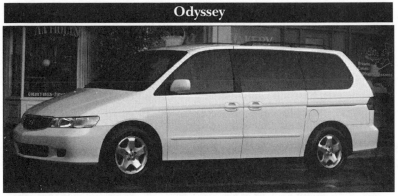

Odyssey

RATING: Above Average. Vehicle rating has been downgraded because quality has slipped as evidenced by the disturbingly frequent reports of safety-related and performance-related failures. Of particular concern are airbag malfunctions, automatic sliding door failures, transmission breakdowns and erratic shifting, and sudden brake loss. **Strong points:** Standard ABS and traction control (EX model only), car-like ride and handling, easy entry/exit, second driver-side door, quiet interior, lots of passenger and cargo room, and an extensive list of standard equipment. **Weak points:** A high base price; premium fuel is required for optimum performance; a decline in quality; and rear seat head restraints impede side and rear visibility.

NEW FOR 2001: Second- and third-row seats get new child seat tether anchors. Upgraded stereo speakers, an intermittent rear window wiper, and floor mats are standard. LX models get a driver's seat height adjuster and traction control, while EX will offer a new remote-controlled alarm. An optional GPS navigation system is also new this year.

OVERVIEW: When it was first launched in 1995, the Odyssey was a sales dud simply because Canadians and *Lemon-Aid* saw through Honda's ruse in trying to pass off an underpowered mid-sized, four-door station wagon with a raised roof as a minivan. However, several years ago the Odyssey was redesigned, and now represents one of the better minivans on the Canadian market.

No longer simply an Accord masquerading as a minivan, the redesigned front-drive, Alliston, Ontario–built Odyssey is longer, wider, taller, and more powerful than ever before. In fact, it compares well with the Ford Windstar as the longest front-drive minivan on the market. It has a lean look, yet the interior is wide enough and long enough to accommodate a 4' x 8' plywood sheet laid flat. Sliding doors are offered as standard equipment and, if you buy the EX version, they will both be power assisted.

You can only get one engine—a powerful 210-hp V6 that easily handles most driving chores. Odyssey also offers an upgraded, fully independent suspension, front and rear AC, second-row captain's chairs that can be shoved side by side to create a bench seat, and a convenient third-row bench seat that folds into the floor when not in use.

Cost analysis/best alternatives: Despite its high price, the Odyssey is more reliable and handles more easily than its American competition. Forget about finding a bargain-priced 2000 model; they're long gone. Incidentally, a fully loaded EX does run $3,000 more than the base model. For the additional money you get traction control, failure-prone power rear doors, remote entry, a power driver's seat, fore-and-aft adjustment for the middle seats, a climate control system that's hard to access and calibrate (the LX version is more user-friendly), and an upgraded sound system. I suggest you bite the bullet and buy your Odyssey before the second round of price increases are announced early next year. There is room for some price negotiation, with savings in the $1,500–$2,000 range, but make sure you have a specific delivery date spelled out in the contract along with a protected price, in case there's a price increase while you're waiting for delivery. The Nissan Quest is also worth considering if you plan mostly light-duty urban commuting. However, if you want better handling and reliability, the closest competitor to the Odyssey is Toyota's Sienna minivan. The Pontiac Montana and Chevrolet Venture from GM are good front-drive choices—they're only a bit less reliable, but are still acceptable. If you're looking for lots of towing "grunt," then the rear-drive GM Astro, Safari, or full-sized vans would be good buys. **Options:** Traction control. **Rebates:** Are you kidding? These minivans are hot! **Delivery/PDI:** $500. **Depreciation:** Slower than average. **Insurance cost:** Higher than average. **Annual maintenance cost:** Average. **Parts supply/cost:** Supply is better than average because the Odyssey uses many generic Accord parts. **Warranty:** Bumper-to-bumper 3 years/60,000 km; powertrain 5 years/100,000 km; rust perforation 5 years/unlimited km. **Supplementary warranty:** Not needed. **Highway/city fuel economy:** 8.5–13.2L/100 km. Premium fuel is recommended, but the Odyssey will run on regular, with a slight loss of power (about five horses).

Quality/Reliability/Safety

Pro: Reliability: Much better than average, but Honda still has a few problems to work out. **Warranty performance:** Comprehensive base warranty that's usually applied fairly with lots of "wiggle room" that the service manager can use to apply "goodwill" adjustments for post-warranty problems. **Safety:** Honda claims it's the only automaker to offer head restraints and three-point seatbelts at all seven seating positions. Plus, the body structure has been extensively reinforced to protect occupants from all kinds of collisions, including rollovers.

Con: Quality control: Component quality and assembly are similar to the Accord: usually first class, although there are more complaints of poor-quality components this year than ever before. **Owner-reported problems:** Premature front brake wear; automatic transmission failures; excessive front brake noise; sliding side door frequently malfunctions; electrical glitches; and accessory items that come loose, break away, or won't work. Plastic interior panels have rough edges and are often mis-aligned. **Service bulletin problems:** Clunk or bang when engaging Reverse; bulletin confirms Honda USA is currently investigating complaints of pulling or drifting (Service Bulletin Number: 99165, Bulletin Sequence Number: 802, Date of Bulletin: 9909 NHTSA Item Number: SB608030); excessive front brake noise; dash ticking or clicking; details on wire harness safety recall; information relating to closing sliding door with care to prevent outward dents or avoid damaging the the slide motor gears. **NHTSA safety complaints/safety:** While fueling, fuel tank exploded; in a frontal collision, van caught fire due to a cracked brake fluid reservoir; sudden acceleration when approaching a stop sign; while travelling at 90 km/h, accelerator jammed; when shifting into fourth gear, engine almost stalls out and engine produces a noise like valve clattering; many reports of sudden transmission and torque converter failure; while stopped on an incline of about 35 degrees, van rolled backwards; brakes made a loud screeching noise and lost effectiveness; when Reverse is engaged, car makes a popping or clunking sound; sudden loss of brakes, preceded by a loud rumbling noise; due to a power booster failure, brakes didn't work properly, producing extended stopping distances; loud squeaking noise from both front wheels, caused by premature wear (at 2,000 km) of brake pads and rotors; cracked wheel rim; Check Engine light constantly on (suspect faulty gasoline filler neck); engine knocks when vehicle reaches 90 km/h; entire vehicle shakes excessively at highway speeds and van pulls to the right (dealer said some type of bar adjustment was needed); passenger-side door window suddenly exploded while driving on the highway; erratic power sliding door that won't open with the remote control, opens and closes on its own, or fails to open and close properly; power sliding doors are hard to open and cannot be locked with remote due to computer failure; sliding door opens intermittently when van is parked (of twenty incidents only two occurred when engine was running); sliding door doesn't have a safety stop—this allows gas cap to get jammed, damaging the gas flap hinge and tank; a woman was loading the van and the power sliding door pinned her against the frame; child's fingers were mashed; driver's power seat will suddenly recline on its own, squeezing rear occupant's legs and falling on child; rear seatbelt tightened up so much that a child had to be cut free; too much play in rear lapbelts, which won't tighten adequately, making it difficult to install a child safety seat securely; inoperative driver seatbelt buckle; faulty speedometer and tachometer; remote wouldn't open or lock vehicle; placement of the gear shift lever interferes with the radio's controls; unable to depress accelerator pedal on cold days; can hear gasoline sloshing in tank while driving; frequent static electricity shocks. Many owners report that the rear head restraints seriously hamper rear and forward visibility.

Road Performance

Pro: Emergency handling: Predictable and well controlled. **Acceleration/torque:** Quiet yet powerful V6 engine performance with plenty of torque throughout the power band (0–100 km/h: just over 9 seconds). In fact, only the Toyota Sienna exceeds the Odyssey in powertrain refinement. **Transmission:** Usually smooth and quiet shifting (note exception below), though a bit slow to downshift at full throttle. **Routine handling:** Better handling than most of the competition, with a short turning circle, making it quite nimble; akin to driving a large, quiet, sport family sedan. Steering is light to the touch and responsive on the highway. **Braking:** Better-than-average braking, with little fading after repeated stops. The ABS-equipped front disc/rear drum setup is the best you'll find among minivans; even with a full load and after repeated stops they perform quite well—most of the time (see "NHTSA safety complaints/safety").

Con: Steering: A bit heavy at low speeds; sometimes feels over-boosted at highway speeds. Column-mounted shift lever tends to slide past Drive into third gear when shifted out of Park. Automatic transmission clunks and jolts the occupants when shifted into Reverse. The taut suspension is also a bit jolting over bumps, but the ride smooths out as the load is increased. Braking is often accompanied by front and rear brake squealing in low-speed stops.

Comfort/Convenience

Pro: Standard equipment: Well appointed. **Driving position:** Comfortable, commanding driving position. **Controls and displays:** Controls and displays are easy to reach and read. **Climate control:** Much improved. Quiet and efficient. Each seat has its own AC and heating vent. **Entry/exit:** Low step-up. The Odyssey provides car-like room in the front two rows of seats; getting in is no more difficult than climbing into an Accord. **Interior space/comfort F/R:** It's easy to strap a child seat into the Odyssey because there's far less lifting and reaching. The bench seat in the centre row is more practical than the captain's chairs, which can't be removed. It's more like a seven-seater station wagon than a minivan. All passengers have their own reading light, air vent, and power rear vent window controls. **Trunk/liftover:** There's space enough for groceries, and the edging around the storage area will help keep your apples from rolling around. **Cargo space:** Lots of little storage areas. A handy storage tray between the front seats folds down when not in use. If you need to expand the cargo area, the third seat folds flat into the floor. **Quietness:** The interior is quiet in most situations.

Con: Styling isn't to everyone's taste: colour and model selection are limited, carpeting looks cheap, and some find the Odyssey looks too bus-like. The sun visor extensions cover up the rear view mirror. Rear washer dribbles rather than squirts and doesn't have an intermittent setting. Standard issue winter wiper won't clean the front and rear windshields adequately (get upgraded wipers at Canadian Tire). **Driving position:** The driver's seat has backrest bolstering that is too padded for some, not enough for others (try before you buy). **Interior space/comfort F/R:** Front-seat passenger leg room is marginal due to the restricted seat travel; you can't slide your legs comfortably under the dash. Some passengers bump their shins on the glove box. Third row seat is only suitable for children; the narrow back bench seat provides little leg room, unless the middle seats are pushed far forward, inconveniencing others. **Controls and displays:** Radio control access is blocked by the shift lever and it's difficult to calibrate the radio without taking your eyes off the road. Power outlet, located at the base of the centre console, is awkward to access. Sealed centre windows. Power-sliding doors are slow to retract. Huge interior is slow to warm up and rear side windows fog up with a full passenger load. **Climate control:** AC controls and pictograms on the EX aren't very user-friendly and are confusing to adjust. **Cargo space:** Stowing the "hideaway" third seat exposes metal sidewall anchors that can easily damage cargo. The storage well won't take any tire larger than a "space saver"—meaning you'll carry your flat in the back. **Quietness:** Some tire rumble and body drumming at highway speeds.

COST				
List Price (negotiable)	**Residual Values (months)**			
	24	**36**	**48**	**60**
Odyssey LX: $30,800 (19%)	$25,000	$21,000	$17,000	$14,000
Odyssey EX: $33,800 (19%)	$26,000	$22,000	$18,000	$15,000

TECHNICAL DATA	
Powertrain (front-drive)	Head room F: 41.2/R1: 40/R2: 38.9 in.
Engine: 3.5L V6 (210 hp)	Leg room F: 41/R1: 40/R2: 38.1 in.
Transmission: 4-speed auto.	Wheelbase: 118.1 in.
Dimension/Capacity	Turning circle: 41 ft.
Passengers: 2/2/3	Cargo volume: 67 cu. ft.
Height/length/width:	GVWR: 5,565 lb.
68.5/201.2/75.6 in.	Payload: 1,227–1,332 lb.
	Tow limit: 2,000 lb.
	Fuel tank: 65L/prem.
	Weight: 4,245 lb.

SAFETY FEATURES/CRASHWORTHINESS		
	Std.	**Opt.**
Anti-lock brakes (4W)	■	❑
Seatbelt pretensioners	—	—

Side airbags	—	—
Traction control	❏	◼
Head restraints F/R	**	*
Visibility F/R	*****	*
Crash protection (front) D/P	*****	*****
Crash protection (side) D/P	*****	*****
Crash protection (off-set)	*****	

HYUNDAI

Hyundai doesn't make top-quality cars—a fact repeated time and again by consumer groups on both sides of the border. But Hyundai quality is improving, its vehicles are now backed by a more comprehensive warranty, and they're reasonably priced—three reasons Canadians are giving Hyundai products more consideration.

Interestingly, Hyundai's complaint ratio has dropped considerably in the past several years, concomitant with the company's more comprehensive warranty. Safety-related complaints have fallen to a level where they're less than frequent than ever before. One complaint that constantly resurfaces is owners' inability to get seatbelt extenders for large occupants, a free service provided by almost all other automakers.

For its 2001 model year lineup, Hyundai has enhanced the Elantra's engine performance and enlarged its interior dimensions. Its other cars are carried over without any significant changes.

Accent

Accent

RATING: Above Average. Think of it as a more refined Metro/Sprint from South Korea. **Strong points:** Reasonably priced and well appointed; adequate engine and automatic transmission performance in most situations; comfortable driving position with good visibility; cheap on gas; and a low base price. **Weak points:** Primitive manual transmission; passing power comes up short, especially with the automatic transmission;

mediocre braking; excessive engine, road, and wind noise; and uncertain long-term reliability.

NEW FOR 2001: A 1.6L replaces the 1.5L engine, adding 13 more hp.

OVERVIEW: This front-drive 4-cylinder sedan retains most of the Excel's underpinnings while dropping the Mitsubishi powerplant in favour of its own homegrown 1.5L 4-cylinder. It's better than the old Excel, though, with its upgraded, smoother-shifting automatic transmission, stiffer, better-performing suspension, stronger and quieter-running engine, dual airbags, and optional ABS. The three-door matches the Excel in length; the four-door is six inches shorter. Interior space was increased by an inch last year.

Cost analysis/best alternatives: Get a 2001 model for the extra horsepower. Other vehicles worth considering: the Chevrolet Metro, Honda Civic, Nissan Sentra, Suzuki Swift, Toyota Corolla, and VW Golf. **Options:** An automatic transmission and power steering are essential. **Rebates:** Expect $1,500 rebates to clear out year 2000 models as this year's cars are trucked in. **Delivery/PDI:** $350. **Depreciation:** Slower than average, now that fuel prices have soared. **Insurance cost:** Average. **Parts supply/cost:** Parts aren't hard to find and they're reasonably priced. **Annual maintenance cost:** Average. **Warranty:** Bumper-to-bumper 3 years/60,000 km; powertrain 5 years/100,000 km; rust perforation 5 years/unlimited km. **Supplementary warranty:** A good idea, since every Hyundai redesign has brought with it a number of first-year factory-related deficiencies. **Highway/city fuel economy:** 6.1–9.0L/100 km.

Quality/Reliability/Safety

Pro: Quality control: Average. Repairs are straightforward because of a fairly simple design, and parts are less expensive than average. **Reliability:** Average. Accents have overcome a lot of the early bad karma caused by the failure-prone Excel. **Warranty performance:** Average. **Service bulletin problems:** Nothing published yet—an encouraging sign.

Con: Owner-reported problems: The engine cooling system and cylinder head gaskets aren't very durable; premature front brake wear and excessive noise when braking; wheel bearings, fuel system, and electrical components also fail prematurely. Body assembly is mediocre and paint is poorly applied. **NHTSA safety complaints/safety:** Airbags failed to deploy; fire caused by alternator failure; main and secondary hood latches failed while vehicle was under power; inability to shift into first gear when decelerating from second gear; sudden transmission and brake failure; accelerator jammed when driving 100 km/h; sudden acceleration accompanied by complete brake loss; chronic stalling; premature suspension strut failure; electrical system failure caused by loose solenoid wire; horn controls may be hard to find in an emergency; windshield wipers and headlights won't work; the rear seatbelt configuration complicates the installation of a child safety seat; engine burns two quarts of oil a month.

Road Performance

Pro: Although the 1.6L engine is no pocket rocket, it performs adequately in city traffic. **Emergency handling:** Slow, but predictable. **Steering:** The non-power steering is precise and transmits plenty of road feedback at higher speeds. **Transmission:** Surprisingly, this is one car where the automatic transmission performs better than the manual gearbox. **Routine handling:** Above average. The Accent rides comfortably and handles responsively.

Con: Acceleration/torque: Last year's 1.5L engine provides glacial acceleration (0–100 km/h: 11.2 sec.). The manual transmission is hard to shift correctly due to its balky linkage and long lever movements. Uneven pavement makes for a busy, jittery ride that's accentuated as passengers are added. Steering without the power-assist option takes a lot of effort around town and when parking. **Braking:** Unacceptably long stopping distances (100–0 km/h: 139 ft.).

Comfort/Convenience

Pro: Driving position: Very good. Multiple front seat adjustments and a well-appointed interior make for a pleasant driving environment with a good view of the road. **Controls and displays:** Well laid-out dashboard and controls. **Climate control:** Efficient, easy-to-understand climate control system. **Entry/exit:** Front and rear access is impressively easy. **Interior space/comfort F/R:** Room for two adults in the rear. Plenty of front head room. Fairly comfortable but very firm and narrow front seats. **Cargo space:** Reasonable amount of luggage space, but the hatchback is more versatile with its folding rear seatbacks. **Trunk/liftover:** Average-sized trunk with a low liftover.

Con: Standard equipment: Few standard features, and there aren't a lot of options to choose from. Limited front leg room for tall passengers. Temperature controls aren't within easy reach. **Quietness:** Excessive engine, road, and wind noise.

COST				
List Price (negotiable)	**Residual Values (months)**			
	24	**36**	**48**	**60**
Accent L: $11,995 (11%)	$7,000	$5,500	$4,500	$3,500

TECHNICAL DATA

Powertrain (front-drive)
Engine: 1.6L 4-cyl. (105 hp)
Transmissions: 5-speed man.
• 4-speed auto.
Dimension/Capacity
Passengers: 2/3
Height/length/width:
54.9/162.1/63.8 in.

Head room F/R: 38.7/38 in.
Leg room F/R: 42.6/32.7 in.
Wheelbase: 94.5 in.
Turning circle: 35 ft.
Cargo volume: 11 cu. ft.
Tow limit: N/A
Fuel tank: 46L/reg.
Weight: 2,100 lb.

SAFETY FEATURES/CRASHWORTHINESS

	Std.	Opt.
Anti-lock brakes	❑	■
Seatbelt pretensioners	—	—
Side airbags	—	—
Traction control	—	—
Head restraints F/R	*	*
Visibility F/R	*****	*****
Crash protection (front) D/P	***	****
Crash protection (side) D/P	N/A	N/A
Crash protection (off-set)	N/A	

Elantra

Elantra

RATING: Average. **Strong points:** Reasonably priced and well appointed. Nimble handling. **Weak points:** Noisy, weak engine; passing power comes up short with the crude automatic transmission; a jittery ride; mediocre braking; lots of wind noise; difficult entry/exit; hard rear seats; below average crashworthiness scores; and a high insurance claim rate for injuries.

NEW FOR 2001: The redesigned, larger sedan arrives this fall. Hyundai keeps the 2.0L engine but has tweaked it to reduce noise, vibration, and harshness. No more Elantra wagon.

OVERVIEW: This Italian-designed, front-drive, conservatively styled sub-compact is only marginally larger than the discontinued Excel. Nevertheless, its 2.0L 140-hp 4-cylinder powerplant supplies the much-needed power that you won't find with the Excel. The ride and hand-ling are also improved, due mainly to the Elantra's longer wheelbase and more sophisticated suspension.

Elantra comes in two body styles: the base model and the GLS. As with most Asian cars, the Elantra is loaded with standard equipment, including standard AC and seatbelt pretensioners, intermittent wipers, full centre console, dual remote control outside mirrors, remote fuel-filler door and trunk release, reclining bucket seats, and tinted glass. Upgrading to the GLS will get you more instruments, power acces-sories, better tires, a tilt steering wheel, and a premium sound system.

Cost analysis/best alternatives: Get this year's model for the engine upgrades and additional interior space. Other cars worth considering are the Honda Civic, Nissan Sentra, and Toyota Corolla. **Options:** None. **Rebates:** Expect $1,500–$2,000 rebates to clear out last year's models and about half that early next year to boost sales of the 2001s. **Delivery/PDI:** $300. **Depreciation:** Average. **Insurance cost:** A bit higher than average. **Parts supply/cost:** Easy-to-find and reasonably priced parts, with heavy discounting by dealers. **Annual maintenance cost:** Average. **Warranty:** Bumper-to-bumper 3 years/60,000 km; powertrain 5 years/100,000 km; rust perforation 5 years/unlimited km. **Supplementary warranty:** A wise investment. **Highway/city fuel economy:** 7.1–10.8L/100 km.

Quality/Reliability/Safety

Pro: Quality control: Few quality control problems, so far. **Warranty performance:** Average. Hyundai customer relations staff usually deal with customer claims in a fair and efficient manner. **Service bulletin problems:** Nothing important.

Con: Reliability: Overall reliability has been slightly below average after the fifth year of ownership. **Owner-reported problems:** Powertrain and electrical system failures. **NHTSA safety complaints/safety:** Airbags failed to deploy; accelerator pedal floored, but vehicle failed to pick up speed; chronic stalling with cruise control engaged and brakes applied; faulty transmission/ignition harness; frequent transmission failures; automatic transmission slips; transmission goes into low gear periodi-cally and gets stuck there; vehicle rolled forward even though emer-gency brake was applied; clutch slave cylinder failure; transmission produces clunking and whining noises; brakes not very efficient; brake master cylinder failure; vehicle pulls left continuously; sudden steering failure; loose steering; low beam doesn't light up driver's view— instead, the light reflects outward to the left or right; AC circulates bad air; tire jack is too small and weak; defective side moulding.

Road Performance

Pro: Emergency handling: Better than average. **Steering:** Accurate and responsive. **Routine handling:** Independent suspension helps make for a pleasant ride with exceptional handling and control.

Con: Acceleration/torque: Leisurely acceleration (0–100 km/h: 10.5 sec.). Around town this is no problem, but highway cruising and hilly terrain bring out the worst in this low-torque engine. **Transmission:** The optional 4-speed automatic transmission robs the base engine of at least 10 horses, and it isn't as smooth as it should be. It shifts frequently, trying to keep up with the overburdened engine. **Braking:** Worse than average without anti-lock brakes (100–0 km/h: 146 ft.). Brakes are difficult to modulate.

Comfort/Convenience

Pro: Driving position: Good driving environment with excellent all-around visibility and comfortable front seats. **Controls and displays:** The attractive interior includes an easy-to-read dashboard with large analogue gauges that are complete and clear, and climate and radio controls that are effective and easy to operate. **Climate control:** The climate control system works without a hitch. Comfortable rear seating for two adults. **Entry/exit:** Good up front; difficult access to the rear. Rear seating is relatively roomy. **Cargo space:** Average. **Trunk/liftover:** Average, with a low liftover. **Standard equipment:** Reasonably well equipped.

Con: Firm rear seats are uncomfortable for long trips. Small radio controls. **Interior space/comfort F/R:** Interior room is snug, and head room is particularly tight for tall drivers. **Quietness:** Excessive high-speed engine and road noise.

COST				
List Price (negotiable)	**Residual Values (months)**			
	24	**36**	**48**	**60**
Elantra GL: $14,875 (13%)	$9,000	$7,000	$5,500	$4,500

TECHNICAL DATA	
Powertrain (front-drive)	Head room F/R: 38.6/37.6 in.
Engine: 2.0L 4-cyl. (140 hp)	Leg room F/R: 43.2/34.6 in.
Transmissions: 5-speed man.	Wheelbase: 100.4 in.
• 4-speed auto.	Turning circle: 36 ft.
Dimension/Capacity	Cargo volume:11.9 cu. ft.
Passengers: 2/3	Tow limit: N/A
Height/length/width:	Fuel tank: 55L/reg.
54.9/174/66.9 in.	Weight: 2,500 lb.

SAFETY FEATURES/CRASHWORTHINESS

	Std.	Opt.
Anti-lock brakes	❑	◼
Seatbelt pretensioners	◼	❑
Side airbags	—	—
Traction control	—	—
Head restraints F/R	***	***
Visibility F/R	*****	*****
Crash protection (front) D/P	****	****
Crash protection (side) D/P	***	*
Crash protection (off-set)	***	

Sonata

Sonata

RATING: Average, but only with an extended warranty. **Strong points:** Well equipped, stylish, and reasonably priced. **Weak points:** Base engine lacks sufficient torque for highway cruising, clunky automatic transmission, primitive ride and handling, substandard braking, uncomfortable rear seating, excessive cabin noise, and inadvertent airbag deployment.

NEW FOR 2001: Nothing significant. The V6 will get a horsepower boost for the 2002 model year.

OVERVIEW: Give Hyundai credit; it's trying to make more refined cars, and this year's Sonata, fresh from last year's redesign, is the best product to come out of South Korea to date. It has a more rigid structure, a double-wishbone front suspension (like the Accord), and more attractive styling. Unfortunately, this mid-sized sedan still lacks the powertrain, handling, and ride refinements to cut it in the Honda Accord, Mazda 626, and Toyota Camry league. Nevertheless, its recent upgrades and significantly longer, more comprehensive warranty make it a contender when compared to the second-tier mid-sized sedans represented by Ford's Taurus and Sable and Chrysler's Cirrus and Stratus.

Like Hyundai's other models, the Sonata is loaded with standard features that are optional or not found on competitive makes. Some of those standard features include air conditioning, power steering, and a 2.4L 149-hp 4-cylinder engine. It also features an optional 2.5L twin-cam 170-hp V6 and ABS.

Hyundai has again put the accent on safety this year, giving buyers a lot more safety features for their money than competing models. Standard features include: side airbags, seatbelt pretensioners, an integrated rear child safety seat, and a "smart" passenger-side airbag that won't deploy if the passenger weighs less than 66 lb (30 kg). An optional ABS/traction control is also offered.

Cost analysis/best alternatives: Buy a deeply discounted second series 2000 model (built after March) and plan to keep it at least five years to shake off the additional year's depreciation. Other cars worth considering are the Honda Accord, Mazda 626, and Toyota Camry. **Options:** The V6 engine; if you get the 4-banger version, keep in mind that good fuel economy means putting up with an engine that's rougher and noisier than the V6. Be wary of the sunroof; it eats up a lot of head room. **Rebates:** Expect $2,000 rebates to clear out the 2000 models. **Delivery/PDI:** $300. **Depreciation:** Average. **Insurance cost:** Average. **Parts supply/cost:** Easy to find and relatively inexpensive. Large engine compartment for easy servicing. **Annual maintenance cost:** Higher than average. **Warranty:** Bumper-to-bumper 3 years/60,000 km; powertrain 5 years/100,000 km; rust perforation 5 years/unlimited km. **Supplementary warranty:** A good idea to get you through the critical fifth year of ownership, when major components start to self-destruct. **Highway/city fuel economy:** 7.7–11.4L/100 km with the 2.4L and 7.8–11.7L/100 km with the 2.5L engine.

Quality/Reliability/Safety

Pro: Quality control: Much improved quality control. No serious problems reported with the 2.5L powerplant. Repair is straightforward because of the Sonata's simple design. **Reliability:** No serious reliability problems have appeared over the last several years. **Warranty performance:** Average.

Con: Owner-reported problems: Poor engine performance (hard starting, poor idling, stalling). Excessive front brake pulsation and premature wear. Steering defects (when the steering wheel is turned to either extreme, it makes a sound like metal cracking). Cruise control malfunctions and electrical short circuits; poor door and window sealing (water leaking into the interior when the car is washed); and premature paint peeling and rusting. **Service bulletin problems:** Diagnostic tips for troubleshooting no-starts or hard starting after gassing up. **NHTSA safety complaints/safety:** Driver's side airbag deployed when door was shut; airbags failed to deploy in a collision; sudden brake failure; transmission shifting causes vehicle to stall; transmission shifter will not lock into place and slips into Neutral if bumped.

Road Performance

Pro: Emergency handling: Average. **Steering:** Very good. Predictable, with lots of road feedback. **Acceleration/torque:** Reasonably good acceleration, but the base engine's insufficient torque makes the optional V6 a prerequisite for highway cruising, especially over hilly terrain (0–100 km/h: 9.8 sec.). **Transmission:** The 4-speed automatic transmission with Overdrive (a fuel-saving feature) works smoothly and is well adapted to the engine's power range. An improved electronic automatic transmission uses "fuzzy logic" to make shifting smooth and predictable. **Routine handling:** Better than average. Hyundai has changed the suspension setting to provide a less bouncy ride.

Con: The V6 engine is still a bit rough-running and noisy despite last year's improvements. Harsh slow-speed or Forward to Reverse shifting. An overly soft, wallowing ride produces significant body roll. Ride quality deteriorates as load increases. **Braking:** Substandard braking accompanied by excessive brake fade—the 151 feet required for a 100 km/h stop is 10–15 feet more than the competition.

Comfort/Convenience

Pro: Standard equipment: Well equipped for the price. **Driving position:** Very good. Great visibility and fairly supportive front seats are set high off the floor. **Controls and displays:** Well laid-out dashboard and controls. Easy-to-read gauges. **Climate control:** Good heating-defrosting-ventilation system. **Entry/exit:** Easy front and rear access. **Interior space/comfort F/R:** Up front, this is one of the roomiest mid-sized vehicles around. **Cargo space:** Many storage bins.

Con: Trunk/liftover: Rear head room is tight for tall passengers and the low, short rear seat cushions forces occupants into a painful knees-to-chin position. Surprisingly shallow trunk has a low liftover. **Quietness:** Excessive wind, road, and suspension noise.

COST				
List Price (very negotiable)	**Residual Values (months)**			
	24	36	48	60
Base: $19,995 (15%)	$15,000	$13,000	$10,500	$8,500
TECHNICAL DATA				
Powertrain (front-drive)	Head room F/R: 38.5/37.7 in.			
Engines: 2.4L 4-cyl. (149 hp)	Leg room F/R: 43.3/36.6 in.			
• 2.5L V6 (170 hp)	Wheelbase: 106.3 in.			

Transmissions: 5-speed man.	Turning circle: 38 ft.
• 4-speed auto.	Cargo volume: 13.2 cu. ft.
Dimension/Capacity	Tow limit: N/A
Passengers: 2/3	Fuel tank: 65L/reg.
Height/length/width:	Weight: 3,100 lb.
55.3/185/69.7 in.	

SAFETY FEATURES/CRASHWORTHINESS

	Std.	Opt.
Anti-lock brakes	☐	■
Seatbelt pretensioners	■	☐
Side airbags	■	☐
Traction control	☐	■
Head restraints F/R	***	***
Visibility F/R	*****	*****
Crash protection (front) D/P	N/A	N/A
Crash protection (side) D/P	****	*****
Crash protection (off-set)	***	

Tiburon

Tiburon

RATING: Average. **Strong points:** Well equipped; impressive 2.0L performance with a manual gearbox; exceptional ride and handling. **Weak points:** Base 2.0L engine's passing power is seriously handicapped by the automatic transmission. Restricted rear visibility, uncomfortable seating, not for six-footers or portly occupants.

NEW FOR 2001: No significant changes. A redesign is scheduled for the 2002 model year.

OVERVIEW: Although the Tiburon (it means shark in Spanish) is a stylish, two-door spinoff of the Elantra sedan, it does deliver sports car thrills in a compact coupe. Powered by a base 140-hp 2.0L and mated to a 4-speed electronically controlled automatic or a 5-speed manual transmission, the Tiburon is a competent performer for both city and highway driving. It handles well, with gas-charged shocks inside coil springs at all four corners, and front MacPherson struts. Steering is light and responsive with a minimum of body flex. Standard brakes consist of discs up front and drums in the rear; the FX package includes four-wheel discs and ABS.

Cost analysis/best alternatives: Get the identical 2000 model if it's discounted sufficiently. Other vehicles worth considering: the GM Cavalier and Sunfire and Honda Civic. **Options:** The FX package with better-gripping tires, four-wheel disc brakes, and ABS. **Rebates:** Hyundai is expected to offer attractive rebates on the 2000s early in 2001. **Delivery/PDI:** $350. **Depreciation:** Average. **Insurance cost:** Higher than average. **Parts supply/cost:** Parts aren't hard to find and they're less expensive than average. Repair is straightforward because of a fairly simple design. **Annual maintenance cost:** Average. **Warranty:** Bumper-to-bumper 3 years/60,000 km; powertrain 5 years/100,000 km; rust perforation 5 years/unlimited km. **Supplementary warranty:** A smart buy. **Highway/city fuel economy:** 7.4–10.5L/100 km.

Quality/Reliability/Safety

Pro: Quality control: Average, but much improved. **Reliability:** Better than average. **Warranty performance:** Average. **Service bulletin problems:** Nothing published, yet. **Safety:** Impressive headlight illumination (take heed, Chrysler).

Con: Owner-reported problems: Premature front brake wear and excessive brake noise. Some electrical glitches. **NHTSA safety complaints:** Airbag deployed when it shouldn't have; airbag didn't deploy when it should have; reflection of the sun on the dash distracts vision; horn controls may be hard to find in an emergency; rear head restraints appear to be too low to protect occupants; front seatbelts are difficult to latch and tighten or loosen on their own; and the rear seatbelt configuration complicates the installation of a child safety seat. The rear spoiler is distracting and cuts rearward vision.

Road Performance

Pro: The 2.0L gives respectable power (0–100 km/h: 9.1 sec.). **Emergency handling:** Very good. Well controlled, with minimal body roll. **Steering:** The light, responsive steering is precise and predictable. **Transmission:** The 5-speed manual transmission shifts smoothly and is well adapted to the engine's power range. The ride is reasonably soft on good roads. **Braking:** Acceptable, though not impressive (100–0 km/h: 132 ft.).

Con: Acceleration/torque: The 4-speed automatic transmission shifts roughly under full throttle and is noisy at high revs. **Routine handling:** Uneven pavement makes for a busy, jittery ride that's accentuated as passengers are added. Poor braking on wet pavement.

Comfort/Convenience

Pro: Attractive styling and a well-appointed interior. **Controls and displays:** Well laid-out dashboard and controls (except for the radio). **Climate control:** Efficient, easy-to-understand climate control system. **Interior space/comfort F/R:** Comfortable seatbacks. Multiple front seat adjustments. Plenty of front head room. **Cargo space:** Average. **Trunk/liftover:** Reasonable amount of luggage space, but the hatchback is more versatile with its folding rear seatbacks. **Standard equipment:** Fairly well equipped for a vehicle in this price range.

Con: Rear view is obstructed by the Tiburon's high tail and wide pillars. Tiny radio controls and temperature controls aren't within easy reach. **Entry/exit:** Front and rear access isn't easy. **Interior space/comfort F/R:** Low, firm, narrow, and short seat cushions give little thigh support. Limited front leg room for tall passengers, and rear head room is tight. Barely enough back seat room for two adults. **Trunk/liftover:** High liftover to the cargo area. **Quietness:** Plenty of engine, road, and wind noise.

COST

List Price (very negotiable)	Residual Values (months)			
	24	36	48	60
Base: $18,995 (15%)	$12,000	$10,000	$8,000	$7,000
SE: $21,295 (17%)	$14,000	$12,000	$10,500	$9,500

TECHNICAL DATA

Powertrain (front-drive)
Engine: 2.0L 4-cyl. (140 hp)
Transmissions: 5-speed man.
• 4-speed auto.
Dimension/Capacity
Passengers: 2/2
Height/length/width:
51.3/170.9/68.1 in.

Head room F/R: 38/34.4 in.
Leg room F/R: 43.1/29.9 in.
Wheelbase: 97.4 in.
Turning circle: 37 ft.
Cargo volume: 12.8 cu. ft.
Tow limit: N/A
Fuel tank: 55L/reg.
Weight: 2,600 lb.

SAFETY FEATURES/CRASHWORTHINESS

	Std.	Opt.
Anti-lock brakes	❏	■
Seatbelt pretensioners	—	—
Side airbags	—	—
Traction control	—	—
Head restraints F/R	**	*
Visibility F/R	*****	**
Crash protection (front) D/P	N/A	N/A
Crash protection (side) D/P	N/A	N/A
Crash protection (off-set)	N/A	

INFINITI

Infiniti has historically stressed performance over comfort and opulence. Lately, though, it's become a more mainstream luxury automaker and has lost its performance edge, particularly after dropping the J30 and J30t. When Nissan launched its Infiniti line, it promised that Infinitis wouldn't be merely restyled Nissans selling at a premium. It lied.

Infiniti makes four vehicles: the G20, a luxury wannabe; the I30, an entry-level luxury sedan; the top-of-the-line Q45 four-door sedan; and the QX4 sport-utility. All Infinitis come fully equipped and offer owners the prestige of driving a reliable and nicely styled luxury car, with lots of standard features. Interestingly, though, Infiniti can't make head restraints that are deemed acceptable by IIHS; its restraints are rated either "marginal" or "poor" by that insurance agency for their ability to protect occupants in a collision.

Infinitis are sold and serviced by dozens of dealers across Canada. This small number doesn't affect either the availability or quality of servicing, since any Nissan dealer can carry out most non-warranty maintenance work.

Infiniti's G20 will be dropped in the fall of 2001 and the I30 isn't likely to last more than another model year. The rest of the Infiniti lineup is carried over this year relatively unchanged.

G20

RATING: Not Recommended. **Strong points:** Standard side airbags; ABS; competent steering and handling; well laid-out controls and instruments; good overall visibility. **Weak points:** Slow acceleration, mediocre automatic transmission performance, inadequate passenger head room and rear leg room, lots of engine and road noise, not very well appointed (want some plastic wood?), limited side and visibility, and a "marginal" head restraint rating by IIHS.

NEW FOR 2001: No significant changes. This model will be dropped in the fall of 2001.

OVERVIEW: After pulling its original G20 off the market in 1996 after a 5-year run, Nissan has been lusting after the entry-level luxury car niche it abandoned. It hoped the G20 launched three years ago would fit the bill.

It didn't. Nissan's "spirited performance" claim is pure hype. Looking a lot like its poor-selling predecessor, the front-drive G20 is merely an entry-level Sentra disguised as a luxury car. Nissan should be ashamed of itself for attempting this automotive charade. The 145-hp 2.0L 4-cylinder engine (most entry-level luxury cars have V6s) and live-axle rear suspension are borrowed from the Sentra, and the rest of its underpinnings are derived from the European Nissan Primera. Owners have complained that the car has numerous squeaks and rattles (addressed by a service bulletin), and that the driver's seat reclines involuntarily when the vehicle is put into Reverse. **Service bulletin problems:** Rotten egg smell from the exhaust and various squeaks and rattles. **NHTSA safety complaints/safety:** Nothing significant.

Slightly larger than its 1996 iteration, the G20 comes with additional features like four-wheel ABS, side-impact airbags, front seatbelt pretensioners, and a Bose 100-watt sound system. Interestingly, Infiniti doesn't charge for shipping or the pre-delivery inspection, and throws in a free tank of gas along with a comprehensive 4-year/100,000 km warranty. A G20t "touring" model adds a viscous limited-slip differential, fog lights, and a spoiler—all for $29,950. Competitive models you may wish to look at are the Audi A4 1.8T and the Lexus ES 300.

I30

RATING: Above Average. Even though this is a redesigned model, Infinitis don't have as many "teething" problems with newly launched models as do other automakers. **Strong points:** Fully equipped with lots of innovative safety features, excellent engine and transmission match-up, comfortable ride, impressive handling, and first-class quality control. **Weak points:** An upscale, roomier, more conservatively styled Maxima; rear headrests obstruct visibility; and it has poor fuel economy (premium fuel suggested).

NEW FOR 2001: Steering wheel-mounted controls, anti-glare mirror, and an emergency trunk release.

OVERVIEW: The I30's $38,000 base price makes it the world's most expensive Maxima, incorporating many of that car's chassis and drive-train components, including the 227-hp 3.0L V6 engine and rear multi-link suspension.

You can choose either the base or sportier I30t Touring models. The I30t gives you larger, 17-inch wheels, a firmer suspension, power moon roof and rear-window sunshade, a Comfort and Convenience Package, and Xenon high-intensity headlights. You won't get a manual transmission; it was dropped last year.

Alternative vehicles that compete with the I30: those costing $40,000–$50,000, like the BMW 328, Lexus ES 300, Mazda Millenia, Mercedes-Benz C230, and Volvo S90; and those costing $50,000 or more, such as the BMW 5-series. For my money, the recently redesigned Maxima looks like the better buy.

Cost analysis/best alternatives: Get last year's discounted models since they're identical to this year's version. The redesigned Maxima is a worthy competitor from a price/performance standpoint. **Options:** None worth the extra money. **Rebates:** Not likely. **Delivery/PDI:** $350. **Depreciation:** Average. **Insurance cost:** Higher than average. **Parts supply/cost:** Moderately priced parts are available only from Nissan or Infiniti dealers. **Annual maintenance cost:** Much less than average. **Warranty:** Bumper-to-bumper 4 years/100,000 km; powertrain 6 years/100,000 km; rust perforation 7 years/unlimited km. **Supplementary warranty:** Not necessary. **Highway/city fuel economy:** *I30:* 7.8–11.4L/100 km.

Quality/Reliability/Safety

Pro: Quality control: Excellent. **Reliability:** Much better than average. **Warranty performance:** Very good. **Owner-reported problems:** Nothing significant, although you can expect some electrical, fuel injection, and fit and finish problems.

Con: Service bulletin problems: Front brakes produce a loud groaning noise when braking; after a cold start, some vehicles exhibit a ticking or humming noise, rear parcel shelf buzz or rattle, and blower noise. **NHTSA safety complaints/safety:** ABS failure; sudden acceleration;

engine surges; transmission shifts erratically; gauges wash out in bright sunlight; faulty keyless entry device.

Road Performance

Pro: Emergency handling: Better than average. Little body lean or front-end plow during high-speed cornering. **Steering:** Exceptionally quick and precise. **Acceleration/torque:** First class for a car of this heft. The engine performs well throughout the power band (0–100 km/h: 8.9 sec.). **Transmission:** The automatic transmission is imperceptible, and the viscous limited-slip differential assists traction over slippery roads. **Routine handling:** Handles better thanks to last year's upgrades and provides a quiet, comfortable ride when cruising. **Braking:** Braking is acceptable, with little fading or loss of directional stability (100–0 km/h: 131 ft.).

Con: The I30t's suspension may be too firm for some. Rear headrests obstruct visibility.

Comfort/Convenience

Pro: Standard equipment: The I30 has many standard features that are optional on other cars in its class. **Driving position:** Excellent driving position with good front visibility. **Controls and displays:** Very well laid out, accessible, and easy to understand. **Climate control:** Efficient and quiet. **Entry/exit:** Large door openings make access a breeze. Rear passengers have a bit more leg room than before. **Trunk/liftover:** The spacious trunk has a pass-through for carrying long items. **Cargo space:** Lots of small storage areas. **Quietness:** Extra damping makes for an exceptionally quiet interior.

Con: Interior space/comfort F/R: Rear middle passenger will still be squeezed. Rear seat backrest is too inclined for comfort.

COST				
List Price (firm)	**Residual Values (months)**			
	24	**36**	**48**	**60**
I30: $38,000 (20%)	$31,000	$25,000	$21,000	$16,000

TECHNICAL DATA	
Powertrain (front-drive)	Head room F/R: 40.5/37.4 in.
Engine: 3.0L V6 (227 hp)	Leg room F/R: 43.9/36.2 in.
Transmission: 4-speed auto.	Wheelbase: 108 in.
Dimension/Capacity	Turning circle: 40 ft.
Passengers: 2/3	Cargo volume: 14 cu. ft.
Height/length/width:	Tow limit: N/A
56.5/193.7/70.2 in.	Fuel tank: 70L/prem.
	Weight: 3,410 lb.

SAFETY FEATURES/CRASHWORTHINESS		
	Std.	**Opt.**
Anti-lock brakes	■	❏
Seatbelt pretensioners	■	❏
Side airbags	■	❏
Traction control	■	❏
Head restraints F/R	****	****
Visibility F/R	*****	*****
Crash protection (front) D/P	****	****
Crash protection (side) D/P	****	****
Crash protection (off-set)	***	

Q45

✓ **BEST BUY**

Q45

RATING: Recommended. A nice compromise between luxury and performance; a Japanese BMW with good rear seating. **Strong points:** Well appointed, stylish, pleasant ride, quiet, plenty of rear leg room, excellent braking, and first-class workmanship. **Weak points:** Limited trunk space, below average offset crash rating, and requires premium fuel.

NEW FOR 2001: Everything's on hold for the big, bad, and beautiful redesigned 2002 model.

OVERVIEW: Infiniti has shifted the Q45's emphasis from performance to luxury and comfort. This is unfortunate, because it reduces the distinction between the Q45 and Lexus LS 400. In fact, since the engine was downsized a few years ago from a 4.5 to a 4.1L, one wonders if the Q45 moniker isn't misleading advertising. Nevertheless, this luxury sedan is faster and more glitzy than many cars in its category in spite of its less powerful engine.

The Q45 uses a 32-valve 266-hp 4.1L V8 not frequently found on Japanese luxury compacts. It's a refined powerplant that has been both reliable and durable over the years. Standard safety features include side airbags for both driver and right front passenger, dual-locking shoulder belts, and front seatbelt pretensioners that activate in a crash to reduce belt slack. Additionally, you get electronically modulated shocks, upgraded headlights, an upgraded moon roof switch, a power-assisted rear-window sunshade, and a remote-closing trunk lid.

Cost analysis/best alternatives: Get the 2000 model if it's sufficiently discounted, or wait until 2002 when the redesigned, more powerful Q45 arrives. **Options:** Forget about the active suspension option; it doesn't improve the handling or ride very much. **Rebates:** Not likely. **Delivery/PDI:** $350. **Depreciation:** Much slower than average. **Insurance cost:** Much higher than average. **Parts supply/cost:** Parts may be more expensive than other cars in this class, and they're available only from Nissan or Infiniti dealers. **Annual maintenance cost:** Much less than average. **Warranty:** Bumper-to-bumper 4 years/100,000 km; power-train 6 years/100,000 km; rust perforation 7 years/unlimited km. **Supplementary warranty:** Not necessary. **Highway/city fuel economy:** 9.2–13.5L/100 km.

Quality/Reliability/Safety

Pro: Quality control: High-quality components and superior workmanship. **Reliability:** No reliability problems reported. **Warranty performance:** Better than average. **NHTSA safety complaints/safety:** Nothing significant.

Con: Owner-reported problems: Tire thumping, some interior rattles, and excessive wind noise around the A-pillars. **Service bulletin problems:** Excessive steering wheel and brake vibration when braking and centre console top lid comes loose.

Road Performance

Pro: Emergency handling: Very good. Standard traction control works well in preventing the car's rear end from sliding out on slippery roads. **Steering:** Precise, with plenty of road feedback. **Acceleration/torque:** Impressive acceleration and plenty of torque (0–100 km/h: 8.6 sec.). The car accelerates without a hint of noise or abrupt shifting. The engine supplies plenty of upper-range torque as well. **Transmission:** Smooth-shifting and quiet automatic transmission. **Routine handling:** Quite nimble handling for such a heavy car. **Braking:** Incredibly short stopping distances, thanks to four-wheel ABS (100–0 km/h: 121 ft.).

Comfort/Convenience

Pro: Standard equipment: Incredibly well appointed, with lots of standard safety and convenience features. **Driving position:** Excellent. Unobstructed front and rear visibility. **Controls and displays:** Well positioned and easy to decipher. Complete instrumentation. **Climate control:** Efficient, quiet, and very easy to adjust. **Entry/exit:** Both the front and rear seats can be easily accessed without undue acrobatics. **Interior space/comfort F/R:** Luxury seating both fore and aft. Rear seating is particularly comfortable. **Trunk/liftover:** Trunk has a low liftover. **Quietness:** Cocoon-like quiet.

Con: **Cargo space:** Limited room for storage of bulky items. **Trunk/liftover:** Small trunk.

COST				
List Price (negotiable)	**Residual Values (months)**			
	24	**36**	**48**	**60**
Q45t: $70,000 (21%)	$56,000	$46,000	$39,000	$30,000

TECHNICAL DATA	
Powertrain (front-drive)	Head room F/R: 37.6/36.9 in.
Engine: 4.1L V8 (266 hp)	Leg room F/R: 43.6/35.9 in.
Transmission: 4-speed auto.	Wheelbase: 111.4 in.
Dimension/Capacity	Turning circle: 40 ft.
Passengers: 2/3	Cargo volume: 12.6 cu. ft.
Height/length/width:	Tow limit: N/A
56.9/199.2/71.7 in.	Fuel tank: 81L/prem.
	Weight: 3,900 lb.

SAFETY FEATURES/CRASHWORTHINESS		
	Std.	**Opt.**
Anti-lock brakes	■	❑
Seatbelt pretensioners	■	❑
Side airbags	■	❑
Traction control	■	❑
Head restraints F/R	*****	*****
Visibility F/R	*****	*****
Crash protection (front) D/P	N/A	N/A
Crash protection (side) D/P	N/A	N/A
Crash protection (off-set)	**	

KIA

After going bankrupt in 1998, Kia has been bought by Hyundai (it's also partly owned by Ford through its Mazda affiliation) and continues to sell the Sephia and Sportage sport-utility in the United States. Unlike Daewoo, Kia has the money and backing to build a solid, stable dealer organization in Canada, but it'll take a great deal of time. Presently, it only has 31 stores in Canada.

What could stop its expansion? Kia's own low-quality cars and sport-utilities.

All of the consumer and government feedback I've seen paints a very poor picture of Kia's quality control. Add in that this is the company's second year in Canada, few dealers can be found outside of large urban areas, and its vehicles haven't been tested in our environment, and you have all the ingredients to make any Kia purchase a risky buy.

At "Don't Buy a Kia" at *members.tripod.com/aiki_joe/kia/index.html,* you'll find a wonderfully comprehensive site set up by a dissatisfied Kia Sephia owner. It offers a compendium of Kia reviews and owner comments from diverse sources around the world.

Kia's $11,995 Rio arrived too late this year to be rated.

Sephia, Spectra

X RISKY BUY

Sephia

RATING: Not Recommended. The Sephia has sold its products in the States since 1994, in Canada since the early '90s—the Aspire and Festiva—marketed under the Ford nameplate. **Strong points:** Cheap, cheap, and cheap. **Weak points:** Crude and weak engine performance, harsh ride, poor handling, noisy engine, lots of road and wind noise, subpar fit and finish, and a small dealer network that may complicate servicing and warranty performance.

OVERVIEW: The front-drive, five-passenger Sephia is about the size of a Toyota Corolla and sells for $12,995 (base model) and $14,945 (LS). It comes with an underpowered twin-cam 125-hp 1.8L 4-cylinder engine hooked to a standard 5-speed manual or an optional 5-speed automatic transmission, and seated on a four-wheel independent suspension. Other standard features with the base models: power steering, an AM/FM cassette sound system, and split-folding rear seatbacks.

On the road, the Sephia is a modest performer, accelerating from 0–100km/h in about 9+ seconds with a manual and two seconds more with an automatic transmission. There's little power left for passing or merging with traffic, and fuel economy is unimpressive (highway/city fuel economy: 7.1–10.3L/100 km).

Launched this summer, the Spectra is really a Sephia with two less doors and different front-end styling. It's hyped and equipped as a sportier, more upscale version of the Sephia.

Kia's products, unlike Daewoo's, do have a track record—and it's not good. In fact, *Consumer Reports* says in its April 1999 New Car edition, "You'd have to search far and wide to find a car that's worse than this small Korean model." CRs conclusion is confirmed by the proportionally large number of safety-related complaints recorded by NHTSA below.

Service bulletin problems: Nothing reported, yet. **NHTSA safety complaints/safety:** Airbags failed to deploy; seatbelts failed to lock in a collision; faulty driver's airbag cover; fuel fumes invade the vehicle's interior; 1-month-old car had a transmission failure; transmission shifts erratically; many reports of early automatic transmission replacement; when coming out of first gear, vehicle will stall; vehicle hesitates when it reaches 60–80 km/h; car suddenly loses all power, no matter what the speed, at idle, in gear, or in Neutral; sudden brake failure; brakes overheated badly; brake pedal went to the floor with no effect, even when pumping it hard; steering wheel and brakes vibrate and squeal excessively when braking; many complaints of brake rotor warpage and premature brake pad wear; door locks become jammed from the inside and the outside; child safety lock can't be released and vehicle has to be opened from the outside; windshield moulding falls off; front windshield glass sealing keeps coming off and glass trembles while driving; weather stripping peels off side of vehicle; loud noise from the engine area when starting vehicle; horn doesn't work properly and when it does work, the sound is weak; defroster doesn't defrost the side windows; engine wiring harness and starter failures; vehicle won't start properly, and has to be constantly switched on and off; headlight design makes high beam about 10 percent off to the left, causing a huge blind spot when turning left.

LEXUS

Unlike cash-strapped Nissan—and Infiniti, which has just been acquired by Renault—this has been another year of record sales for Toyota and Lexus. Lexus has become a luxury automaker on its own merits, even though it started out selling dressed-up Camrys as upscale models (only the ES 300 fits that description now). But so did Acura and Infiniti, right? Unlike Infiniti, though, Lexus isn't morphing into anything other than what it's always been: the epitome of luxury and comfort, with a small dab of performance thrown in. While Infiniti engineers see the highway as a challenge, Lexus sees it as an irritant, successfully isolating the driver from the driving experience. And guess what? It's a winning formula. No matter how often car enthusiast magazines say that drivers want "road feel," "responsive handling," and "high-performance" thrills, the truth of the matter is that most drivers simply want to travel from point A to point B in safety and comfort, without interruption, in cars that are more than fully equipped Sentras or warmed-over Maximas.

Infiniti bucked that concept, and lost.

Although these luxury imports do set advanced benchmarks for quality control, they're not engineering perfection (they do average about half a defect per car during the first 90 days of ownership). Cheaper luxury cars like the Acura 3.0L CL, Mazda Millenia, Nissan Maxima, and Toyota Avalon give you almost as much comfort and reliability, but without the Lexus cachet.

Dealer service bulletins show that these cars are affected by some minor body fit and trim glitches. Most owners haven't heard of these problems, because Lexus dealers have been particularly adept at fixing many of them before they become chronic.

In summary, the Lexus lineup is geared more to the luxury cruiser crowd, which prefers comfort over performance thrills. All models come with such important standard safety features as side airbags, automatically adjusted head restraints, an automatic transmission shifter interlocked with the ignition and brakes, childproof door locks, and easily adjusted three-point seatbelts.

Holding a winning hand, Lexus won't make any major changes to its existing line except for the redesigned LS 430. Last spring, however, it did come out with the IS 300, a V6-equipped, rear-drive sedan targeting BMW's 3-series.

IS 300

RATING: Above Average. *Lemon-Aid* rarely rates a first-year vehicle, but Lexus's previous new models have been launched without the first year glitches found with other automakers. **Strong points:** Nice array of standard features, good acceleration, handling, and braking, pleasant riding, and first-class workmanship. **Weak points:** Automatic transmission manual E-shifter is awkward to use; excessive road noise and tire thump; seat cushions don't provide adequate thigh support; cramped rear seating; trunk hinges eat up trunk space and may damage luggage; and car requires premium fuel.

OVERVIEW: Targeting BMW's 3-series, Lexus's latest $40,830 rear-drive sports-compact sedan comes with similar power and features to the BMW 328I—for about $5,000 less. The only engine is a 215-hp inline six (borrowed from the GS 300), mated to a 5-speed automatic transmission, incorporating Lexus's E-shift feature for manual shifting. Other important features: four-wheel, ABS-equipped disc brakes, 17-inch wheels, performance tires, and traction control.

Just a bit narrower than the BMW 3-series, the IS 300 is a competent performer both for routine tasks and in emergency situations.

NEW FOR 2001: A manual shifter will be phased in during the 2001 model-year run.

Cost analysis/best alternatives: Other cars worth considering are the Acura TL, Audi A4, BMW 3-series, Infiniti I30, and Mercedes-Benz C-Class. **Options:** Limited-slip differential is a good idea. Don't waste money on the sunroof, heated seats, or leather upholstery. **Rebates:** None. **Delivery/PDI:** $400. **Depreciation:** Depreciation predicted to be much lower than average. **Insurance cost:** Higher than average. **Parts supply/cost:** Average availability, though parts may be expensive until independent resellers come on stream. **Annual maintenance cost:** Below average. **Warranty:** Bumper-to-bumper 4 years/

80,000 km; powertrain 6 years/110,000 km; rust perforation 6 years/ unlimited km. **Supplementary warranty:** Not necessary. **Highway/city fuel economy:** N/A.

ES 300

RATING: Recommended. **Strong points:** Standard side airbags, good acceleration, pleasantly quiet ride, quiet running, top-quality components, impressive crashworthiness ratings and favourable accident injury claim data, and excellent quality control and warranty performance. **Weak points:** Primarily a four-seater; three adults won't sit comfortably in the rear. Muted steering feel, some nosedive in panic stops, automatic transmission is reluctant to kick down for passing, and overall handling isn't as nimble as its BMW or Mercedes rivals. Trunk space is limited (low liftover, though) and rear corner visibility is hampered by the high rear end.

NEW FOR 2001: Returns this year virtually unchanged.

OVERVIEW: A Camry clone with some additional features, this $43,995 entry-level Lexus front-drive carries a 210-hp V6 mated to an electronically controlled 4-speed automatic transmission that handles the 3.0L engine's horses effortlessly—making for 0–100 km/h times in the low 8s—without sacrificing fuel economy. All ES 300s feature dual front and side airbags, anti-lock brakes, improved double-piston front brake calipers, 60/40 split-folding rear seats, and one of the rarest features of all: a conventional spare tire.

Cost analysis/best alternatives: Get the 2000 model if you can find one discounted by about 10 percent. Other cars worth considering are the Acura TL, Audi A6, BMW 3-series, Infiniti I30, Mercedes-Benz E420, Mazda Millenia, Toyota Avalon, and Volvo S70 and S90 series. **Options:** Antiskid VSC is worthwhile. I don't recommend the Adaptive Variable

Suspension option; it's mostly a gimmick with little functional improvement. **Rebates:** None. Some discounting on the 2001's MSRP by about 5 percent. **Delivery/PDI:** $350. **Depreciation:** Depreciation is much lower than average. **Insurance cost:** Much higher than average. **Parts supply/cost:** Average availability, and parts are moderately priced. **Annual maintenance cost:** Below average. **Warranty:** Bumper-to-bumper 4 years/80,000 km; powertrain 6 years/110,000 km; rust perforation 6 years/unlimited km. **Supplementary warranty:** Not necessary. **Highway/city fuel economy:** 8.4–12.5L/100 km.

Quality/Reliability/Safety

Pro: Quality control: Impressive; top-quality mechanical and body components. **Reliability:** Dependable reliability. **Warranty performance:** Excellent; Toyota is generous in interpreting its warranty and postwarranty responsibilities.

Con: Owner-reported problems: Some interior fit and finish deficiencies. **Service bulletin problems:** Tips on eliminating front suspension noise. **NHTSA safety complaints/safety:** Instrument panel lights aren't bright enough at night; poor visibility due to poor rear view mirror design; middle rear shoulder belt locks up, making it difficult to get the occupant out from the middle seat.

Road Performance

Pro: Emergency handling: Very good, though not as nimble as the Acura TL. **Acceleration/torque:** Fast acceleration and lots of torque (0–100 km/h: 7.5 sec.); beats out the Infiniti Q45. **Transmission:** Shifts smoothly in all gear ranges. **Routine handling:** Capable handling, with little body roll. **Braking:** Better than average braking (100–0 km/h: 121 ft.).

Con: Considerable body lean when cornering under power. Transmission kickdown when passing is slower than what one would expect. Steering is a bit numb and over-assisted. Lots of nosedive when braking.

Comfort/Convenience

Pro: Standard equipment: Although the ES 300 is a Camry V6 twin, it does have its own styling, a bit more power, and more standard features. **Driving position:** Better than average. **Controls and displays:** User-friendly and fairly complete instrumentation. **Climate control:** Efficient and easy to adjust. **Entry/exit:** Easy access. **Interior space/comfort F/R:** Comfortable seating with plenty of head and leg room. **Trunk/liftover:** Modest-sized trunk has a low liftover. **Quietness:** Quiet, with little road or engine noise.

COST

List Price (firm)	Residual Values (months)			
	24	**36**	**48**	**60**
ES 300: $43,295 (20%)	$36,000	$32,000	$27,000	$22,000

TECHNICAL DATA

Powertrain (front-drive)
Engine: 3.0L V6 (210 hp)
Transmission: 4-speed auto.
Dimension/Capacity
Passengers: 2/3
Height/length/width:
54.9/190.2/70.5 in.

Head room F/R: 36.8/36.2 in.
Leg room F/R: 43.5/34.4 in.
Wheelbase: 105.1 in.
Turning circle: 40 ft.
Cargo volume: 13 cu. ft.
Tow limit: N/A
Fuel tank: 70L/prem.
Weight: 3,300 lb.

SAFETY FEATURES/CRASHWORTHINESS

	Std.	Opt.
Anti-lock brakes	■	❑
Seatbelt pretensioners	■	❑
Side airbags	■	❑
Traction control	■	❑
Head restraints F/R	***	***
Visibility F/R	*****	**
Crash protection (front) D/P	****	****
Crash protection (side) D/P	*****	****
Crash protection (off-set)	N/A	

GS 300, 400

GS 430

RATING: Recommended. **Strong points:** Standard side airbags, and Vehicle Stability Control anti-skid system. Excellent high-performance powertrain setup, pleasantly quiet ride, superb handling and braking, and exceptional quality control and warranty performance. **Weak points:** Primarily a four-seater with limited head room for six-footers; high window line impedes rear visibility; poor fuel economy (premium fuel); some instruments hidden by the steering wheel; trunk and fuel-door releases hidden at the base of the dash; and the fuel gauge may give inaccurate readings (there's a service bulletin on this problem). Dash-mounted GPS navigator; climate control and entertainment system tries to do too much.

NEW FOR 2001: V8 engine will be boosted to 4.3 litres, matching the LS 430. *GS300:* E-shift (steering shift switch), door glass repellent (front), auto door lock (shift)/unlock (collision), adoption of immobilizer in card key, extra front assist grip (driver seat), odour removal feature added to clean air filter, front curtain shield SRS airbag, RDS feature on audio, and occupant detecting cut-off mechanism on passenger-side airbag. *GS430:* Torque up from 310 to 325 (+15), steering wheel mounted audio controls (balance of equipment changes are same as GS300 except E-shift is deleted from the 2001 GS430). *LS 430:* A larger, 4.3-litre engine, a restyled aerodynamic shape that allows for more cabin space, and a new suspension that enhances stability and gives a smoother ride. The interior is more richly styled and includes more advanced safety features.

OVERVIEW: Redesigned in 1999, these rear-drives are shorter, the wheelbase is longer, the trunk is larger, and there's a lot more interior room. Two models are available: one carries the inline 6-cylinder engine and the other is V8-powered. Both engines have VVT-i (Variable Valve Timing with intelligence), a feature that continually changes the engine timing to achieve peak horsepower with low emissions and high fuel economy. Other innovative features include Vehicle Stability Control (VSC), dual side airbags, and dual-zone climate controls. **Service bulletin problems:** Rattles from the glove box, the garage door opener cover, and the centre seat belt retractor cover. **NHTSA safety complaints/safety:** Faulty Bridgestone tires.

Cost analysis/best alternatives: Buy the 2001 for the engine upgrade and enhanced features. Other cars worth considering are the Acura RL, BMW 5-Series, and Mercedes-Benz E-class. **Options:** 17-inch tires. Stay away from the in-dash navigator; it complicates the calibration of the sound system and climate controls. **Rebates:** Not likely. Look for discounting on the MSRP by about 5 percent. **Delivery/PDI:** $350. **Depreciation:** Much slower than average. **Insurance cost:** Much higher than average. **Parts supply/cost:** Parts aren't easily found outside of the dealer network; prices tend to be on the high side. **Annual maintenance cost:** Less than average. **Warranty:** Bumper-to-bumper 4 years/80,000 km; powertrain 6 years/110,000 km; rust perforation 6 years/unlimited km. **Supplementary warranty:** Not necessary. **Highway/city fuel economy:** 8.5–11.8L/100 km for the GS 300 and 9.0–13.4L/100 km for the GS 400.

Road Performance

Pro: Acceleration/torque: Hot rod acceleration with lots of torque (0–100 km/h: 6.1 sec. with the V8). **Braking:** Exceptional braking for a car this heavy (100–0 km/h: 122 ft.).

COST				
List Price (firm)	**Residual Values (months)**			
	24	**36**	**48**	**60**
GS 300: $60,015 (30%)	$45,000	$39,000	$34,000	$29,000
GS 400: $69,585 (30%)	$49,000	$44,000	$39,000	$35,000

TECHNICAL DATA	
Powertrain (rear-drive)	Head room F/R: 39.2/37 in.
Engines: 3.0L 6-cyl. (225 hp)	Leg room F/R: 44.5/34.3 in.
• 4.3L V8 (325 hp)	Wheelbase: 110.2 in.
Transmissions: 5-speed auto.	Turning circle: 39 ft.
• 5-speed auto.	Cargo volume: 15 cu. ft.
Dimension/Capacity	Tow limit: N/A
Passengers: 2/3	Fuel tank: 70L/prem.
Height/length/width:	Weight: 3,300 lb.
56.7/189/70.9 in.	

SAFETY FEATURES/CRASHWORTHINESS		
	Std.	**Opt.**
Anti-lock brakes	■	❑
Seatbelt pretensioners	■	❑
Side airbags	■	❑
Traction control	■	❑
Head restraints F/R	***	***
Visibility F/R	*****	**
Crash protection (front) D/P	N/A	N/A
Crash protection (side) D/P	N/A	N/A
Crash protection (off-set)	*****	

MAZDA

Ford is putting Mazda through the wringer—and Mazda executives appreciate the punishment. Teetering on the verge of bankruptcy in 1994, Ford stepped in to turn the company around (Mazda was a major Ford supplier) and two years later bought a controlling interest of 34 percent of the company's shares.

Now with Ford effectively running Mazda, it has decreed that the Japanese automaker must close 40 percent of its unprofitable North American dealerships this year, in order to reward those dealers who are market leaders in an effort to stem costs and increase profits. The company's profits have declined mainly because of fluctuating currency rates, lackluster earnings, higher dealer incentives and customer rebates, less utilization of its Michigan factory, and revolving-door management.

Now that Mazda's Canadian sales have picked up a bit this year, the company remains more vulnerable to downturns than other Japanese automakers because it doesn't have the huge cash reserves of Toyota (almost $30 billion) and has only one overseas plant (a Michigan plant co-owned by Ford) to which it can shift production. The company had been hit hard by a lack of new products and a softening in the entry-level market, both in North America and in Japan. Mazda's 2000 MPV minivan has been a sales flop, making this year's freshening of the Miata and Millenia all the more important. Later this year we'll see the debut of Mazda's new Tribute sport-utility, a twin of the small Ford Escape, but with sportier suspension tuning and quicker transmission gear ratios. If successful, the Tribute will become the "cash cow" Mazda needs so badly (see *Lemon-Aid New 4X4s, Vans and Trucks 2001* for a full report on the Tribute and Escape).

Protegé

Protegé

RATING: Recommended. **Strong points:** Good engine performance (manual transmission), comfortable ride, plenty of interior room, good fuel economy, few safety-related complaints, and quality workmanship. **Weak points:** Limited highway passing power is further compromised by the automatic transmission; there is excessive engine, road, and wind noise; ride is a bit harsh in the SE version.

NEW FOR 2001: Carried over without any significant changes.

OVERVIEW: Protegé is Mazda's least costly model. It shares platforms with the recently discontinued Escort and Tracer, but keeps its own sheet metal, engine, and interior styling. Powered by a standard, fuel-efficient 105-hp 1.6L engine mated to a manual 5-speed transmission, and offering an optional Miata-based 1.8L powerplant, the Protegé is one of the roomiest and most responsive small cars around.

Cost analysis/best alternatives: Get the 2000 model if it's discounted by about 15 percent. Other cars worth considering are the 2000 Ford Escort and Tracer (Protegé clones), redesigned 2001 Honda Civic, Hyundai Accent, Suzuki Swift, Toyota Corolla, and VW Golf and Jetta. **Options:** The 1.8L engine and anti-lock brakes. **Rebates:** $1,000–$1,500 on the 2000s. **Delivery/PDI:** $400. **Depreciation:** Average. **Insurance cost:** Average. **Parts supply/cost:** Mazda parts costs are more reasonable since the company cut prices last year and they aren't difficult to find. Plus, Ford dealers or independents can easily service these cars if you're not satisfied with your Mazda dealer's servicing. In fact, most Ford dealers have parts that can be used on Mazda products because the Ford Escort uses lots of Mazda mechanical components. This knowledge may be useful if you find your Mazda dealer jacking up parts prices or providing lousy service (same thing applies to Ford dealers who give poor servicing to Escorts and Tracers). **Annual maintenance cost:** Below average. **Warranty:** Bumper-to-bumper 3 years/80,000 km; powertrain 5 years/100,000 km; rust perforation 5 years/unlimited km. **Supplementary warranty:** A good idea while waiting for improved service. **Highway/city fuel economy:** 6.9–9.3L/100 km with the base 1.6L engine and an automatic transmission, and 7.1–9.7L/100 km with the 1.8L engine and an automatic transmission.

Quality/Reliability/Safety

Pro: Quality control: Very good. Few quality control complaints. **Reliability:** Better than average. **Warranty performance:** Better than average; a big improvement by Ford customer relations, though a lot depends on the dealer going to bat for you. ABS is standard on the ES and optional on the LX.

Con: Owner-reported problems: The front brakes tend to wear out quickly, and MacPherson struts and rear shock absorbers don't last as long as they should. Some complaints of poor fit and paint defects. **Service bulletin problems:** Excessive exhaust resonance noise at 2200–2300 rpms. **NHTSA safety complaints/safety:** Brake pedal pushed almost to the floor before brakes work, and they produce excessive noise; inadequate high beam illumination; random hard shifting at moderate speed; erratic speedometer movement; driver sprained knee when got caught by the handle underneath seat; passenger seatbelt won't disengage, forcing occupant to "slither" out of the seat; passenger seatbelt broke; seatbelt case and release button broke while trying to release belt.

Road Performance

Pro: Emergency handling: Comfortable, firm, no-surprise ride doesn't deteriorate as passenger load increases or when cornering at high speed. **Steering:** Predictable, well-controlled, and transmits good road feedback. **Acceleration/torque:** Excellent overall performance with either engine. The 1.6L twin-cam 4-cylinder engine is surprisingly responsive and quiet. Impressive acceleration with the 1.8L optional powerplant. **Transmission:** Both transmissions shift smoothly. The 5-speed manual has a handy "Hold" feature that allows the driver to select and hold any of the three lower gears through the shift lever. Two other advantages: the automatic transaxle can be driven away in second gear, an asset on snow and ice; and you can lock out Overdrive with the push of a button, allowing you to traverse hilly terrain or urban traffic without constant shifting. **Routine handling:** Although the base suspension is less firm this year, handling is quite nimble.

Con: The automatic transmission robs the base engine of much-needed power. Some body roll in turns. SE suspension is a bit too firm for some. **Braking:** Average braking without ABS.

Comfort/Convenience

Pro: Driving position: Better than average. The driver and front passenger are pampered with firm, comfortable front bucket seats and multiple-seat steering wheel adjustments. Great all-around visibility. **Controls and displays:** Clear and well laid-out controls. **Climate control:** Efficient, quiet heating and defrosting, although controls are not as user friendly as they could be. **Entry/exit:** Large doors make for easy access to the front and rear. **Interior space/comfort F/R:** One of the roomiest small cars on the market, although the rear seating is better suited for two average-sized adults. **Cargo space:** Lots of interior space to store large and small items. **Trunk/liftover:** Trunk space is expanded with locking, folding rear seatbacks. A low liftover facilitates loading.

Con: Standard equipment: Cheap-looking, sober interior. The sunroof drastically reduces head room. Even with a tilt steering column, the steering wheel may be too low for some tall drivers. Others may find the gearshift lever a bit too far away when shifting into fifth gear. **Quietness:** Excessive engine, road, and wind noise intrusion into the interior.

COST				
List Price (negotiable)	**Residual Values (months)**			
	24	**36**	**48**	**60**
DX: $15,095 (12%)	$11,000	$9,000	$7,500	$6,000

TECHNICAL DATA

Powertrain (front-drive)
Engines: 1.6L 4-cyl. (105 hp)
• 1.8L 4-cyl. (122 hp)
Transmissions: 5-speed man.
• 4-speed auto.
Dimension/Capacity
Passengers: 2/3
Height/length/width:
55.5/174/67.1 in.

Head room F/R: 37.9/36.7 in.
Leg room F/R: 42.2/35.6 in.
Wheelbase: 102.8 in.
Turning circle: 38 ft.
Cargo volume: 13.1 cu. ft.
Tow limit: N/A
Fuel tank: 50L/reg.
Weight: 2,350 lb.

SAFETY FEATURES/CRASHWORTHINESS

	Std.	Opt.
Anti-lock brakes	❏	■
Seatbelt pretensioners	—	—
Side airbags	—	■
Traction control	—	—
Head restraints F/R	**	**
Visibility F/R	*****	*****
Crash protection (front) D/P	****	****
Crash protection (side) D/P	***	****
Crash protection (off-set)	***	

626

626

RATING: Recommended. These sedans provide room for five along with a high level of luxury and comfort, making the 626 one of the best and most reasonably priced mid-sized cars on the market. **Strong points:** Strong V6 acceleration, pleasant handling, roomy interior, comfortable front and rear seating, easy entry/exit, few safety-related or bulletin-related problems reported, and good overall reliability. **Weak points:** Sluggish 4-cylinder performance, jerky automatic transmission, and excessive road noise.

NEW FOR 2001: No significant changes this year.

OVERVIEW: Restyled three years ago to resemble the more luxurious Mazda Millenia, the 626 is a stylish front-drive compact sedan that does everything well. It comes in three trim levels with a choice of two engines, coupled to either a 5-speed manual or a 4-speed automatic transmission. The base DX is touted as the price leader, but you have to take the 4-cylinder engine and few standard features with the low price. The top-of-the-line ES has more bells and whistles in addition to a V6 engine. A good compromise model is the LX: it's cheaper than the ES, yet offers many of its amenities.

Cost analysis/best alternatives: Get the cheapest 2000 model available; it's practically identical to this year's version. Alternative vehicles: Honda Accord and Toyota Camry. Now that there's so little difference between the 626 and the upscale Millenia, consider the 626 as a cheaper alternative. **Options:** The LX's V6 engine, traction control, and various power accessories. **Rebates:** Expect $1,500 rebates to clear out the 2000s. **Delivery/PDI:** $400. **Depreciation:** Faster than average. **Insurance cost:** Slightly higher than average. **Parts supply/cost:** Reasonably priced parts aren't difficult to find, and independent garages easily service the cars. **Annual maintenance cost:** Less than average. **Warranty:** Bumper-to-bumper 3 years/80,000 km; powertrain 5 years/100,000 km; rust perforation 5 years/unlimited km. **Supplementary warranty:** Not necessary. **Highway/city fuel economy:** 7.5–10.7L/100 km with the base 4-banger and 8.5–12.2L/100 km with the 2.5L.

Quality/Reliability/Safety

Pro: Quality control: Few quality control complaints. Assembly and component quality are high. **Reliability:** Better than average. **Warranty performance:** Not generous, but fair.

Con: Owner-reported problems: Complex electronics cause trouble with age; air conditioning defects; head gasket leaks; automatic transmission malfunctions; excessive hydraulic lifter noise; sunroof rattles; and premature wearout of the front brakes. **Service bulletin problems:** A rear end tapping noise may be heard during the first ten minutes after a cold start. **NHTSA safety complaints/safety:** Surging and stalling; transmission shift shock; noisy fuel pump; knocking noise while driving.

Road Performance

Pro: Emergency handling: Very good. The 626 is sure-footed, responds well to sudden corrections, and has little body roll or front-end plow when cornering under speed. **Steering:** Power steering is a bit light, but very accurate and predictable. **Acceleration/torque:** The V6 powerplant is a road burner with a fair amount of torque once it gets up to speed (0–100 km/h: 7.8 seconds). **Transmission:** The manual transmission and clutch work very well, though downshifts are sometimes jerky. Handling is very good, but not quite as crisp and responsive as the Toyota and Honda competitors. The 4-speed Overdrive automatic shifts smoothly most of the time. **Routine handling:** Nimble handling, and the steady, soft ride doesn't deteriorate as passenger load increases. Overall, a less jittery ride than one finds with the competition. **Braking:** Good braking (100–0 km/h: 119 ft.).

Con: The standard 2.0L 4-cylinder engine is smooth and peppy for urban duties, but it's at a disadvantage when pressed into more demanding service, like passing other vehicles on the highway or merging with fast-moving traffic. It works best with the manual gearbox. Equipped with the V6, power is channelled just a bit less smoothly than what you'd find with the Toyota Camry or Honda Accord.

Comfort/Convenience

Pro: Standard equipment: Many standard performance and convenience features. **Driving position:** The front seats are exceptionally comfortable with lots of head and leg room for tall drivers. **Controls and displays:** Well-positioned gauges and instruments. **Climate control:** Heating and ventilation are above reproach. **Entry/exit:** Easy as pie. **Interior space/comfort F/R:** The rear seat will hold two adults easily and comfortably. **Cargo space:** The hatchback version has a versatile cargo area and lots of handy storage bins. **Trunk/liftover:** Large trunk can be easily expanded with the sedan's locking, folding rear seatbacks. **Quietness:** Body rigidity has been increased, making the car more comfortable and preventing many of the creaks and groans common to all small cars.

Con: The driver's seat may be too low for some. Rear middle passenger will find it a tight fit. **Quietness:** Excessive road noise in the passenger compartment.

COST				
List Price (negotiable)	**Residual Values (months)**			
	24	**36**	**48**	**60**
DX: $23,175 (17%)	$18,000	$14,000	$12,000	$10,000

TECHNICAL DATA	
Powertrain (front-drive)	Head room F/R: 39.2/37 in.
Engines: 2.0L 4-cyl. (125 hp)	Leg room F/R: 43.6/34.6 in.
• 2.5L V6 (170 hp)	Wheelbase: 105.1 in.
Transmissions: 5-speed man.	Turning circle: 39 ft.
• 4-speed auto.	Cargo volume: 14.2 cu. ft.
Dimension/Capacity	Tow limit: 2,000 lb.
Passengers: 2/3	Fuel tank: 60L/reg./prem.
Height/length/width:	Weight: 3,100 lb.
55.1/186.8/69.6 in.	

SAFETY FEATURES/CRASHWORTHINESS

	Std.	Opt.
Anti-lock brakes	❑	■
Seatbelt pretensioners	—	—
Side airbags	—	■
Traction control	❑	■
Head restraints F/R	*	*
Visibility F/R	*****	*****
Crash protection (front) D/P	****	*****
Crash protection (side) D/P	***	***
Crash protection (off-set)	***	

Millenia

Millenia

RATING: Above Average. **Strong points:** Well appointed; lots of power (S version); good handling, steering, and braking; comfortable ride; quiet running; no safety-related and few performance-related complaints; and top-quality, sophisticated mechanical components. **Weak points:** Just so-so acceleration with the base powerplant, some S-model throttle lag, limited rear seating room, and restricted rear visibility.

NEW FOR 2001: Slight restyling of the front and rear end. Millenia is living on borrowed time.

OVERVIEW: Despite its late entry into the luxury market—Lexus and Infiniti have had years to fortify their position—Millenia has sold fairly well; unfortunately, sales have now plateaued, forcing Mazda to look for a replacement for 2002.

Smaller than the Mazda 929, the front-drive Millenia carries the same 2.5L 170-hp V6 used by the 626. An optional 2.3L Miller Cycle "S" 6-cylinder engine, although smaller than the base powerplant, still manages to pump out 210 horsepower. Both engines use a standard 4-speed automatic transmission.

As with all luxury cars, the Millenia comes with a wide array of standard features that would normally cost thousands of dollars more. Although billed as a five-passenger car, the middle occupant in the rear seat would be cramped and have to sit on a hump—a problem with which 929 owners are familiar.

Cost analysis/best alternatives: Get a discounted 2000 model, if this year's restyling isn't important to you. From a performance standpoint, the Camry V6, with its less complicated powertrain, outruns the Millenia; and the redesigned 626 gives you practically all the same features for less money. Other cars worth considering are the Acura TL, Infiniti I30, Lexus ES 300, and Mercedes-Benz E420. **Options:** Traction control. Get the dealer to change the limited spare tire for a full-service tire that can easily fit in the trunk well. Be wary of the sunroof option on the sedan if you're a tall driver; it takes away much-needed head room. **Rebates:** Instead of rebates, Mazda has announced hefty price cuts of $2,000 for the base model and over $5,000 on the Miller version. **Delivery/PDI:** $600. **Depreciation:** Slower than average. **Insurance cost:** Higher than average. **Parts supply/cost:** Parts are costly and frequently back-ordered. **Annual maintenance cost:** Average. **Warranty:** Bumper-to-bumper 3 years/80,000 km; powertrain 5 years/100,000 km; rust perforation 5 years/unlimited km. **Supplementary warranty:** Not necessary. **Highway/city fuel economy:** 8.0–12.2L/100 km with the 2.3L, and 8.3–12.3L/100 km with the 2.5L.

Quality/Reliability/Safety

Pro: Quality control: Assembly and component quality are high. **Reliability:** No serious reliability problems noted. **Warranty performance:** Acceptable. **Owner-reported problems:** Nothing of any significance. **NHTSA safety complaints/safety:** No safety-related incidents have been recorded.

Con: Some complaints of poor servicing and long waits for parts, sidelining vehicle for days at a time. **Service bulletin problems:** Tips for eliminating a musty, mildew-type odour from the AC.

Road Performance

Pro: Emergency handling: Very good. Electronic traction control performs flawlessly. **Steering:** Smooth, precise steering. **Acceleration/torque:** The 170-hp V6 engine provides plenty of power in most driving situations, but the supercharged version is a real road burner (0–100 km/h: 8.3 sec.) that provides gobs of mid-range torque. **Transmission:** Quiet and smooth-shifting. **Routine handling:** Fun to drive, due to the Millenia's crisp handling and comfortable ride, which doesn't deteriorate as passenger load increases. **Braking:** Relatively short braking distance without any fading after successive application (100–0 km/h: 130 ft.).

Con: The Miller Cycle engine is a bit slow to get up to speed.

Comfort/Convenience

Pro: Standard equipment: Plenty of standard amenities. Great sound system. Firm, comfortable driver's seat has lots of control for height and tilt. **Climate control:** Works well with little noise. **Cargo space:** Above average storage space in the passenger compartment. **Trunk/liftover:** Spacious trunk has a low liftover. **Quietness:** Very little engine or road noise intrudes into the interior.

Con: Bland exterior styling. Front seat may be too low for some. **Driving position:** Tall drivers may find head and leg room a bit limited. Insufficient thigh support with the bucket seats. **Controls and displays:** Controls aren't sufficiently lit. Radio controls aren't user-friendly. **Climate control:** Erratic temperature control can't keep a consistent setting. **Entry/exit:** Narrow rear doors complicate rear seat access. **Interior space/comfort F/R:** Rear seating isn't very comfortable for three.

COST				
List Price (negotiable)	**Residual Values (months)**			
	24	**36**	**48**	**60**
Base: $39,595 (21%)	$28,000	$22,000	$18,000	$14,000

TECHNICAL DATA

Powertrain (front-drive)
Engines: 2.5L V6 (170 hp)
• 2.3L V6 (210 hp)
Transmission: 4-speed auto.
Dimension/Capacity
Passengers: 2/3
Height/length/width:
54.9/189.8/69.7 in.

Head room F/R: 37.9/36.5 in.
Leg room F/R: 43.3/34.1 in.
Wheelbase: 108.3 in.
Turning circle: 42 ft.
Cargo volume: 13.3 cu. ft.
Tow limit: 2,000 lb.
Fuel tank: 68L/prem.
Weight: 3,400 lb.

SAFETY FEATURES/CRASHWORTHINESS

	Std.	Opt.
Anti-lock brakes	■	❏
Seatbelt pretensioners	—	—
Side airbags	—	—
Traction control	❏	■
Head restraints F/R	*	*
Visibility F/R	*****	**
Crash protection (front) D/P	*****	*****
Crash protection (side) D/P	N/A	N/A
Crash protection (off-set)	***	

MX-5 (Miata)

Miata

RATING: Recommended. An exceptional, reasonably priced roadster. **Strong points:** Good powertrain setup provides better than expected acceleration for such a small engine, nice handling, impressive braking, good fuel economy, no safety-related and few performance-related complaints, and a high resale value. **Weak points:** Limited passenger and cargo room, a firm ride, excessive road, wind, and engine noise intrudes, restricted rear visibility, and no crashworthiness or injury claim data available.

NEW FOR 2001: No significant changes.

OVERVIEW: The Miata is a stubby, rear-drive, two-seater sports car that combines new technology with old British roadster styling reminiscent of the Triumph, Austin-Healy, and Lotus Elan.

This is a fun car to drive, costing much less than other vehicles in its class. Built on a shortened 323 platform, the Miata is shorter than all other sports cars except the Porsche 911 (although it's almost eight inches longer than the old Honda CRX). The 1.8L twin-cam 4-cylinder engine, borrowed from the Protegé, is coupled to a 5-speed manual gearbox, and the rear suspension is a copy of the discontinued RX-7's.

Cost analysis/best alternatives: A discounted 2000 model (if you can find one) would be a great buy, since it offers practically everything you'll find in this year's model. Other cars worth considering are the BMW Z3 series, Ford Mustang, GM Camaro and Firebird, Honda Prelude, and Toyota Celica. No, the Honda S2000 isn't a credible alternative; check out its rating. **Options:** Anti-lock brakes, power steering, and a limited-slip differential. Original equipment 185/60R14 winter tires are poor performers; go for the Sport Package's 195/50VR15 rubber, instead. Goodyear Ultra Grip brand is also a good alternative. **Rebates:** $1,500 on the 2000s early in 2001. **Delivery/PDI:** $300. **Depreciation:** Much slower than average. **Insurance cost:** Higher than average. **Parts supply/cost:** Parts are easy to find, but often cost more than average. **Annual maintenance cost:** Less than average. **Warranty:** Bumper-to-bumper 3 years/80,000 km; powertrain 5 years/100,000 km; rust perforation 5 years/unlimited km. **Supplementary warranty:** Not needed. **Highway/city fuel economy:** 7.5–10.5L/100 km.

Quality/Reliability/Safety

Pro: Quality control: Excellent workmanship and exceptional quality. **Reliability:** Nothing reported that would take these cars out of service. **Warranty performance:** Average, although a lot depends on dealer servicing. **NHTSA safety complaints:** Nothing significant. If you must carry an infant, the Miata has a factory-installed airbag cut-off switch.

Con: Owner-reported problems: Specialty replacement batteries have been hard to find, and dirt and debris can clog up side door sill holes, allowing water to collect and corrosion to occur. Ask the dealer to drill larger drain holes. **Service bulletin problems:** Tips for eliminating a musty, mildew-type odour from the AC. **Safety:** Shoulder belts may chafe your neck; seatbelt's low anchor causes the belt to pull down against the shoulder.

Road Performance

Pro: Emergency handling: No surprises. Performs emergency manoeuvres predictably and almost as quickly as the Porsche Boxster. Exceptionally responsive, with minimal body roll; the rigid chassis gives the car a solid feeling. **Steering:** Steering is crisp and predictable. **Acceleration/torque:** Brisk acceleration with a good amount of low-end torque (0–100 km/h: 8.5 seconds). **Transmission:** Easy, precise throws with the manual and smooth, quiet shifting with the automatic. The 6-speed gearbox is helpful in keeping the noise level down. **Routine handling:** Lightness and 50/50-weight distribution make it an easy car to toss around corners without tossing your cookies. **Braking:** Impressive braking performance on dry pavement with little brake fading after successive stops (100–0 km/h: 102 ft.).

Con: Although the ride is a bit choppy, it's not as harsh as previous versions. The rear end tends to swing out when cornering under speed.

Comfort/Convenience

Pro: Standard equipment: The base model is well equipped. The round dash air vents heighten the sports car image, giving the cockpit a 1960s British roadster allure. The convertible top is easily lowered from inside or outside of the car, and the optional hardtop is quite practical and easy to install. An innovative wind block flips up behind the rear seats. **Controls and displays:** Gauges are simple to comprehend and well positioned. **Climate control:** Efficient, quiet heating and defrosting system is easy to adjust. **Entry/exit:** Not difficult once you get used to stepping down into your Miata. **Cargo space:** Storage areas include a relatively large locking glove compartment and centre console bin (with cupholder), net pouches behind the seats, and small map pockets in each door. However, storage space for large objects is practically non-existent, and there's almost no room behind the rear seats. **Trunk/liftover:** A low liftover makes for easy loading, although the trunk itself is quite small and shallow.

Con: Driving position: Not for six-footers. The steering wheel is set too close to the driver, isn't height-adjustable, and blocks your view of the ignition switch and power mirror control. Seats are set too low for short drivers. Unusually small inside door releases are mounted too far back to be accessed comfortably. With the top in place, rear visibility is obstructed by the wide rear panels, the small rear window, and small side view mirrors. Small bucket seats give marginal lateral support and could use a bit more padding. **Interior space/comfort F/R:** Interior is a bit small for tall occupants, who must sit bolt upright when pushing their seat all the way back. Insufficient lower back and thigh support. Inadequate head and leg room for tall adults. If you have large thighs, you may need a month at Weight Watchers to fit them between the steering wheel and seat cushion. **Quietness:** Better get used to road, tire, and engine noise that increases as the Miata picks up speed.

COST				
List Price (negotiable)	**Residual Values (months)**			
	24	**36**	**48**	**60**
Base Miata: $26,995 (19%)	$18,000	$15,000	$12,000	$10,000

TECHNICAL DATA	
Powertrain (rear-drive)	Head room: 37.1 in.
Engine: 1.8L 4-cyl. (140 hp)	Leg room: 42.7 in.
Transmissions: 5-speed man.	Wheelbase: 89.2 in.
• 4-speed auto.	Turning circle: 33 ft.
Dimension/Capacity	Cargo volume: 5 cu. ft.
Passengers: 2/0	Tow limit: N/A
Height/length/width:	Fuel tank: 45L/reg.
48.2/155.4/65.9 in.	Weight: 2,300 lb.

SAFETY FEATURES/CRASHWORTHINESS		
	Std.	**Opt.**
Anti-lock brakes	❏	■
Seatbelt pretensioners	—	—
Side airbags	—	—

Traction control	—	—
Head restraints F/R	*	N/A
Visibility F/R	*****	*
Crash protection (front) D/P	N/A	N/A
Crash protection (side) D/P	N/A	N/A
Crash protection (off-set)	N/A	

MPV

RISKY BUY

MPV

RATING: Not Recommended. This underpowered, lumbering, under-sized, and overpriced minivan is an Odyssey wannabe that simply comes across as odd. **Strong points:** Comfortable ride and easy handling, good driver's position, responsive steering, and lots of gadgets and innovative storage spots. Not many factory-related defects reported, yet, and seatbelts are the main safety-related complaint. **Weak points:** The small V6 engine is performance-challenged; it gives the impression that there's nothing in reserve, with barely enough power for highway use and leisurely acceleration from a stop (like the first Odysseys). Mediocre automatic transmission performance. Smaller than most of the competition. Dealer servicing and head office support have been problematic in the past.

NEW FOR 2001: Carried over unchanged.

OVERVIEW: Mazda's only minivan quickly became a bestseller when it first came on the market in 1989, but during the past few years, its popularity has fallen off. Mazda sales bounced back last year as a result of price cutting and the popularity of the automaker's small cars and pickups. This infusion of cash has allowed the company (33 percent owned by Ford) to put additional money into its MPV redesign. Mazda hoped to get a fresh start with its redesigned MPV, thus ending a minivan drought that has plagued the company for almost a year.

Unfortunately, the latest MPV iteration appears to embody all the mistakes made by Honda's first Odyssey—its 170 horses aren't adequate for people hauling and it's too expensive for what is essentially a smaller van than its predecessor. For example, the MPV is over a foot shorter than the Ford Windstar and a half foot shorter than the Toyota Sienna and Nissan Quest.

Manufactured in Hiroshima, Japan, this redesigned seven-passenger minivan switches from rear-drive to front-wheel drive and includes a number of innovative features, like "theatre" seating (rear passenger seat is slightly higher), and a third seat that pivots rearward to become a rear-facing bench seat—or folds into the floor for picnics or tailgate parties. Another feature unique among minivans is Mazda's Side-by-Slide removable second-row seats that move fore and aft as well as side-to-side while a passenger is seated. Sliding door crank windows are standard on the entry model and power assisted on the LS and ES versions.

All-wheel-drive models have been dropped, and this year's MPV comes equipped with a standard Ford 170-hp 2.5L V6, assembled in Ohio and shipped to Japan (a homegrown 3.0L V6 is scheduled for 2002). A 4-speed automatic transmission is the only gearbox available—which is unfortunate, because it shifts erratically and robs the MPV engine of power it badly needs.

Standard DX equipment includes AC, dual sliding doors, intermittent rear wiper/washer, 100-watt audio system, and tilt steering wheel. The higher trim levels don't offer much of value, except for power windows and door locks and an ignition immobilizer/alarm/keyless entry system. Side airbags are optional on the LX and standard on the ES model. This being only their second year in service, buyers should be wary of these airbags until their reliability and safety have been ascertained.

Cost analysis/best alternatives: Go for a discounted 2000 model, but make sure it's a second-series version to keep factory-induced glitches to a minimum. Other minivans worth considering are the Honda Odyssey, Nissan Quest, and the Toyota Sienna. **Options:** Higher trim option includes an ugly, orange, fake wood dash. An integrated child safety seat isn't available. Rear AC and seat height-adjustment mechanisms are recommended convenience features. **Rebates:** Expect $2,000 rebates by spring as dealer inventory piles up. **Delivery/PDI:** $900. **Depreciation:** Predicted to be worse than average. **Insurance cost:** Likely to be higher than average. **Parts supply/cost:** Likely to be backordered and cost more than average. **Annual maintenance cost:** Too early to say. **Warranty:** Bumper-to-bumper 3 years/80,000 km; powertrain 5 years/100,000 km; rust perforation 5 years/unlimited mileage. **Supplementary warranty:** An extended warranty is worth having, particularly in view of the fact that this is a totally redesigned vehicle that's in its second year on the market. **Highway/city fuel economy:** 9.9–13.6L/100 km.

Quality/Reliability/Safety

Pro: Quality control: High-quality workmanship and rugged construction. **Service bulletin problems:** Insufficient air flow at bi-level setting, door key difficult to insert or rotate, and troubleshooting of a broken console sunglass holder. **NHTSA safety complaints/safety:** Airbags failed to deploy; excessive drivetrain vibration at 90 km/h; seatbelts lock up when vehicle is moving; seatbelts are too short; difficult keeping child safety seat secured properly due to the anchor placement.

Con: Reliability: Expect transmission failures, ABS malfunctions, and premature wearout of the front and rear brakes. **Warranty performance:** Inadequate base warranty. Mediocre past servicing will likely be put to a severe test as the new model's problems emerge. **Owner-reported problems:** Too early to report. This new model will likely have some engine, transmission, and brake problems, judging by the mechanical specs given out at press time. Rear visibility obstructed by high seatbacks.

Road Performance

Pro: Ford's Duratec V6 (essentially the same engine that powers the Mercury Cougar) has plenty of power for in-town use. Excellent steering feedback. **Routine handling:** Acceptable at low speeds. **Braking:** Adequate.

Con: Acceleration/torque: Insufficient power for highway use. Slow acceleration makes merging with traffic and passing other cars a bit scary. Little low-end torque, insufficient with a full load. Excessive engine whine and vibration when passing the 4500 rpm mark. **Transmission:** The primordial automatic transmission shifts roughly and constantly. It lumbers through first and second gear, and then bangs when going from second to third. Drivetrain is particularly rough when cold. **Emergency handling:** This minivan's highway performance doesn't inspire confidence. Some brake fade after successive stops. **Steering:** Fights to stay on-centre, even when trying to make a turn.

Comfort/Convenience

Pro: Standard equipment: Lots of standard features, but the 180-watt, nine-speaker audio system that stores up to six CDs is particularly impressive. **Driving position:** Driver sits comfortably high with excellent forward visibility and lots of head room. **Controls and displays:** Instrumentation is easy to read, with large gauges, buttons, and knobs. Controls are within easy reach. **Climate control:** Good heating/defrosting/ventilation system. **Entry/exit:** Easy entry/exit up front. **Interior space/comfort F/R:** Without a doubt, the MPV manages its limited interior space far better than the competition. All seats are well bolstered with plenty of head room in all seating positions. Middle row seating converts easily from bench, with an aisle on each side, to buckets, with an aisle down the middle. Third row seat flips and folds into a floor well. Side doors have windows that drop down, rather than swing out, which tends to be rattle prone. **Cargo space:** Adequate; large door bins. Seats can be easily removed for additional cargo room and they weigh 13 lb. (6 kg) less than the Odyssey's seats. **Trunk/liftover:** Easy to load or unload.

Con: The sliding side door openings are narrow and doors only operate manually. **Interior space/comfort F/R:** Elbow room is at a premium and it takes a lithe figure to move down the front- and middle-seat aisle. Don't believe for a minute the MPV will hold seven passengers in comfort—six is more like it. The flip and fold third-row seat, when flipped 90 degrees backward for tailgate parties, puts the passenger-side occupant dangerously close to the hot exhaust pipe and leaves adult legs dangling uncomfortably. **Quietness:** Excessive engine and road noise.

COST

List Price (negotiable)	Residual Values (months)			
	24	**36**	**48**	**60**
DX: $25,095 (20%)	$16,000	$12,000	$10,000	$8,000

TECHNICAL DATA

Powertrain (rear-drive)	Head room F: 41/R1: 39.3/R2: 38 in.
Engine: 2.5L V6 (170 hp)	Leg room F: 40.8/R1: 37/R2: 35.6 in.
Transmission: 4-speed auto.	Wheelbase: 111.8 in.
Dimension/Capacity	Turning circle: 37.4 ft.
Passengers: 2/2/3	Cargo volume: 54.6 cu. ft.
Height/length/width:	GVWR: N/A
68.7/187/72.1 in.	Payload: N/A
	Tow limit: N/A
	Fuel tank: 70L/reg.
	Weight: 3,662 lb.

SAFETY FEATURES/CRASHWORTHINESS

	Std.	Opt.
Anti-lock brakes (2W; 4W)	■	■
Seatbelt pretensioners	❑	❑
Side airbags	❑	■
Traction control	—	—
Head restraints F/R	***	***
Visibility F/R	*****	***
Crash protection (front) D/P	****	****
Crash protection (side) D/P	*****	*****
Crash protection (off-set)	***	

NISSAN

In the following year, Nissan will showcase both performance and styling with the return of the Z Car. In the meantime, for the 2001 year models, Nissan will carry over most of its models with minimal changes and rev up production of its popular Xterra SUV and Frontier pickup.

Nissan, or should I say, Renault's Nissan division, is one sick puppy. It has had only one profitable year in the past nine and last year's losses were horrific—losing about $6.6 billion U.S. from $261 million a year earlier. Now, with Renault's controlling interest in the automaker, Nissan executives are seeking to turn the company around this year by closing plants, reducing the supplier base, slashing costs, paying off Nissan's huge debts, and coming up with a new product mix. Undoubtedly, the new vehicles are said to combine dramatic styling, high-performance and sport-utility and truck versatility.

Nissan does make good cars, trucks, and minivans, and the public is slowly catching on to this fact. Its Tennessee manufacturing plant is running at full capacity to meet demand for its new Xterra sport-utility and Crew Cab pickup. Most of this year's production of both vehicles has been sold and orders for the Crew Cab, with its four full-sized doors, represent 28 percent of pickup sales, whereas Nissan predicted only 12 percent.

On the other hand, Renault France's acquisition of a controlling interest in Nissan may not be the godsend that was first thought. The French automaker is known for making lousy marketing decisions and producing low quality vehicles (think back to the Alliance, Encore, Premier, and Medallion). The first sign of Renault's effect upon Nissan will be seen in the Altima's replacement, expected for the summer of 2001. Here's to hoping that Renault will show some styling flair without compromising performance or reliability. Nevertheless, many industry watchers still suspect Renault's purchasing of a controlling interest in Nissan may only be a ploy for the French automaker to re-enter the American market under another name. Such is the bad rep and suspicion Renault has earned subsequent to its dealings with Chrysler.

Sentra

Sentra

RATING: Recommended. Unlike many bare-bones economy cars, entry-level Sentras offer dependable motoring at little cost. **Strong points:** Both engines provide plenty of power, comfortable ride and easy handling, good quality control, few safety-related or performance-related defects reported by owners. On top of that, the cars are reasonably priced. 2.0L-equipped versions provide much better acceleration, handling, and ride. **Weak points:** Difficult rear access; average crashworthiness, but much higher than average accident injury claims.

NEW FOR 2001: A supercharged, 160-hp SE-R with upgraded tires and a sport-tuned suspension to compete against the Honda Civic Si and the Mazda Protegé.

OVERVIEW: Nissan's entry-level small sedans come in three trim levels: the XE and GXE, housing a perky 126-hp 1.8L 4-cylinder engine, and the sporty SE, carrying the same 2.0L engine with five additional horses. A manual 5-speed transmission is standard; a 4-speed is optional. Now that the car is classed by the U.S. government as a compact rather than sub-compact, the exterior design is a mixture of the Altima and Maxima. The base model comes with standard 14-inch wheels, instead of last year's 13s, and a height-adjustable driver's seat. The SE has a more taut suspension, 4-wheel disc brakes, and 15-inch wheels, rather than 14s. ABS and front side airbags are optional.

Cost analysis/best alternatives: Get the year 2001 model; it's the last new model launched before Renault's cost-cutters arrived. You may wish to opt for a second-series version sometime in the new year, not for rebates, which will be rare, but for a Sentra with fewer redesign glitches. Another reason to avoid last year's leftover models is the woefully underpowered 1.6L engine. Sentra's engine and body dimension improvements have made it a good competitor to the Honda Civic and Toyota Corolla.

Other worthwhile cars to consider are the GM Cavalier and Sunfire and Mazda Protegé. **Options:** If you do a lot of highway driving, spend the extra money for the SE's stronger engine, four-wheel disc brakes, and better-grade, quieter tires. **Rebates:** $2,000 to clear out the leftover 2000s. **Depreciation:** Average. **Insurance cost:** Average. **Parts supply/cost:** Inexpensive parts can be found practically anywhere. **Annual maintenance cost:** Less than average. Uncluttered under-hood layout makes servicing easy. **Warranty:** Bumper-to-bumper 3 years/80,000 km; powertrain 5 years/100,000 km; rust perforation 5 years/unlimited km. **Supplementary warranty:** Not needed. **Highway/city fuel economy:** 6.6–8.9L/100 km with the 1.8L and an automatic, and 7.5–10.3L/100 km with the 2.0L and an automatic.

Quality/Reliability/Safety

Pro: Quality control: Sentras are almost trouble-free. First-class body assembly. Sentra production has been moved to Mexico—however, this hasn't affected quality control. **Reliability:** Overall reliability is better than average. **Warranty performance:** Average. **Service bulletin problems:** Causes for a slow fuel fillup, water on the front carpet, and a faulty front seatbelt latch plate.

Con: Owner-reported problems: Some reports of 1.6L engine cylinder head and gasket failures (2000 model). Clutch, exhaust system, and fuel system problems are fairly common after the first three years. Front pads and rotors wear out quickly. **NHTSA safety complaints/safety:** Airbag failed to deploy; ABS brake failure.

Road Performance

Pro: Acceleration/torque: Both the 1.8L and 2.0L 4-cylinder engines provide plenty of power for all driving situations. **Transmission:** Both manual and automatic transmissions shift very smoothly. **Routine handling:** Good manoeuvrability around town. Firm but well-mannered ride on most roads. **Steering:** Predictable, with little understeer, but slow. **Braking:** Average; minimal fading after successive stops.

Con: SE version has sportier handling, but ride comfort is compromised. **Emergency handling:** High-speed handling is a bit sloppy, and emergency handling is sluggish.

Comfort/Convenience

Pro: Standard equipment: Average for an entry-level small car. **Driving position:** Spartan, though acceptable instruments and controls. Standard tilt wheel and height-adjustable seat creates a comfortable driving position. **Controls and displays:** Easy-to-read dash gauges and convenient controls. Neatly finished interior. **Climate control:** Efficient and uncomplicated heating, defrosting, and ventilation. **Interior space/comfort F/R:** Comfortable, supportive seats. Up front, there's good all-around head room and leg room. In the rear, you have to move the front seats all the way forward to be comfortable. **Cargo space:** Average for this size of car. **Trunk/liftover:** Average-sized, but a bit smaller than the Honda Civic or Ford Focus trunk; has a low liftover.

Con: Entry/exit: Small rear doors make access a bit difficult. **Interior space/comfort F/R:** Don't believe Nissan's claim of five-passenger seating: the four-door sedan only accommodates four people comfortably. All seats could use extra padding. **Quietness:** Lots of wind and tire noise.

COST				
List Price (very negotiable)	**Residual Values (months)**			
	24	**36**	**48**	**60**
Base XE: $15,298 (12%)	$11,000	$9,000	$7,500	$6,500
GXE: $17,698 (14%)	$13,000	$11,000	$9,500	$8,500

TECHNICAL DATA

Powertrain (front-drive)
Engines: 1.8L 4-cyl. (126 hp)
• 2.0L 4-cyl. (145 hp)
Transmissions: 5-speed man.
• 4-speed auto.
Dimension/Capacity
Passengers: 2/3
Height/length/width:
55.6/177.5/67.3 in.

Head room F/R: 39.9/37 in.
Leg room F/R: 41.6/33.7 in.
Wheelbase: 99.8 in.
Turning circle: 38 ft.
Cargo volume: 12 cu. ft.
Tow limit: 1,000 lb.
Fuel tank: 50L/reg./prem.
Weight: 2,548 lb.

SAFETY FEATURES/CRASHWORTHINESS

	Std.	Opt.
Anti-lock brakes (4W)	❏	■
Seatbelt pretensioners	■	❏
Side airbags	■	❏
Traction control	—	—
Head restraints F/R	**	**
Visibility F/R	*****	***
Crash protection (front) D/P	N/A	N/A
Crash protection (side) D/P	N/A	N/A
Crash protection (off-set)	***	

Altima

RATING: Above Average. **Strong points:** Handles well, good braking, reliable, well laid-out instruments and controls, and better-than-average craftsmanship. **Weak points:** Delayed, harsh shifting; uncomfortable rear seating; vague steering requires frequent correction, and disappointing crashworthiness scores and accident injury claim data.

NEW FOR 2001: Nothing much: next year, it goes onto the same platform as the redesigned Maxima and gets more powerful engines.

OVERVIEW: Nissan's latest mid-size sedan, this yuppie-mobile is a four-door, front-drive, 4-cylinder aimed at Chrysler's LH series and GM's best-selling Cavalier/Sunfire. The engine is a spinoff of the discontinued 240SX's 16-valve 150-hp 2.4L 4-banger. Three models are available: the GLE, GXE, and SE. Front side airbags are standard on the GLE, along with standard 16-inch wheels on the GLE and SE. GXE is available with a new Limited Edition package, which includes side impact airbags, an eight-way power driver's seat, remote keyless entry, floor mats, and a security system.

Cost analysis/best alternatives: For the money, last year's identical 2000 version is your best choice. Other cars worth considering are the Honda Accord, Mazda 626, Toyota Camry, and VW Passat. **Options:** 16-inch wheels are a plus for a better ride and easier handling. Nissan tends to option-load its Altimas, forcing you to take a number of unwanted, unnecessary optional features along with the one you want. Can you get by without the optional automatic transmission? I say it's not refined enough for pleasurable shifting; however, test-drive an Altima yourself to judge your own tolerance for its shifting eccentricities. **Rebates:** $2,000 to clear out the leftover 2000s. **Delivery/PDI:** $500. **Depreciation:** A bit slower than average. **Insurance cost:** Higher than average. **Parts supply/cost:** Parts are easy to find, but dealer prices can be steep. Independent suppliers often sell them at discount prices. **Annual maintenance cost:** Less than average. Uncluttered under-hood layout makes servicing easy. **Warranty:** Bumper-to-bumper 3 years/80,000 km; powertrain 5 years/100,000 km; rust perforation 5 years/unlimited km. **Supplementary warranty:** Not needed. **Highway/city fuel economy:** 7.1–9.9L/100 km with the manual transmission and 7.2–10.6L/100 km with an automatic.

Quality/Reliability/Safety

Pro: Quality control: Good body assembly and powertrain components. **Reliability:** No reliability problems have been reported. **Warranty performance:** Average. Nissan staffers aren't particularly generous in handling premature brake wear complaints or in giving out post-warranty "goodwill."

Con: Owner-reported problems: Minor electrical glitches and excessive brake wear, noise, and pulsations. **Service bulletin problems:** Excessive steering wheel vibration and brake pedal pulsation; no-starts caused by ignition key not properly programmed for the immobilizer control unit; squeak and rattle troubleshooting guide; missing seatbelt latch plate stopper button; and jammed sunroof. **NHTSA safety complaints/safety:** Fire ignited in fuse box area; accelerator stuck three times; driver approached red light and vehicle suddenly accelerated with no brakes; exhaust fumes enter the interior; windshield cracked three times; the driver hit a telephone pole head-on and neither airbag deployed; design of door caused consumer to hit eye on sharp door edge; malfunctioning power door locks re-lock doors; rear seatbelts malfunction; front passenger shoulder/lapbelt won't pull out of seatbelt assembly; tiny horn buttons may be hard to locate in an emergency.

Road Performance

Pro: Acceleration/torque: Good acceleration (0–100 km/h: 8.9 sec.). **Emergency handling:** The SE's sporty handling is way overrated, but it does handle sudden corrections quite well. **Routine handling:** Good manoeuvrability around town, and highway cruising is quite comfortable. Suspension handles rough pavement without jostling passengers. **Braking:** Average.

Con: Engine a bit noisy. The 4-banger has insufficient top-end torque and gets buzzier the more it's pushed. This car cries out for a V6 like the one used in the Maxima. **Steering:** Responsive, but with insufficient road feedback. **Transmission:** The automatic transmission hesitates, and then shifts abruptly. The 5-speed manual transmission is sloppy.

Comfort/Convenience

Pro: Standard equipment: Fairly well appointed. Infiniti J30 styling. **Controls and displays:** Most controls are easy to understand and access, and instruments are easy to read and understand. **Climate control:** Good heating, defrosting, and ventilation. **Interior space/comfort F/R:** Up front, you'll find comfortable, supportive seats and good all-around head room and leg room. **Cargo space:** Acceptable. Trunk pass-through allows for storage of long items. **Trunk/liftover:** Good-sized trunk with a low sill to facilitate loading. **Quietness:** Very little engine, road, and tire noise gets into the passenger compartment

Con: Driving position: Rear roof pillars and high-tail styling obstruct rear/side visibility. Audio controls aren't easily reached. **Entry/exit:** Rear seat access is difficult to master due to the slanted roof pillars, inward-curving door frames, and narrow clearance. **Interior space/comfort F/R:** The small cabin seats only four comfortably, with limited rear leg room and a short uncomfortable rear seat. Trunk loading is made difficult by the wide bumper shelf; trunk lid hinges can damage cargo.

COST				
List Price (very negotiable)	**Residual Values (months)**			
	24	36	48	60
XE: $19,998 (15%)	$14,000	$11,000	$9,000	$7,500

TECHNICAL DATA	
Powertrain (front-drive)	Head room F/R: 39.4/37.7 in.
Engine: 2.4L 4-cyl. (155 hp)	Leg room F/R: 42/33.9 in.
Transmissions: 5-speed man.	Wheelbase: 103.1 in.
• 4-speed auto.	Turning circle: 41 ft.
Dimension/Capacity	Cargo volume: 14 cu. ft.
Passengers: 2/3	Tow limit: N/A
Height/length/width:	Fuel tank: 60L/reg.
55.9/183.5/69 in.	Weight: 3,050 lb.

SAFETY FEATURES/CRASHWORTHINESS		
	Std.	**Opt.**
Anti-lock brakes	❑	■
Seatbelt pretensioners	—	—
Side airbags	—	—
Traction control	—	—
Head restraints F/R	**	**
Visibility F/R	*****	**
Crash protection (front) D/P	****	*****
Crash protection (side) D/P	***	***
Crash protection (off-set)	**	

Maxima

Maxima

RATING: Recommended. A high-quality, reasonably priced luxury sedan that's hidden by all the Infiniti hype. Even though this is a redesign, Nissans don't have as many "teething" problems with newly launched models, as do other automakers. Nevertheless, check out the headlights at night to verify if illumination is adequate. **Strong points:** Impressive powertrain performance, comfortable ride, pleasant handling, and above average reliability. **Weak points:** Loose clutch and stiff shift with the manual transmission, some automatic transmission glitches, cramped rear seating, night visibility compromised by poor headlight design.

NEW FOR 2001: A 20th Anniversary edition includes the 227-horsepower version of the standard 3.0-litre V6, bronze-lensed headlight covers, and some features normally optional on the SE. GXE and SE can now be equipped with a Meridian package, which includes side-impact airbags, heated front seats, and side mirrors.

OVERVIEW: The front-wheel drive mid-sized Maxima soldiers on as Nissan's luxury flagship, one step removed from the briefly discontinued and recently resuscitated Infiniti G20. The 222-hp 24-valve DOHC V6 is a real dazzler and the Maxima comes with an impressive array of standard features like standard anti-lock brakes, a bit more interior space (mostly rear leg room) and trunk volume, and a standard engine immobilizer anti-theft system. The sportier SE offers a firmer suspension, an optional spoiler, 17-inch wheels, and traction control.

Cost analysis/best alternatives: Get a second-series, discounted 2000 model for the upgrades (check headlight illumination, though). Other cars worthy of consideration are the BMW 3-series, Ford Crown Victoria and Grand Marquis, Honda Accord, Lexus ES 300, Mazda Millenia, and Toyota Camry and Avalon. **Options:** Form-fitting SE seats. The optional sonar suspension found on the GXE is an unnecessary gadget; it will give the average mechanic nightmares. Be wary of the sunroof option (it eats up head room) and don't buy the optional instrument panel: it's distracting, confusing, and more suitable to a video arcade than a luxury automobile. **Rebates:** $2,500 to clear out the leftover 2000s. **Delivery/PDI:** $500. **Depreciation:** Average. **Insurance cost:** Higher than average. **Parts supply/cost:** Reasonably priced parts aren't hard to find from dealers or independent suppliers. **Annual maintenance cost:** Less than average. **Warranty:** Bumper-to-bumper 3 years/80,000 km; powertrain 5 years/100,000 km; rust perforation 5 years/unlimited km. **Supplementary warranty:** Not needed. **Highway/city fuel economy:** 7.7–11.4L/100 km with the 3.0L engine.

Quality/Reliability/Safety

Pro: Quality control: Better than average. **Reliability:** Maximas have always had an impressive reliability history. **Safety:** Integrated child safety seat anchors have been added to the rear parcel shelf. Except for headlight design, safety complaints don't fall into any pattern, nor are they disproportionate to the number of vehicles sold.

Con: Warranty performance: The company's claims handlers can be rather obtuse in interpreting Nissan's warranty obligations to Maxima owners. (I'm reminded of the ongoing battle that some customers are waging in order to get the company to pay for exhaust manifold components.) **Owner-reported problems:** Scattered reports of automatic transmission and electrical system malfunctions, as well as paint defects and assorted body clunks and rattles. **Service bulletin problems:** No Low or idle when shifting into Drive or Reverse, slow or delayed shifting from first to second gear, groaning brakes when applied, a light ticking or humming heard from the blower motor, sources for a variety of squeaks and rattles, a click or clunk noise heard from the right front strut, vehicle won't start due to miscalibrated ignition key, traction control light may come on for no reason, door cloth inserts may be rough or uneven. **NHTSA safety complaints:** While driving, the front wheels locked up, causing extensive undercarriage damage; unable to control engine speed with the accelerator pedal; vehicle stalls without warning in cold weather (suspect the computer module); airbags failed to deploy; fuel leaks from seal when over-filled; excessive front end vibrations; strong "bleach-type" odour permeates the interior; many complaints that the headlights are poorly designed, placing the high beams too high for adequate visibility; drivers complain they can't see between the high and low beams; trunk lid and latch are hazardous when raised.

Road Performance

Pro: Emergency handling: A bit slow, but well controlled. **Steering:** Accurate and predictable. **Acceleration/torque:** The powerful and smooth standard V6 engine provides substantial power without excessive noise (0–100 km/h: 8.7 sec.). This year's engine upgrade doesn't make the car accelerate faster from a stop, but it does get better mid-range passing ability. **Transmission:** The smooth-shifting automatic transmission has an Auto position that switches the transmission from normal to power mode when accelerating. It also has a switch to let you lock out fourth gear to assist in trailer towing and to prevent frequent gear changes over hilly terrain. **Routine handling:** Very good, with lots of control. The ride is fairly firm but comfortable, due to the refined suspension that handles rough roads well if the car is lightly loaded. The SE's sport suspension makes the handling a bit crisper. **Braking:** Good braking with or without ABS (optional on last year's models) thanks to rear disc brakes (100–0 km/h: 131 ft.).

Con: Manual transmission's clutch action is vague and the shifting is a bit stiff. Some torque steer (a steering wheel tug upon acceleration) is still present.

Comfort/Convenience

Pro: More rearward seat travel for tall drivers, power seat controls are more user friendly, and a lower windshield line adds to fore and aft visibility. Impressive theft deterrent system sounds an alarm, flashes the lights, and disables the car if the vehicle is disturbed. The system is automatically armed whenever the Maxima's doors are locked with a key. **Driving position:** Very good. Firm, supportive, and comfortable front seating, plenty of head and leg room, and good all-around visibility. **Controls and displays:** Although some controls are a bit fussy, the dashboard is designed well, with easily read analogue gauges that don't wash out in sunlight. **Climate control:** Efficient and quiet. **Entry/exit:** Easy front and rear access. **Interior space/comfort F/R:** Lots of front and rear head room and leg room. **Cargo space:** Lots of little storage bins for odds and ends. **Trunk/liftover:** Trunk has a low liftover to facilitate loading and is a bit larger this year. **Quietness:** Much improved this year, with little wind and road noise invading the passenger compartment.

Con: Rear visibility is blocked by rear side pillars. **Standard equipment:** Disappointing. High-tech luxury interior with emphasis on electronic gadgets. Head restraints in the rear are too low for average-sized adults. **Interior space/comfort F/R:** Only two adults will fit comfortably in the rear; three adults will adopt a knees-to-chin posture. Low, flat seats give inadequate thigh support, and obtrusive side wing bolsters push passengers into the middle. **Trunk/liftover:** The trunk isn't very deep.

COST				
List Price (negotiable)	**Residual Values (months)**			
	24	**36**	**48**	**60**
Maxima GXE: $29,000 (20%)	$23,000	$18,000	$15,000	$13,000

TECHNICAL DATA

Powertrain (rear-drive)
Engines: 3.0L V6 (222 hp)
• 3.0L V6 (227 hp)
Transmissions: 5-speed man.
• 4-speed auto.
Dimension/Capacity
Passengers: 2/3
Height/length/width:
55.7/187.7/69.7 in.

Head room F/R: 40.1/37.4 in.
Leg room F/R: 43.9/34.3 in.
Wheelbase: 106.3 in.
Turning circle: 39 ft.
Cargo volume: 15 cu. ft.
Tow limit: N/A
Fuel tank: 70L/prem.
Weight: 3,050 lb.

SAFETY FEATURES/CRASHWORTHINESS

	Std.	Opt.
Anti-lock brakes	■	❑
Seatbelt pretensioners	■	❑
Side airbags	❑	■
Traction control	■	■
Head restraints F/R	***	***
Visibility F/R	*****	*****
Crash protection (front) D/P	****	****
Crash protection (side) D/P	****	****
Crash protection (off-set)	***	

Quest

Quest

RATING: Above Average. Nissan reliability and Ford styling. **Strong points:** Plenty of passenger and cargo room, and a comfortable ride with lots of seating choices. **Weak points:** Adequate powertrain setup trails Windstar and Odyssey in acceleration and passing. Soggy base suspension, difficult rear seat access, and horrendous gas consumption.

NEW FOR 2001: Styling, never a strong point for this mini-minivan, has been revised in hopes of boosting sagging sales. Modifications to the suspension improve handling, and top-grade versions get more luxury features. A new entertainment system with overhead monitor is optional. The Quest will be discontinued in August of 2001.

OVERVIEW: Smaller and more car-like than most minivans, the Quest is built by Ford at its truck factory in Avon Lake, Ohio, and sized comfortably between the regular and extended Chrysler minivans. This front-drive, five- or seven-passenger minivan is the most economical to maintain and the most fun to whip around the city in. Its strongest assets are car-like handling, modular seating, and reliable mechanical components that have been tested for years on the Maxima.

The 170-hp 3.3L V6 engine gives this minivan car-like handling, ride, and cornering. Nissan borrowed the powertrain, suspension, and steering assembly from its Maxima, mixed in some creative sheet metal, and left the job of outfitting the sound system, climate control, dashboard, steering column, and wheels to Ford. This has resulted in an attractive and not overly aero-styled minivan.

Cost analysis/best alternatives: Get the 2001 model for the handling. Other minivans worth considering are the Honda Odyssey, or the Toyota Sienna. **Options:** The integrated child safety seat is a must-have and the seat height adjuster will benefit short drivers. A separate rear air conditioner/heater and power side windows are also worth considering. The optional performance handling equipment makes little improvement to the standard suspension. **Rebates:** $1,000 on the 2000s. **Delivery/PDI:** $900. **Depreciation:** Average. **Insurance cost:** Above average. **Parts supply/cost:** Good supply and reasonable costs. **Annual maintenance cost:** Average. **Warranty:** Bumper-to-bumper 3 years/80,000 km; powertrain 5 years/100,000 km; rust perforation 5 years/unlimited km. **Supplementary warranty:** An extended warranty isn't needed. **Highway/city fuel economy:** 8.9–13.8L/100 km.

Quality/Reliability/Safety

Pro: Quality control: Good quality control—Nissan designs and develops the minivans while Ford manufactures them. **Reliability:** The engine and drivetrain are borrowed from the Nissan Maxima, a very reliable vehicle. Excellent fit and finish. A large dealer network means that servicing and parts are readily available. Parts are less expensive than most other cars in this class. Plenty of glass provides excellent front and rear visibility.

Con: Warranty performance: Average. **Owner-reported problems:** Most owner-reported problems involve excessive brake noise and premature brake wear, door lock malfunctions, interior noise, and driveline vibrations. **Service bulletin problems:** Front brake groan; grinding noise when braking; rear suspension rattling; cycling, or self-activating front door locks; missing seatbelt latch plate stopper button. **NHTSA safety**

complaints/safety: ABS failures; brake and accelerator pedals are the same height, so driver's foot can easily slip and step on both at the same time; 22-month-old child was able to pull the clasp apart on integrated child safety seat; many complaints that the mid-row passenger bench seat vibrates uncomfortably; rear window on liftgate door shattered for unknown reason (dealer was aware of problem and replaced window under warranty); power steering fluid leakage due to O-ring at rack gear splitting; door hinge allows the door to damage the fender during average wind storms; windshield wipers are noisy when put in the "high" mode. Safety investigators are also looking into reports of electric door lock and power window failures that have trapped occupants in their vehicles.

Road Performance

Pro: Emergency handling: Impressive highway stability. **Steering:** Precise steering makes the Quest quite responsive at highway speeds and in emergency manoeuvres. **Acceleration/torque:** Upgraded V6 engine delivers plenty of power for city and highway driving needs (0–100 km/h: 11.5 seconds). **Transmission:** The 4-speed automatic transmission is much quieter and smoother this year—you can switch from Economy to Power shift mode by pressing a dashboard button. Fourth gear can be locked out to prevent constant gear hunting when going over hilly terrain. **Routine handling:** Handles and manoeuvres like a large station wagon. Agile (the short wheelbase and revised suspension help in this area) and easy to drive. The smooth, quiet ride on the highway isn't compromised by a full load. **Braking:** Braking performance is excellent, because four-wheel ABS improves directional control by eliminating wheel lockup (100–0 km/h: 138 ft.).

Con: Long-legged drivers may find the leg room a bit short. Not the minivan for high-speed cruising or carrying lots of cargo or passengers. Don't make too much of the Quest's car-like handling pretensions. Sure, it handles much better than truck-based minivans like the GM Astro and Ford Aerostar, but it isn't superior to other front-drive minivans. It requires a rather wide turning circle. Towing capacity of 3,500 lb. (1,590 kg) is possible only with an optional towing package.

Comfort/Convenience

Pro: Standard equipment: Comfortable and well-appointed interior. The standard radio gives great sound. The Quest offers a large array of standard safety features that include airbags, side-impact beams, reinforced centre pillars, front and rear impact absorbing zones, rear outboard three-point safety belts, ABS, and a childproof door lock in the sliding door. An integrated child seat is optional. **Driving position:** Car-like driving position and comfortable seats, which include a power lumbar support in the driver's seat. **Controls and displays:** Most controls and instruments are generally easy to use and read. **Climate control:** Efficient, powerful system; you can turn on the AC and control the air outlet location separately. All side windows can be opened for maximum ventilation. **Entry/exit:** Easy. Helpful assist grab handles over the front and sliding doors. The front captain's chairs are easily removed, and the modular interior allows 14 possible seating and cargo configurations, making for better seating for three adults in the rear than with most other small vans or wagons. An additional 4.8 inches in length gives second row passengers an extra inch of leg room and two more inches of cargo space. **Cargo space:** Expanded this year. Flexibility and the easy-to-use sliding rear seat make up for the Quest's modest cargo-carrying capacity. Middle seatback folds flat, and the rear seats have tracks that allow them to slide forward all the way to the front. **Trunk/liftover:** Low liftover height makes for convenient loading from the rear.

Con: Interior space/comfort F/R: Front seats could use more lateral support. **Quietness:** Some wind and road noise.

COST

List Price (negotiable)	Residual Values (months)			
	24	36	48	60
Quest: $30,498 (20%)	$21,000	$17,000	$15,000	$13,000

TECHNICAL DATA

Powertrain (front-drive)
Engine: 3.3L V6 (170 hp)
Transmission: 4-speed auto.
Dimension/Capacity
Passengers: 2/2/3
Height/length/width:
64.2/194.8/74.9 in.

Head room F: 39.7/R1: 39.9/R2: 37.6 in.
Leg room F: 39.9/R1: 36.4/R2: 36.3 in.
Wheelbase: 112.2 in.
Turning circle: 39.9 ft.
Cargo volume: 56.5 cu. ft.
GVWR: 5,445 lb.
Payload: 1,290 lb.
Tow limit: 2,000–3,500 lb.
Fuel tank: 75L/reg.
Weight: 3,850 lb.

SAFETY FEATURES/CRASHWORTHINESS

	Std.	Opt.
Anti-lock brakes (4W)	■	❑
Seatbelt pretensioners	—	—
Side airbags	—	—
Traction control	—	—
Head restraints F/R	**	*
Visibility F/R	*****	**
Crash protection (front) D/P	****	***
Crash protection (side) D/P	*****	****
Crash protection (off-set)	*	

SUBARU

In 1995, Subaru realized it was in a losing battle with Honda and Toyota for buyers of its front-drive compact cars and bet the farm on all-wheel drive, versatile Outback and Forester models, and "Crocodile Dundee," an Australian actor cum Subaru pitchman. Since then, sales have soared, with most cars selling close to MSRP.

Subaru's overall product lineup for the year 2001 reinforces the company's return to its four-wheel drive off-roading roots with a continued emphasis put on its 4X4 capabilities and Outback versatility. This year the 3.0 6-cylinder engine is added as an option on selected Outback models.

Are Subarus good buys? Yes, if you can get good servicing. If not, get something less complicated and more reliable, like an equivalent Honda or Toyota.

All Subarus provide reliable, reasonably priced 4X4 capability, but most owners could care less about their Outback's off-road prowess; only 5 percent will ever use their Subaru for that purpose. The other 95 percent just like knowing they have the option of going wherever they please, whenever they please. Even if they stay home.

Impreza

RATING: Above Average. If you don't need the AWD capability, you're wasting your money. **Strong points:** One of the most refined and reliable AWD drivetrains you'll find. Good acceleration with the 2.5 RS, excellent handling, lots of storage space with the wagons, and better than average quality control. **Weak points:** 2.2L engine has little reserve power for highway cruising, especially when hooked to an automatic transmission; both engines are rough-running and noisy; limited rear seat room; difficult entry/exit, and very dealer-dependent for parts and servicing.

NEW FOR 2001: Nothing significant until early 2001, when the 2002 model arrives on a shortened Legacy platform.

OVERVIEW: The full-time four-wheel drive Impreza is essentially a shorter Legacy with additional convenience features. It comes as a two-door coupe, a four-door sedan, a wagon that resembles the old American Motors Pacer, and an Outback Sport wagon also powered by the 2.2L engine and dressed more aggressively in GT cladding.

The base engine is a peppy (with a manual transmission) 2.2L 142-hp 4-cylinder, but the optional 2.5L powerplant provides an extra dose of power for highway passing and additional torque when traversing rough or hazardous terrain. Buyers may choose either a 5-speed manual or a 4-speed automatic transmission.

Cost analysis/best alternatives: Get a discounted 2000 model. If you really don't need a 4X4, here are some front-drives worth considering: Honda Civic, Mazda Protegé, and Toyota Corolla. **Options:** Anti-lock brakes. The RS version's safety and performance upgrades are well worth the extra cost. **Rebates:** $1,000 rebates to clear out last year's models. **Delivery/PDI:** $500. **Depreciation:** Slower than average. **Insurance cost:** Higher than average. **Parts supply/cost:** Parts aren't easy to find and can be costly. **Annual maintenance cost:** Higher than average. Mediocre, expensive servicing is hard to overcome because independent garages can't service key 4X4 powertrain components. Warranty: Bumper-to-bumper 3 years/60,000 km; powertrain 5 years/100,000 km; rust perforation 5 years/unlimited km. **Supplementary warranty:** A good idea. **Highway/city fuel economy:** 7.5–10.7L/100 km with the 2.2L engine and 7.7–10.5L/100 km with the 2.5L.

Quality/Reliability/Safety

Pro: Quality control: Better than average. Above average quality mechanical components. **Reliability:** Powertrain components should be durable, and there are few mechanical problems that take these Subarus out of service. **Warranty performance:** Base warranty is fairly applied, but servicing quality is spotty. **Safety:** Huge, fold-away side mirrors.

Con: Body panel and trim fit and finish is inconsistent. **Owner-reported problems:** Poor engine idling, frequent cold weather stalling, manual transmission malfunctions, premature exhaust system rust-out and brake wear, minor electrical short circuits, catalytic converter failures, and paint peeling. **Service bulletin problems:** Automatic transmission light comes on. **NHTSA safety complaints:** Driver burned from airbag deployment; clunking noise when brakes are applied; soft pedal and late brake engagement—pedal goes almost to the floor.

Road Performance

Pro: The 2.5L is the engine of choice. It's smooth and powerful with lots of low-end torque if you really need to go off-roading. The 2.2L engine is quite peppy with a manual gearbox when travelling over level terrain or darting in and out of city traffic. **Emergency handling:** Better than some sport-utilities. Tight cornering at highway speeds is done with minimal body lean and no loss of control. **Steering:** Precise and predictable. **Transmission:** The automatic transmission shifts smoothly. The all-wheel drive system is a boon for people who often need extra traction, and it works well with either a manual or an automatic transmission. The manual transmission's "hill holder" clutch prevents the car from rolling backwards when starting out. **Routine handling:** Smooth and nimble. Hurtles through corners effortlessly with a flat, solid stance and plenty of grip.

Con: Acceleration/torque: The 2.2L lacks sufficient mid-range torque to traverse hilly terrain without straining. When harnessed to an automatic transmission, it quickly loses steam. Uncomfortable ride with a full load. Larger tires would improve handling. Non-assisted steering requires maximum effort when parking. **Braking:** Average braking (100–0 km/h: 133 ft.). Barely adequate with the L models. Non-ABS braking may lead to loss of directional stability that causes the car to spin out of control.

Comfort/Convenience

Pro: Standard equipment: Well-appointed base models have a nice array of standard safety and convenience features. **Driving position:** Very good. Comfortable front seat and plenty of head and leg room. **Controls and displays:** Clear and simple dashboard and gauges. Very firm and supportive front seats. Versatile hatchback design. **Trunk/liftover:** Trunk has a low liftover.

Con: The coupe's narrow rear window and large rear pillars hinder rear visibility. Radio has awkward-to-access, poorly marked, tiny buttons. **Climate control:** The heater is insufficient and air distribution is inadequate. Tiny, confusing radio controls. **Entry/exit:** Small doors and entryways restrict rear access. **Interior space/comfort F/R:** Front shoulder belts are uncomfortable and rear seatbelts are hard to buckle up. Front and rear seat leg room may be insufficient for tall drivers. Rear seating is uncomfortable and limited to two small passengers. **Cargo space:** Not exceptional. Even though the wagon has extra storage capacity, overall capacity is a bit limited. **Trunk/liftover:** Small trunk. **Quietness:** This is not a quiet car. The clutch pedal and the dash click, the engine roars, and the fan whirs.

COST

List Price (negotiable)	Residual Values (months)			
	24	**36**	**48**	**60**
Base: $21,995 (18%)	$15,000	$12,000	$10,000	$8,000

TECHNICAL DATA

Powertrain (AWD)
Engines: 2.2L 4-cyl. (142 hp)
• 2.5L 4-cyl. (165 hp)
Transmissions: 5-speed man.
• 4-speed auto.
Dimension/Capacity
Passengers: 2/3
Height/length/width:
60/172.2/67.1 in.

Head room F/R: 39.2/37.4 in.
Leg room F/R: 43.1/32.4 in.
Wheelbase: 99.2 in.
Turning circle: 36 ft.
Cargo volume: 19.5 cu. ft.
Tow limit: 1,500 lb.
Fuel tank: 50L/reg.
Weight: 2,900 lb.

SAFETY FEATURES/CRASHWORTHINESS

	Std.	Opt.
Anti-lock brakes	❏	■
Seatbelt pretensioners	—	—
Side airbags	—	—
Traction control	—	—
Head restraints F/R	N/A	N/A
Visibility F/R (coupe)	*****	**
Crash protection (front) D/P	****	****
Crash protection (side) D/P	N/A	N/A
Crash protection (off-set)	N/A	

Legacy Outback, Forester

Legacy Outback

RATING: *Legacy Outback:* Average. *Forester:* Above Average. The AWD is what this car is all about. Without it, the Legacy is just a mediocre, middle-of-the-road sedan. **Strong points:** A refined and reliable AWD system, a powerful, optional 6-cylinder engine, a comfortable ride, and better-than-average crashworthiness ratings, as well as fewer-than-average accident injury claims. **Weak points:** The reworked 2.5L is only a so-so; problematic manual and automatic transmissions; mediocre handling; excessive engine and road noise; cramped back seat; seatbelts may be too short for large occupants; and very dealer-dependent for parts and servicing.

NEW FOR 2001: *Outback:* Two new models, the H6-3.0 L.L. Bean Edition and the H6-3.0 VDC, both featuring a more-powerful 3.0-litre engine. *Forester:* The 2001 Forester gets a slight restyling of the front and rear end and interior upgrades.

OVERVIEW: A competent, full-time 4X4 performer for drivers who want to move up in size, comfort, and features. Available as a four-door sedan or five-door wagon, the Legacy is cleanly and conventionally styled, with even a hint of the Acura Legend in the rear end.

Owners who prize Subaru's rugged reliability and distinctive styling may find the Legacy too "modern." Nowhere is there any sign of the excessive reliance on chrome moulding and oddball styling that has turned off buyers in the past. Another plus is that the Legacy's interior dimensions are similar to the Accord's—the benchmark for comfortable four-door sedans.

The Legacy Outback is a marketing coup that stretches the definition of sport-utility by simply customizing the AWD Legacy wagon to give it more of an outdoorsy flair. American Motors tried the same marketing approach with the Eagle several decades ago and failed miserably due to poor quality control, lousy marketing, and a passive public whose concept of off-road thrills was a night at the drive-in.

Another Subaru spinoff, the Forester, is a cross between a wagon and a sport-utility. Based on the shorter Impreza, the Forester uses the Legacy Outback's 2.5L 165-hp engine coupled to a 5-speed manual transmission, or an optional 4-speed automatic. Its road manners are more subdued and its engine provides more power and torque for off-roading.

Cost analysis/best alternatives: Get this year's model for the upgrades. Front-drives worth considering: Honda Accord, Toyota Camry, and VW Passat. Worthwhile 4X4s: the Honda CR-V, second-series Nissan Xterra, Suzuki Grand Vitara, and Toyota RAV4. **Options:** four-wheel disc brakes. **Rebates:** $1,000 rebates to clear out the 2000s. Matching dealer incentives are also applicable. **Delivery/PDI:** $500. **Depreciation:** Slower than average. **Insurance cost:** Higher than average. **Parts supply/cost:** Parts aren't easily found and can be costly. **Annual maintenance cost:** Average. **Warranty:** Bumper-to-bumper 3 years/60,000 km; powertrain 5 years/100,000 km; rust perforation 5 years/unlimited km. **Supplementary warranty:** A good idea. **Highway/city fuel economy:** 7.8–11L/100 km with the 2.5 L engine. No info on the 3.0L, yet.

Quality/Reliability/Safety

Pro: Quality control: Average, though powertrain defects have begun cropping up. Above average body assembly and finish.

Con: Reliability: Powertrain defects can sideline the car for days. Engine and transmission problems keep showing up. One owner of a '98 Legacy Outback has replaced his engine twice, at 800 km and 4,000 km. There are several reports of the transmission jumping out of first gear, or using first gear to slow down or to descend a steep grade. **Warranty performance:** Servicing quality is spotty. **Owner-reported problems:** The above-mentioned powertrain deficiencies and minor electrical, fuel system, and automatic transmission problems are common. Owners report that the front brakes require more attention than average. Premature surface rust and exhaust system rust-out are common. Servicing can be awkward because of the crowded engine compartment, particularly on turbocharged versions. Small horn buttons may be hard to find in an emergency. **Service bulletin problems:** Probable causes for the automatic transmission temperature light flashing. **NHTSA safety complaints/safety:** Igniter failure allowed unburned gasoline to flow into catalytic converter and resulted in chronic stalling; sudden acceleration when in Reverse; ABS brake failure; brakes feel spongy and take too much time to stop vehicle; braking pedal goes to the floor before braking effect, resulting in extended stopping distances; vehicle suddenly veers to the right when braking; cruise control failed to disengage when brake pedal was depressed; fuel sloshes in fuel tank due to the absence of baffles; during a collision, airbags deployed but failed to inflate; the suspension's design causes severe pulling to one side; excessive steering and vehicle vibration when passing over uneven pavement; steering lockup while driving; knocking and clunking noise heard when turning; vehicle's rear end bounces about when passing over bumps; engine failure due to a cracked #2 piston; frequent surging from a stop; hard to shift from Park to Reverse; cracked seatbelt buckle; seatbelts are too short for large occupants and Subaru won't supply an extension; rear centre seatbelt prevents the secure attachment of child safety seats; misadjusted door strikers make for hard closing/opening; snow storm ice builds up in the wheel well making turning difficult; sudden tire blowout.

Road Performance

Pro: Steering: Acceptable steering response and average handling at moderate speeds. **Acceleration/torque:** The 2.5L engine is a competent performer only with a manual gearbox (0–100 km/h: 9.7 seconds). **Transmission:** The electronically controlled automatic has a power mode and a manual button that holds the lower gears a bit longer to reduce irritating gear hunting. **Routine handling:** Fairly soft and comfortable ride on smooth pavement. The GT's firmer suspension exhibits above average handling. **Braking:** A bit better than average (100–0 km/h: 126 ft.).

Con: Base engine is noisy and rough-running. It's tuned more for low-end torque than speedy acceleration. The automatic transmission shifts into too high a gear to adequately exploit the engine's power and is reluctant to downshift into the proper gear. Manual transmission's shift linkage isn't suitable for rapid gear changes. **Emergency handling:** Vehicle bounces around on uneven pavement, rear end tends to swing out during high-speed cornering, and there's too much body lean in turns at lesser speeds.

Comfort/Convenience

Pro: Standard equipment: Well appointed. **Driving position:** Low but comfortable driving position, with plenty of head and leg room. Good fore and aft visibility. The left footrest prevents cramping. Adjustable driver's seat on the deluxe model. **Controls and displays:** Well designed, sweeping dashboard (similar to the Accord's) and control layout. Easy-to-read analogue gauges. **Climate control:** Excellent climate control system that's both efficient and quiet. **Entry/exit:** Tall doors make for easy front and rear access. **Interior space/comfort F/R:** Seating for four adults offers good front and rear head and leg room. Comfortable cloth-covered seats with plenty of side and shoulder support. **Cargo space:** Better-than-average cargo capacity. **Trunk/liftover:** The wagon's cavernous trunk is expandable with split rear seatbacks.

Con: It's a tight fit for the middle rear seat passenger. Power window and lock switches aren't easily accessible. Limited-service spare tire. Sedan has a small trunk, which is expandable only through a rear-seat pass through. **Quietness:** Excessive engine noise.

COST				
List Price (firm)	**Residual Values (months)**			
	24	**36**	**48**	**60**
Forester: $26,895 (20%)	$20,000	$17,000	$13,000	$11,000
Legacy Outback:				
$34,695 (20%)	$24,000	$21,000	$17,000	$15,000

TECHNICAL DATA	
Powertrain (AWD)	Head room F/R: 40.2/39.5 in.
Engines: 2.5L 4-cyl. (165 hp)	Leg room F/R: 43/33.4 in.
• 3.0L 6-cyl. (212 hp)	Wheelbase: 99.4 in.
Transmissions: 5-speed man.	Turning circle: 39 ft.
• 4-speed auto.	Cargo volume: 13 cu. ft.
Dimension/Capacity	Tow limit: 1,500 lb.
Passengers: 2/3	Fuel tank: 60L/reg.
Height/length/width:	Weight: 3,140 lb.
65/175/68 in.	

SAFETY FEATURES/CRASHWORTHINESS		
	Std.	**Opt.**
Anti-lock brakes (4W)	■	❑
Seatbelt pretensioners	■	❑
Side airbags	❑	■
Traction control	■	❑
Head restraints F/R	**	*
Visibility F/R	*****	*****
Crash protection (front) D/P	****	****
Crash protection (side) D/P	N/A	N/A
Crash protection (off-set)	*****	

SUZUKI

Thanks to its new Vitara and Grand Vitara sport-utilities launched last year, Suzuki's sales have been on the upswing over the past year. Actually, with the exception of its ill-fated X-90 sport-utility, Suzuki has been making very good entry-level small cars and sport-utility vehicles for over a decade. But most buyers aren't familiar with the company's products because they're mostly sold under GM's name. In fact, the company makes only three mainstream vehicles: the soon-to-be-discontinued Swift (GM's Metro twin), the Esteem, and the Vitara—a vehicle sold by General Motors of Canada as the Tracker. All of the above vehicles return this year relatively unchanged.

Early in 2001, Suzuki will bring out a new compact sport-utility based upon its XL6 concept vehicle first shown at the Detroit auto show last January. About the size of a Chevrolet Blazer, the new SUV will accommodate seven occupants with three rows of seats. Powertrain will consist of a 6-cylinder engine coupled to a part-time four-wheel-drive system.

Esteem, Swift

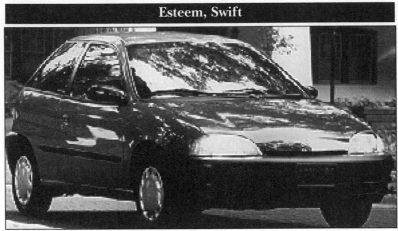

Swift

RATING: *Swift:* Average, for city use. *Esteem:* Above Average, for city and some highway use. Both the Swift and Esteem are best used as urban commuter cars. However, the Esteem, with its larger engine, upgraded brakes, and more comfortable interior, is the better choice. **Strong points:** Nimble handling around town, plenty of cargo room (wagon), good fuel economy, and better-than-average quality control. **Weak points:** Weak, noisy base engine; poor rear visibility; poor braking and ride; excessive engine, road and wind noise; rear seat room limited to two passengers in comfort; and insufficient crashworthiness and accident injury claim data.

NEW FOR 2001: Both vehicles return this year relatively unchanged. The Swift will be dropped at the end of the 2001 model year.

OVERVIEW: The Esteem is Suzuki's small four-door imported sedan; Swift is its Canadian-made two-door hatchback twin. Smaller than the Honda Civic and Dodge Neon, both cars have a fairly spacious interior, offering comparable or better rear accommodation for two full-sized adults than many cars in their class.

The base GA and upscale GL come loaded with standard features that cost extra on other models. The GL, for example, comes with power steering, rear-window defroster, remote trunk and fuel-filler door releases, tinted glass, and a fold-down rear seat (great for extra cargo space). Esteem GLX shoppers can look forward to standard ABS, power windows and door locks, and a host of other interior refinements.

Cost analysis/best alternatives: Try to get a discounted, fully loaded 2000 Esteem GLX Plus. Other cars worth considering are the GM Metro, Honda Civic, Hyundai Accent, and Nissan Sentra. **Options:** Think twice about adding an automatic transmission to the Swift; as with so many other small cars with small engines, it shifts harshly and cuts fuel economy. Also, ditch the 13-inch tires for ones that are larger. Rear-wheel lockup when braking is a certainty without ABS. **Rebates:** $500 on the 2000 models. **Delivery/PDI:** $450. **Depreciation:** Slower than average. **Insurance cost:** Average. **Parts supply/cost:** Suzuki parts are occasionally expensive, but not that hard to find. **Annual maintenance cost:** Average. Servicing can be done by any independent garage, and maintenance is made simple by an uncluttered under-hood layout. **Warranty:** Bumper-to-bumper 3 years/80,000 km; rust perforation 5 years/unlimited km. **Supplementary warranty:** A good idea if you plan to keep the car longer than three years. **Highway/city fuel economy:** 6.2–7.8L/100 km with the Swift; 6.3–9.0L/100 km with the 1.8L Esteem wagon.

Quality/Reliability/Safety

Pro: Quality control: Better than average. **Reliability:** Many of the mechanical components have been used on Suzuki's other models with few reliability problems reported. **Warranty performance:** Average.

Con: Body panels and trim are flimsy, and wind and water leaks may be a problem. **Owner-reported problems:** Problems include noisy front metallic brake pads, wind and water intrusion into the passenger compartment, and fragile body panels and trim items. **Service bulletin problems:** Dead batteries in remote keyless entry devices. **NHTSA safety complaints/safety:** Sudden acceleration from a stop; excessive steering wheel vibration.

Road Performance

Pro: Acceleration/torque: The ugraded engine delivers respectable acceleration. **Emergency handling:** Average. **Steering:** Predictable and precise. **Transmission:** The manual gearbox performs flawlessly. **Routine handling:** Better than average, thanks to the Esteem's 4-wheel independent suspension, which gives just the right balance between a comfortable ride and no-surprise handling.

Con: Small tires compromise handling. Power steering doesn't transmit much road feedback. The Esteem's automatic transmission shifts harshly and vibrates excessively between gear changes. **Braking:** mediocre braking for cars this light (100–0 km/h: 149 ft.).

Comfort/Convenience

Pro: Standard equipment: Many standard features that would cost extra on other small cars. **Driving position:** Very comfortable. Everything's within reach and there's plenty of head and leg room. **Controls and displays:** Nicely laid-out instruments and controls. **Climate control:** Efficient, quiet-running heater, defroster, and AC. **Interior space/comfort F/R:** Despite sitting on a small wheelbase, the interior space beats out most of the competition. Roomy cabin has lots of front and rear head room and leg room for four adults. **Cargo space:** Fairly good with the sedan; exceptional with the wagon's rear seats folded. **Trunk/liftover:** Average trunk space; a low sill makes for easier loading.

Con: Boring, bland styling. Vinyl upholstery. A narrow windshield and thick pillars hinder rear visibility. Thinly padded rear bench seat. **Entry/exit:** Narrow rear doors complicate rear seat access. **Trunk/liftover:** Sedan's trunk opening is a bit small. **Quietness:** Excessive wind, road, and engine noise.

COST

List Price (negotiable)	Residual Values (months)			
	24	**36**	**48**	**60**
Esteem GL: $15,495 (10%)	$11,000	$9,000	$7,000	$6,000
Swift DLX: $11,595 (9%)	$8,500	$7,000	$5,000	$4,000

TECHNICAL DATA

Powertrain (front-drive)
Engines: 1.0L 3-cyl. (55 hp)
• 1.3L 4-cyl. (70 hp)
• 1.8L 4-cyl. (122 hp)
Transmissions: 5-speed man.
• 4-speed auto.
Dimension/Capacity (Esteem)
Passengers: 2/3
Height/length/width:
53.9/165.2/66.5 in.

Head room F/R: 39.1/37.2 in.
Leg room F/R: 42.3/34.1 in.
Wheelbase: 97.6 in.
Turning circle: 35 ft.
Cargo volume: 12 cu. ft.
Tow limit: N/A
Fuel tank: 51L/reg.
Weight: 2,200 lb.

SAFETY FEATURES/CRASHWORTHINESS

	Std.	Opt.
Anti-lock brakes	❏	■
Seatbelt pretensioners	—	—
Side airbags	—	—
Traction control	—	—
Head restraints F/R	**	**
Visibility F/R	*****	**
Crash protection (front) D/P	N/A	N/A
Crash protection (side) D/P	N/A	N/A
Crash protection (off-set)	N/A	

Vitara, Grand Vitara/Tracker (GM)

Grand Vitara

RATING: *Vitara/Tracker:* Below Average. *Grand Vitara/V6-equipped Tracker:* Average. These truck-based sport-utilities' lack of refinement relegates them primarily to off-road use. A more comprehensive rating is given in *Lemon-Aid New 4X4s, Vans and Trucks 2001.*

NEW FOR 2001: *Vitara/Grand Vitara:* Nothing significant. *Tracker:* Finally, GM gets the Suzuki V6 it has been lusting for, since many buyers find the 4-banger way underpowered.

OVERVIEW: The Vitara/Tracker is longer, wider, taller, and handles much better (read: less tippy) than the Sidekick it replaced. Essentially an entry-level version of the Grand Vitara, the Vitara carries a smaller 2.0L 127-hp 4-cylinder engine, less standard equipment, and a smaller price tag. It's Canadian-built at Suzuki's CAMI factory in Ingersoll, Ontario, alongside its Tracker twin. It's slow, tippy, loud, and hard riding.

Suzuki's top-line entry, the Grand Vitara, is an import that arrives with a competent, though not very powerful, 24-valve, 2.5L 155-hp V6 powerplant, shared with GM's Tracker this year. Other standard features include a full-sized spare tire and four-wheel ABS on any "+" model.

Selling for $23,995, the Grand Vitara is a versatile truck-base, body-on-frame sport-utility that may not provide as much car-like handling as the Honda CR-V and Toyota RAV4, but its V6 power and shift-on-the-fly capability make it a worthy contender in the small sport-utility segment. Furthermore, its plastic lower body and wheel-well covers effectively ward off rust and parking lot dents. Inside, there's plenty of head room, arm room, and leg room, but like the RAV4, the interior is somewhat narrow—hips and thighs are pressed uncomfortably against the armrests. The rear seats and seatbacks fold flat, adding to cargo capacity, and there are plenty of small trays, bins, and compartments in which to store things.

Neither model has been crash-tested by NHTSA. However, the Vitara was given an "acceptable" rating by the IIHS for offset-impact collision protection. **Highway/city fuel economy:** 8.4–10.3L/100 km with the 2.0L engine; 10.2–12.6L/100 km with the V6.

COST				
List Price (negotiable)	**Residual Values (months)**			
	24	**36**	**48**	**60**
Tracker 4X4 convert.:				
$19,825 (15%)	$14,000	$12,000	$10,000	$8,000
Vitara 2.0L: $19,895 (13%)	$16,000	$14,000	$12,000	$10,000
Grand Vitara JLX:				
$26,995 (13%)	$20,000	$18,000	$16,000	$13,000

TECHNICAL DATA

Powertrain (rear-drive/p.t. 4X4)
Engines: 1.6L 4-cyl. (97 hp)
• 2.0L 4-cyl. (127 hp)
• 2.5L V6 (155 hp)
Transmissions: 5-speed man.
• 3-speed auto.
• 4-speed auto.
Dimension/Capacity (Vitara)
Passengers: 2/3
Height/length/width:
66.3/162.4/66.7 in.

Head room F/R: 39.9/39.6 in.
Leg room F/R: 41.4/35.9 in.
Wheelbase: 97.6 in.
Turning circle: 37 ft.
Cargo volume: 30 cu. ft.
GVWR: 3,373–3,593 lb.
Payload: N/A
Tow limit: 1,000 lb.
Fuel tank: 66L/reg.
Weight: 2,450 lb.

SAFETY FEATURES/CRASHWORTHINESS

	Std.	Opt.
Anti-lock brakes (4W)	❏	■
Safety belt pretensioners	—	—
Side airbags	—	—
Traction control	—	—
Head restraints F/R	***	***
Visibility F/R	*****	*
Crash protection (front) D/P	N/A	N/A
Crash protection (side) D/P	N/A	N/A
Crash protection (off-set)	***	

TOYOTA

Toyota's cars, trucks, sport-utilities, and minivans are the epitome of first-class quality and long-term durability. But this hasn't always been the case, as owners of the company's deservedly discontinued LE Van or readers of *Lemon-Aid Used Cars* will attest.

Nevertheless, most Toyotas do hold up very well over the years, are especially forgiving of owner neglect, and cost very little to service at independent garages. Also, warranty performance is outstanding; customers are treated generously even after the warranty has expired. But the kicker for most buyers is how little their vehicles depreciate; it's not unusual to see a 5-year-old sedan selling for almost half its original selling price—a value reached by most Big Three American vehicles between the second and third year of ownership.

On the downside, Toyotas have been plagued by engineering mistakes, much like Honda, that result in serious safety-related defects. A perusal of *Lemon-Aid* readers' letters, emails, and NHTSA reports confirms the problem. Consequently, I have lowered the ratings on some vehicles to reflect this deficiency and warn buyers of the potential for harm.

Additionally, there are some generic factory-related problems with Toyotas, but they're all mostly minor glitches affecting the front brakes, electrical system, AC, and accessories like the sound system and trim items.

Apart from launching the MR2 Spyder sports car, the Prius hybrid, and a convertible Solara, and slightly restyling the Corolla, Toyota's product lineup remains practically unchanged this year.

MR2 Spyder

MR2 Spyder

RATING: Not Recommended during its first year on the market. **Strong points:** Excellent acceleration; impressive steering, handling, and braking; user-friendly instruments and controls. **Weak points:** Entry/exit a bit difficult; top pillars obstruct rear visibility; limited shoulder room and cargo space; low seats and tall doors create a claustrophobic feeling; first year on the market with a limited production run of less than 7,000 units for all of North America. Prices weren't available at press time.

OVERVIEW: Toyota's mid-engine, rear-drive, 2-seat sports car is back, but only as a convertible. Its only powertrain configuration uses a 138-hp 1.8L 5-cylinder engine coupled to a 5-speed manual transmission. Fully loaded; there are no options available.

Extensive standard features include: 4-wheel disc ABS; AC; tilt steering with power assist; power windows, locks, and mirrors; a complete audio system; and 15-inch alloy wheels.

This first-year car is a sure winner despite its high price, which will likely be amortized by a similarly high resale value. Most of the MR2's mechanical and electronic components can be found in Toyota's generic parts bin, so servicing shouldn't be a problem.

Prius

RATING: Not Recommended. **Strong points:** Excellent fuel economy, five-passenger capacity, comprehensive powertrain warranty. **Weak points:** Way overpriced at $29,990; underpowered—Honda Insight is more fuel efficient; rear seating is not for three adults; sales and servicing may not be available outside of Montreal, Toronto, Ottawa, and Vancouver; and there's no long-term reliability data.

NEW FOR 2001: Nothing important.

OVERVIEW: Larger and more refined than the Honda Insight, the five-passenger, front-drive Prius is Toyota's year-old gas/electric hybrid that employs both a gasoline engine and an electric motor for maximum fuel economy and power. Two other major differences from the Insight: An electric motor, not the gasoline engine, is the Prius's main source of power; and, the Insight uses a 5-speed manual gearbox, while the Prius employs an innovative and more complex continuously-variable transmission.

The Prius uses its electric motor for acceleration, with the gasoline engine kicking in when needed. Once underway, the 1.4L 70-hp 4-cylinder gasoline engine (Insight's 3-cylinder engine produces 73 hp) takes over to provide power and recharge the battery pack. Braking automatically shuts off the engine, as the electric motor acts as a generator to replenish the nickel-metal-hydride battery pack.

Clearly, Toyota's hybrid is engineered to be as versatile and hassle-free as possible, based as it is on the Echo's dimensions and designed to never need recharging. Interestingly, due to its primary reliance upon electrical energy, fuel economy is higher in the city than on the highway—the opposite of what one finds with gasoline-powered vehicles.

Going hybrid doesn't mean that drivers have to forsake modern conveniences and safety features. Each Prius comes with standard ABS (Hydraulic Antilock Braking System with Generative Braking Assist), airbags, power windows, locks, and mirrors, and air conditioning. Only options are cruise control and front side airbags.

Cost analysis/best alternatives: Honda's Insight two-seater isn't much of an alternative. It's not as refined and doesn't provide much interior room. On the other hand, it does cost $4,000 less and uses less fuel (U.S. estimates are 88 mpg versus about 50 mpg for the Prius). Other small cars that represent good investments are the GM Metro, Honda Civic, Suzuki Swift, and Toyota Echo (see following report). **Options:** Nothing worth the extra money. **Rebates:** Expect considerable discounting as these cars fail to catch on. **Delivery/PDI:** $500. **Depreciation:** Too early to tell. **Insurance cost:** Average. **Parts supply/cost:** Parts will likely be hard to find and costly. **Annual maintenance cost:** Unknown. **Warranty:** Bumper-to-bumper 3 years/60,000 km; powertrain 5 years/100,000 km; hybrid-related components (HV battery, battery control module, inverter with converter) 8 years/160,000 km; major emission components 8 years/130,000 km; rust perforation 5 years/unlimited km. **Supplementary warranty:** Not needed. **Highway/city fuel economy:** 4.5–4.6L/100 km.

COST				
List Price (very negotiable)	**Residual Values (months)**			
	24	**36**	**48**	**60**
Prius: $29,990 (15%)	$21,000	$18,000	$14,000	$10,000

TECHNICAL DATA	
Powertrain (front-drive)	Head room F/R: 38.8/37.1 in.
Engine: 1.5L 4-cyl. (52 hp)	Leg room F/R: 41.1/35.4 in.
Transmission: CVT.	Wheelbase: 100.4 in.

Dimension/Capacity		Turning circle: N/A
Passengers: 2/3		Cargo volume: 11.8 cu. ft.
Height/length/width:		Tow limit: N/A
57.7/169.5/66.7 in.		Fuel tank: 45L/reg.
		Weight: 2,767 lb.

SAFETY FEATURES/CRASHWORTHINESS

	Std.	Opt.
Anti-lock brakes	■	❏
Seatbelt pretensioners	■	❏
Side airbags	■	❏
Traction control	—	—
Head restraints F/R	N/A	N/A
Visibility F/R	*****	*****
Crash protection (front) D/P	N/A	N/A
Crash protection (side) D/P	N/A	N/A
Crash protection (off-set)	N/A	

Echo

Echo

RATING: Recommended. An incredibly practical small car, if you can get by the tall, function-over-form styling. **Strong points:** More usable power than the Tercel, excellent fuel economy, and lots of interior space that provides for plenty of passenger room along with an incredible array of storage areas, including a huge trunk and standard 60/40 split-folding rear seats. Reasonably well equipped with good quality materials, well-designed instrument and controls, comfortable seating, easy rear access, excellent visibility fore and aft, quite nimble when cornering, and very stable on the highway. Surprisingly quiet for an economy car. **Weak points:** Tall profile and light weight makes the Echo vulnerable to side wind buffeting, base tires provide poor wet traction, excessive torque steer (sudden pulling to one side when accelerating), narrow body width limits the rear bench seat to two adult passengers, unorthodox styling "cute" to some but ugly to others.

NEW FOR 2001: Nothing significant.

OVERVIEW: Toyota scrapped its stripped-down Tercel in favour of the $13,835 Echo, a new entry-level five-passenger model that uses some of the same engine technology as the Lexus to give great fuel economy without sacrificing performance.

Both two- and four-door models are available, and the car costs substantially less than the Corolla. Echo offers about the same amount of passenger space as the Corolla, thanks to a high roof and low floor height.

Cockpit controls and instrumentation are particularly user-friendly—located high on the dash and more toward the centre of the vehicle, rather than directly in front of the driver, where many gauges and controls are hidden by the steering column. Toyota says the repositioning of the instrument cluster farther away from the driver requires less refocusing of the eyes from far to near. This produces less driving fatigue and eye strain.

Echo is powered by an all-new, 108-hp 1.5L DOHC 4-cylinder engine featuring Variable Valve Timing cylinder head technology. It's the same design used in Lexus to combine power and fuel economy in a low-emissions vehicle. Normally, an engine this small would provide wimpy acceleration for most cars, but, thanks to the Echo's light weight, acceleration is more than adequate with a manual gearbox, and acceptable with the automatic.

Standard safety features: five three-point seatbelts (front seatbelts have pretensioners and force limiters), two front airbags (side airbags are not available), four height-adjustable head restraints, rear child seat tether anchors, and rear child door locks.

Service bulletin problems: Probable causes for interior squeaks and rattles; wheel covers may click or squeak; excessive wind noise; fuel gauge and speedometer malfunctions. **NHTSA safety complaints/safety:** Vehicle drifted off the highway at 110 km/h.

For a better idea of what makes the Echo a winning choice, *Lemon-Aid* correspondent George Rutkay, from Brampton, Ontario, has these observations to offer:

> ...I bought the new Toyota Echo (it now has 15,000 km) and just wanted to give you information about how it's been so far.
>
> 1) Fuel economy: During first several thousand km, fuel economy runs about 30 MPG. You can expect about 650 km out of a tank of gas in city driving.
>   If you stay under 110 km/h, you can expect 900 km. If you boot it though, you can expect your economy to fall to

about 25–30 MPG. And this is one little engine that CAN! The faster you go, the more power you seem to find! Even at 150, there was no sign that the engine was straining.

2) Construction: It's a rattle-free, solid little car. No wind noise, though in high winds, being a very light car, you can feel the wind.

3) Repairs: I had to replace (under warranty) one of the hub-caps. Three plastic claws broke and when I hit a pothole, it would rattle. Around 7000 km the transmission seemed to make a bit of a clicking noise during parking attempts, only while shifting from Reverse to Drive, or from Drive to Reverse. It went away.

4) Beefs:

   a) Reposition the Overdrive switch. During long high-way drives, big passengers like me may relax their legs and the right thigh may bump against the Overdrive switch. At 100 km/h the engine jumps to higher rpm (though certainly well within it's operating limits) and causes a bit of a suprise.

   b) Winter: The Echo warms up rapidly. I live about 1 km from Hwy 410 in Brampton. If I enter the high-way and the blue light is still on, indicating the engine is still 'cold', the computer won't allow the transmission to shift higher than third gear. Kinda sucks to push the engine that hard during the cold weather, though Toyota told me that it's not a prob-lem, the engine can take it.

6) My opinion: The Echo is a GREAT car!

Roomy, very fuel efficient yet will pin you to the seat back when you give her the gas, handles great in the snow, great visi-bility, comfortable seats, great sound system. Solid car, built like a brick, fun to drive and a very consistent performer.

You know how it is: with an older North American car, how every time you start it, you notice it performs, sounds and feels just a little bit different from the day before, how it seems to loosen up and wear out in noticeable ways?

Well, my 2000 Saturn did that too but this little car hasn't!

Yeah, she looks like a hippo on roller-skates but from inside, it's a great view!

Note that not all Toyota dealers and their service depart-ments are equal. The dealership where I bought my Echo seems to have at least one ex-GM or ex-Chrysler fellow in the service department and it's his attitude towards customer service, which turned me off from going back there.

Mississauga Toyota, on the other hand, they're very cool about service and are extremely helpful. I should've bought my car from THEM!…

Cost analysis/best alternatives: If you can find a discounted 2000 left-over, go for it, but most are long gone. Other cars worth considering are the GM Metro, Honda Civic, Hyundai Accent, Mazda Protegé, Nissan Sentra, and Suzuki Swift. **Options:** Consider snow tires and better quality 14-inch tires for improved traction in inclement weather. Forget the silly-looking rear spoiler. Beware of option loading where you have to buy a host of overpriced non-essential, impractical features in order to get one or two amenities you require. For example, an automatic transmission is available for $1,000. Included in the Toyota Style Package, automatic transmission and air conditioning boosts an Echo sedan's price to $17,815. Air conditioning cuts horsepower; test-drive before you buy. **Rebates:** Not likely. **Delivery/PDI:** $500. **Depreciation:** Expected to be much slower than average. **Insurance cost:** Average. **Parts supply/cost:** Easily found and reasonably priced. **Annual maintenance cost:** Costs over the long term are predicted to be low. **Warranty:** Bumper-to-bumper 3 years/60,000 km; powertrain 5 years/100,000 km; rust perforation 5 years/unlimited km. **Supplementary warranty:** Not needed. **Highway/city fuel economy:** 5.5–7.0L/100 km with an automatic transmission.

COST

List Price (very negotiable)	Residual Values (months)			
	24	36	48	60
Echo: $13,835 (8%)	$12,000	$10,000	$8,500	$7,000

TECHNICAL DATA

Powertrain (front-drive)	Head room F/R: 39.3/36.9 in.
Engine: 1.5L 4-cyl. (108 hp)	Leg room F/R: 42.5/33.2 in.
Transmissions: 5-speed man.	Wheelbase: 93.3 in.
• 4-speed auto.	Turning circle: N/A
Dimension/Capacity	Cargo volume: 14 cu. ft.
Passengers: 2/3	Tow limit: 1,000 lb.
Height/length/width:	Fuel tank: 50L/reg.
59.1/163.2/65.4 in.	Weight: 2,035 lb.

SAFETY FEATURES/CRASHWORTHINESS

	Std.	Opt.
Anti-lock brakes	❏	■
Seatbelt pretensioners	■	❏
Side airbags	❏	❏
Traction control	—	—
Head restraints F/R	N/A	N/A
Visibility F/R	*****	*****
Crash protection (front) D/P	N/A	N/A
Crash protection (side) D/P	N/A	N/A
Crash protection (off-set)	N/A	

Corolla

RATING: Above Average. **Strong points:** Effective powertrain setup, pleasant ride, good braking, better-than-average quality control and crashworthiness scores, and a high resale value. **Weak points:** Few standard features; rear seating is not for three adults; clumsy emergency handling; some reports of airbags deploying inadvertently or failing to deploy; and only hard-to-find stripped versions are reasonably priced.

NEW FOR 2001: A slight facelift and the addition of a new sport-oriented variant called the Corolla S. The VE has been dropped and the formerly mid-level CE is now the entry-level model. The CE's lower price means you get less standard features, like a tilt steering wheel, cassette player, rear defogger, and split-fold rear seat. LE drops to the CE's former level and is also "decontented," losing its standard AC and power windows, locks, and mirrors.

OVERVIEW: A step up from the Tercel/Echo, the Corolla has long been Toyota's standard-bearer in the compact sedan class. Over the years, however, the car has grown in size, price, and refinement to the point where it can now be considered a small family sedan. All Corollas ride on a front-wheel drive platform with independent suspension on all wheels.

Cost analysis/best alternatives: Because the 2001 models have fewer standard features, you would do well to look for a discounted 2000 model. Other small cars that represent good investments are the Honda Civic, and Mazda Protegé. **Options:** Be wary of the new S model. For your extra bucks you get fancy trim, fog lights, a sport steering wheel, and tachometer. The optional 4-speed automatic is worth consideration. Stay away from the 3-speed; it's mainly for rental agencies and driving schools. Also, consider the built-in rear child seat. Air conditioning saps horsepower considerably; test-drive an AC- and automatic transmission–equipped Corolla before making a final decision. For better steering response and additional high-speed stability, order the optional 185/65R14 tires that come with the LE. **Rebates:** Expect $1,000 rebates early in the new year. **Delivery/PDI:** $500. **Depreciation:** Much slower than average. **Insurance cost:** Higher than average. **Parts supply/cost:** Parts are easily found and reasonably priced. **Annual maintenance cost:** Lower than average. **Warranty:** Bumper-to-bumper 3 years/ 60,000 km; powertrain 5 years/100,000 km; rust perforation 5 years/ unlimited km. **Supplementary warranty:** Not needed. **Highway/city fuel economy:** 6.8–8.5L/100 km with the 1.8L and an automatic transmission.

Quality/Reliability/Safety

Pro: Quality control: Better-than-average component and assembly quality. **Reliability:** The Corolla is one of the most reliable cars sold. **Warranty performance:** Fair and generous in interpreting warranty obligations, even after the base warranty expires.

Con: The Corolla has fallen from its Recommended status, due mainly to the flurry of safety complaints reported to government safety officials. This may mean that Toyota has gone too far in "decontenting" its cars over the past several years. **Owner-reported problems:** Premature front brake wear and vibrations, suspension and steering malfunctions, airbag failures, and electrical glitches are the more common problems. **Service bulletin problems:** Front brake vibration (corrective kit available) and a malfunctioning speedometer and tachometer. **NHTSA safety complaints/safety:** When the vehicle was parked the parking brake was released and both airbags deployed; both airbags deployed right after driver turned on the ignition switch; airbags deployed after car passed over a bump in the road; in a rear-end collision, front airbag came out, but failed to deploy; side airbag failed to deploy in a side impact; faulty seatbelt wiring could cause a fire; floor mat catches accelerator pedal; brake failure when decelerating; when brakes are applied, pedal goes soft, resulting in extended stopping distances; when coming to a gradual stop, brakes locked up, causing extended stopping distance; rear welding broke away from the frame resulting in complete loss of control; sudden collapse of the rear axle; rear control arm broke while driving at 110 km/h; shifter refused to go into gear while driving; transmission sometimes goes from Drive to Neutral while driving; vehicle pulls to the left or right at moderate speeds; in windy conditions, vehicle becomes hard to steer, veering left or right; suspension bottoms out when passing over small bumps in the road; centre console has insufficient padding.

Road Performance

Pro: Acceleration/torque: Good, but not impressive, acceleration times. **Transmission:** Both manual and automatic transmissions shift smoothly. The automatic permits you to lock out fourth gear for towing or when climbing long grades. The manual transmission gives the Corolla extra pep and uses a light clutch for effortless shifting. **Routine handling:** Average handling under normal driving conditions; the ride is busy, but comfortable. This is characteristic of Toyota products, where handling takes second place to comfort. **Braking:** Better-than-average performance without ABS (100–0 km/h: 123 ft.).

Con: AC and an automatic transmission can seriously reduce engine horsepower. **Emergency handling:** A bit clumsy, with some body roll, and sometimes the car plows straight ahead in hard cornering. Ride quality deteriorates as the load increases. **Steering:** Not much road feel. The sedan's ABS braking isn't impressive—too much weaving and veering to one side.

Comfort/Convenience

Pro: Controls and displays: The instrument panel and control layout are exceptionally user friendly. **Climate control:** First-class heating, defrosting, and ventilation system. **Entry/exit:** Wide rear doors facilitate access to the rear. **Interior space/comfort F/R:** Comfortable front seating; the wagon's rear seat will hold two comfortably. **Cargo space:** Spacious cargo area on the wagon. The rear seatback can be folded down. **Trunk/liftover:** Large trunk on the sedan has a low sill for easy loading. **Quietness:** Very little noise intrudes into the passenger compartment.

Con: Standard equipment: Disappointing. Many features that were standard last year are now optional. **Driving position:** Short drivers may have trouble seeing over the wagon's hood. Rear seating is compromised by insufficient toe and leg room. **Climate control:** Climate controls aren't user friendly and there's no automatic shutoff for the rear defroster. **Interior space/comfort F/R:** Tight rear seating and limited rear foot room. Trunk lid hinges can damage luggage. Base models don't have the handy split folding seatbacks that increase storage space.

COST				
List Price (very negotiable)	**Residual Values (months)**			
	24	**36**	**48**	**60**
Corolla: $15,625 (9%)	$12,000	$10,000	$8,500	$7,000

TECHNICAL DATA	
Powertrain (front-drive)	Head room F/R: 39.3/36.9 in.
Engine: 1.8L 4-cyl. (125 hp)	Leg room F/R: 42.5/33.2 in.
Transmissions: 5-speed man.	Wheelbase: 97 in.
• 3-speed auto.	Turning circle: 34 ft.
• 4-speed auto.	Cargo volume: 12.1 cu. ft.
Dimension/Capacity	Tow limit: 1,000 lb.
Passengers: 2/3	Fuel tank: 50L/reg.

Height/length/width: 54.5/174/66.7 in.	Weight: 2,400 lb. (est.)	

SAFETY FEATURES/CRASHWORTHINESS

	Std.	Opt.
Anti-lock brakes	❏	■
Seatbelt pretensioners	■	❏
Side airbags	■	❏
Traction control	—	—
Head restraints F/R	***	***
Visibility F/R	*****	*****
Crash protection (front) D/P	****	****
Crash protection (side) D/P	***	***
Crash protection (off-set)	***	

Camry, Solara

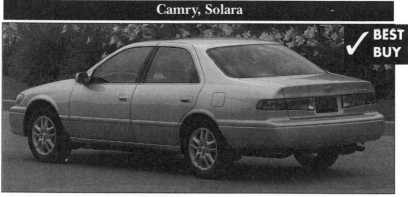

✓ **BEST BUY**

Camry

RATING: Recommended. **Strong points:** Excellent powertrain setup (V6), 4-cylinder is also a competent performer, pleasant ride, quiet interior, well-laid-out instrumentation and controls, legendary reliability, and a high resale value. *Solara:* More attractively styled than the sedan. **Weak points:** Suspension may be a bit too soft for some and noisy at times, limited over-the-shoulder visibility, little steering feedback, inadequate rear seating for three adults due to insufficient head and shoulder room, and annoying windshield reflections at night. Also, an unusually large number of safety-related complaints registered by government safety investigators may show that Toyota went too far in its cost-cutting, "decontenting" strategy adopted several years ago. *Solara:* Tricky entry/exit, and trunk has a small opening and high sill.

NEW FOR 2001: New headlights, a restyled front end, and an inside-trunk safety release. The LE and new sporty S model carry 4-speed automatics, while the entry-level CE will come with a 3-speed transaxle. The

16-valve, 1.8L, 125-hp dual overhead cam 4-cylinder engine is carried over from the 2000 model year. A convertible Solara arrived last spring.

OVERVIEW: The Camry is available only as a four-door sedan—gone is the station wagon variant, and the coupe and convertibles have been given the Solara moniker (see below). The Camry is powered by a peppy 2.2L 136-hp 16-valve 4-cylinder engine (taken from the Celica), and an optional 3.0L 24-valve V6 that unleashes 194 horses. Either engine can be coupled to a 5-speed manual or an electronically controlled 4-speed automatic. The suspension features MacPherson struts up front, dual-link mounted struts at the rear, gas-pressurized shocks for better damping, and stabilizer bars in the front and rear. Control is further maintained through speed-sensing variable power steering.

Camrys have fallen behind in the standard equipment offered in base models, obviously a result of Toyota's "decontenting" its products to keep prices down. For example, all 4-cylinder Camrys still use rear drum brakes while most of the competition use disc brakes; variable intermittent wipers are found only on top-of-the-line Camrys while the competition spread them throughout their lineup; the Camrys' MacPherson strut suspension is no match for the Accords' double-wishbone suspension at all four corners; and Camrys now have single-seal doors while Accords use double seals—and the Taurus uses triple.

But there is a nice array of safety features: ABS and traction control are standard on all V6-equipped models; rear seats have shoulder belts for the middle passenge; low beam lights are brighter; headlights switch on and off automatically as conditions change; and front side airbags are optional.

The Solara's small, but it's not cheap. Built in Cambridge, Ontario, a base model Solara costs $26,655, but put in the Sienna and Lexus ES 300's V6 powerplant and you can expect to pay thousands more.

Introduced in the summer of 1998, the Solara is essentially a longer, lower, bare-bones, two-door coupe or convertible Camry with a sportier powertrain and suspension and a more stylish exterior. But don't let this put you off. Most new Toyota model offerings, like the Sienna, Avalon, and RAV4s, are Camry derivatives.

You have a choice of either a 4- or 6-cylinder powerplant. Unfortunately, if you choose the V6, you also get a gimmicky rear spoiler and a head room-robbing moon roof. The stiff body structure and suspension, as well as tight steering, make for easy sports car-like handling, with lots of road feel and few surprises.

Cost analysis/best alternatives: A 2000 model Camry or Solara would be your best bet if discounted by about 10 percent. Prices are at their highest during the fall, and most of the initial supply will be snapped up by leasing agencies and rental car firms, creating delays of 90 days or more for everyday buyers (make sure you have a specific delivery date spelled out in the contract along with a protected price, in case there's a price increase while you're waiting for delivery). Other cars worth considering are the Honda Accord, Lexus ES 300, and Nissan Maxima. **Options:** The built-in child safety seat ($150). Stay away from the optional sunroof; it robs you of much-needed head room. Toyota's base radio and tape player have been failure prone in the past; buy a better sound system from an independent supplier. **Rebates:** Not likely. **Delivery/PDI:** $500. **Depreciation:** Slower than average. **Insurance cost:** Higher than average. **Parts supply/cost:** Parts are easily found and moderately priced. **Annual maintenance cost:** Less than average. **Warranty:** Bumper-to-bumper 3 years/60,000 km; powertrain 5 years/100,000 km; rust perforation 5 years/unlimited km. **Supplementary warranty:** Not needed. **Highway/city fuel economy:** 7.2–10.4L/100 km with the 2.2L and automatic transmission, and 7.8–11.9L/100 km with the 3.0L and an automatic transmission.

Quality/Reliability/Safety

Pro: Quality control: Better than average for most components. **Reliability:** One of the most reliable cars on the market. **Warranty performance:** Much better than average. Customers usually get a fair shake, even if the warranty has expired.

Con: Owner-reported problems: Chronic braking problems even though pads and calipers are replaced repeatedly, suspension failures, and body/accessories glitches. The unusually large number of safety-related complaints seen during the past two years raises concerns that Toyota's last Camry redesign has cheapened the product. **Service bulletin problems:** Front suspension support noise and malfunctioning speedometer and tachometer. *Solara:* Poor durability of rear view mirrors. **NHTSA safety complaints/safety:** Under-hood fire (left side) while vehicle was parked overnight; fire ignited from underneath vehicle while driving; airbags failed to deploy; inadvertent airbag deployment; faulty cruise control caused vehicle to suddenly accelerate; sudden acceleration without braking effect; excessive grinding noise and long stopping distances associated with ABS braking; pedal went to floor but no braking effect; ABS brakes suddenly locked up when coming to a gradual stop; defective rear brake drum; vehicle tends to drift to the right at highway speeds; excessive steering wheel vibrations at speeds over 100 km/h; entire vehicle shakes excessively when cruising; vehicle's weight is poorly distributed, causing the front end to lift up when the vehicle speed exceeds 90 km/h; suspension bottoms out too easily, damaging the undercarriage; too-compliant shock absorbers make for a rough ride over uneven terrain; rear suspension noise at low speeds; automatic transmission slippage; engine was running with transmission in Park position and the car rolled down a hill—the two small girls inside of the car jumped out, but one was run over. Car rolled backwards after driver put it into Park and removed ignition key; vehicle parked overnight had its rear window suddenly blow out; windshield distortion is a strain on the eyes; floor-mounted gear shift indicator is hard to read; seatbelts are too tight on either side and tighten up uncomfortably with the slightest movement; shoulder belt twists and won't lie straight; leaking suspension struts and strut rod failure; trunk lid may suddenly collapse; faulty driver-window track; driver-side door latch sticks; sulfuric acid odour enters the interior; fuel tank makes a sloshing noise when three-quarters full; clunking noise heard from rear of vehicle when gas tank is half full; tire jack collapsed while changing tire.

Road Performance

Pro: Emergency handling: Very good. Minimal body roll and front-end plow. Responds well to sudden steering corrections. **Steering:** Quick to respond and predictable. **Acceleration/torque:** Better than average (0–100 km/h: 8.7 seconds with the V6), with sufficient reserve torque for passing. Both the 4- and 6-cylinder powerplants are more powerful and offer better fuel economy than do previous years' engines. The smooth and flexible 2.2L 4-cylinder engine is best mated to the 5-speed manual transmission and should be relegated to city commuting, although it's surprisingly peppy in the lower gear ranges. This car shines on long drives, and for that you must have the exceptionally quiet-running 3.0L V6. **Transmission:** Smooth-shifting automatic gearbox with a dual-mode feature that allows the driver to choose either a power or economy setting. **Routine handling:** Nimble and predictable handling. Supple but steady ride on all but the worst roads. **Braking:** Better-than-average braking with the optional anti-lock brakes (100–0 km/h: 128 ft.).

Con: Neither the 4-banger nor the V6 are high-performance engines, but the Camry doesn't pretend to be a high-performance car. The torque converter disengages noisily when traversing hilly terrain. Overly compliant suspension makes for a busy ride when passing over bumps, even for the more tightly sprung coupes. Little road feel with power steering.

Comfort/Convenience

Pro: Standard equipment: Fully equipped. **Controls and displays:** Well-designed instrument layout is both practical and attractive. Heater and climate controls are well situated and easy to use, with large buttons and logical placement. **Climate control:** Efficient heating, defrosting, and ventilation. **Entry/exit:** Front and rear seats are easily accessible. **Interior space/comfort F/R:** Firm and supportive seats. Roomy interior includes comfortable front seats, and large rear seats will easily accommodate three adults, though rear head room is a bit tight for six-footers. **Cargo space:** Better than average. Huge glove box and lots of little storage bins and door map pockets. Huge but narrow cargo area on the wagon. **Trunk/liftover:** Reasonably sized trunk has a low liftover sill and carries a full-size spare tire. All models have split-folding rear seatbacks with in-trunk security locks.

Con: Standard equipment: Squarish, angular, and conservatively styled, the Camry lacks distinctintion. Rear taillights look to be the wrong size for the allocated space. Side-view mirrors don't spring back (if you clip your garage door, kiss your insurance deductible good-bye). You can get the manual transmission and V6, but only with the CE model. **Driving position:** The side-view mirrors can't be adjusted from inside unless you go for the power option. Front seat centre console armrest is set too far back to be comfortable. Limited over-the-shoulder visibility, worse with the Solara. **Entry/exit:** Difficult with the Solara's narrow rear passageway and the lack of a driver's seat slide-forward mechanism. **Cargo space:** Tall rear suspension towers cut into luggage space. Trunk hinges can damage cargo. Solara's trunk isn't user-friendly with its small opening and high sill. **Quietness:** Noisy suspension transmits lots of shock absorber clunk and tire rumble into the passenger cabin.

COST

List Price (negotiable)	Residual Values (months)			
	24	36	48	60
Camry CE: $23,310 (12%)	$19,000	$17,000	$14,000	$12,000
Solara: $26,655 (12%)	$20,000	$18,000	$15,000	$13,000

TECHNICAL DATA

Powertrain (front-drive)
Engines: 2.2L 4-cyl. (136 hp)
• 2.2L 4-cyl. (138 hp)
• 3.0L V6 (194 hp)
• 3.0L V6 (200 hp)
Transmissions: 5-speed man.
• 4-speed auto.
Dimension/Capacity (Camry)
Passengers: 2/3
Height/length/width:
55.4/188.5/70.1 in.

Head room F/R: 38.7/37.6 in.
Leg room F/R: 43.5/35.6 in.
Wheelbase: 105.2 in.
Turning circle: 40 ft.
Cargo volume: 14.1 cu. ft.
Tow limit: 2,000 lb.
Fuel tank: 70L/reg.
Weight: 3,200 lb.

SAFETY FEATURES/CRASHWORTHINESS

	Std.	Opt.
Anti-lock brakes	■	■
Seatbelt pretensioners	■	❑
Side airbags	❑	■
Traction control	❑	■
Head restraints F/R	***	***
Visibility F/R	*****	*
Crash protection (front) D/P	****	*****
Crash protection (side) D/P		
Camry	***	***
Solara	***	*****
Crash protection (off-set)	*****	

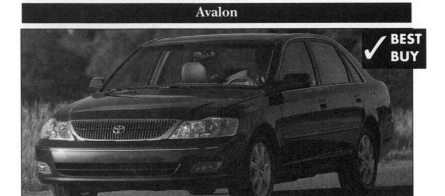

Avalon

RATING: Recommended. Essentially an all-dressed Camry or an entry-level Lexus. **Strong points:** Excellent powertrain performance, a roomy interior with plenty of storage space, and easy access to comfortable rear seats. Exceptional reliability, quiet interior, and a high resale value. Sportier handling than the Camry. **Weak points:** Rear corner blind spots, mushy brake pedal, and a bit fuel thirsty.

NEW FOR 2001: Carried over unchanged.

OVERVIEW: Toyota's largest model, this six-passenger near-luxury four-door offers more value and reliability than do other cars in its class that cost thousands of dollars more. A front-engine, front-drive, mid-sized sedan, based on a stretched Camry platform, the Avalon is similar in size to the Ford Taurus and bigger than the rear-drive Cressida it replaced.

The Avalon offers a 210-hp version of the Camry's 3.0L V6 power-plant coupled to a 4-speed electronically controlled automatic transaxle. Base models give a nice array of standard comfort and convenience features, including air conditioning, power windows, power door locks, cruise control, and an AM/FM cassette sound system. Safety features include standard ABS and a three-point shoulder belt for the rear centre seat passenger.

Cost analysis/best alternatives: Look for a discounted, second-series 2000 Avalon. If you want a more driver-involved experience in a Toyota/Lexus, consider a Lexus ES 300 or GS 300. Other cars you may wish to look at: the Ford Crown Victoria and Mercury Grand Marquis, Mazda Millenia, Nissan Maxima, and Toyota Camry V6. **Options:** The engine-immobilizing, anti-theft system. **Rebates:** $2,000 on the 2000s. **Delivery/PDI:** $500. **Depreciation:** Slower than average. **Insurance cost:**

Higher than average. **Parts supply/cost:** Parts are relatively inexpensive and easily found. **Annual maintenance cost:** Less than average. **Warranty:** Bumper-to-bumper 3 years/60,000 km; powertrain 5 years/100,000 km; rust perforation 5 years/unlimited km. **Supplementary warranty:** Not needed. **Highway/city fuel economy:** 7.4–11.2L/100 km.

Quality/Reliability/Safety

Pro: Quality control: Top-quality powertrain and body components. Much-improved brake durability. **Reliability:** The Avalon uses conventional mechanical components employed on Toyota's other models, which explains why there are no major reliability or durability problems. **Warranty performance:** Better than average. Warranty claims are handled in a fair and professional manner.

Con: Owner-reported problems: Owners report excessive wind noise intruding into the passenger compartment, and some fragile trim items. **Service bulletin problems:** Door rattling and malfunctioning speedometer and tachometer. **NHTSA safety complaints/safety:** Sudden acceleration with no brakes; airbag deployed for no reason; side airbags failed to deploy in a side impact; airbag warning light comes on constantly; transmission failure; transmission failed to hold vehicle on a hill while waiting for a red light; fuel dampener and fuel pump failure caused fuel leak and fumes to enter interior; Bridgestone tire failure; upper steering knuckle broke; steering wheel turned to the right, yet car fails to respond; dashboard lighting reflects into the windshield; inaccurate speedometer gives a 10 percent lower reading.

Road Performance

Pro: Emergency handling: Slow, but sure footed. **Acceleration/torque:** Brisk acceleration with the smooth, powerful, and quiet V6 engine; and there's plenty of torque for passing and traversing hilly terrain (0–100 km/h: 7.8 sec.). **Transmission:** The electronically controlled 4-speed automatic transmission is well matched to its power without sacrificing performance. In fact, the powertrain setup is one of the smoothest, best-integrated combinations available. **Routine handling:** Better-than-average handling, thanks to the stiffened suspension. Ride quality is flawless, providing living-room comfort on virtually any kind of road. **Braking:** Better than average (100–0 km/h: 130 ft.).

Con: Steering: Power steering is over-assisted at all speeds, and the car has a tendency to oversteer. Tends to plow ahead when cornering at high speed.

Comfort/Convenience

Pro: Standard equipment: Loaded with standard safety and convenience features. **Driving position:** Plenty of room and comfortable, supportive seating. **Controls and displays:** Well-designed instrument layout is both practical and attractive, with controls that are both easy to see and well within reach (instruments are similar to the Camry's, with controls placed in all the familiar places). **Climate control:** Powerful climate control system—efficient heating, defrosting, and ventilation. User-friendly controls. **Entry/exit:** Easy access to both the front and rear seating areas. **Interior space/comfort F/R:** Roomier than the Camry; front and rear seats are exceptionally comfortable, with plenty of thigh support and more room as a result of this year's lengthened wheelbase. Large rear seat will easily seat three people. **Trunk/liftover:** Enormous trunk has a low liftover sill. **Quietness:** Lots of sound insulation makes for an interior that's quieter, generally speaking, than the Camry's.

Con: Bland styling, with a hint of Lexus' GS 300. Limited rear corner visibility. **Controls and displays:** Radio controls are busy, with lots of identical buttons that are difficult to operate while driving. The cupholders are flimsy, and the fuzzy headliner has a cheap appearance. **Cargo space:** The Avalon doesn't have fold-down rear seats for trunk access and hauling long objects.

COST				
List Price (negotiable)	**Residual Values (months)**			
	24	**36**	**48**	**60**
Avalon XL: $37,000 (15%)	$28,000	$23,000	$19,000	$16,000

TECHNICAL DATA	
Powertrain (front-drive)	Head room F/R: 39.2/37.8 in.
Engine: 3.0L V6 (210 hp)	Leg room F/R: 44.2/38.3 in.
Transmission: 4-speed auto.	Wheelbase: 107.1 in.
Dimension/Capacity	Turning circle: 40 ft.
Passengers: 3/3	Cargo volume: 15 cu. ft.
Height/length/width:	Tow limit: 2,000 lb.
55.9/190.2/70.3 in.	Fuel tank: 70L/reg.
	Weight: 3,300 lb.

SAFETY FEATURES/CRASHWORTHINESS		
	Std.	**Opt.**
Anti-lock brakes	■	❑
Seatbelt pretensioners	■	❑
Side airbags	■	❑
Traction control	❑	■
Head restraints F/R	***	***
Visibility F/R	*****	**
Crash protection (front) D/P	****	*****
Crash protection (side) D/P	****	*****
Crash protection (off-set)	*****	

Celica

RATING: Recommended. Last year's redesign addressed almost all of the Celica's earlier shortcomings. **Strong points:** Exceptionally well-matched engine and transmission, great road holding and handling, comfortable front seating, impressive reliability, reasonably priced GT, and a high resale value. **Weak points:** Automatic transmission compromises GT engine performance, difficult rear seat access, rear seating not for three adults, and rear bucket seats aren't suitable for long drives. Pricey GT-S, noisy 180-hp engine at high rpms, no crashworthiness data, and a higher than average rate of accident injury claims.

NEW FOR 2001: Nothing significant.

OVERVIEW: The front-wheel drive Celica is a four-passenger, two-door hatchback that offers benchmark reliability, good handling, and great fuel economy in an attractive sports car package that's almost $10,000 cheaper since its last redesign. The GT and GT-S have a firm suspension, well-equipped interior, ABS brakes, and a more sporting feel than do other versions. All handle competently and provide the kind of sporting performance expected from a car of this class. The extra performance in the higher-line versions does come at a price, but this isn't a problem given the high resale value and excellent reliability for which Celicas are known. Overall, it's one of the best choices in the sporty car field.

Cost analysis/best alternatives: Buy a second-series year 2000 model for the engine and body upgrades. For a base price of $23,980, the GT is your best value. There's a generous array of standard equipment, performance is excellent, and it looks much like the more expensive GT-S. If you miss the GT version, try the Acura Intregra SE, Ford Mustang, GM

Camaro and Firebird, Honda Prelude, Mazda Miata, and Subaru Impreza RS Coupe. GT-S rivals include the Acura Integra GS-R, and BMW 323Ci. **Options:** Not much worth buying. The Celica comes fairly well equipped. GT models have standard front disc/rear drum brakes, which offer excellent braking performance; anti-lock brakes are not available on the GT, and judging by their high failure rate on other cars, this doesn't seem to be much of a loss. **Rebates:** Not likely. **Delivery/PDI:** $500. **Depreciation:** Slower than average. **Insurance cost:** Higher than average. **Parts supply/cost:** Parts are relatively inexpensive and easily found. **Annual maintenance cost:** Less than average. **Warranty:** Bumper-to-bumper 3 years/60,000 km; powertrain 5 years/100,000 km; rust perforation 5 years/unlimited km. **Supplementary warranty:** Not necessary. **Highway/city fuel economy:** 7.3–10.2L/100 km with an automatic transmission.

Quality/Reliability/Safety

Pro: Quality Control: The best among automakers, but has declined of late. **Reliability:** The Celica uses the same mechanical components that are employed on Toyota's other models, and this explains why there are few reliability or durability problems. **Warranty performance:** Warranty claims are dealt with in an efficient, professional, and fair manner. Safety features include dual front airbags, height-adjustable front head restraints, impact absorbing materials on the roof and doors, three-point seatbelts with pretensioners and force limiters for front passengers, three point seatbelts for rear passengers, and rear child seat anchors. When the airbags are deployed, a sensor disconnects the fuel pump to minimize the risk of fire.

Con: Owner-reported problems: The front brakes are troublesome; some audio systems and trim items have also been failure prone. **Service bulletin problems:** Interior squeaks and rattles (troubleshooting tips), malfunctioning speedometer and tachometer, and wind noise at the left front mirror. **NHTSA safety complaints/safety:** Passenger wheel suddenly locked up, causing a collision; cruise control may suddenly disengage, causing vehicle to lose power; transmission is too easy to accidentally shift from fifth to second gear; automatic transmission won't shift into Overdrive; fuel leak from faulty hose; engine clicks and stalls.

Rear head restraints aren't available and the audible reverse alarm isn't Toyota's brightest idea. Audible only inside the vehicle, it adds a forklift cachet to your Celica. For info on disabling this feature, log onto *celica.net/home.html*, an excellent site for technical advice and owners' unbiased reviews.

Road Performance

Pro: Emergency handling: Better than average. **Steering:** Responsive, predictable power steering also transmits plenty of road feel.

Acceleration/torque: Both the 140- and 180-hp variants of the 1.8L provide plenty of high-performance thrills. GT engine has more torque at lower rpms than the GT-S, which only delivers sporty performance after hitting 6000 rpms. **Transmission:** Standard 5-speed manual transmission has easy throws and light clutch action. The GT-S' E-Shift automatic transmission is very user-friendly, and shifting times are reasonably quick. **Routine handling:** Nimble and predictable handling in all conditions. Sportier handling on GT and GT-S models makes for a firm but not uncomfortable ride. **Braking:** Excellent performance (100–0 km/h: 120 ft.).

Con: Automatic transmission saps GT's engine performance. Suspension may be too firm for some.

Comfort/Convenience

Pro: Standard equipment: Long on standard, innovative features. For example, the 10-speaker 200-watt "System 10" radio is one of the most advanced systems currently on the market. Restyled exterior resembles a Lexus coupe from the front and a Supra from the rear. **Driving position:** Very good. The driver's seat has a manual adjustment that's easy to use. **Controls and displays:** Complete and well-designed controls. **Climate control:** Works well and is easy to calibrate while driving. **Interior space/comfort F/R:** Basically a two-seater; front seats are particularly comfortable, especially on the GT and GT-S. Long objects can be accommodated by folding down the 50/50 split rear seatbacks. **Quietness:** Fairly quiet, well-insulated interior.

Con: Tacky-looking plastic cover for the storage bin. **Entry/exit:** Very poor rear access forces you to practically crawl into the cramped back seat. **Interior space/comfort F/R:** Models equipped with the sunroof offer minimal head room for tall front-seat passengers. Limited outward vision. The high beltline and low seating position induce claustrophobia. **Cargo space:** Rather limited. **Trunk/liftover:** Small trunk has a high liftover. Some road noise and transmission whine may intrude into the interior.

COST				
List Price (firm)	**Residual Values (months)**			
	24	36	48	60
Celica GT: $23,980 (13%)	$18,000	$16,000	$14,000	$11,000
GT-S: $31,675 (15%)	$25,000	$22,000	$19,000	$15,000

TECHNICAL DATA	
Powertrain (front-drive)	Head room F/R: 38.4/35 in.
Engines: 1.8L 4-cyl. (140 hp)	Leg room F/R: 44/27 in.
• 1.8L 4-cyl. (180 hp)	Wheelbase: 102.3 in.

Transmissions: 5-speed man.
• 6-speed man. (4-speed automatic
  E-shift)
Dimension/Capacity
Passengers: 2/2
Height/length/width:
51.4/170.4/68.3 in.

Turning circle: 38 ft.
Cargo volume: 12.9 cu. ft.
Tow limit: N/A
Fuel tank: 60L/prem.
Weight: 2,500 lb.

SAFETY FEATURES/CRASHWORTHINESS

	Std.	Opt.
Anti-lock brakes	❑	■
Seatbelt pretensioners	■	❑
Side airbags	❑	■
Traction control	—	—
Head restraints F/R	***	**
Visibility F/R	*****	*****
Convertible	*****	**
Crash protection (front) D/P	N/A	N/A
Crash protection (side) D/P	N/A	N/A
Crash protection (off-set)	N/A	

Sienna

Sienna

RATING: Above Average, but still outclassed by the brawnier, more innovative Odyssey. **Strong points:** Incredibly smooth powertrain; a comfortable, stable ride; a fourth door; a good amount of passenger and cargo
room; and quiet interior. **Weak points:** V6 performance compromised by
AC and automatic transmission power drain; lacks the trailer-towing
brawn of rear-drive minivans; poor rear visibility; and an unusually large
number of body rattles and safety-related complaints, including power
sliding door dangers and automatic transmission defects.

NEW FOR 2001: A driver's side sliding door and standard rear defroster. Optional dual power sliding doors, side airbags, and stability control system. The JBL audio, heated front seats, and an electrochromic rearview mirror with integrated compass are optional on XLE models.

OVERVIEW: Toyota's Camry-based front-drive Sienna replaced the Previa three years ago. It's built in the same Kentucky assembly plant as the Camry and comes with lots of safety and convenience features that include side airbags, anti-lock brakes, and a low-tire-pressure warning system.

Sienna abandoned the Previa's futuristic look in favour of a more conservative Chevrolet Venture styling. It seats seven, and offers dual power sliding doors with optional remote controls and a V6 powerplant. As with most minivans and vans, you can save money by buying the Sienna's cargo version, but you won't get as many features.

Cost analysis/best alternatives: Get this year's model for the upgrades. Other minivans worth considering are the Honda Odyssey and Nissan Quest. **Options:** Power windows and door locks, rear heater, and AC unit. Be wary of the power sliding door. As with the Odyssey and GM minivans, these doors can injure children and pose unnecessary risks to other occupants. **Rebates:** Not likely. Toyota favours discounts instead. **Delivery/PDI:** $900 (est.). **Depreciation:** Much slower than average. **Insurance cost:** A bit higher than average. **Parts supply/cost:** Excellent supply of reasonably priced parts taken from the Camry parts bin. **Annual maintenance cost:** Like the Camry, much lower than average. **Warranty:** Bumper-to-bumper 3 years/60,000 km; powertrain 5 years/100,000 km; rust perforation 5 years/unlimited mileage. **Supplementary warranty:** An extended warranty isn't really necessary. **Highway/city fuel economy:** 8.8–12.9L/100 km.

Quality/Reliability/Safety

Pro: Reliability: Better than average, but on the decline. **Warranty performance:** Above average.

Con: Quality control: What is happening to Toyota quality control? Although mechanical and body components are generally reliable, there's been a disturbing increase in factory-related defects reported by owners during the past few years. **Owner-reported problems:** Premature brake wear, automatic transmission failures, distracting windshield reflections, power sliding door malfunctions, and interior squeaks and rattles. **Service bulletin problems:** Power sliding door malfunctions (troubleshooting tips); false activation of the security alarm; power windows rattling; and faulty speedometer and tachometer. **NHTSA safety complaints/safety:** Automatic transmission suddenly went into Neutral while on the highway; defective transmission torque converter causes the engine warning light to come on; sudden unintended acceleration; sudden stalling when the AC is turned on; vehicle rolled away, with shifter in Park on a hill, and ignition shut off; vehicle constantly pulls to the right, even after several alignments; power sliding door unlocks when vehicle is underway or door can close on children because it requires too much pressure to stop when closing. Next to the power sliding door there's a power door switch that continues to operate even if the child door lock is on—a child can easily activate the switch; rear brakes make a loud clunking noise when backing up or accelerating; reflection of the dashboard on the windshield impairs visibility; when turning the steering wheel to the left, the steering wheel doesn't return smoothly; rear seatbelts can't be adjusted; slope of the windshield makes it hard to gauge where the front end stops; excessive door rattling; rear window exploded as front door was closed.

Road Performance

Pro: Emergency handling: No problem. Sienna can change course abruptly without wallowing or losing directional stability. **Steering:** Excellent steering feel and quick response. **Acceleration/torque:** Toyota's V6 handles most driving chores effortlessly without noise or vibration (0–100 km/h: 10.2 sec.). **Transmission:** Quiet and smooth shifting. **Routine handling:** A pleasure. Handling is crisp and effortless. **Braking:** Excellent for a minivan (100–0 km/h: 139 ft.), with minimal brake fade after successive stops.

Con: Engine struggles a bit when carrying a full load uphill. **Braking:** Rear drum brakes cheapen the vehicle and will surely require early replacement—they should be discs.

Comfort/Convenience

Pro: Standard equipment: Very well appointed. **Driving position:** Comfortable seating with excellent forward visibility. **Controls and displays:** Easy-to-read displays and user friendly controls. **Climate control:** Easy to adjust and operates efficiently. **Entry/exit:** Easy entry/exit up front. **Interior space/comfort F/R:** First-class seating with plenty of head and leg room. **Cargo space:** Adequate. Seats can be removed for additional cargo room. **Trunk/liftover:** Easy to load or unload. **Quietness:** No engine or road noise.

Con: There's a confusing array of stalks sprouting out from the steering column. Rear visibility obstructed by middle roof pillars and rear head restraints. Radio speakers are set too low for acceptable acoustics. **Interior space/comfort F/R:** The wide centre pillars make for difficult access to the middle seats. Removing middle- and third-row seats is a two-person chore. **Cargo space:** Third-row seats lack a fore/aft adjustment to increase cargo space. **Trunk/liftover:** The rear hatch is inordinately heavy. **Quietness:** A proliferation of body rattles undermines Toyota quality claims.

COST				
List Price (negotiable)	**Residual Values (months)**			
	24	**36**	**48**	**60**
Sienna: $28,655 (15%)	$21,000	$18,000	$15,000	$13,000
Sienna LE: $31,590 (16%)	$23,000	$20,000	$17,000	$15,000

TECHNICAL DATA

Powertrain (front)
Engine: 3.0L V6 (194 hp)
Transmission: 4-speed auto.
Dimension/Capacity (LE)
Passengers: 2/2/3
Height/length/width:
67.3/193.5/73.4 in.

Head room F: 40.6/R1: 40.3/R2: 38.7 in.
Leg room F:42/R1: 36.4/R32: 8 in.
Wheelbase: 114.2 in.
Turning circle: 44 ft.
Cargo volume: 63.5 cu. ft.
GVWR: 5,247 lb.
Payload: N/A
Tow limit: 3,759 lb.
Fuel tank: 79L/prem.
Weight: 3,990 lb.

SAFETY FEATURES/CRASHWORTHINESS

	Std.	**Opt.**
Anti-lock brakes (4W)	■	❑
Seatbelt pretensioners	■	❑
Side airbags	❑	■
Traction control	—	—
Head restraints F/R	*	*
Visibility F/R	*****	**
Crash protection (front) D/P	*****	*****
Crash protection (side) D/P	****	*****
Crash protection (off-set)	*****	

European Vehicles

European hatchbacks, sedans, convertibles ("cabriolets"), and sport-utilities are hot in Canada. For the most part, they *are* more fun and comfortable to drive than most American vehicles, they're loaded with high-tech gadgets, most have a relatively slow rate of depreciation, and they're not much more expensive than the Japanese and American competition.

Volkswagen and Audi have managed to do relatively well as a result of their comprehensive warranties, improved quality control (don't mention the Rabbit or the Fox), price cuts, and the launching of less expensive entry-level models (for example, Audi's A4 1.8T, a spinoff of the A4 2.8).

Over the next five years we're likely to see more European makes and models imported into North America. First off the mark will be Alfa Romeo, Maserati, and the BMW Mini (a holdover from its Rover acquisition). BMW and Mercedes-Benz will develop a new line of smaller cars; Porsche, Volvo, and Volkswagen will launch new sport wagons; and VW will bring out the D1, a $70,000 (U.S.) luxury sedan, cobbled together from two VR6 engines set on a longer, wider Passat platform.

On the other hand, some European automakers have abandoned the U.S. and Canadian markets altogether, while others are barely hanging on. Fiat, Renault, and Peugeot were the first to turn tail, while Saab and Rover continue to struggle with losses that have drained GM's and BMW's cash reserves. Why? Because buyers are still wary of European automakers' reputation for poor quality, high parts and servicing costs, and weak dealer networks. As heretical as it sounds, some of the luxury makes have indeed proved to be surprisingly problematic. One MIT report, for example, concluded that European automakers fail to build quality into every step of the production process, as do Japanese manufacturers. Instead, they waste time and money correcting mistakes at the end of the assembly line rather than preventing them at the beginning. The Mercedes M-series sport-utilities are only the latest example of this European manufacturer malady.

Canadian drivers have their own examples of spotty European-built quality. *Lemon-Aid* readers who own pricey European imports invariably tell me of nightmarish electrical glitches that run the gamut from the annoying to the life-threatening. Other problems noted by owners include premature brake wear and excessive brake noise, AC malfunctions, faulty computer modules leading to erratic shifting, poor driveability, hard starts, and frequent stalling.

Although the servicing problem is usually more acute with vehicles that are new on the market, it has long been the Achilles heel of European importers. Owners give them low ratings for mishandling complaints, inadequately training service representatives, and hiring an insufficient number of service representatives—not to mention the abrasive, arrogant attitude typified by some automakers and dealers who bully customers because they have a virtual monopoly on servicing in their region. Look at their dealer networks and you'll see that most European automakers are crowded into Quebec and Ontario, leaving their Eastern and Western Canada customers to fend for themselves. This makes the chance of finding competent repairs somewhat akin to winning the lottery.

In light of all their shortcomings, why are European vehicles still so popular? Because they make driving so much fun and so comfortable that you quickly forget about Franz, Ingmar, and Luigi waiting for your return for servicing at Marquis de Sade Motors Inc.

The purchase of Jaguar and Saab by Ford and GM has gradually improved the quality and servicing of these European makes over the past five years. I would expect Volvo customers to also benefit. An improvement of Land Rover quality and servicing, on the other hand, leaves me skeptical.

AUDI

Sudden acceleration? That phrase is now only used to describe Audi sales over the past five years. Audi sales plummeted in the '80s amid controversy over the 5000's reputation for sudden, unintended acceleration, poor reliability, and sky-high maintenance costs. But Audi refused to follow Fiat and Peugeot back to Europe and has staged a spectacular comeback in North America with well-built, moderately priced front-drive and AWD Quattro sedans. Through a limited lineup of just three vehicles (the A4, A6, and A8), Audi has gained a reputation for making sure-footed, all-wheel drive luxury cars that are loaded with lots of high-tech bells and whistles. This reputation will no doubt be enhanced when the S4 Avant, a high performance wagon version of the A4, hits the streets along with an AWD Quattro TT Coupe, and a redesigned A4 sedan.

As with most European makes, Audis excel in comfort and performance. But servicing and warranty support remains problematic, especially now that VW/Audi has closed down its Canadian headquarters and runs its Canadian operations from the U.S. and Germany.

European Vehicles

TT Coupe

RATING: Recommended. This year's more powerful engine and upgraded rear brakes are important improvements. **Strong points:** Impressive acceleration with the optional 225-hp powerplant; first-class handling and road holding; very well-appointed and tastefully designed interior; comfortable, supportive seats; plenty of passenger and cargo space (especially with rear seatbacks folded); standard ABS; "smart" dual front airbags; and a predicted high resale value. **Weak points:** Poor rear and side visibility; ride may be too firm for some; limited rear seat room; difficult rear seat access; lots of engine and road noise; and limited availability.

NEW FOR 2001: An optional 225-hp engine, a 6-speed manual transmission, the Quattro AWD system, and ventilated rear brakes.

OVERVIEW: Costing an estimated $50,000, the TT Coupe debuted in the spring of 1999 as a sporty front-drive hatchback with 2+2 seating and set on the same platform used by the A4, Golf, Jetta, and New Beetle. A two-seat convertible version, the Roadster, was launched in the spring of 2000. The base 180-hp 1.8L engine (lifted from the A4) is coupled to a manual 5-speed, while the optional engine uses a 6-speed manual transaxle. Shorter and more firmly sprung than the A4, the TT's engines are turbocharged, though only the optional engine comes with standard AWD.

More beautifully styled and better handling than the Prowler, the TT comes with lots of high-tech standard features that include 4-wheel disc brakes, airbags everywhere, traction control (FWD models), a power top (Quattro), a heated-glass rear window, and a power-retractable glass windbreak between the roll bars (convertible). An alarm system employs a pulse radar system to catch prying hands invading the cockpit area.

In a safety recall following reports that the car is dangerous at high speeds, Audi announced in late 1999 that it would make key suspension modifications and add a rear spoiler.

Cost analysis/best alternatives: Choose the upgraded year 2001 model for the better-performing engine and upgraded rear brakes. Other vehicles worth taking a look at: the BMW Z3 Series, Honda S2000, and Mazda Miata. **Options:** All-wheel drive is recommended if it's essential for your driving needs.

A6

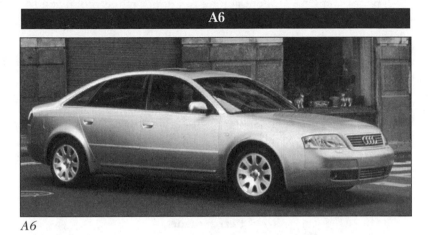

A6

RATING: Above Average. **Strong points:** Standard ABS "smart" dual front airbags, superb handling, comfortable seating, plenty of passenger and cargo room (beats out both BMW and Mercedes in this area), easy front and rear access, and very good build quality. The Avant wagon performs like a sporty sport-utility with side airbags and intense HID Xenon headlights. IIHS considers head restraint protection to be "acceptable," and accident injury claim rates are far lower than average. **Weak points:** Limited availability; firm suspension can make for a jittery ride; some tire thumping and engine growling; low-mounted climate controls aren't user friendly; outside mini-mirrors make side and rear vision a bit tricky; the wagon's two-place rear seat is rather small; door-mounted stowage compartments frequently open inadvertently; and servicing can be problematic.

NEW FOR 2001: The 2.7T and the 4.2 models get Audi's electronic stabilization program, which prevents fishtailing and enhances traction control. A new all-road version, featuring AWD, the 2.7L engine, and adjustable air suspension, will arrive in showrooms late this year.

OVERVIEW: The $49,835 A6 is essentially a larger, fully equipped A4. It's a comfortable, spacious, front-drive or all-wheel drive luxury sedan or wagon that comes with standard dual front side airbags and ABS. It can be ordered with a base 200-hp 2.8 V6, a biturbo, 250-hp 2.7L V6 or a 300-hp 4.2L V8. Its Tiptronic automatic transmission also has a manual gearshift capability.

Cost analysis/best alternatives: Choose the upgraded year 2001 model for the improved suspension and handling. Other vehicles worth taking a look at: the Acura TL, Infiniti I30, and Lexus ES 300. **Options:** All-wheel drive. Think twice about getting the power moon roof if you're a tall driver. **Rebates:** Look for $1,000 rebates by late spring, as Audi clears out dealer stocks in preparation for its new arrivals. **Delivery/PDI:** $650. **Depreciation:** Slower than average. Audi values no longer plummet when the base warranty expires, and high repair costs have been brought under control. **Insurance cost:** Higher than average. **Parts supply/cost:** Very dealer-dependent and expensive. Independent suppliers carry few Audi parts. **Annual maintenance cost:** Low during the warranty period, then it climbs steadily. **Warranty:** Bumper-to-bumper 3 years/80,000 km; powertrain 3 years/80,000 km; rust perforation 10 years/unlimited km. **Supplementary warranty:** A prerequisite to Audi ownership, and it guarantees a good resale price. **Highway/city fuel economy:** 7.8–13.5L/100 km and 8.4–13.9L/100 km for the Quattro version.

Road Performance

Pro: Acceleration/torque: So-so acceleration with the base engine and automatic transmission. Impressive performance is delivered by the 2.7T, however, with 0–100 km/h times under seven seconds. **Braking:** Better than average braking performance (100–0 km/h: 125 ft.).

Con: Service bulletin problems: Transmission slips into limp mode; won't change gears. **NHTSA safety complaints/safety:** Faulty gas tank sensors transmit wrong indication of remaining fuel. Also, one report of sudden tire failure. Average off-set crash protection and acceptable head restraint performance.

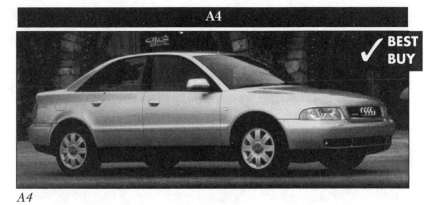

A4

RATING: Recommended. **Strong points:** "Smart" airbags, ABS, traction control (front-drive 2.8), optional AWD, powerful and smooth-running base engine, comfortable ride, exceptional handling, cargo room (wagon), front and rear seatbelt pretensioners, and impressive build quality. **Weak points:** Not as fast as its rivals; plain, functional interior; an obtrusive centre console limits leg movements; quite limited rear seat room; climate controls mounted too low; some tire drumming and engine noise; and servicing remains a problem. Limited availability (S4).

NEW FOR 2001: Base 1.8L engine gets 20 extra horses. An all-new 2001 S4 sedan and Avant, featuring a 250-hp 2.7L twin-turbocharged V6.

OVERVIEW: The A4 bills itself as Audi's family sport sedan and targets the BMW 3-series and Volvo S70 customer by featuring a roomy interior; standard multi-link suspension; an efficient automatic climate control; a light body; low-speed traction enhancement; an optional 5-speed automatic/manual transmission; and all-wheel drive—all for about an extra $2,000. Equipped with standard dual and side airbags, ABS, and a 170-hp 1.8L turbo or a 200-hp 2.8L V6 engine coupled to an electronic 5-speed Tiptronic automatic transmission, this entry-level four-door is reasonably powerful, easy to handle, and holds its value very well.

Cost analysis/best alternatives: Get the year 2000 A4 if the MSRP has been discounted by at least 10 percent. Other vehicles worth taking a look at: the BMW 3-Series, Infiniti I30, Lexus ES 300, Mazda Millenia, Mercedes C-series, Toyota Avalon, and Volvo C70 and S70. **Options:** An automatic transmission and all-wheel drive. Think twice about getting the power moon roof if you're a tall driver. **Rebates:** Not likely; instead, Audi gives out dealer incentives to encourage discounting. **Delivery/PDI:** $500. **Depreciation:** Very slow. Audi values no longer nosedive when the base warranty expires, and repair costs become the owner's responsibility. **Insurance cost:** Higher than average. **Parts supply/cost:** Often back-ordered and expensive. Forget about saving money by getting parts from an independent supplier; they carry few Audi parts. **Annual maintenance cost:** Higher than average, but not exorbitant. **Warranty:** Bumper-to-bumper 3 years/80,000 km; power-train 3 years/80,000 km; rust perforation 10 years/unlimited km. **Supplementary warranty:** Don't leave home without it. **Highway/city fuel economy:** 7.0–11.4L/100 km with the 1.8L, and 7.4–13.1L/100 km with the 2.8L. 2.7L twin turbo V6: N/A.

Quality/Reliability/Safety

Pro: Quality control: Better than average. Overall quality control has improved over the past several years, with fewer body, trim, accessory, brake, and electrical glitches than exhibited by previous models. **Reliability:** No major headaches. Electrical problems have taken these cars out of service for extended periods in the past. The jury is still out on the new 2.8L's long-term reliability. **Warranty performance:** Better than average over the past few years. **Service bulletin problems:** Nothing for this model year. Acceptable head restraint performance.

Con: Owner-reported problems: Long servicing delays and minor brake, electrical, and powertrain glitches. **Service bulletin problems:** N/A. **NHTSA safety complaints/safety:** Chronic complaints of delayed braking; no brakes in rainy weather; premature replacement of the front brake rotors.

Road Performance

Pro: Emergency handling: Better than average. **Steering:** Crisp and predictable, with lots of road feedback. **Acceleration/torque:** Surprisingly, the base 1.8L engine provides gobs of low-end torque and accelerates better with the automatic transmission than with the manual gearbox. The turbocharger works well with no turbo delay or torque steer. The 2.8L V6 engine needs full throttle for adequate performance. Nevertheless, it provides respectable acceleration times and plenty of torque for passing and traversing hilly terrain (0–100 km/h: 8.7 sec.). The S4's high-performance engine performs flawlessly with plenty of high- and low-end torque and impressive 0-100 km/h acceleration times (around six seconds). **Transmission:** Both the manual and Tiptronic automatic transmission perform flawlessly. AWD is extended to entry-level models at a time when most automakers are dropping the option on passenger cars. **Routine handling:** Handling is exceptional, with no passenger discomfort. **Braking:** Impressive braking performance (100–0 km/h: 118 ft.).

Con: The A4's rivals provide better acceleration. The ride is a bit firm (particularly the S4 versions and those models equipped with Sport packages), and the car still exhibits some body roll and brake dive under extreme conditions. Braking is a bit twitchy at times.

Comfort/Convenience

Pro: Standard equipment: A nice array of functional, though not lavish, features. **Driving position:** Acceptable. Comfortable, firm seating and a telescopic steering column help you easily find the right driving position. Excellent visibility fore and aft. **Controls and displays:** Most major controls can be easily reached and the instrument layout is both practical and complete. **Climate control:** Efficient climate control system, although some of the controls take getting used to. **Entry/exit:** Easy front and rear access. **Interior space/comfort F/R:** Plenty of head room and interior space for passengers up front. **Cargo space:** Average cargo space for a vehicle this size. **Trunk/liftover:** Large trunk is easy to load and unload. **Quietness:** Exceptionally quiet interior.

Con: Don't mistake Audi's automatic locking differential for traction control. It's not as effective. The wide centre console robs the driver of much-needed leg and knee room, and the optional, power moon roof cuts head room by almost two inches. Rear passenger room is very limited. **Controls and displays:** Radio and climate controls aren't intuitive; keep the owner's manual handy.

COST				
List Price (negotiable)	**Residual Values (months)**			
	24	**36**	**48**	**60**
A4 1.8: $35,050 (21%)	$24,000	$20,000	$16,000	$14,000

TECHNICAL DATA	
Powertrain (front/AWD)	Leg room F/R: 41.3/33.5 in.
Engines: 1.8L 4-cylinder (170 hp)	Head room F/R: 38.2/36.8 in.
• 2.8L V6 (200 hp)	Wheelbase: 103 in.
• 2.7L V6 (250 hp)	Turning circle: 36 ft.
Transmissions: 5-speed man.	Cargo volume: 14 cu. ft.
• 5-speed auto.	Tow limit: 2,000 lb.
Dimension/Capacity	Fuel tank: 62L/prem.
Passengers: 2/3	Weight: 3,000 lb.
Height/length/width:	
55.8/178/68.2 in.	

SAFETY FEATURES/CRASHWORTHINESS		
	Std.	**Opt.**
Anti-lock brakes	■	❑
Seatbelt pretensioners	■	❑
Side airbags	■	❑
Traction control	❑	■
Head restraints F/R	***	***
Visibility F/R	*****	*****
Crash protection (front) D/P	****	*****
Crash protection (side) D/P	N/A	N/A
Crash protection (off-set)	N/A	

BMW

BMW's 1994 purchase of the Rover Group was a major mistake. It drained the German automaker's cash reserves, delayed the upgrading of its models, and weakened management through dismissals and resignations, Now, BMW is counting upon its upgraded 3-series and the newly launched X5 sport-utility to buy it the time it needs to reorganize and upgrade its offerings.

While Audi improves its product mix, BMW continues to build well-appointed cars that excel at handling and driving comfort. Its vehicles have excellent road manners, depreciate slowly, and have an "I got mine!" cachet that buyers find hard to resist. Unfortunately, they also have limited interior room (except for the high-end models) and are difficult and expensive to service. But these drawbacks haven't discouraged BMW's loyal following of young professionals and people who want something prestigious, but not priced entirely beyond reach.

Tapping this growing popularity over the past several decades, BMW has brought out a larger and much more expensive line of sedans known as the 3.0, the Bavaria, and (since 1976) different combinations of the 5-series, 6-series, 7-series, and 8-series. Over the past few years, however, BMW has concentrated its efforts to trim its model lineup, introduce a sporty entry-level roadster, produce larger interiors, introduce wagon versions of its best-selling 3- and 5-series, and engineer handling improvements to give their vehicles better traction on slippery roads.

There are three good reasons for buying one of these German cars: high-performance road handling, prestige value, and a low rate of depreciation. Keep in mind, though, that there are plenty of other cars that cost less, offer more interior room (VW Passat and Audi come to mind), and are safer, more reliable, and better performing. So if you're buying a BMW, remember that the entry-level versions of these little status symbols are more show than go, and that just a few options can blow your budget. The larger, better-performing high-end models are more expensive and don't give you the same standard features as do many Japanese imports. Also, be prepared to endure long servicing waits, body and trim glitches, and brake, electrical, and accessory problems.

For the 2001 model year changes are modest: new additions to the 3-series line, the launch of a new Z8 rear-drive sports car priced at $128,000 (U.S.), with 400 allocated to the states and a few dozen earmarked for Canada, and a 5-series facelift.

BMW X5 sport-utility
Basically a tall wagon with all-wheel drive and extra ground clearance, the X5 runs circles around all the other luxury SUVs, particularly the Mercedes M-Class, which has gained the unenviable reputation for poor quality control. South Carolina production can't keep up with

demand. The plant is expected to produce 50,000 units annually for a world market only supplied by one factory in the U.S.

Z3

RATING: Recommended. **Strong points:** Attractively styled, standard traction control, impressive acceleration, excellent handling, exceptional braking, top quality fit and finish, and a "good" rating for head restraint protection by IIHS. **Weak points:** Some rear-end instability upon acceleration and when cornering; excessive engine, road, and wind noise filters through the soft top; difficult rear access; and limited rear leg room. Limited availability in Canada.

NEW FOR 2001: The addition of new 2.5L and 3.0L 6-cylinder engines.

OVERVIEW: BMW's Z3 3.0L is an attractive, rear-drive, $55,900 roadster made with parts cobbled together from the 318ti hatchback. Its modern interior, head-turning body, and affordable base price makes the Z3 a tough competitor in a market niche heretofore monopolized by the cheaper and less distinctive Mazda Miata. It comes with a 170-hp 2.5L inline six, borrowed from the 3-series, and an optional 193-hp 2.8 six, coupled to either a 5-speed manual or 4-speed automatic transmission. The M Roadster and Coupe come with a high-performance 3.2L 240-hp 6-cylinder powerplant.

On the plus side are the Z3's generally excellent handling and braking, a firm ride, and its uniquely German styling. Safety features include smart airbags and three-point seatbelts with pretensioners. Accident injury data shows far fewer claims than the average for this type of vehicle and for small vehicles overall.

The base 2.5L six is slower than the 2.8L inline six, but it's more fuel efficient. The new 2001 6-cylinders offer better acceleration times without sacrificing much fuel economy. Unlike some other convertibles, the

Z3 has few body rattles and groans; the climate system works well; and lowering the top, assisted by an electric motor, is a breeze. Resale value remains high, primarily because the Z3 is still relatively rare in Canada.

Some of the Z3's less impressive features: a handling problem all too familiar to Mustang owners—the rear end can slide out upon acceleration or during hard cornering; braking performance is about 20 feet longer than what the Miata can do; and the transmission is slow to upshift when cold.

The small interior also has its minuses. For example: six-footers will find the seats don't retract far enough and the low windshield blocks their view of overhead traffic lights; other drivers may have difficulty seeing over the non-adjustable steering wheel. Visibility is further hampered by side mirrors that are set too far back on the doors and by the plastic rear window, which is easily damaged and lacks a defroster. As with many convertibles, there's plenty of noise that intrudes into the interior at highway speeds, and storage capacity is limited to a small glove compartment and mini storage bins.

Service bulletins highlight the following two problems: Original equipment Michelin tires may be defective and headliner fastening clips may be faulty. **NHTSA safety complaints/safety:** Inaccurate speedometer and jammed passenger-side seatbelt shoulder retractor.

Other deficiencies mostly concern poor ergonomics, a surprising oversight for a German-engineered car. Examples are: inside door handles are located too far back on the doors; getting the spare tire from under the vehicle is a chore; and shoulder belts are uncomfortable.

Service bulletin problems: N/A. Best alternatives: Honda S2000, Mazda Miata, Mercedes-Benz SLK230, and Porsche Boxster.

328

RATING: Recommended. **Strong points:** Standard traction control, good acceleration (except for the 318ti), excellent handling, impressive braking, and top-notch quality control. **Weak points:** Limited rear seat room and cargo area; tricky entry/exit, even on sedans; and excessive tire noise.

NEW FOR 2001: The addition of a 325xi sedan, an AWD 330xi sedan, and a 325xi sport wagon. 2.8L 6-cylinder engines will be replaced by the X5 sport-utility's 3.0L six, while the 325xi sedan and wagon eventually will give up their 2.3L 6-cylinder engines for a new 2.5L inline six. A revamped M3 coupe housing a new 3.2L 330-hp 6-cylinder engine will appear at year's end.

The 323Ci convertible is longer, wider, and taller than last year's model. This gives it about 10 percent more interior room. It also wrings two more horses out of its 2.5L, 170-hp inline 6-cylinder engine. BMW's optional rollover-protection system, a $2,000 option last year, is a standard feature on the 2001 model. Other additional features on this year's convertible: a more rigid body structure to reduce shudder (a common fault with convertible flexing); upgraded front bucket seats with integrated seatbelts; the freeing up of more trunk space; and a glass rear window to replace the tacky-looking plastic window used in previous years.

The sport wagon is a couple of hundred pounds heavier and about a third of an inch longer than the four-door sedan. Through its versatile seat setup the wagon has over twice the cargo space as that of the 323i sedan. Plus, BMW has added a firmer suspension and larger brakes to handle the extra weight.

OVERVIEW: With BMW's recent mechanical upgrades, styling changes, and increased exterior and interior dimensions, the 3-series has come to resemble its more expensive big brothers with super-smooth powertrain performance and enhanced handling. The 323Ci and 328Ci coupes now come with 2.5L and 2.8L 6-cylinder engines used in BMW's entry-level sedans and standard Sport suspension. These new four-seaters are also lower, longer, and wider than their four-door equivalents, use different body panels, and present a more aero appearance. 323 convertible and wagon versions (launched last spring) have been made over in a similar fashion. The 2.8L 4-valves-per-cylinder 193-hp inline 6-cylinder engine is borrowed from the 525 and will be phased out shortly.

Recently upgraded cockpit amenities include a standard tilt/telescope steering wheel and optional power memory seats, power lumbar adjustments, an in-dash CD player, and steering wheel audio and cruise controls.

Cost analysis/best alternatives: Get the 2001 version for the upgrades; you're also unlikely to find any leftover year 2000 models. Other cars worth considering are the Audi A4, Lexus ES 300, and Mercedes-Benz C-Class and SLK. **Options:** If you buy a convertible, invest $1,500 in the rollover protection system that pops up from behind the rear seat. The optional Sport suspension does enhance handling and steering, but it also produces an overly harsh, jiggly ride on rough pavement. Plus, the wider tires compromise traction in snow. **Rebates:** Not likely. **Delivery/PDI:** $500. **Depreciation:** Slower than average. Insurance cost: Higher than average. **Parts supply/cost:** Parts are less expensive than for other cars in this class. Unfortunately they aren't easily found outside of the dealer network, where they're often back-ordered. **Annual maintenance cost:** Average, until the warranty runs out; then your mechanic starts sharing your pay cheque. **Warranty:** Bumper-to-bumper 4 years/80,000 km; powertrain 4 years/80,000 km; rust perforation 6 years/unlimited km. **Supplementary warranty:** A prerequisite to Bimmer ownership. **Highway/city fuel economy:** *Base 323:* 7.8–12.3L/100 km.

Quality/Reliability/Safety

Pro: Quality control: Better than average. Body assembly and workmanship is quite good. **Reliability:** No serious reliability problems have been reported. **Warranty performance:** Average. BMW usually resolves disputes through individual "goodwill" settlements. **Service bulletin problems:** Nothing reported on this year's models. **Safety:** All 3-series models are pre-wired for an alarm system and use a Coded Driveaway Protection system that won't allow the car to start unless the ignition key matches the ignition switch code, which changes each time the car is started.

Con: Parts are scarce outside major metropolitan areas, and independent mechanics are rare. **Owner-reported problems:** Brakes, electrical system, and some body trim and accessories are the most failure-prone components. **NHTSA safety complaints:** *323:* Premature failure of the magnesium-alloy control arms and steering damper; airbag light stays on for no reason; poor steering when braking at slow speeds; sudden acceleration while cruising; in rainy weather brakes stiffen as they are applied, leading to extended stopping distance; faulty sunroof. *328:* Premature tire failure (bubbles in the tread); sudden acceleration; when accelerating, engine cuts out, then surges forward (suspected failure of the throttle assembly); severe engine vibrations after a cold start as Check Engine light comes on; if driver wears a size 12 shoe or larger, when foot is flush against the accelerator pedal, the top of the shoes rubs up against the panel above the pedal, preventing full pedal access. Rear quarter blind spot with the convertibles.

Road Performance

Pro: Emergency handling: No-surprise suspension and steering makes for crisp high-speed and emergency handling. Much better rear-end stability. **Steering:** Exceptionally accurate and sensitive. Lots of road feedback. **Acceleration/torque:** The inline 6-cylinder engines and transmissions are the essence of harmonious cooperation, even when coupled to an automatic transmission; there's not actually that much difference between the two from a performance perspective. **Transmission:** Light and precise gear shifting with easy clutch and shift action. **Routine handling:** Competent and predictable handling on dry surfaces. **Braking:** Smooth, efficient braking produces short stopping distances with the 328i (100–0 km/h: 120 ft.).

Con: The ride is firm and occasionally uncomfortable on rough roads. Mediocre acceleration with the heavier 323Ci ragtop coupled to an automatic transmission. Some body flexing and shake when the convertible is run over rough pavement.

Comfort/Convenience

Pro: Driving position: Comfortable driving position enhanced by firm, supportive seats, a tilt/telescope steering wheel, nice ergonomics, plenty of front head and passenger leg room, and good all-around visibility. **Controls and displays:** Excellent control layout and design, though it could use additional gauges. Wiper action automatically drops from constant to intermittent when you slow down or stop. All power windows have an express down and up. **Climate control:** The 325i's additional room and separate driver and passenger climate controls make for a more hospitable interior. **Interior space/comfort F/R:** Plenty of space and comfort for four occupants—not five, as BMW would like you to believe. More toe, leg, and knee room for rear occupants this year. **Trunk/liftover:** Trunk has a low liftover for easy loading. **Quietness:** A rigid body design keeps rattles and clunks to a minimum.

Con: Standard equipment: Competitors offer more (can you believe the convertible's power soft top is a $2,000 option?). Bland styling and very austere, narrow interior. Interior plastics look tacky. **Controls and displays:** Confusing switches on the dual climate-control system. **Entry/exit:** Tight rear access with coupes, despite the front seats' automatic forward positioning feature. The four-door model offers marginally improved access to the rear seat. **Interior space/comfort F/R:** Seats are too firm for some. Limited head room when equipped with a sunroof. Centre console cuts into driver's leg and knee room. Not much knee or leg room for rear seat passengers with the front seats pushed rearward (particularly bad with the convertible) Rear seating is limited to two adults. **Cargo space:** At a premium. **Trunk/liftover:** Limited trunk space. **Quietness:** Noisy high-performance tires.

COST				
List Price (firm)	**Residual Values (months)**			
	24	**36**	**48**	**60**
323: $35,900 (18%)	$27,000	$23,000	$19,000	$16,000
330: $45,900 (20%)	$33,000	$29,000	$24,000	$20,000

TECHNICAL DATA

Powertrain (rear-drive)
Engines: 2.5L 6-cyl. (170–185 hp)
• 3.0L 6-cyl. (225 hp)
• 3.2L 6-cyl. (330 hp)
Transmissions: 5-speed man.
• 4-speed auto.
Dimension/Capacity (328i)
Passengers: 2/3
Height/length/width:
55.7/176/68.5 in.

Head room F/R: 37.2/36.7 in.
Leg room F/R: 41/34 in.
Wheelbase: 107.3 in.
Turning circle: 36 ft.
Cargo volume: 15 cu. ft.
Tow limit: 1,000 lb.
Fuel tank: 62L/prem.
Weight: 3,100 lb.

SAFETY FEATURES/CRASHWORTHINESS

	Std.	Opt.
Anti-lock brakes	■	❏
Seatbelt pretensioners	■	❏
Side airbags	■	❏
Traction control	■	❏
Head restraints F/R	***	***
Visibility F/R	*****	*****
Crash protection (front) D/P	N/A	N/A
Crash protection (side) D/P	N/A	N/A
Crash protection (off-set)	*****	

MERCEDES-BENZ

Mercedez-Benz has long made it a point to design and engineer cars at the forefront of technology and safety, and to clothe them in conservative, though attractive, garb. So what has it done for Chrysler since buying the company? Not much, except for sending hundreds of Detroit executives running for the doors and their pensions. I'm confident that Mercedes will eventually instill a quality control ethic into Chrysler's executive ranks, but I also realize it'll take many more years.

On the other hand, maybe Chrysler's daring designers (read Viper, Prowler, and PT Cruiser) will convince Mercedes to freshen its model lineup with vehicles that are both striking and conservative.

In an attempt to respond to critics' charges that its cars were priced out of most buyers' reach and that its styling was antiquated, Mercedes tried out its own new aero look in the beginning of this decade with the entry-level 190 ("baby Benz") series. It was a flop.

But the aero look was retained and refined, and is now what makes these luxury imports distinctive, along with a revamped model lineup full of high-tech safety and convenience features. This has worked well in attracting younger buyers, while keeping Mercedes's older, more conservative clientele.

C-Class, CLK, SLK

CLK320

RATING: Recommended. **Strong points:** Standard "smart" airbags, side airbags, traction control (optional on the C230), "brake assist," and ABS. Good powertrain match-up enhanced with a supercharger. Comfortable ride, easy handling, good braking, excellent quality control, innovative anti-theft system, and a high resale value. **Weak points:** Limited rear seat and cargo room; small, oddly shaped trunk; tight entry/exit; a choppy ride; some tire thumping, engine, and wind noise.

NEW FOR 2001: A redesigned C-Class, aimed right at the BMW 3-series, will debut by year's end with the introduction of the C240 and C320 sedans. The cars will be equipped with a 2.6L V6 and a 3.2L V6, respectively. Although the wheelbase is only about an inch longer, interior space has been increased almost everywhere (particularly in the back seat). A number of new features will be offered for the first time as standard features. These include side curtain airbags and video-screen controls. A hatchback and an AWD sedan and wagon will debut a year later as 2002 models.

The CLK returns relatively unchanged, while the SLK gets a facelift, an optional V6, and a six-speed manual transmission (first manual transmission in Mercedes's North American lineup since 1993).

OVERVIEW: The CLK320 coupe and convertible are styled a bit like the larger E-Class and use a 3.2L version of the C280 6-cylinder as the base engine. A 275-hp 4.3L V8 equips the CLK430, and the C230, redesignated as the C230 Kompressor, uses a 185-hp supercharged 4-banger, taken from the SLK roadster.

CLK

The $58,350 CLK320 is a stylish, four-passenger, roomy coupe that's both practical and well appointed, with technically advanced features that enhance high performance and comfort. Standard safety features include front and side airbags; a BabySmart sensor that disconnects the passenger airbag when a special child seat is in place; and a "smart" passenger airbag that won't deploy if no one is seated, cutting repair costs. An innovative brake assist feature is tied into the anti-lock brake system to provide an extra boost upon hard braking. Surprisingly, the CLK has been given a "marginal" rating for head restraint protection by IIHS.

In addition to a high degree of comfort and safety, the CLK's 215-hp V6 engine posts a 0–100 km/h time of less than seven seconds—with an automatic 5-speed transmission. The multi-link suspension and optional Electronic Stability Program (ESP) allow for high-speed, sure-footed cornering in quiet comfort.

Keep in mind that this is a heavy car that accelerates slowly and then rockets to an impressive 0–100 km/h finish in under seven seconds. The V8's performance tires still have trouble finding sufficient traction in snow, despite traction control. Some tire thump and rough-road rumble. Convertibles flex and shake a bit on uneven roads.

SLK230

Taking its cue from BMW's 318ti and Audi's 1.8t, the SLK230, Mercedes-Benz's entry-level model, returns this year with few changes. This rear-drive roadster isn't cheap ($54,350), but you can get one for almost half the cost of M-B's other roadsters. In addition to a great price, there are a number of amenities one would expect to find only with a far costlier SL, including a one-button full-power top, rollover protection, side airbags, ABS, and traction control. Add to this a 185-hp 2.3L supercharged inline four hooked to a 5-speed automatic transmission pulling only 3,000 pounds (1,360 kg), and you can expect swift performance and superb handling. Additionally, the SLK has earned from IIHS an "acceptable" rating for head restraint protection.

Cost analysis/best alternatives: Don't bother looking for a discounted 2000 model; most have been sold. Other cars worth considering are the Audi A4, BMW 3-series, and Volvo C70, S70, or V70. Rivals to the CLK and the SLK230 would be the BMW Z3, Chevrolet Corvette, Mazda Miata (OK, I am reaching a bit here), Porsche Boxster, and other models in the Mercedes-Benz SL-Class stable. **Options:** Generally, you'll get a better price and more standard features if you choose one of the 4-cylinder versions. Seriously consider the traction control option. **Rebates:** Not likely. **Delivery/PDI:** $600. **Depreciation:** Average. **Insurance cost:** Higher than average. **Parts supply/cost:** Limited availability, but parts aren't that expensive. **Annual maintenance cost:** Less than average. **Warranty:** Bumper-to-bumper 4 years/80,000 km; powertrain 4 years/80,000 km; rust perforation 5 years/unlimited km. **Supplementary warranty:** Not needed. **Highway/city fuel economy:** 7.6–11L/100 km with the 2.3L; 8–11.2L/100 km with the 2.8L V6; 9.6–13.1L/100 km with the 4.3L.

Quality/Reliability/Safety

Pro: Quality control: Above average. **Reliability:** Major components that would affect reliability are relatively trouble-free. **Safety:** Standard three-point seatbelts, side airbags, and high-tech, anti-theft alarm.

Con: Service bulletin problems: Hesitation following a cold start. **NHTSA safety complaints:** *C230:* Transmission slips in cold weather; speedometer calibration goes beyond what's legal in Canada, making for a smaller, hard-to-see readout; driver side seatbelt buckle attachment located between the seat and console is set too far down, making it impossible for driver to latch or release buckle.

Road Performance

Pro: Emergency handling: Excellent. Hard cornering produces very little body roll and sudden corrections don't compromise handling or comfort. **Steering:** Quick, precise, and predictable. **Acceleration/torque:** The supercharged 2.3L engine is a bit lethargic, and produces some throttle lag until the turbos kick in. But, the new 3.2L V6 powerplant is a real powerhouse in this small car. Its power is used most effectively when coupled to a manual transmission. **Transmission:** With its smooth and quiet shifting, the 6-speed manual outclasses the 5-speed it replaces. **Routine handling:** Exemplary. The C-Class combines superb handling with enhanced passenger comfort. **Braking:** First-class braking that produces incredibly short stopping distances (100–0 km/h: 106 ft.) for a car of this heft.

Con: The firm ride is a bit choppier than what you would find with the E-class.

Comfort/Convenience

Pro: Standard equipment: These cars are lavishly equipped with safety, convenience, and high-performance features. **Driving position:** Very good; everything is within easy reach. **Controls and displays:** Well laid-out displays and complete instrumentation. **Climate control:** Efficient, quiet, and innovative. Large buttons calibrate the system; a "rest" setting circulates warm air with the engine off. **Entry/exit:** Easy access to the front seats. **Interior space/comfort F/R:** Has as much room up front as the E-Class sedan. Comfortable, supportive front and rear seats. **Cargo space:** Average. **Trunk/liftover:** Average-sized trunk has a low liftover. **Quietness:** Better than most cars.

Con: CLK's wide rear roof pillars obstruct visibility. **Interior space/comfort F/R:** Rear seat is a squeeze for three adults and access is a bit tricky. The coupe's rear seat is configured for two adults only. Storage of the convertible top robs the trunk area of much needed space. **Quietness:** Some road noise intrudes into the passenger compartment.

COST

List Price (firm)	Residual Values (months)			
	24	**36**	**48**	**60**
C230: $38,450 (21%)	$27,000	$22,000	$18,000	$15,000

TECHNICAL DATA

Powertrain (rear-drive)
Engines: 2.6L 4-cyl. (168 hp)
• 2.3L 4-cyl. (185 hp)
• 3.2L V6 (215 hp)
• 4.3L V8 (275 hp)
Transmissions: 5-speed man.
• 4-speed auto.
• 5-speed auto.
Dimension/Capacity (C230)
Passengers: 2/3
Height/length/width:
56.1/177.4/67.7 in.

Head room F/R: 37.2/37 in.
Leg room F/R: 41.5/32.8 in.
Wheelbase: 105.9 in.
Turning circle: 35 ft.
Cargo volume: 13 cu. ft.
Tow limit: 2,000 lb.
Fuel tank: 62L/prem.
Weight: 3,200 lb.

SAFETY FEATURES/CRASHWORTHINESS

	Std.	**Opt.**
Anti-lock brakes	■	❑
Seatbelt pretensioners	■	❑
Side airbags	■	❑
Traction control	■	❑
Head restraints F/R	***	**
Visibility F/R	*****	**
Crash protection (front) D/P	****	****
Crash protection (side) D/P	***	****
Crash protection (off-set)	N/A	

E-Class

E-Class

RATING: Recommended. **Strong points:** Standard "smart" airbags, traction control, "brake assist," and ABS. Excellent engine and transmission combo, all-wheel drive available, easy handling, good braking, comfortable ride, roomy interior, cargo room (wagon), innovative anti-theft system, excellent quality control, a high trade-in value, and an "acceptable" rating by IIHS for off-set crashworthiness and head restraint protection. **Weak points:** Handling not quite as crisp as the BMW 5-series; really a four-seater, though touted to seat five; a surprisingly small trunk; and tall drivers may be bothered by the knee bolsters.

NEW FOR 2001: These cars return with upgraded option packages and other minor refinements. The 2002 models will get additional rear room and storage space, more high-performance features, a wagon, and an AWD sedan and wagon.

OVERVIEW: Mercedes's best-selling sedans offer inline 6-cylinder engines, but a V8 powerplant is offered on the E320 ($67,150; the wagon is only $800 more) with a 217-hp 3.2L and on the E430 ($74,750) with its 275-hp 4.3L V8.

Redesigned twice in the past eight years, the E-Class is considered to be state of the art in German auto technology. These cars do everything well, and manage to hold five people in relative comfort. They're first class in combining performance, road manners, and comfort. True, they're not the best riding, handling, or accelerating cars available, but they're able to perform each of these tasks almost as well as the best cars in each specific area, without sacrificing some other important element in the driving equation.

The E-Class continues to offer standard traction control that prevents wheelspin upon acceleration. Another interesting feature is the

remarkably smooth and quiet base 24-valve 217-hp high-performance
version of the inline 6-cylinder engine that powers the 300 series.

Mercedes E-Class models have front and side airbags for both driver
and right front passenger, plus dual-locking shoulder belts. The front
airbags are designed to deploy at higher crash speeds when occupants
are belted than when they're unbelted. Belts in the front seat have ten-
sioners that activate in a crash to reduce belt slack. Sensors in the seat
and belt deactivate the airbags and belt pretensioner on the passenger
side if no occupant is riding in this seat. The middle back seat has a
lap/shoulder belt. Energy-absorbing padding between the footwell and
floor carpet is designed to reduce the forces on drivers' legs in serious
frontal crashes. IIHS has given the E-Class an "acceptable" rating for
off-set crash protection.

Cost analysis/best alternatives: Get the 2000 model if you can find one
that's been sufficiently discounted. I'd suggest, however, that you wait
for the upgraded 2002 versions for the additional interior space and
performance enhancements. Other cars worth considering are the
Audi A6, BMW 5-series, Lexus GS 300 or 400, or Volvo S90 and V90.
Options: None. **Rebates:** Not likely. **Delivery/PDI:** $500. **Depreciation:**
Slower than average. **Insurance cost:** Higher than average. **Parts sup-
ply/cost:** Hard to find outside of the dealer network, and can be expensive at times (body parts especially). **Annual maintenance cost:** Less
than average. **Warranty:** Bumper-to-bumper 4 years/80,000 km; powertrain 4 years/80,000 km; rust perforation 5 years/unlimited km.
Supplementary warranty: Not needed. **Highway/city fuel economy:**
7.5–11.4L/100 km with the 3.2L V6 engine, and 6.1–8.9L/100 km with
the 3.2L V6 diesel powerplant.

Quality/Reliability/Safety

Service bulletin problems: Brake pedal may be hard to apply. **NHTSA
safety complaints/safety:** *320:* Stalling, hesitation, leakage, and noise
due to the failure of the transmission's electronic circuit board; ABS
light comes on for no reason; faulty electrical wires; centre console mirror fell out of the console unit.

Road Performance

Acceleration/torque: Better than average acceleration with the base
engine, but the 4.2L V8's performance is dazzling (0–100 km/h: 8 sec.).
Transmission: Flawless. The 5-speed automatic is the only shifter available, now that Mercedes has incorporated Touch Shift capability for
manual shifting. **Braking:** It'll be hard to find better braking with any
other car in this class (100–0 km/h: 114 ft.).

VOLKSWAGEN

Like most European cars, Volkswagens are practical and offer excellent handling and great fuel economy without sacrificing interior comfort. While overall reliability isn't spectacular (particularly after their fifth year of ownership), the entry-level models are reasonably priced. And they're not all that difficult to service at independent garages, which have grown increasingly popular as owners flee more expensive VW dealerships. Although parts are fairly expensive, independent repair agencies usually have no trouble finding them.

The only continuing concern is how the closure of its Canadian headquarters will affect Volkswagen's supply of new vehicles, warranty administration, and parts availability. In a recent Canadian Federation of Automobile Dealer Associations dealer survey, done before VW relocated, VW dealers blasted Volkswagen management for being insensitive to their concerns.

So far, the company's move to the States hasn't showed VW to be insensitive to its Canadian customers' concerns: its toll-free, bilingual customer service line is easily accessed and the few staffers I spoke with were friendly, helpful, and forthcoming.

This year, Volkswagen introduces a new Jetta wagon, a restyled Passat, a Passat Plus sedan and coupe with an 8-cylinder, 370-hp, 3.7L engine, and a repowered, upgraded EuroVan.

New Beetle

RATING: Average. The New Beetle is an expensive ($21,950) trip down memory lane. Personally, I don't think it's worth it—with or without its speed-activated spoiler and dash-mounted bud vase. **Strong points:** Powerful 1.8L turbocharged engine; easy handling; sure-footed and

comfortable, though firm, ride; impressive braking; most instruments
and controls are user friendly; comfortable and supportive front seats
with plenty of head and leg room; cargo area can be expanded by folding down the front seats; and top-quality mechanical components and
workmanship. **Weak points:** Serious safety defects reported by owners;
base engine runs out of steam around 100 km/h; diesel engine lacks
pep and produces lots of noise and vibration; delayed shifts from Park
to Drive; easily buffeted by crosswinds; large head restraints and large
front roof pillars obstruct front visibility; limited rear leg and head
room; excessive engine noise; skimpy interior storage and trunk space.

NEW FOR 2001: Larger and lower side mirrors. A redesigned version
will come out next year as a 2002 model.

OVERVIEW: A car that has less space for people and cargo and less
performance than cars that cost 15–20 percent less, the New Beetle has
been a hands-down marketing and public relations winner since it was
reintroduced after being absent since 1979.

Why so much enthusiasm for an ugly German import that never had
a functioning heater, was declared "Small on Safety" by Ralph Nader
and his Center for Auto Safety, and carried a puny 48-hp engine? The
simple answer is that it was cheap, and it represented the first car most
of us could afford as we went through school, got our first job, and
dreamed of getting a better car. Time has taken the edge off the mem-
ories of the hardship the Beetle made us endure—like having to scrape
the inside windshield with our nails as our breath froze—and left us
with the cozy feeling that the car wasn't that bad, after all.

But it was.

Now VW has resurrected the Beetle and produced a competent
front engine, front-drive, compact car—set on the chassis and running
gear of the Golf hatchback—that's much safer than its predecessor, but
oddly enough is still afflicted by many of the same deficiencies we
learned to hate with the original.

Again, without the turbocharger, the 115-hp base engine is under-
whelming (the 90-hp turbodiesel isn't much better) when you get it
up to cruising speed, there's still not much room for rear passengers,
engine noise is disconcerting, radio buttons and power accessory switches
located on the door panels aren't user-friendly, front visibility is hin-
dered by the car's quirky design, and storage capacity is at a premium.

On the other hand, the powerful, optional 1.8L turbocharged
engine makes this Beetle an impressive performer; the heater works
fine; steering, handling, and braking are quite good; and the interior is
not as spartan or tacky as it once was.

Cost analysis/best alternatives: Don't bother looking for a discounted
2000 model, they're long gone. Other cars worth considering are the
Acura CL, Chrysler Sebring, Honda Prelude, Mazda Protegé, Nissan

Sentra, Toyota Corolla, and VW Cabrio. **Options:** A turbocharged engine is essential if you plan lots of highway use. **Rebates:** Until the novelty wears off, price cuts will be ephemeral. **Delivery/PDI:** $525. **Depreciation:** Much slower than average, especially during the first two years. **Insurance cost:** Higher than average. **Parts supply/cost:** Not hard to find since they're taken from the Golf/Jetta parts bin, but they may be more expensive than parts for most other cars in this class. **Annual maintenance cost:** Less than average during the first three years. After this, expect repair costs to start to climb dramatically. **Warranty:** Bumper-to-bumper 2 years/40,000 km; powertrain 5 years/80,000 km; rust perforation 6 years/unlimited km. **Supplementary warranty:** A good idea. **Highway/city fuel economy:** 4.8–6.9L/100 km with the 1.9L turbodiesel, 7.9–10.5L/100 km with the 1.8L, and 7.7–10.5L/100 km with the 2.0L.

Quality/Reliability/Safety

Pro: Quality control: Better than average. Major components are relatively trouble-free. **Reliability:** Good overall reliability during the first few years. **Warranty performance:** Slow, but fair treatment of warranty claims by customer service staff located in the States. **Safety:** Standard three-point seatbelts and anti-theft alarm (thieves just adore these cars). The Insurance Institute for Highway Safety has given the Beetle a "good" rating for off-set crashworthiness and front seat head restraint protection, and an "acceptable" rating for the rear.

Con: Service bulletin problems: A front end humming noise during cornering and no air flow adjustment at centre air adjustment. **NHTSA safety complaints/safety:** Sudden acceleration; delayed acceleration; inoperative driver power window; driver door and trunk won't shut; premature radio failure; chronic stalling; Check Engine comes on for no reason; temperature gauge warning light malfunctioned and reservoir tank sensor failed, causing vehicle to overheat; side impact airbags did not deploy, resulting in death; in another incident, driver side airbag didn't deploy; airbag light won't go off; busted fuel tank leaked fuel; headrest is six inches too high to fit driver's head and obstructs rear visibility; horn failure; malfunctioning dashboard gauges; the left front strut slipped down through the spindle, causing the spindle to hit the wheel well; axle oil pan failure; oil pump failure.

COST				
List Price (firm)	**Residual Values (months)**			
	24	**36**	**48**	**60**
Base model: $21,950 (17%)	$16,000	$14,000	$11,000	$9,000

TECHNICAL DATA

Powertrain (front-drive)
Engines: 2.0L 4-cyl. (115 hp)
• 1.9L TD 4-cyl. (90 hp)
• 1.8L T 4-cyl. (150 hp)
Transmissions: 4-speed auto.
• 5-speed man.
Dimension/Capacity
Passengers: 2/2
Height/length/width:
59.5/161.1/67.9 in.

Head room F/R: 42/34 in.
Leg room F/R: 45.5/23 in.
Wheelbase: 98.9 in.
Turning circle: 36. ft.
Cargo volume: 12 cu. ft.
Tow limit: N/A
Fuel tank: 55L/reg.
Weight: 2,769 lb.

SAFETY FEATURES/CRASHWORTHINESS

	Std.	Opt.
Anti-lock brakes	■	❑
Seatbelt pretensioners	■	❑
Side airbags	■	❑
Traction control	❑	■
Head restraints F/R	*****	***
Visibility F/R	**	*
Crash protection (front) D/P	****	****
Crash protection (side) D/P	*****	***
Crash protection (off-set)	*****	

Golf, Jetta, Cabrio

Jetta

RATING: Above Average. Price hikes are putting these cars out of most people's reach. **Strong points:** Superb all-around front-drive performers that offer power to spare with the manual shifter (GTI VR6, GLX), first-class handling, a comfortable ride, and good fuel economy. **Weak points:** Poor acceleration with the 4-cylinder engine, powerful V6 produces excessive torque steer, harsh automatic transmission downshifts, difficult entry/exit, restricted rear visibility, limited rear leg room, and a high number of safety-related complaints. Keep in mind that maintenance costs increase dramatically after the fifth year of ownership.

NEW FOR 2001: The Golf gets optional sports suspension on the GLS with the 1.8LT engine option. GTI gets the same sports suspension and new alloy wheels for the GLX. A new Jetta wagon arrives in the spring.

OVERVIEW: Practical and fun to drive. That pretty well sums up the main reasons why these VWs continue to be so popular. Yet they offer much more, including lots of front interior room, a peppier engine than what you'll find in most cars this size, responsive handling, great fuel economy, and better than average reliability over the first three years.

The Jetta is a more expensive Golf with a trunk (probably why Jettas outsell Golfs five to one), and the Cabrio is a much more expensive Golf without a roof. The Golf GTI V6 is a sporty performer that comes with lots of standard equipment, including air conditioning, an upgraded sound system, and a split folding rear seat. Jettas offer standard cruise control, power mirrors, and alloy wheels.

Four engines are available: a 115-hp 2.0L base 4-cylinder, a 150-hp 1.8L 4-cylinder turbo, a 90-hp 1.9L turbo diesel variant, and a 174-hp 2.8L V6 borrowed from the Corrado and Passat. A manual 5-speed transmission is also offered as a standard feature, along with an optional 4-speed automatic. Power steering is optional on base-level models. Although the entry-level Golf's engine is no tire burner, it's well mated to the base manual transmission.

Cost analysis/best alternatives: These vehicles were extensively redesigned two years ago and this year's models are coasting on those upgrades. For this reason, discounted year 2000 models offer the same features for less money. Other cars worth considering are the Honda Civic, Mazda Protegé, Nissan Sentra, and Toyota Corolla. Cabrio shoppers might also want to test-drive a convertible Chevrolet Cavalier or Sunfire. **Options:** Stay away from the electric sunroof; it costs a bundle to repair and offers not much more than the well-designed manual sunroof. Plus, you lose too much head room. The Jetta TDI isn't a good idea. Why in the world would you invest in a diesel engine, unless you want to get your gas at truck stops? Granted, there are fewer things to go wrong with diesel engines, but gasoline-powered VW engines already have an excellent track record. Less fuel cost isn't a strong enough argument to weigh against the extra noise and smellier emissions associated with diesel engines. And there's no guarantee that diesel prices won't get boosted again this year. **Delivery/PDI:** $525. **Rebates:** Not likely. **Depreciation:** Slower than average, especially the Jetta and all Cabriolet versions. **Insurance cost:** Higher than average. **Parts supply/cost:** Not hard to find, but parts can be more expensive than most other cars in this class. **Annual maintenance cost:** Less than average while under warranty. After that, repair costs start to climb dramatically. **Warranty:** Bumper-to-bumper 2 years/40,000 km; powertrain 5 years/80,000 km; rust perforation 6 years/unlimited km. **Supplementary warranty:** A good idea. **Highway/city fuel economy:** 4.8–6.9L/100 km with the 1.9L TDI; 7.7–10.5L/100 km with the 2.0L; and 8.4–12.6L/100 km with the 2.8L V6.

Quality/Reliability/Safety

Pro: Quality control: Better than average; Golfs made for the Canadian market are made in Wolfsburg, Germany. Major components are relatively trouble free. No rusting due to a galvanized body and stainless steel exhaust system. **Reliability:** Good overall reliability during the first few years (that's why so many are used as taxis). **Warranty performance:** Slow, but fair treatment of warranty claims by customer service staff located in the States. **Safety:** Standard three-point seatbelts and anti-theft alarm (thieves just adore these cars).

Con: Ownership costs rise dramatically after the fifth year of ownership. **Owner-reported problems:** The brakes and the electrical, fuel, and exhaust systems are especially troublesome. Owners report that doors are poorly hung, rattles are omnipresent, and dashboard controls and interior and exterior trim items aren't very durable. Poor radio reception. Convertible top storage obstructs rear vision.

Service bulletin problems: Vehicle may exhibit throttle pedal vibration at idle; transmission goes into limp mode; vibrating transmission shifter; and poor radio reception. **NHTSA safety complaints/safety:** *Golf:* Intermittent stalling; uncomfortable driver's seat creates excessive fatigue on long trips; horn can't be located when wheel is turned; improper lug nuts allow wheel to separate from the car. *Jetta:* When the brakes are released, vehicle suddenly accelerates; airbag warning light comes on for no apparent reason and shuts down the airbag system; ABS failure; driver's seat faulty wiring caused a fire; passenger-side airbag deployed seconds after impact; exhaust pipe extends underneath the bumper, revealing raw edge of pipe; car hit the curb and airbag deployed, hitting driver's head and killing him; fuel tank leaks; adhesive that secures the brake light in the rear window can melt in sunlight; shoulder and lapbelt disengaged during a collision; restraints failed, allowing driver to hit the windshield even though the airbag deployed; vehicle was hit from all sides and neither front nor side airbags deployed; intermittent stalling; when vehicle is driven at speeds over 35 mph (57 km/h), tachometer registers 4700 rpm before downshifting; gear console gives an inaccurate gear reading; interior and instrument lights fail intermittently.

Road Performance

Pro: Emergency handling: Acceptable, despite the softer suspension creating additional body roll. **Steering:** Precise and predictable steering. **Acceleration/torque:** The standard 2.0L 4-cylinder engine is acceptable for city driving and leisurely highway cruising with the manual gearbox, thanks mainly to the car's light weight and improved fuel injection. The V6 is the prerequisite engine for performance thrills (0–100 km/h: 8 sec.). **Routine handling:** Excellent handling. Ride quality is less firm than with previous models. **Braking:** Acceptable (100–0 km/h: 130 ft.).

Con: The base 4-cylinder engine provides sluggish acceleration when hooked to an automatic transmission. Excessive torque steer with the V6. Diesel engines equipped with cruise control can't handle small hills very well, and usually drop 10–15 km/h. **Transmission:** Manual 5-speed transmission is imprecise and requires long lever throws to change gear. Harsh automatic transmission downshifts at full throttle. The soft suspension produces lots of body roll when cornering under power.

Comfort/Convenience

Pro: TDI comes with impressive features like standard cruise control, side airbags, pretensioning seatbelts, a full-sized spare, four-wheel disc brakes, ABS, tilt/telescoping steering column, heated mirrors, anti-theft alarm system, central power locking system, and air conditioning. **Driving position:** Excellent. Front seat head room is adequate for most drivers, even with a sunroof. Ergonomics are impressive. **Controls and displays:** The dash is well laid out and gauges are easy to read. Most controls are easy to find and use. **Climate control:** Generally works well and is easy to adjust. However, some owners have complained that heating is barely sufficient. Check this out on the dealer's lot before accepting delivery. **Interior space/comfort F/R:** Although the interior is austere, it's well finished and fairly spacious up front. The rear seats include headrests. **Cargo space:** The Golf's hatchback design is a bit more versatile for diverse cargo. **Trunk/liftover:** Spacious trunk has a low liftover.

Con: Standard equipment: Basic amenities are disappointing, such as the crank windows and cloth upholstery. Rear visibility somewhat restricted. The front seats are too firm for some and the low-profile tires make small bumps unusually harsh. The rear seats are too narrow and there's not enough knee room. Radio and power window buttons are too small. The lack of a centre console cuts down on storage space. The Cabrio's trunk is too small. The odd way the trunk opens compromises loading. **Entry/exit:** A bit tricky. **Quietness:** Despite additional sound deadening, the TDI's engine is fairly noisy and tends to produce excessive vibrations.

COST

List Price (firm)	Residual Values (months)			
	24	36	48	60
Golf 2d: $19,040 (13%)	$13,000	$11,000	$9,000	$7,000
Golf 4d: $21,910 (14%)	$15,500	$13,500	$11,500	$9,500
Jetta GL: $21,280 (14%)	$16,000	$14,000	$12,000	$10,000

TECHNICAL DATA

Powertrain (front-drive)
Engines: 2.0L 4-cyl. (115 hp)
• 1.8LT 4-cyl. (150 hp)
• 1.9L 4-cyl. diesel (90 hp)
• 2.8L V6 (174 hp)
Transmissions: 5-speed man.
• 4-speed auto.
Dimension/Capacity (GTI VR6)
Passengers: 2/3
Height/length/width:
56.7/163.3/68.3 in.

Head room F/R: 37.1/36.5 in.
Head room F/R: 37.9/36.5 in.
Leg room F/R: 41.3/33.3 in.
Wheelbase: 98.9 in.
Turning circle: 36 ft.
Cargo volume: 18 cu. ft.
Tow limit: 1,000 lb.
Fuel tank: 55L/reg.
Weight: 2,723 lb.

SAFETY FEATURES/CRASHWORTHINESS

	Std.	Opt.
Anti-lock brakes	■	❏
Seatbelt pretensioners	■	❏
Side airbags	■	❏
Traction control	■	■
Head restraints F/R	**	*
Cabrio	*	*
Visibility F/R	*****	**
Crash protection (front) D/P	*****	*****
Crash protection (side) D/P	****	****
Crash protection (off-set)	***	

Passat

Passat

RATING: Recommended. **Strong points:** Refined road manners; sophisticated, user-friendly all-wheel drive; quiet running; plenty of passenger and cargo room; exceptional driving comfort; and top-quality construction and mechanical components. Well appointed, with standard side airbags, traction control, and ABS. **Weak points:** Mediocre acceleration (automatic transmission-equipped GLS 1.8T and TDI), rear corner blind spots, serious safety complaints, and poor fuel economy.

NEW FOR 2001: Curtain-style side airbags and steering wheel–mounted controls for the radio and the cruise control.

OVERVIEW: Volkswagen's largest front-drive compact, the Passat is an attractive mid-sized car that rides on the same platform as the Audi A4, giving it a 3-inch larger wheelbase and more passenger room. It has a more stylish design than the Golf or Jetta, but still provides a comfortable, roomy interior and gives good all-around performance for highway and city driving. The car's large wheelbase and squat appearance give it a massive, solid feeling, while its aerodynamic styling makes it look sleek and clean. Most Passats come fully loaded with air conditioning, tinted glass, power-assisted disc brakes on all four wheels, front and rear stabilizer bars, full instrumentation, and even a roof rack with the wagon. Engine offerings include a new 150-hp 1.8L turbocharged inline four and a 190-hp 2.8L V6 hooked to either a 5-speed manual or a 5-speed Tiptronic automatic transmission.

Cost analysis/best alternatives: Get a discounted 2000 model, if you can find one; otherwise, you'll have to wait until the new year to get the upgrades. Other cars worth considering are the BMW 3-series, Honda Accord, Mazda 626, Nissan Altima, and Toyota Camry. **Options:** The 2.8L V6 and a good anti-theft system. The AWD is an excellent investment, if you need the extra surefootedness and traction. **Rebates:** Not likely. **Delivery/PDI:** $500. **Depreciation:** Slower than average. **Insurance cost:** Higher than average. These cars are favourites with thieves—whether for radios, wheels, VW badges, or the entire car. **Parts supply/cost:** Not hard to find. Parts and service are much more expensive than average. **Annual maintenance cost:** Higher than average. **Warranty:** Bumper-to-bumper 2 years/40,000 km; powertrain 5 years/ 80,000 km; rust perforation 6 years/unlimited km. **Supplementary warranty:** A must-have. Maintenance costs are higher than average once the warranty expires, which is all the more reason to buy the optional warranty from VW. **Highway/city fuel economy:** 7–11.4L/100 km with the 1.8L engine, 7.5–13.3L/100 km with the 2.8L, and 8.2–13.7L/ 100 km with the 2.8L Synchro.

Quality/Reliability/Safety

Pro: Quality control: So far, so good. The new Passat uses mechanical parts and underpinnings borrowed from Audi, so overall reliability and problem areas should be similar to those of the Audi A4. **Reliability:** Predicted above average reliability during the first three years. **Warranty performance:** Apparently good. VW staffers in the States (there's no office in Canada) have been particularly sensitive to Passat complaints.

Con: Owner-reported problems: Some electrical malfunctions, premature brake wear, and noisy braking. **Service bulletin problems:** Poor AM reception. **NHTSA safety complaints/safety:** Hard starts and chronic stalling. This appears to be a generic problem caused by premature "carbon deposits" as the following *Lemon-Aid* reader relates in a recent email:

> I have just been told that VW has issued a bulletin to dealers regarding the V6 model Passat, (I have a two-month-old 2000 model). It seems there is carbon building up on the valves due to incompatibility of the engine requirements and across the board blended gasolines available to the US consumer (I don't know about other countries). I have been told that the problem exists with Audi models as well. My car is in the shop and cannot be repaired until the dealership receives a "special" machine which will clean the carbon off the valves without a major engine disassembly (!?) I have been told that the dealerships will not be getting these machines for at least a month. Even then the problem will not be solved as available gasoline will continue to cause a carbon build-up. They have suggested that the engine be adjusted so it burns hotter and this "may" solve the problem. They do not know what if anything this would do to the engine block. Again, I have been told that this is an across-the-board problem for all V6 models with this particular engine. My 2000 Passat is only two months old…

Road Performance

Pro: Emergency handling: Better than average; impressive, with the AWD system. **Steering:** Quick, precise, and predictable. **Acceleration/torque:** Decent acceleration with the base 1.8L turbocharged engine, unless saddled with an automatic transmission. Better acceleration times with more torque can be wrung from the V6 (0–100 km/h: 7.9 sec.). Diesel power is relatively quick and quiet. **Transmission:** Great performance with the manual gearbox. Smooth and quiet shifting with the automatic gearbox. The 4Motion full-time all-wheel drive shifts effortlessly into gear. **Routine handling:** Suspension is both firm and comfortable; precise handling outclasses most of the competition.

Con: 4-cylinder engine power is seriously compromised by the automatic transmission. **Braking:** Less than impressive (100–0 km/h: 141 ft.).

Comfort/Convenience

Pro: Standard equipment: This is VW's most luxurious car, so it comes fairly well appointed. Heated outside mirror. **Driving position:** Very good. Comfortable seating and good fore and aft visibility. Fairly good dashboard layout. **Controls and displays:** User-friendly instrument panel. **Climate control:** Efficient and quiet operation. Includes a dust and pollen filter. **Entry/exit:** Relatively easy front and rear access. **Interior space/comfort F/R:** Spacious interior seats four in comfort, as long as the rear passengers aren't too tall. All seats are supportive and comfortable. **Cargo space:** Average for the sedan. Many small storage spaces. **Trunk/liftover:** Large and accessible trunk has an innovative latch and low liftover. **Quietness:** Additional sound-deadening material keeps interior noise to a minimum.

Con: The styling of the rear pillars compromises rear visibility. Cheap-looking cupholders. Limited rear head room. Rear seatbacks don't fold for added storage. **Quietness:** Excessive tire noise.

COST				
List Price (firm)	**Residual Values (months)**			
	24	**36**	**48**	**60**
Passat GLS 1.8:				
$30,345 (18%)	$23,500	$19,500	$16,500	$13,500

TECHNICAL DATA	
Powertrain (front-drive)	Head room F/R: 39.7/37.8 in.
Engines: 1.8L 4-cyl. (150 hp)	Leg room F/R: 41.5/35.3 in.
• 2.8L V6 (190 hp)	Wheelbase: 106.4 in.
Transmissions: 5-speed man.	Turning circle: 38 ft.
• 5-speed auto.	Cargo volume: 15 cu. ft.

Dimension/Capacity	Tow limit: 1,000 lb.
Passengers: 2/3	Fuel tank: 47L/prem.
Height/length/width:	Weight: 3,250 lb.
57.4/184.1/68.5 in.	

SAFETY FEATURES/CRASHWORTHINESS		
	Std.	**Opt.**
Anti-lock brakes	■	❑
Seatbelt pretensioners	■	❑
Side airbags	■	❑
Traction control	■	❑
Head restraints F/R	**	*
Visibility F/R	*****	**
Crash protection (front) D/P	*****	*****
Crash protection (side) D/P	****	****
Crash protection (off-set)	*****	

VOLVO

The Ford Volvo. Kinda sticks in your craw, doesn't it, pardner?

Volvo has always distinguished itself from the rest of the automotive pack through its much-vaunted standard safety features, crashworthiness, and engineering that emphasized function over style. But unfortunately these noteworthy features were eclipsed by bland styling, ponderous highway performance, inconsistent quality control that compromised long-term reliability and drove up ownership costs, and chancy servicing by a small dealer network.

Well, times have changed and Volvo has changed with them. While the mainstream U.S. automakers go retro with creased styling and dashes of chrome, Volvo has dumped its boxy station wagons and rediscovered rounded edges. The automaker's curvy 2001 V70 is the latest example of a styling change that is already in full swing with the company's S80 sedan, C70 coupe, and smaller 40-series cars. This was the last design by Volvo before the company was purchased by Ford (thank goodness— just imagine a Volvo/Taurus restyling!).

As far as quality control and dealer servicing are concerned, Volvo has improved service and warranty relations by accelerating service training programs and allowing its dealers to carry out most warranty and extra-warranty repairs without obtaining prior authorization from the company. Ford's impact upon the dealer network has been minimal and is likely to stay that way as long as Volvo products continue to be hot.

The downside to all this good news?

Ford is counting on Volvo to garnish its corporate wallet with immediate profits (not like Jaguar and Land Rover), so don't be surprised to see Volvo pushing new car prices through the roof. One gets the impression that Ford will milk the company for all it can get and keep prices high to do so. Furthermore, Ford's involvement may mean some sharing of components—a good idea for Jaguar, a bad idea for Volvo. Such a scheme will likely make Fords safer and more reliable and Volvos less so (I doubt Ford's failure prone automatic transmission, aluminum forward clutch piston, or fuel pumps would have ever found their way onto a Volvo assembly line. I hope they won't be used in future Volvo production, either).

S60

A new sporty sedan due to arrive in October, the S60 is set on the same large-car platform as the V70 and S80, but provides more interior room. Drivers will have the choice of three inline 5-cylinder engines: a 236-hp high pressure turbo, a 197-hp low-pressure turbo, and a 168-hp naturally aspirated version.

V40

Volvo S40 and V40

A Mitsubishi Volvo? That's right, the S40/V40, Volvo's new small sedan and wagon that went on sale last September, are built in the Netherlands through a joint venture with Mitsubishi. Priced much less than the V70, Volvo's $29,995 entry-level model comes with a 1.9L 150-hp turbocharged 4-cylinder engine coupled to an automatic transmission. Two side airbags, anti-lock brakes, air conditioning, cruise control, and power windows are also standard. Both of these small Volvos are Recommended buys.

   The 2001 model will get a minor facelift, side-curtain airbags, and some handling improvements; there won't be a redesign before 2004.

   Service bulletin problems: *S40:* Engine oil filler neck may be faulty; a ticking noise may be heard from the canister purge valve; and the malfunction light (MIL) stays on while driving. **NHTSA safety complaints/safety:** *S40:* When applying the brakes in cold weather, pedal won't depress, causing extended stopping distance (dealer confirmed vacuum pump motor was defective) and vehicle pulls to the left when accelerating or coming to a stop. *V40:* More complaints that the pedal won't depress, causing total brake loss or extended stopping distance and premature wearout of the front brake pads (around 20,000 km).

C70

RATING: Above Average. **Strong points:** Good acceleration with lots of torque, exceptional steering and handling, first-class body construction and finish, predicted better than average reliability. **Weak points:** Difficult rear-seat entry/exit, some engine turbo lag, excessive engine noise, a jarring suspension, and an uncertain future.

NEW FOR 2001: No significant changes; future is uncertain.

OVERVIEW: Seating four comfortably, this $52,995 luxury coupe and convertible is based on the 850 (pardon, S70) platform, and marketed as a high-performance Volvo. It comes with two turbocharged engines: a base 2.4L 190-hp inline 5-cylinder and a 2.3L 236-hp variant. Either engine can be hooked to a 5-speed manual or a 4-speed automatic transmission. Of the two engines, the 190-hp appears to offer the best response and smoothest performance.

Acceleration is impressive, despite the fact that the car feels underpowered until the turbo kicks in at around 1,500 rpm—a feature that drivers will find more frustrating with a manual shifter than with an automatic. Steering and handling are first class, fit and finish above reproach, and mechanical and body components are top quality.

The only things not to like are a high base price, turbo lag, tire thumping caused by the high-performance tires, excessive engine and wind noise, and power-sliding rear seats that require lots of skill and patience.

Safety features include dual driver/passenger airbags, side airbags, ABS, traction control, and a platform designed to give maximum passenger protection in a collision. IIHS has awarded the C70 its highest rating for front and rear seat head restraint protection.

V70

RATING: Recommended. **Strong points:** Practical to the extreme. Plenty of power, good handling, lots of carrying capacity, top-quality mechanical and body components, many standard safety features, and impressive crashworthiness ratings and accident injury claim data. **Weak points:** A jarring ride with vehicles equipped with 16- and 17-inch wheels; limited rear visibility; excessive engine, wind, and road noise; fuel-thirsty (turbo models); and limited availability, causing soaring base prices with little room for negotiating.

NEW FOR 2001: The S70 sedan has been dropped and a V70 wagon, based on the S80 platform, was added to the lineup last April. Also added is a Cross Country V70, which is essentially a wagon with extra body cladding, AWD, and bigger tires.

OVERVIEW: There are two variants of the V70 wagon: a base front-drive and an AWD. Both versions use a 2.4L 197-hp 5-cylinder engine hooked to a 5-speed automatic. These cars are loaded with safety and convenience features that include four-wheel disc brakes, head/chest front and side airbags, and high-tech seatbacks designed to minimize whiplash.

On sale since last August, the Cross Country's all-wheel drive and truck-like appearance distinguish it from last year's front-drive V70 wagon that it replaces. However, its mechanical components are practically identical to those of Volvo's other sedans. The original front-drive V70 Cross Country debuted in 1997 and was panned by auto critics as a pseudo-SUV. The 2001 iteration corrects its predecessor's performance deficiencies by adding all-wheel drive and a 5-speed automatic gearbox; raising the ground clearance and seating position; and installing more muscular body cladding. The upgraded interior includes a versatile "40/20/40" split rear seat. Safety improvements include side-curtain and dual-stage (less forceful) airbags. Volvo says the Cross Country's yet-to-be-announced price will be about $1,500 less than last year's less-equipped model. If Volvo does hold the line on prices, expect some dealer price gouging and increased prices in the new year.

Cost analysis/best alternatives: The 2000 versions have a greater choice of powertrains and models; however, they won't likely be discounted, if you can find one. Other cars worth considering are the Acura TL, Audi A4 or A6, Infiniti I30, Lexus ES 300, or the Toyota Camry. Other wagons you may wish to consider: the BMW 5-series Touring and Mercedes-Benz E-Class wagon. **Options:** Integrated child safety seats, seat heaters, and a full-sized spare tire. The turbo's traction control isn't worth the extra cost. **Rebates:** Are you kidding? These cars are so hot that dealers are refusing to budge from the MSRP, and some are tacking on unwarranted "administrative" fees and inflated PDI/destination charges. **Delivery/PDI:** $700. **Depreciation:** Slower than average. **Insurance cost:** Higher than average. **Parts supply/cost:** Parts are highly dealer-dependent. Volvos are well serviced by the small dealer body, and parts aren't hard to find. **Annual maintenance cost:** Average. Higher than average predicted after the fourth year. **Warranty:** Bumper-to-bumper 4 years/80,000 km; powertrain 4 years/80,000 km; rust perforation 8 years/unlimited km. **Supplementary warranty:** Not needed. The most frequent complaint concerns the brakes, an item excluded from most supplementary warranties. This latest generation of Volvos hasn't shown any major reliability weaknesses yet, but it's still too early to tell how they'll perform on a long-term basis, now that Ford owns the company ("Have you driven a Ford, lately?"). **Highway/city fuel economy:** 7.7–11.6L/100 km with the 2.4L, and 8.1–12L/100 km with the turbocharged engine.

Quality/Reliability/Safety

Pro: Reliability: No serious reliability problems have been encountered. **Warranty performance:** Much better than average. Many warranty claims are settled through "goodwill" on a case-by-case basis. **Safety:** Standard side-impact airbags and standard traction control with the T5R version are a nice touch. Other safety features include rear head restraints; reinforced anti-roll bars; front and rear crumple zones; a practical, roof-mounted interior cargo net that protects passengers from being hit by objects stored in the rear; and rear three-point seatbelts. As with Volvo's other models, IIHS has awarded the V70 its highest rating for front and rear seat head restraint protection.

Con: Body assembly and paint quality are better than average, but they can't match the Japanese competition. **Owner-reported problems:** Problem areas are limited to the front brakes, electrical system, and minor body faults. Some servicing delays reported. **Service bulletin problems:** Automatic transmission lockup (engagement/disengagement) while driving at cruising speed, vehicle may experience rear axle whine, and Check Engine and throttle system lights may come on for no reason. *Cross Country:* In addition to the above bulletin problems, drivers may hear a persistent squeaking noise coming from the rear suspension between the rear spring bump stop and the spring seat. **NHTSA safety complaints/safety:** Fuel line may leak fuel; fuse blows whenever turn signal lights are activated; car may have been delivered with an undersized spare tire.

Road Performance

Pro: Emergency handling: Better than average, with minimal body roll and good control. **Steering:** Predictable, rapid steering response. Handles sudden steering corrections very well. **Acceleration/torque:** Plenty of high-range power with the base engine, especially with a manual gearbox. With an automatic transmission, the normally aspirated base engine has a 0–100 km/h time of 9.5 seconds. No turbo lag. The 197-hp engine posted better than average acceleration times (0–100 km/h: 8.8 sec.) with plenty of torque. **Transmission:** Smooth and quiet automatic and manual gearboxes. **Routine handling:** Nimble handling doesn't sacrifice passenger comfort. **Braking:** Despite some complaints of poor braking, tested braking performance is quite good (100–0 km/h: 115 ft.) on dry or wet pavement.

Con: Moderate torque steer when accelerating. The soft ride deteriorates progressively as the road gets rougher and passenger weight is added.

Comfort/Convenience

Pro: Standard equipment: Lots of standard safety and performance features. **Driving position:** Excellent driving position and plenty of seat adjustments to accommodate almost any size of driver. **Controls and displays:** Everything is in plain sight, accessible, and intuitive. **Climate control:** Excellent. The system operates flawlessly and is simple to comprehend. **Entry/exit:** Easy front and rear access. **Interior space/comfort F/R:** Passenger space, seating comfort, and trunk and cargo space are unmatched by the competition. **Cargo space:** The wagon's rear seatbacks fold flat and the seat cushion can be removed for additional cargo space. **Trunk/liftover:** Spacious trunk has a low liftover.

Con: Rear head restraints limit rear visibility. **Quietness:** Excessive engine noise upon acceleration, as well as some wind and tire noise at highway speeds.

COST				
List Price (firm)	**Residual Values (months)**			
	24	**36**	**48**	**60**
Base V70: $37,495 (20%)	$27,000	$22,000	$17,000	$13,000

TECHNICAL DATA

Powertrain (front-drive/AWD)   Head room F/R: 39.3/38.9 in.
Engines: 2.4L 5-cyl. (197 hp)   Leg room F/R: 42.6/35.2 in.
• 2.4L 5-cyl. turbo (247 hp)   Wheelbase: 108.5 in.
Transmission: 5-speed auto.   Turning circle: 40 ft.
Dimension/Capacity   Cargo volume: N/A
Passengers: 2/3   Tow limit: 2,000 lb.
Height/length/width: Fuel tank: 73L/prem.
58.6/185.4/71 in.   Weight: 3,366 lb.

SAFETY FEATURES/CRASHWORTHINESS

	Std.	Opt.
Anti-lock brakes	■	❏
Seatbelt pretensioners	■	❏
Side airbags	■	❏
Traction control	■	❏
Head restraints F/R	*****	*****
Visibility F/R	*****	**
Crash protection (front) D/P	*****	*****
Crash protection (side) D/P	****	N/A
Crash protection (off-set)	*****	

S80

✓ BEST BUY

S80

RATING: Recommended. **Strong points:** Powerful turbocharged engine; generally comfortable ride; quiet running; handles well; good amounts of passenger and cargo room; excellent build quality with first-class materials; and many standard safety features. **Weak points:** Base engine a so-so performer; driving position not for everyone; ride comfort deteriorates as load is increased; steering feels over-assisted; fuel thirsty; and high base prices demanded by dealers who won't negotiate.

NEW FOR 2001: Dual-stage airbags have been added this year.

OVERVIEW: Volvo has replaced the rear-drive S90 sedan with the front-drive S80, equipped with a twin-cam 2.9L straight-six engine. The S80 T6 employs two turbochargers to boost the 2.8L engine's power to 268 horses and mate it to a 4-speed automatic transmission equipped with a Geartronic manual-shift feature.

Both models are well equipped with safety and convenience features that include standard ABS, front side airbags and Inflatable Cushion side airbags that extend from the front to the rear roof pillars, seatbelt pretensioners, traction control, a "WHIPS" seatback and head restraint whiplash protection system, and an optional Dynamic Stability and Traction Control System. Furthermore, IIHS has awarded its highest rating to the S80 for front and rear seat head restraint protection.

Cost analysis/best alternatives: Safer airbags on the 2001 model is sufficient reason to steer clear of any leftover 2000 versions. Other cars worth considering are the Acura RL, BMW 5-series, or Lexus GS 300 and LS 400. **Options:** The turbocharged engine is the better performer for highway driving. Also consider built-in child safety seats and seat heaters. Think twice about buying the optional navigation system: the map screen rises from the centre of the dashboard, controls are on the steering wheel, and calibrating or reading the device takes patience and an MIT degree. **Rebates:** Not likely. Get ready for some real sticker shock. These cars are so hot that dealers are tacking on unwarranted "administrative" fees and inflated PDI/destination charges. **Delivery/PDI:** $700. **Depreciation:** Less than average. **Insurance cost:** Higher than average. **Parts supply/cost:** Parts availability is very dealer-dependent; a high-volume dealer is your best bet. Volvos are well served by the small dealer body, and reasonably priced parts aren't generally hard to find. **Annual maintenance cost:** Average during the warranty period; expected to rise when the warranty expires. **Warranty:** Bumper-to-bumper 4 years/80,000 km; powertrain 4 years/80,000 km; rust perforation 8 years/unlimited km. **Supplementary warranty:** Not necessary. This latest generation of Volvos hasn't shown any major reliability weaknesses yet, but it's still too early to tell how they'll perform on a long-term basis. **Highway/city fuel economy:** 8.0–12.2L/100 km with the 2.9L 6-cylinder, and 7.9–12.8L/100 km with the turbocharger.

Quality/Reliability/Safety

Pro: Quality control: Volvo's quality control is better than most European automakers'. **Reliability:** Nothing that would sideline these cars for an extended period of time. Body assembly and finish is comparable to the Japanese competition. **Warranty performance:** Better than average. Volvo staffers have been fair and professional in handling warranty claims.

Con: Owner-reported problems: Failure-prone air conditioning, premature brake wear and noisy braking, and electrical and fuel system malfunctions. Parts shortages and delivery delays are commonplace. **Service bulletin problems:** Cruise control may not hold the desired speed when driving downhill; transmission 2–3 upshift shudder; engine oil filler neck service campaign; and Check Engine light comes on for no reason. **NHTSA safety complaints/safety:** Steering wheel recoils when accelerating; after a cold start brakes fail to stop the car for the first few seconds; front seat head restraints cannot be removed, and they block the driver from seeing around the car's blind spot.

Road Performance

Pro: Emergency handling: Very good. The multi-link rear suspension and front engine placement make for crisp handling. **Steering:** Good steering response, although it sometimes feels over-assisted and road feel is a bit muted. **Acceleration/torque:** The 2.9L 201-hp 6-cylinder puts out lots of low-end and mid-range torque that meets all driving conditions with a minimum of strain or engine noise (0–100 km/h: 9.2 sec.). The turbocharged version is the engine of choice, however. It delivers plenty of high-speed cruising power and torque. **Transmission:** Smooth and quiet automatic transmission. **Routine handling:** Acceptable handling prioritizes passenger comfort. **Braking:** Better than average. Braking is short and straight with minimal fading after successive brake application (100–0 km/h: 120 ft.).

Con: Some torque steer upon acceleration. Comfort and handling diminishes as passenger/cargo load increases.

Comfort/Convenience

Pro: Very good driving position for most. User-friendly cockpit. **Controls and displays:** Well laid-out dash and analogue gauges are easy to read. Controls are within easy reach. **Climate control:** Climate control system is efficient, quiet, and unobtrusive. **Entry/exit:** Easy front and rear access. **Interior space/comfort F/R:** Capable of carrying five people in comfort, and the wagon variant provides lots of cargo space. Front and rear seats are supportive and comfortable. Three passengers can sit in the rear in comfort. **Cargo space:** Plenty of cargo space. **Trunk/liftover:** Spacious trunk has a low liftover. **Quietness:** Whisper quiet.

Con: Not enough room for driver's left leg to stretch. Small trunk opening. **Standard equipment:** Bland exterior and interior styling. **Driving position:** Short-statured drivers may find it necessary to lower the seat in order to decrease the leg room to reach the accelerator comfortably. This makes it difficult to see over the steering wheel.

COST

List Price (firm)	Residual Values (months)			
	24	**36**	**48**	**60**
S80: $53,795 (22%)	$38,000	$32,000	$26,000	$22,000

TECHNICAL DATA

Powertrain (front-drive)
Engine: 2.9L 6-cyl. (201 hp)
• 2.8L 6-cyl. (268 hp)
Transmission: 4-speed auto.
Dimension/Capacity
Passengers: 2/3
Height/length/width:
57.2/189.8/72.1 in.

Head room F/R: 39.1/37.9 in.
Leg room F/R: 41.4/35.2 in.
Wheelbase: 109.9 in.
Turning circle: 40 ft.
Cargo volume: 14 cu. ft.
Tow limit: 2,000 lb.
Fuel tank: 73L/prem.
Weight: 3,630 lb.

SAFETY FEATURES/CRASHWORTHINESS

	Std.	Opt.
Anti-lock brakes	■	❏
Seatbelt pretensioners	■	❏
Side airbags	■	❏
Traction control	■	❏
Head restraints F/R	*****	*****
Visibility F/R	*****	*****
Crash protection (front) D/P	N/A	N/A
Crash protection (side) D/P	*****	*****
Crash protection (off-set)	*****	

Appendix
HELPFUL INTERNET GRIPE SITES

Websites come and go. Please email *lemonaid@earthlink.net* if you find a site has closed down or moved. Also let me know if you have discovered a website that should be included in next year's *Lemon-Aid* guides. Incidentally, gripe sites can be very useful in showing you how to set up your own protest/gripe site.

Consumer Protection

1. Lemon-Aid *(www.lemonaidcars.com)*
The official website sponsored by the *Lemon-Aid* guides. Quick, easy, and free access to confidential service bulletins, owner complaints, recalls, and defect investigations. A Secret Warranty Watch is updated monthly, paint delamination jurisprudence is supplied, and tips for making a successful claim are given in The Art of Complaining (even a sample complaint letter is included).

2. "Lemon Aid or How to Get Carmakers to Call You and Beg You for Mercy!" (*www.saabnet.com/aas/1997.W26/1344522661.26426.html*)
Although not affiliated with the *Lemon-Aid* guides, this site contains a hilarious listing of tactics to use in getting auto manufacturers to return your calls, listen to your complaints, and give you compensation.

3. Center for Auto Safety *(www.autosafety.org)*
Consumers Union and Ralph Nader founded the Center for Auto Safety (CAS) in 1970 to provide consumers a voice for auto safety and quality in Washington and to help lemon owners fight back across the United States. CAS has a small budget but a big impact on the auto industry. It collects complaints and provides a lawyer referral service to its members.

4. Automobile Protection Association *(www.apa.ca)*
Phil Edmonston and the Center for Auto Safety founded this non-profit national consumers association in Montreal in the late '60s. Since then, the group has fought for safer vehicles and exposed many scams associated with new-car sales, leasing, and repairs. The association fights for its members through mediation and makes invoice prices for new vehicles available to non-members for a small fee.

5. CBC *Marketplace* (*cbc.ca/consumers/market/files/cars/index.html*)
Marketplace has been the Canadian Broadcasting Corporation's premiere national consumer show for almost three decades. It pulls no punches in exposing scams and reporting upon automaker mistakes. In

fact, its site has extensive links and in-depth reports on Chrysler paint delamination, ABS brake failures, and a host of other automotive topics that private broadcasters are afraid to touch. *Marketplace* is also useful for giving consumer groups national exposure in their battles with automakers. Recently, it covered Chris Ekstrom's battles with Chrysler paint problems, which led to the founding of CLOG Alberta.

6. *Consumer Reports* and Consumers Union *(consumerreports.org/)*
It costs $3.95 a month to subscribe on-line, but CR's database is chock full of comparison tests and in-depth stories on products and services. It's also a great place to get replacement tire ratings. Canadians may be disappointed that many of the rated tires and other products either aren't sold in Canada or are sold under a different name.

7. Chrysler Lemon Owners Group (CLOG) Alberta (email: *clog_alberta@ hotmail.com*)
If you own a Chrysler vehicle with paint, automatic transmission, engine head gasket, ABS brake, or air conditioning problems, contact CLOG Alberta founder Chris Ekstrom. He's been helping Chrysler owners across the country through referrals to the company and "Lemon Parades" in front of Chrysler and Mercedes dealerships. He also works closely with Sandra Knipple (tel. 306-651-2164) and Kim Shalinko (tel. 306-665-5805), the two coordinators of CLOG Saskatchewan.

8. Chrysler Lemon Owners Group (CLOG) B.C. (email: *underdog@ Lynx.bc.ca)*
Although not as active as it once was, CLOG B.C. continues to refer Chrysler complaints to Chrysler Canada on a case-by-case basis. Contact CLOG founder Patricia Wong at the above email address.

Auto Safety

9. Transport Canada *(www.tc.gc.ca/roadsafety/Recalls/search_e.asp)*
Cybersurfers can access the recall database for 1970–2000 model vehicles, but, unlike the NHTSA's website, owner complaints aren't listed, defect investigations aren't disclosed, and service bulletin summaries aren't provided. And you can't complain on-line. Buyers wishing to know if a vehicle can be imported into Canada from Europe or the States can get a list of admissible vehicles (those that conform to Canadian federal safety and pollution regulations) at *www.tc.gc.ca/ roadsafety/rsimp_e.htm#US,* or can call the Registrar of Imported Vehicles at 1-800-511-7755.

10. U.S. NHTSA *(www.nhtsa.dot.gov/cars/problems)*
Run by the Big Daddy of federal government auto safety regulators, the National Highway Traffic Safety Administration, this site has a comprehensive database covering owner complaints, recall campaigns, defect

Appendix

investigations initiated by the department, and automaker service bulletin summaries that may not be found in the ALLDATA database. Best of all, this data is easily accessed by typing in your vehicle's year, make, and model.

11. Insurance Institute for Highway Safety *(www.hwysafety.org)*
A dazzling site that's long on crash photos and graphs that show which vehicles are the most crashworthy. Lots of safety info that eschews the traditional "nut behind the wheel" dialectic. (Let owners deactivate their airbags if they feel at risk, and beware of driving schools: they don't make kids better drivers.)

12. The Safety Forum *(www.safetyforum.com)*
An awesome kick-butt site that shines a light on corporate weasels who make unsafe products. I especially like the "dirty Hoar" award (yes, it's pronounced like it's written) given out by Ralph Hoar, the Forum's founder, to deserving companies and individuals. The Forum also contains comprehensive news archives and links to useful sites, plus, names of court-recognized experts on unsafe Chrysler minivan latches, failure-prone tires, dangerous van conversions, and much more.

13. Strategic Safety *(www.strategicsafety.com/mainindex.html)*
These are the people who blew the whistle on dangerous Firestone Wilderness and ATX tires. This firm was founded by a former "Nader Raider" in partnership with a trial lawyer specializing in product liability cases. Strategic Safety provides research, investigation, analysis, and education on safety issues. Unintended sudden acceleration of Jeep Cherokees and Grand Cherokees is presently a priority dossier under investigation.

14. Consumerama *(www.consumerama.org/index.html)*
News and commentary on corporate wrongdoing. Includes links to protest sites, boycotts, and class actions by company name.

15. *Perez-Trujillo v. Volvo Car Corp.* *(www.law.emory.edu/1circuit/mar98/97-1792.01a.html)*
This U.S.-initiated lawsuit provides an interesting, though lengthy, dissertation on the safety hazards that airbags pose and why automakers are ultimately responsible for the injuries and deaths caused by their deployment.

16. Airbag killer sites *(www.plescia.org/indexair.htm; www.gov.on.ca/health/english/program/pubhealth/phero/phero_199906.html)*
After reading the dispassionate legal dissertation in *Perez-Trujillo*, the above sites will give you anecdotal evidence of drivers and passengers who have been severely injured by airbags in low-speed collisions or who have had loved ones that were killed. The last website is a recent

Canadian study that concludes airbags are dangerous to women, even those who wear their seatbelts.

Information/Mediation/Protest

17. The Unofficial BMW Lemon Site *(www.bmwlemon.com)*
Everything you wanted to know, or maybe didn't want to know, about factory-related defects affecting the 3-series, 5-series, and 7-series V8-equipped models. Plus a useful link to Dodge Dakota lemon sites (go figure).

18. Chrysler Owner Review Committee (email: *rar17@daimlerchrysler.com*)
No, you won't read about Chrysler Canada's consumer complaint committee in your owner's manual or see it touted anywhere at your local dealership. Chrysler's Review Committee was set up in February 1998 by Chrysler Canada VP Robert Renaud in response to the bad publicity and threats of court action coming from *Lemon-Aid* and about six hundred Chrysler owners who helped form Chrysler Lemon Owners Groups (CLOG) in British Columbia and New Brunswick (now established in Alberta and Saskatchewan and organizing in Ontario). These groups have succeeded in getting sizeable refunds for brake, transmission, AC, and paint repairs. Canadians who have had any of these problems and want "goodwill" repairs or a refund for repairs already carried out, should go through Chrysler's regular customer relations hotline. If you're not satisfied by the response you get, phone, fax, or email Mr. Larry Latta, Vice President Sales and Marketing; or Lou Spadotto, National Service Manager, Parts, Service, and Engineering, at: tel.: 519-973-2300; fax: 519-561-7005; email: *rar17@daimlerchrysler.com*.

19. Chrysler Products' Problem Web Page *(www.wam.umd.edu/ ~gluckman/Chrysler/)*
This page was designed to be a resource for Chrysler owners who have had problems in dealing with Chrysler, including issues with peeling paint, transmission failure, the Chrysler-installed Bendix-10 ABS, and other maladies.

20. Chrysler-Plymouth-Dodge Central *(www.allpar.com)*
This is an excellent website that's jam-packed with historical information, tips on fixing common problems inexpensively, and advice on how to deal with Chrysler representatives and dealer service managers. Lots of useful links.

21. Chrysler Peeling Paint Page *(peelingpaint.homestead.com)*
Just set up (July 2000), this is an incredibly comprehensive site that gives you easy, step-by-step procedures to follow (with all the documents, court cases, service bulletins, and links to other helpful groups) in order to get Chrysler to repaint your vehicle for free.

Set up by a 1992 Plymouth Grand Voyager minivan owner (with just a little bit of my input) who got Chrysler to pay for a $4,000 paint job with a lifetime warranty just a few months after filing his small claims papers, this site *must* be your starting point in dealing with Chrysler for paint problems—or any other problems, for that matter. Just the small claims court complaint statement that you can copy is well worth the visit.

22. Daewoo Complaints *(www.badcustomerservice.co.uk/press.htm)*
This 2000 Galant owner set up this site after his new Daewoo burned up and the automaker wouldn't make good on its claim that it would replace the vehicle.

23. Ford Insider Info *(www.blueovalnews.com)*
Set up by a Ford Mustang enthusiast living in the Detroit area who has contacts with lots of Ford employee whistleblowers, this website is the place to go for all the latest insider info on the company's activities. The website is still operating although Ford got a temporary restraining order preventing it from publishing certain internal documents that Ford considers to be confidential.

24. Ford Automatic Transmission Victims *(members.aol.com/MKBradley/index.html)*
A great site for learning about Ford's biodegradable automatic transmissions (1991–99) from owners and expert mechanics.

25. Dead Ford Page *(www.mindspring.com/~ics_mak/deadford.html)*
An amusing and informative gathering place for Ford car, truck, sport-utility, minivan, and van owners who discuss common problems and solutions. A fun site just to see the FORD VENT page, where an animated character walks across the screen, drops his shorts, and takes a leak up against a thinly disguised Ford logo.

26. Ford Contour/Mystique *(www.contour.org/FAQ/)*
This website provides a comprehensive listing of common problems and fixes affecting the Ford Contour, Mercury Mystique, and European-sold Mondeo (especially, engine overheating and stalling). It's particularly useful, now that Ford has taken these cars off the market, making technical info hard to find.

27. Ford Suckz *(members.xoom.com/fordsuckz/index.html)*
An excellent site set up by an Alberta Sable owner who succeeded in getting Ford to refund his engine repair costs. Lots of helpful links to other sites.

28. Ford Windstar Faulty Engine Head Gaskets *(home.att.net/~ccatanese/ford/)*
This is the most comprehensive site relating to faulty engine gaskets on Ford's 3.8L and 4.2L engines. Plenty of technical help supported by

internal service bulletins and extended warranties you can download. Many links to other helpful sites.

29. Ford Diesel Website *(www.Ford-diesel.com)*
Everything from engine cavitation repairs, servicing tips, discounted parts, to lots of other diesel links are found on this independently run site.

30. Ford Paint Delamination/Peeling *(www.ihs2000.com/~peel)*
Everything you should know about the cause and treatment of Ford paint delamination. Useful links to other sites and tips on dealing with Ford and GM paint problems.

31. GMAC Sucks *(www.gmacsucks.com)*
An online complaint forum about GMAC and General Motors set up by an army veteran whose vehicle was repossessed while he was stationed in Kosovo. Lot of links to other gripe sites as well as complaint summaries relating to both GM and GMAC.

32. GMC Safari Paint Delamination *(members.home.net/ssbassi/index.htm)*
A pictorial presentation of the paint delamination problem affecting this man's 1992 Safari minivan. Some useful links and owner feedback pages.

33. GM Saturn Exposed *(www.saturnexposed.com)*
Go beyond the GM Saturn hype and learn why Saturn owners call their car "a different kind of headache." Plenty of owner summaries, service tips, and links to other Saturn gripe sites.

34. GM Suburban Lemons *(www.gmclemon.com)*
Thrill to the excitement of faulty brakes. Experience the wonder of breaking down in Utah on a Sunday afternoon. Marvel at the cut and thrust of verbal duels with callous GM reps. Enter the 'which piece of crap is going to fall off next' sweepstakes. Cringe in terror at a tale of driving around with a fuel leak, corroded battery cables and a short circuit. Lot of links to other gripe sites, copies of service bulletins relating to Suburban defects (brakes, especially), and summaries of complaints from other owners. Incidentally, GM bought back this owner's Suburban, shortly after his website went up.

35. Don't Buy a Kia! Page *(members.tripod.com/aiki_joe/kia/index.html)*
A wonderfully comprehensive site set up by a dissatisfied Kia Sephia owner. No fancy graphics or elaborate frames, just a compendium of Kia reviews and owner comments from diverse sources around the country.

36. Neon Enthusiasts Page *(neons.org/index.html)*
Good source for technical information and troubleshooting tips. Lots of service bulletins categorized by component failure can be accessed.

Chrysler's engine head gasket service bulletin can be downloaded to reinforce your claim for a free engine repair on many of Chrysler's 1995–99 4-cylinder engines *(neons.org/neontsb/TSB/09/090598.htm)*.

Information/Services

37. ALLDATA Service Bulletins *(www.alldata.com/consumer/TSB/yr.html)*
Free summaries of automotive recalls and technical service bulletins are listed by year, make, model and engine option. Like the NHTSA summaries, ALLDATA's summaries are so short and cryptic that they're of limited usefulness. You can't see the contents of individual bulletins unless you purchase, for about $30 U.S., a CD-ROM that holds all the bulletins that pertain to your vehicle. Considering that many vehicles have over three hundred bulletins, the ALLDATA fee is a real bargain.

38. The Auto Channel *(www.theautochannel.com/)*
This website gives you comprehensive information useful in choosing a new or used vehicle, filing a claim for compensation, or linking up with other owners. Lots of background info on ABS defects and paint delamination/peeling, with an update as to where the paint class actions are before the courts.

39. Automobile News Groups
These news groups are compilations of email raves and gripes and cover all makes and models. They fall into four distinct areas: *rec.autos.makers.chrysler* (you can add any automaker's name at the end); *rec.autos.tech; rec.autos.driving;* and *rec.autos.misc*. The following news group bulletin board is particularly helpful to owners with minivan and van problems: *www.he.net/~brumley/family/vanboard.html*.

40. Autopedia *(autopedia.com/index.html)*
An automotive encyclopedia, Autopedia offers a compendium of information related to automobiles.

41. Canadian Driver *(www.canadiandriver.com/reviews/index.htm)*
An up-to-date collection of well-written articles, test drives, website critiques, Canadian MSRP prices, and links to other sites that should appeal to drivers on both sides of the border.

42. CarCalculator, "Why leasing can be a sucker's bet." *(www.carcalculator.com/)*
This is an excellent site to learn about the dark side of leasing from leasing expert and consumer advocate Bob Lo Presti. Another well-done and easily accessed site is the U.S. Federal Reserve Bank's "Leasing" site, which contains more information about leasing (in easy to understand terms) than you're ever to likely need. Geared to an American audience, most of the info applies to Canadian leasees as well. Click on at: *www.bog.frb.fed.us/pubs/leasing/*.

43. Cartrackers *(www.cartrackers.com)*
This is a large site that has a nice balance of the pros and cons of car ownership. Its technical resources are impressive and there are experts to advise you on everything from secret warranties to simple maintenance. Plenty of useful links, particularly the one to the Ford Explorer message board for SUV owners, at: *www.4x4central.com.*

54. Kelley Blue Book Prices *(www.kbb.com)*
Providing over 9 million free reports every month, the Kelley Blue Book site is an excellent repository of vehicle reviews. *www.edmunds.com* provides a similar service.

55. Metro Credit *(www.metrocu.com/about/news/default.asp?load=97)*
What, a credit union that puts a car broker at its members disposition to negotiate a new- or used-car sale? Or, better yet, finds you a reliable new or used vehicle at the right price? That's what this Toronto-based credit union has been doing for many years. If you'd like to try this service, join the group. If you'd like your own credit union to provide similar services, recommend this site to the board of directors.